SOMETHING ABOUT THE AUTHOR

SOMETHING ABOUT THE AUTHOR

Facts and Pictures about Contemporary Authors.
and Illustrators of Books for Young People

Anne Commire

VOLUME 14

GALE RESEARCH
BOOK TOWER
DETROIT, MICHIGAN
48226

Also Published by Gale

CONTEMPORARY AUTHORS:

*A Bio-Bibliographical Guide to Current Writers in
Fiction, General Nonfiction, Poetry, Journalism,
Drama, Motion Pictures, Television,
and Other Fields*

(Now Covers More Than 50,000 Authors)

Associate Editor: Agnes Garrett

Assistant Editor: Linda Shedd

Consultant: Adele Sarkissian

Sketchwriters: Rosemary DeAngelis Bridges, D. Jayne Higo,
Deci Lowry, Susan L. Stetler, Jo Ann Tedesco, Ruth Toms

Research Assistants: Cathy Coray, Elisa Ann Sawchuk,
Anna Deavere Smith

Library of Congress Catalog Card Number 72-27107

ISBN 0-8103-0095-8

GRATEFUL ACKNOWLEDGMENT

is made to the following publishers, authors, and artists, for their kind permission to reproduce copyrighted material. ■ **ABELARD-SCHUMAN.** Illustration by Marc Simont from *American Riddle Book* by Carl Withers and Sula Benet. Copyright © 1954 by Carl Withers and Dr. Sula Benet. Reprinted by permission of Abelard-Schuman. ■ **ABINGDON PRESS.** Drawings and photographs by Tom Tichenor from *Tom Tichenor's Puppets* by Tom Tichenor. Copyright © 1971 by Abingdon Press. Reprinted by permission of Abingdon Press. ■ **ADDISON-WESLEY PUBLISHING CO.** Illustration by Marc Tolon Brown from *Super Sam and the Salad Garden* by Patty Wolcott. Text © 1975 by Patty Wolcott Berger. Illustrations © 1975 by Marc Brown./ Illustration by Irma Webber from *Up Above and Down Below* by Irma Webber. Both reprinted by permission of Addison-Wesley Publishing Co. (Young Scott Books) ■ **AMERICAN LIBRARY ASSOCIATION.** Sidelight excerpts from *British Children's Authors* by Cornelia Jones and Olivia R. Way. Copyright © 1976 by the American Library Association. Reprinted by permission of the American Library Association. ■ **ATHENEUM PUBLISHERS.** Illustration by Ron Barrett from *Benjamin's 365 Birthdays* by Judi Barrett. Text © 1974 by Judi Barrett. Illustrations copyright © 1974 by Ron Barrett./ Illustration by Erik Blegvad from *Mittens for Kittens* chosen by Lenore Blegvad. Copyright © 1974 by Erik Blegvad./ Illustration by Eliza Moon from *The Leopard* by Cecil Bodker. Translation copyright © 1975 by Gunnar Poulsen./ Drawings by Peter Warner from *Zomo the Rabbit* by Hugh Sturton. Copyright © 1966 by H.A.S. Johnston./ Illustration by David McPhail from *One Winter Night in August* by X.J. Kennedy. Copyright © 1975 by X.J. Kennedy./ Illustration by Joseph Low from *Boo to a Goose* by Joseph Low. Copyright © 1975 by Joseph Low. All reprinted by permission of Atheneum Publishers. ■ **ATRIUM VERLAG** (Switzerland). Illustration by Horst Lemke from *When I Was a Boy* by Erich Kästner. Translation by Isabel and Florence McHugh. Copyright © 1957 by Atrium Verlag. Reprinted by permission of Atrium Verlag. ■ **BAKER BOOK HOUSE.** Photograph by James P. Barry from *The Fate of the Lakes* by James B. Barry. Copyright © 1972 Baker Book House. Reprinted by permission of Baker Book House. ■ **BETHANY PRESS.** Jacket illustration by Arthur Fitzsimmons from *Island in the Mist* by Ellen Jane MacLeod. Copyright © 1965 by The Bethany Press. Reprinted by permission of The Bethany Press. ■ **BOBBS-MERRILL CO.** Illustration by Maxfield Parrish from *Mother Goose in Prose* by L. Frank Baum. Copyright © 1901 by George M. Hill Co. Reprinted by permission of The Bobbs-Merrill Co. ■ **THE BODLEY HEAD, LTD.** Illustration by Ezra Jack Keats from *The Snowy Day* by Ezra Jack Keats. Copyright © 1962 by Ezra Jack Keats. Reprinted by permission of The Bodley Head, Ltd. ■ **R.R. BOWKER CO.** Sidelight excerpts from an article entitled "Geoffrey Household," April 4, 1977, *Publishers Weekly.* Copyright © 1977 by Xerox Corporation. Reprinted by permission of R.R. Bowker Co. ■ **CURTIS BROWN, LTD.** Illustration by Barbara Bottner from *Jungle Day* by Barbara Bottner. Copyright © 1978 by Barbara Bottner. Reprinted by permission of Curtis Brown, Ltd. ■ **JONATHAN CAPE, LTD.** Illustration by Walter Trier from *Emil and the Detectives* by Eric Kästner. Copyright © 1959 by Jonathan Cape./ Illustration by Patrick Williams from *Jeff Dickson: Cowhand* by David Severn. Copyright © 1963 by Jonathan Cape, Ltd. Both reprinted by permission of Jonathan Cape, Ltd. ■ **CHATTO & WINDUS, LTD.** Illustration by Fritz Wegner from *Wizards and Witches* by Frances Wilkins. Copyright © 1965 by Frances Wilkins. Reprinted by permission of Chatto & Windus, Ltd. ■ **CHILDREN'S PRESS.** Illustration by De Grazia from *Little Sky Eagle and the Pumpkin Drum* by Mildred Feague. Copyright © 1972 by Regensteiner Publishing Enterprises, Inc. Reprinted by permission of Children's Press. ■ **WILLIAM COLLINS SONS & CO. LTD.** (London). Illustration by Martin Thomas from *The Wooden Horse* by Eric Williams. Reprinted by permission of William Collins Sons & Co. Ltd. ■ **DAVID C. COOK PUBLISHING CO.** Illustration by Seymour Fleishman from *Turkey Red* by Esther Loewen Vogt. © 1975 by David C. Cook Publishing Co. Reprinted by permission of

I

1961 by Jack Aistrop./ Illustration by Theodore McClintock from *The Underwater Zoo* by Theodore McClintock. Copyright 1938 by Vanguard Press Inc. Both reprinted by permission of Vanguard Press Inc. ■ **VIKING PRESS.** Illustration by Valenti Angelo from *The Acorn Tree* by Valenti Angelo. Copyright © 1958 by Valenti Angelo./ Illustration by Kate Seredy from *Finnegan II: His Nine Lives* by Carolyn Sherwin Bailey. Copyright 1953 by Carolyn Sherwin Bailey./ Illustration by Taro Yashima from *Umbrella* by Taro Yashima. Copyright © 1958 by Taro Yashima./ Illustration by Ezra Jack Keats from *The Snowy Day* by Ezra Jack Keats. Copyright © 1962 by Ezra Jack Keats./ Illustration by Laszlo Gal from *The Moon Painters* by Selve Maas. Copyright © 1971 by Selve Maas. All reprinted by permission of Viking Press. ■ **HENRY Z. WALCK, INC.** Illustration by Charles Robinson from *Once a Bright Red Tiger* by Alex Whitney. Text copyright © 1973 by Alex Whitney. Illustrations copyright © 1973 by Charles Robinson. Reprinted by permission of Henry Z. Walck, Inc. ■ **FREDERICK WARNE & CO., LTD.** Illustration by K. Nixon from *Animals and Birds in Folklore* by K. Nixon. Copyright © 1969 by Frederick Warne and Co., Ltd. Reprinted by permission of Frederick Warne & Co., Ltd. ■ **WATSON-GUPTILL PUBLICATIONS.** Sidelight excerpts from *Maxfield Parrish* by Coy Ludwig. Reprinted by permission of Watson-Guptill Publications. ■ **FRANKLIN WATTS, INC.** Illustration from *The Concise Encyclopedia of Sports* edited by Keith W. Jennison. Copyright © 1970 Grolier Incorporated./ Illustration by Horst Lemke from *When I was a Boy* by Erich Kästner. Translation by Isabel and Florence McHugh. Copyright © 1957 by Atrium Verlag./ Illustration by Ulrick Schramm from *Let's Find Out About Sound* by David Knight./ Pictures by Steven Kellogg from *The Boy Who Was Followed Home* by Margaret Mahy. Text copyright © 1975 by Franklin Watts. Illustrations copyright © 1975 by Steven Kellogg./ Illustration by Dorothy Marino from *Buzzy Bear's First Day at School* by Dorothy Marino. Copyright © 1970 by Dorothy Marino./ Illustration by John Hamberger from *Vanishing Wings* by Griffing Bancroft. Copyright © 1972 by Griffing Bancroft. All reprinted by permission of Franklin Watts, Inc. ■ **ALBERT WHITMAN & CO.** Illustration by Kurt Wiese from *Connecticut* by Bernadine Bailey. Copyright © 1966, 1955 by Albert Whitman & Co. Reprinted by permission of Albert Whitman & Co. ■ **OSWALD WOLFF, LTD.** Sidelight excerpts from *Erich Kästner: Modern German Authors,* Volume III, by R.W. Last. Reprinted by permission of Oswald Wolff, Ltd. ■ **WORLD'S WORK, LTD.** Picture by Frances Zweifel from *Alligator* by Evelyn Shaw. Pictures copyright © 1972 by Frances W. Zweifel. Reprinted by permission of World's Work, Ltd. ■ **WREN PUBLISHING.** Illustration by Jeff Hook from *Animal Olympics* by Stan Marks. Reprinted by permission of Wren Publishing. Sidelight excerpts from an article "Robert Frost Remembered" by Lesley Frost in *American Way,* March, 1974. Reprinted by permission of *American Way,* inflight magazine of American Airlines./ Sidelight excerpts from an article "Successful Light Verse Writing" by Richard Armour, *The Writer,* February, 1973. Reprinted by permission of Richard Armour./ Photograph by Sarah M. Elliott from *Our Dirty Land* by Sarah M. Elliott. Reprinted by permission of The Environmental Protection Agency./ Illustration by Boris Artzybasheff from *Creatures* by Padraic Colum. Reprinted by permission of Emmet M. Greene./ Illustration from *The World Awakes: The Renaissance in Western Europe* by Polly Schoyer Brooks and Nancy Zinsser Walworth. Reprinted by permission of the Italian Government Travel Office./ Photograph by Jerry Wainwright from *Native Funk and Flash* by Alexandra Jacopetti. Reprinted by permission of Alexandra Jacopetti./ Illustration by W.H.D. Koerner from *The Time of the Indian* by Kenneth Ulyatt. Reprinted by permission of Mrs. Ruth Koerner Oliver./ Illustration from *Demeter's Daughters* by Selma R. Williams. Reprinted by permission of Pioneer Village, Salem, Mass./ Illustration from *The Second Book of True Animal Stories* by Eric Delderfield. Reprinted by permission of the *Sunday Independent* newspaper./ Photograph by Suzanne Szasz from *Little League to Big League* by Jim Brosnan. Reprinted by permission of Suzanne Szasz./ Photograph by Kathryn Tucker Windham from *Jeffrey Introduces 13 More Southern Ghosts* by Kathryn Tucker Windham. Reprinted by permission of Kathryn Tucker Windham./ Photo from *Reflections on a Gift of Watermelon Pickle* by Stephen Dunning, Edward Lueders and Hugh Smith. Reprinted by permission of Jurg Klages photographer./ Illustration by Harold Jones from *The Fairy Stories of Oscar Wilde.* Reprinted by permission of Harold Jones.

PHOTOGRAPH CREDITS

Boris Artzybasheff: New York Public Library Picture Collection; Carolyn Sherwin Bailey: Arni; Lorna Beers: Dorsey Studio; Suzanne Bladow: James Evans Mueller; Eric Delderfield: Edward Lucas; Edith Fowke: Jean Gainfort Merrill (Toronto); Carl Glick: Courtesy of the University of Iowa Libraries; William C. Grimm: Delmar Studios; Erich Kästner: Atrium Press, Ltd.; Ezra Jack Keats: Weston Woods; Ethel and Leonard Kessler: Parents' Magazine Press; Phyllis La Farge: Ronald Steel; Matthew Lipman: Ed Kamper; Joseph Low: New York Public Library Picture Collection; Elizabeth Spencer: Sam Tata; Allan C. Stover: Rams Manila; Margaret Pitcairn Strachan: Howard Reynolds; Ruth

Tabrah: Modern Camera Center; Walter Terry: Martha Swope; Norman Thelwell: Thomas Wilkie; Agnes Sligh Turnbull: Richard's Studio Art; John Verney: Stefan Buzas; David Russell Wagner: Pat Wagner; Elizabeth M. Whelan: Barry Bartle; Brenda Wilkinson: Archie Hamilton; Carol Woodard: Oubre Photographers; Edward Wynter: J.C. Watts and Partner.

SOMETHING ABOUT THE AUTHOR

She cradled the cigar-box violin in her arms. ■ (From *Fidelia* by Ruth Adams. Illustrated by Ati Forberg.)

ADAMS, Ruth Joyce

CAREER: Author and teacher. Worked as a music teacher in Los Angeles schools.

WRITINGS: Mr. Picklepaw's Popcorn (illustrated by Kurt Werth), Lothrop, 1965; *Fidelia* (illustrated by Ati Forberg), Lothrop, 1970; (with Guy Adams) *Mr. Picklepaw's Puppy* (illustrated by K. Werth), Lothrop, 1970.

SIDELIGHTS: Ruth Joyce Adams' first book, *Mr. Picklepaw's Popcorn,* was a humorous tale about a harvest of popcorn and what became of it on an unseasonably hot autumn day. "A tellable tall tale, illustrated with appropriately breezy double spreads," commented a *Horn Book* reviewer.

ADDONA, Angelo F.   1925-

PERSONAL: Born November 18, 1925, in Connecticut; son of Frank and Mary Addona; married Micheline Couturier, August, 1950; children: Babette, Jacqueline. *Education:* Student at University of Connecticut and St. John's University, Jamaica, N.Y.; Brooklyn Law School, LL.B., 1951, J.D., 1967. *Residence:* Connecticut and Italy. *Agent:* Marilyn Marlow, Curtis Brown Ltd., 575 Madison Ave., New York, N.Y. 10022.

CAREER: International attorney. Special assistant and financial attorney to a commissioner at the U.S. Securities and Exchange Commission; attorney for the Banking and Currency Commission of the U.S. Senate; has practiced law in Connecticut, Europe, and various federal courts; admitted to practice in the U.S. Supreme Court; former diplomat in U.S. Foreign Service. *Military service:* U.S. Army Air Forces, World War II; served in China-Burma-India Theater.

WRITINGS: The Organization of African Unity (juvenile), World Publishing, 1969. Contributor to Literary Review, Laurel Review, Encyclopedia Britannica, Friends Magazine, Experience in Language Series, Xerox publications, among others.

WORK IN PROGRESS: An adventure book for children, set in Africa; a book about living abroad; a suspense novel; a book on African history as it relates to the United States; travel articles.

SIDELIGHTS: Angelo Addona is fluent in Italian and French and has lived and traveled through most of Europe, North and East Africa, and the Middle and Far East.

HOBBIES AND OTHER INTERESTS: Classical music, especially piano concertos; photography, reading.

ADLER, David A.   1947-

PERSONAL: Born April 10, 1947, in New York, N.Y.; son of Sidney G. (a teacher) and Betty (a social worker; maiden name, Straus) Adler; married Renee Hamada (a school psychologist), April 8, 1973. Education: Queens College of the City University of New York, B.A., 1968; New York University, M.B.A., 1971. Religion: Jewish. Home: 84-23 Manton St., Briarwood, N.Y. 11435.

WRITINGS—All for children: 3D, 2D, 1D (mathematics book), Crowell, 1975; Base Five (mathematics book), Crowell, 1976; A Little at a Time (fiction), Random House, 1976; Hanukkah Fun Book, Puzzles, Riddles, Magic and More, Bonim Books, 1976; Roman Numerals (mathematics book), Crowell, 1977; Passover Fun Book, Bonim Books, 1977; Redwoods Are the Tallest Trees in the World (science book), Crowell, 1978; The Children's Concise Bible, Bonim Books, 1978; Hanukkah Game Book, Bonim Books, 1978. Contributor of reviews to journals.

WORK IN PROGRESS: A juvenile novel; more mathematics, fiction and puzzle books for children.

SIDELIGHTS: "I grew up on Long Island in a large house filled with brothers, sisters, and books. I have been a professional artist with more than two hundred drawings and cartoons published in magazines and newspapers. My artwork has been publicly exhibited in New York and Florida and is contained in private collections in the United States and Europe. I now devote full time to teaching and writing for children and illustrate only my Fun books."

(From A Little at a Time by David A. Adler. Illustrated by N.M. Bodecker.)

DAVID ADLER

AISTROP, Jack 1916-

PERSONAL: Born August 22, 1916; married Josephine Hunter; children: Jennifer, Josepha. *Home:* 36A Townshend Rd., London, N.W. 8, England. *Agent:* James Brown Associates, 22 East 60th St., New York, N.Y. 10022.

CAREER: Writer. British Information Services, New York, N.Y., director of radio and television divisions, 1947-55; British Broadcasting Corp., London, England, External Service, 1946-63, representative in United States, 1963-66; head of production, Gramophone Records and Tapes, a division of the BBC., 1966-76; head of copyright, Music Sales Ltd. and Omnibus Ltd., London, England, 1976—. *Military service:* British Army, 1939-45. *Member:* Zoological Society (London, fellow). *Awards, honors:* Tom Gallon Award, 1946-47; *Atlantic* award in literature, 1947.

WRITINGS: Backstage with Joe, Farrar, Straus, 1948; *The Lights Are Low,* Roy, 1948; *Pretend I Am a Stranger,* Roy, 1950. Editor, *Triad;* co-editor, *Bugle Blast.*

Factual nature books for children: *Every Child's Book of Pets,* Dobson, 1949; *Fun at the Zoo,* Roy, 1951; *Animals Around Us,* Dobson, 1953; *Enjoying Pets,* Vanguard, 1955; *Enjoying Nature's Marvels,* Dobson, 1961, Vanguard, 1962; *Pet Lover's Dictionary,* Arco, 1961; *The Mongolian Gerbil,* Dobson, 1968; *Budgerigars and Other Cage Birds,* Arco, 1968.

Author of radio scripts for BBC Overseas Services, BBC Radio 4, National Broadcasting Company and others. *Pretend I Am a Stranger* was adapted as a television play by NBC.

WORK IN PROGRESS: The Animals in our House; revision and updating of some of the earlier books.

SIDELIGHTS: "My life has been almost equally divided between England, those parts of Europe through which the Second World War cut its swathe, and North America. I still speak with a touch of Cockney but use more American colloquialisms than British. I get homesick for places dotted around the globe and sometimes suffer from that awful state of being able to visualise a town without being able to give a name to it. In my working life I have been fortunate in knowing many of the world's unique people—the greatest bonus from an investment of time in broadcasting, gramophone record production and writing.

"My wife, who is half Californian, half British is a product of Roedean, a very proper English school and UCLA. She is now head of a school in the centre of London's vice district—Soho—and copes with Chinese, Asian and children of many other nationalities in a little old schoolhouse surrounded by shops and clubs of dubious character. Our own children, two girls, have lost their American accents and are now British to all intents and purposes.

"Our home has always been full of animals from the exotic to the ordinary and for some years, my wife had a spot on a BBC television show on which unwanted pets were given, to carefully checked homes, for adoption. They all lived with us for a few weeks before facing the cameras where they generally romped (or slithered) around with our own pets."

JACK AISTROP, with Mongolian gerbil

(From *Enjoying Nature's Marvels* by Jack Bentley Aistrop. Picture by Lynwood M. Chase.)

ALBERTS, Frances Jacobs 1907-

PERSONAL: Born January 14, 1907, in Lennox, S.D.; daughter of Henry H. and Annie (Plucker) Jacobs; married Arnold A. Alberts (now college professor of chemistry), September 14, 1931; children: Ann Amelia, Brechter Arnold. *Education:* General Beadle State Teachers College, certificate; additional study at Purdue University. *Politics:* Republican. *Religion:* Presbyterian. *Home:* 1119 North Elm, Hastings, Neb.

CAREER: Taught grade school in South Dakota, 1928-31; Radio station WBAA, West Lafayette, Ind., script writer, Purdue School of the Air, 1950-52; Radio station KCRS, Midland, Tex., committee on continuity, 1955-56; Young Women's Christian Association, Hastings, Neb., instructor, creative writing course, 1962-63. *Member:* National Federation of Press Women, International Platform Association, Nebraska Writers (chairman, membership committee, 1961-63), Nebraska Folklore Society (vice-president, 1964-65), National Pen Women of America, Sod House Society of Nebraska, Sons and Daughters of the Soddies, Delta Kappa Gamma. *Awards, honors:* Puss 'n Boots Bronze Award for article about cat; first prize, Pennsylvania Federation of Women's Clubs, for poem, "Soliloquy," 1940.

WRITINGS: A Gift for Genghis Khan, Whittlesey House, 1961; (editor) *Sod House Memories,* Cornhusker Press, 1963; *Sod House Memories,* Volume II, Cornhusker Press, 1967; *Nebraska Writers Guild Anthology,* Service Press, 1967; *Sod House Memories,* Volume III, Service Press, 1972; (contributor) *Adams County Centennial History* (comprising *The People,* Volume I, and *The History,* Volume II), 1973.

Contributor to textbooks: *New Friends and Neighbors,* Scott, 1953; *Friends About Us,* Seventh Day Adventists, 1957; *Open the Gates,* Ginn, 1959. Sonnet in *Beyond the Night,* Scribner, 1944; "Lucky Antlers" serial in *Children's Activities;* juvenile stories in *Child Life, Instructor, Jack and Jill, Trailblazer, Golden Magazine, Children's Friend.* Articles have appeared in *P.E.O. Record, Midlands Magazine, Omaha World Herald, Focus Magazine, Lincoln Star.* Also author of many nature articles and poems.

WORK IN PROGRESS: The Snow Leopard, a juvenile book laid in the period of history when Genghis Khan was about to besiege the countries beyond the Himalayas; *Samarkand Summer,* third in Genghis Khan series; *Indian Days to Soddy Days; Bolo, the Arabian Mare; Speed, the Boy from M 31;* and *Wayfarer at El Charman.*

SIDELIGHTS: "Writing is one of those things held closely to you and as personal as the color of your eyes and hair. The lowest common denominator of a child as well as an adult is to love and be loved, and that is the springboard for my juveniles—I try to give them a tenderness, an insight, that can be felt. . . . I write for the child I once was.

"When I was four years old my father homesteaded in Canada, in Alberta near a small settlement called Amisk. There we lived in a soddy and had all the usual pioneer experiences. That first year as we were getting our first Canadian Christmas tree from the sandhills near our claim, I stood by myself for many long moments in complete communication with a small grey rabbit which sat under an evergreen. We looked at each other with love and understanding and trust, speaking to each other wordlessly.

"Now that I am grown with a family of my own, I still have a violent love for all wild creatures, be they large or small, bird or animal. I also seem to have a complete understanding of why they act as they do. This is due I think to my early closeness to nature.

"We have a cabin at a lakeside thirty miles out in the country just a mile or so south of the Platte River which is noted for its shallow water which is a haven to the migrating sandhill cranes twice yearly. The waters of the Platte are, and I quote from early pioneer records, 'a mile wide and a foot deep.' For centuries this has drawn the cranes annually."

FOR MORE INFORMATION SEE: Hastings Daily Tribune (Hastings, Neb.), April 20, 1963.

FRANCES JACOBS ALBERTS

(From *Gift for Genghis Khan* by Frances Jacobs Alberts. Illustrated by Rafaello Busoni.)

ALDRIDGE, Josephine Haskell

MARRIED: Richard Aldridge (a poet), October, 1958; children: Abigail Nancy. *Home:* Sebasco Estates, Maine.

CAREER: Artist and author of books for children. *Awards, honors: Reasons and Raisins* was selected as one of the books in the American Institute of Graphic Arts Children's Book Show, 1971-72.

WRITINGS: A Penny and a Periwinkle (illustrated by Ruth Robbins), Parnassus Press, 1961; *The Best of Friends* (illustrated by Betty F. Peterson), Parnassus Press, 1963; *Fisherman's Luck* (illustrated by R. Robbins), Parnassus Press, 1966; (with husband, Richard Aldridge) *Reasons and Raisins* (illustrated by John Larrecq), Parnassus Press, 1972.

SIDELIGHTS: The *Horn Book* review of *A Penny and a Periwinkle* said, "Old Sy lives in a little house on the edge of the sea. A penny in his pocket for a sharp new fishhook and a periwinkle hiding in the seaweed are all he needs to have comfort and contentment. The story is slight, but the overtones are great and . . . little children . . . will feel the charm and reassurance of this lovely picture book. Black and white, red, and a great deal of sea blue are used effectively to create the Maine scene and atmosphere in pictures completely in harmony with the poetic text." *Commonweal* described it as, "A few rhythmical lines to a page illustrated with beautiful spareness and delicacy. A serene and distinguished book." The *New York Herald Tribune* added, "The charming little story exalts the satisfactions of the simple life in a delightful fashion." The comments of the *Kirkus* reviewer included, "Miss Aldridge chooses the poetic form to demonstrate the simple philosophy of the old New England Yankee and Ruth Robbins appealingly etches it in our thoughts with sturdy illustrations."

ALEXEIEFF, Alexandre A.   1901-

PERSONAL: Born April 18, 1901, in Kazan, Russia; married Claire Parker. *Education:* Studied oriental languages in Paris, and later stage design with Serge Soudeikine.

CAREER: Illustrator, animator, and stage designer. Designed stage sets for the Theatre Pitoeff in Paris and the Ballet Russe de Monte Carlo, and costumes, 1922-25. Conducted research on the application of wood, copper, and stone engravings to graphic art, and in 1931, invented the pinboard process for making animated cartoons, using this technique for his first film, "Night on Bare Mountain," and for book illustration in 1959 for *Doctor Zhivago.* He made advertising and other films, 1934-40, and a pinboard film, "En Passant," in the United States. Invented animated totalisée technique, 1947-58, using it for advertising films. Was a film judge at Tours, 1957, and at Brussels, 1958. *Member:* Founder-member of Cinematheque Francaise; also member of Artistes et Amis du Cinema d'Animation, Studio Alexeieff, Academie du Cinema (Paris).

ILLUSTRATOR: Jean Genbach, *L'Abbe de Abbaye* (poems), [Paris], 1927; Aleksandr S. Pushkin, *The Queen of Spades* (translated from the Russian by J. E. Pouterman and C. Bruerton), Blackamore Press, 1928; Fedor Dostoevskii, *Les Freres Karamasov* (French translation from the Russian), Schiffrin, 1929; Nikolai Vasilevich Gogol, *The Diary of a Madman* (translated from the Russian by Prince Mirsky), Cresset Press, 1929; Edgar Allan Poe, *Colloques entre Monos et Una* (French translation from the English), Orion, 1930; Poe, *The Fall of the House of Usher,* A. A. M. Stols, 1930; Charles Baudelaire, *Poemes,* Exemplaires, 1931; L. P. Fargue, *Poemes,* Gallimard, 1942; Lev N. Tolstoi, *What*

ALEXANDRE ALEXEIEFF

In a certain town there lived a cobbler, Martin Avdeich by name. ■ (From *Russian Stories and Legends* by Leo Tolstoy. Illustrated by Alexander Alexeieff.)

Men Live By: Russian Stories and Legends (translated from the Russian by Louise and Aylmer Maude), Pantheon Books, 1943, reprinted as *Russian Stories and Legends,* 1967; Aleksandr N. Afanasev, *Russian Fairy Tales* (translated from the Russian by Norbert Guterman), Pantheon Books, 1945; *Chant du Prince Igor,* Eynard, 1949; Boris Pasternak, *Docteur Jivago* (French translation from the Russian), Gallimard, 1959; F. Dostoevskii, *The Gambler [and] Notes from Underground* (translated from the Russian by Constance Garnett), Limited Editions, 1967; *Alexandre Alexeieff* (catalog of book illustrations), National Library of Scotland, 1967.

Contributor to art magazines.

SIDELIGHTS: "My first language was French, learned in Constantinople (Istanbul) where my family lived in 1903, 1904. I started drawing at the age of four the procession of boats sailing on the Bosphorus.

"At the age of five I tried to render the movement of my tin soldiers and learned Russian. At the age of ten I drew Indians on galloping horses in profile and at the age of twelve, succeeded in drawing locomotives and galloping horses seen from the front.

"I learned to paint theatrical sets in Paris at the age of twenty. At twenty-five, learned etching by myself discovering techniques of my own invention.

"At thirty I learned English with my second wife. Together we invented the Pinboard techniques to illustrate music. We then learned by trial and error to make motion picture with pinboard engravings. When I was 58 we applied our pinboard technique to the book by illustrating *Doctor Zhivago.*

"Now, at 75, I am building my sixth Pinboard with 'only' 250,000 pins (the first had 3,000, the second 500,000, the fourth 1,140,000).

"My love for reading is a passion developed during childhood. I read French, Russian and English fluently. Although acquired in childhood, my German is timid for lack of practice.

"I am interested in psychology, neurology, physiological optics and languages. I like Tolstoy's philosophy although I am wary of its schematic excesses. From Tolstoy I borrowed a taste for manual work. In my view manual work is to the human psyche what the pendulum is to the clock.

"I think a great deal about movement and time.

"As to my aesthetic views, I hate all mannerisms for their lack of sincerity and spontaneity. (Between the two I make a distinction: 'one may lie spontaneously—when afraid of saying the truth, as they seem to do nowadays in Russia.' But could one 'lie sincerely?')

"What about style and stylisation?—in my opinion stylisation is mannerism, whereas style comes as naturally, as unconsciously to an artist as his way of walking.

"I have practiced all graphic techniques except serigraphy. My preference goes to etching and the Pinboard. I've been influenced by Georges Seurat.

"I have traveled extensively."

ALLISON, Bob

CAREER: Author and teacher. Allison left teaching and has worked in radio as Special Events Officer with the "Voice of America."

WRITINGS: (With Frank Ernest Hill) *The Kid Who Batted 1.000* (illustrated by Paul Galdone), Doubleday, 1951, reissued, Scholastic Book Services, 1972.

SIDELIGHTS: The Kid Who Batted 1.000 told the story of Dave King, a small town Oklahoma boy, who possessed a rare talent that nearly upset American League baseball. A *New York Times* critic wrote, "Here's the zaniest laugh-loaded baseball story since rhubarb stopped being a vegetable. There are even surprises in it for Dodger fans. . . . If there's one story likely to survive the competition among teen agers this year, *The Kid Who Batted 1.000* may well be it." *Horn Book* described it as, "A baseball story that is different in that it has a good deal of fresh humor and a hero who has no ambition to be a baseball star. He does play big league baseball one season for a purpose, but no amount of money or persuasion can swerve him from his real ambition; puzzled commercial baseball managers are up against something they cannot believe. Here is a boy worth knowing." The *Christian Science Monitor* called it, "A good yarn. . . . Good reading for anyone who enjoys fun and humorous situations, whether or not they are interested in baseball." *Atlantic Monthly* added, "Some of the dialogue is slightly reminiscent of Elmer the Great, and people who saw 'It Happens Every Spring' may note a familiar ring, but the story itself has freshness and fast, authentic baseball jargon."

ANGELO, Valenti   1897-

PERSONAL: Born June 23, 1897, in Massarosa, Tuscany, Italy; came to the United States, 1905; son of Augustino and Viclinda (Checchi) Angelo; married Maxine Grimm, July 23, 1923; children: Valdine, Peter. *Education:* Attended schools in Italy and California. *Religion:* Catholic. *Home:* Bronxville, New York.

CAREER: Author and illustrator. Worked in a paper mill at the age of fifteen; later worked as a laborer in rubber, steel, and glass works; employed for three years at a photoengraving firm; began illustrating books for Grabhorn Press, 1926; became a free-lance artist, 1933; turned to writing children's books, 1937. *Awards, honors:* Since 1927, thirty-seven books illustrated by Angelo have been included in the American Institute of Graphic Arts' Fifty Books of the Year Exhibits; *Roller Skates,* written by Ruth Sawyer and illustrated by Angelo, won the Newbery Medal, 1937.

WRITINGS—All self-illustrated; all published by Viking, except as noted: *Nino,* 1938; *Golden Gate,* 1939, reprinted, Arno, 1975; *Paradise Valley,* 1940; *A Battle in Washington Square,* Golden Cross Press, 1942; *Hill of Little Miracles,* 1942; *Look Out Yonder,* 1943; *The Rooster Club,* 1944; *The Bells of Bleecker Street,* 1949, reissued, 1969; *The Marble Fountain,* 1951; *Big Little Island,* 1955; *The Acorn Tree,* 1958; *The Honey Boat,* 1959; *The Candy Basket,* 1960; *Angelino and the Barefoot Saint,* 1961; *The Merry Marcos,* 1963; *The Tale of a Donkey,* 1966.

Illustrator: Walt Whitman, *Leaves of Grass,* Random House, 1930; Alexander Dumas, *Three Musketeers,* Illustrated Editions Co., 1935; Nathaniel Hawthorne, *House of*

VALENTI ANGELO

the Seven Gables, Limited Editions Club, 1935; Ruth Sawyer, *Roller Skates,* Viking, 1936; Charles George Soulie, editor and translator, *Chinese Love Tales,* Illustrated Editions Co., 1936; Richard Francis Burton, *F. Kasidah of Haji Abdu el-Yezdi: A Lay of the Higher Law,* Limited Editions Club, 1937; Clement Clarke Moore, *Visit from St. Nicholas,* Hawthorne, 1937; Charles K. Scott Moncrieff, translator, *Song of Roland,* Limited Editions Club, 1938; Marguerite Vance, *Paula,* Dodd, 1939.

John Fante, *Dago Red,* Viking, 1940; R. Sawyer, *Long Christmas,* Viking, 1941; Bret Harte, *Luck of Roaring Camp and Other Stories,* Peter Pauper Press, 1943; Bible, *Psalms of David in the King James Version,* Peter Pauper Press, 1943; Annie Thaxter Eaton, *The Animals' Christmas,* Viking, 1944, reissued, 1966; Elizabeth Barrett Browning, *Sonnets from the Portuguese,* Heritage Press, 1945; Edwin Arnold, *Light of Asia,* Peter Pauper Press, 1946; R. F. Burton, translator, *Book of the Thousand Nights and a Night,* Heritage Press, 1946; Floy Perkinson Gates, *Hey, Mr. Grasshopper!,* privately printed, 1949.

Clyde Robert Bulla, *Song of St. Francis,* Crowell, 1952; Sterling North, *Birthday of Little Jesus,* Grosset, 1952; Delos Wheeler Lovelace, *Journey to Bethlehem,* Crowell, 1953; Francis Thompson, *Hound of Heaven,* Peter Pauper Press, 1953; A. T. Eaton, *Welcome Christmas,* Crowell, 1955; William Shakespeare, *The Tragedy of Hamlet,* Peter Pauper Press, 1956; C. R. Bulla, *Benito,* Crowell; Bible (Old Testament, English), *The Book of Proverbs,* Heritage Press, 1963; C. R. Bulla, *St. Valentine's Day,* Crowell, 1965; N. Hawthorne, *Twice-Told Tales,* edited by Wallace Stegner, Limited Editions Club, 1966.

SIDELIGHTS: Valenti Angelo first became interested in drawing as a child growing up in Italy. His earliest encouragement to pursue a career in art came from the village

wood-carver. The future author-illustrator came to the United States at the age of eight and briefly attended schools in California before joining the labor force. In 1916, Angelo left his parent's home to live in San Francisco. While there, he frequently visited the museums and libraries to further his education in the field of art.

Since 1926, Angelo has decorated and illustrated over two hundred books. At the age of forty, he decided to try his hand at writing books for children—with nearly all stories based on his own experiences. Angelo's first book, *Nino,* was about the childhood of an Italian boy, and closely resembled the author's own boyhood. "The artist-author has painted a vivid word picture of Italian country life, with a wealth of color and detail and a real affection for the people and the place," commented a reviewer for *Library Journal.* Angelo continued the adventures of the young Italian boy in a sequel entitled, *Golden Gate.* A *New York Times* critic wrote, "The book, like its predecessor, is designed with beauty and distinction. . . ."

The author had only a brief stay on New York's Bleecker Street as a child, but his memory of the Little Italy was so sharp and colorful, that he used the location as the backdrop for a later book, *Bells of Bleecker Street.* A reviewer for the *New York Herald Tribune* noted, "Here Mr. Angelo's many abilities combine in a complete success: his feeling for a place . . . , his remarkable insight into the hearts of small boys . . . , his keen artist's eye for detail and his ability to write fluid, lively good English."

A more recent Angelo story, *The Candy Basket,* told the adventures of a little mouse who accidently arrived at a ladies luncheon. "Valenti Angelo can spin a tale as fragile and colorful as his cooks can fashion a basket," observed a *Christian Science Monitor* critic.

Angelino and the Barefoot Saint is one of the author's latest works. Focusing on the kind and good-natured spirit of a little boy, the story has become a particular favorite for the Christmas season. A *Horn Book* reviewer commented, "The author illumines the spirit of the Italian village, particularly the faith and the action of a friendly child to make this excellent for reading aloud."

HOBBIES AND OTHER INTERESTS: Painting and sculpting.

For all his scolding, the squirrels and chipmunks and the other bluejays went on gathering acorns. ▪ (From *The Acorn Tree* by Valenti Angelo. Illustrated by the author.)

FOR MORE INFORMATION SEE: Olga Peragallo, *Italian-American Authors and Their Contribution to American Literature,* S. E. Vanni, 1949; (for children) Stanley J. Kunitz, editor, *Junior Book of Authors,* revised edition, H. W. Wilson, 1951.

ARENELLA, Roy   1939-

PERSONAL: Born July 3, 1939, in Brooklyn, N.Y.; son of John James and Ann (Aguanno) Arenella; married Martine Hahn, December 14, 1973; children: Kenneth. *Education:* Columbia College, B.A., 1961. *Home:* 410 Westminster Road, Brooklyn, N.Y. 11218.

CAREER: New York City Department of Social Services, New York, N.Y., family caseworker, 1962-67, 1969-71; The Tutoring School of New York, New York, N.Y., tutor, 1968; New York City Human Resources Administration, New York, N.Y., trainer, 1971—. *Exhibitions:* The Darkroom, one-man show, New York, N.Y., 1968; "Woodstock," The Public Theater, group show, New York, N.Y., 1970; The Little Photo Gallery, one-man show, New York, N.Y., 1974; "The First Post Card Show," group show, New York, N.Y., 1975; "Language as Structure," Kensington Arts Association, group show, Toronto, Canada, 1976; Foto, one-man show, New York, N.Y., 1976; The Ameri-

can Cultural Center, one-man show, Paris, France, 1976; Musee Francais de La Photographie, group show, Versailles, France, 1976; Galleria Nadar, one-man show, Pisa, Italy, 1977-78. *Military service:* U.S. Army, private first class, Signal Corps, 1963-65.

ILLUSTRATOR: Lee Bennett Hopkins, editor, *City Talk,* Knopf, 1970; Jonathan Eisen, *The Age of Rock, Two* (one of several illustrators), Random House, 1970.

SIDELIGHTS: "I left college wanting to be a writer, but several years later, while in the Army, decided on photography as the way to 'express' my sense of the world. I taught myself in the post's recreation center which had a well-equipped darkroom. Several years after this I studied for six months with David Vestal and began to find my own direction.

"I've always been interested in poetry and wrote it, but not to my satisfaction, until the late sixties when I discovered the concrete or visual poetry movement (which was then coming to the fore in America). My interest in this kind of poetry, some of which appeals very strongly to the eye, has remained constant.

"In the past several years I've combined photography and visual poetry by making photographic prints from hand-

There are
Many street signs.
Signs are many colors
Some say STOP, GO, SLOW, WAIT, and WALK. . .
SLOW DOWN!
■ (From *City Talk* by Lee Bennett Hopkins. Photographs by Roy Arenella.)

ROY ARENELLA

drawn negatives. My interest is in that area where words and images meet and where words, literally, *become,* images.

"I've continued through my 'straight' photography, finding in that direction the most consistently satisfactory way to make sense of the world as I see it."

ARMOUR, Richard 1906-

PERSONAL: Born July 25, 1906 in San Pedro, Calif.; son of Harry Willard and Sue (Wheelock) Armour; married Kathleen Stevens, 1932; children: Geoffrey, Karin. *Education:* Pomona College, California, B.A.; Harvard University, M.A., 1928, Ph.D., 1933. *Politics:* Democrat. *Religion:* Protestant. *Home:* 460 Blaisdell Dr., Claremont, Calif.

CAREER: University of Texas, Austin, instructor, 1928-29; Northwestern University, Evanston, Ill., instructor, 1930-31; College of the Ozarks, Clarksville, Ark., professor, 1932-33; University of Freiburg, Germany, American lecturer, 1933-34; Wells College, Aurora, N.Y., professor, 1934-45; Scripps College, Claremont, Calif., professor of English, 1945—, dean of the faculty, 1961-63; Claremont Graduate School, Claremont, Calif., professor of English, 1946-63, Balch Lecturer in English Literature, 1963-66, dean and professor emeritus, 1966—. Carnegie Visiting Professor, University of Hawaii, 1957; American Specialist Abroad for U.S. State Department in Europe and Asia, 1964-70. Trustee, Claremont Men's College, 1968—. Author and lecturer. *Military service:* U.S. Army, Antiaircraft Artillery, 1942-46, 1950; became colonel; received Legion of Merit with oak leaf cluster. *Member:* P.E.N., California Writers Guild, Modern Language Association, American Association of University Professors, Sunset Club. *Awards, honors:* Harvard research scholar at John Forster Library, Victoria and Albert Museum, London, 1931; Ford Foundation Faculty Fellow; Litt.D., College of Ozarks, 1944, and Pomona College, 1972; L.H.D., Whittier College, 1968, Southern California School of Optometry, 1972; LL.D., College of Idaho, 1969, Claremont Men's College, 1974.

WRITINGS: Barry Cornwall, Meador Publishing Co., 1935; (editor) *The Literary Recollections of Barry Cornwall,* Meador Publishing Co., 1935.

(Editor with Raymond F. Howes) *Coleridge, the Talker,*
Cornell University Press, 1940; (editor) *Young Voices,*
Wells College Press, 1941; *Yours for the Asking,* Humphries, 1942; (with Bown Adams) *To These Dark Steps,*
New York Institute for the Education of the Blind, 1943;
Privates' Lives (verse), Ryerson, 1944; *Leading with My
Left,* Beechurst Press, 1946; *Golf Bawls,* Beechurst Press,
1946; *Writing Light Verse,* Writer, Inc., 1947, revised edition, 1968.

For Partly Proud Parents, Harper, 1950; *It All Started with
Columbus,* McGraw, 1953, revised edition, 1961; *Light
Armour,* McGraw, 1954; *It All Started with Europa,* McGraw, 1955; *It All Started with Eve,* McGraw, 1956;
Twisted Tales from Shakespeare, McGraw, 1957; *It All
Started with Marx,* McGraw, 1958; *Nights with Armour,*
McGraw, 1958; *Drug Store Days,* McGraw, 1959 (published
in England under title *Pills, Potions and Granny,* Hammond, Hammond & Co.)

The Classics Reclassified, McGraw, 1960; *Golf Is a Four-
Letter Word,* McGraw, 1962; *Armour's Almanac,* McGraw,
1962; *The Medical Muse,* McGraw, 1963; *American Lit Relit,* McGraw, 1964; *The Year Santa Went Modern,* McGraw, 1964; *Our Presidents,* Norton, 1964; *Through Darkest Adolescence with Tongue in Cheek and Pen in
Checkbook,* McGraw, 1964; *The Adventures of Egbert the
Easter Egg,* McGraw, 1965; *Going Around in Academic
Circles,* McGraw, 1965; *Animals on the Ceiling,* McGraw,
1966; *Punctured Poems,* Prentice-Hall, 1966; *It All Started
with Hippocrates,* McGraw, 1966; *It All Started with Stones
and Clubs,* McGraw, 1967; *A Dozen Dinosaurs,* McGraw,
1967; *Odd Old Mammals,* McGraw, 1968; *My Life with
Women,* McGraw, 1968; *English Lit Relit,* McGraw, 1969;
On Your Marks: A Package of Punctuation, McGraw, 1969;
A Diabolical Dictionary of Education, World, 1969, McGraw, 1970.

All Sizes and Shapes of Monkeys and Apes, McGraw, 1970;
A Short History of Sex, McGraw, 1970; *Who's in Holes?,*
McGraw, 1971; *Writing Light Verse and Prose Humor,*
Writer, Inc., 1971; *All in Sport,* McGraw, 1972; *Out of My
Mind,* McGraw, 1972; *The Strange Dreams of Rover Jones,*
McGraw, 1973; *It All Started with Freshman English,*
McGraw, 1973; *Going Like Sixty: A Lighthearted Look at
the Later Years,* McGraw, 1974; *Sea Full of Whales,* McGraw, 1974; *The Academic Bestiary,* Morrow, 1974; *The
Spouse in the House,* McGraw, 1975; *The Happy Bookers:
A History of Librarians and Their World,* McGraw, 1976; *It
All Would Have Startled Columbus,* McGraw, 1976; *It All
Started with Nudes: An Artful History of Art,* McGraw,
1977.

Contributor of some six thousand pieces of verse and prose
to more than two hundred magazines in America and England. Member of editorial board, *Writer;* department editor, *Quote.* Author of syndicated features weekly in over
three hundred newspapers.

SIDELIGHTS: "My kind of writing, short humor in light
verse and in prose, uses up ideas fast. This is especially true
of light verse. How I envy the writer of novels. Assuming a
novel requires one basic idea, or one idea to get it off the
ground and moving, a novelist needs only one idea every
twelve months, if he is so prolific as to write a novel a year.
More likely, he needs only one idea every three or four
years. Since I am currently selling slightly over two hundred

RICHARD ARMOUR

pieces a year, about thirty of them prose articles, and the
rest light verse, I must have a new idea a little oftener than
one every other day, seven days a week, or three-fourths of
an idea a day.

"Of course my ideas can be, and usually are, very small
ones, since I am writing only a few lines and not *War and
Peace.* Let me give you an example of a really tiny idea,
nothing more than a stock phrase that I thought I might give
a fresh twist. The phrase that popped into my mind was 'out
of the woods.' Somehow this suggested another much-used
phrase. I rubbed the two together and got this small spark,
which ultimately appeared in *The Wall Street Journal:*

PROGRESS REPORT

I'm out of the woods at last, I say,
And at first it is quite a thrill.
Till I notice that though I am out of the woods
I'm also over the hill.

"That was an easy one, a simple idea and a simple piece of
versification. Playing with words, phrases, and clichés is
probably what I do most. But sometimes I fool around with
rhymes. I find that if I start with an unusual polysyllabic
rhyme, I continue with it, and the rhyming may be more fun
for the reader than the idea. Here is another piece that was
sold to *The Wall Street Journal,* but this time it depended
largely on its rhymes:

Great men have been born in log cabins, great souls;
Great otters, no doubt, have been born in log holes.
■ (From *Who's in Holes?* by Richard Armour. Illustrated by Paul Galdone.)

OH, HORRORS!

Horror movies don't much enlighten me,
They do, however, manage to frighten me.
They tell of happenings weird and miraculous
And ghosts and monsters and horrible Draculas.

The movie ended, I go to my beddy-bye,
Which I stand for a moment slightly unsteady by.
I'm only human, I'm not a Titan. . . .
I go to sleep with my bedside light on.

"The late, wonderful Ogden Nash was, of course, the master when it came to ingenious, unexpected rhymes. He probably would have spelled it not 'Draculas' but 'Draculous,' and I thought of doing it that way, but was afraid of being thought a Nash imitator. Not that I don't imitate him occasionally, as I imitate Samuel Hoffenstein and Arthur Guiterman and David McCord and Phyllis McGinley and Morris Bishop and all the other light verse writers I read and admire. But it is subconscious imitation, as practiced by most writers—imitation which puts your individual mark on what is being imitated and makes it your own. (Think of the dramatists who have imitated, or been influenced by, Shakespeare; the novelists who have imitated Hemingway.)

"In the verse about horror movies, I didn't depend entirely on rhymes. Rhymes alone, I realized, would not have been enough. I had a little more to say in the second stanza. In a sense, I made into a very short story what began only as a statement. You will also notice that I pictured myself as something of a coward—which happens to be the truth. The humor writer—whether in verse or prose—frequently reveals some personal weakness, he can't make a hero of himself.

"But at the same time you need to link yourself with others. You will notice my reference to being 'only human.' My guess is that I am not alone in being so frightened by a horror movie that I leave my bedside light on. If I were, my idea wouldn't be a good one—or a saleable one, the two perhaps being synonymous.

"I keep a rhyming dictionary close at hand, but seldom use it. Once I used it a good deal, but after twenty-five years of tinkering with rhymes every day I get along pretty well on my own. Also, I like now and then to think up a rhyme that isn't listed. A couple of years ago I was going abroad and had to have the usual shots. Inoculation is an experience that always leaves marks not only on my arm, but on my psyche. While I was waiting in the doctor's office (a place where I get quite a bit of writing done, trying to keep my mind off what is ahead of me), I wrote these lines (without benefit of a rhyming dictionary), which I placed with *Family Health:*

TRAVEL SHOTS

Shots for cholera, shots for tetanus,
Thanks to hypos, vaccines getinus,
Shots for typhoid, shots for diphtheria,
Shots for algae found in Algeria. . . .
Arms enlarge like red flags unfurled
From shots that hurt around the world.

"I think light verse should be fun all the way, but it helps to have something a little extra at the end. That is why I pushed the needle a bit harder in that last line with the double punning, first with 'shots' and then with 'hurt.'

"Puns (and all kinds of wordplay) are the stock-in-trade of the light verse writer, but the stock should be kept as fresh as possible. Also, anything of the sort should be an extra embellishment, along with playful, unusual rhymes. At the heart of the thing is still the idea.

"To emphasize this, let me give you an example of a piece of light verse that has no puns and no out-of-the-ordinary rhymes. It has only an idea, along with a figure of speech, a mixture of metaphor and personification. Except for that touch of whimsy in the last line, it is simply the straight statement of an idea in verse. Here it is, as it appeared in *Family Weekly:*

FOOLED AGAIN

I must confess I look askance
At plastic flowers, plastic plants,
The ones that look so very real
That I must sidle up and feel.
It really doesn't seem quite right,
Infringing on the copyright.
And making false so much like true:
If I were Nature, I would sue.

"In the fourth line, I originally had 'get up close,' but I think you will agree that 'sidle up' is an improvement. There is something appropriately unsure and sly about it. Someone might be watching me, say the owner of the plant, and it might be the real thing, after all.

"When I leave the house, I feel in my pockets to make sure I have three things; my keys, my wallet, and my notebook and pen. This last is the most important. I can never tell when an idea may spring up, and it is always a struggle to keep it in mind until materials are available for writing it down. Sometimes an idea has come to me and, not having my notebook and pen, I have lost the thought and never been able to dredge it up again, hard as I might try. I have stopped while jogging to write down an idea or a first line. I have had an idea or a rhyme or a full-blown quatrain while shaving, while taking a shower, and in church.

"Next to the doctor's office, I find church my most creative place. Usually, my mind wanders, and what I write has no connection with the sermon. On one occasion, however, I wrote a piece of light verse after hearing a sermon our minister gave about the conscience. I can't remember what he said, but I remember what I wrote:

ON MY CONSCIENCE

My conscience is a small, weak thing.
Unhandsome, too. So be it.
I'm glad, unlike my nose and hair,
It's hidden deep within me where
My friends and foes can't see it.

"It must have been on my conscience that I wrote this when I should have been listening. Anyhow, as I left the church and shook hands with the minister and congratulated him on his inspiring sermon (it had inspired me five lines worth), I handed him a copy of my little poem.

"Apparently I didn't make clear to him that it was my own composition, written in church. The next Sunday, when I shook hands with him and complimented him on his sermon, he thanked me for the poem I had given him the Sunday before and asked me who wrote it. He thought it was something I had run across somewhere and was stimulated by his sermon into reading. I tried to tell him I was the author, but by that time he was shaking hands with the next person in line. Perhaps it is just as well for him to think I am jotting down the best parts of his sermons when I scribble in that little notebook I always have with me.

"As I said at the outset, humor writing uses up ideas at a frightening rate. I try not to use the same idea twice, though I have probably done so (I hope giving it a different treatment each time). I must confess, however, that I have occasionally used the same idea for a prose article and a piece of light verse. Once, for instance, I came across the following item in a newspaper; 'Always approach a strange dog with the back of the hand outstretched.' From this I got an article for 'The Phoenix Nest' of the old *Saturday Review* and a piece of light verse for *Quote*. They were so different, both in technique and in approach to the subject, that there was not the slightest repetition.

"It is the shortness of light verse that causes this eating up of ideas. And yet it is the shortest light verse that is usually the easiest to sell, since it is often used, as cartoons are used, as a filler. A couplet or a quatrain has more chance of sale than something sixteen or twenty lines long. At the height, and I do mean height, of miniskirts, I sold this two-liner to the *Reader's Digest:*

If fashions change, you'll find, in most cases,
Girls with long skirts and men with long faces.

"I had never thought of it until now, but I suppose short verse and short skirts have something in common. I don't know what that is, but when I figure it out I'll write a piece of verse about it.

"Always looking. For an idea, that is."

FOR MORE INFORMATION SEE: Library Journal, November 1, 1964; *Book Week,* December 13, 1964, May 16, 1965.

ARTZYBASHEFF, Boris (Miklailovich) 1899-1965

PERSONAL: Surname is pronounced Art-zee-*bash*-eff; born May 25, 1899, in Kharkov, Ukraine, Russia; came to the United States in 1919; naturalized in 1926; son of Michael Petrovich (an author and playwright) and Anna Vasilievna (Koboushko) Artzybasheff; married Elisabeth Southard Snyder, February 22, 1930. *Education:* Attended Prince Tenishev's School, St. Petersburg (now Leningrad). *Religion:* Russian Greek Orthodox. *Home:* Old Lyme, Connecticut.

CAREER: Author and illustrator. Became a seaman after the Russian Revolution, 1919; worked for a brief time in an engraver's shop in New York; began designing restaurant murals and stage sets, 1922; commissioned to illustrate books, beginning 1922; served as a consultant of graphic presentation of facts for the U.S. Department of State and the Psychological Warfare Department during the Second World War; started illustrating magazine covers for *Life, Fortune,* and *Time,* 1937. His works have been in numerous exhibitions in New York, Boston, and Paris. *Military service:* Served as a machine gunner in the Ukrainian Army, 1918-19. *Member:* Institute of Graphic Arts, Society of Illustrators, Royal Society of Arts (fellow; London), Grolier

BORIS ARTZYBASHEFF, 1960

Club, Century Club. *Awards, honors:* New York Herald Tribune Spring Book Festival Award, 1937, for *Seven Simeons;* runner-up for the Caldecott Medal, 1938, for *Seven Simeons; Gay-Neck* written by Dhan Gopal Mukerji and illustrated by Boris Artzybasheff won the Newbery Medal in 1928.

WRITINGS—All self-illustrated: *Poor Shaydullah,* Macmillan, 1931; *Seven Simeons: A Russian Tale,* Viking, 1937, reprinted, 1965; *As I See,* Dodd, 1954.

Illustrator: Dmitrii Narkisovich Mamin, *Verotchka's Tales,* Dutton, 1922; Harriet Martineau, *Feats on the Fiord,* Macmillan, 1924; Padraic Colum, *Forge in the Forest,* Macmillan, 1925; Margery Bianco, *Apple Tree,* Doran, 1926; Sonia Lustig, *Roses of the Winds,* Doubleday, 1926; Theodore A. and Winifred M. Harper, *Siberian Gold,* Doubleday, 1927; Alfred Kreymborg, *Funnybone Alley,* Macaulay, 1927; Dhan Gopal Mukerji, *Gay-Neck,* Dutton, 1927, reprinted, 1968; Ella Young, *Wonder Smith and His Son,* Longmans, 1927, reissued, 1957; *Fairy Shoemaker, and Other Fairy Poems,* Macmillan, 1928; D. G. Mukerji, *Ghond, the Hunter,* Dutton, 1928; *Herodotus,* edited by Gordon King, Doubleday, Doran, 1929; Jacques Dorey, *Three and the Moon,* Knopf, 1929.

P. Colum, *Orpheus: Myths of the World,* Macmillan, 1930; George Edward Bock, *What Makes the Wheels Go 'Round,* Macmillan, 1931; Henriette Celairie, *Behind Moroccan Walls,* Macmillan, 1931, reprinted, Books for Libraries, 1970; (and editor) *Aesop's Fables,* Viking, 1933; Hugh J. Chisholm, *This Casual Glory,* Ashlar Press, 1934; Robert Nathan, *Jonah; or, The Withering Vine,* Knopf, 1934; Charles Grandison Finney, *Circus of Dr. Lao,* Viking, 1935; Maude Barrows Lynch, *Henry the Navigator,* Thomas Nelson, 1935; *Arabian Nights,* edited by Edward L. Thorndike, Appleton-Century, 1937; Helen Haskell, *Nadya Makes Her Bow,* Dutton, 1938; Honore de Balzac, *Droll Stories,* translated by Jacques Le Clercq, Heritage Press, 1939, reissued, 1965; Youel Benjamin Mirza, *Rug That Went to Mecca,*

Stokes Publishing, 1939; Anna Gertrude Hall, *Nansen,* Viking, 1940; Ruth P. Smith, editor, *Tree of Life,* Viking, 1942.

SIDELIGHTS: Artzybasheff arrived in New York Harbor in 1919. He had no friends or relatives with whom he could stay, no knowledge of the English language, and only a few Turkish coins in his pocket. However, through the aid of an immigration official, the young Russian managed to find work in an engraving shop. It wasn't long before Artzybasheff was given the opportunity to demonstrate his skill as an illustrator, and within three months some of his caricatures were published by the New York *World.* Encouraged by his success, the young artist approached the engraver for an increase in pay only to be turned down.

A disappointed Artzybasheff went back to sea on an oil tanker bound for Mexico and South America. During the five months spent on board, the Russian artist learned to speak English from his fellow sailors. Upon his return to New York, Artzybasheff's attempts to establish himself as an independent artist brought an assortment of assignments ranging from designing stage sets for Michel Foline's ballets to fashioning inexpensive clothing for women.

In 1926, the illustrator became a United States citizen. This permitted him to spend an extensive period of time in Paris to further his career as an artist. Artzybasheff held two one-man shows in Paris between 1926 and 1930 and at one point was even commissioned to design a cathedral altar.

The Russian-American's talent for designing statistical charts, graphs, and maps in an attractive yet simplified manner was brought to the attention of United States government officials during the Second World War. In addition to his duties as a graphic consultant to the Department of State, Artzybasheff also supervised the production of an atlas used by the Army Training Command and designed insignias for several units of the armed forces.

Although the author-illustrator used a number of different methods and materials in his works, he was perhaps most noted for his *Time* magazine illustrations of humanized machines and portraits of people in the news. The artist designed his first cover for *Time* magazine in 1941. In all, Artzybasheff's art work appeared on two hundred and nineteen covers of *Time* from 1941 through 1965.

HOBBIES AND OTHER INTERESTS: Boating, fishing, and hunting.

FOR MORE INFORMATION SEE: Howard Simon, *500 Years of Art in Illustration,* Garden City Publishers, 1942; *Current Biography Yearbook,* 1945; (for children) Stanley J. Kunitz, editor, *Junior Book of Authors,* second edition, H. W. Wilson, 1951; L. S. Bechtel, "Boris Artzybasheff," *Horn Book,* April, 1966.

Obituaries: *New York Times,* July 18, 1965; *Time,* July 23, 1965; *Newsweek,* July 26, 1965; *Library Journal,* September 15, 1965; *Current Biography Yearbook,* 1965.

(Died July 16, 1965)

ATKINSON, Margaret Fleming

PERSONAL: Born in Washington, D.C. *Education:* Studied art in college. *Home:* Washington, D.C.

CAREER: Author and illustrator of books for young people. Has worked as a department store art director and as an organizer of Cooperative Handicrafts, Inc., in Puerto Rico, 1936.

WRITINGS: How to Raise Your Puppy (self-illustrated), Greenberg, 1944; *Care for Your Kitten,* Greenberg, 1946; *It's Fun to Help at Home* (self-illustrated), 1947; (with Nancy Draper) *Ballet for Beginners,* Knopf, 1951, reprinted, 1964; (with May Hillman, pseudonym of May B. Hipshman) *Dancers of the Ballet,* Knopf, 1955, 3rd edition, 1965.

SIDELIGHTS: The *Library Journal* review of Margaret F. Atkinson's *How to Raise Your Puppy* said, "[The] book covers everything a small child needs to know about care and training of a young dog. Also, much information that adults will welcome. Clever pictures dramatize instructions in how to pick up a puppy, what and when to feed him, how to housebreak, train and care for him."

Horn Book's description of *Ballet for Beginners* included, "Photographs and charts along with clearly-written text show the basic ballet positions and tell children how to practice. Included also are several pages with music adapted and arranged by Beatrix B. Woolard; photographs and brief biographical sketches of a few famous ballerinas; a history of the ballet; synopses of some of the ballets especially appeal-

The daws on the elms
Kept tribal speech,
And he perched there,
Within a hand's reach--
■ (From *Creatures* by Padraic Colum. Illustrated by Boris Artzybasheff.)

Their backs are not yet strong, and they have difficulty keeping their balance. ■ (From *Ballet for Beginners* by Nancy Draper and Margaret F. Atkinson. Photos by Fred Lyon.)

ing to young people; and a dictionary of ballet terms." The *New York Herald Tribune* added, "Probably no little girl should try to follow all this at home. But it may persuade more parents to let their young daughters join similar classes, and will supplement them most hopefully. Also, it is a charming introduction for non-dancers to this art, and to its basic techniques."

"The mere sight of this volume," wrote *New Yorker* of *Dancers of the Ballet*, "with its stunning photographs of forty outstanding dancers of the United States, England, and France, is likely to raise girls of over eight sur les pointes. The accompanying biographies are written in a chatty and somewhat breathless style, though less disturbingly so than most books on the subject." *Horn Book* commented, "The authors have written in a lively style, with many anecdotes.... An exceptionally good photograph of the star dancing accompanies each biography and the book is so well designed that it is one of the most attractive—and will no doubt be also one of the most popular—of the many ballet books...." The *San Francisco Chronicle* added, "Obviously designed for the young adult market, it is apt to smack of the sugar-plum-fairy backstage atmosphere in the hands of the mature reader. However, for its very scope alone, it is not without a certain value to the adult balletomane."

BAILEY, Bernadine Freeman

PERSONAL: Born in Mattoon, Ill.; daughter of Thomas Oscar and Nellie (Voigt) Freeman; married John Hays Bailey (divorced). *Education:* Wellesley College, B.A.; University of Chicago, M.A., Sorbonne, University of Paris, certificate. *Home:* 777 N. Michigan Ave., Chicago Ill. 60611.

CAREER: Laidlaw Brothers, Chicago, Ill., assistant editor; W. F. Quarrie Co. (now part of Field Enterprises), Chicago, Ill., directing staff editor of *Childcraft;* free-lance writer, mainly of books for young people, whose travel picture files form the basis for a business, 'Round the World Photos, Chicago, Ill. *Member:* National Woman's Book Association, Society of Midland Authors, Mystery Writers of America, Alliance Francaise, Press Club (London), Chicago Press Club, Women's Athletic Club, Arts Club (Chicago). *Awards, honors:* French decoration, Commander of the Order of Arts, Science and Letters, 1975.

WRITINGS: The Follett Picture-Story of Indians, Follett, 1936; (with Zabeth Selover) *Homes of Long Ago,* Follett, 1937; (with Selover) *Homes of Today,* Follett, 1937; *Puckered Moccasins: A Tale of Old Fort Dearborn,* Whitman,

The charm of colonial days can still be found in winding roads and old covered bridges.
■ (From *Connecticut* by Bernadine Bailey. Illustrated by Kurt Wiese.)

1937; (with Selover) *Cave, Castle, and Cottage*, Follett, 1937; (photographs by author) *Little Greta of Denmark*, Grosset, 1939.

(Photographs by author) *Little Lauri of Finland*, Grosset, 1940; (photographs by author) *The Little Woodsman of the North*, Grosset, 1940; *Abe Lincoln's Other Mother*, Messner, 1941; *The Story of Abraham Lincoln*, Rand McNally, 1942; *The Youngest WAAC*, Messner, 1943; *The Youngest WAAC Overseas*, Messner, 1944; *The Youngest WAAC Comes Home*, Messner, 1946; (adapter with Frank Lee Beals) *Story of Treasure Island*, Sanborn, 1947; (adapter with Beals) *The Story of the Three Musketeers*, Sanborn, 1948.

Forest and Fiords, Beckley-Cardy, 1952; *Maureen Marshall, Private Eye*, Dodd, 1953; *To London, to London*, Beckley-Cardy, 1954; *Einar: The Story of an Icelandic Boy*, Hutchinson, 1954; *Here's Carlos of Mexico*, Beckley-Cardy, 1955; *Carol Carson: Books Across the Border*, Dodd, 1956; *Paris, I Love You*, Dodd, 1958; *Juan Ponce de Leon: First in the Land*, Houghton, 1958; *Famous Latin-American Liberators*, Dodd, 1960; *Abraham Lincoln: Man of Courage*, Houghton, 1960; *Christopher Columbus: Sailor and Dreamer*, Houghton, 1960; *Famous Modern Explorers*, Dodd, 1963; *Denmark: Wonderland of Work and Play*, Dodd, 1966; *Austria and Switzerland: Alpine Countries*, Thomas Nelson, 1969; *The Captive Nations: Our First Line of Defense*, Hallberg, 1969; *José*, Houghton, 1969; *Wonders of the World of Bears*, Dodd, 1975.

"Picture Story Series": *Bolivia in Story and Pictures*, and five other books with similar titles, on Ecuador, Greenland, Iceland, Peru, Venezuela, all published by Whitman, 1942, books on Bolivia and Greenland reissued by Sterling, 1974, new books on Malawi, Madagascar, and Rhodesia published by Sterling, 1974; *Picture Book of Illinois*, and fifty-one other books with similar titles for each state of the Union plus Puerto Rico and Washington, D.C., all published by Whitman, 1949-1962, revised editions, illustrated by Kurt Wiese, 1964-71.

Contributor of some two hundred articles to publications, including *Reader's Digest, Today's Health, Travel, Ford Times, News Digest International* (Australia), *Lady* (England), *Christian Science Monitor, New York Times, Chicago Tribune, Wide World* (England).

SIDELIGHTS: "I have been very fortunate in having the opportunity to travel all over the world, first with my mother and uncle, and later by myself. After seeing how the people in Europe, Russia, Africa, South America, and the Orient live and work and play, I like to tell other people about them. Also, I like adventure of all kinds, even though it may have an element of danger. That is why I spent a night with the head-hunters in Borneo, why I went to the bottom of Lake Geneva (Switzerland) in Piccard's new mesoscaph, why I went on a seal-hunting trip in the frozen Arctic, why I went down the Mississippi in the old stern-wheeler, the Delta Queen, why I traveled in England in an old-time 'coach and four,' why I crossed Kansas in a covered wagon, why I went down the Nile to see the building of the Aswan Dam, and many more exciting experiences all over the globe. I've written articles about these adventures and may put them all in a book some day. In the course of all these travels and adven-

BERNADINE BAILEY

tures I have met some fabulous people: the Queen Mother of England, the oil-rich Ibn Saud of Saudia, Arabia, the mayor of Paris, the Archbishop of Canterbury, the Prime Minister of Rhodesia, and many others.

"When I'm not traveling I stay home and write about the places and people I have seen. For fun, I like to dance and go to the theatre. As a young woman, I won the woman's tennis championship in my home town of Mattoon, Illinois. Now I like to swim, play golf, and ice skate, but am not very good at any of them. Recently I've taken up Yoga, which I think is wonderful."

Several of Bernadine Bailey's books have been translated into Spanish and one into German; more than sixty currently are in print.

FOR MORE INFORMATION SEE: Chicago Schools Journal, Supplement, May, 1951.

BAILEY, Carolyn Sherwin   1875-1961

PERSONAL: Born October 25, 1875, in Hoosick Falls, New York; daughter of Charles Henry (a scientist and traveler) and Emma Frances (a teacher and writer; maiden name, Blanchard) Bailey; married Eben Clayton Hill (a radiologist), 1936. *Education:* Educated at home until age 12; attended Lansingburgh Academy, and later Teachers College, Columbia University (graduated, 1896), Montessori School (Rome), and the New York School of Social Work. *Politics:* Republican. *Religion:* Episcopalian. *Home:* "Hillcrest," Temple, New Hampshire.

CAROLYN SHERWIN BAILEY

CAREER: Author and editor of books for children. Worked as a teacher in New York and as a principal in Springfield, Massachusetts; did social work at Warren Goddar House in New York. Editor of the children's department of *Delineator,* and of *American Childhood,* 1924-35. *Member:* Pen and Brush Club (New York); Mount Vernon Town Club (Baltimore). *Awards, honors:* Newbery Medal, 1947, for *Miss Hickory.*

WRITINGS—For children: *The Peter Newell Mother Goose* (illustrated by Peter Newell), Holt, 1905; (editor with Clara M. Lewis) *For the Children's Hour* (illustrated by G. William Breck), M. Bradley, 1906, reprinted, Gale, 1974; *Firelight Stories* (illustrated by Diantha W. Horne), M. Bradley, 1907; *Stories and Rhymes for a Child* (illustrated by Christine Wright), M. Bradley, 1909; *Girls' Make-at-Home Things,* F. A. Stokes, 1912; (with sister Marian Elizabeth Bailey) *Boys' Make-at-Home Things,* F. A. Stokes, 1912; *For the Story Teller,* M. Bradley, 1913, reprinted, Gale, 1975; *The Children's Book of Games and Parties,* M. A. Donohue, 1913; *Every Child's Folk Songs and Games,* M. Bradley, 1914; *Stories for Sunday Telling,* Pilgrim Press, 1916; (editor) *Stories Children Need,* M. Bradley, 1916; *For the Children's Hour,* two volumes (illustrated by Frederick A. Nagler), M. Bradley, 1916; *Stories for Any Day,* Pilgrim Press, 1917; *Boys and Girls of Colonial Days* (illustrated by Uldene Shriver), A. Flanagan, 1917.

What to Do for Uncle Sam, A. Flanagan, 1918; *Stories for Every Holiday,* Abingdon Press, 1918, reprinted, Gale, 1974; (editor) *Tell Me Another Story,* M. Bradley, 1918; *Once upon a Time Animal Stories,* M. Bradley, 1918; *The Outdoor Story Book,* Pilgrim Press, 1918; *Stories of Great Adventures (Adapted from the Classics)* (illustrated by Clara M. Burd), M. Bradley, 1919; *Folk Stories and Fables* (illustrated by F. A. Nagler), M. Bradley, 1919; *Hero Stories* (illustrated by Frederick Knowles), M. Bradley, 1919; *Broad Stripes and Bright Stars: Stories of American History* (illustrated by Power O'Malley), M. Bradley, 1919, reissued as *Boy Heroes in Making America* (illustrated by Lea Norris and P. O'Malley), A. Flanagan, 1931; *Everyday Stories* (illustrated by F. Knowles), M. Bradley, 1919.

The Enchanted Bugle, and Other Stories, F. A. Owen, 1920; *Wonder Stories: The Best Myths for Boys and Girls* (illustrated by Clara M. Burd), M. Bradley, 1920; (editor) *Merry Tales for Children: Best Stories of Humor for Boys and Girls,* M. Bradley, 1921; *The Torch of Courage, and Other Stories,* M. Bradley, 1921; *Flint: The Story of a Trail* (illustrated by Charles Lassell), M. Bradley, 1922; *Friendly Tales: A Community Story Book,* M. Bradley, 1923; *Bailey's In and Outdoor Play-Games: Boys' and Girls' Book of What to Play and Make* (illustrated by Cobb Shinn), A. Whitman, 1923; *When Grandfather Was a Boy,* Pilgrim Press, 1923; *Reading Time Stories,* A. Whitman, 1923; *Stories from an Indian Cave: The Cherokee Cave Builders* (illustrated by Joseph Eugene Dash), A. Whitman, 1924; *Boys and Girls of Pioneer Days, from Washington to Lincoln,* A. Flanagan, 1924; *Little Men and Women Stories,* A. Whitman, 1924; *Lincoln Time Stories,* A. Whitman, 1924; (editor) *In the Animal World,* M. Bradley, 1924; *All the Year Play Games: Boys' and Girls' Book of Merry Pastimes* (illustrated by C. Shinn), A. Whitman, 1924.

The Wonderful Tree and Golden Day Stories (illustrated by J. E. Dash), A. Whitman, 1925; *The Wonderful Days* (illustrated by C. B. Falls), 1925; *Boys and Girls of Discovery Days* (illustrated by Dorothy Dulin), A. Flanagan, 1926; *The Wonderful Window, and Other Stories* (illustrated by

She lit the skies to charm their eyes with many Christmas tapers.
She spread the ground with snowy rugs to help their merry capers.
■ (From *A Christmas Party* by Carolyn Sherwin Bailey. Pictures by Cyndy Szekeres.)

Katherine R. Wireman), Cokesbury Press, 1926; *Untold History Stories* (illustrated by Lillian O. Titus), F. A. Owen, 1927; *Forest, Field, and Stream Stories* (illustrated by D. Dulin), A. Flanagan, 1928; *Sixty Games and Pastimes for all Occasions* (illustrated by C. Shinn), A. Whitman, 1928; *Boys and Girls of Today: A First Book of Citizenship,* A. Flanagan, 1928; *Read Aloud Stories* (illustrated by Hildegard Lupprian), M. Bradley, 1929; *Boys and Girls of Modern Days* (illustrated by D. Dulin), A. Flanagan, 1929; *Garden, Orchard, and Meadow Stories* (illustrated by Dulin), A. Flanagan, 1929.

Plays for the Children's Hour, M. Bradley, 1931; (editor) *Stories Children Want* (illustrated by Jack Perkins), M. Bradley, 1931; (editor) *Schoolroom Plans and Projects,* M. Bradley, 1932; (editor) *The Story-Telling Hour,* Dodd, 1934; *Tell Me a Birthday Story* (illustrated by Margaret Ayer), F. A. Stokes, 1935; *Children of the Handcrafts* (illustrated by Grace Paull; Junior Literary Guild selection), Viking Press, 1935, reissued, 1962; *Tops and Whistles: True Stories of Early American Toys and Children* (illustrated by Paull), Viking Press, 1937; *From Moccasins to Wings: Stories of Our Travel Ways* (illustrated by Margaret Ayer), M. Bradley, 1938; *Li'l' Hannibal,* Platt & Munk, 1938.

Homespun Playdays (illustrated by G. Paull), Viking Press, 1941; *Country-Stop* (illustrated by Paull), Viking Press, 1942 (published in England as *Wishing-Well House,* Muller, 1950); *Pioneer Art in America* (illustrated by G. Paull; Junior Literary Guild selection), Viking Press, 1944, reissued, 1966; *The Little Rabbit Who Wanted Red Wings* (illustrated by Dorothy Grider), Platt & Munk, 1945, reissued, 1961; *Miss Hickory* (illustrated by Ruth Gannett; Junior Literary Guild selection), Viking Press, 1946, reissued, 1968; *Merry Christmas Book* (illustrated by Eunice Young Smith), A. Whitman, 1948; *Old Man Rabbit's Dinner Party* (illustrated by Robinson), Platt & Munk, 1949, reissued, 1961; *Enchanted Village* (illustrated by Eileen Evans), Viking Press, 1950; *Finnegan II, His Nine Lives* (illustrated by Kate Seredy), Viking Press, 1953, reissued, 1968; *A Candle for Your Cake: Twenty-Four Birthday Stories of Famous Men and Women* (illustrated by M. Ayer), Lippincott, 1952; *The Little Red Schoolhouse* (illustrated by Dorothy Bayley Morse), Viking Press, 1957; *Flickertail* (illustrated by Garry McKenzie), H. Z. Walck, 1962; *A Christmas Party* (poem; illustrated by Cyndy Szekeres), Pantheon, 1975.

Other: (With Clara M. Lewis) *Daily Program of Gift and Occupation Work,* M. Bradley, 1904; *Montessori Children,*

FINNEGAN II
His Nine Lives
BY CAROLYN SHERWIN BAILEY
ILLUSTRATED BY KATE SEREDY
THE VIKING PRESS
New York

Not having known any home but the Alley, or any family except dim memories of his mother, who had lived across the way on MacDougal Street in a delicatessen shop, he had always shifted for himself. ■ (From *Finnegan II: His Nine Lives* by Carolyn Sherwin Bailey. Illustrated by Kate Seredy.)

Holt, 1915; (with E. Hershey Sneath, George Hodges, and Henry H. Tweedy) *The Way of the Gate,* Macmillan, 1917; *The Carolyn Sherwin Bailey Historical Collection of Children's Books: A Catalogue,* edited by Dorothy R. Davis, Southern Connecticut State College Press, 1966.

Also editor of editions of *The Three Musketeers* by Alexandre Dumas, *Lorna Doone* by Richard D. Blackmore, and *Evangeline* by Henry Wadsworth Longfellow. General editor, with Alice Hanthorn, of "Little Readers" series (illustrated by Ruth M. Hallock), McLoughlin Brothers, beginning 1934.

A dramatization of *Miss Hickory* was adapted by Ray Fowler and Barrett Clark as a Viking recorded book in 1972.

SIDELIGHTS: "The new-old art of story telling is being rediscovered. We are finding that the children's daily story hour in school, in the neighborhood house, and at home is a real force for mental and moral good in their lives. . . . There are good stories and there are poor stories for children. The story that fits a child's needs to-day may not prove a wise choice for him to-morrow. Some stories teach, some stories only give joy, some stories inspire, some stories just make a child laugh.

"Apperception is a formidable and sometimes confusing term for a very simple and easy-to-understand mental process. I once told Seumus MacManus' deliciously humorous story of Billy Beg and his Bull to a group of foreign boys and girls in one of New York's East Side Settlement Houses. The children listened with apparent appreciation, but, halfway along in the story, it occurred to me to ask them if they had ever seen a bull. No one answered me at first. Then Pietro, a little dusky-eyed son of Italy, raised a grimy hand.

"'I seen one last summer when we was on a *fresh-air,*' he said. 'It's a bigger cow, a bull is, with the bicycle handlebars on her head.'

"Pietro's description of a bull was an example of apperception, the method by means of which a new idea is interpreted, classified, 'let into' the human mind. He knew the class, *cows.* He also knew the class, *bicycles.* He did not know the class, *bulls*—at least vividly enough to be able to put the idea into terms of a verbal explanation and description. So he did the most natural thing in the world, the only possible mental process in fact by means of which children or adults classify the *new.* He interpreted it in terms of the old, explaining the unfamiliar idea, bull, by means of the familiar ideas, cow and a bicycle.

"This, then, is apperception. *It is the involuntary mental process by means of which the human mind makes its own the strange, the new, the unfamiliar idea by a method of fitting it into the class of familiar ideas already known.* Apperception is a means of quick mental interpretation. It is the welcoming of strangers to the mind-habitation, strangers who come every day in the guise of unfamiliar names, terms, scenes, and phrases, and determining in which corner of the brain house they will fit most comfortably. The most natural process is finally to give these new ideas an old mind corner to rest in, or an old brain path in which to travel.

"A child's mind at the age when he is able to concentrate upon listening to a story, three or four years of age—kindergarten age—is not a very crowded house. It is a mind-house tenanted by a few and very simple concepts

which he has made his own through his previous home, mother and play experiences. He is familiar with his nursery, his pets, his family, his toys, his food, his bed. If he is a country child he knows certain flowers, birds and farm animals, not as classes—flower, bird and animal—but as *buttercup, robin* and *sheep.* If he is a city child his mind has a very different tenantry, and he thinks in terms of *street, subway, park, fire engine, ambulance.* These to the city child are also individual ideas, not classes. He knows them as compelling, noisy, moving ideas which he has seen and experienced, but they do not at all appeal to him as classes. . . .

"*The apperceptive basis of story telling consists in study on the part of the story teller to discover what is the store of ideas in the minds of the children who will listen to the story.*

"Has the story too many new ideas for the child to be able to classify them in terms of his old ideas? On the other hand, has it one or two new thoughts so carefully presented through association with already familiar concepts that the child will be able to make them his own and give them a permanent place in his mind with the old ones?

"The story teller must ask herself these questions:

"'What do these children *know?*'

"'Have they any experience other than that of the home on which to bank?'

"'Do they come from homes of leisure or homes of industry?'

"'Have they had a country or a city experience?'

"'Have they passed from the stage of development when toys formed their play interest to the game stage in which chance and hazard interest them more deeply?'

"'Are they American children, familiar with American institutions, or are they little aliens in our land, unfamiliar with and confused by our ways?'

"When she has satisfactorily answered these questions, the story teller will select her story having for its theme, atmosphere and *motif* an idea or group of ideas that will touch the child's mental life as she has discovered it and by means of which it will find a permanent place in his mind through its comfortable friendliness and familiarity." [Carolyn Sherwin Bailey, *For the Story Teller,* Milton Bradley Co., 1913.[1]]

Bailey commented on story construction: "Cutting out unnecessary description, avoiding any explanation as to why you are telling the story, introducing your thunder clap, your trumpet, your story hero in the first sentence—this is the way to begin a story.

"Each emotion that will prevail over and influence human action in adult life may be appealed to in childhood through stories.

"Instinct may be defined as inherited memory.

"Suspense is the story quality that stimulates curiosity and in this way develops concentrated thinking on the part of the child.

"It seems to be almost impossible to find many instances of well constructed climax in the short story for children. The story teller must look for climax and in the event of not being able to find it in the story that she selects for telling, it will be necessary for her to make over her story ending that it may be a complete surprise to her listeners, in this way strengthening the plot greatly. Many stories just *stop*, giving one a feeling of dissatisfaction. There has been no climax to make of the whole a finished picture, complete in its minutest detail of light and shade and forming an unerasable vignette, on the child's mind.

"Climax knots the thread of the narrative."[1]

In 1947 Baldwin received the Newbery Medal for *Miss Hickory.* "Miss Hickory had her beginnings in a Victorian childhood. I had many dolls, among them an enchanting small creature named Elsie for the *Elsie* books. Her real hair was golden. Her small body was French bisque and her features were amiable. At an early age I decided to stitch up a dress for Elsie. I cut a straight piece of silk with slits for armholes and a gathering at the neck. Then I began a sleeve, an impossible task, for her arms were tiny and my skill slight. At that point I decided to have a tantrum.

"I see now the large red roses on the carpet that I kicked, watered with my tears, and among which I then lay and writhed. The house became still; no one paid heed to me. After a while a door opened and my grandmother came in. She did not speak to me. She gathered up Elsie and began putting the sleeves in the dress—so fascinating an occupation that it quieted me. I got up and leaned on her knee to watch. When the sewing was done, she spoke: 'My child, there is something we always have to keep in mind. A lady never expresses her feelings.'

"About that time the grandmother made me the first Miss Hickory, probably from the design of a pioneer childhood. I found Miss Hickory a stout companion. We lived under a lilac bush. Then she must have broken, and the years forgot her." ["Miss Hickory: Her Genealogy," by Carolyn Sherwin Bailey, *Newbery Medal Books: 1922-1955,* edited by Bertha Mahony Miller and Eleanor Whitney Field, The Horn Book, Inc., 1955.[2]]

"Two years ago I was sent to Florida. My typewriter took another route and disappeared. I developed hay fever; an argument for California. And I was homesick for the small mountain town in New Hampshire where for ten years I have spent the apple seasons. It is an austere land. They say, 'You don't plant in New Hampshire. You excavate!' It is also a beautiful and lovable land. They brought Willa Cather to a nearby God's Acre. One of her summer neighbors said, 'Fittin'! It's a good place for her to spend her time until 'The Day.' It is, for anyone.

"Well, there in Florida, sneezing and weeping hay-fever tears, I sharpened a pencil and got out some yellow paper. I knew I should write something, but I had no ideas. Suddenly I remembered Miss Hickory and she wrote her own story with very little help from me."[3]

Of one of her characters, Mr. T. Willard-Brown, *a cat,* she said: "I shall tell all Hillsborough what your given name is, *Tippy,* because you have a white tip to your tail. Willard is for the barn where you were born. Brown is pretense. The hyphen is putting on airs." ["Books and An Apple Orchard," by Jennie D. Lindquist, *Newbery Medal Books: 1922-1955,* edited by Bertha Mahony Miller and Elinor Whitney Field, The Horn Book, Inc., 1955.[3]]

Hers was a simple direct philosophy: "Touching a child's life through the medium of a story is like a friendly hand clasp."[1]

FOR MORE INFORMATION SEE: Jennie D. Lindquist, "Books and an Apple Orchard," *Horn Book,* July, 1947; May Massee, "Carolyn Sherwin Bailey Awarded Newbery Medal," *Library Journal,* July, 1947; (for children) Stanley J. Kunitz and Howard Haycraft, editors, *Junior Book of Authors,* second revised edition, H. W. Wilson, 1951; Dorothy R. Davis, *Carolyn Sherwin Bailey, 1875-1961: Profile and Bibliography,* Eastern Press, 1967; Obituaries—*New York Times,* December 25, 1961; *Publishers Weekly,* January 8, 1962.

(Died December, 1961)

BARRETT, Ron   1937-

PERSONAL: Surname "rhymes with carrot"; born July 25, 1937, in Bronx, N.Y.; son of James Aloysius (a liquor store clerk) and Lillian (Platzner; a bank clerk) Barrett; married Judi Bauman, June 20, 1962 (divorced March 8, 1976). *Education:* Pratt Institute, Brooklyn, N.Y., B.F.A., 1959. *Home:* 344 West 72nd St., New York, N.Y. 10023.

RON BARRETT

Now he had the world's largest and nicest birthday present. ■ (From *Benjamin's 365 Birthdays* by Judi Barrett. Illustrated by Ron Barrett.)

CAREER: William Douglas McAdams Pharmaceutical Advertising, New York, N.Y., designer, 1960-61; Brown & Maffei Advertising, New York, N.Y., art director, 1961-62; Young & Rubicam Advertising, New York, N.Y., art director, 1962-65; Carl Ally Advertising, New York, New York, art group head/vice-president, 1965-73; Pratt Institute, Brooklyn, N.Y., instructor, 1970-72; Electric Company Magazine, Children's Television Workshop, New York, N.Y., consulting art director and editor, 1973-75. *Exhibitions:* Musee Des Arts Decoratifs, The Louvre, Paris, France, 1973; Children's Book Exhibit, 1974. *Military service:* U.S. Army, six months active duty; National Guard, 1959-63. *Awards, honors:* American Institute of Graphic Arts, Childrens Books Show, certificate of excellence, for *Old MacDonald Had an Apartment House,* 1969, and *Benjamin's 365 Birthdays,* 1974; Children's Book Council Showcase Title, *Benjamin's 365 Birthdays,* 1975.

ILLUSTRATOR: Judith Barrett, *Old MacDonald Had an Apartment House,* Atheneum, 1969; Judith Barrett, *Animals Should Definitely Not Wear Clothing,* Atheneum, 1970; Judith Barrett, *Benjamin's 365 Birthdays,* Atheneum, 1974;

Marshall Efron and Alfa-Betty Olsen, *Bible Stories You Can't Forget No Matter How Hard You Try,* Dutton, 1976; Judith Barrett, *Cloudy with a Chance of Meatballs,* Atheneum, 1978.

SIDELIGHTS: "When I draw a children's book, I think of Richie Rich comics. They're very entertaining and they're available at newsstands everywhere for only thirty-five cents. I also think of donuts."

BARRY, James P(otvin)   1918-

PERSONAL: Born October 23, 1918, in Alton, Ill.; son of Paul A. (a U.S. army officer) and Elder (Potvin) Barry; married Anne Jackson (an education librarian), April 16, 1966. *Education:* Ohio State University, B.A. (cum laude with distinction), 1940; U.S. Army Command and General Staff College, honor graduate, 1959. *Home and office:* 353 Fairway Blvd., Columbus, Ohio 43213.

JAMES P. BARRY

CAREER: U.S. Army, Artillery, 1940-66, with world-wide assignments ranging from adviser to Turkish Army to staff and editorial work in the Pentagon; became colonel; Capital University, Columbus, Ohio, administrator, 1967-71; freelance writer and editor, 1971—. *Member:* Marine Historical Society, Great Lakes Historical Society, Ohio Historical Society, Phi Beta Kappa, Royal Canadian Yacht Club.

WRITINGS: (Illustrated with photographs by author) *Georgian Bay: The Sixth Great Lake* (adult), Clarke, Irwin, 1968; *The Battle of Lake Erie* (juvenile), Watts, 1970; *Bloody Kansas* (juvenile), Watts, 1972; *The Noble Experiment* (juvenile), Watts, 1972; (illustrated with photographs by author) *The Fate of the Lakes* (adult), Baker Book, 1972; (illustrated with photographs by author) *Ships of the Great Lakes* (adult), Howell-North, 1973; *The Louisiana Purchase* (juvenile), Watts, 1973; *Henry Ford and Mass Production* (juvenile), Watts, 1973; *The Berlin Olympics* (juvenile), Watts, 1975; (illustrated with photographs by author) *The Great Lakes: A First Book* (juvenile), Watts, 1976. Contributor of articles and reviews to journals and magazines. Former editor of military publications.

SIDELIGHTS: "I took my first voyage on a Great Lakes freighter at the age of eight, and soon afterward learned to sail in a Mackinaw boat—a sailboat of the kind once used in the commercial fisheries of the Lakes. Among my early hobbies were marksmanship and photography. My father taught me how to sail and how to shoot. My mother's family home was in Canada and I spent most of my growing-up summers on the Canadian shores of the Great Lakes.

"While I was in university I wrote my first published article. It told about the old Great Lakes fishing boats and appeared in *Yachting* magazine; some of the illustrations for it were from my own photographs. I have been writing and taking pictures ever since.

"I went into the army at the beginning of the Second World War, fought in the European Theater of Operations, and then stayed in the service for over twenty-five years. During that time I wrote articles for military magazines, and when I was in the Pentagon I also edited and helped write a number of official army publications. Wherever I went, whenever I could, I took photos.

"Not until I retired from the army was I able to start writing books, and I've written them steadily ever since. My wife, who is a high school librarian, first suggested that I write books for young people. She often goes with me on my research trips (she took the picture showing me on a lake freighter) and she conceived the subjects for several of the books.

"My army travels have helped with many of the books: a tour of duty in Kansas made me familiar with the scene of *Bloody Kansas,* for example, and two tours of duty in Germany provided background for *The Berlin Olympics.* A strong interest in history lies behind many of them. The Great Lakes still are one of my major concerns and I have been on them in boats and ships, around them in cars, and over them in airplanes, taking pictures and gathering information. My research for books has ranged from studying private collections of old letters and pictures, through working in libraries, to such on-the-spot research as visiting a shipyard on Georgian Bay or a gas-drilling platform offshore in Lake Erie."

HOBBIES AND OTHER INTERESTS: Photography, beagling, sailing, theater, travel.

(From *The Fate of the Lakes* by James P. Barry. Illustrated by the author.)

BEECHING, Jack 1922-
(James Barbary)

PERSONAL: Born 1922, in Sussex, England; married Amy Brown (an author and translator), 1950 (divorced, 1970); married Charlotte Mensforth (a painter), 1971; children: (first marriage) John Rutland, Laura Caroline. *Agent:* Georges Borchardt, Inc., 145 East 52nd St., New York, N.Y. 10022; and, Hope Leresche & Steele, 11 Jubilee Pl., Chelsea, London S.W. 3, England.

CAREER: Professional writer ("poetry is my avocation; the other forms of writing are a means of livelihood"); since mid-fifties has lived outside of England and traveled widely; formerly poet-in-residence at North Dakota State University, Fargo. *Military service:* Navy service during World War II. *Awards, honors:* Arts Council of Great Britain award, 1967.

WRITINGS: Aspects of Love (poetry), A. Swallow, 1950; *Paper Doll* (novel), Heinemann, 1950; *Truth Is a Naked Lady* (poetry), Myriad, 1957; *Let Me See Your Face* (novel), Heinemann, 1959; *The Dakota Project,* Delacorte, 1968; *The Polytheme Maidenhead* (poetry), Penguin, 1970; (contributor) *Jack Beeching, Harry Guest, Matthew Mead* (poetry), Penguin, 1970; (editor and author of introduction) *Voyages and Discoveries: The Principal Navigations, Voyages, Traffiques and Discoveries of the English Nation,* Penguin, 1972; *The Chinese Opium Wars,* Harcourt, 1976. Also author of *Personal and Partisan* (poetry), 1940.

Juveniles; with Amy Baumann, under pseudonym James Barbary: *The Fort in the Forest,* Parrish, 1962, published as *The Fort in the Wilderness,* Norton, 1965; *The Engine and the Gun,* Meredith Press, 1963; *Ten Thousand Heroes,* Parrish, 1963, Roy, 1964; *The Student Buccaneer,* Roy, 1963; *The Pike and the Sword,* Parrish, 1963; *The Young Cicero,* Roy, 1964; *Lawrence and His Desert Raiders,* Parrish, 1965, Meredith Press, 1968; *The Young Lord Byron,* Roy, 1965; *The Young Mutineer,* Parrish, 1966; *1066,* Parrish, 1966.

> Cardigan was now riding quietly at the trot, his back erect, sword held high, never turning in the saddle. During a charge, a cavalry officer, like a runner, must control himself never to glance over his shoulder--a backward glance discourages the men behind.
> ■ (From *The Crimean War* by James Barbary. Illustrated by Ned Glattauer.)

Sole author under pseudonym James Barbary: *The Boer War,* Hawthorn, 1968; *Captive of the Corsairs,* Macdonald & Co., 1969; *The Crimean War,* Hawthorn, 1970; *Puritan and Cavalier: The Stories of the English Civil War,* Thomas Nelson, 1976. Also translator from French and Spanish of poetry and of several plays for the London stage.

BEERS, Lorna 1897-

PERSONAL: Born May 10, 1897, in Maple Plain, Minn.; daughter of John Henry (a pioneer) and Sarah (James) Beers; married Clyde Ray Chambers (an economist), December 27, 1919; children: Richard (deceased). *Education:* University of Minnesota, B.A., 1919. *Politics:* Independent. *Religion:* United Church of Christ. *Home:* 687 East Beverly, Staunton, Va. 24401.

CAREER: Teacher for two years in a prairie town. *Member:* Author's Guild, Pen and Brush, Phi Beta Kappa. *Awards, honors:* Avery Hopwood Award, 1932, for *The Mad Stone;* National Library Association citation for *The Crystal Cornerstone.*

WRITINGS: Prairie Fires (novel), Dutton, 1925; *A Humble Lear* (novel), Dutton, 1929; *The Mad Stone* (novel), Dutton, 1932; *The Book of Hugh Flower* (ALA Notable Book), Harper, 1952; *The Crystal Cornerstone* (novel), Harper, 1953; *Wild Apples and North Wind,* Norton, 1966; *My Brothers, My Country, My World,* United Church

LORNA BEERS

Press, 1969. Contributor of short stories and essays to *Yankee, Harper's, Christian Science Monitor,* and *New England Galaxy.*

WORK IN PROGRESS: Two books with Minnesota settings.

SIDELIGHTS: "The village in which I was born would now be thought drab and its standard of living low, but it was my beautiful world and I was free to wander along the banks of its lakes and streams and through its meadows, pastures and woods. And the people! No two alike, and the stories they told of the wars and home-steading!

"Then high school in Minneapolis. The discipline was severe, we were worked hard. I still have the texts, Professor West's histories. They represent the liberalism and solid scholarship of the first decade of this century. We were considered children in the process of being educated, and we wore our hair in braids all four years.

"The great dark awakening was World War I. I loved the German language. I could recite *Immensee* by heart. I could not and would not believe the fury and hatred in the papers—it was a terrible catastrophe in which we were all involved. On Armistice Day, I being a junior at the University of Minnesota, my roommate and the other students carried on a victory celebration, but I lay on my cot alone having a vision of endless lines of men rising from the trenches and walking, walking,—where? That war and that vision gave me forever a tragic sense of life.

"I have never thought of myself as a 'writer.' I have always liked to make things with water color, with yarns, to create a home with an atmosphere of harmony and repose. Sometimes I made things with words. Whatever the medium I tried to make as beautiful a thing as my talents permitted.

"I do not think the events of my life much different from the events of other peoples' lives: marriage, accepting the role expected of women of my generation, having children and losing them, the battering of the depression, widowhood. All this is the common stuff of life.

"However I have thought much about the art of writing and perhaps what I have observed might be of value to young writers. Aside from the clean spare use of words, the writer must have a set of values with which to select and sort out his subject matter.

"The values I learned at the University of Minnesota were those of humanism. They are still my values. In the 1920's there was a shift in America to a post-war hedonism. In the 1930's that was gone and there was grim realism. There were many talented writers in the 1920's who petered out. I believe it was not because of a lack of talent, but a shift in the social ethos lost them their public and they fell into confusion. It is the agony of the writer in this civilization that there are no generally accepted enduring values. He has to find his own values and cling to them even though they are 'out,' or adapt himself to an ever shifting market.

"As an example: in the 1920's, fairy stories were in. In the 1930's, they were out. In the late 1940's, fictionalized history was in. In the 1960's, because of a general pessimism, it was out and the personal adventure was in.

"Since publishing houses have to survive, the problem of the writer is how to ride through these cultural upheavals with integrity. Perhaps, it is best done simply by mastering the craft and then trying to be the best human being one can."

BEHRMAN, Carol H(elen) 1925-

PERSONAL: Born August 24, 1925, in Brooklyn, N.Y.; daughter of Louis (a postman) and Sylvia (Leventhal) Bostwick; married Edward Behrman (an accountant), January 22, 1949; children: Bonnie, Joseph, Linda. *Education:* City College (now City College of the City University of New York), B.S.Ed. (cum laude), 1947; graduate study at Columbia University. *Home:* 325 Howard Ave., Fair Lawn, N.J. 07410. *Office:* Glen Ridge Middle School, Glen Ridge, N.J.

CAREER: Teacher of business education in public schools in New York, N.Y., 1949-54; free-lance writer, 1954-70; teacher of adult secretarial studies in public schools in Fair Lawn, N.J., and River Edge, N.J., both 1970-73; Glen Ridge Middle School, Glen Ridge, N.J., teacher of typing and language arts, 1973—. Has conducted private creative writing workshops. *Member:* Society of Children's Book Writers, New Jersey Education Association, New Jersey Business Education Association.

WRITINGS: There's Only One You (juvenile), Southern Publishing, 1973; *Catch a Dancing Star* (juvenile), Dillon, 1975. Contributor to professional, poetry, and juvenile magazines.

WORK IN PROGRESS: An Indian legend for children in verse, *Little Dreamer,* for Oddo.

Then Ellen's wishes and fantasies took off on magic wings into lovely daydreams about Elena Santiago.
■ (From *Catch a Dancing Star* by Carol H. Behrman. Illustrated by Judy King Rieniets.)

SIDELIGHTS: "I write poetry because it provides an emotional release. A considerable amount of my other writing is directed toward young children . . . because communicating with them seems to 'come naturally' to me, and because, while a tremendous responsibility, it is also just plain fun."

BERRY, William D(avid) 1926-

PERSONAL: Born May 20, 1926, in California; son of Harvey R. (an electrical engineer) and Ruth (Black) Berry; married Elizabeth M. Lambert (a potter), April 27, 1952; children: Mark Fraser, Paul Norman. *Education:* Attended Art Center School of Los Angeles, 1943, School of Allied Arts, Glendale, Calif., 1947-50, Glendale Junior College, 1949-50, and University of Alaska, Fairbanks, 1971. *Politics:* "No hard line." *Religion:* "No organized religion." *Home and office:* Miller Hill, Star Rt. Box 20063, Fairbanks, Alaska 99701.

CAREER: California Junior Museum, Sacramento, curator of science, 1951-52; National Park Service, Western Museum Laboratory, San Francisco, Calif., preparator, 1958-60; Denver Museum of Natural History, Denver, Colo.,

staff artist, 1973-74; Tanana Valley Community College, Fairbanks, Alaska, instructor in art, 1975-77. Free-lance artist and writer. Technical consultant to Walt Disney Enterprises, 1956-57. *Military service:* U.S. Army, 1944-47; received Bronze Star. *Member:* Alaska Conservation Society. *Awards, honors:* Has received several prizes for paintings and prints in regional shows.

WRITINGS—All self-illustrated: (With wife, Elizabeth M. Berry) *Mammals of the San Francisco Bay Region*, University of California Press, 1959; *Buffalo Land*, Macmillan, 1961; *Deneki*, Macmillan, 1965.

Illustrator: George Willett, *Birds of the Southern California Deserts*, Los Angeles County Museum, 1951; Fran Hubbard, *Animal Friends of the Sierra*, Awani, 1955; Hubbard, *Animal Friends of· the Northwest*, Awani, 1957; Vinson Brown, *How to Understand Animal Talk*, Little, Brown, 1958; Charles A. McLaughlin, *Mammals of Los Angeles County*, Los Angeles County Museum, 1959; Herbert H. Wong, *Ducks, Geese, and Swans*, Lane, 1960; William O. Pruitt, *Animals of the North*, Harper, 1966.

Contributor of articles to *Audubon* and *North American Review*.

WORK IN PROGRESS: A book on drawing animals and humans; a book using his wildlife sketches; two picture books for children.

SIDELIGHTS: "From early childhood until the age of thirty-five I had one overriding interest: animals. Starting about age three, I drew them, studied books about them, kept them as pets, observed them in zoos and in the wild. Unable to make up my mind whether I wanted to be a wildlife artist or a biologist, I settled on a sort of compromise between the two. As a child I loved the magic worlds of Dr. Doolittle, and the Oz Kingdom, where no hard line separated human beings from the rest of the animal world. I collected all the *National Geographic* magazines and *Nature* magazines—then illustrated largely with paintings of wildlife rather than photographs—I could lay my hands on. But my enthusiasm was not without criticism. If the living animals did not turn out to look as they had been depicted in the illustrations, I felt as if I had been misled somehow, and resolved that any paintings I did would attempt to show animals and birds as accurately as possible. (I was as keen on imaginary animals as real ones, and although I separated the world of fantasy from the world of science, the scientific attitude crept into the fantasy world to produce a kind of science-fiction result.) Above all, I was enchanted with Walt Disney's animated films, and the possibilities that movie animation offered the artist to create his own moving, speaking world. Second choice lay in the field of comic strips, much more accessible to individual effort. Another type of 'world' existed in the museum diorama, with its painted background and mounted animals. As a child I spent many hours trying to construct miniature dioramas; my room was always a combination of a museum collection and cartoon factory.

"With adolescence the world of human beings began increasingly to invade my interest, but, like Mowgli, it was as if I had been raised in the forest and had never quite learned the language of humanity. The behavior of animals seemed to make much more 'sense' to me than the behavior of my own species. When I met the girl I was to marry, it was her background in biology and her own love of animal life that enabled us to communicate, and certainly it was her training in the sciences that, coupled with my own mania for 'accura-

Cow and calf now cropped the bare, dormant twigs--willow, dwarf birch, and sometimes older-- that made up their diet almost nine months of the year. ■ (From *Deneki* by William D. Berry. Illustrated by the author.)

WILLIAM D. BERRY and family

cy,' tended to steer my work, at the beginning of my professional career, into scientific and natural history illustration with an educational intent. Not until *Buffalo Land* and *Deneki* was I allowed the freedom to present the material in my own way, however.

"Just after the completion of *Buffalo Land,* events in my own life brought the 'conversion to humanity' to completion. Suddenly I could identify wholly with my fellow man, and animals—which had always seemed more individual to me, somehow, than the masses of people—were just as suddenly seen in a different light: a host of hoofed, furred, and feathered creatures whose minds could never be truly known to me, and in fact whose world had much less to offer than my 'own.' *Deneki* was produced just at this time, and is in a sense a fond look back at a world I had once pretended to inhabit, but now seen from the outside, from the viewpoint of Man trying to look objectively at another species and its environment. Most 'animal stories,' enchanting as they may be, are myths about mankind given animal form, and I suppose *Deneki* was an attempt to create a primarily visual book (with traces of museum-exhibit, animation, and comic-strip-sequence style) that would tell the 'true' story about a young moose's growing-up: that there is no 'moral lesson' to be learned by us from any other species, for their individual struggles are not ours. 'Deneki' is just a moose, no more (except, possibly, in a very general metaphorical sense), but his world and his means of coping with his environment are of interest in themselves, valuable to us because in our attempts to understand them, we develop ways of understanding ourselves."

"It may be of interest that *Deneki* was conceived and illustrated on the spot where the story takes place, so that although the book is fiction based on many facts, it is in a sense a portrait of an area done from life, for the land, the weather, the vegetation, and the animals surrounded my studio, daily shaping the nature of the book during the three years it was in progress.

"For the past ten years most of my work—although still dealing primarily with wildlife—has been devoted to individual paintings, drawings, or sculpture, or to a series of limited-edition prints, almost all dealing with Alaskan subjects."

FOR MORE INFORMATION SEE: Alaska Journal, summer, 1973.

BISHOP, Claire Huchet

PERSONAL: Born in Brittany, France; later became an American citizen; married Frank Bishop (a pianist). *Education:* Attended the Sorbonne, Paris. *Religion:* Catholic. *Home:* New York City.

CAREER: Author and poet. Instrumental in opening "L'-Heure Joyeuse," the first children's library in France, 1924; worked on the staff of the *Nouvelle Revue Francaise;* joined the staff of the New York Public Library upon her arrival to the United States; served for a time as children's book editor for the *Commonweal;* has traveled all over America as a lecturer and storyteller. Actively involved as lecturer and writer for various social movements in France. *Awards, honors: Pancakes-Paris* was a prize winner in the New York Herald Tribune Spring Book Festival, 1947, and a runner-up

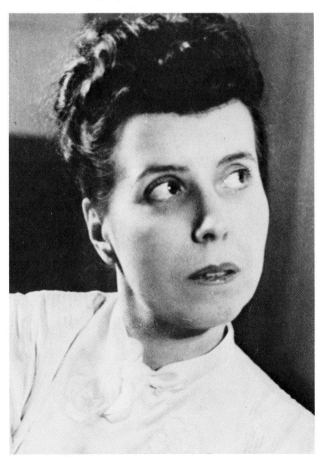

CLAIRE HUCHET BISHOP

Under the arcades of the Plaza de Armas, a young handsome Indian sat next to the public writer. From time to time he drew a few notes from his hand-made Pan-pipe of llama bones, beautifully decorated. ■ (From *Martin de Porres, Hero* by Claire Huchet Bishop. Illustrated by Jean Charlot.)

for the Newbery Medal, 1948; Well-Met Children's Book Award, 1952, for *Twenty and Ten; All Alone* was chosen as best-liked book by the Boys' Club of America, 1953, and a runner-up for the Newbery Medal, 1954.

WRITINGS—Fiction: *The Five Chinese Brothers* (illustrated by Kurt Wiese), Coward-McCann, 1938, reissued, Scholastic Book Services, 1965; *The Kings' Day* (illustrated

by Doris Spiegel), Coward-McCann, 1940; *The Ferryman* (illustrated by K. Wiese), Coward-McCann, 1941, reissued, Viking, 1974; *The Man Who Lost His Head* (illustrated by Robert McCloskey), Viking, 1942; *Augustus* (illustrated by Grace Paull), Viking, 1945; *Pancakes-Paris* (illustrated by Georges Schreiber), Viking, 1947; *Blue Spring Farm,* Viking, 1948; *Christopher the Giant* (illustrated by Berkeley Williams, Jr.), Houghton, 1950; *Bernard and His Dogs* (illustrated by Maurice Brevannes), Houghton, 1952; (with Janet Joly) *Twenty and Ten* (illustrated by William Pene du Bois), Viking, 1952; *All Alone* (illustrated by Feodor Rojan-kovsky), Viking, 1953; *The Big Loop* (illustrated by Charles Fontsere), Viking, 1955; (editor) *Happy Christmas: Tales for Boys and Girls* (illustrated by Ellen Raskin), Stephen Daye Press, 1956; *Toto's Triumph* (illustrated by Claude Ponsot), Viking, 1957; *A Present from Petros* (illustrated by Dimitris Davis), Viking, 1961; *Twenty-Two Bears* (illustrated by K. Wiese), Viking, 1964; *The Truffle Pig* (illustrated by K. Wiese), Coward-McCann, 1971; *Georgette* (illustrated by Ursula Landshoff), Coward-McCann, 1973.

Biographies: *Martin de Porres: Hero* (illustrated by Jean Charlot), Houghton, 1954; *Lafayette: French American Hero* (illustrated by M. Bevannes), Garrard, 1960; *Yeshu: Called Jesus* (illustrated by Donald Bolognese), Farrar, Straus, 1966; *Mozart: Music Magician* (illustrated by Paul Frame), Garrard, 1968; *Johann Sebastian Bach: Music Giant* (illustrated by Russell Hoover), Garrard, 1972.

Nonfiction: *French Children's Books for English Speaking Children,* Sheridan Square Press, 1938; *France Alive,* McMullen, 1947; *All Things Common,* Harper, 1950; *French Roundabout,* Dodd, 1960, revised edition, 1966; *Here Is France,* Farrar, Straus, 1969; *How Catholics Look at Jews,* Paulist Press, 1974.

Also contributor of poetry to French avant-garde literary magazines and other periodicals.

SIDELIGHTS: Claire Huchet Bishop became a children's author as a direct result of being an oral storyteller. She told the story, "The Five Chinese Brothers" to a New York audience, was pleased with her English translation, and decided to write it down. Its publication began her writing career.

Commonweal called *Mozart: Music Magician* "a sensitive introduction to the bitter-sweet history of one of the very greatest composers who ever lived. Young readers will pay this gifted biographer the best compliment of all by consulting the 'listening choices' she appends. . . ." Another biography, *Yeshu, Called Jesus* was described by *Young Readers' Review* as ". . . the day to day and year to year life as Jesus, a Jewish boy in a small village, might have lived it . . . an objective, logical, and carefully developed book which breathes the spirit of ecumenism. . . ."

HOBBIES AND OTHER INTERESTS: Music, cooking, gardening, and reading.

FOR MORE INFORMATION SEE: Stanley J. Kunitz, editor, *Junior Book of Authors,* second edition, H. W. Wilson, 1951; Lee Bennett Hopkins, *Books Are by People,* Citation, 1969.

BLADOW, Suzanne Wilson   1937-

PERSONAL: Born October 2, 1937, in Des Moines, Iowa; daughter of Roy R. (a pharmacist) and Dorothy (Inabnet) Wilson; married Terrence Bladow (a pediatrician), June 26, 1960; children: Craig Wilson, Amy Lynn. *Education:* University of Missouri, B.J., 1959. *Home and office address:* Route 5, Box 140-A, Joplin, Mo. 64801.

CAREER: Better Homes and Gardens, Des Moines, Iowa, copywriter in advertising sales promotion, 1959-60; Chris-

tian College (now Columbia College), Columbia, Mo., writer for public relations office, 1960-62, editor of *Christian College Alumnae,* 1961-62; University of Missouri, Columbia, writer for publications section of department of alumni activities, 1963-64; free-lance writer, 1971—.

WRITINGS: The Midnight Flight of Moose, Mops, and Marvin (juvenile), McGraw, 1975. Contributor to *Scouting* and *Missouri Life.*

WORK IN PROGRESS: A sequel to *The Midnight Flight of Moose, Mops, and Marvin,* and a manuscript for older children.

SIDELIGHTS: "My career as an unpublished writer is much more long-standing and impressive by volume than my career as a published one. Just for warm-ups there was a second grade poem about a bird that ended, 'It didn't matter if he satter in a little breeze.' As a teenager, I typed my poems and stories on my father's tall, ancient typewriter and sent them to magazines, hoping editors would believe me to be an older person. I don't believe they did. I learned early in life about rejection slips. But now, I think a person with poems and stories in a drawer is as much a writer as one with poems and stories in a book. The writing that stays unsold is still of value. I have a lot of that sort of writing, and consider it rehearsal for some unknown production to come.

"I like photography and watercolor painting, and sometimes try combining these with writing.

SUZANNE BLADOW

There were animals with cotton insides (Mops peeked) and small people--like creatures, some stuffed and some solid and some that would say "Mama" if you bumped them over (Moose did). ■ (From *The Midnight Flight of Moose, Mops, and Marvin* by Suzanne Wilson Bladow. Illustrated by Joseph Matthieu.)

"This is the way an idea happens. It doesn't matter what else is going on. An idea sinks its teeth in and shakes you and shakes you. Then you take the idea and shake it and shake it, until it sits down and begins to mind. Then you are writing, and the experience of it is exhilarating. One April, the idea for a book happened to me—there it was. After that, there was writing, and no real concept of passing time. I only knew I was writing a book, or it was writing me, for it was in control of my life.

"Ideas emerge from strange hiding places. One came to me while I was standing under a maple tree, hoping my son, then eight, would not fall in his first attempt to climb it. (He didn't.) A poem about a calico cat bloomed in my mind as I was chauffeuring my daughter to a dancing lesson. So I know where ideas come from. They are in clouds and under rocks, they fall out of trees and hang around cars waiting for someone to climb in. You have to be ready for them, and welcome them to your notebook immediately.

"Several years ago I was given the task of cheering up our two tired and cranky children as my husband tried to take their picture for a family Christmas card. For a while it seemed the camera was destined to record only chaos or boredom. I launched into 'Once upon a time . . . there were three mice . . . and they lived in a funny old house in the far North . . .' The pictures were taken, and in a rambling, sketchy way, Moose, Mops and Marvin were brought into the world.

"Every story, article or poem I write is like a challenging puzzle. After the first writing, it becomes apparent certain parts must be exchanged, moved, slightly reshaped to fit. And miraculously they do fit, and more easily and logically than in the first try. The excitement of the first writing is almost equaled by the revelation of a better way to write it.

"For some time I have suspected a good laugh to be one of the essentials for human survival. Children deserve humor in their books, anywhere from a little to a lot. *Midnight Flight* has its share. It was a story so enjoyable in the writing, the time spent with it seemed a gift to myself.

"There is joy in the writing, and joy when the writing is done."

HOBBIES AND OTHER INTERESTS: Painting.

BLEGVAD, Erik 1923-

PERSONAL: Born March 3, 1923, in Copenhagen, Denmark; son of Harald Blegvad (a marine biologist for the Danish government); married Lenore Hochman (a painter and writer), 1950; children: Peter, Kristoffer. *Education:* Attended Copenhagen School of Arts and Crafts, 1941-44. *Home:* London, England.

CAREER: Artist and illustrator. Employed with a Copenhagen advertising agency during the Second World War; worked as a free-lance artist in London, 1947; became a free-lance artist for book and magazine publishers in Paris, 1948-51; began illustrating children's books after arriving in the United States, 1951. His works have been in several exhibitions of the American Institute of Graphic Arts. *Military service:* Royal Danish Air Force, interpreter with the British Forces in Germany, 1945-47. *Awards, honors:* The Mushroom Center Disaster and The Winter Bear were Children's Book Showcase Titles, 1975, and 1976.

ILLUSTRATOR: Thomas Franklin Galt, *Story of Peace and War,* Crowell, 1952; Lee Kingman, *Village Band Mystery,* Doubleday, 1956; Lillian Pohlmann, *Myrtle Albertina's Secret,* Coward, 1956; Dan Wickenden, *Amazing Vacation,* Harcourt, 1956; Edward Anthony, *Oddity Land,* Doubleday, 1957; Mary Norton, *Bed-Knob and Broomstick,* Harcourt, 1957; Jean Fritz, *Late Spring,* Coward-McCann, 1957; (and translator) Hans Christian Andersen, *The Swineherd,* Harcourt, 1958; (and translator) H. C. Andersen, *The Emperor's New Clothes,* Harcourt, 1959; Isabella Holt, *The Adventures of Rinaldo,* Little, Brown, 1959; Carol Kendall, *The Gammage Cup,* Harcourt, 1959; Betty Miles, *Having a Friend,* Knopf, 1959.

Margaret (Glover) Otto, *The Little Old Train,* Knopf, 1960; Robert Paul Smith, *Jack Mack,* Coward-McCann, 1960; Rona Jaffe, *The Last of the Wizards,* Simon & Schuster, 1961; Myra Cohn Livingston, *I'm Hiding,* Harcourt, 1961; Marjorie Winslow, *Mud Pies and Other Recipes,* Macmillan, 1961; Jane Langton, *The Diamond in the Window,* Harper, 1962; M. C. Livingston, *See What I Found*, Harcourt, 1962; Miska Miles, *Dusty and the Fiddlers*, Little, Brown, 1962; Jean Stafford, *Elephi*, Farrar, Straus, 1962; Barbara Brenner, *The Five Pennies*, Knopf, 1963; Felice Holman, *Elizabeth the Bird Watcher*, Macmillan, 1963; Richard Webber Jackson, *A Year in a Window*, Doubleday, 1963; F. Holman, *Elizabeth the Treasure Hunter*, Macmillan, 1964; M. C. Livingston, *Happy Birthday!*, Harcourt, 1964.

William Allingham, *The Dirty Old Man*, Prentice-Hall, 1965; Lenore Blegvad, *Mr. Jensen and Cat*, Harcourt, 1965; F. Holman, *Elizabeth and the Marsh Mystery*, Macmillan, 1966; M. C. Livingston, *I'm Waiting*, Harcourt, 1966; Doris Orgel, *The Good-Byes of Magnus Marmalade*, Putnam, 1966; Sally Clithero, editor, *Beginning-to-Read Poetry*, Follett, 1967; J. Langton, *The Swing in the Summer House*, Harper, 1967; L. Blegvad, *One Is for the Sun*, Harcourt, 1968; L. Blegvad, *The Great Hamster Hunt*, Harcourt, 1969; D. Orgel, *Phoebe and the Prince*, Putnam, 1969; Max Steele, *The Cat and the Coffee Drinkers*, Harper, 1969; Monica Stirling, *The Cat from Nowhere*, Harcourt, 1969; Janice (May) Udry, *Emily's Autumn*, Albert Whitman, 1969.

Edith (Nesbit) Bland, *The Conscience Pudding*, Coward-McCann, 1970; Margery Sharp, *Miss Bianca in the Orient*, Heinemann, 1970; Alvin R. Tresselt, *Bonnie Bess: The Weathervane Horse*, Parents' Magazine Press, 1970; J. Langton, *The Astonishing Stereoscope*, Harper, 1971; Judith Viorst, *The Tenth Good Thing about Barney*, Atheneum, 1971; Roger Drury Wolcott, *The Finches' Fabulous Furnace*, Little, Brown, 1971; L. Blegvad, *Moon-Watch Summer*, Harcourt, 1972; M. Sharp, *Miss Bianca and the Bridesmaid*, Little, Brown, 1972; E. N. Bland, *The Complete Book of Dragons*, Macmillan, 1973; Mark Taylor, *The Wind's Child*, Atheneum, 1973; L. Blegvad, editor, *Mittens for Kittens and Other Rhymes about Cats*, Atheneum, 1974; N. M. Bodecker, *The Mushroom Center Disaster*, Atheneum, 1974; Ruth Craft, *The Winter Bear*, Collins, 1974, Atheneum, 1975; Joan Phipson, *Polly's Tiger*, Dutton, 1974; Jan Wahl, *The Five in the Forest*, Follett, 1974; L. Blegvad, editor, *Hark! Hark! the Dogs Do Bark and Other Rhymes*, Atheneum, 1975; Charlotte (Shapiro) Zolotow, *May I Visit?*, Harper, 1976; Nancy Dingman Watson, *Blueberries Lavender*, Addison-Wesley, 1977; Jan Wahl, *The Pleasant Fieldmouse Storybook*, Prentice-Hall, 1977; Jan Wahl,

She rode on a high bicycle with a basket in front, and she visited the sick and taught the piano. ■ (From *Bed-Knob and Broomstick* by Mary Norton. Illustrated by Erik Blegvad.)

ERIK and LENORE BLEGVAD

Pleasant Fieldmouse Valentine Trick, Windmill, 1977; *Burnie's Hill*, Collins, 1977, Atheneum, 1977; Charlotte Zolotow, *Someone New*, Harper, 1978; L. Blegvad, editor, *This Little Pig-a-wig*, Atheneum, in press; Robert Louis Stevenson, *A Child's Garden of Verses*, Random House, in press.

Also illustrator of a book for Editions Ode, entitled *Les Pays Nordique*; Madame Prunier's *Fish Cook Book; The Margaret Rudkin Pepperidge Farm Cook Book;* several works on fishing written by his father, Dr. Harald Blegvad; various periodicals in France (including *France Soir, Elle*, and *Femina*) and the United States (including *Esquire, McCall's, Saturday Evening Post*, and the *Woman's Day* serialization of Mary Norton's *The Borrowers* and *The Magic Bed Knob*).

SIDELIGHTS: Blegvad was enrolled in an art school during the years Germany occupied Denmark, and travelled throughout Europe after his home country was liberated. He does art work in both pen and ink, and watercolor. Known mostly as an artist and illustrator, Blegvad has also co-authored two books with his wife, Lenore.

Commenting on *Mr. Jensen and Cat*, which Blegvad illustrated, *Library Journal* noted, "Much loving care and artistic skill has been lavished on this charming little book, which gives a lovely picture of Copenhagen...." Blegvad illustrated and wrote (with his wife) *The Great Hamster Hunt*, in which a *Saturday Review* critic found "... [the drawings] add to the pleasure of a realistic and satisfying story that is written with grace and humor."

FOR MORE INFORMATION SEE: F. Whitaker, "Illustration of Erik Blegvad," *American Artist*, September, 1961; Doris De Montreville, editor, *Third Book of Junior Authors*, H. W. Wilson, 1972.

BLEGVAD, Lenore 1926-

PERSONAL: Born May 8, 1926, in New York, N.Y.; daughter of Julius C. (a mechanical engineer) and Ruth (a teacher; maiden name, Huebschman) Hochman; married Erik Blegvad (an illustrator), September 12, 1950; children: Peter, Kristoffer. *Education:* Vassar College, B.A., 1947. *Home:* 4 Crescent Mansions, 113 Fulham Rd., London S.W.3, England.

CAREER: Painter and writer.

RINDLE, RANDLE

Rindle, randle,
Light the candle,
The cat's among the pies;
No matter for that,
The cat'll get fat,
And I'm too lazy to rise.

(From *Mittens for Kittens* chosen by Lenore Blegvad. Illustrated by Erik Blegvad.)

WRITINGS—All illustrated by her husband, Erik Blegvad: *Mr. Jensen and the Cat*, Harcourt, 1965; *One Is for the Sun*, Harcourt, 1968; *The Great Hamster Hunt*, Harcourt, 1969; *Moon-Watch Summer*, Harcourt, 1972; *Mittens for Kittens*, Atheneum, 1974; *Hark Hark the Dogs Do Bark*, Atheneum, 1975; *This Little Pig-a-Wig*, Atheneum, in press.

SIDELIGHTS: "I divide my time between writing and painting, and which one I do at any given moment is dictated by various things: mood, inspiration, location (we live half the year in London and half in the South of France). I find the creative effort for each equally exciting, arduous, and absorbing. The change from one occupation to the other brings new insights every time and somehow suits me to perfection."

FOR MORE INFORMATION SEE: Doris De Montreville, editor, *Third Book of Junior Authors*, H. W. Wilson, 1972.

BOCK, William Sauts Netamux'we

PERSONAL: Born September 18, 1939, in Hatfield, Pa.; son of William Albert (a mechanic) and Louise Elsie (Rauch) Bock; married Barbara Ann Schmauch Lunapexkway; children: David Ashiih Kalumpexeng, Sandra Nijonih Netamataexkway. *Education:* Philadelphia College of Art, B.F.A., 1962; Lutheran Seminary, Philadelphia, Pennsylvania, Master of Theology, 1972. *Religion:* "I see Christianity as possibly a *fulfillment* of the ancient Lenape religion, rather than an alternative to it." *Home and office:* 252 E. Summit St., Souderton, Pa. 18964.

CAREER: Artist, painter, illustrator. Commissioned by Merck, Sharp and Dohme, Pharmaceuticals to create a series of Bicentennial illustrations for posters and theatre programs, 1975-76. *Exhibitions:* Paintings are in many collections in the United States and Europe, and the offices of Marriott Corp. *Member:* Philadelphia Children's Reading Round Table. *Awards, honors:* Named honored illustrator by the American Institute of Graphic Arts for illustrations in *The Crusader King: Richard the Lionhearted*, 1974; Philadelphia Children's Reading Round Table monthly choice award, 1978, for *Malcolm Yucca Seed*.

WRITINGS—Self-illustrated: *Coloring Book of the First Americans, Lenape Indian Drawings*, Middle Atlantic Press, 1974.

Illustrator: Jean Stanley, *The Horse with a One Track Mind*, Westminster, 1963; *The Vinlanders' Saga*, Holt, 1965; Elizabeth Campbell, *The Carving on the Tree*, Little, Brown, 1968; Daniel Jacobson, *The First Americans*, Ginn, 1969; Walter Edmonds, *Wolf Hunt*, Little, Brown, 1970; Walter Edmonds, *Seven American Stories*, Little, Brown, 1970; Joseph and Edith Raskin, *Tales our Settlers Told*, Lothrop, 1971; Alex Bealer, *Only the Names Remain: The Cherokees and the Trail of Tears*, Little, Brown, 1972; C. Weslager, *Magic Medicine of the Indians*, Middle Atlantic Press, 1973; Joseph and Edith Raskin, *Ghosts and Witches Aplenty: More Tales our Settlers Told*, Lothrop, 1973; Richard Suskind, *Crusader King: Richard the Lionhearted*, Little, Brown, 1973.

Walter Edmonds, *The Story of Richard Storm*, Little, Brown, 1974; Elizabeth Campbell, *Jamestown: The Beginning*, Little, Brown, 1974; Joseph and Edith Raskin, *Guilty or Not Guilty*, Lothrop, 1975; Richard Richardson, *Sam Adams: The Boy Who Became Father of the American Revolution*, Crown, 1975; Mark Twain, *Tom Sawyer*, Field Enterprises Educational Corp/World Book, 1975; Joseph and Edith Raskin, *Spies and Traitors*, Lothrop, 1976; James McCloy and Ray Miller, Jr., *The Jersey Devil*, Middle Atlantic Press, 1976; Joseph and Edith Raskin, *Strange Shadows: Spirit Tales of Early America*, Lothrop, 1977; Joseph and Edith Raskin, *Tales of Land and Sea*, Lothrop, 1978;

Malcolm Yucca Seed, Harvey House, 1977; *An Alaskan Flingit (Indian) Story*, Lippincott, 1978; Joseph and Edith Raskin, *Tales of Indentured Servants*, Lothrop, in press; C. Weslager, *Migrations of the Delaware Indians*, Middle Atlantic Press, in press. Articles and illustrations have appeared in *Animals, M.S.P.C.A., Royal S.P.C.A.* and *Bucks County Panorama*.

Filmstrip: "The White Fang," color, composed of 42 paintings by William Sauts Bock, Spoken Arts, 1978.

SIDELIGHTS: "I was born in the country, but raised in Philadelphia where my father was a mechanic and engineer. My mother, an artistic person was a basketmaker. Many weekdays, and most weekends were spent deep in the wooded foothills of Montgomery County, Pennsylvania where our family's summer estate was located. My favorite hours and years were spent here, roaming and learning the ways of nature, and aware that this is the heart of the ancient Lenápe country that extends from Hudson River to Delaware Bay, from the Atlantic Ocean to the Coast. I've always felt the presence of the Spirit-Forces (Lenápe: Mani'towak).

"In Philadelphia, my third grade teacher asked what we wanted to be as adults, I said 'artist' without hesitation and have never for an instant wavered from that passion. I remember her sending me to show a picture I'd done to a class down the hall. I returned and said I had shown it, but in truth, being shy, I stood in the hall. Still under pressure, I gave 'performances' on the piano and accordian in the school auditorium and today play the old-time Lenápe love-flute and water drum as well. But my native disposition as a reclusive hermit has never left me.

"Father walked me around Center City to the Art Museum, never failing to describe how he had walked over the spot when only the Museum foundation was there. Here, from my earliest days, I saw the 'old masters.' I absorbed and studied them tirelessly and in details and began my now large library of art books. I was sparked by the *magic* of art—and still regard it as a magical-spiritual affair. It's a magic that keeps after a person too—for if I attempt to vacation without brushes, pen, ink and paint, I get itchy and irritable. My work is my vacation.

"Before his marriage, my father knew the artist Albert Jean Adolph who painted the stage sets for the Philadelphia Academy of Music and steamship murals early in the twentieth century. Pa often spoke of Albert's roof top parties under the stars in Philadelphia. Albert had angels painted on his ceilings; and had painted Mussolini, the art school model, before he became Mussolini leader of Italy.

The ceilings of my home are covered with copies of pictographs of animals, spirits and gods of aboriginal North America.

"Much of Lenápe religion is celestial, concerned with the twelve levels of heavenly light, and the spirit *forces* (mani' tuwak) who occupy the levels below the creator. Thus, my paintings (not those done for books) have strong celestial, cosmic, surreal elements, and range in size from tiny watercolor miniatures to giant gold-leaf on plexiglass and acrylic-on-panel murals. I've had plenty of mural experience in preparation for this latter work, having worked for a Philadelphia mural and design studio for years. So I work both real and surreal, depending upon the subject matter. But I much prefer the natural earth colors and traditional media to the synthetic ones that cause allergic reactions.

Cheered and eager to help other children, she threw on her mantle and hurried off to town, knocking on doors and offering her remedy. ■ (From *Ghosts and Witches Aplenty* by Joseph and Edith Raskin. Illustrated by William Sauts Bock.)

WILLIAM SAUTS BOCK

"In the late 1960's I walked, bus-rode and horse backed my way to and around the Navaho country in Arizona and New Mexico; following the routes taken by Lenápe scouts as early as the 1840's. This I did as part of some private research I do for my paintings—and because of the Lenápe-Navaho connection we've given Navaho middle names to our two children.

"My family of four was visited by one of our old tribal visionaries from Oklahoma. (Where many Lenápes found a home under anglo pressure in the 1860's). She performed the naming-rites for us, the first time this was done here in the homeland in probably 200 years. My family belong to the Red Paint division of the Lenápe wolf phratry. In former times husband and wife belonged to different phratries, the children joining the mothers. History has disrupted this phase of our culture.

"In accordance with ancient Lenápe tradition, I do not remember or count birthdays and our celebrations and events are observed in accordance with positions of sun, moon and stars. We feel that it is not natural to be concerned in any exact, mechanical way with the passage of time. Nevertheless, I consistently meet, in fact beat publisher's deadlines.

"My approach to illustrating children's books is to remain, as I always have, unconscious of the audience's age, and just go ahead in my own way as if the work were for my own pleasure alone.

"It takes a lot of control to use watercolor, and especially pen and ink the way I do it. Even in the winter I'll often break the ice and swim in our pool to get the blood into my fingers and warm them for work. The old time Lenápes did this and it helps. I'd prefer a natural pond, or creek, but, of course, pollution has taken over Lenápe country.

"For as long as I can recall I've loved books, the smell of the printers ink, the blopping sound when a book is briskly closed. I've often bought a book because I liked the look and

smell of it, without much regard for what the subject matter was. I've always sensed that a choice book sends out waves of ideas and power, by just lying there. When I'm working on a book I'm not performing for an audience. My idea of professionalism is concerned with the work not my dress habits; which is why summer days see me working in, indeed living in, one of my swimsuits. It's my personal version of air-conditioning. Our oldtime men wore breech clouts. Newspaper reporters and photographers and other guests have often appeared at my garden studio (I call it "wik-wam"), or home to find me at work dressed just so. I figure whatever helps me work is O.K. Sometimes fasting helps. I did it once for twelve days straight with only water to consume—and worked on a book all the while. Once again, this thing of fasting is of Lenápe origin for sharpening the senses.

"While working as a book illustrator I earned a Masters Degree in theology and was ordained to be a Lutheran minister. However I do not want to be a minister. What I want is theological insight that will help my paintings by penetrating what similarities and differences there might be between European and American Indian world views, and so that I can weed out foreign elements that have crept into the native way.

"I remember as I worked on the rooftop scene on the cover of *Sam Adams* how my mind filled with memories of climbing ladders and scaffolds with a paint spattered face in the mural studio in Philadelphia where I worked while in art school—and of the earlier years when my father took me to the rooftops along Delaware Avenue in Philadelphia; overlooking docked ships and others floating in. It also reminded me of the good feeling of working on a vast surface with a broad brush one day and then on a tiny book illustration with a sharp pen point the next. I recalled what Robert Riggs, the great illustrator and my teacher had said—that in his view there were two sorts of artist—the line sort, and the mass sort—and that he believed I saw things in a linear way, that even when I worked on a large painting the line and edge of forms would be more obvious than the mass. I think he was right.

"I listen to music, whether it is a classical concert at the Philadelphia Academy of Music; Temple Universities Summer Festival at Ambler, or Rock music—this in addition to my deep attachment to the Lenápe tribal music and chant, which I practice myself, along with my knowledge of herbal medicine.

"I am enthralled by whatever creates *visual* excitement and music does this for me. My imagination is also turned loose by the smells of a hickory and cedar woods in fall and many another event.

"I study North Eastern United States bird and animal life too, for my paintings, and spend lots of time at bird sanctuaries at Island Beach, New Jersey, Hawk Mountain, Pennsylvania and in the big marshlands around Philadelphia International Airport, and calling native birds into our own wooded premises. In the fall I like to track black bears through the hickory and cedar-swamps near my home—though it's as an observer, not a hunter. In October we celebrate a variant of the ancient Lenápe Big Horse Ceremony of Thanksgiving, over a period of nearly two weeks, which of course, pre-dates the arrival of Europeana, and concerns vision-songs."

FOR MORE INFORMATION SEE: Bucks County Panorama Magazine, February, 1976.

BODKER, Cecil 1927-

PERSONAL: Born March 27, 1927, in Fredericia, Denmark; daughter of H. P. (an author and artist) and Gertrude (Mathiesen) Jacobsen; married; children: (daughters) Dorete, Mette, Tadjure, Madena. *Education:* Completed four year apprenticeship to a silversmith in Fredericia, Denmark. *Agent:* V. Allen Jensen, International Children's Book Service, Kildeskovsvej 21, Gentofte, Denmark DK-2820.

CAREER: Silversmith Georg Jensen (silversmith workshop), Copenhagen, Denmark, silversmith, 1948-51; Silversmith Markstroems, Stockholm, Sweden, silversmith, 1951-52; writer, 1955—.

AWARDS, HONORS: Edith Rodes grant, 1956, for *Luseblomster* and *Fygende Heste;* Morten Nielsens Memorial Award, 1960; Critics' Prize, 1961, for *Oejet;* Otto Benzon's author fellowship, 1963; anniversary prize from Arena, 1963; Louisiana Prize, 1964; state arts grant, 1965; first and only prize ever bestowed by Danish Academy for a children's book, 1967, and best children's book of the year award from Danish Ministry of Cultural Affairs, 1968, both for *Silas og den sorte hoppe;* nominated for International Board on Books for Young People (IBBY) Hans Christian Andersen Medal, 1970, received diploma as highly commended author, 1974, and awarded IBBY Hans Christian Andersen Medal, 1976, for her works for children; second prize from Danish Mission Society, 1970, for short story "Hyaenenatten"; received Silver Pencil from Netherlands, 1972, and the 1975 Mildred L. Batchelder Award from American Library Association, 1977, both for *Leoparden;* Drachmann prize, 1973, for her poetry, prose, and children's books; Ingrid Jespersen Prize from Danish Women's Organization, 1974; Tagea Brandts travel fellowship, 1975.

WRITINGS—Juveniles in English translation: *Silas og den sorte hoppe,* Branner & Korch, 1967, translation published as *Silas and the Black Mare,* Seymour Lawrence, in press; *Leoparden,* Branner & Korch, 1970, translation by Gunnar Poulsen and Solomon Deressa published as *The Leopard,* Atheneum, 1975, and as *Leopard,* Oxford University Press, 1977.

Other juveniles: *Silas og Ben-Godik* (title means "Silas and Foot-Godik"), Branner & Korch, 1969; *Timmerlis* (title means "Timanna"), Branner & Korch, 1969; *Dimma Gole* (collection of short stories), illustrated by Arne Bodker, Branner & Korch, 1971; *Silas fanger et firspand* (title means "Silas Rescues Two Four-in-Hand"), Branner & Korch, 1972; *Barnet i sivkurven* (title means "The Child in the Basket of Rushes"), P. Hasse & Soens, 1975; *Jerutee fra Raeveroed* (title means "Jerutte of Fox Clearing"), Arena, 1975; *Jerutte redder Tom og Tinne* (title means "Jerutte Saves Tom and Tinne"), Arena, 1975; *Da jorden forsvandt* (title means "When the Earth Disappeared"), P. Haase & Soens, 1975; *Jerutte og bjornen paa Raeverod* (title means "Jerutte and the Bear at Fox Clearing"), Arena, 1976; *Silas stifter familie* (title means "Silas Starts a Family"), Branner & Korch, 1976; *Silas paa Sebastianbjerget* (title means "Silas on Sebastian Mountain"), Branner & Korch, 1977; *Jerutte besoger Hundejens* (title means "Jerutte Visits Dog-Jens"), Arena, 1977; *Den udvalgte* (title means "The Chosen One"), P. Haase & Soens, 1977.

Poems: *Luseblomster* (title means "Lice Flowers"), Arena, 1955; *Fygende heste* (title means "Drifting Horses"), Arena, 1956; *Anadyomene* (title means "Aphrodite"), Arena,

CECIL BODKER

1959, 2nd edition, 1961; *Samlede digte* (title means "Collected Poems"), S. Hasselbalch, 1964; *I vaedderens tegn* (title means "In the Sign of the Ram"), Arena, 1968.

Short Stories: *Oejet* (title means "The Eye"), Arena, 1961; *Tilstanden Harley* (title means "The State of Harley"), Arena, 1965; *Fortaellinger Omkring Tavs* (title means "Stories About Tav"), Arena, 1971.

Novels: *Pap* (title means "Cardboard"), Arena, 1967; *Salthandlerskens Hus* (title means "The Salt Dealer's House"), Arena, 1972; *En Vrangmaske I Vorherres Strikketoej* (title means "A Wrong Stitch in Our Lord's Knitting"), Arena, 1974.

Plays: *Latter* (radio play; title means "Laughter"), Arena, 1964; "Badekarret" (radio play; title means "The Bathtub"), 1965; "Dukke Min" (radio play; title means "Doll of Mine"), 1968; "Kvinden Som Gik Bort Over Vandet" (radio play; title means "The Woman Who Walked Away over the Water"), 1971; "Skyld" (stage play; title means "Guilt"), first produced in Denmark, 1972.

WORK IN PROGRESS: More English translations of Bodker's "Silas" books are in preparation by Sheila Le Farge for Seymour Lawrence and Oxford University Press.

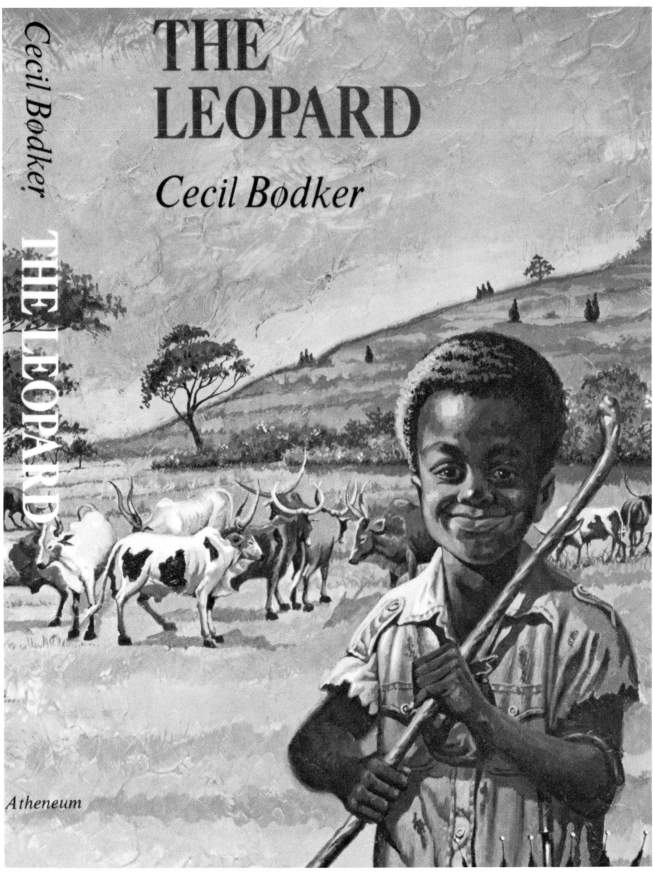

Tibeso was happy. The day augured well. On the green slope above him the animals were grazing--the horses and donkeys high up on the slope and the cattle almost down at the watercourse. ■ (From *The Leopard* by Cecil Bodker. Cover illustration by Eliza Moon.)

SIDELIGHTS: "People frequently ask me why I almost always write about boys and hardly ever about girls. Perhaps it is because my childhood was full of boys—or perhaps because I found what boys did more interesting than what girls did.

"When I was young, most children's books were written especially for boys or especially for girls—at least, that was true in Denmark where I live. I preferred to read the books for boys until I began reading adult books. Those written for girls usually seemed boring and sentimental.

"I never played with dolls for I found them boring, too. Once I was given a doll buggy. I used it as a soapbox car until it fell apart.

"I liked skating, sledding, sailing, biking, and camping. We lived out in the country, near the sea and not far from a town, with a beach to one side and open fields and the forest to the other.

"We were six children, five of them boys. I wore boy's clothing at a time when other girls wore only dresses; slacks and jeans didn't exist. Since we had a long, cold bike ride to school, my mother reasoned that I should be warmly dressed for the winter. So I was outfitted with knickers, a lumberjacket, a dark brown sheepskin cap, and leather boots that laced to the knees—just like my brothers.

"Was I teased about my clothes?

"To be honest, I don't remember, but probably.

"In Denmark people have titles according to their occupations and so people used to ask me *what* my father was. I didn't know how to answer, not because I didn't *know* what he was but because he was so many things. He was trained as a house painter and he was an author and an artist, but he earned a living as a designer in a silversmith's factory. He called himself 'draftsman.' Many people thought that was a strange thing to be. I could see it on their faces.

"After I finished high school, I became an apprentice at the factory where my father worked but this didn't change my situation. Counting all of us in the various workshops at the factory, there were fifty apprentices and I was the only girl. We attended technical schools in the evenings, where—again—I was the only girl. At the time I must have seen the world with the eyes of a boy.

"After four years as an apprentice, I received a silversmith's certificate and moved to Copenhagen, where I worked in the Georg Jensen silversmith workshop. I stayed there for three years and later spent one year as a silversmith at Markstroem's model workshop in Uppsala, Sweden.

"All this time I was writing and my poetry was piling up. I don't think I was more than ten when I wrote the first poem, but not until I was twenty-eight were any of my poems published. By then I had assembled an impressive number from which to choose the first collection.

"The critics gave this first volume an excellent reception and as a result I received my first writer's grant: five hundred Danish crowns. I decided to buy a typewriter with the money, to drop my work as a silversmith, and to concentrate on writing. Something inside me said that this was the right thing to do.

"Apparently that 'something' advised me well.

"My husband is a farmer. We are a good match. Half of his life is books and half of mine is the soil. We have just bought a good-sized farm in a beautiful part of Jutland. Now both of us must work very hard to develop it the way we want it to be, but we enjoy doing it together.

"I am often asked why I began to write and I must answer truthfully that I do not know. I just did. On the other hand, I do know why I continue to write: partly because I cannot help it and partly because I want to produce books so tightly-knit and so exciting that the children and young people who read them will experience them as intensely as I experienced books when I was their age. Even though my stories are mostly about boys, I hope that they will be read by both boys and girls, and sometimes by grownups, too."

FOR MORE INFORMATION SEE: Bookbird, Number 2, 1976, Number 4, 1976; *Top of the News,* Summer, 1977.

BOND, Gladys Baker 1912-
(Jo Mendel, a house pseudonym; Holly Beth Walker)

PERSONAL: Born May 7, 1912, in Berryville, Ark.; daughter of Coy Ernest and Clara (Clark) Baker; married Floyd James Bond (linoleum mechanic), September 3, 1934 (died August 3, 1973); children: Nicholas Peter. *Education:* Blair Business College, graduate, 1933; Kansas City Art Institute, 1936; Montana State University, student, 1954, 1956; University of Idaho, extension work, 1961-66. *Politics:* Republican. *Religion:* Lutheran. *Home:* 1425 Eighth St., Clarkston, Wash. 99403, and Vagabond Hill, Hayden Lake, Idaho.

GLADYS BAKER BOND

CAREER: Newswriter; free-lance short story writer, lecturer and teacher of art. Library board, Kellogg, Idaho, 1960-63. *Member:* Idaho Writers League (organized local chapter, twice president), Pacific Northwest International Writers, Gallery Board, Valley Art Center, Lewis-Clark Art Association (three time president). *Awards, honors:* Edith Kempthorne Award, Camp Fire Girls; Idaho's Writer of the Year, 1967.

WRITINGS: Little Stories on Big Subjects, B'nai B'rith, 1955; *Blue Chimney,* Holiday House, 1959; (as Jo Mendel) *Special Secret,* A. Whitman, 1961; (as Jo Mendel) *Cottage Holiday,* A. Whitman, 1962; *A Head on Her Shoulders,* Abelard-Schuman, 1963; (as Jo Mendel) *Here Comes A Friend,* A. Whitman, 1963; (as Jo Mendel) *That Kitten Again,* A Whitman, 1964; (as Jo Mendel) *Here Comes the Tuckers,* A. Whitman, 1964; (as Jo Mendel) *Toby Tucker,* A. Whitman, 1965; (as Jo Mendel) *Tom and the Dickie Bird,* A. Whitman, 1965; *Adventures with Hal,* A. Whitman, 1965; *Chap and Chirpy,* A. Whitman, 1965; *On Hoofs and Paws in High Country,* A. Whitman, 1965; (with Florence Baker Bertram) *The Secret at Rocky Ridge,* Abelard-Schuman, 1965; *Animal Babies Wild and Free,* A. Whitman, 1965; *Fawn Baby,* A. Whitman, 1966; *Timmy's New Bed,* A. Whitman, 1966; *Beth's Rock,* A. Whitman, 1966; *Patrick Will Grow,* A. Whitman, 1966; *The Magic Friend Maker,* A. Whitman, 1966, Little Golden Book, 1976.

(As Holly Beth Walker) *Meg and the Disappearing Diamonds,* A. Whitman, 1967; *Lassie and the Four White Ducks,* A. Whitman, 1967; (with Florence Bertram) *The Mystery at Far Reach,* Abelard-Schuman, 1967; *Corey Baker's Show and Tell,* A. Whitman, 1969; *Buffy and the New Girl,* A. Whitman, 1969; *My Widening World,* Childcraft's 1969 Annual, Field Enterprises, 1969; *On the Stranger's Mountain,* Abelard-Schuman, 1969; *Buffy Finds a Star,* A. Whitman, 1970; *Album of Cats,* Rand McNally, 1971; *Boy in the Middle,* Ginn and Co., 1972; *The Penny Sale* ("The Waltons"), A. Whitman, 1975; *Up She Rises* ("The Waltons"), A. Whitman, 1976. Sold more than 200 short stories to children's papers and magazines between 1945 and 1955.

WORK IN PROGRESS: Novels for A. Whitman.

SIDELIGHTS: "I was four when I stood on a chair and read a recipe from an oatmeal box. My reward? Cookies, of course. Cookies, too, for the young uncle and aunt who had taught me to read and spell from building blocks. From that day I've read, read, read. With all of those words rolling around in my head, what could I do but write short stories and books? My first published story was read by everybody in the block when I was twelve. I had to wait until I had a son in college before *Blue Chimney* came off the press. I suppose I had to wait to be old enough to have something to say.

"I am the eldest of five children born in the Arkansas Ozarks and transplanted to Idaho and Washington. I married an only child, have one son [who has one son (Brook) whose mother (Kelly) is an only child]. That makes good story material. I use it.

"In fact, I use everything that has ever happened to me, good and bad, happy and sad. I place people in places I've been. I watch the movie behind my eyes and report it to you, my reader. I have not traveled widely, but I have lived a long time in each of several places: on a southern farm, in a western lumber town, in an Idaho mining community, in Washington's cow country, and in a few cities. Quite often I write about lakeside summer living because my brothers and sisters still share swimming, boating, hiking, fishing, beachfires and huckleberrying on the same bay of Hayden Lake, Idaho, we knew as children.

"I am a triple-professional. Besides writing, I paint and teach art at the college level. I was married thirty-nine years. A lot can happen in thirty-nine years. I am a widow, but I am never bored and seldom lonely. There is much, too much to do!

"I write for children because I know what it is like to be a child . It is like being one drop of water in the oceans of the world, when you want to be the biggest wave that ever tossed a ship in a storm. One learns to blend with other drops of water to form that wave. At long last there comes the storm that tosses that wave up, up and up. With any luck you find yourself flung high and far, all alone in space before dropping back to become part of the ocean again. I write about that one dizzying moment when the self is on its own to win or fail.

"I like both people and animals and always have a Siamese cat to boss me around. Right this minute Girl is napping on my desk, barely beyond the reach of the moving carriage of my electric Royal. A squirrel on the patio roof likes the hum of my typewriter, too, and peers across space while eating peanuts I toss in the eave trough.

"Service to Camp Fire Girls has taken twenty-five years of my time. I share the Career Education Program and visit hundreds of grade school children each year.

Even when they look alike, no two siamese cats have the same voice, though all talk long and loudly. ■ (From *Album of Cats* by Gladys Baker Bond. Illustrated by Marge Opitz Burridge.)

"When it snows, I shovel the walks. When it storms, I get wet. I never wear a hat to cover my head from sun. I just get freckles and enjoy the heat in my bones. But wind bothers me. I am allergic to dust.

"I like rocks, hills, pine trees and brown-eyed boys. I listen for a frog chorus at night. My favorite roads wind up mountains. I like quails in snow, cool spring sun on yellow roses, the warmth of a cat in my lap while I read. I like crossword puzzles, Scrabble games and children's fan letters. I like to lie flat on a smooth boulder after swimming in cold water. I like to fly, but I don't like to drive in heavy traffic on a hot day.

"I like life. That's what writing is all about, isn't it? Sharing life's experiences with a friend?"

HOBBIES AND OTHER INTERESTS: Painting, handcrafts, Indian lore, a grandson, long summers at Hayden Lake, Idaho, and people.

BOND, Ruskin 1934-

PERSONAL: Born May 19, 1934, in Kasauli, India; son of Aubrey Alexander (in Royal Air Force) and Edith (Clerke) Bond. *Education:* Attended Bishop Cotton School, Simla, India, 1943-50. *Home:* Maplewood Lodge, Bala Hissar, Mussoorie, Uttar Pradesh, India.

CAREER: Worked at one period for Cooperative for American Relief Everywhere (CARE), but has been a full-time writer since the age of twenty-two. *Awards, honors:* John

...she woke up to this terrible sound and looked about her, and there in the moonlit glade, up to his belly in water, stood a young elephant, his trunk raised as he trumpeted his predicament to the forest.... ■ (From *Angry River* by Ruskin Bond. Illustrated by Trevor Stubley.)

Llewellyn Rhys Memorial Prize for the most memorable work of 1957 by a writer under thirty, for *The Room on the Roof.*

WRITINGS: The Room on the Roof (novel), Deutsch, 1956, Coward, 1957; *The Neighbour's Wife and Other Stories,* Higginbotham (Madras), 1967; *Grandfather's Private Zoo,* India Book House, 1967; *Panther's Moon,* Random House, 1969; *The Last Tiger,* Publications Division (New Delhi), 1970; *Angry River,* Hamish Hamilton (London), 1972; *The Blue Umbrella,* Hamish Hamilton, 1974. Stories included in *World's Best Contemporary Stories,* Ace Books, and *Young Winter's Tales 1970,* Macmillan. Contributor of short stories and articles to *Reader's Digest, Christian Science Monitor, Lady, Times of India, Illustrated Weekly of India, Statesman, Hemisphere, Cricket* and *The Asia Magazine.* Edits *Impoint,* a magazine published from Bombay.

WORK IN PROGRESS: A novel; a children's book; autobiography; poetry; commissioned by the Nehru Memorial Fund to write a biography (for children) of Nehru, First Prime Minister of independent India.

RUSKIN BOND

SIDELIGHTS: All of Ruskin Bond's books to date have dealt with life in India—*The Room on the Roof* about growing up in a changing India, *The Last Tiger* about the disappearance of wild life in India, and *Panther's Moon* about a remote Himalayan village. "My interests (mountains, animals, trees, wild flowers) are embodied in these and other writings.

"I live in the foothills of the Himalayas, and my window opens out on the forest and the distant snow-peaks—the highest mountains in the world. . . . I sit here and, inspired by the life of the hill people and the presence of birds and trees, write my stories and poems." Bond is an Indian national.

BORNSTEIN, Ruth 1927-

PERSONAL: Born April 28, 1927, in Milwaukee, Wis.; daughter of Adolph and Bertha (Friedman) Lercher; married Harry Bornstein (a designer and builder), January 7, 1951; children: Noa, Jonah, Adam, Jesse. *Education:* University of Wisconsin, Madison, B.S., 1948; graduate study at Art Students League, 1949, and at Cranbrook Academy of Art, 1951. *Home:* 14912 McKendree Ave., Pacific Palisades, Calif. 90272.

MEMBER: Society of Children's Book Writers, Southern California Council on Literature for Children and Young People. *Awards, honors:* Southern California Council on Literature for Children and Young People award for significant contribution to illustration, 1974, for *Son of Thunder,* 1977, for *Little Gorilla.*

WRITINGS—Juvenile fiction; self-illustrated: *Indian Bunny,* Childrens Press, 1973; *Little Gorilla* (Junior Literary Guild selection), Seabury, 1976; *The Dream of the Little Elephant,* Seabury, 1977; *Jim,* Seabury, 1978; *Annabelle,* Crowell, 1978; *The Dancing Man,* Seabury, 1978.

Illustrator: Ethel K. McHale, *Son of Thunder,* Children's Press, 1974; Crescent Dragonwagon, *Your Owl Friend,* Harper, 1977.

His grandma and grandpa, and his aunts and uncles loved him.

(From *Little Gorilla* by Ruth Bornstein. Illustrated by the author.)

RUTH BORNSTEIN

SIDELIGHTS: "When I was ten years old we moved from Milwaukee to New London, Wisconsin, a very small town. I liked it because right in town were rivers and woods and I loved exploring the countryside. This is something I still love to do wherever I am.

"After college and a year in New York City, teaching art in a settlement house and painting at the Art Students League, I went to Israel. For over a year I wandered around, painted and worked at various jobs, including herding goats on a kibbutz for four months.

"My husband and I met in Paris where we were both painting. Eventually we came to California where our daughter, Noa, and sons, Jonah, Adam, and Jesse were born. I enjoyed reading books with my children, I even enjoyed reading books without them. But I didn't dream of doing books myself.

"Through the years I continued to paint, had four solo art exhibits and participated in many group and juried exhibitions. I still exhibit with a group of artists about once a year.

"Then gradually, about eight years ago, my painting changed. I found that I was drawing little elephants talking to flowers, flowers flying through the air, rabbits underground, little gorillas talking to rabbits—I didn't know what was happening but I let it happen—because it was fun! In 1971 I grew my first vegetable garden. I was so moved by the life cycle of the garden that I began to write. Words became very important suddenly. I filled sketchbooks with words and pictures and that's what I've been doing ever since.

"Of course, it's been my hard work but I love what I do. Not only is it tremendously challenging, but it involves all of me."

HOBBIES AND OTHER INTERESTS: Folk dancing, hiking, reading, and vegetable gardening.

BOTTNER, Barbara 1943-

PERSONAL: Born May 25, 1943, in New York, N.Y.; daughter of Irving (a business executive) and Elaine (Schiff) Bottner. *Education:* Attended Boston University, 1961-62, and Ecole des Beaux Arts, 1963-64; University of Wisconsin, B.S., 1965; University of California, Santa Barbara, M.A., 1966. *Religion:* Bio-energetics. *Home:* 34 West 28th St., New York, N.Y. 10001.

CAREER: Actress, kindergarten teacher, animation producer, writer, and artist; Parsons School of Design, New York, N.Y., instructor, 1973—. *Member:* Graphic Artists Guild, Art Directors Club, Society of Illustrators, Association International of Film Animation, Association of Independent Filmakers and Video. *Awards, honors:* Best Film for Television award from International Animation Festival, Annecy, France, 1973, for "Goat in a Boat"; Cine Golden Eagle for animated film, "Later That Night." Has been represented in film festivals in London, Melbourne, Ottawa and New York City.

WRITINGS—Juvenile: *What Would You Do with a Giant?,* Putnam, 1972; *Fun House,* Prentice-Hall, 1975; *Eek, a Monster,* Macmillan, 1975; *The Box,* Macmillan, 1975; *What Grandma Did on Her Birthday,* Macmillan, 1975; *Jungle Day,* Delacorte, 1977; *There Was Nobody There,* Macmillan, in press; *Messy,* Delacorte, in press; *The Mickey Mouse Ring that Honks When You Squeeze It,* Random, in press.

Author of film, "Goat in a Boat." Children's book reviewer for *New York Times* Sunday Section. Editorial illustrator for *New York Times, Ms., Viva,* and *Intellectual Digest.* Cartoonist for *Viva* and *Penthouse.*

WORK IN PROGRESS: Juvenile novel; short animated film; feature length script.

SIDELIGHTS: "It's been a long trek for me to learn who it was inside me that wanted to speak to children, but I feel like I've finally begun to tap 'her.' I like to use the disgruntled

BARBARA BOTTNER

(From *Jungle Day* by Barbara Bottner. Illustrated by the author.)

child who nonetheless has tremendous fight and spirit. Childhood wasn't the sweet melody it might have been, but it was probably a fairly universal type of struggle. I believe it's extremely important for children to accept all their difficult and angry feelings, so they don't feel they're 'bad' for being who they are. On the other hand, my illustrations, al-though they portray this child exactly, seem to have the warmth and cozy ambiance I *would* have liked to have, but didn't.

''I have an almost mystical respect for children, they come into this world perfect. If we, as adults, cannot manage to leave them unscarred, the least we can do is give them a place to let their wild and intractable feelings roam free. I admire Sendak's *Wild Things* for exactly this reason, although I'm sure he didn't write it in as analyzed a process as I'm describing here. I also like to entertain children, because 'going down to their level' is climbing up to rather dizzy heights."

HOBBIES AND OTHER INTERESTS: Jogging, travel, dancing, cooking.

FOR MORE INFORMATION SEE: Rita Xanthoudakis, "All About Time and No Time" (film), New York University, 1974, distributed by Filmmakers Library.

BRENT, Stuart

PERSONAL: Surname was originally Brodsky; born in Chicago, Illinois.

CAREER: Former university philosophy teacher; lecturer; critic; TV and radio reviewer, and host of "Books and Brent," 1959-60, a series of book reviews presented on WBKB television and WLS radio of the American Broadcasting Co., Chicago; author of children's books; and bookseller since 1946.

WRITINGS: The Seven Stairs (autobiographical), Houghton, 1962; *The Strange Disappearance of Mr. Toast* (illustrated by Leslie Goldstein), Viking, 1964; *Mr. Toast and the Woolly Mammoth* (illustrated by Lillian Obligado), Viking, 1966; *Mr. Toast and the Secret of Gold Hill* (illustrated by George Porter), Lippincott, 1970.

SIDELIGHTS: Stuart Brent's love for good books is what made him want to be a bookseller. In 1946, with a G.I. loan, Brent bought $300 worth of books, borrowed some more, and opened a small store fifteen feet long and nine feet wide. The original store, called The Seven Stairs, also sold records, with the idea being, according to Brent, that anyone with literary taste would have the equivalent taste in music. With the help of newspaper columnists, the word was spread about Brent's bookstore. In 1968, the store, located at 670 Michigan Ave. in Chicago, was remodeled into what Brent described as an American version of Blackwell's in Oxford, England.

FOR MORE INFORMATION SEE: Stuart Brent, *The Seven Stairs,* Houghton, 1962; "Brent's New Shop Has Literary Ambience," *Publishers Weekly,* September 30, 1968; S. Brent, "There's Nobody There: a Bookseller Looks at Publishing Today," *Publishers Weekly,* March 12, 1973; S. Brent, "How Alexander Solzhenitsyn Brightened a Day in the Life of a Chicago Bookseller," *Publishers Weekly,* March 11, 1974.

BROSNAN, James Patrick   1929-
(Jim Brosnan)

PERSONAL: Born October 24, 1929, in Cincinnati, Ohio; son of John Patrick and Rose (Brockhoff) Brosnan; married Anne Stewart Pitcher, June 23, 1952; children: Jamie, Timothy, Kimberlee. *Education:* Xavier University, student, 1947. *Politics:* Independent. *Home:* 7742 West Churchill St., Morton Grove, Ill. 60053. *Agent:* Max Wilkinson, Littauer & Wilkinson, 500 Fifth Ave., New York, N.Y. 10036.

CAREER: Professional baseball player, 1947-63, with Chicago Cubs, St. Louis Cardinals, and Cincinnati Reds; Arthur Meyerhoff, Inc. (advertising and merchandising), research and publicity, 1949-57; American Broadcasting Co. radio network and Station WBKB, Chicago, Ill., sports commentator, 1963-65; *Chicago Daily News,* Chicago, Ill., sports columnist, 1965—. *Awards, honors:* National Association of Independent Schools Award for *The Long Season,* 1961; *Playboy* article, "The Short Season," included in *Best Sports Stories of 1977.*

WRITINGS—Under name Jim Brosnan: *The Long Season,* Harper, 1960; *Pennant Race,* Harper, 1962; *Great Baseball Pitchers,* Random, 1965; *Great Rookies of Major Leagues,* Random, 1966; *Little League to Big League,* Random, 1968; *Ron Santo, 3b,* Putnam, 1974; *Ted Simmons,* Putnam, 1977. Short stories in *Boy's Life.* Articles in *Sports Illustrated, Life, New York Times Magazine, National Review, St. Louis Post-Dispatch, Atlantic Monthly, MacLean's, Saturday Evening Post, Boy's Life, Sport, Playboy.*

WORK IN PROGRESS: Nine Innings, a novel; *The Last Season,* non-fiction journal about a current major league ball club.

SIDELIGHTS: "I became a writer by accident rather than design. When I was pitching for the Chicago Cubs in 1968 a *Time* magazine reporter, Robert Boyle, said to me: 'The trouble with most sportswriting is the lack of basic knowledge, an insider's point of view. People who play sports professionally don't write about their business. Why don't you take a crack at it?

"So I did. He read it, liked it, and helped persuade *Sports Illustrated* to publish it. That article, a brief journal covering three weeks in the lives of some big league ballplayers, was expanded into a book, *The Long Season,* concerning an entire year of my professional career. A sequel, *Pennant Race,* covered the 1961 season when the Cincinnati Reds won the National League championship.

"That experience, those happy circumstances made me THE ATHLETE WHO WROTE BOOKS. It did not, of course, make me a professional writer. All I had going for

JAMES PATRICK BROSNAN

(From *Little League to Big League* by Jim Brosnan. Photo by Suzanne Szasz.)

me was a point of view, a candid style, and a facility with words. Constructive criticism from editors of magazines, newspapers and publishing houses helped me to understand that writing is a craft, not a magical gift. And the advice of Red Smith, America's best sportswriter, was invaluable. Said Red: 'What you have to do is attach the seat of your pants to a chair, roll the paper in your typewriter, put your hands on the keys, and write 'til you bleed!' Doing it for a living is better than digging ditches, but pitching to Hank Aaron was more fun.

"Having my by-line on seven books, a hundred magazine articles, several newspaper columns, and many radio and television sports programs, I can get pretty glib about WHAT, WHERE, WHEN and HOW to write. Pick a subject, research it, find an angle, and 'attach your self to the chair, etc.' One important question about the craft remains: 'WHY WRITE?' Modern philosophers like Marshall Mc-Cluhan claim that the printed word has lost its power and relevance in a world of oral and visual communication. I doubt it's true, but the possibility is chilling. As a boy I found delight and joy in literature and was just as happy with a book in my hands as I ever was with a bat or a ball. Young readers who think reading is a chore rather than a pleasure are missing out on life's great satisfactions. A culture that would discourage the production and consequent enjoyment of the printed word has, it seems to me, taken an unfortunate point of view.

"It's enough to make me keep writing. Madly."

FOR MORE INFORMATION SEE: Time, September 5, 1960; *New York Times Book Review,* October 16, 1960; *Saturday Evening Post,* May 13, 1961.

BROWN, Robert Joseph 1907- (Bob Brown)

PERSONAL: Born August 19, 1907, in Rockwood, Tenn. *Home:* 20 Vandalia St., Asheville, N.C.

CAREER: Onetime editor; currently lecturer-demonstrator of "Science Circus," appearing at school assemblies throughout eastern and southern United States. *Member:* American Association for Advancement of Science, National Education Association, National Science Teachers Association, International Brotherhood of Magicians, North Carolina Academy of Science.

WRITINGS: Science Circus, Fleet, 1960; *Science Circus No. 2,* Fleet, 1964; *Take 100,000 Volts,* Vow Labs, 1964; *Science Treasures,* Fleet, 1968; *Science Circus, No. 3,* Fleet, 1972; *Two Hundred Illustrated Science Experiments for Boys and Girls,* Collins-World, 1974; *How to Fool Your Friends,* Western Publishing, 1978; *"666" Science Experiments,* TAB Books, 1978. Author of syndicated newspaper panel, "Science for You," syndicated by the Los Angeles Times Syndicate.

WORK IN PROGRESS: A book of fiction based on the happiness and tragedy of a coal mining town.

SIDELIGHTS: "I was born and went through high school in Rockwood, Tennessee, a coal mining and iron making town. In high school I was privileged to attend the Scopes evolution trial which was only 25 miles from my home. There I mingled with reporters from around the world, and the desire to be one of them was born.

"Earlier my grandfather had given me a typewriter, and earlier still my father had given me an electrical toy and my uncle had given me Erector sets. I was undecided as to whether I liked science or writing better. Two explosions in the Rockwood mine provided me with tragic material for a book. A congenial superintendent, aware of my writing interest, allowed me to go into the mine for a day to see the destruction.

"Then, for two summers, while in high school, I worked in McRoberts mines in Eastern Kentucky. This gave me much good background.

"In Cincinnati I asked editors of the four newspapers what courses I should take at the University to prepare me for a reporting job. All said "take anything *except* journalism if you want to work for us." The result was that I had many non-credit courses in physics and psychology that have been useful.

"Jay Hensley, chief reporter for the Asheville, N.C., 'Citizen' is collaborating with me on the coal mine novel. We hope to make it the best coal mine novel ever written. Meantime, I am busy with my column, which combines writing and science, and with books on science for children.

"My family has been an encouraging factor in my life. My son is a scientist. My daughter is beautiful and talented enough to work as a model in New York. My four grandchildren are the greatest in the world. My wife has always been tolerant, understanding, and most helpful. I expect to work until senility sets in. Then my wife, hopefully, can continue to bring in a few dollars as a television personality."

This photograph shows Robert Brown's daughter Betty with high voltage Tesla currents streaming from her fingers. A piece of untreated wood held in the hand will catch fire from this discharge. ■ (From *Science Treasures* by Bob Brown.)

TREVOR CAIRNS

CAIRNS, Trevor   1922-

PERSONAL: Born April 17, 1922; son of John Thomas and Emily (Wisbach) Cairns; married Heather Mary Bowman, April 2, 1956; children: Conrad, Edmund. *Education:* Balliol College, Oxford, B.A., 1943, M.A., 1947.; King's College, Newcastle upon Tyne, M.Ed., 1953. *Politics:* "Convinced floating voter." *Religion:* "Unconvinced." *Home:* 4 Ashmore Ter., Sunderland, SR2 7DE, Tyne and Wear, England. *Office:* Polytechnic, Sunderland, Tyne and Wear, England.

CAREER: History master at secondary schools in Bristol, England, 1944-45, Midhurst, England, 1945-49, and Newcastle upon Tyne, England, 1950-54; Training College, Bedford, England, lecturer in history, 1955-60; College of Education, Sunderland, England, lecturer in history and head of department, 1960-75; Polytechnic, Sunderland, England, lecturer in history and head of section, 1975—. *Member:* Historical Association (president of Sunderland branch, 1963-66), Association of Teachers in Colleges and Departments of Education (member of executive, 1958-66), Society for Nautical Research. *Awards, honors: Men Become Civilized* and *The Romans and Their Empire* received bronze medals at International Book Fair in Leipzig, 1971.

WRITINGS: (General editor) "Cambridge Introduction to the History of Mankind" (series of secondary school texts), Cambridge University Press, Volume I: *Men Become Civilized,* 1969, Volume II: *The Romans and Their Empire,* 1970, Volume III: *Barbarians, Christians and Muslims,*

1971, Volume IV: *The Middle Ages,* 1972, Volume V: *Europe Finds the World,* 1973, Volume VI: *The Birth of Modern Europe,* 1975, Volume VII: *The Old Regime and the Revolution,* 1976, Volume VIII: *Power for the People,* in press. General editor of over twenty books on special topics.

WORK IN PROGRESS: Europe Rules the World, Volume IX of "Cambridge Introduction to the History of Mankind."

SIDELIGHTS: "Some of our sillier educationalists persist in trying to tell us that children do not like history, cannot understand it and get nothing out of it. What nonsense!—I wonder if they have ever known any normal children. In my experience most children, like most people generally, are very ready to be interested in history. Certainly I was, as long ago as I can remember.

"Stories, pictures, buildings, models and other things in museums—I liked them all. Why? Of course, I never bothered to ask myself what would have seemed, then, such an unnecessary question. Now that the question does not seem to me unnecessary, I have to try to forget what I have since learnt if I want to know what made history seem so interesting then. Perhaps it was that historical people seemed to lead more colourful lives than the people I met every day. Their clothes and houses, towns and ships all looked so much more attractive than those of the 1920's and 1930's, and they seemed to spend their lives doing things that were much more worthwhile than earning a twentieth-century living. Indeed it often seemed that they were, quite simply, better people. And there was the endless fascination of entering into so many new ways of life, each of them strange, but not too strange to believe.

"In some respects it is still the same. I still value very highly the enormous variety of people we meet in history—to adapt Dr. Johnson, the man who is tired of history is tired of life. I still prefer the architecture, costume and arts of many other periods to our own, and often admire the standards of behaviour that past generations tried to maintain. But I admit to being much more conscious of the hardships, limitations and monotony of a great deal of life in previous centuries, and have become more interested in the problems our forefathers faced and in how they solved them. I have come to view the history of the human race as one great continuing story, with civilizations, nations and individuals making their contributions in sub-plots and episodes. There is no saga to equal it.

"In the books I write and edit, I am always aware that each one, even when it seems complete in itself, is a piece of this greater story. I accept that different writers will emphasise different parts of the story. For instance, I usually take the development of Western European civilization as the most useful central theme, while a writer brought up in a different cultural tradition (and writing for readers also brought up in his tradition) would naturally work with his own civilization at the centre. He would be right—as I am right, too. Without a guiding thread, the story would be too labyrinthine for most of us to learn. But there is another reason: anyone who has not first learnt to understand and respect his own civilization is unlikely to understand or respect others.

"It is beginning to sound as if I am preoccupied with theories about the vast sweep of history. That would be a misleading impression. It is rather in the details that I find most pleasure and new insights—in reading accounts of personal experiences or in handling the things made and used by people who were so like ourselves, but placed in such different circumstances. That is the real stuff of history; I have no time for those computerised statisticians who have apparently forgotten that numbers and machines are excellent servants, but execrable masters. History is not about vague trends, or graphs, or social or political or economic doctrines. It is about the real men and women who made the world we live in.

"One of my favourite ways of trying to get closer to these people is through their possessions. Private Wheeler can tell us much about what it was like to be one of Wellington's soldiers, but we can still learn something more if we pick up a Brown Bess musket. Some of my students once decided to try to reproduce, as nearly as resources allowed, the full equipment of a Norman knight. They did very well, though at the cost of many fingernails worn down in the task of interlocking the hundreds of steel rings that made up the coat of mail. It was good practical research, for it helped us to offer explanations of several things that looked puzzling on the Bayeux Tapestry. It has also proved a huge success in another way. Many students have borrowed it when they have been teaching in schools, and it has never failed to stimulate keen interest, sensible questions and imaginative comments.

"That armour, in its own way, does what a history book should also do: give information, generate interest, stir imagination and provoke questions."

Trevor Cairns specialized interests are in the sixteenth-century, in Spain and Spanish America, in naval and nautical history, and in military architecture. He collects weapons and used to make models ("not enough time nowadays").

CROSHER, G(eoffry) R(obins) 1911-
(G. R. Kesteven)

PERSONAL: Born May 5, 1911, in Hampstead, London. *Home:* 99 Langley Way, Watford, Hertfordshire WD1 3ED, England.

CAREER: Has worked in insurance, advertising, fire-fighting, gardening and for many years in teaching (often of retarded teenagers); now full-time author.

WRITINGS—All for children, except as indicated; under name G. R. Crosher: *Ken and the Kidnappers*, Cassell, 1954; *The Limping Smuggler*, Cassell, 1954; *The Strange Lodger*, Cassell, 1954; *The Robbery at Blairs*, Cassell, 1954, Fearon, 1969; *Fire at Brean House*, Cassell, 1954; *Castaway on Green Rock*, Cassell, 1954, published in the United States under the title *Devil's Rock*, Fearon, 1969; *Fireman Joe*, Methuen, 1955; *Cowboy Dave*, Methuen, 1955; *Footballer Steve*, Methuen, 1955; *Lone Eagle*, Methuen, 1955; *Island Adventure*, Methuen, 1955, Fearon, 1963; *House on Fire*, Methuen, 1955, published in the United States under the title *Fire on the Second Floor*, Fearon, 1966; *A Convict Has Escaped*, Methuen, 1955, published in the United States under the title *Catch Tom Rudd*, Fearon, 1966; *Treasure in the Ruins*, Methuen, 1955, Fearon, 1965; *Mail-Bag Robbery*, Cassell, 1956; *Attack on a Stranger*, Cassell, 1956; *A Spy on the Falcon*, Cassell, 1956; *Trail to Adventure*, Cassell, 1956, Fearon, 1963; *Night Chase*, Cassell, 1956, published in the United States under the title *Night Adventure*, Fearon, 1969; *A Bomb in the Submarine*, Cassell, 1956, Fearon, 1965; *Laughter from the Past* (one-act plays based on European folk tales), Methuen, 1956; *Mystery at Camp*, Methuen, 1957, published in the United States under the title *Trouble on the Farm*, Fearon, 1969; *A Night*

in the Old House, Methuen, 1957, published in the United States under the title *The Haunted House*, Fearon, 1966; *A Man Without Memory*, Methuen, 1957, Fearon, 1966; *A Gun from Nowhere*, Methuen, 1957, Fearon, 1965; *A Drive into Danger*, Cassell, 1959, published in the United States under the title *Ride on a Rainy Afternoon*, Fearon, 1965; *Mystery Cottage*, Cassell, 1959, Fearon, 1963; *The Man from the Sea*, Cassell, 1959; *Blackmailer's Hide-Out*, Cassell, 1959; *Hunt the Necklace!*, Cassell, 1959; *The Drifting Yacht*, Cassell, 1959; (with D. R. Crawford) *Problem Practice* (arithmetic books), three volumes, Methuen, 1959-60.

More Laughter from the Past (one-act plays), Methuen, 1961; *Holiday Mystery*, Methuen, 1961, published in the United States under the title *Mystery at Camp Sunshine*, Fearon, 1965; *Uncle Bill Comes Home*, Methuen, 1961, Fearon, 1963; *Adventure in the Snow*, Methuen, 1961, Fearon, 1965; *The Strange Artist*, Methuen, 1961, Fearon, 1963; *Country Stories*, Cassell, 1962; *Seaside Days*, Cassell, 1962, published in the United States under the title *By the Sea*, Fearon, 1969; *At Home*, Cassell, 1962, published in the United States under the title *Around Home*, Fearon, 1969; *Round the Town*, Cassell, 1962, Fearon, 1963; (with N.W.N. Sagar) *Pilot English*, three volumes, Methuen, 1965-66; *Along the Chiltern Ways* (adult travel book), Cassell, 1973; *The Match on the Patch*, Cassell, 1975; *A Find on the Patch*, Cassell, 1975; *Christmas on the Patch*, Cassell, 1975; *A Pinch on the Patch*, Cassell, 1975; *Along the Cotswold Ways* (adult travel book), Cassell, 1976; *No Sun at Sunnyside*, Cassell, 1976; *Attack in Dark Lane*, Cassell, 1976; *Runaway into Danger*, Cassell, 1976; *Strangers in the Village*, Cassell, 1976.

Under pseudonym G. R. Kesteven: *The Peasants' Revolt*, Chatto & Windus, 1965; *The Reformation in England*, Chatto & Windus, 1965; *The Armada*, Chatto & Windus, 1965; *The Mayflower Pilgrims*, Chatto & Windus, 1966; *The Execution of the King*, Chatto & Windus, 1966; *The Glorious Revolution of 1688*, Chatto & Windus, 1966; *1485, from Plantagenet to Tudor*, Chatto & Windus, 1967; *Peterloo, 1819*, Chatto & Windus, 1967; *The Triumph of Reform, 1832*, Chatto & Windus, 1967; *The Forty-Five Rebellion*, Chatto & Windus, 1968; *The Loss of the American Colonies*, Chatto & Windus, 1968; *1851, Britain Shows the World*, Chatto & Windus, 1968; *1870, Year of Change*, Chatto & Windus, 1970; *The Boer War*, Chatto & Windus, 1970; *1914*, Chatto & Windus, 1970; *The Why of Our Towns and Villages*, Chatto & Windus, 1972; *The Pale Invaders* (futuristic fiction), Chatto & Windus, 1974, Atheneum, 1975; *Where Do You Live?: The Story Behind English Place-Names*, Chatto & Windus, 1976; *The Awakening Water* (futuristic fiction), Chatto & Windus, 1977.

WORK IN PROGRESS: Four books in the "Onward Books" series, for Cassell.

SIDELIGHTS: "I can remember at quite an early age trying verses, usually intended to be humorous; . . . by my teens I was trying more ambitious stories and essays; I was, I think, drawn by the challenge of giving shape to often-vague ideas, fascinated by the variety and subtlety of words, and intrigued by working out the intricacies of a plot. . . .

"When asked to try teaching retarded youngsters, I found that almost the only simply written books then available were those for five-year-olds. My teenagers were not encouraged by such books, so I wrote . . . exciting stories in a controlled vocabulary and a deliberately repetitive style. . . . The forty-eighth is due early in 1977, and many have been published . . . in European countries where they are used in teaching English as a second language.

"The writing of those stories taught me much. Their simple language and controlled sentence construction make them, of course, of no literary value . . . though some stories are more than mere adventures. But . . . that these stories have enjoyed a long life, and many have been given a more up-to-date appearance and re-issued, suggests that they did their job well.

"Meanwhile, perhaps to relieve the strain of teaching retarded children, I had been asked to take Social Studies with brighter classes. As part of this work I tried to get away from the conventional and often superficial approach to History by taking a series of incidents and trying to discover what contemporaries thought about them. The results often gave very different impressions from the text-book summary . . . and so I wrote my findings.

"A few years ago, on my doctor's advice, I left teaching. Since then I have written two adult travel books. . . . I have also written two futuristic (definitely not Science Fiction) novels for children. . . . To me, these last seem unexpected works, and I'm unsure of my reasons for attempting them . . . perhaps partly an extension of my interest in History, partly a distrust of those futuristic works which appear to me suspect in their assumptions and improbable in their conclusions, partly a feeling which many of us must share of being subjected to forces too large for our comprehension, partly a belief that, whatever comes, we humans will retain our essential humanity."

CROWTHER, James Gerald 1899-

PERSONAL: Born in 1899, in Lightcliffe, Yorkshire, Eng. *Education:* Attended local schools. *Address:* West Cottage, Flamborough Head, Nr. Bridlington, E. Yorks. YO15 1AN, England.

CAREER: Manchester Guardian, scientific correspondent, 1928-48; British Council, director of the science department, 1941-46; free-lance writer. *Member:* Association of Scientific, Technical, and Managerial Staffs.

WRITINGS: Science for You, Brentano's, 1928; *Short Stories in Science,* Routledge, 1929; *Science in Soviet Russia,* Williams & Norgate, 1930; *An Outline of the Universe,* Dodd, 1931; *The ABC of Chemistry,* Kegan Paul, 1932; *Osiris and the Atom,* Routledge, 1932; *Industry and Education in Soviet Russia,* Heinemann, 1932; *The Progress of Science: An Account of Recent Fundamental Researches in Physics, Chemistry, and Biology,* Kegan Paul, 1934; *British Scientists of the Nineteenth Century,* Kegan Paul, 1935, reissued, 1962, published in America as *Men of Science: Humphry Davy, Michael Faraday, James Prescott Joule, William Thomson, James Clerk Maxwell,* Norton, 1936; *Famous American Men of Science,* Norton, 1937, reprinted, Books for Libraries, 1969; *Science and Life,* V. Gollancz, 1938; *About Petroleum,* Oxford University Press, 1938.

The Social Relations of Science, Macmillan, 1941, revised edition, Dufour, 1967; (with Richard Whiddington) *Science at War,* McLeod, 1948; *Science in Liberated Europe,* Pilot, 1949; *Six Great Inventors: Watt, Stephenson, Edison, Marconi, Wright Brothers, [and] Whittle,* H. Hamilton, 1954, reissued, 1961; *Sciences of Energy,* Muller, 1954; *Discoveries and Inventions of the Twentieth Century,* 4th edition

JAMES GERALD CROWTHER

(Crowther was not associated with earlier editions), Dutton, 1955, 5th edition, 1966; *Nuclear Energy in Industry,* Pitman, 1956; *Science Unfolds the Future,* Muller, 1956; *Six Great Doctors: Harvey, Pasteur, Lister, Pavlov, Ross, [and] Fleming,* H. Hamilton, 1957; *The Story of Agriculture,* H. Hamilton, 1958; *Six Great Engineers: De Lesseps, Brunel, Westinghouse, Parsons, Diesel, [and] Hinton,* H. Hamilton, 1959.

Francis Bacon, the First Statesman of Science, Cresset, 1960; *Founders of British Science: John Wilkins, Robert Boyle, John Ray, Christopher Wren, Robert Hooke, Isaac Newton,* Cresset, 1960; *Six Great Scientists: Copernicus, Galileo, Newton, Darwin, Marie Curie, Einstein,* H. Hamilton, 1961; *Radioastronomy and Radar* (illustrated by David A. Hardy), Criterion, 1961; *Six Great Astronomers: Tycho Brahe, Kepler, Halley, Herschel, Russell, Eddington,* H. Hamilton, 1961; *Electricity* (illustrated by D. A. Hardy), Methuen, 1961; *Scientists of the Industrial Revolution: Joseph Black, James Watt, Joseph Priestley, Henry Cavendish,* Cresset, 1962, Dufour, 1963; *The Young Man's Guide to Civil Engineering,* H. Hamilton, 1963; *Statesmen of Science: Henry Brougham, William Robert Grove, Lyon Playfair, the Prince Consort, the Seventh Duke of Devonshire, Alexander Strange, Richard Burdon Haldane, Thomas Tizard, [and] Frederick Alexander Lindemann,* Cresset, 1965, Dufour, 1966.

Science in Modern Society, Cresset, 1967, Schocken Books, 1968; *Scientific Types,* Cresset, 1968, Dufour, 1970; *A Short History of Science,* Methuen, 1969; *Fifty Years with Science,* Barrie & Jenkins, 1970; *Alexander Fleming,* Heron Books, 1971; *Ernest Rutherford,* Methuen, 1972; *Charles Darwin,* Methuen, 1972; *Josiah Wedgwood,* Methuen, 1972; *The Cavendish Laboratory, 1874-1974,* Science History Publications, 1974.

Editor, *Science and Mankind,* 1949.

SIDELIGHTS: "A volume like this," wrote the *New York Times* of James Gerald Crowther's *Famous American Men of Science,* "is worth a dozen of the usual histories of science and invention. For we are given more than a chronicle. It is important to show why scientists attack just the particular problems that they do.... When this is done, as Mr. Crowther does it, the 'flash of genius' turns out to be as much a social phenomenon as the mark of an exceptional man's way of thinking and we realize more truly what the real significance of a discovery or an invention may be." *Nature* added, "Only as an integral part of the story of man's social relationships can the history of science give them understanding. As such Mr. Crowther's book has a wide appeal and claims a large audience. Among men of science it should arouse a new sense of social responsibility. Among those who have received a humanistic education, it should stimulate a new interest in science."

About Petroleum was described by *New Republic* as, "Definitely the best short general account of a major natural resource available in English. Sound information, well organized and lucidly presented." The *Manchester Guardian* commented, "No book of this kind can be written in non-technical language, and even if it was possible such an achievement would defeat its own ends, for the explanation of technicalities is the reason for the work, but Mr. Crowther gives an account which is easily read and as easily understood."

Crowther wrote *Radioastronomy and Radar* for young readers. *Library Journal* called it an, "Excellent ... book with good style and tone despite a tendency toward hyperbole.... Section on radar is clearly written and includes specific examples of radar engineering. Addressed to a British audience, language and point of view are occasionally disconcerting to an American reader." The *New York Times* noted that the author "... brings considerable experience, as one of Britain's pioneering science writers, to the task of making highly technical subjects clear, understandable, and exciting to young readers.... As always, his tale is fascinating.... Mr. Crowther's clear text is complemented by photographs and by David Hardy's good line illustrations."

Crowther has lectured in Canada, the United States, and many other countries, and has made several trips to the U.S.S.R.

DARBY, Patricia (Paulsen)

MARRIED: Raymond Darby, October 26, 1954; children: Glen, Jessica, Grant, Raymond, Jr., Edward, Rebecca. *Address:* 2527 Hereford Rd., Thousand Oaks, Calif. *Agent:* August Lenniger, Lenniger Literary Agency, 11 W. 42nd St., New York, N.Y. 10036.

CAREER: Physical therapist and author.

WRITINGS—With husband, Ray Darby: *Your Career in Physical Therapy* (Junior Literary Guild selection), Messner, 1969; *Conquering the Deep Sea,* McKay, 1971.

SIDELIGHTS: Patricia and Ray Darby's book, *Conquering the Deep Sea,* "... is one of the best descriptive analyses of man's exploration of the ocean ...," wrote a reviewer for *Science Books.* "Perhaps the one shortcoming of the book is that the authors do not cover more of the technically and economically important areas of man's involvement with the oceans...." The critic added, "[The Darbys] also present an interesting description of the career opportunities in these areas.... The book provides a good mechanism for helping a student plan for a career in ocean technology."

FOR MORE INFORMATION SEE: Science Books, September, 1972.

DELDERFIELD, Eric R(aymond) 1909-

PERSONAL: Born May 4, 1909, in London, England; married Dora Hedgethorn; married Dena Ward; children: (first marriage) one daughter; (second marriage) two daughters. *Education:* Attended schools in Selhurst, London, England. *Home:* 10 Sarlsdown Rd., Exmouth, Devonshire, England. *Office:* Erd Publications Ltd., 53 Strand, Exmouth, Devonshire, England.

ERIC DELDERFIELD

(From *Eric Delderfield's Second Book of True Animal Stories* by Eric Delderfield.)

CAREER: Manager of printing, stationery, and photography, Rotol Airscrew Co., 1940-45; managing director, *Exmouth Chronicle* (newspaper), 1945-60; Erd Publications Ltd., Exmouth, England, managing director, 1964—. Member of board of directors of David & Charles (publishers), 1964-70. *Member:* Rotary International (president of Exmouth branch, 1935, 1946, 1955, 1971).

WRITINGS: Cavalcade by Candlelight, Raleigh, 1950; *Exmouth Yesterdays,* Raleigh, 1952; *North Devon Story,* Erd Publications, 1952; *Lynmouth Flood Disaster,* Erd Publications, 1953; *Exmoor Wanderings,* Erd Publications, 1956.

The Cotswolds: Its Villages and Churches, Erd Publications, 1961; *British Inn Signs and Their Stories,* David & Charles, 1965; *Yorkshire Sketches,* Erd Publications, 1966; *Cotswold Sketches,* Erd Publications, 1966; *Kings and Queens of England and Great Britain,* Stein & Day, 1966; *Church Treasure,* David & Charles, 1966; *Cotswold Countryside and Its Characters,* David & Charles, 1967; *Fascinating Facts and Figures of the Bible,* Erd Publications, 1967; *West Country Historic Houses and Their Families,* David & Charles, Volume I, 1968, Volume II, 1970, Volume III, 1970; *Introduction to Inn Signs,* David & Charles, 1969.

Eric Delderfield's True Animal Stories, Volume I, Taplinger, 1970, Volume II, Taplinger, 1972, Volume III, Pan Books, 1975; *Stories of Inns and Their Signs,* David & Charles, 1974; *Alphabetical Guide to Inns and Their Signs,*

David & Charles, 1975; *West Country Historic Houses,* Erd Publications, 1976.

Contributor: G. Frere Cook, editor, *Decorative Arts of the Christian Church,* Cassell, 1972; *New Book of the Road,* Reader's Digest, 1974. Author of a series of twenty topographical brief guides for Erd Publications, 1956-73; contributor to magazines and newspapers.

SIDELIGHTS: "Born in London, May 4, 1909. Transferred to Exmouth, Devonshire where my father purchased and we all ran a weekly newspaper. My brother R. F. Delderfield left the business for full time writing which made him famous.

"Our mother's love of literature inspired us for writing, she was a great storyteller and could quote Dickens and Shakespeare ad infinitum. My father, a forceful character, was a tremendous admirer of Abraham Lincoln who he was apt to quote regularly. At an early age I knew the Gettysburg address by heart.

"It was not until I was thirty and had disposed of the newspaper business that I wrote, first a history of our town, then a general love of history led me to travel extensively all over the British Isles, hence my loves—ancient churches, historic houses and British inn signs on which subjects I have written numerous books. A great animal lover, I have for twenty-nine years been accompanied on my travels by a succession of Border collies.

"Generally I have written about anything which I become enthusiastic about, including individuals as tramps, bishops and gypsies. Have for years carried out lecture tours and my hope is that one day I will be able to do the same in America."

HOBBIES AND OTHER INTERESTS: Walking, history.

DELTON, Judy 1931-

PERSONAL: Born May 6, 1931, in St. Paul, Minn.; daughter of A. F. (a plant engineer) and Alice (Walsdorf) Jaschke; married Jeff J. Delton (a school psychologist), June 14, 1958; children: Julie, Jina, Jennifer, Jamie. *Education:* Attended School of Associated Arts, 1950, and College of St. Catherine, 1954-57. *Home:* 511 Sixth St., Hudson, Wis. 54016.

CAREER: Elementary school teacher in private schools of St. Paul, Minn., 1957-64; free-lance writer. Lecturer at University of Wisconsin, 1973, and at Lakewood Community College, Minnesota Metropolitan State College, and Minneapolis schools, all 1974—. *Awards, honors: Two Good Friends* was named an American Library Association Notable Book, 1975; outstanding teacher award, January, 1977.

WRITINGS: Two Good Friends (Junior Literary Guild selection), Crown, 1974; *Rabbit Finds a Way,* Crown, 1975; *Two is Company,* Crown, 1976; *Three Friends Find Spring* (Junior Literary Guild selection), Crown, 1977; *Penny-Wise, Fun-Foolish,* Crown, 1977; *My Mom Hates Me in January,* A. Whitman, 1977; *Mariko Goes to Camp,* Scott, Foresman, 1978; *On a Picnic,* Doubleday, 1978; *Brimhall Comes to Stay,* Lothrop, 1978. Contributor of about two hundred essays, articles, poems, and short stories to popular magazines including *Wall Street Journal, Saturday Review, Humpty Dumpty, Instructor* and *Highlights for Children.*

WORK IN PROGRESS: Four children's books pending publication.

SIDELIGHTS: Judy Delton began writing when she was forty. "Suddenly I had reached middle age and I sat down and took stock of the situation. I asked myself what I'd done with my life besides raise four children, bake cakes for the PTA, and donate blood. I began to put my thoughts on paper, and a city newspaper published a very poor verse of mine. The check for six dollars looked like six hundred at the time and I was inspired to plunge ahead, oblivious to pitfalls, competition, rejection, and depression.

"Without a writing class or a textbook on the subject, I unknowingly was saved from the hazards of structure and confinement, however many editors shuddered at my abuse of the English language. I was admonished that one must 'know the rules before breaking them' and phone calls from editors said, 'Your spelling is atrocious, your grammar poor, and the way you change tense in the middle of a paragraph makes me extremely nervous.' Their reluctant words, however, said 'I'll buy.'

"So through trial and error, kind help of editors, and mainly *experience,* I sold, in two and a half years, 115 of my essays,

It seemed to take a long time to get to Bear's house. ■ (From *Rabbit Finds a Way* by Judy Delton. Pictures by Joe Lasker.)

JUDY DELTON

LAVINIA DERWENT

articles, verse, short stories, children's stories, and newspaper features. *Two Good Friends* was my first hardcover book.

"I lecture regularly at colleges, workshops, clubs, and other organizations around the Midwest. Ten students in my workshop are publishing regularly now. My classes and lectures are inspirational and motivational in theme, and stress not only marketing, but the joy of self-fulfillment through self-expression and communication of the written word."

FOR MORE INFORMATION SEE: Junior Literary Guild, March, 1974; *Hudson Star-Observer,* June 20, 1974, April, 1977; *St. Paul Sunday Pioneer Press,* August 11, 1974; *St. Paul Dispatch,* April 2, 1977.

DERWENT, Lavinia

PERSONAL: Born in Jedburgh, Scotland. *Education:* Attended grammar school in Jedburgh. *Home:* 1 Great Western Ter., Glasgow G12 0UP, Scotland. *Agent:* Campbell, Thomson & McLaughlin, 31 Newington Green, London, England.

CAREER: Writer, 1950—. Has appeared on television; storyteller in schools. *Member:* International P.E.N., Society of Authors, Writer's Guild, Soroptimists. *Awards, honors:* Member of Order of the British Empire.

WRITINGS—For children: *Joseph and the Coat of Many Colors,* Scholastic Book Services, 1963; *A Breath of Border Air,* Hutchinson, 1975; *Sula,* four volumes, Gollancz, 1976-77; *Another Breath of Border Air,* Hutchinson, 1977.

WORK IN PROGRESS: Children's book; another volume of childhood reminiscences, to be published by Hutchinson, 1978.

SIDELIGHTS: Lavinia Derwent spent her childhood on a Scottish farm; her books deal with her experiences of farm life.

HOBBIES AND OTHER INTERESTS: Travel.

DE SELINCOURT, Aubrey　1894-1962

PERSONAL: Born June 7, 1894, in London, Eng.; son of Martin De Selincourt; married Irene Rutherford McLeod, 1919; children: two daughters. *Education:* University College, Oxford, M.A.

CAREER: Dragon School, Oxford, senior Classical master, 1924-29; Clayesmore School, Hampshire (later Dorset), vice-master, 1929-31, headmaster, 1931-35, resigned in 1935 to serve as headmaster of another school; author and translator. *Military service:* During World War I served in Italy and in France with the Royal Air Force. *Member:* P.E.N., Royal Cruising Club, Oxford University Authentics.

WRITINGS: Streams of Ocean, Heinemann, 1923; *Family Afloat* (illustrated by Eileen Verrinder and Guy de Selincourt), Routledge, 1940; *Three Green Bottles* (illustrated by G. de Selincourt), Routledge, 1941; *One Good Tern* (illustrated by G. de Selincourt), Routledge, 1943; *One More Summer* (illustrated by G. de Selincourt), Routledge, 1944; (with wife, Irene) *Six o' Clock and After, and Other Rhymes for Children* (illustrated by John Morton Sale), Muller, 1945; *Calicut Lends a Hand* (illustrated by G. de Selincourt), Routledge, 1946; *Dorset* (illustrated by Barbara Jones), Elck, 1947; *Micky* (illustrated by G. de Selincourt), Routledge, 1947; *A Capful of Wind* (illustrated by G. de Selincourt), Methuen, 1948; *Isle of Wight* (illustrated by Kenneth Rowntree), Elck, 1948; *The Young Schoolmaster* (illustrated by F. M. Middlehurst), Oxford University Press, 1948; *Kestrel* (illustrated by G. de Selincourt), Routledge & Kegan Paul, 1949; *Mr. Oram's Story: The Adventures of Captain James Cook* (illustrated by John Baynes), Methuen, 1949; *The Ravens Nest* (illustrated by G. de Selincourt), Routledge & Kegan Paul, 1949; *Sailing: A Guide for Everyman* (illustrated by G. de Selincourt), Lehmann, 1949.

(Reteller) *Odysseus the Wanderer* (illustrated by Norman Meredith), G. Bell, 1950; *The Schoolmaster,* Lehmann, 1951; *On Reading Poetry,* Swallow, 1952, reprinted, Folcroft, 1970; *The Channel Shore,* R. Hale, 1953; *Six Great Englishmen,* Hamish Hamilton, 1953; (translator and author of introduction) Herodotus, *Herodotus: The Histories,* Penguin, 1954, revised edition, 1972; *Horatio Nelson,* Hamish Hamilton, 1954; *Cat's Cradle,* M. Joseph, 1955; *Six Great Poets,* Hamish Hamilton, 1956, reprinted, Folcroft, 1973; *Nensen* (illustrated by Ian Ribbons), Oxford University Press, 1957; (translator) Flavius Arrianus, *The Life of Alexander the Great,* Penguin, 1958, reissued as *The Campaigns of Alexander,* 1976; *Six Great Thinkers,* Hamish Hamilton, 1958, reissued, Folcroft, 1977; *Six Great Playwrights,* Hamish Hamilton, 1960, reprinted, Folcroft, 1974; (translator and author of introduction) Titus Livius, *The Early History of Rome: Books I-V of The History of Rome from Its Foundation,* Penguin, 1960, reissued, Heritage Press, 1972; (editor) *The Book of the Sea,* Eyre & Spottiswoode, 1961, Norton, 1963; *The World of Herodotus,* Secker & Warburg, 1962, Little, Brown, 1963; (translator) T. Livius, *The War with Hannibal: Books XXI-XXX of The History of Rome from Its Foundation,* edited by Betty Radice, Penguin, 1965.

Editor, *Oxford Magazine,* 1927-29.

SIDELIGHTS: De Selincourt's *Odysseus the Wanderer* was described by a critic for the *New York Times* as "an exhilarating, smooth-paced retelling of the epic marked by unerring taste in the selection and treatment of incidents and the haunting echoes of Homeric phraseology...." In reviewing the same book, a *Horn Book* critic noted, "For children still too young for a translation of the Odyssey, this is an excellent introduction.... Mr. de Selincourt uses the English language with a strength and sincerity which makes it very good to read."

For *The Book of the Sea,* De Selincourt selected literary passages that dealt with the briny deep from writings by Conrad, Melville and others. "Readers will not have to be possessed of sea fever to enjoy this delightful and tasteful anthology of writings about the sea ...," observed a reviewer for *Library Journal.*

To accompany his translation of Herodotus' *The Histories,* De Selincourt wrote *The World of Herodotus.* Of the latter book a critic for the London *Times Literary Supplement* wrote, "[The owners of the Penguin edition of Herodotus' *Histories*] will surely welcome this volume written by the author of that translation, for their understanding of Herodotus will be enlarged, and they can share an enthusiasm based on a close familiarity with the original...."

HOBBIES AND OTHER INTERESTS: Yacht cruising.

FOR MORE INFORMATION SEE: Brian Doyle, editor, *Who's Who of Children's Literature,* Schocken, 1968.

(Died, 1962)

ELLIOTT, Sarah M(cCarn) 1930-

PERSONAL: Born March 6, 1930, in Chicago, Ill.; daughter of Davis Glessner (a manufacturer) and Ruth (an assistant dean of students at University of Chicago; maiden name, O'Brien); married Paul M. Elliott (a free-lance writer and editor), June 16, 1961. *Education:* Student at Stephens College, 1948-49, and National College of Education, 1949-50; Northwestern University, B.S. in Ed., 1952. *Politics:* "Independent-liberal." *Religion:* "Independent." *Home and office:* 333 East 34th St., New York, N.Y. 10016.

CAREER: Elementary teacher in Washington State, New York, and Illinois, 1952-54, 1958; commercial artist in garment industry, New York, N.Y., 1954-55; text and trade book editor in Chicago, Ill., and New York, N.Y., 1957-63, working for Scott, Foresman, Prentice-Hall, Macmillan, Harcourt, Brace & World, and other publishers; Community Gallery, New York, N.Y., curator and coordinator of art shows, 1969-72. Artist, with work in group shows in New York, 1968, 1970, 1976, 1977, and book illustrator; teacher of course on children's classics at New School for Social Research. Conductor of radio series on children's classics; has appeared on other radio and television programs, including "Today" and "Johnny Carson" shows. *Member:* American Begonia Society, Forum of Writers for Young People (president, 1976-77). *Awards, honors:* Children's Book Council–National Science Teachers Association award, Outstanding Science Books for Children for *Our Dirty Land,* 1976.

WRITINGS—Self-illustrated: *Our Dirty Air* (juvenile; Library of Congress selection for *Books 1971*), Messner, 1971; *Our Dirty Water* (juvenile), Messner, 1973; *Our Dirty Land,* Messner, 1976.

HOBBIES AND OTHER INTERESTS: Gardening on city roof ("despite pollution"), bird watching, jazz.

SARAH M. ELLIOTT

At Anza-Barego State Park in California these throwaway cans litter the land and can harm any barefoot hikers. ■ (From *Our Dirty Land* by Sarah M. Elliott. Photos by the author.)

FEAGUE, Mildred H. 1915-

PERSONAL: Surname is pronounced Fayg; born May 30, 1915, in Sharon, Pa.; daughter of Carl Isaac (a pattern-maker) and Mildred (Jones) Hickox; married Robert Feague, July 11, 1941 (deceased); children: Robert Carl. *Education:* Hiram College, A.B., 1937; Westminster College, New Wilmington, Pa., M.S.Ed., 1947. *Residence:* 523 Glastonbury Manor, Davison, Mich. 48423.

CAREER: Elementary teacher in Prescott, Ariz., 1952-55; U.S. Bureau of Indian Affairs, Gallup, N.M., counselor, 1955-57; teacher of English, French, and Latin at Orme School, Mayer, Ariz., 1957-58, at Leelanau School, Glen Arbor, Mich., 1958-60, in Traverse City, Mich., 1960-67; Arizona State University, Tempe, administrator, 1967-68. *Member:* American Association of University Women, Author's Guild.

WRITINGS—Juvenile: *Little Indian and the Angel,* illustrated by Ted DeGrazia, Childrens Press, 1970; *Little Sky Eagle and the Pumpkin Drum,* illustrated by DeGrazia, Childrens Press, 1972; *True Book of Rodeos,* Childrens Press, 1972.

WORK IN PROGRESS: Children of the Canyon; The Christmas Tree Ship.

And he walked down the wellworn path, carrying it with both arms. ■ (From *Little Sky Eagle and the Pumpkin Drum* by Mildred Feague. Illustrated by De Grazia.)

MILDRED FEAGUE

FOWKE, Edith (Margaret) 1913-

PERSONAL: Surname is pronounced like "folk"; born April 30, 1913, in Lumsden, Saskatchewan; daughter of William Marshall (a garage proprietor) and Margaret (Fyffe) Fulton; married Franklin George Fowke (an engineer), October 1, 1938. *Education:* University of Saskatchewan, B.A. (with high honors), 1933, M.A., 1937. *Home:* 5 Notley Pl., Toronto M4B 2M7, Ontario, Canada. *Office:* Room S706, York University, 4700 Keele St., Downsview, Ontario, Canada.

CAREER: Has worked as an editor, prepared radio programs for CBC, and worked for various magazines; York University, Downsview, Ontario, professor of English, 1971—; editor of the *Canadian Folk Music Journal,* 1973—. *Member:* Canadian Folk Music Society (director, 1960—), American Folklore Society, English Folk Dance and Song Society, Association of Canadian University Teachers of English, Canadian Authors Association, Mensa Canada, Folklore Studies Association of Canada, Writers Union of Canada. *Awards, honors:* Medal from Association of Canadian Children's Librarians, for *Sally Go Round the Sun,* 1970; elected a fellow of the American Folklore Society, 1974, LL.D., Brock University, 1974; D.Litt., Trent University, 1975.

WRITINGS: (With Richard Johnston) *Folk Songs of Canada,* Waterloo Music Co., 1954; (with Johnston) *Folk Songs*

Queenie, Queenie, Caroline
Washed her face in turpentine.
Turpentine made it shine,
Queenie, Queenie, Caroline.
■ (From *Sally Go Round the Sun* by Edith Fowke. Illustrated by Carlos Marchiori.)

EDITH FOWKE

of Quebec, Waterloo Music Co., 1957; (with Alan Mills) Canada's Story in Song, Gage, 1960; (with Joe Glazer) Songs of Work and Freedom, Roosevelt University, 1960; Traditional Singers and Songs from Ontario, Folklore Associates, 1965; (with Johnston) More Folk Songs of Canada, Waterloo Music Co., 1967; Sally Go Round the Sun (juvenile), McClelland & Stewart, 1969; Lumbering Songs from the Northern Woods, University of Texas Press, 1970; The Penguin Book of Canadian Folk Songs, Penguin, 1973; Folklore of Canada, McClelland & Stewart, 1976; Ring Around the Moon, McClelland & Stewart, 1977.

SIDELIGHTS: Edith Fowke has produced the following recordings: "Folk Songs of Ontario," "Irish and British Songs from the Ottawa Valley," "Lumbering Songs from the Ontario Shanties," "Songs of the Great Lakes," "La-Rena Clark: Canadian Garland," "Tom Brandon of Peterborough," "Ontario Ballads and Folksongs," and "Far Canadian Fields: companion to The Penguin Book of Canadian Folk Songs."

FROST, Lesley 1899-

PERSONAL: Born in Lawrence, Mass., April 28, 1899; daughter of Robert (the poet) and Elinor M. (White) Frost; married James Dwight Francis, 1928 (divorced); married Joseph W. Ballantine (retired Foreign Service Consul General; lecturer on American foreign policy and Far Eastern cultures at New School for Social Research and New York University), 1952 (died, 1973); children—first marriage: Eli-

nor (Mrs. Malcolm Wilber), Lesley Lee. Education: Attended Wellesley College, one year; attended Barnard College after World War I; attended University of Michigan; attended University of Mexico, one year. Home: 129 East 10th St., New York, N.Y. 10003; La Granja, Segovia, Spain.

CAREER: After World War I, worked as a journalist in New York, N.Y.; owned and operated, with her sister Marjorie, The Open Book, Pittsfield, Mass., 1923-34, and, from this shop, operated a bookshop-on-wheels throughout New England and then around the world on the S.S. Franconia, 1928-29; Rockford College, Rockford, Ill., assistant professor and director of Maddox House Cultural Center, 1935-37; King-Smith Studio School, Washington, D.C., director, three years; owner and director of Frost Studio School for adult education. Was associated with Office of War Information in Madrid, Spain as cultural officer and director of U.S. Information Library, 1945-47, then with the State Department as a lecturer on American literature in Latin America, 1949-50. Regular lecturer, formerly for Columbia Lecture Bureau, then for Wide World Lecture Bureau in New York. Wartime activity: During World War I, worked in the Curtis airplane factory in Marblehead, Mass.; during World War II, served as an electrical mechanic in the Washington airport of the Air Transport Command. Member: Women's Press Club of New York City (chairman of literature), Women's National Republican Club, National Association of New England Women, International P.E.N., Daughters of the American Revolution (New York City chapter), New York Browning Society.

LESLEY FROST at Barnard College, 1919

I walk and I talk to myself
I am practicing what I shall say
When they come and tell me I can't
Get covered with mud this way.
■ (From *Going on Two* by Lesley Frost. Drawings by
Robin Hudnut.)

WRITINGS: (Editor) *Come Christmas* (anthology), Coward, 1929; *Murder at Large* (fiction), Coward, 1932; *Not
Really!* (stories for children), introduction by Louis Untermeyer, Coward, 1939; (with John Caldwell) *The Korea Story,* Regnery, 1952; *Really Not Really* (juvenile), Channel,
1962; *Digging Down to China* (juvenile), Devin-Adair, 1966;
(edited with Dr. Arnold Grade) *New Hampshire's Child:
The Derry Journals of Lesley Frost,* State University of
New York Press, 1969; *The Family Letters of Robert and
Elinor Frost,* State University of New York Press, 1972;
Going on Two (verse), Devin-Adair, 1973. Author of various introductions and articles. Has, also, recorded a collection of her father's poems, entitled "Derry Down Derry,"
for Folkways Records.

SIDELIGHTS: "In 1934, I crossed the Atlantic as a member of the crew of an 85-foot schooner-rigged sailing ship, the
Wonder Bird, Skipper Warwick Tompkins, minus engine—Gloucester, Massachusetts to Sean Saira. In 1963 I
purchased an estate in La Granja, Sequoia, Spain and
opened a summer school, La Escuela de la Tahona, for
sixteen-eighteen year old girls, two months of language and
history. After eight or nine years I have now changed to op-
erating as a guest house, July 1-September 1.

"Of course, as time marches on I become more involved in
the affairs of my descendants! The eldest daughter, Elinor
Wilber, is a third term member of the Connecticut State Leg-
islature from the thirty-third district in Fairfields. Her four
children, two boys, two girls, are up and away, the girls married, and I have a great-grandchild in Houston. My youngest
daughter, is a staff member of the AAUP (American Association of University Professors), Dupont Circle,
D.C.—three daughters are still in preparatory schools. My
children's books have, naturally, grown out of the family
tradition of reading and story telling at bedtime. The verses
in 'Going on Two' are the result of a vivid ESP happening
with a two-year-old grandson.

"Every year since 1964 I have been presenting a segment of
my father's library to New York University's Division of
Special Collections. On May 22, 1977 the Derry Farm, a
National Monument and a part of the Parks Division of the
state of New Hampshire, was officially dedicated.

"I am busy with many library collections of Frost throughout the country and in gathering material for a book relating
the incidents in the three years, 1912-1915, that the family
spent in England. The core of which will be the monthly
home publication (that is *I* did the typing) of *The Banquet,*
carrying on the tradition exemplified by the earlier *New
Hampshire Child* and the *Derry Journals of Lesley Frost.*"

LESLEY FROST

FROST, Robert (Lee) 1874-1963

PERSONAL: Born March 26, 1874, in San Francisco, California; died January 29, 1963, in Boston, Massachusetts; son of William Prescott (a newspaper reporter and editor) and Isabel (a teacher; maiden name Moodie) Frost; married Elinor Miriam White, December 28, 1895 (died, 1938); children: Eliot (deceased), Lesley (daughter), Carol (son; deceased), Irma, Marjorie (deceased), Elinor Bettina (deceased). *Education:* Student, Dartmouth College, 1892, Harvard University, 1897-99.

CAREER: Poet. Held various jobs between college studies, including bobbin boy in a Massachusetts mill, cobbler, editor of a country newspaper, schoolteacher, and farmer. Lived in England, 1912-15, returning to America as an established poet. Tufts College, Medford, Massachusetts, Phi Beta Kappa poet, 1915, 1940; Amherst College, Amherst, Massachusetts, professor of English and poet-in-residence, 1916-20, 1923-25, 1926-28, Simpson Lecturer in Literature; Middlebury College, Middlebury, Vermont, co-founder of the Bread-Loaf School and Conference of English (for writers), 1920, annual lecturer, beginning 1920; University of Michigan, Ann Arbor, professor and poet-in-residence, 1921-23, fellow in letters, 1925-26; Columbia University, New York City, Phi Beta Kappa poet, 1932; Pierson College, Yale University, New Haven, Connecticut, associate fellow, beginning 1933; Harvard University, Cambridge, Massachusetts, Phi Beta Kappa poet, 1916, 1941, Charles Eliot Norton Professor of Poetry, 1936, board overseer, 1938-39, Ralph Waldo Emerson Fellow, 1939-41, honorary

ROBERT FROST in England, 1913

fellow, 1942-43, associate of Adams House; fellow in American civilization, 1941-42; Dartmouth College, Hanover, New Hampshire, George Ticknor Fellow in Humanities, 1943-49, visiting lecturer; member of the advisory board of *Seven Arts* magazine, 1916-17. *Member:* National Institute of Arts and Letters (elected, 1916), American Academy of Arts and Letters (elected, 1930), American Philosophical Society, International P.E.N.

AWARDS, HONORS: Pulitzer Prize for poetry, 1924, for *New Hampshire,* 1931, for *Collected Poems,* 1937, for *A Further Range,* and 1943, for *A Witness Tree;* Loines Prize for poetry, 1931; Mark Twain medal, 1937; Gold Medal of the National Institute of Arts and Letters, 1938; Silver Medal of the Poetry Society of America, 1941; Huntington Hartford Foundation award, 1958; unanimous resolution in his honor and gold medal from the U.S. Senate, March 24, 1950; participated in President John F. Kennedy's inauguration ceremonies, 1961, by reading his poems, *Dedication* and *The Gift Outright;* chosen poet laureate of Vermont by the State League of Women's Clubs; over forty honorary degrees from colleges and universities, including Oxford and Cambridge Universities, Amherst College, and the University of Michigan.

*WRITINGS—*Poems: *Twilight,* [Lawrence, Massachusetts], 1894, reprinted, University of Virginia, 1966; *A Boy's Will,* D. Nutt, 1913, Holt, 1915 (includes *The Tuft of Flowers*); *North of Boston,* D. Nutt, 1914, Holt, 1915 (includes *Death of the Hired Man* and *The Mending Wall*); *Mountain Interval,* Holt, 1916 (includes *Birches* and *The Road Not*

ROBERT LEE FROST, age seven months

FROST, LESLEY, MARJORIE, and CAROL with two friends on Mt. Lafayette, c. 1916

Taken); *New Hampshire,* Holt, 1923, reissued, New Dresden Press, 1955 (includes *Stopping by Woods on a Snowy Evening*); *West-Running Brook,* Holt, 1928; *The Lone Striker,* Knopf, 1933; *Two Tramps in Mud-Time,* Holt, 1934; *The Gold Hesperidee,* Bibliophile Press, 1935; *Three Poems,* Baker Library Press, 1935 (contains *The Quest of the Orchis, Warning,* and *Caesar's Lost Transport Ships*); *A Further Range,* Holt, 1936; *From Snow to Snow,* Holt, 1936; *A Witness Tree,* Holt, 1942; *A Masque of Reason* (verse drama), Holt, 1945; *Steeple Bush,* Holt, 1947; *A Masque of Mercy* (verse drama), Holt, 1947; *Greece,* Black Rose Press, 1948; *Hard Not to Be King,* House of Books, 1951; *Aforesaid,* Holt, 1954; *The Gift Outright,* Holt, 1961; *Dedication* [and] *The Gift Outright* (poems read at the presidential inaugural, 1961; published with the inaugural address of J. F. Kennedy), Spiral Press, 1961; *In the Clearing,* Holt, 1962. Also author of *The Lovely Shall be Choosers,* 1929; *And All We Call American,* 1958.

Poems issued as Christmas greetings: *Christmas Trees,* Spiral Press, 1929; *Neither Out Far nor In Deep* (illustrated by J. J. Lankes), Holt, 1935; *Everybody's Sanity,* [Los Angeles], 1936; *To a Young Wretch,* Spiral Press, 1937; *Triple Plate,* Spiral Press, 1939; *Our Hold on the Planet,* Holt, 1940; *An Unstamped Letter in Our Rural Letter Box,* Spiral Press, 1944; *On Making Certain Anything Has Happened,* Spiral Press, 1945; *One Step Backward Taken,* Spiral Press, 1947; *Closed for Good* (illustrated by Thomas W. Nason), Spiral Press, 1948; *On a Tree Fallen across the Road to Hear Us Talk,* Spiral Press, 1949; *Doom to Bloom,* Holt, 1950; *A Cabin in the Clearing,* Spiral Press, 1951; *Does No One but Me at All Ever Feel This Way in the Least,* Spiral Press, 1952; *One More Brevity,* Holt, 1953; *From a Milkweed Pod,* Holt, 1954; *Some Science Fiction,* Spiral Press, 1955; *Kitty Hawk, 1894,* Holt, 1956; *My Objection to Being Stepped On,* Holt, 1957; *Away* (illustrated by Stefan Martin), Spiral Press, 1958; *A-Wishing Well* (illustrated by T. W. Nason), Spiral Press, 1959; *Accidentally on Purpose,* Holt, 1960; *The Woodpile* (illustrated by T. W. Nason), Spiral Press, 1961; *The Prophets Really Prophesy as Mystics, the Commentators Merely by Statistics,* Spiral Press, 1962; *The Constant Symbol,* [New York], 1962.

Other: *A Way Out* (one-act play), Harbor Press, 1929; *The Cow's in the Corn* (one-act play in rhyme), Slide Mountain Press, 1929; (contributor) "Maturity No Object," in *Writing Poetry,* edited by John Holmes, Writer, Inc., 1960; (contributor) "On Emerson," in *Emerson,* edited by Milton R. Konvitz and Stephen E. Whicher, Prentice-Hall, 1962; *Robert Frost on "Extravagance"* (the text of Frost's last college lecture, Dartmouth College, November 27, 1962), [Hanover, New Hampshire], 1963.

Collections: *Collected Poems of Robert Frost,* Holt, 1930, new edition, 1939 (Frost's preface to this edition, "The Figure a Poem Makes," reprinted in *Discovering Modern Poetry,* edited by Elizabeth A. Drew and George Connor, Norton, 1963); *The Letters of Robert Frost to Louis Untermeyer,* Holt, 1963; *Complete Poems of Robert Frost,* Holt, 1968; *The Poetry of Robert Frost,* edited by Edward Connery Lathem, Holt, 1969; *Family Letters of Robert and Elinor Frost,* edited by Arnold Grade, State University of New York Press, 1972.

Selections: *Selected Poems,* Holt, 1934; *Come In, and Other Poems* (illustrated by John O'Hara Cosgrave II; edited by Louis Untermeyer), Holt, 1943, reissued, F. Watts, 1967, enlarged edition published as *The Road Not Taken: An Introduction to Robert Frost,* 1951, reissued as *The*

The Poet using his homemade writing-board in his parlor, Franconia, N.H., 1915

Pocket Book of Robert Frost's Poems, Pocket Books, 1956; *The Poems of Robert Frost,* Modern Library, 1946; *You Come Too: Favorite Poems for Young Readers* (illustrated by T. W. Nason), Holt, 1959, reissued, 1967; *A Remembrance Collection of New Poems by Robert Frost,* Holt, 1959; *Poems,* Washington Square Press, 1961; *Selected Letters* (edited by Lawrance Thompson), Holt, 1964; *Longer Poems: The Death of the Hired Man,* Holt, Rinehart, 1966; *Selected Prose* (edited by Hyde Cox and E. C. Lathem), Holt, 1966, reissued, Collier Books, 1968; *Robert Frost: Poetry and Prose* (edited by L. Thompson and E. C. Latham), Holt, 1972; *Selected Poems* (edited by Ian Hamilton), Penguin, 1973.

ADAPTATIONS—Movies: "The Tuft of Flowers" (motion picture), read by Robert Frost, Creative Film Society, 1971; "Reading Poetry: Mending Wall" (motion picture), read by Leonard Nemoy, Oxford Films, 1972; "Autumn: Frost Country" (9 min. color), BFA Educational Media.

Recordings: "Robert Frost: Reading His Poetry," recorded at the Kaufmann auditorium, 1953-54, Caedmon.

SIDELIGHTS: Lesley Frost writes of her father: "Robert Lee Frost was born March 26, 1874, but the location—San Francisco—was an accident of birth. His forefathers had been Englanders and New Englanders since they came ashore in 1632 and established themselves in the clipper ship business in Kittery, Maine—twelve years after my mother's ancestor, Peregrine White, had arrived.

"My father's father, William Prescott Frost, a brilliant student and athlete at Harvard—he had run away to join the army of General Robert E. Lee, whom he admired, but was brought home—had heeded the going advice of post-Civil War days: 'Go West, young man.' During his year as principal of Lewisburg Academy, Lewistown, Pennsylvania, he met and married Isabelle (Belle) Moodie, the only other teacher in the Academy.

"William Prescott Frost went into journalism and politics in San Francisco, and, following an erratic but promising career, fell ill with tuberculosis and died at the age of thirty-six, leaving a wife and two children completely penniless. Robert was ten; his sister, Jeanie, eight.

"Belle Moodie Frost returned East to Lawrence, Massachusetts, and the Frost family homestead. But being an independent spirit, she left to open a private school, which was attended by a large group of children from first through eighth grades. By educating other people's children, my grandmother was able to put her own through grade and high schools. . . ." [*The American Way*, "Robert Frost Remembered," Lesley Frost, March, 1974.[1]]

"Like any true Highlander or Celt, she was a mystic. She 'heard voices.' She believed in 'second sight.' She dwelt in the 'double lives' of Emanuel Swedenborg, her mentor: the outer and the inner, the actual and the spiritual (which he claims is the more actual of the two). The lines he and she faintly drew between fact and fantasy, nature and the nature of man, were all but invisible. . . .

"From poetry to life and back again to poetry was Belle Moodie's way of taking things, of accepting the uncertainties and tragedies that were to be her lot. And the poetry, the reading aloud, was her way of educating her children. She was a born teacher. And either because she did not think too well of the schools in San Francisco (she herself had been a teacher in Columbus, Ohio), or because she believed her son was not strong enough to attend, she let him stay at home when not roaming the street or being companion to his political father. . . ." [*Forum*, "Somewhat Atanistic," Lesley Frost Ballantine, Volume XI, Number 3, Summer, 1974.[2]]

"The first poem Robert Frost wrote at fourteen was in ballad form; history (this early ballad-poem told of Cortez as he fled from Mexico City. . . .)

"It was in his class at the Lawrence High School (now known as the Robert Frost High School) that Robert met Elinor Miriam White. Their graduations marked an innovation: Robert and Elinor were judged co-valedictorians. His essay, entitled 'Monument to After Thoughts Unveiled,' and hers, 'Conversation as a Force in Life,' have been preserved.

"The two young people had been seeing a great deal of each other; on his part it had been love at first sight:

Meeting and Passing

As I went down the hill along the wall
There was a gate I had leaned at for the view
And had just turned from when I first saw you
As you came up the hill. We met. But all
We did that day was mingle great and small
Footprints in summer dust as if we drew
The figure of our being less than two
But more than one as yet. Your parasol
Pointed the decimal off with one deep thrust.
And all the time we talked you seemed to see
Something down there to smile at in the dust.
(Oh, it was without prejudice to me!)
Afterward I went past what you had passed
Before we met, and you what I had passed.

The Telephone

"When I was just as far as I could walk
From here today,
There was an hour
All still
When leaning with my head against a flower
I heard you talk.
Don't say I didn't, for I heard you say–
You spoke from that flower on the windowsill–
Do you remember what it was you said?"

"First tell me what it was you thought you heard."

"Having found the flower and driven a bee away,
I leaned my head,
And holding by the stalk,
I listened and I thought I caught the word–
What was it? Did you call me by my name?
Or did you say–
Someone said 'Come'–I heard it as I bowed."

"I may have thought as much, but not aloud."

"Well, so I came."

"Still, of course, both families were against an early marriage. So Elinor went off to St. Lawrence University in Canton, New York, on full scholarship, and Robert to Dartmouth. But he soon found he could not endure the fear that he might lose her, and he dropped out of college, going to Canton to persuade her to leave with him. Her answer, expressed years later in a letter, was: 'I always told him that if he found work and could even support us in *one room*, I would marry, but until then I would have to stay in college, since above all we *must* not be a burden to either of our families.' Not that she also wasn't eager to marry. In proof, she redoubled her courses at St. Lawrence and was graduated in two-and-a-half years, in high academic standing.

"By this time, the private school in Salem needed more teachers, and, of course, Robert's mother was delighted to take them both on her staff. Their marriage took place on December 19, 1895. As well as carrying his classes in his mother's school, Robert was able to enter Harvard and for two or more years commuted to Cambridge. His particular scholastic work was in the classics, Greek and Latin, and he won the same honors his father had received before him. However, already having the makings of a poet, he dreamed of a place of peace removed from the pressures of classrooms. My mother, who understood his restlessness (in fact, felt likewise), persuaded Robert's grandfather to buy them a small farm near Derry, New Hampshire. I'm sure the old gentleman was thinking, 'Good riddance,' with a sense of relief that they might not worry him further. I doubt he ever saw the poem my father wrote at the time:

In Neglect

They leave us so the way we took,
As two in whom they were proved mistaken,
That we sit sometimes in the wayside nook,
With mischievous, vagrant, seraphic look,
And try if we cannot feel forsaken.

"So it was my great good fortune (privilege, not lack of it) to have been brought up on a farm, at least until I was nine. Was it Freud who said that the intimations of what we are to

ROBERT FROST, his daughter Lesley, and her two daughters

be and do are determined by the age of six? I had till nine and the intimations were all there.

"I think of my childhood, even my life, as an education by poetry. Held by the hands of two loving parents, I was led into the realm of nature, closeness to the earth itself. (My father preferred to call it love *in* nature.) The farm was our answer to Fate, to Poetry, to Prayer . . .

"Robert Frost said, 'Say something we can learn by heart and when alone respect.' And, 'A poem begins in delight and ends in wisdom; the figure is the same as for love.' Let's not forget: 'the figure is the same as for love.'

"My father wrote 'The Pasture' for my mother when we moved to the farm. I was only six months old. But when I was old enough, I thought he wrote it for me. And I let my children think he wrote it for them.

The Pasture

I'm going out to clean the pasture spring;
I'll only stop to rake the leaves away
(And wait to watch the water clear, I may):
I shan't be gone long.—You come too.

I'm going out to fetch the little calf
That's standing by the mother. It's so young
It totters when she licks it with her tongue.
I shan't be gone long.—You come too.

The Last Word of a Bluebird

As I went out a Crow
In a low voice said, 'Oh,
I was looking for you.
How do you do?
I just came to tell you
To Tell Lesley (will you?)
That her little Bluebird
Wanted me to bring word
That the north wind last night
That made the stars bright
And made ice on the trough
Almost made him cough
His tail feathers off.

He just had to fly!
But he sent her Good-by,
And said to be good,
And wear her red hood,
And look for skunk tracks
In the snow with an ax–
And do everything!
And perhaps in the spring
He would come back and sing.'

". . . As luck, good luck, would have it, we lived too far from town to go to school, and since my parents were already accredited teachers, the town excused us. . . .

ROBERT FROST

"My mother taught the organized subjects, reading (the phonetic method), writing (then known as penmanship), geography, spelling. My father took on botany and astronomy. They both went over our stories for criticism, though it was my mother who scanned them first for spelling and grammar (a word that I believe is rarely heard today).

"Reading was most important. *Learning* to read and *being read to*. Reading aloud was taught in our family. Every evening of our lives we sat before the Franklin stove in the front room, under the rather dim light of the kerosene lamps, while my mother read and my father whittled, or my father read and my mother mended. . . .

"We were allowed to take part in whatever our parents did, whether it was haying, going down to John Hall's farm for a setting of white Leghorn eggs, naming the constellations at all hours of the night, clearing the pasture spring, seeking the rare orchid or rarer fern or conversing around the table at mealtime. Living was as uncomplicated, as simple, as it was humanly possible to make it. 'We love the things, we love for what they are,' Robert Frost said.[1]

". . . The family became a part of Pinkerton Academy where my father was teaching. We attended the ball games played by the team he helped coach. We made the costumes for the plays he directed: Milton's *Comus,* Yeats' *Cathleen ni Houlihan* and *The Land of Heart's Desire,* Lord Dunsany's *The Golden Hoop,* and an adaptation of Marlowe's *Doctor Faustus.* For days on end our house was a shambles of cloth and paper cuttings.

"Then there were the themes my father brought home for his correcting and our criticism. I was well up on this! It was at Pinkerton that my father was to discover his particular genius as a teacher. He *founded* students. To them in turn was revealed what it means to see, to think, to write.

"A letter my father wrote me when I was at Barnard reads: 'Let's feel darned friendly toward your psychology teacher

for liking you to think. People deserve almost more credit for appreciating what we do than we deserve for doing it.

"'The great things are direct thought and emotion and never to be put off our natural thought and emotion in any circumstances however disturbing—not even in examinations. I never got so I was serenely myself in examinations. I have to pick and choose my circumstances. The Carter Goodrich kind of boy is the ideal kind of examinee. No Faculty can muddle his faculties.

"'Powerful flight the CN 4 made to the Azores. It makes me feel strong myself. I almost wish Hawker hadn't tried it. It was too wild an adventure. But he was a brave man.'

"How my father liked bravery! And how he appreciated 'unforced natural thought.' Again he was to write me (dated Franconia, N.H., 18 March 1920):

"'[People] have been allowed to think that declaring for a more or less new idea is the same as thinking. It would be hard to explain to them what thinking is unless you could catch them sometime in the act of thinking. We all start accidentally and unconsciously. We grow in the power to think as we become aware of ourselves by circumstances and by other people. I suppose it starts in the realm of plain observation. There is sight and there is insight. You learn first to know what you see and to put fresh words to it. That's the whole story. I don't believe there is anything in literature that that doesn't cover.'

"So I was always having it pointed out to me that poetry is an education in analogous thinking—in the metaphor—in seeing one thing in terms of another—getting on paper what such relationships convey in ideas. Unless you are at home in the metaphor, he preached, you are nowhere on safe ground, whether in poetry history, science, or even politics. . . . Not that there are not plenty of weaknesses in analogous thinking, he would add, but it is being quick on the uptake to be able to rescue oneself with another analogy that counts." [*Forum,* "Certain Intensities," Lesley Frost, Volume XV, Number 3, Summer, 1974.[3]]

"My father once told a class: 'Columbus didn't cross the Atlantic. He didn't suffer hardships and privations. At least not for these is he Columbus. Why is he immortal, then? Can't you tell. Well, because he had the faith so few people are capable of: the faith of an idea. Not for him to feel his

The city had withdrawn into itself
And left at last the country to the country...
■ From *You Come Too: Favorite Poems for Young Readers* by Robert Frost. Wood engravings by Thomas W. Nason.)

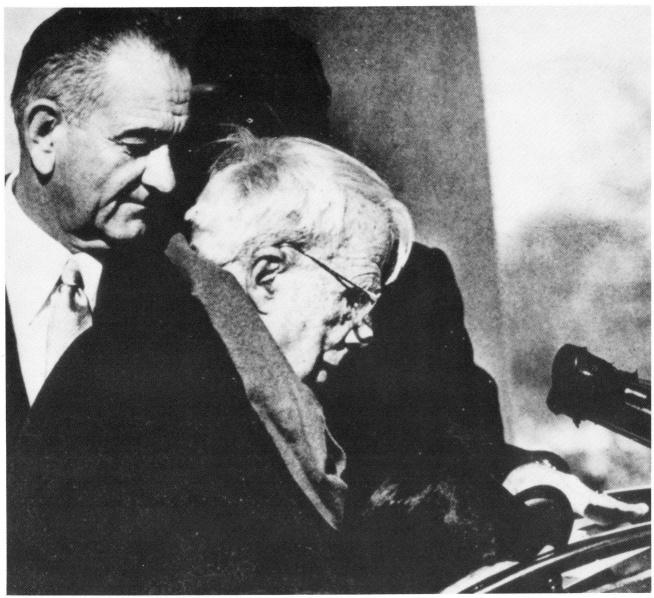

At the Kennedy Inauguration, a dramatic moment came when Frost stumbled over his lines which were obscured by the sun's glare. Lyndon Johnson offered a top hat for shade.

way around Africa to India. He launched out into space with the supreme confidence of reason. Great in his confidence, great in his justification. And the only ones near him are the Wright Brothers.'

". . . [Robert Frost] left a heritage, not only of poetry, but of descendants: seven grandchildren, eleven great-grandchildren. One of the last, aged five, after his first experience hearing his great-grandfather speak in public, was heard to say: 'Great-grandfather, he's really a great man too. That makes him a great-great-grandfather.'

"Now Robert Frost has gone, but he left a poem, 'Take Something Like a Star,' which closes with the lines:

> *It asks a little of us here.*
> *It asks of us a certain height,*
> *So when at times the mob is swayed*
> *To carry praise or blame too far,*
> *We may take something like a star*
> *To stay our minds on and be staid.*"[1]

FOR MORE INFORMATION SEE: Amy Lowell, "Robert Frost," in her *Tendencies in Modern American Poetry,* Macmillan, 1917; Gorham B. Munson, *Robert Frost: A Study in Sensibility and Good Sense,* G. H. Doran, 1927, reprinted, Haskell House, 1969; G. R. Elliott, "The Neighborly Humor of Robert Frost," in his *The Cycle of Modern Poetry,* Princeton University Press, 1929; Lawrance R. Thompson, *Fire and Ice: The Art and Thought of Robert Frost,* Holt, 1942, reprinted, Russell & Russell, 1961; Marshall Louis Mertins and Esther Mertins, *Intervals of Robert Frost: A Critical Bibliography,* University of California Press, 1947, reprinted, Russell & Russell, 1975; Herbert Faulkner West, *Mind on the Wing,* Coward-McCann, 1947; W. G. O'Donnell, "Robert Frost and New England: A Revaluation," *Yale Review,* Summer, 1948; Yvor Winters, "Robert Frost; or, The Spiritual Drifter as Poet," *Sewanee Review,* October, 1948; Sidney Cox, "Some Educational Beliefs and Practices of Robert Frost," *Educational Record,* October, 1948.

J. W. Beach, "Robert Frost," *Yale Review,* Winter, 1954;

The cabin where Robert Frost lived his last twenty-five years.

"Poet and a Plight," *Life,* November 28, 1955; Louis Untermeyer, *Makers of the Modern World,* Simon & Schuster, 1955; S. Cox, *Swinger of Portraits: A Portrait of Robert Frost* (with an introduction by Robert Frost), New York University Press, 1957; "Poet's Pilgrimage," *Life,* September 23, 1957; Reginald Lansing Cook, *Dimensions of Robert Frost,* Rinehart, 1958; M. Bracker, "Quietly Overwhelming Robert Frost," *New York Times Magazine,* November 30, 1958; Frank Magill, *Cyclopedia of World Authors,* Harper, 1958; James Nelson, editor, *Wisdom,* Norton, 1958; J. Ciardi, "Robert Frost: Master Conversationalist at Work," *Saturday Review,* March 21, 1959; Loring Holmes Dodd, *Celebrities at Our Hearthside,* Dresser, 1959; C. Morrison, "Visit with Robert Frost," *Look,* March 31, 1959; L. Thompson, *Robert Frost,* University of Minnesota Press, 1959; L. Untermeyer, *Lives of the Poets,* Simon & Schuster, 1959.

R. Kahn, "Visit with Robert Frost," *Saturday Evening Post,* November 19, 1960; M. Drury, "Robert Frost," *McCall's,* April, 1960; Elizabeth Shepley Sergeant, *Robert Frost: The Trial by Existence,* Holt, 1960; R. A. Greenberg, "Frost in England: A Publishing Incident," *New England Quarterly,* September, 1961; A. Whitridge, "Robert Frost and Carl Sandburg," *New York Public Library Bulletin,* March, 1962; James M. Cox, editor, *Robert Frost: A Collection of Critical Essays,* Prentice-Hall, 1962; Emily Elizabeth Isaacs, *Introduction to Robert Frost,* A. Swallow, 1962, reprinted, Haskell House, 1972; C. Anderson and others, "Robert Frost," *Saturday Review,* February 23, 1963; Mar-

garet Anderson, *Robert Frost and John Bartlett: The Record of a Friendship,* Holt, 1963; Edward C. Lathem and L. Thompson, editors, *Robert Frost: Farm-Poultryman,* Dartmouth Publishers, 1963; J. M. Irving, "Parting Visit with Robert Frost," *Hudson Review,* Spring, 1963; Edna H. Byers, compiler, *Robert Frost at Agnes Scott College,* Agnes Scott College, 1963.

Jean Gould, *Robert Frost: The Aim Was Song,* Dodd, 1964; John F. Kennedy, "Poetry and Power," *Atlantic Monthly,* February, 1964; L. Untermeyer, *Robert Frost: A Backward Look,* U.S. Government Printing Office, 1964; Franklin D. Reeve, *Robert Frost in Russia,* Little, Brown, 1964; M. L. Mertins, *Robert Frost: Life and Talks-Walking,* University of Oklahoma Press, 1965; John R. Doyle, Jr., *Poetry of Robert Frost: An Analysis,* Hafner, 1965; L. R. Thompson, *Robert Frost: The Early Years, 1874-1915,* Holt, 1966; Elizabeth Jennings, *Frost,* Barnes & Noble, 1966; Philip L. Gerber, *Robert Frost,* Twayne, 1966; E. C. Lathem, editor, *Interviews with Robert Frost,* Rinehart, 1966; J. Dickey, "Robert Frost, Man and Myth," *Atlantic Monthly,* November, 1966; David A. Sohn and Richard Tyre, *Frost: The Poet and His Poetry,* Holt, 1967; R. L. Cook, "Robert Frost," in *Fifteen Modern American Authors,* edited by Jackson Bryer, Duke University Press, 1969; Lesley Frost, *New Hampshire Child: Derry Journals of Lesley Frost,* State University of New York Press, 1969; Radcliffe Squires, *Major Themes of Robert Frost,* University of Michigan Press, 1969.

15 Sunset Avenue, the Frost home in Amherst, 1931-1938.

L. Thompson, editor, *Robert Frost: The Years of Triumph, 1915-1938,* Holt, 1970; C. E. Lathem, editor, *A Concordance to the Poetry of Robert Frost,* Holt Information Systems, 1971; Robert Francis, recorder, *A Time to Talk: Conversations and Indiscretions,* University of Massachusetts Press, 1972; Elaine Barry, *Robert Frost,* Ungar, 1973; E. Barry, compiler, *Robert Frost on Writing,* Rutgers University Press, 1973; Kathleen Morrison, *Robert Frost: A Pictorial Chronicle,* Holt, 1974; Donald J. Greiner and Charles Sanders, *Robert Frost: The Poet and His Critics,* American Library Association, 1974; R. L. Cook, *Robert Frost: A Living Voice,* University of Massachusetts Press, 1974; Jac Tharpe, editor, *Frost: Centennial Essays II,* University Press of Mississippi, 1976; Lawrance Thompson and R. H. Winnick, *Robert Frost: The Later Years, 1938-1963,* Holt, 1976; Lentricchia, *Robert Frost: A Bibliography, 1913-1974,* Scarecrow, 1976.

For children: Laura Benét, *Famous American Poets,* Dodd, 1950; Frances Helmstadter, *Picture Book of American Authors,* Sterling, 1962; Doris Faber, *Robert Frost: America's Poet,* Prentice-Hall, 1964; Ellen J. Wilson, *Robert Frost: Boy with Promises to Keep,* Bobbs-Merrill, 1967; Norman Richards, *Robert Frost,* Childrens Press, 1968; Reuben Brower, *Poetry of Robert Frost: Constellations of Intention,* Oxford University Press, 1968; John T. Winterich, *Writers in America,* Davey, Daniel, 1968; Emery Kelen, *Fifty Voices of the Twentieth Century,* Lothrop, 1970; Lucas Longo, *Robert Frost: Twentieth Century Modern American Poet Laureate,* edited by Steve D. Rahmas, Samhar Press, 1972.

Obituaries: *New York Times,* January 30, 1963; *Illustrated London News,* February 9, 1963; *Newsweek,* February 11, 1963; *Publishers' Weekly,* February 11, 1963; *National Review,* February 12, 1963; *Senior Scholastic,* February 13, 1963; *Reporter,* February 28, 1963; *Current Biography,* March, 1963; *Current Biography Yearbook 1963; Britannica Book of the Year 1964.*

Movies: "Small World: Frost, Herbert, Vasconellos" (28 minutes, sound, black & white), Columbia Broadcasting System, 1959; "Robert Frost" (10 minutes, sound, color, with a study guide), Oxford Films, 1972.

GILLETTE, Henry Sampson 1915-

PERSONAL: Born January 29, 1915, in New York, N.Y.; son of Curtenius (a physician) and Annie (Sampson) Gillette; married Gertrude Wachtell (an artist). *Education:* Studied at St. Mark's School, National Academy of Design, Art Students League of New York, and other art schools. *Home:* Battery Pl., Crugers, N.Y.

CAREER: Illustrator of magazines and books; writer. Teacher of art at St. Mary's School, Peekskill, N.Y. and Westchester Art Center, White Plains, N.Y. *Exhibitions*—Group shows: National Academy of Design, Audu-

HENRY SAMPSON GILLETTE

bon Artists, Allied Artists, California Watercolor Society, Texas Watercolor Society, Herron Institute, American Watercolor Society. One-Man Shows: Harrison, N.Y. and Croton, N.Y. *Military service:* U.S. Army Air Forces, 1943-46; served in Pacific Theater. *Member:* American Water Color Society, Art Students League (life membership).

WRITINGS: (Self-illustrated) *Leonardo da Vinci, Pathfinder of Sciences* (juvenile), Watts, 1962; *Raphael, Painter of the Renaissance*, Watts, 1967.

Illustrator: *Mark Twain: Boy of Old Missouri,* Bobbs, 1939; *The Green Cockade,* Longmans, 1939; *Old Wolf: The Story of Israel Putnam,* Farrar, Straus, 1940; Mildred M. Pace, *Early American: The Story of Paul Revere,* Scribner, 1940; *Stark of the North Country,* Farrar, Straus, 1941; *Jogging Around New England,* Appleton-Century, 1943; Opal Wheeler, *Paganini: Master of Strings,* Dutton, 1950; *Findlay: The Story of a Community* (adult), Findlay Printing, 1961; Irmengarde Eberle, *Benjamin Franklin: Man of Science,* Watts, 1961; *The First Book of The Star Spangled Banner,* Watts, 1961; Herbert E. Arntson, *Adam Gray: Stowaway,* Watts, 1961; *The First Book of China Clippers,* Watts, 1962; *A Civil War Sampler,* Watts, 1963; Donald J. Sobol, *Two Guns in Old Oregon* (fiction), Watts, 1964; *Hernando De Soto,* Garrard, 1964; Charles and Mary Shapp, *Let's Find Out About Our Flag,* Watts, 1964; Donald J. Sobol, *An American Revolutionary War Reader,* Watts, 1964; David C. Knight, *Let's Find Out About Insects,* Watts, 1967; Irmengarde Eberle, *Edward Jenner and Smallpox Vaccination,* Watts.

WORK IN PROGRESS: An adventure story.

SIDELIGHTS: "My household upbringing as a child was among authors, artists and musicians, as my father (my mother died when I was seven) surrounded himself in the cultural milieu of his time. Leaving for boarding school (age

ten), these influences continued in my studies. I had always drawn pictures, persuaded by the early illustrations in the classic childrens' stories of those years. Piano was a concomitant study, also, as was the necessity of learning a foreign language (French). Good writing, of course, was a prerequisite for any communication—be it a letter home or a composition in English class. I became editor of the literary magazine and in due course illustrated the year book. Upon graduation I entered the National Academy of Design for four years and studied at night schools.

"My first jobs illustrating were for *Coronet* and the old *St. Nicholas* magazine for children. In books I started with a man who was then New York City's poet, Charles Hanson Towne.

"As for writing, I was approached by Watts to try my hand at *Leonardo*—having spent three years in Italy—and the manuscript was accepted. The readers were determined by the nature of the book itself. Leonardo as a *scientist* automatically predetermined the age group."

Henry Gillette has resided in Mexico and Italy; speaks Italian and French. Has travelled around the world on a freighter.

GLICK, Carl (Cannon) 1890-1971 (Captain Frank Cunningham, Peter Holbrook)

PERSONAL: Born September 11, 1890, in Marshalltown, Iowa; son of Charles and Myra (Cannon) Glick; married Sue Ann Wilson, June 27, 1936. *Education:* Northwestern University, B.S., 1915. *Politics:* Republican. *Religion:* Episcopalian. *Address:* c/o Russell Burns, 1144 Hollyhock St., Livermore, Calif. 94550.

CAREER: Fairmount College, Wichita, Kan., instructor in drama, 1915-17; Community Theatre, Waterloo, Iowa, director, 1917-20; University of Colorado, Boulder, English instructor, 1923-25; University of Montana, Missoula, assistant professor, 1925-27; Little Theatre, San Antonio, Tex., director, 1927-31; Players Club, Sarasota, Fla., director, 1933-34; Little Theatre, York, Pa., director, 1934-35; Town Theatre, Columbia, S.C., director, 1938-40; New York University, New York, N.Y., instructor in playwriting, 1943-54; California Western University, San Diego, assistant professor of drama and English, 1955-61. *Military service:* U.S. Army, 1918-19, intelligence office. *Member:* Drama League of New York (member of advisory committee), California Writers Guild, Phi Kappa Psi, Chinese Athletic Club, Royal Arch Masons. *Awards, honors: Mickey, the Horse that Volunteered* selected as honor book, *New York Herald Tribune* Children's Spring Book Festival, 1945.

WRITINGS—Adult books: *The Laughing Buddha* (fiction), Lothrop, 1937; (with Albert McCleery) *Curtains Going Up: The Community Theatres of America,* Pitman, 1939; *Shake Hands with the Dragon* (non-fiction), Whittlesey House, 1941: *Three Times I Bow* (non-fiction), Whittlesey House, 1943; *Double Ten: Captain O'Banion's Story of the Chinese Revolution of 1911,* Whittlesey House, 1945; (with Hong Sheng-Hwa) *Swords of Silence: Chinese Secret Societies–Past and Present,* Whittlesey House, 1947; *I'm a Busybody* (non-fiction), Crowell, 1949; *The Secret of Serenity* (non-fiction), Crowell, 1951; (compiler) *A Treasury of Masonic Thought,* Crowell, 1953; *Death Sits In* (mystery novel), Washburn, 1954.

CARL GLICK

Children's books: *Oswald's Pet Dragon,* Coward, 1943; (ghost writer) *The Good Luck Horse,* Whittlesey House, 1943; (ghost writer) *The Magic Monkey,* Whittlesey House, 1944; *Mickey, the Horse that Volunteered,* Whittlesey House, 1945; (ghost writer) *Mary Jane and Little Lu,* Whittlesey House, 1945; *Mickey Wins His Feathers,* Whittlesey House, 1948; (with Ollie Rogers) *The Story of Our Flag,* Putnam, 1964.

Published plays: (With Mary Hight) *The Police Matron,* Walter H. Baker, 1918; *Outclassed,* Samuel French, 1928; *The Fourth Mrs. Phillips,* Samuel French, 1928; *It Isn't Done,* Samuel French, 1928; *Sun-Cold,* Samuel French, 1929; *The Devil's Host* (first produced in London), Diana Verlag, 1929; *The Dragon Znee Zee,* National Play Bureau, Federal Theatre Project, 1936; (adapter with Kent Wilson) *Everyman,* Drama Shop, 1956.

Other plays produced: "Little Girls," Regent Theatre, New York, N.Y., 1920; "Enemies at Home," New York, N.Y., 1932; "The Unconquered," Federal Portable Theatre, 1934.

Motion pictures: "Modern Love," Universal, 1913; "Unto the Weak," American, 1914; "The Pursuer Pursued," American, 1914; "A Murderous Elopement," Nestor, 1914; "Like Father, Like Son," American, 1914; "Business Versus Love," American, 1914; "The Ingrate," American, 1914; "The Girl in Question," American, 1914; "The Pipe Rush," Unique, 1914; "Pioneers of Today," Willard, 1938; "Coast Guard," Willard, 1941.

More than a hundred short stories in magazines, including *Smart Set, Delineator, This Week, Saucy Stories, Breezy Stories, College Humor;* almost a hundred articles in *Bookman, Collier's, Coronet, Esquire, Pageant,* other magazines. Columnist on theater under pseudonym Peter Holbrook in *Parisienne* and *Follies,* 1921-22; columnist on community theaters, *Springfield Republican,* 1931-40; book reviewer under pseudonym Captain Frank Cunningham, *Black Mask* Magazine, 1920-22; more than twenty other reviews in *Philadelphia Inquirer, New York Times, Saturday Review of Literature,* 1945-50.

SIDELIGHTS: "Any idiot can write a book (and many do), but it takes a genius to sell one. I've known a number of professional writers who have sold stories after twenty or more rejections." A few years ago, Glick turned his own collection of rejection slips (from the days when editors wrote letters) into cash by selling notes from Robert Benchley, David Belasco, H. L. Mencken, and others to an autograph agency.

The author's widow, Sue Glick, writes: *"The Devil's Host* was produced first in England where it had a good run in London. That, I believe, was in 1929, then in New York in 1931 or 1932. It was the first time an American play, by an American, was produced in London before the United States.

"If you remember, the early 30's was no time to get financial backing or to 'achieve' audiences. I was, at that time, National Director of the Drama League of America. We moved our office from Chicago to New York in the fall of 1929. Had a brief 'honeymoon' with the National Council of Churches as Church and Drama League, then I 'split,' as they would say. Carl had been a chairman of Playwriting contest and later of Drama Week. As we had branches all over the country, we were often amused later when he'd find a letter from me about some committee matter ending 'When you come to New York be sure to visit the office.' He did.

"In some cases, Carl became best known for his books about the Chinese in America. *Shake Hands* was on the best seller list for a short time, but the book had a definite influence on the Chinese New York community (by the way, it tells how Carl came to know them and write about them). When we first knew the Chinese, so many of the young men were college educated but could not find employment except as waiters. The book opened doors. Also, it and *Three Times I Bow* were required reading for all the hush-hush boys who operated behind the Japanese lines. *Three Times* was also published by the government for the armed forces.

"Both books are about *real* people and were our experiences with them. Carl had to simplify by using one view point and the same character for all stories for the readers benefit.

"The small boys in *Shake Hands* are now grown up and fathers with families, the older 'boys' grandfathers. We keep in touch and so many still do—you should see my Christmas cards!

"Among the short stories, 'My Song Yankee Doodle,' became almost a classic. It has been reprinted in many anthologies for children.

"When Carl was fulfilling a book or story contract, he observed a strict schedule for writing. At his typewriter by 9:30 or 10:00 a.m.—maybe a short rest for a light lunch. Then at 2:30 or 3:00 he would close his typewriter, even if in the middle of a thought—he'd then relax, read, maybe go for a walk to think out the next day's work and be ready for a happy hour with me when I returned from my office. He would play solitare for some time while he thought out his ideas—playing the victrola as *loud* as possible—Wagner, Strauss, Beethoven and when ready, attack the typewriter furiously. Even during 'dry spells' he would follow the same routine.

"As you know, he was born in the midwest and grew up in Marshalltown. He was an asthmatic child which prevented his participation in team games. So he took to reading and music, was at one time an accomplished pianist, but did not keep up practice. His father was a manufacturer and would have liked Carl to enter the firm, but he never could hit a nail straight! His father was also a baseball fan. However, his mother had been a school teacher, so she encouraged him in his reading, writing, acting in high school and music. One thing his mother made him promise was never to write anything she would be ashamed of and Carl always was happy to know he had kept the promise. He also was writing and selling all during college—stories, movies, etc.

"Carl was a gay gregarious soul. When I first knew him, my 'British' would often shudder, for he would talk to anyone—anytime—anyplace. As he said, 'that's how I get stories and characters.' I got used to it and liked it. When my father died in 1948, he had lived with us since our marriage, we went to Florida for a month 'vacation.' I wanted to take a stateroom on the train. Carl would not hear of it, two lowers.

'I'd never get to meet the people in the car shut away in a room.' By the time we reached Philadelphia, he knew half of them.

"Carl had a delightful sense of humor, one reason he got along so well with the Chinese. For instance, he never resented my father, who being of the 'old school,' would 'throw him out of the house' about once a week. Why didn't he go out to business every day as a man should instead of sitting typing! When a book was finished, Carl would show him a copy, 'This, Herb, is what I have been doing.' Father would then look it over and say, 'Nice pictures.' Of course, Carl never illustrated anything.

"You can see we had a very happy married life—and the only 'fight' we ever had was over a kitten, as he was as fond of cats as I was. I'd promised one of our last litter to Charlie, our Chinese laundry man, and when mother cat finally disowned the last of the litter, I gave him to Charlie, when he brought the laundry. Carl returned from a walk, 'Where was the kitten?' Fireworks!! He'd never had a cat of his own—father had his—I had the mother cat—now his was gone!!

"Another memory of Carl and cats is later. We had to put our cream color Persian pet of eleven years to sleep. That was in 1965. We had left the California Western campus when Carl retired in 1961. A friend, who had property adjacent to the campus gave us permission to bury her there. Carl was not physically able to dig the grave. So while I dug, he sat on a log with Imogene cradled in his arms and the tears rolling down his cheeks. But we left her where she had spent many days playing. A brother and sister adopted us a little later and lived with us till I left home."

FOR MORE INFORMATION SEE: This Week, August 1, 1937; *Northwestern Alumni News,* October 1, 1943; *Wilson Library Journal,* October, 1945; *Christian Science Monitor,* December 21, 1946; *San Diego Sentinel,* July 4, 1963.

(Died March 7, 1971)

GODE von AESCH, Alexander (Gottfried Friedrich) 1906-1970 (Alexander Gode)

PERSONAL: Gode pronounced *Go*-dah; born October 30, 1906, in Bremen, Germany; son of Heinrich and Anna (von Aesch) Gode; married Johanna Roser, 1930; married second wife, Janet Alison Livermore, 1963; children: (first marriage) Anna Johanna (Mrs. Richard Merritt), Marilyn. *Education:* Columbia University, M.A., 1929, Ph.D., 1939. *Home:* Finney Farm, Croton-on-Hudson, N.Y. *Office:* Interlingua Division, Science Service, Inc., 80 East 11th St., New York, N.Y. 10003.

CAREER: T. Y. Crowell Co. (publishers), New York, N.Y., editor of linguistic works, 1943-46; International Auxiliary Language Association, New York, N.Y., director of research, 1949-53; Storm Publishers, Inc., New York, N.Y., president, 1946-70; Science Service, Inc., Interlingua Division, New York, N.Y., chief, 1953-70, New York University, New York, N.Y., adjunct professor of German, 1959-70.

MEMBER: International Society for General Semantics, International Society of Aviation Writers, Modern Language Association, American Medical Writers Association,

American Association for Advancement of Science, National Society for Study of Communication, American Translators Association (past president; executive director), American Interlingua Society, Association of Technical Writers and Publishers (past president, New York chapter), Union Mundial pro Interlingua (president). *Awards, honors:* American Medical Writers Association citation and award for distinguished contributions to medical communication, 1959; Mildred L. Batchelder Award, 1973, for translation of *Pulga.*

WRITINGS: Natural Science in German Romanticism, Columbia University Press, 1941; (with E. Clark Stillman) *Spanish at Sight,* Storm Publishers, 1943; *Portuguese at Sight,* Storm Publishers, 1944; (with Chassia Heldt) *French at Sight,* Storm Publishers, 1946, 2nd revised edition, Ungar, 1963; (with Hugh E. Blair) *Interlingua Grammar,* Storm Publishing, 1951; *El Romanticismo Aleman y las Ciencias Naturales,* Espasa-Calpe, 1953; *Interlingua at Sight,* Storm Publishers 1954; (with Merrill Moore) *Homo Sonetticus Moorensis,* Storm Publishers, 1956; *Dece Contros,* Storm Publishers, 1958.

Editor: *Roget's Thesaurus,* Crowell, 1946; *Bulfinch Mythology,* Crowell, 1946; (with Frederick Ungar) *An Anthology of German Lyric Poetry Through the 19th Century* (in German and English), Ungar, 1950; *Interlingua-English Dictionary,* Storm Publishers, 1951.

Translator: Fulop-Miller, *Saints that Moved the World,* Crowell, 1945; Selye, *Le Major Phases de Recerca in Le Historia del Syndrome de Adaptation,* Science Service, 1953; Frankl, *Theodore Herzl,* Storm Publishers, 1956; Nettl, *National Anthems,* Storm Publishers, 1958; *Pulga* (juvenile), Morrow, 1973. Also translator of volumes of abstracts of various international congresses into Interlingua.

Columnist, "Just Words," *Journal of American Medical Association,* "Of Words and Things," Science Service, and "Live Chitchat," *Lebende Sprachen.* Contributor to more than twenty linguistic and science journals. Editor, *Buten und Binnen, Der Reading Deutsche,* 1932-35, *Scientia International,* 1952-70, *Novas de Interlingua,* 1954-70, *ATA Notes,* 1960-70.

WORK IN PROGRESS: Translating summaries for some twenty medical journals into Interlingua.

(Died August 10, 1970)

GRANT, Neil   1938-
(David Mountfield)

PERSONAL: Born June 9, 1938, in the United Kingdom; son of Alastair and Margaret (Sims) Grant. *Education:* St. Johns College, Cambridge, B.A., 1961. *Home:* 2 Avenue Road, Teddington, Middlesex, England.

CAREER: American Peoples Encyclopedia, New York, N.Y., associate editor, 1962-67.

WRITINGS: Benjamin Disraeli: Prime Minister Extraordinary, F. Watts, 1969; *Charles V: Holy Roman Emperor,* F. Watts, 1970; *Victoria: Queen and Empress,* F. Watts, 1970; *English Explorers of North America,* Messner, 1970; *The Renaissance: A First Book,* F. Watts, 1971; *Munich, 1938: Appeasement Fails to Bring Peace for Our Time,* F. Watts, 1971; *Cathedrals: A First Book,* F. Watts, 1972; *Guilds: A*

First Book, F. Watts, 1972; *The Easter Rising: Dublin, 1916,* F. Watts, 1972; *The Industrial Revolution,* F. Watts, 1973; *The Partition of Palestine, 1947: Jewish Triumph, British Failure, Arab Disaster,* F. Watts, 1973; *The New World Held Promise: Why England Colonized North America,* Messner, 1974.

Under pseudonym David Mountfield: *A History of Polar Exploration,* Dial, 1974; *A History of African Exploration,* Domus Books, 1977.

GRIMM, William C(arey)   1907-

PERSONAL: Born July 1, 1907, in Pittsburgh, Pa.; son of Charles and Harriet Elizabeth (Carey) Grimm; married Ruth Fahr Curtis (a school librarian), July 12, 1941. *Education:* University of Pittsburgh, B.S., 1935. *Home:* 15 Strawberry Dr., Route 9, Greenville, S.C. 29609.

CAREER: Wildlife biologist; teacher of science in Georgetown, S.C., 1951-55, Pickens, S.C., 1955-56, and Greenville, S.C., 1956-60. *Military service:* U.S. Army, 1942-45; became sergeant. *Member:* National Audubon Society, American Forestry Association, National Wildlife Federation. Southern Appalachian Botanical Club, Carolina Bird Club. South Carolina Retired Educators Association. *Awards, honors: Indian Harvests* was a Children's Book Showcase Title, 1975.

WRITINGS: Book of Trees, Stackpole, 1957, published as *How to Recognize Trees,* Castle, 1972; *Recognizing Native Shrubs,* Stackpole, 1966, published as *How to Recognize Shrubs,* Castle, 1972; *Familiar Trees of America,* Harper, 1967; *Recognizing Flowering Wild Plants,* Stackpole, 1968, published as *How to Recognize Flowering Wild Plants,* Castle, 1972; *Home Guide to Trees, Shrubs, and Wildflowers,* Stackpole, 1970; (with M. Jean Craig) *The Wondrous World of Seedless Plants,* Bobbs-Merrill, 1973; *Indian Harvests,* McGraw, 1974.

WILLIAM C. GRIMM

Indian children gathering walnuts. ■ (From *Indian Harvests* by William C. Grimm. Illustrated by Ronald Himler.)

GUY, Rosa (Cuthbert) 1928-

PERSONAL: Born September 1, 1928, in Trinidad, West Indies; came to U.S. in 1932; daughter of Henry and Audrey (Gonzales) Cuthbert; married Warner Guy (deceased); children: Warner. *Agent:* Curtis Brown Ltd., 575 Madison Ave., New York, N.Y. 10019.

CAREER: Writer. *Member:* Harlem Writer's Guild (president).

WRITINGS: Bird at My Window (novel), Lippincott, 1966; (editor) *Children of Longing* (anthology), Holt, 1971; *The Friends* (novel), Holt, 1973; *Ruby* (novel), Viking, 1976; *Edith Jackson* (novel), Viking, in press. Author of one-act play, "Venetian Blinds," 1954. Contributor to *Cosmopolitan* and *Freedomways.*

WORK IN PROGRESS: A book, *Alexander Hamilton; Benidine,* a novel dealing with a Trinidadian family in New York; research in African languages; *Sun, Sea, a Touch of the Wind; Dorine Davis,* biography of a step-mother.

SIDELIGHTS: "[I am] interested in the historical and cultural aspects of all peoples of African descent. Have been to Haiti and back to Trinidad to study the ways, customs, and languages retained over the years from Africa. Have traveled to Africa five times: Senegal, Gambia, Ivory Coast, Nigeria and Algeria." Rosa Guy speaks French and Creole.

FOR MORE INFORMATION SEE: Horn Book, April, 1974, December, 1976.

I did not like her. Edith always came to school with her clothes unpressed, her stockings bagging about her legs with big holes, which she tried to hide by pulling them into her shoes but which kept slipping up.... ■(From *The Friends* by Rosa Guy.)

ROSA GUY

HAINING, Peter 1940-

PERSONAL: Born April 2, 1940, in Enfield, Middlesex, England; son of William (a manager) and Joan (Pattrick) Haining; married Philippa Waring, October, 1965; children: Richard, Sean, Gemma. *Education:* Educated in Buckhurst Hill, England. *Home:* The Hideaway, Birch Green, near Colchester, Essex, England.

CAREER: Journalist and magazine writer, 1957-63; New English Library, London, England, 1963-72, began as editor, became senior editor, then editorial director; editorial consultant, writer, and anthologist, 1972—. *Member:* International P.E.N.

WRITINGS: (With Arthur V. Sellwood) *Devil Worship in Britain,* Transworld Publishers, 1964; *Holiday Guide to the Channel Islands,* New English Library, 1966; *The Warlock's Book: Secrets of Black Magic from the Ancient Grimoires,* University Books, 1972; *The Hero,* New English Library, 1973; *Ghosts: The Illustrated History,* Macmillan, 1974; *An Illustrated History of Witchcraft,* New English Library, 1976, Pyramid, 1977; *Terror: A History of Horror Illustrations from the Pulp Magazines,* Souvenir Press, 1976; *The Great English Earthquake,* Hale, 1976; *The Compleat Birdman: A History of Man-Powered Flight,* Hale, 1977.

Editor or compiler: *The Craft of Terror: Extracts from the Rare and Infamous Gothic 'Horror' Novels,* New English Library, 1966, MEWS Books, 1976; *The Gentlewomen of Evil: An Anthology of Rare Supernatural Stories from the Pens of Victorian Ladies,* Taplinger, 1967; *The Evil People: Being Thirteen Strange and Terrible Accounts of Witchcraft, Black Magic and Voodoo,* Frewin, 1968; *Dr. Caligari's Black Book: An Excursion into the Macabre, in Thirteen Acts,* W. H. Allen, 1968; *The Future Makers: A*

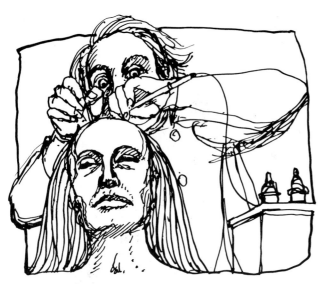

(From *The Monster Makers* by Peter Haining. Illustrated by David Smee.)

Selection of Science Fiction from Brian Aldiss [and Others], Sidgwick & Jackson, 1968; *The Midnight People: Being Eighteen Terrifying and Bizarre Tales of Vampires,* Frewin, 1968, published in America as *Vampires at Midnight: Seventeen Brilliant and Chilling Tales of the Ghastly Bloodsucking Undead,* Grosset, 1970; *The Witchcraft Reader,* Dobson, 1969, Doubleday, 1970; *The Satanist,* N. Spearman, 1969, Taplinger, 1970; *The Unspeakable People: Being Twenty of the World's Most Horrible Horror Stories,* Leslie Frewin, 1969.

The Freak Show: Tales of Fantasy and Horror, Rapp & Whiting, 1970, published in America as *The Freak Show: Freaks, Monsters, Ghouls, Etc.,* Thomas Nelson, 1972; *The Hollywood Nightmare: Tales of Fantasy and Horror from the Film World,* Macdonald, 1970, Taplinger, 1971; *A Thousand Afternoons,* Cowles. 1970 (published in England with introduction and preface by Haining, under title *A Thousand Afternoons: An Anthology of Bullfighting*), P. Owen, 1970; *The Wild Night Company: Irish Stories of Fantasy and Horror,* Gollancz, 1970, Taplinger, 1971; *A Circle of Witches: An Anthology of Victorian Witchcraft Stories,* Taplinger, 1971; *The Clans of Darkness: Scottish Stories of Fantasy and Horror,* Taplinger, 1971; *The Ghouls,* Stein & Day. 1971; *The Necromancers: The Best of Black Magic and Witchcraft,* Hodder and Stoughton, 1971, Morrow, 1972; *Gothic Tales of Terror: Classic Horror Stories from Great Britain, Europe, and the United States, 1765-1840,* Taplinger, 1972 (published in England as *Great British Tales of Terror: Gothic Stories of Horror and Romance, 1765-1840,* Gollancz, 1972); *The Magicians: Occult Stories,* P. Owen, 1972, published in America as *The Magicians: The Occult in Fact and Fiction,* Taplinger, 1973; *The Lucifer Society: Macabre Tales by Great Modern Writers,* Taplinger, 1972 (published in England as *The Lucifer Society,* W. H. Allen, 1972); *The Nightmare Reader,* Gollancz, 1972, Doubleday, 1973; *The Anatomy of Witchcraft,* Taplinger, 1972; *Nightfrights: Occult Stories for All Ages,* Taplinger, 1973; *The Monster Makers: Creators and Creations of Fantasy and Horror,* Taplinger, 1974; *The Witchcraft Papers,* University Books, 1974; *The Ancient Mysteries Reader,* Doubleday, 1975; *The Penny Dreadful,* Gollancz, 1975; *The Fantastic Pulps,* St. Martin's, 1976; *The Black Magic Omnibus,* Taplinger, 1976; *The Ghost's Companion,* Taplinger, 1976.

WORK IN PROGRESS: Deadly Nightshade, a new anthology for younger readers; two works of non-fiction.

SIDELIGHTS: "Although I have written on a wide variety of topics from bullfighting to ballooning, earthquakes to manpowered flight, the majority of my books have been collections of ghost, horror and macabre stories which have been successfully published in many countries in both English and translation. These anthologies have been primarily assemblies of rare and unknown tales by writers of distinction, many of them household names in the fantasy and science fiction fields. I have always been dismayed at the number of books of this kind which have been published over the years which only reprint the same classic stories over and over again. My research has convinced me that much good material lies forgotten—and still does—and that there is an ever growing army of readers who welcome such 'discoveries.' The continuing success of my books has seemingly proved me right.

"My own interest in this kind of material stems back to my childhood and perhaps even one extraordinary incident. I distinctly remember that the first adult television programme I was allowed to stay up and view by my parents was a particularly frightening production of Robert Louis Stevenson's classic horror tale, 'Dr. Jekyl and Mr. Hyde.' I was both terrified and attracted by the story and thereafter began to search out similar material—a quest that has continued to this day and also become the source of my livelihood.

"I have also written studies of witchcraft and black magic. These books stem from my early working days in journalism

PETER HAINING

when, as a young reporter, I was sent to write a story about a church that had been desecrated during one night. When the possibility that those responsible might have been practitioners of black magic emerged, I began research of my own in both printed material and by consulting experts. As a result I have subsequently written several books on both witchcraft and black magic, describing my beliefs in what they are, their differences, and their prevalence in the world today.

"Although much of my work has been directed towards adults, I have of late compiled several collections for children and am even now writing a book of true mysteries particularly for a younger audience. Most of the same principles that I apply to selecting material for adults I use for children, believing strongly that it is a grave mistake to 'talk down' to youngsters as I have seen some other writers do. I like, too, for each of my books to have a theme—not be just general collections of stories—and for the stories to progress naturally from one to the next, although they may be by quite different types of writers. A good anthology, I believe, should develop the way an exciting novel or story does, and I always take the utmost care in the structure and selection of my material. I always greatly appreciate the letters I get from readers of all ages on my books—one letter genuinely felt is worth columns of newspaper praise to me.

"My wife is a great helpmate in my work and a fine critic. My younger brother is also a writer of macabre short stories and has been published in several collections. Also my eldest son is both showing interest in this material and writing his own tales. Long may we all continue, I trust!"

Peter Haining, whose family lived for many generations in the lowlands of Scotland, now makes his home in English folklore's "witch country." His researches have prompted a curse from a group of devil worshippers in London, but he has nonetheless completed several studies of witchcraft and black magic. *The Warlock's Book* is based on records he discovered about his own ancestor, who was burned at the stake for possessing a "book of spells."

HOBBIES AND OTHER INTERESTS: Sports, travel, book collecting.

HAMBERGER, John   1934-

PERSONAL: Born August 17, 1934, in Jamaica, N.Y.; son of Michael and Pearl (Wandolowski) Hamberger; married Rita Backer (an agent), November 29, 1975; children: Christopher, Matthew. *Education:* Attended School of Visual Arts. *Home and office:* 120 East 34th St., New York, N.Y. 10016.

CAREER: Writer and illustrator. *Military service:* U.S. Army, 1952-56. *Member:* Society of Animal Artists (member of Jury of admissions), Society of Illustrators. *Awards, honors:* Christopher Award, 1973, for illustrating *Vanishing Wings.*

WRITINGS—Self-illustrated: *The Day the Sun Disappeared,* Norton, 1964; *The Wish,* Norton, 1967; *The Peacock Who Lost His Tail,* Norton, 1967; *Hazel Was an Only Pet,* Norton, 1968; *The Call of a Loon: Story and Pictures,* Four Winds Press, 1969; *This Is the Day,* Grosset, 1971; *The Lazy Dog,* Four Winds Press, 1971; *A Sleepless Day,* Four Winds Press, 1973; *Birth of a Pond* (juvenile), Coward, 1975.

He was hungry so he landed on the twelfth story perch overlooking the park to take stock. ▪ (From *Vanishing Wings* by Griffing Bancroft. Illustrated by John Hamberger.)

Illustrator: Kay Hill, *Badger: The Mischief Maker,* Dodd, 1965; Elizabeth Jane Coatsworth, *The Fox Friend,* Macmillan, 1966; Charles House, *The Biggest Mouse in the World,* Norton, 1968; Millen Brand, *This Little Pig Named Curly,* Crown, 1968; Margaret Rau, *The Penguin Book,* Hawthorn, 1968; Helen Ross Russell, *Clarion the Killdeer,* Hawthorn, 1970; Bernice Kohn, *Chipmunks,* Prentice-Hall, 1970; Hill, *More Glooscap Stories,* Dodd, 1970; Daniel Cohen, *Watchers in the Wild,* Little, Brown, 1971; Patricia Miles Martin, *Navajo Pet,* Putnam, 1971; Griffing Bancroft, *Vanishing Wings: A Tale of Three Birds of Prey,* F. Watts, 1972; Jane Annixter, *Sea Otter,* Holiday House, 1972; Julian May, *Wild Turkeys,* Holiday, 1973; Irmengarde Eberle, *Prairie Dogs in Prairie Dog Town,* Crowell, 1974; Wilda S. Ross, *Can You Find the Animal?,* Coward, 1974; Ralph Louis Woods, editor, *Wit and Wonder of the Animal World,* C. R. Gibson, 1974; Joan Joseph, *Pet Birds,* F. Watts, 1975; Cohen, *Animal Territories,* Hastings House, 1975; Millicent Selsam, *Animals of the Sea,* Four Winds, 1975; Dorothy Edwards Shuttlesworth, *The Hidden Magic of Seeds,* Rodale

JOHN HAMBERGER

Press, 1976; Millicent Selsam, *See Monsters of Long Ago*, Four Winds, 1977.

WORK IN PROGRESS: Macmillan Dictionary for Children.

SIDELIGHTS: "I love nature and travel throughout the country to study animals. This is what I write about and what I illustrate—anything to do with nature."

FOR MORE INFORMATION SEE: Illustrators of Children's Books: 1957-1966, Horn Book, 1968.

HAMIL, Thomas Arthur 1928-
(Tom Hamil)

PERSONAL: Born in 1928. *Education:* University of Washington, Ph.D.

CAREER: Painter and author. *Awards, honors: Brother Alonzo,* 1957, was chosen for the American Institute of Graphic Arts exhibit of outstanding children's books.

WRITINGS: Brother Alonzo (self-illustrated), Macmillan, 1957; *Hans and the Golden Flute* (self-illustrated), Macmillan, 1958.

Illustrator: James Kendrick Noble, *Ploob: A Midshipman's First Year at Annapolis,* Noble, 1949, revised edition pub-

lished as *Ploob: The Fortunes and Misfortunes of a Midshipman's First Year at the United States Naval Academy,* Noble, 1957; Ashraf Siddiqui, *Bhombal Dass: The Uncle of Lion,* Macmillan, 1959; Patricia Miles Martin, *Calvin and the Cub Scouts,* Putnam, 1964; Patricia M. Martin, *The Pumpkin Patch,* Putnam, 1966; Patricia M. Martin, *Kumi and the Pearl,* Putnam, 1968; Patricia M. Martin, *There Goes the Tiger!,* Putnam, 1970.

SIDELIGHTS: Hamil lived for a time in California. His book, *Hans and the Golden Flute* told the story of a shepherd boy, his magical flute, and the lesson he learned about humility. A reviewer for *Kirkus* noted, "Tom Hamil . . . both in his text and in his illustrations happily combines whimsy with morality." In describing the same book, a critic for the London *Times Literary Supplement* commented, "This gentle tale is illustrated . . . by pert line drawings coloured very boldly with what seems to be chalk or crayon laid sideways. . . ."

She dropped to the ground and ran stumbling, pushing against the wind. ■ (From *Kumi and the Pearl* by Patricia Miles Martin. Pictures by Tom Hamil.)

HOUSEHOLD, Geoffrey (Edward West) 1900-

PERSONAL: Born November 30, 1900, in Bristol, Eng.; son of Horace W. (a lawyer) and Beatrice (Noton) Household; married Elisaveta Kopelanoff, 1930; married second wife, Ilona Zsoldos-Gutman, 1942; children: Geoffrey Andrew, Nicolette Ilona, Anna Celia. *Education:* Attended Clifton College, Bristol, 1914-19, Magdalen College, Oxford, 1919-22, first class honors in English literature, 1922. *Address:* Church Headland, Whitchurch, Aylesbury, Buckinghamshire, England.

CAREER: Engaged in commerce in Europe, the United States, South America, and the Near East, 1922-35; professional writer, 1935—. *Military service:* Served in the Intelligence Corps, 1939-45; attained rank of lieutenant colonel; awarded a Territorial Decoration and mentioned in dispatches.

WRITINGS—Novels: *The Third Hour,* Chatto & Windus, 1937, Little, Brown, 1938; *Rogue Male,* Little, Brown, 1939, reissued, 1971; *Arabesque,* Little, Brown, 1948, reissued, International Publications Service, 1969; *The High Place,* Little, Brown, 1950, reissued, White Lion, 1972; *A Rough Shoot* (originally appeared serially in the *Saturday Evening Post,* March, 1951, under the title *Run from the Hangman*), Little, Brown, 1951; *A Time to Kill,* Little, Brown, 1951; *Fellow Passenger,* Little, Brown, 1955; *Watcher in the Shadows,* Little, Brown, 1960, reissued, M. Joseph, 1972; *Thing to Love,* Little, Brown, 1963; *Olura,* Little, Brown, 1965; *The Courtesy of Death,* Little, Brown, 1967; *Dance of the Dwarfs,* Little, Brown, 1968; *Doom's Caravan,* Little, Brown, 1971; *The Three Sentinels,* Little, Brown, 1972; *The Lives and Times of Bernardo Brown,* M. Joseph, 1973, Little, Brown, 1974; *Red Anger,* Little, Brown, 1975; *Escape into Daylight,* Little, Brown, 1976; *Hostage London: The Diary of Julian Despard,* Little, Brown, 1977.

Short stories: *The Salvation of Pisco Gabar, and Other Stories,* Chatto & Windus, 1938, Little, Brown, 1940; *Tales of Adventurers,* Little, Brown, 1952; *The Brides of Solomon, and Other Stories,* Little, Brown, 1958; *Sabres on the Sand, and Other Stories,* Little, Brown, 1966.

For children: *The Spanish Cave* (illustrated by Henry C. Pitz), Little, Brown, 1936, reissued, Longmans, 1965 (published in England as *The Terror of Villadonga,* Hutchinson, 1936); *The Exploits of Xenophon* (illustrated by Leonard E. Fisher), Random House, 1955 (published in England as *Xenophon's Adventure,* Bodley Head, 1961); *Prisoner of the Indies* (illustrated by Warren Chappell), Little, Brown, 1967.

Autobiography: *Against the Wind,* M. Joseph, 1958, Little, Brown, 1959.

SIDELIGHTS: For a man who has himself led a life laced with adventure, particularly during World War II, Household now lives quietly and happily in the English countryside with his wife, Ilona, some charming cats, a frisky dog, and in a neighboring field the horse his daughter rides when she comes for hunt weekends. The Households occupy what was once a farmhouse, one-story and rambling, with softly faded oriental carpets, shelves of books and, just outside the windows, the extensive garden in which Household "putters" every day from 2:30 to 5 p.m. He writes mornings, in longhand, from 10 to 1 and again in the evenings from 5 to 7.

GEOFFREY HOUSEHOLD

Leaving Oxford in the halcyon days between World Wars I and II with a First Class degree in English Literature, through "a great friend who was the son of the managing director" he found himself posted to Rumania as an assistant confidential secretary to the management of the Bank of Rumania, a big consortium representing Rumanian, Greek and Anglo-Austrian interests. For a young man, learning to speak Rumanian and to type with two fingers, "it was a marvelous four years. You could get the best lunch in Europe in Rumania in those days for half a crown. I well remember the first time I realized I could actually speak French, too. There was the most charming French cabaret girl in Bucharest and I suddenly thought, 'I'm talking to her in her own language and she's enjoying it.'"

From Rumania young Household moved on to Spain and a job with the European end of the United Fruit Company. Although for most of us today bananas and Spain may seem almost synonymous, it was Household's job to launch them in that country as a diet staple for the poor. "I think I can actually say," he declares, "that I introduced bananas to the masses in Spain."

He also picked up "quite good Spanish," wrote and published his first short stories and found the setting for his first book, *The Spanish Cave,* a tale for youngsters that he wrote in America a year later. The only distinction he makes between his adventure writing for youngsters and for adults is "to make it faster and simpler for children. I also like to think I'm helping unobtrusively to educate them in the proper use of the English language."

(From the movie "Man Hunt" based on *Rogue Male* by Geoffrey Household, starring Walter Pidgeon and Joan Bennett. Copyright 1941, Twentieth Century-Fox.)

Newly arrived in America from Spain, and determined to support himself by writing, Household collided head on with the Depression and was lucky enough to get a job as a junior editor at $100 a week producing very simple entries on famous figures for a children's encyclopedia. "I became an expert at writing about people I'd never heard of before," he says, "and I also wrote a whole series of little radio plays for children for the Columbia Broadcasting Company."

Still combining business with writing on the side, Household travelled widely in the Middle East, all over Europe and through South America, representing printing ink manufacturers, and acquiring background atmosphere he would use in book after book. It was about this time that he came into contact with Edward Weeks at the *Atlantic Monthly,* and found it so happy an association editorially that even though Weeks is long retired, Household remains today an Atlantic-Little, Brown author and wouldn't dream of going anywhere else.

"I am one of the few British writers who loves American editing," he says. "When Ted Weeks said of my first book, 'It's about 60% right but the rest needs work,' I had sense enough to say to myself, 'You'd better listen to what he has to say. You won't get this kind of careful attention every place.'"

During World War II Household had a busy career in British military intelligence, going in as a captain and coming out as a major. He served first in Rumania, not surprisingly, officially as a legation clerk but knowing that when the time came he would be one of those expected "to go out and blow up the Rumanian oil fields." What happened instead was the fall of France. The Germans walked into Rumania and the Britons "were expelled bell, book and candle." Subsequently Household served in intelligence in Greece, Syria, Palestine and Iraq, becoming in the process himself "a damn good revolver shot, learning how to pot a chap before he could pot you." Many of the fascinating "insider's" experiences he actually lived through in his own intelligence career are recounted in the autobiographical *Against the Wind.* Of the terrible campaign in Greece he has written that he managed to get his men out "nearly naked but reasonably unashamed."

Summing up a long and very happy writing career that sees him in his 70s able to write about youthful contemporary anarchists as if he mingled with them every day, Household says, simply: "I think I began to write because I was so anxious to try to put into English some of the same sense of excitement, adventure, man pitted against his fate that I had first encountered in reading classical Greek and Latin." [*Publishers Weekly,* April 4, 1977.]

Rogue Male is perhaps Household's best known work. It is a psychological novel of an English sportsman from a family of excellent financial standing who suddenly desires to assassinate a European dictator. "*Rogue Male*," commented a *Books* critic, "is one of the most original adventure tales of recent times, a book with a delightfully dry, bitter tang of intelligent dramaturgy.... Mr. Household's dish is a pungent combination of dramatic and lyric ingredients. It is exciting to consume...." The *New York Times* added, "The author is thoroughly adroit, but what the reader feels is not deftness or 'swift pace,' but a breath-taking, uninterrupted concentration. As a work of imagination *Rogue Male* is an almost overpowering tour de force. And in its spare, tense, desperately alive narrative it will keep, long after the last page is finished, its hold from the first page upon the reader's mind. Its deepest and broadest suggestion the reader must find for himself, if he will."

In 1941, Twentieth-Century Fox adapted Household's *Rogue Male* into a motion picture, "Man Hunt," and in 1953, United Artists produced "Shoot First," based on *A Rough Shoot.*

FOR MORE INFORMATION SEE: Stanley J. Kunitz and Howard Haycraft, editors, *Twentieth Century Authors,* H. W. Wilson, 1942; S. J. Kunitz, editor, *Twentieth Century Authors,* first supplement, H. W. Wilson, 1955; Geoffrey Household, *Against the Wind,* Little, Brown, 1959; Brian Doyle, editor, *Who's Who of Children's Literature,* Schocken Books, 1968.

IWAMATSU, Jun Atsushi 1908-
(Taro Yashima)

PERSONAL: Born September 21, 1908, in Kagoshima, Japan; emigrated to the U.S. in 1939; son of a country doctor; married wife, Mitsu (an artist); children: Mako (son; an actor), Momo (daughter). *Education:* Studied art at the Imperial Art Academy, Tokyo, 1927-30, and at the Art Students League, New York City, 1939-41. *Residence:* Los Angeles, Calif.

CAREER: Author and illustrator of books for children. *Military service:* Served in the U.S. Army in the Office of War Information and in the Office of Strategic Services during World War II. *Awards, honors:* Runner-up for the Caldecott Medal, 1956, for *Crow Boy,* 1959, for *Umbrella,* and 1968, for *Seashore Story;* Child Study Association of America/Wel-Met Children's Book Award, 1955, for *Crow Boy;* New York Times Choice of Best Illustrated Children's Books of the Year, 1967, for *Seashore Story;* Southern California Council on Literature of Children and Young People Award for significant contribution in the field of illustration, 1968.

WRITINGS—Under pseudonym Taro Yashima; all self-illustrated: *The New Sun,* Holt, 1943; *Horizon Is Calling,* Holt, 1947; *The Village Tree,* Viking, 1953, reissued, 1972; (with Mitsu Yashima, pseudonym of wife, Tomoe Iwamatsu) *Plenty to Watch,* Viking, 1954; *Crow Boy* (Junior Literary Guild selection), Viking, 1955, reissued, 1969; *Umbrella* (Junior Literary Guild selection), Viking, 1958; (with M. Yashima) *Momo's Kitten,* Viking, 1961; *Youngest One,* Viking, 1962; *Seashore Story,* Viking, 1967.

Illustrator: Eleanore M. Jewett, *Which Was Witch?,* Viking, 1953; (and translator) Hatoju Muku, pseudonym of Hikoho Kubota, *The Golden Footprints,* World Publishing, 1960;

JUN ATSUSHI IWAMATSU

June Behrens, *Soo Ling Finds a Way,* Golden Gate Junior Books, 1965.

SIDELIGHTS: Jun Iwamatsu began using the name Taro Yashima during World War II. Because of his involvement with the Office of Strategic Services, he could not use his real name.

His first book, *The New Sun,* is an autobiography. The *New York Times* called it, "A simple and moving document.... It is particularly in his account of [his] jail experience, of its anguish and degradation and the indomitable courage and comradeship of the underground fellowship, that the artist's talent achieves its best dimensions. The black and whites tell the story with an economy and eloquence that might readily have turned into melodrama in an idiom less personal and stenographic than Mr. Yashima's own."

His first book for children was written in answer to his daughter's question about what he did as a boy in Japan. *Horn Book* described *The Village Tree* as, "A strikingly beautiful interpretation in poetic prose and picture of the author's childhood in Japan portrayed as he recalls the fun he enjoyed with other boys by the river where a great tree still stretches its branches. The brief text and full-color sketches illustrate, in an atmosphere of great peace and happiness, the kind of tree-play, diving, and underwater fun that boys anywhere might invent. Of ageless interest." A *New York Times* critic wrote, "The work of Taro Yashima leaves this reviewer with a strong feeling that here is an artist-writer who knows children, respects and loves them deeply. With both words and pastel-and-ink strokes he has captured their simplicity, gaiety, and sense of wonder."

Crow Boy was a runner-up in 1959 for the Caldecott Medal. A *Horn Book* reviewer wrote, "Children will love his story; adults will be deeply moved by it; it is a remarkable accom-

On her umbrella, the raindrops made the wonderful music. ■ (From *Umbrella* by Taro Yashima. Illustrated by the author.)

plishment to have got so much into so few words. The beautiful pictures linger in one's memory as if one had been in the village and walked with little Chibi, morning and night, the long walk between his home and school. The *New York Times* added, "The sensitive, penetrating touch of the artist is ever present in the pages of this book.... As in *The Village Tree* and *Plenty to Watch,* this picture book about childhood in Japan is a gentle reminder that children are much the same everywhere." *Saturday Review* commented, "From page to page [the story] flows, revealing a deeper meaning to life as a child blossoms under the understanding eye of a true teacher. One is left refreshed at its close as though touched by the mountain air which is the source of Crow Boy's individuality."

The comments of a *Saturday Review* critic on *Umbrella* included, "It seems . . . that Taro Yashima makes his picture books live through the special gift of love with which he endows them. The simple charm and delicacy of his text and

his impressionistic drawings always communicate more than is seen on the page. *Umbrella* was made for his daughter for her eighth birthday, but it is also a gift for every child—and grown-ups as well—so tenderly does it convey the excitement and pleasure of a small child with her first umbrella and red rubber boots, and the wonder of life itself." *Horn Book* added, "It is only unfortunate, that, at the end, the author swings forward, then backward again in time. Young children cannot make these rapid transitions and the adult reader will have a good deal of explaining to do. But the beauty of the book makes this worth while."

Taro Yashima has had several one-man shows of his works in such cities as New York, Los Angeles, and Pasadena. His paintings have been bought for permanent collections in several museums, including the Phillips Memorial Museum in Washington, D.C. Yashima also directs the Yashima Art Institute where he teaches fundamental techniques and methods of art instruction. His son, Mako, is an actor and was nominated for an Academy Award in 1967 as best supporting actor for his performance in "The Sand Pebbles."

Crow Boy, The Village Tree, and *Umbrella* have all been adapted into educational movies and filmstrips for children.

FOR MORE INFORMATION SEE: Taro Yashima, *The New Sun,* Holt, 1943; T. Yashima, *Horizon Is Calling,* Holt, 1947; T. Yashima, "On Making a Book for a Child," *Horn Book,* February, 1955; Bertha E. Miller and others, compilers, *Illustrators of Children's Books, 1946-1956,* Horn Book, 1958; Muriel Fuller, editor, *More Junior Authors,* H. W. Wilson, 1963; Lee Kingman and others, compilers, *Illustrators of Children's Books, 1957-1966,* Horn Book, 1968.

JACOPETTI, Alexandra 1939-

PERSONAL: Born August 1, 1939, in Preston, Idaho; daughter of Newell Scheib (a musician, carpenter, and writer) and Ruth (a store manager; maiden name, Cutler) Hart; married Gregory L. Williams, May, 1957 (divorced November, 1958); married Roland Jacopetti (a radio producer), October 8, 1960; children: Hobert, Lucas, Natalia. *Education:* Attended University of Utah, 1956-57. *Politics:* Feminist. *Religion:* Subud. *Home and office:* Folkwear, P.O. Box 98, Forestville, Calif. 95436.

CAREER: Atelier Alexandra Jacopetti (weaving), Forestville, Calif., fibre artist, 1967—. Member of board of direc-

A great way to recycle a chair! ■ (From *Native Funk and Flash* by Alexandra Jacopetti. Photos by Jerry Wainwright.)

ALEXANDRA JACOPETTI

tors and gallery director of Berkeley Experimental Arts Foundation, 1965-66; director of apprentices in weaving for Baulines Craftsman's Guild, Marin Co., Calif., 1972-76, member of board of directors, 1972-74; partner in Folkwear Ethnic Patterns, Forestville, Calif., 1976—.

WRITINGS: (With collaborator and photographer, Jerry Wainwright) *Native Funk & Flash: An Emerging Folk Art* (ALA Notable Book), Scrimshaw Press (California), 1974.

WORK IN PROGRESS: Research in ethnic clothing fashions; paper patterns for ethnic clothing for current use, including a book of information and instruction.

SIDELIGHTS: "I never thought that I would be an author; I am primarily a craftsperson—a fibre artist, weaver, and needleperson. But, as the book which I most hoped to find on the shelves of the library or local bookstore never seemed to appear, I knew I had to put it together myself. *Native Funk & Flash* shows the work and tells about people like myself—their work shown in full color photos by my friend, Jerry Wainwright.

"I love to make beautiful things, mostly with yarns and threads, and my work has been centered around finding a way to earn a living doing what I enjoy doing, and sharing it with others. This has led me through building a 12 foot high x 12 foot square ropework playground and taking apprentices as a tapestry weaver for corporate clients such as United Gas & Pipeline (twelve tapestries in their Pennzoil Towers, Houston Texas offices) and Carter Hawley Hale (seven tapestries in their Los Angeles offices) to being instrumental in the creation of Folkwear, my current near full time occupation.

"Folkwear Ethnic Patterns prints and distributes full-size paper clothing patterns for authentic clothes from other countries and cultures, including the handwork designs and instructions which are my special interest.

"I . . . have found that those who are most productive and satisfied with their lives . . . are people who are actively involved with making inner states material through an art or craft."

An exhibit of material from *Native Funk & Flash* toured several western states under arrangements made by Western Association of Art Museums.

FOR MORE INFORMATION SEE: Saturday Review of Education, May, 1973; "The Saga of Macrame Park" (film), Eccentric Circle Films, 1973; *Sunset,* June, 1974; *Art Week,* September 28, 1974; *Fibrearts,* September-October, 1976; *Shuttle Spindle & Dyepot,* Spring, 1977.

JENNISON, Keith Warren 1911-

PERSONAL: Born December 12, 1911, in Winnipeg, Manitoba, Canada. *Education:* Attended Williams College, Williamstown, Mass., and the University of Toronto.

CAREER: Following an apprenticeship to a Vermont printer and a job in the shipping room of A. S. Barnes & Co., Cranbury, N.J., Jennison held a variety of positions with several New York publishers, including salesman with Harcourt, Brace, 1935-41, sales manager, Henry Holt, 1941-46, vice-president, Sloane Associates, 1946-49, editor, Viking Press, 1949-58, and vice-president and editor-in-chief, David McKay Co., 1959-62; assistant director, New York University Graduate Institute of Book Publishing, beginning 1958. *Military service:* Served in the Office of War Information during World War II.

WRITINGS: Vermont Is Where You Find It, Harcourt, 1941; *The Maine Idea,* Harcourt, 1943; (editor) *Dedication: Text and Pictures of the United Nations,* Holt, 1943; *New Hampshire,* Holt, 1944, reissued, R. Smith, 1961; *New York and the State It's In,* Sloane Associates, 1949; *The Half-Open Road: A Handy Guide to Chaos on the Highway* (illustrated by George Price), Doubleday, 1953; *The Green Place* (novel), Funk & Wagnalls, 1954; *Green Mountains and Rock Ribs,* Harcourt, 1954; *The Boys and Their Mother,* Viking, 1956; (with John Tebbel) *The American Indian Wars,* Harper, 1960; *From This to That* (illustrated by Kathleen Elgin), McKay, 1961; *Remember Maine,* Durrell, 1963; (with Kathryn Sisson Phillips) *My Room in the World,* Abingdon, 1964; *The Humorous Mr. Lincoln,* Crowell, 1965; *To Massachusetts with Love,* Durrell, 1970; (editor) *The Concise Encyclopedia of Sports,* Watts, 1970; *Yup . . . Nope, and Other Vermont Dialogues,* Countryman Press, 1976.

SIDELIGHTS: Keith W. Jennison's first book, *Vermont Is Where You Find It,* prompted this comment from *Christian Century:* "The total number of words in this book is not far from 500. Yet it is a treasure of verbal wit and pictorial beauty. Vermonters are not loquacious; they can say a good deal in 500 words." *New Republic* added, "These fifty-eight full-page pictures taken in Vermont get closer to the character of the state and its people than all the stuff that's been written about them. Nothing spectacular or tricky, just excellent photography inspired by good sense."

The *Chicago Tribune's* comments on *Half-Open Road: A Handy Guide to Chaos on the Highway* included, "In Benchley style mock solemnity, Jennison analyzes nearly every problem which may confront a motorist, and outlines carefully the procedure which is surest to land this motorist in a pine box and all others in the nut houses—a procedure which comes naturally to a lot of people. George Price's superb drawings could not be more fitting or hilarious." The *Spring-*

Contestants leap forward with their iceboats from the lineup for a race on Lake St. Clair, Michigan, as the official on the right gives the starting signal by firing a small cannon. ■ (From *The Concise Encyclopedia of Sports* **edited by Keith W. Jennison.)**

field Republican noted, "If you've ever driven, dodged, or ridden in an automobile you'll get a few hours of pleasure reading *The Half-Open Road.* This is a zany, totally facetious little book."

Jennison's novel, *Green Place,* received mixed reviews. *Kirkus* called it, "A slight story, written with grace and a sensitivity to pertinent concerns." *Library Journal* described it as, "A short novel which is entertaining although a bit contrived.... The author uses his plot as a framework for his opinions on some of modern life's larger issues. Well written." The *New York Herald Tribune* commented, "That no man can escape the violence of life, no matter where it is staged, is the obvious moral of the story. It is well told in swiftly moving incidents but somehow fails to jell into character conviction." The *New York Times* wrote, "Mr. Jennison has written an artificial story that suggests but one moral: a park is no place to try to think in."

Jennison has also written *Boys and Their Mother* which, through a series of incidents, shows how the author and his wife coped with the problems of raising their two sons. The comments of the *New York Times* critic included, "A little book which is whimsical without a single whimsy, tender but not mushy, witty but not comic, it should raise no blood pressure, stir no emotions—just make one feel good while reading it. Seeing the parents through their boys, they must be a fine couple. Seeing the boys through their parents, don't worry about them; they'll do." *Saturday Review* added, "Essentially Mr. Jennison stands in the place all parents occupy—constantly irritated by the brilliance their offspring show in evading responsibility from day to day, yet proud and somewhat amazed by their response to a crisis. This is a good book for parents who despair of ever changing the little monsters into human beings. It will also make you laugh aloud."

JOHNSTON, H(ugh) A(nthony) S(tephen) 1913-1967
(A Fighter Pilot; Hugh Sturton)

PERSONAL: Born December 7, 1913, in Belfast, Northern Ireland; son of James (in Indian Civil Service) and Edith Alma (Sturton) Johnston; married Berrice Jacqueline Lincoln, October 3, 1942; children: Carolyn, Robin (son). *Education:* King's School, Canterbury, England, scholar, 1922-32; Brasenose College, Oxford, B.A., 1935, M.A., 1943. *Home:* 40 Middleway, London N.W. 11, England.

CAREER: H. M. Overseas Civil Service, various posts in Nigeria, 1936-40, 1945-60, including deputy governor, 1960; Overseas Services Resettlement Bureau, London, England,

director, 1961-65; City Parochial Foundation (charitable organization), London, England, chief executive, 1965-67. *Military service:* Royal Air Force, pilot, 1940-45; commanded a flight in the American Eagle Squadron, 1941-42; shot down over Malta in 1942 and wounded; became wing commander; received Distinguished Flying Cross and bar. *Member:* Royal Commonwealth Society, East India Sports Club (London). *Awards, honors:* Companion of St. Michael and St. George, 1959; Officer of Order of the British Empire, 1964.

WRITINGS: (Under pseudonym A Fighter Pilot) *Tattered Battlements,* P. Davies, 1943; (editor and translator) *A Selection of Hausa Stories,* Clarendon Press, 1966; (under pseudonym Hugh Sturton) *Zomo the Rabbit* (children's book), Atheneum, 1966; *The Fulani Empire of Sokoto,* Oxford University Press, 1967.

(Died December 9, 1967)

JONES, Harold 1904-

PERSONAL: Born February 22, 1904, in London, England; son of William Edward and Ethel (Susie) Jones; married Mollie Merry, July, 1933; children: Stephanie Angela, Gabrielle Pamela. *Education:* Attended St. Dunstans College, 1914-20; Goldsmith's College, 1920-21; Camberwell School of Arts & Crafts, 1922-23; Royal College of Art, diploma (A.R.C.A.), 1929. *Home:* Doune Lodge, 27 Oxford Road, Putney, London, SW15 2LG, England. *Agent:* Laura Cecil, 10 Exeter Mansions, 106 Susxusbury Avenue, London, W1V 7DH, England.

CAREER: Illustrator. Bermondsey Central School for Boys, London, England, teacher, 1930-34; Ruskin School of Drawing, Ashmolean Museum, Oxford, England, teacher, 1937-40; The Working Men's College, London, England, head of evening art school, 1937-40; Chelsea School of Art, London, England, teacher, 1945-58; Sunningdale School of Ballet, Sunningdale, England, teacher, 1945-46. *Exhibitions:* Royal Academy, N.E.A.C., Leichester Gallery, National Book League, Piccadilly Gallery, (one-man show) Green & Abbott, 1974, 1975. *Military service:* Royal Engineers, lithographic draftsman, 1939-45. *Awards, honors:* Work has been purchased by the Tate Gallery, the Victoria and Albert Museum, and the London County Council.

WRITINGS—All self-illustrated: *The Visit to the Farm,* Faber, 1939; *The Enchanted Night,* Faber, 1947; *The Child-*

When Kada finds he can't get out, he starts threatening Zomo with all the nasty things he will do to him and his family if he doesn't open the door. ▪ (From *Zomo the Rabbit* by Hugh Sturton. Drawings by Peter Warner.)

Why had they not left him in the forest, where there was no mirror to tell him how loathsome he was? ■ (From *The Fairy Stories of Oscar Wilde*. Illustrated by Harold Jones.)

hood of Jesus, Gollancz, 1964; *There and Back Again,* Atheneum, 1977.

Illustrator: Cecil A. Joll, *Diseases of the Thyroid Gland,* Heinemann, 1932; H. G. Wells, *The Croquet Player* (book jacket), Chatto & Windus, 1936; James Hanley, *The Secret Journey* (book jacket), Chatto & Windus, 1936; M. E. Atkinson, *August Adventure,* Jonathan Cape, 1936; H. G. Wells, *Star Begotten* (book jacket), Chatto & Windus, 1937; M. E. Atkinson, *Mystery Manor,* Bodley Head, 1937; Walter de la Mare, *This Year: Next Year,* Faber, 1937, Holt, 1937; H. G. Wells, *The Brothers* (book jacket), Chatto & Windus, 1938; C. S. Lewis, *Out of the Silent Planet* (book jacket), Bodley Head, 1938; M. E. Atkinson, *The Compass Points North,* Bodley Head, 1938; M. E. Atkinson, *Smuggler's Gap,* Bodley Head, 1939; M. E. Atkinson, *Crusoe Island,* Bodley Head, 1947; John Pudney, *Selected Poems,* Bodley Head, 1947.

Kathleen Lines, *Four to Fourteen,* Oxford University Press, 1950; Kathleen Lines (compiler), *Lavender's Blue* (ALA Notable Book), Oxford University Press, 1954; Kathleen Lines (compiler), *Once in Royal David's City,* Oxford University Press, 1956, Watts, 1956; Henry Fagen, *Nikya,* Jonathan Cape, 1956; Donald Suddaby, *Prisoners of Saturn,* Bodley Head, 1957; Kathleen Lines (compiler), *A Ring of Tales,* Oxford University Press, 1958, Watts, 1958; W. Blake, *Songs of Innocence,* Faber, 1958; Elfrida Vipont (compiler), *Bless This Day* (ALA Notable Book), Collins, 1958, Harcourt, 1958; Kathleen Lines, *Noah and the Ark,* Oxford University Press, 1961; *Songs from Shakespeare,* Faber, 1961; Charles Kingsley, *The Water Babies,* Gollancz, 1961, Watts, 1961; Robert Browning, *The Pied Piper of Hamelin,* Oxford University Press, 1962, Watts, 1962, Angus Robertson, 1977; *The Complete Greek Stories of Nathaniel Hawthorne,* Gollancz, 1964; Lewis Carroll, *The Hunting of the Snark* (limited edition), Whittington Press, 1975; *The Fairy Stories of Oscar Wilde,* Gollancz, 1976; Paul Ries Collin, *Calling Bridge,* Oxford University Press, 1976; Ruth Manning-Sanders, *The Town Mouse and the Country Mouse,* Angus Robertson, 1977.

An illustration has appeared in T. E. Gregory, *The Westminster Bank,* Oxford University Press, 1936; Colin Brooks, *The First Hundred Years (of the Woolwich Equitable Society),* Curwen Press, 1947; M. Fisher, *Open the Door,* Brockhampton, 1965.

SIDELIGHTS: "I studied wood engraving, etching, line engraving, lithography at the Royal College of Art, which influenced my style in pen drawings for illustration. I admire the work of Rembrandt, Cruikshank, Heinrich, Huffman, Beardsley, Jean de Brunhoff, and Beatrix Potter.

"To me the three essentials of an illustrator's education are the study of drawing, the technicalities of engraving—to get the feeling of print upon paper—and the great Italian frescoes; to which I think illustration very comparable in spite of the difference of scale. In them too the artist has had a feeling for the flat white surface—plaster instead of paper—and achieved a marriage of three-dimensional form and two dimensional design.

"My long apprenticeship of drawing—which is the background of all illustration—has been the basis of my work and my whole artistic conviction.

"It's impossible to dodge that apprenticeship. The most difficult thing is: to draw with the economy of simple line all

HAROLD JONES

the forms in the human figure, so that when the drawing is finished, it has the same simplicity that nature has.

"I don't think you can paint in a very simple way until you've got a very big knowledge. To be able to put a line exactly in the right place is the result of forty or fifty years' work: to put on colour is a question of sheer knowledge. That's why I deplore this lack of fundamental knowledge today.

"You face a blank sheet of paper with a pen that's going to make a precise line. You've got a concept in your mind—you want to draw a strange bird in a strange land. Where do you begin? Out of airy nothing you've got to produce a local habitation and a name.

"Then that background of knowledge comes to your mind. This must be so, that can only go this way. One knows what one can and can't do: you find yourself putting down what you want to put down.

"Curiously enough, I think one's sense of rhythm—one's joy in painting—is increasing all the time: because in the early days there was so much mortification. When you want a thing to look beautiful—and it looks ugly that is extraordinary mortification. And I'm sure no genuine work of art can come from uncertainty and fear. You've got to have that absolute conviction that assurance born of knowledge, to get the sense of inevitability—that this is the one and final solution, that it could not be otherwise—that you get in all great works of art.

"Drawing is to me a pleasurable thing, and a form of escapism. Half the world I distinctly want to escape from."

FOR MORE INFORMATION SEE: The Junior Bookshelf, December, 1948; *Third Book of Junior Authors,* edited by Doris de Montreville and Donna Hill, H. W. Wilson, 1972; *Arts Guardian,* December 6, 1974; *The Times,* August 27, 1975; William Feaver, *When We Were Young,* Thomas & Hudson, 1977.

His nightly song will scarce be missed:
Nine times death claimed our alley cat.
Good-by, you old somnambulist!--
A long word, that.

■ (From *Take Sky* by David McCord. Illustrated by Henry B. Kane.)

KANE, Henry Bugbee   1902-1971

PERSONAL: Born January 8, 1902, in Cambridge, Mass.; children: one son, one daughter. *Education:* Attended Massachusetts Institute of Technology. *Home:* Lincoln, Mass.

CAREER: Worked in a variety of fields, including lighting engineering, kitchen design, advertising, and public relations; Massachusetts Institute of Technology, Cambridge, Mass., director of Alumni Fund, 1940-66; author, photographer, and illustrator for adult and juvenile magazines and books. *Military service:* Served in the U.S. Navy as a flyer. *Awards, honors: The Tale of a Wood* was chosen by the *New York Times* as one of the best illustrated children's books of the year, 1962.

WRITINGS: The Alphabet of Birds, Bugs, and Beasts (self-illustrated), Houghton, 1938; *Wings, Legs, or Fins* (self-illustrated), Knopf, 1965; *Four Seasons in the Woods* (self-illustrated), Knopf, 1968; *A Care for Nature,* W. W. Norton, 1971.

"Wild World Tales" series, self-illustrated, published by Knopf: *The Tale of the Whitefoot Mouse,* 1940; . . . *the Bullfrog,* 1941; . . . *the Promethea Moth,* 1942; . . . *the Crow,* 1943; . . . *the White-Faced Hornet,* 1943; . . . *the Wild Goose,* 1946; *Wild World Tales: The Tale of the Mouse, the Moth, and the Crow,* 1949; *The Tale of a Meadow,* 1959; . . . *a Pond,* 1960; . . . *a Wood,* 1962.

Illustrator: Sally Carrighar, *One Day on Beetle Rock,* Knopf, 1944; Henry David Thoreau, *Thoreau's Walden: A Photographic Register,* Knopf, 1946; John James Rowlands, *Cache Lake Country,* W. W. Norton, 1947; H. D. Thoreau, *Maine Woods,* W. W. Norton, 1950; H. D. Thoreau, *Cape Cod,* W. W. Norton, 1951; H. D. Thoreau, *Walden,* W. W. Norton, 1951; David Thompson Watson McCord, *Far and Few,* Little, Brown, 1952, reissued, Dell, 1971; S. Carrighar, *Icebound Summer,* Knopf, 1953; Edwin Way Teale, *Wilderness World of John Muir,* Houghton, 1954; H. D. Thoreau, *Concord and the Merrimac,* Little, Brown, 1954; Bud Helmericks, *Arctic Hunter,* Little, Brown, 1955; D.T.W. McCord, *Take Sky,* Little, Brown, 1962; Dudley Cammett Lunt, *The Woods and the Sea: Wilderness and Seacoast Adventures in the State of Maine,* Knopf, 1965; D.T.W. McCord, *All Day Long: Fifty Rhymes of the Never Was and Always Is,* Little, Brown, 1966; Louise and Norman Dyer Harris, *Flash: The Life Story of a Firefly,* Little, Brown, 1966; D.T.W. McCord, *For Me to Say: Rhymes of the Never Was and Always Is,* Little, Brown, 1970.

SIDELIGHTS: Though Kane became attracted to drawing and photography as a child, he only pursued his interest in the arts as an avocation until he retired from the Massachusetts Institute of Technology in 1966. The author's earlier books in the "Wild World Tales" series, examined the lifecycle of various insects, birds, and animals. Kane's book, *The Tale of the Whitefoot Mouse,* traced the animal's life from birth through its first year. "Beautiful and unusual photographs, exquisite in detail and masterly in composition, make a distinguished picture book which will be enjoyed at any age," commented a reviewer for *Horn Book.*

The author-illustrator's book, *Tale of the Bullfrog,* told the life story of a frog from its tadpole stage to that of a full grown adult. A critic for the *New York Times* noted the book's "graphic text, distinguished for its simplicity and conciseness, which nevertheless has room for flashes of humor. . . ." In reviewing the same book, a critic for *Books* noted, "The reproduction does justice to split second photography: the pictures of the grown-up bullfrog . . . are amazing."

In *The Tale of the White-Faced Hornet* Kane traced the development and lifestyle of a hornet. "Unusually fine photographic illustrations and pen-and-ink sketches as tailpieces go far to enhance format," observed a reviewer for *Library Journal.*

The later books in the author-illustrator's "Wild World Tales" series looked at nature's plant and animal life from a small boy's viewpoint. Kane's book, *The Tale of a Pond,* gave an account of the wildlife that inhabits a pond's environment. A reviewer for the *Christian Science Monitor* noted, "Mr. Kane's unusual nature photographs are highly educational in themselves. Added are penciled decorations and accurate sketches. . . ."

In his book, *The Tale of a Wood,* the writer-photographer observed wildlife in a forest surrounding. "The book is worth owning for its exceptional photography. . . . Fine drawings, with many caption details, supplement the camera work in adding information . . . ," commented a *Horn Book* critic.

One of Kane's last books on nature was *Four Seasons in the Woods.* A critic for *Saturday Review* wrote, "With clearly defined photographs and precise drawings of flora and fauna, the author effectively describes the changing patterns of the woods. He conveys an appreciation of the beauty there without being didactic, and he succeeds in discussing many topics very simply in an easy quiet style."

FOR MORE INFORMATION SEE: Lee Kingman, editor, *Illustrators of Children's Books: 1957-1966,* Horn Book, 1968. Obituaries—*New York Times,* February 16, 1971.

(Died February, 1971)

KÄSTNER, Erich   1899-1974

PERSONAL: Born February 23, 1899, in Dresden, Saxony (now part of East Germany); son of Emil (a harnessmaker) and Ida Amalia (Augustin) Kästner. *Education:* Attended schools in Dresden, with the desire to become a teacher; later attended the Universities of Leipzig, Rostock, and Berlin, receiving a Ph.D., 1925. *Politics:* Liberal Democrat. *Religion:* Protestant. *Home:* Munich, Germany.

CAREER: Novelist, poet, playwright, essayist, editor, social critic, and author of children's books. Early jobs included those of bookkeeper, publicist, researcher, and journalist. Drama critic and associate feuilleton editor of *Neue Leipziger Zeitung,* in Leipzig, 1925-27; feuilleton editor of *Neue Zeitung,* 1945-47; founder and editor of *Pinguin,* a children's magazine, 1946; founded two literary cabarets, "Schaubude," 1945, and "Die Kleine Freiheit," 1951. *Military service:* Drafted into the Imperial Army, 1917; discharged, 1918, as an artillery corporal. *Member:* International P.E.N. (past vice-president; past president of German P.E.N. center), Deutsche Akademie fuer Sprache und Dichtung, Akademie der Wissenschaft und Literatur of Mainz, Akademie der Schoenen Kuenste of Bavaria. *Awards, honors:* Literature Prize of Munich, 1956; Buechner Prize, 1957; Hans Christian Andersen Award, 1960;

Mildred L. Batchelder Award, 1968, for *The Little Man* (translated by James Kirkup).

WRITINGS—For children: *Emil und die Detektive,* 1928, translation by May Massee published as *Emil and the Detectives* (illustrated by Walter Trier), Doubleday, Doran, 1930; *Puenktchen und Anton,* 1931, translation by Eric Sutton published as *Annaluise and Anton* (illustrated by W. Trier), J. Cape, 1932, Dodd, 1933; *Der 35 Mai; oder, Konrad Reitet in die Suedsee,* 1931, translation by Cyrus Brooks published as *The 35th of May; or, Conrad's Ride to the South Seas* (illustrated by Trier), J. Cape, 1933, Dodd, 1934; *Das Fliegende Klassenzimmer,* F. A. Perthes, 1933, translation by C. Brooks published as *The Flying Classroom* (illustrated by Trier), J. Cape, 1966; *Emil und die Drei Zwillinge: Die Zweite Geschichte von Emil und den Detektiven,* Atrium-Verlag, 1935, translation by Brooks published as *Emil and the Three Twins: Another Book about Emil and the Detectives,* J. Cape, 1935, reissued, F. Watts, 1961; *Das Doppelte Lottchen,* Atrium-Verlag, 1949, translation by Brooks published as *Lottie and Lisa* (illustrated by Trier), J. Cape, 1950, Little, Brown, 1951; *Die Konferenz der Tiere,* Europa Verlag, 1949, translation by Zita de Schauensee published as *The Animals' Conference* (illustrated by Trier), D. McKay, 1949.

Der Gestiefelte Kater, C. Ueberreuter, 1950, translation by Richard and Clara Winston published as *Puss in Boots* (Charles Perrault's fairy tale, retold by Kästner; illustrated by Trier), J. Messner, 1957; (translator) Jonathan Swift, *Gulliver's Reisen* ("Gulliver's Travels"), C. Ueberreuter, 1961; *Der Kleine Mann,* C. Dressler, 1963, translation by James Kirkup published as *The Little Man* (illustrated by Rick Schreiter), Knopf, 1966; *Der Kleine Mann und die Kleine Miss,* C. Dressler, 1967, translation by J. Kirkup published as *The Little Man and the Little Miss* (illustrated by Horst Lemke), J. Cape, 1969; *The Little Man and the Big Thief* (translated from the German by J. Kirkup; illustrated by Stanley Mack), Knopf, 1969; (editor) *Die Lustige Geschichtenkiste,* A. Betz, 1972.

Poems: *Herz auf Taille,* C. Weller, 1928; *Laerm im Spiegel,* C. Weller, 1929; *Ein Mann Gibt Auskunft,* Deutsche Verlags-Anstalt, 1930; *Gesang Zwischen den Stuehlen,* Deutsche Verlags-Anstalt, 1932; *Kurz und Buendig: Epigramme,* Atrium-Verlag, 1950; *Let's Face It* (a selection of Kästner's poems translated from the German by Patrick Bridgwater and others), J. Cape, 1963; *Von Damen und Anderen Weibern,* Fackeltraeger-Verlag, 1963; (editor) *Heiterkeit in Vielen Versen,* Fackeltraeger-Verlag, 1965; *Grosse Zeiten, Kleine Auswahl,* Fackeltraeger-Verlag, 1969.

Other writings: *Fabian: Die Geschichte eines Moralisten* (semi-autobiographical novel), Deutsche Verlags-Anstalt, 1931, translation by C. Brooks published as *Fabian: The Story of a Moralist,* Dodd, 1932, reissued, Ace Books, 1961; *Drei Maenner im Schnee* (novel), Rascher, 1934, translation by Brooks published as *Three Men in the Snow,* J. Cape, 1935; *Die Verschwundene Miniatur; oder auch, Die Abenteuer eines Empfindsamen Fleischermeisters,* [Vienna], 1936, translation by Brooks published as *The Missing Miniature; or, The Adventures of a Sensitive Butcher,* J. Cape, 1936, Knopf, 1937; *Georg und die Zwischenfaelle* (novel), Atrium-Verlag, 1938, translation by Brooks published as *A Salzburg Comedy* (illustrated by W. Trier), F. Unger, 1957; *Bei Durchsicht Meiner Buecher,* Atrium-Verlag, 1946; *Zeltbuch von Tumilad,* Insel-Verlag, 1949.

ERICH KÄSTNER

Die Kleine Freiheit: Chansons und Prosa, 1949-1952, Atrium-Verlag, 1952; *Die Dreizehn Monate,* C. Dressler, 1955; *Die Schule der Diktatoren: Eine Komoedie in Neun Bildern* (play), C. Dressler, 1956; *Eine Auswahl,* C. Dressler, 1956; *Leben und Taten des Scharfsinnigen Ritters Don Quichotte,* Ueberreuter, 1956, translation by R. and C. Winston published as *Don Quixote* (Miguel de Cervantes' novel, retold by Kästner; illustrated by H. Lemke), J. Messner, 1957; *Als Ich ein Kleiner Junge War,* C. Dressler, 1956, translation by Isabel and Florence McHugh published as *When I Was a Little Boy* (illustrated by H. Lemke), J. Cape, 1959, F. Watts, 1961; *Rede zur Verleihung des Georg Buechner-Preises 1957,* C. Dressler, 1958; *Der Gegenwart ins Gaestebuch,* Buechergilde Gutenberg, 1958; *Gesammelte Schriften,* seven volumes, Buechergilde, 1958; (editor) *Heiterkeit in Dur und Moll* (German wit and humor), Fackeltraeger-Verlag, 1958; *Ueber das Verbrennen von Buechern,* C. Dressler, 1959; *Heiteres von Walter Trier,* Fackeltraeger-Verlag, 1959.

(Editor) *Heiterkeit Kennt Keine Grenzen* (German wit and humor), Fackeltraeger-Verlag, 1960; *Notabene 45: Ein Tagebuch,* C. Dressler, 1961; (editor) *Heiterkeit Braucht Keine Worte* (German wit and humor), Fackeltraeger-Verlag, 1962; *Das Schwein beim Friseur und Anderes,* C. Dressler, 1962; *Das Erich-Kästner-Seemaennchen,* E. Seeman, 1963; *Kurz und Buendig,* Kiepenheuer & Witsch, 1965; *Der Taegliche Kram: Chansons und Prosa, 1945-19 ,* C. Dressler, 1965; *Zwei Schueler sind Verschwunden,* Longmans, Green, 1966; *Kästner fuer Erwachsene,* S. Fischer, 1966; *Unter der Zeitlupe,* Hyperion-Verlag, 1967; "*. . . was Nicht in Euren Lesebuechern Steht*" (selections from Kästner's works), Fischer-Buecherei, 1968; *Kästner fuer Studenten,* Harper, 1968; *Kennst Du das Land, wo die Kanonen Bluehn?,* Atrium-Verlag, 1968; (editor) *Heiterkeit aus Aller*

Welt (German wit and humor), Fackeltraeger-Verlag, 1968; *Wer Nicht Hoeren Will, Muss Lesen,* Fischer Taschenbuch, 1971; *Friedrich der Grosse und die Deutsche Literatur,* W. Kohlhammer, 1972.

Also author of works for children, *Das Verhexte Telefon,* 1931; *Arthur Mit dem Langen Arm,* 1932; *Till Eulenspeigel,* 1938; *Der Gestiefelte Kater,* 1950; *Muenchhausen,* 1951; *Die Schildbuerger,* 1954. Author of *Leben in Dieser Zeit* (radio and stage play), 1930; *Lyrische Hausapotheke* (poems), 1936; and *Der Taegliche Kram* (songs and prose), 1948.

ADAPTATIONS: Several motion pictures have been adapted from Kästner's works. "Paradise for Three," an adaptation of *Drei Maenner im Schnee,* starring Robert Young and Mary Astor, was produced by Metro-Goldwyn-Mayer in 1938. "The Parent Trap," an adaptation of *Das Doppelte Lottchen,* starring Hayley Mills, Maureen O'-Hara, and Brian Keith, was filmed by Walt Disney Productions in 1961. "Emil and the Detectives," starring Walter Slezak, was filmed by Walt Disney Productions in 1964. There was also a German version, "Emil und die Detektive," released with English subtitles in the U.S. by the International Film Bureau.

SIDELIGHTS: **February 23, 1899.** Born in Dresden, Saxony, the only child of Emil and Ida Amalia (Augustin) Kästner.

"To tell you 'a little' about my father's ancestors is quite easy, because I know nothing, or next to nothing, about them. Their names and the dates of their births, marriages and deaths were conscientiously entered in church registers by various Protestant pastors throughout Saxony. The men were craftsmen, had many children, and outlived their wives, who generally died in childbirth. And many of the newborn babies died with their mothers. That was the way, not only with the Kästners but all over Europe and America.

"Perhaps it was from them and their forebears that I have inherited the careful craftsmanship which I apply to my calling. And perhaps I owe my talent for gymnastics, which I admit has gone a bit rusty now, to my Uncle Hermann who, at seventy-five, was still head of the older men's team in the Penig Gymnastics Society. But it is quite certain that the Kästners have handed me on one family characteristic which always surprises and often annoys my friends—a chronic aversion to travel.

"We Kästners have no particular curiosity to see the great world. We suffer, not from love of roving, but from love of home. Why should we go the Black Forest, or climb Mount Everest, or see Trafalgar Square? The Chestnut tree in front of the house, the Wolfshügel hill which overlooks Dresden, or the Altmarkt, do us quite well. If we could take our beds and our living-room windows with us, we might perhaps be induced to budge. But as for going off to foreign parts and leaving our home at home. No, thank you! There is not a mountain so high, an oasis so mysterious, a harbour so exciting, a Niagara Falls so loud that we feel we must go and see them. It might be all right if we could go to sleep at home and wake up in Buenos Aires, for instance. The being there would probably be tolerable for a while; but what about the getting there? We would never do it. I'm afraid we're far too set in our ways and fond of our comfort for that. But to offset these doubtful qualities we Kästners have one virtue: we're utterly incapable of being bored. A ladybird on the window-

pane can absorb our attention completely. It doesn't have to be a lion in the jungle.

"I myself have seen a little more of the world than [my father] and our ancestors. I have been in Copenhagen and Stockholm, Moscow and Leningrad, Paris and London, Vienna and Geneva, Edinburgh and Nice, Prague and Venice, Dublin and Amsterdam, Radebeul and Lugano, Belfast and Garmisch-Partenkirchen. But I don't like travelling. Unfortunately, however, it is much the same in my trade too—a man must go away from home if he wants to be a master one fine day at home. And I too would very much like to become a master of my craft.

"[My father's] favourite work was making saddles, bridles, horse-collars, saddle-bags, riding-boots, whips and all leather articles for use with riding-horses, carriage horses and cart-horses.

"He was an excellent craftsman, an artist in his craft . . . [He] who had wanted so much to remain an independent master-craftsman, became an artisan. The machine age rolled like a tank over handwork and independent craftsmanship. The shoe factories vanquished the shoemakers, the furniture factories the cabinet-makers and joiners, the textile factories the weavers, the china factories the potters, and the suitcase and leatherware factories the saddlers. The machines worked more quickly and cheaply than the craftsmen. Soon there were bread factories and sausage factories and hat factories and jam factories and paper factories and vinegar factories and button factories and pickled-cucumber factories and artificial-flower factories. The craftsmen fought a tenacious rearguard action, and they are still putting up a fight today. It is an admirable struggle, but a hopeless one. . . . The hungry years of apprenticeship, the lean years as a journeyman, the three anxious years as a master-craftsman on his own had all been in vain. The dream was finished and so was the money. The debts had to be paid. The machines had won.

". . . Ida Kästner, who was already thirty-five, decided to take up a trade, and she took it up. In spite of her age my mother decided to become a hairdressing apprentice with a view to setting up as a hairdresser on her own when trained.

"The greatness of a human being does not depend on the size of his or her field of action. My mother was no angel, and did not want to be one. Her ideal was more realistic. Her goal was distant, yet not up in the clouds. It was attainable. And as she was more strong-minded than anyone I've ever known and would not allow herself to be dissuaded from anything by anyone, she achieved her aim. Ida Kästner wanted to be that, she had no consideration for anyone, not even for herself, and became the perfect mother. All her love and imagination, all her industry, every moment of her time, her every thought—in fact her whole existence she staked, like a frenzied gambler, on one single card—on me? Her stake was her whole life to its last breath.

"I was the card, so I simply had to win. I dared not disappoint her. That was why I became the best pupil in the school and the best-behaved son possible at home. I could not have borne it if she had lost her great game. Since she wanted to be and was the perfect mother, for me, her trump card, there seemed no choice but to become the perfect son. Did I become this? I certainly tried to. I had inherited her talents—her energy, her ambition and her intelligence. That was at least something to begin with. And when I, her sole

(From the movie "Emil and the Detectives," starring Walter Slezak, Bryan Russell and Roger Mobley. Copyright © 1964, Walt Disney Productions.)

capital and stake, sometimes felt really tired of always winning and of only winning, one thing and one thing only kept me going: I truly loved that perfect mother; I loved her very much indeed.

"Attainable goals are particularly strenuous precisely because we want to attain them. They challenge us and, without looking to the right or to the left, we set out to achieve them. My mother looked neither to the right nor to the left. She loved me, and nobody else. She was kind to me, but that was the limit of her kindness. She treated me to her gaiety, and had none left for others. She thought only of me, she had no other thoughts. Her life and every breath she breathed were dedicated to me, only to me.

"If I were a modern psychiatrist I should ponder the matter deeply and then publish in a psychological journal a paper entitled 'The Back-Pedalling Brake as Complex: An Interpretation,' in which I should say something like this: 'To the above-named patient, Frau Ida K., there existed only an uphill course in life in general, and cycling in particular. The opposite concept, namely, the downhill course, was utterly foreign to the aims and nature of her inexhaustible ambition, which sought in her promising son a compensation for her own frustrations. Since Ida K. categorically rejected the downhill course and was therefore incapable of considering its consequences, she naturally lacked all understanding of the precautionary measures necessary. If she nevertheless

found herself confronted with a downhill course, on a cycling tour for example, her conscious mind refused to apply the rules which she had learned. These were automatically forced over the threshold of the conscious into the subconscious. There, in spite of the fact that excellent back-pedalling brakes are provided by bicycle manufacturers, this gadget passed an existence of which Frau Ida K. remained oblivious in moments of danger, precisely because it had been eradicated from her conscious mind. She was fundamentally incapable of taking cognizance either of the phenomenon of the downhill course or of any techniques whatsoever designed to counteract it. To have done so would have been implicitly to criticize and cast doubt upon her own invincible will to aspire. This was out of the question. She rather chose to doubt the principle that hills go down as well as up. In fine, she preferred, at whatever risk, to ignore reality.'" [Erich Kästner, *When I Was a Boy,* translated from German *Als ich ein kleiner Junge war* by Isabel and Florence McHugh, Watts, 1961.[1]]

Ida Kästner, the dominant figure in the author's life, concerned herself with every aspect of his up bringing, including the theater. "Soon the theatres of Dresden became my home from home, and Father often had to eat his supper alone because Mamma and I were paying homage to the muse Thalia, generally in standing places. We took our supper during the long interval, standing in the corners of the stairs. There we unwrapped our sausage sandwiches, and the sand-

(From the movie "The Parent Trap," starring Hayley Mills, Maureen O'Hara, and Brian Keith. Copyright © 1961, Walt Disney Productions.)

wich papers, neatly folded, disappeared into Mother's brown handbag again.

"We frequented the Albert Theatre, the Playhouse and the Opera. We queued for hours in the street to grab the cheapest places when the box-office opened. When we failed we went home as shattered as if we had lost a battle. But we did not lose many battles. We won our standing places by guile and patience and held out bravely in them. Anyone who has ever literally stood through Goethe's *Faust* or one of Wagner's operas will surely take off his hat to us. Only once did my mother faint, and that was at *The Mastersingers* one hot summer afternoon. By this mishap we actually got two seats—they were on the step of the last row—and we were able at least to hear the dance of the apprentices in the last act.

"My love of the theatre was love at first sight, and it will remain my love until my last breath. I have written many theatrical critiques, and now and then a sketch or a play. Opinions may differ about these efforts, but there is one thing about which I will permit no contradiction—as a spectator I cannot be beaten."[1]

The Kästners were compelled to supplement an inadequate family income by taking in boarders. "Our first lodger was a primary-school teacher named Franke. That his name was Franke was of no importance to my future, but the fact that he was a teacher influenced it deeply. To be sure my parents could not know that then. It was just a chance. Our beautiful sunny room might have been rented by a bookkeeper, or a shop-girl, but it attracted a teacher, and it was this chance which was later to prove so significant.

"So I grew up with teachers. I did not get to know them only when I went to school. I had them at home. I saw the blue exercise books and the corrections in red ink long before I myself could write and make mistakes. Blue mountains of dictation books, arithmetic books and essay books; and before Michaelmas and Easter, mountains of fawn examination papers. And always and everywhere primers, text-books, teachers' journals, periodicals dealing with teaching, psychology, folklore and the history of Saxony. . . . And when people asked me, as they are apt to ask children, 'What do you want to be when you grow up?' I always answered eagerly, 'A teacher!'"[1]

Became youngest member of the Neustadt and Antonstadt Gymnastics Society. "I became a pretty good gymnast. I shone at displays and was leader of the team. But I did not become a very good gymnast because I was terrified of swinging right over the high horizontal bar, and I knew why. I had been present once when another boy had lost his hold in full swing and fallen down head first. The comrades who were standing around had been unable to catch him in time, and he was carried off to hospital. And for the rest of my life

Now and again he glanced over his shoulder, and saw the train still thundering after him. ■ (From *Emil and the Detectives* by Eric Kästner. Illustrated by Walter Trier.)

I sedulously avoided swinging right over the high horizontal bar. That was really a very disgraceful thing, and who likes being disgraced? But I never got that fear out of my system and preferred to bear disgrace rather than risk a fractured skull. Was I right? I was.

"I wanted to do gymnastics because I enjoyed them. I did not want to be a hero. And I did not become one—either false or real. Do you know the difference? False heroes have no fear because they have no imagination. They are stupid, and they have no nerves. Real heroes have fear, but they overcome it. Many and many a time in my life I have been afraid, and God knows I have not overcome my fear every time. If I had done so I might perhaps be a real hero today, but I should certainly be a dead one. Now I do not want to make myself out worse than I really am. I have been quite brave at times, and it was not always easy. But being a hero would never have done as my main calling.

"For a time I was passionately addicted to playing billiards. The father of a school friend of mine had an inn near the Johannstadt Embankment. It was deserted in the afternoon while the father had his nap upstairs in his flat and only the barmaid remained on duty in case any thirsty wanderer should stray in. . . .

"We hung our jackets over the backs of chairs because the coatstand was too high for us. Then we picked the smallest billiard cues we could find among the selection standing by the wall, and stood on our toes to do the marking because the cues were too long and thick and also much too heavy. It was an arduous business. The billiard table was too high and too wide for us. The ivory balls never got properly rolling. To get a right screw into the ball we had to lie half over the

edge of the table with our legs dangling. To write our scores on the slate we had to get up on a chair. We tortured ourselves like Gulliver in the land of the giants, when really we should have been laughing at ourselves. We didn't laugh at all, however, but went about our game with solemn dignity, like grown-up men competing at the tournament for the Central German billiards championship. We found this solemnity great fun."[1]

1906. Began formal education in the higher elementary school. "In school itself there was only one difficulty. I was dreadfully inattentive. School was too slow for me. I was bored stiff. So I carried on entertaining conversations with my neighbours in front, behind and beside me. Clearly young men of seven have a lot to tell each other. Herr Bremser, easy-natured though he was, found my love of chattering most disturbing. His efforts to make thirty little Dresdeners into good readers were sadly hampered by the fact that one-third of the class was carrying on unlawful conversations, and that I was the ringleader. Finally he lost patience one day and told me angrily that if I did not mend my ways he would write to my parents about me.

"When a child has learned to read and likes reading, he discovers and conquers a new world, the world of letters. The land of reading is a mysterious, endless continent. Things, people, spirits and gods we could never see otherwise come to life for us by printer's ink. The child who cannot yet read is only aware of what is under his nose—his parents, the door-bell, the lamplighter, the bicycle, a bunch of flowers; and from the window, perhaps the church tower. The child who can read sits over a book and suddenly he can see Mount Kilimanjaro, or Charles the Great, or Huckleberry Finn on the prairie, or Zeus transformed into a white bull with the fair Europa riding on his back. The child who can read has a second pair of eyes, as long as he takes care that he does not spoil the first pair.

"I read and read and read. Nothing printed was safe from my eyes. I read books and pamphlets, advertisements, titles of firms, name-plates, catalogues, directions for use, inscriptions on tombstones, animal lovers' calendars, menu cards, Mamma's cookery book, greetings on picture postcards, Paul Schurig's teachers' journals, the *Coloured Picture-Book of Saxony* and the wet scraps of newspaper in which I carried home heads of lettuce.

"I read as I breathed—as if I would suffocate if I didn't. It became an almost dangerous passion with me. I read what I could understand and what I could not understand. 'That is not for you' my mother would say; 'you will not understand it.' But I read it all the same. And I thought to myself, 'Do grown-ups understand all they read?' Now I am grown-up myself and I can answer with authority as an expert: grown-ups do not understand everything they read either. If they only read why they understood the printers and compositors in the newspaper offices would be permanently on short time."[1]

1913. Entered the Freiherrlich von Fletscher'sche Lehrerseminar, a teacher training institute, in Dresden.

1914. "The First World War had begun and my childhood was over.[1] Childhood is the quiet, pure light that shines consolingly out of the past into the present and the future. Truly to hold childhood in the memory means to know again, suddenly and without long contemplation, what is genuine and what false, what is good and what bad. Most people forget their childhood like an umbrella and leave it standing somewhere in the past. . . . Childhood is a lighthouse.'' [R. W. Last, *Erich Kästner: Modern German Authors New Series*, Volume III, Oswald Wolff, Ltd., 1974.[2]]

''Memory and recollection are mysterious powers, and recollection is the more mysterious and puzzling of the two. For the memory has only to do with our heads. . . . The pigeonholes for all the things we have ever learned are there. I imagine they are like the drawers in a cupboard or a chest of drawers. They often stick when you try to pull them out. Sometimes there's nothing in them, and sometimes there's the wrong thing. And sometimes they won't pull out at all. Then they and we are 'as if nailed down,' as the saying goes. Our memories are either large or small chests of drawers. In my own head, for instance, the chest of drawers is rather small. The drawers are only half full, but they're fairly tidy. When I was a little boy my chest of drawers looked quite different. In those days my little top storey was a real lumber room.

''Our recollections, on the other hand, do not lie in drawers, nor in cupboards, nor in our heads at all. They live right inside us. They are generally dormant, but they are alive and breathing, and sometimes they open their eyes. They live, breathe and sleep everywhere—in the palms of our hands, in the soles of our feet, in our nostrils, in our hearts, and in the seats of our trousers.

''What we have once experienced suddenly comes back after years and years, and stares us in the face. And we feel that it had never gone away at all, it was only asleep. And when one recollection wakes up and rubs the sleep from its eyes, it often arouses others, and they in turn yet others, like sleepers in a dormitory.''[1]

1917. Drafted into Imperial Army. His brutal experience in army life resulted in a chronic heart condition. ''He was an animal. And he spat and shouted. And the beast was named Sergeant Waurich, that everyone may know.''[2]

1918. Discharged from army as a corporal in the artillery. Entered Strehlener Lehereseminar for completion of his teachers training. ''Lastly—and worst of all—our character building was directed towards dubious objectives. This came over most clearly in the boarding school life. The state channelled our education solely in the one direction which it saw would bring the greatest possible practical return. In the Seminars it was schooling blindly obedient, petty officials with pension rights. . . . The Seminar was an educational barracks.''[2]

Disenchanted with the seminar, he wrote: ''I was no teacher; I was a learner. I wanted not to teach but to learn. I had wanted to be a teacher so that I could remain a pupil as long as possible. I wanted to absorb new knowledge and to keep on absorbing new knowledge. I certainly did not want old knowledge, nor to spend my life passing on old knowledge. I was hungry, but I was no baker. I was thirsty, but I was no innkeeper. I was impatient and restless, and therefore no future educator of youth. For teachers and educators must be calm and patient. They must think not of themselves but of their pupils. And they must not confuse patience with complacency. There are plenty of teachers who have this kind of patience. But authentic, dedicated teachers are as rare as heroes and saints.''[1]

Recalling a meeting with a retired educator, he wrote: ''. . . I was talking to a Basle University professor, a man famous as

''You shouldn't lick the marmalade spoon,'' the Professor warned.
''Today it doesn't matter,'' Maxje claimed. **''When one is as famous as I am, one may do such things.''**
■ (From *The Little Man* by Erich Kästner, translated from the German by James Kirkup. Illustrated by Rick Schreiter.)

a scholar in his subject. He had retired a short time before and I asked him what he was doing now. His eyes shone with sheer delight as he answered: 'I'm studying, now that I have time at last.' At seventy years of age he sat day after day in the lecture halls, learning something new. He was old enough to be the father of the professors to whose lectures he listened, and the grandfather of the students among whom he sat. He was a member of many academies. His name was cited with respect all over the world. He had spent his long life teaching what he knew. Now at last he could learn what he did not know. He was in the seventh heaven of delight. Other people may have laughed at him and thought him a trifle odd, but I understood him as if he were my elder brother.''[1]

1919. Admitted to Koenig-Georg-Gymnasium, Dresden. Awarded the Golden Stipendium scholarship enabling him to enter Leipzig University.

1925. Completed doctoral dissertation—Die Erwiderungen auf Friedrichs des Grossen ''De la Littérature allemande.'' ''I have penned a bulky PhD thesis on this singular topic and can vouch for it. One year before Lessing died, the Prussian monarch knew nothing of him, nor of Wieland, Herder and Goethe. (To name only the most important figures of whom he knew nothing.)''[2]

1928. Published first two volumes of poetry, *Herz auf Taille*, and *Laerm in Spiegel* as well as his first children's book, *Emil und die Detektive (Emil and the Detectives).*

1933. Witnessed burning of his books by the Nazi Regime. Did not choose exile at this time. ''A writer wants to and

[The barmaid] washed glasses behind the counter, made us sugar beer or ordinary beer with raspberry juice in it, gave each of us a long wooden spoon to stir it, and then we retired sedately to the inn parlour. Here there was a billiard table. ■ (From *When I Was a Boy* by Erich Kästner. Translated by Isabel and Florence McHugh. Illustrated by Horst Lemke.)

must experience how the nation to which he belongs endures its fate in hard times. Going abroad at such a moment can only be justified if his life is in extreme danger. Besides, it is his professional duty to run that risk, if he is to remain as a witness and to be able one day to testify to what he has seen.''[2]

1945. ''Munich has become *the* meeting place of those who were not in Berlin when the war finished, but in the west or south of Germany. In the middle of the street they throw their arms round one another. Actors, poets, painters, producers, journalists, singers, people from the film world: day and night they stand in the courtyard of the *Kammerspiele,* greeting new arrivals, hearing news of deaths, discussing the future of Germany and of their craft, wanting to go to Berlin but not being able to, pondering whether it would be better to make a start here or in Hamburg.

''That we have to live like gypsies, behind broken windows, with no books and no change of shirt, facing a winter without coal, worries no one. No one notices. Life has been rescued. That's all we need to make a new start.

''Anyone who can stand on the sidelines now, instead of becoming involved, evidently has stronger nerves than I have. Anyone who is now thinking about his *Collected Works* instead of the daily task will have to come to terms with his conscience. Anyone who is now building castles in the air instead of clearing away the rubble deserves to have Fate put him over its knee. And that doesn't just apply to writers.''[2]

1946. Returned to post-war Dresden. ''Yes, Dresden was a wonderful city. You may take my word for it. And you have to take my word for it, because none of you, however rich your father may be, can go there to see if I am right. For the city of Dresden is no more. It has vanished, except for a few fragments. In one single night and with a single movement of its hand the Second World War wiped it off the map. It had taken centuries to create its incomparable beauty. A few hours sufficed to spirit it off the face of the earth. This happened on the night of February 13th, 1945. Eight hundred planes rained down high explosive and incendiary bombs on it. When they had gone, nothing remained but a desert with a few giant ruins which looked like ocean liners heeling over.

"... 'Prager Strasse,' I deciphered with difficulty. Could it be that I was standing in the Prager Strasse, the world-famous Prager Strasse, the most magnificent street of my childhood? The street with the loveliest shop windows? The most wonderful street at Christmas-time? I was standing in a waste half a mile long by half a mile wide, a desert of broken bricks and rubble and utter desolation.

"To this day the Governments of the great Powers are disputing with each other as to who murdered Dresden. To this day people are arguing as to whether fifty thousand, a hundred thousand or two hundred thousand lie dead under that desert of nothingness. And none of them will admit having done it: each says it was the fault of the others. Ah, what is the use of quarrelling about it? You will not bring Dresden back to life by so doing—neither its beauty nor its dead. Punish the Governments in future and not the people. And don't punish them afterwards, Punish them at once. Does that sound simpler than it is? No, it is simpler than it sounds."[1]

"If a small businessman were to commit a mere hundredth of the errors and blunders which have been perpetrated by the great men of antiquity, the Middle Ages, and, if appearances are anything to go by, more recent times as well, he would spend the rest of his days bankrupt and locked up in prison. If bankers dealt with their clients in a 'statesmanlike' fashion, or doctors their patients, husbands their wives, parents their children or train drivers their passengers, the end of humanity would have come a few thousands of years ago."[2]

1956. Given Literature Prize of Munich.

1957. Won the Büchner Prize.

1958. Addressed the German PEN-Club in Hamburg: "The events of 1923 to 1945 should at the very latest have been combatted in 1928. Later it was too late. One should not wait until fighting for freedom is branded as national treason. One should not wait until the snowball has turned into an avalanche. One must crush the snowball as it rolls along. No one is capable of stopping an avalanche. It only comes to rest when it has buried all beneath it.

"That is the lesson, that is the sum of what happened to us in 1933. That is the conclusion we must draw from our experiences.... The threat of dictatorship can only be countered before the dictator comes to power. It is a matter of timetable, not of heroism."[2]

1960. Received Hans Christian Andersen Award.

1961. Received Lewis Carroll Shelf Award.

July 29, 1974. Died in Munich. "... There are two kinds of time. The one kind can be measured with instruments and calculations, just like streets or plots of ground. But the other chronology, our memory, has nothing to do with metres and months, decades or acres. What we have forgotten is old. The unforgettable was yesterday. The measure here is not the time but the value. And the most precious of all things, whether happy or sad, is our childhood. Do not forget the unforgettable. I believe that this advice cannot be given early enough."[1]

"Should one not in one's own life be able to go up and downstairs as in a house? What use is the most beautiful of first floors without the cellar with its fragrant shelves of fruit and without the ground floor with its front door that bangs closed and tinkling bell? Well—that's how most people live! They stand on the highest step, without a staircase or house beneath them, and parade their self-importance.... Only a man who grows up and remains a child, is a true man!"[2]

FOR MORE INFORMATION SEE: John Winkleman, *Social Criticism in the Early Work of Erich Kästner,* University of Missouri Press, 1953; Erich Kästner, *When I Was a Little Boy* (translated from the German by Isabel and Florence McHugh), F. Watts, 1961; "Erich Kästner," *Current Biography,* H. W. Wilson, 1964; Brian Doyle, editor, *Who's Who of Children's Literature,* Schocken Books, 1968; Doris De Montreville and Donna Hill, editors, *Third Book of Junior Authors,* H. W. Wilson, 1972; Rex W. Last, *Erich Kästner,* Humanities, 1975.

(Died July 29, 1974)

KEATS, Ezra Jack 1916-

PERSONAL: Born March 11, 1916, in Brooklyn, N.Y.; son of Benjamin (a waiter) and Augusta (Podgainy) Keats. *Education:* Attended public schools in New York City, but received no formal training in art. *Address:* 444 E. 82nd St., New York, N.Y. 10028.

CAREER: Worked as a muralist for the Works Progress Administration (W.P.A.) during the Depression; instructor, School of Visual Arts, New York City, 1947-48, and Workshop School, New York City, 1955-57; author and illustrator of books for children. *Military service:* Camouflage expert in the U.S. Air Corps during World War II. *Member:* P.E.N., Author's Guild, Society of Illustrators. *Awards, honors:* Caldecott Medal, 1963, for *The Snowy Day;* runner-up for the Caldecott Medal, 1970, for *Goggles;* Boston Globe-Horn Book Award for Illustration, 1970, for *Hi, Cat!;* Brooklyn Art Books for Children citation, 1973, for *The Snowy Day.*

WRITINGS—All self-illustrated: (With Pat Cherr) *My Dog Is Lost!,* Crowell, 1960; *The Snowy Day,* Viking, 1962, reissued, 1972; *Whistle for Willie,* Viking, 1964; *John Henry, an American Legend,* Pantheon Books, 1965; *Jennie's Hat,* Harper, 1966; (compiler) *God Is in the Mountain,* Holt, 1966; *Peter's Chair,* Harper, 1967; *A Letter to Amy,* Harper, 1968; (compiler) *Night,* Atheneum, 1969; *Goggles,* Macmillan, 1969; *Hi, Cat!,* Macmillan, 1970; *Apt. 3,* Macmillan, 1971; *Pet Show!,* Macmillan, 1972; *Skates!,* Watts, 1973; *Psst! Doggie—,* Watts, 1973; *Dreams,* Macmillan, 1974; *Kitten for a Day,* Watts, 1974; *Louie,* Greenwillow Books, 1975; *The Trip,* Greenwillow Books, 1978.

Illustrator: Elisabeth C. Lansing, *Jubilant for Sure,* Crowell, 1954; Frances Carpenter, *Wonder Tales of Dogs and Cats,* Doubleday, 1955; E. C. Lansing, *Sure Thing for Shep,* Crowell, 1956; George S. Albee, *Three Young Kings,* Watts, 1956; William McKellar, *Wee Joseph,* McGraw-Hill, 1957; Tillie S. Pine, *Indians Knew,* McGraw-Hill, 1957; T. S. Pine and Joseph Levine, *Pilgrims Knew,* McGraw-Hill, 1957; T. S. Pine and J. Levine, *Chinese Knew,* McGraw-Hill, 1958; Dorothea F. Fisher, *And Long Remember,* McGraw-Hill, 1959; Eleanor A. Murphey, *Nihal of Ceylon,* Crowell, 1960; Paul Showers, *In the Night,* Ambassador, 1961, reissued, A. & C. Black, 1971; Patricia M. Martin, *The Rice Bowl Pet,* Crowell, 1962; Solveig P. Russell, *What Good Is a Tail?,* Bobbs-Merrill, 1962; Ruth P. Collins, *The Flying Cow,* Walck, 1963; Lucretia P. Hale, *The Peterkin Papers,* Doubleday, 1963; Ann N. Clark, *Tia Maria's Gar-*

EZRA JACK KEATS

den, Viking, 1963; Millicent E. Selsam, *How to Be a Nature Detective,* Harper, 1963; Maxine W. Kumin, *Speedy Digs Downside Up,* Putnam, 1964; Ann McGovern, *Zoo, Where Are You?,* Harper, 1964; John Keats, *The Naughty Boy,* Viking, 1965; Richard Lewis, editor, *In a Spring Garden,* Dial Press, 1965, reissued, 1976; Esther R. Hautzig, *In the Park,* Macmillan, 1968; *The Little Drummer Boy* (words and music by Katherine Davis), Macmillan, 1968; *Over in the Meadow,* Four Winds Press, 1971; Lloyd Alexander, *The King's Fountain,* Dutton, 1971; Myron Levoy, *Penny Tunes and Princesses,* Harper, 1972.

ADAPTATIONS: "Goggles," "Whistle for Willie," "Peter's Chair," "A Letter to Amy," "Apt. 3," "In a Spring Garden," "The Little Drummer Boy," animated films, Weston Woods (iconographic, color, 6 mm); "The Snowy Day," filmstrip, Miller-Brody Productions (cassette, teacher's guide); "Hi, Cat!," filmstrip, Miller-Brody Productions (color, record, teacher's guide).

SIDELIGHTS: "I think I started painting when I was about four years old. I really dedicated myself to what I did, avidly and lovingly. I drew on and colored in everything that came across my path, with the indulgent approval of my mother. ["A Conversation with Ezra Jack Keats," publicity folder, Macmillan Publishing Co.[1]]

"We had this kitchen table—it was enamel, with two drawers, one for silverware, the other for bread. Anyway, I proceeded to draw on the top of it, all the things kids draw pretty much, a profile of a lady with long lashes and a lot of curls. . . . I filled up the entire table with pictures of little cot-

tages, curly smoke coming out of the chimneys, men's profiles, and kids. I drew an Indian and a Chinese with straw hat and pigtails. . . . [When] I finished, the entire area was covered with sketches, completely covered with them. My mother came in and I expected her to say, 'What have you been doing?' and 'Get that sponge and wash it off!' Instead she looked at me and said, 'Did you do that? Isn't it wonderful!' and she proceeded to look at each thing and clucked her tongue and said, 'Now isn't that nice!' Then she said, 'You know, it's so wonderful, it's a shame to wash it off.' So she got out the tablecloth which we used only on Friday nights and she covered the whole little mural and every time a neighbor would come in, she'd unveil it to show what I had done. They'd all say, 'Mmm, isn't that nice.' They couldn't say anything else, Mother was so proud.

"My father would come in and smell the paints and say, 'You've been painting. Get out and play ball and stop making a fool of yourself.' So I had to go out and play ball. . . . Then one day he came home and said, 'If you don't think artists starve, well, let me tell you. One man came in the other day and swapped me a tube of paint for a bowl of soup.' My father put down a brand-new tube of paint. I thought how lucky I was that the poor man had to make such a swap. The swap happened again and again, and one day my father brought home a package of brushes, very inexpensive brushes which no professional artist would have bought. It dawned on me that my father was buying this stuff for me and had a terrible conflict. He was proud of my painting and he wanted to supply me with paint, but at the same time he lived in real dread of my living a life like that of the artists he had seen.

"My father thought that the most important paintings in the world would be those of important people. He took me to the Metropolitan Museum and showed me Gilbert Stuart's painting of George Washington and Andrew Jackson's portrait and all the colonial paintings.... It was all very nice and it was all really dull, and I was getting tired. Suddenly I looked down the length of the corridor and at the other end was an arched doorway which opened to another gallery, completely bathed in sunlight. Framed in that archway was Daumier's *Third Class Carriage*. I never heard of Daumier and I knew nothing about his painting.... I felt a pounding in my heart and I just turned toward it and walked toward it as though hypnotized. As I got closer to it, it glowed more magnificently.... ["Ezra Jack Keats" by Esther Hautzig, *Horn Book Magazine*, August, 1963[2]]

"I lived in a very, very tough section of Brooklyn, in an old, beat-up tenement, and drawing was really a rather hazardous pursuit. I remember being intercepted once by some tough older neighborhood boys when I was about eight. I had a painting of mine under my arm. They closed in and pulled it out of my hands—I was really scared—and then a very strange thing happened. When they learned that I had done the painting, they began to treat me with great respect. From then on, when they'd see me, I'd be greeted with 'Hi, Doc!,' and I discovered that there was a place for me in my piece of the world.

"When I was about nine, I began to tell stories to the kids. All these little tough kids on my block would follow me around asking, 'Tell me a story, tell me a story.' I'd make them up as I'd go along—sort of a Pied Piper. I was ridiculed by my family when I read an early attempt at poetry. I continued to paint in a serious way, but the notion of writing my stories was put aside. I wanted approval very badly then, and so I just continued to paint.

"I taught myself to paint, using any kind of material I could find. Once I got some paint—just a few colors, two of which were blue and white—and I covered a board with my blue paint. I dipped my brush into the white paint and dabbed it onto the board, shook the brush a little and let it trail off. I

stepped back and got the greatest thrill I can remember. I saw a little cloud floating across a blue sky. It was very real to me, and I'll always remember it. What a tremendous feeling of gratification, to have created something like this! Even today, when I look up and see a tiny cloud floating across the sky with little wispy ends trailing off, I think of that time.

"For about ten years I illustrated other people's books. There were two things that troubled me at that time: one was that in many of the manuscripts I was given there was a peculiar quality of contrivance and rigid structure; the other was that I never got a story about Black people, Black children. I decided that if I ever did a book of my own it would be more of a happening—certainly not a structured thing, but an experience. My hero would be a Black child. I made many sketches and studies of Black children, so that Peter would not be a white kid colored brown. I wanted him to be in the book on his own, not through the benevolence of white children or anyone else.[1]

"The important thing is that the kids in a book have to be real—regardless of color. I don't like to emphasize the race thing, because what's really important is the honesty.

"I think that children look at Peter first of all as a child, who is like themselves in some ways whether they are boy or girl, black, brown or white, fat or skinny or what.

"The essential thing is that we see each other, 'see' as perceive, understand, discover.

"If we all could really see each other exactly as the other is, this would be a different world. But first I think we have to begin to see each other. [*Milwaukee Journal*, March 28, 1974[3]]

"To me Peter is a real child. In my first books I was totally unaware of the fact that he was growing. It was midway through *Peter's Chair*, when he tries to sit in his baby chair, that I was surprised to realize that he was growing up all by himself—even though I was painting the pictures! After that I deliberately continued to have him grow. Now that he has

(From *The Trip* by Ezra Jack Keats. Illustrated by the author.)

(From *Louie* by Ezra Jack Keats. Illustrated by the author.)

actually grown older he plays the role of protective older brother to Archie, who now takes center stage.

"The story comes first, but not in terms of text. I have an image of certain things happening—more of a visual image—and then I hear the characters talking to each other, and the story grows in counterpoint. Sometimes my emphasis is on the pictures and sometimes on the story. The pictures do pace the book, however. As I sketch the children and place them in the various scenes of the story I hear their conversations, and the book grows. I hang my illustrations on my studio wall in rows so that I can see them flow and move in sequence, like a ballet. I guess I'm the choreographer.[1]

"In 1961 I used Peter in *The Snowy Day* which tells about the excitement I felt as a boy when I woke up to see snow outside the Brooklyn apartment where I grew up without a single picture book of my own.

"We were too darn poor, I just never saw a picture book. Really, it wasn't until I was about 35 that I discovered children's books.[3]

"Years ago, long before I ever thought of doing children's books, while looking through a magazine I came upon four candid photos of a little boy about three or four years old. His expressive face, his body attitudes, the very way he wore his clothes, totally captivated me. I clipped the strip of

(From *The Snowy Day* by Ezra Jack Keats. Illustrated by the author.)

photos and stuck it on my studio wall, where it stayed for quite a while, and then it was put away.

"As the years went by, these pictures would find their way back to my walls, offering me fresh pleasure at each encounter.

"In more recent years, while illustrating children's books, the desire to do my own story about this little boy began to germinate. Up he went again—this time above my drawing table. He was my model and inspiration. Finally I began work on *The Snowy Day*. When the book was finished and on the presses, I told Annis Duff, whose guidance and empathy have been immeasurable, about my long association with this little boy. How many years was it? I went over to *Life* magazine and had it checked. To my astonishment they informed me that I had found him twenty-two years ago!

"Now for the technique—I had no idea as to how the book would be illustrated, except that I wanted to add a few bits of patterned paper to supplement the painting.

"As work progressed, one swatch of material suggested another, and before I realized it, each page was being handled in a style I had never worked in before. A rather strange sequence of events came into play. I worked—and waited. Then quite unexpectedly I would come across just the appropriate material for the page I was working on.[2]

"For instance, one day I visited my art supply shop looking for a sheet of off-white paper to use for the bed linen for the opening pages. Before I could make my request, the clerk said, 'We just received some wonderful Belgian canvas. I think you'll like to see it.' I hadn't painted on canvas for years, but there he was displaying a huge roll of canvas. It had just the right color and texture for the linen. I brought a narrow strip, leaving a puzzled clerk wondering what strange shape of picture I planned to paint.

"The creative efforts of people from many lands contributed to the materials in the book. Some of the papers used for the collage came from Japan, some from Italy, some from Sweden, many from our own country.

"The mother's dress is made of the kind of oilcloth used for lining cupboards. I made a big sheet of snow-texture by rolling white paint over wet inks on paper and achieved the effect of snow flakes by cutting patterns out of gum erasers, dipping them into paint, and then stamping them onto the pages. The gray background for the pages where Peter goes to sleep was made by spattering India ink with a toothbrush.

"Friends would enthusiastically discuss the things they did as children in the snow, others would suggest nuances of plot, or a change of a word. All of us wanted so much to see little Peter march through these pages, experiencing, in the purity and innocence of childhood, the joys of a first snow.

"I can honestly say that Peter came into being because we wanted him; and I hope that, as the Scriptures say, 'a little child shall lead them,' and that he will show in his own way the wisdom of a pure heart. ["Caldecott Award Acceptance," by Ezra Jack Keats, *Horn Book Magazine*, August, 1963[4]]

"To me, one of the greatest triumphs in doing a book is to pare down the words, to tell the story as simply as possible. My aim is to imply rather than to overstate. Whenever the

Peter ran to the hideout
and put on the goggles.
"Aren't they great?" he asked.
Archie smiled and nodded.
■ (From the animated film "Goggles" based on the story by Ezra Jack Keats. Copyright Weston Woods.)

reader participates in the experience or fills in his own interpretation, I feel that the book is that much more successful. I love and admire haiku poetry—I appreciate how much can be said with so little—and I work on the premise that less is more.[1]

"I'm an ex-kid. We all have within us the whole record of our childhood. What I do is address the child within myself. And try to be as honest as possible, then hope for the best."[3]

In 1967, the Weston Woods Studio's film version of *Whistle for Willie* was shown at the Second Teheran International Festival of Films for Children in Iran, which Keats attended as a U.S. delegate and as guest of honor of the Empress. Earlier, at the Venice Film Festival, the Weston Woods Studio adaptation of *The Snowy Day* won the prize for the best children's film.

FOR MORE INFORMATION SEE: Bertha Mahony Miller and others, compilers, *Illustrators of Children's Books, 1946-1956*, Horn Book, 1958; *Commonweal*, November 16, 1962; *Saturday Review*, December 15, 1962; *Horn Book*, February, 1963; A. Duff, "Ezra Jack Keats: 1963 Caldecott Medal Winner," *Library Journal*, March 15, 1963; Esther Hautzig, "Ezra Jack Keats," *Horn Book*, August, 1963; "Newbery-Caldecott Medals," *Publishers Weekly*, March 11, 1963; Muriel Fuller, editor, *More Junior Authors*, H. W. Wilson, 1963; E. Keats, "The Artist at Work: Collage," *Horn Book*, June, 1964; Lee Kingman and others, compilers, *Illustrators of Children's Books, 1957-1966*, Horn Book, 1968; Lee Bennett Hopkins, *Books Are by People*, Citation Press, 1969; Florence B. Freeman, "Ezra Jack Keats, Author and Illustrator," *Elementary English*, January, 1969; E. Perry, "Gentle World of Ezra Jack Keats," *American Artist*, September, 1971; J. F. Mercier, "Ezra Jack Keats," *Publishers Weekly*, July 16, 1973; *Horn Book*, December, 1974; Margo Huston, "Honesty Is Author's Policy for Children's Books," *Milwaukee Journal*, March 28, 1974, reprinted in *Authors in the News*, Volume 1, Gale, 1976.

Film: "Ezra Jack Keats" (17 min., color), Weston Woods.

EZRA JACK KEATS

KENNEDY, Joseph   1929-
(X. J. Kennedy)

PERSONAL: Born August 21, 1929, in Dover, N.J.; son of Joseph Francis and Agnes (Rauter) Kennedy; married Dorothy Mintzlaff, 1962; children: Kathleen, David, Matthew, Daniel, Joshua. *Education:* Seton Hall University, B.Sc., 1950; Columbia University, M.A., 1951; University of Paris, certificat, 1956; University of Michigan, graduate student, 1956-62. *Home:* 4 Fern Way, Bedford, Mass. 01730. *Agent:* Curtis Brown, Ltd., 575 Madison Ave., New York, N.Y. 10022. *Office:* Department of English, Tufts University, Medford, Mass. 02155.

CAREER: University of Michigan, Ann Arbor, teaching fellow, 1956-60, instructor in English, 1960-62; Woman's College of University of North Carolina, Greensboro, North Carolina, department of English, 1962-63; Tufts University, Medford, Mass., professor of English, 1963—. Visiting lecturer, Wellesley College, Fall, 1964; University of California, Irvine, 1966-67. Bruern fellow in American civilization, University of Leeds, 1974-75. *Military service:* U.S. Navy, 1951-55, journalist second class. *Member:* John Barron Wolgamot Society, Authors Guild, P.E.N., Phi Beta Kappa. *Awards, honors:* Bread Loaf Fellow in poetry, Middlebury College, 1960; Lamont award of Academy of American Poets for *Nude Descending a Staircase*, 1961; Bess Hokin prize for *Poetry*, 1961; grant, National Council on Arts and Humanities, 1967-68; Shelley Memorial award, 1970; Guggenheim fellow, 1973-74; Golden Rose award, New England Poetry Society, 1974; *One Winter Night in August* was an Outstanding Book of the Year, *New York Times Book Review*, November, 1975.

WRITINGS—Juvenile: *One Winter Night in August and Other Nonsense Jingles*, Atheneum, 1975. Contributor of verse to *Cricket, Allsorts, Children's Digest*, anthologies.

Adult books—poetry: *Nude Descending a Staircase*, Doubleday, 1961; *Growing into Love*, Doubleday, 1969; *Breaking and Entering*, Oxford University Press (London), 1971; *Emily Dickinson in Southern California*, David R. Godine, 1974; *Celebrations After the Death of John Brennan*, Penmaen, 1974; (with James Camp and Keith Waldrop) *Three Tenors, One Vehicle*, Open Places (Stephens College), 1975.

Editor: (With James Camp and Keith Waldrop) *Pegasus Descending, a Book of the Best Bad Verse*, Macmillan, 1971.

College textbooks: (With James Camp) *Mark Twain's Frontier*, Holt, 1963; *An Introduction to Poetry*, Little, Brown, 1966, fourth edition, 1978; *Messages, a Thematic Anthology of Poetry*, Little, Brown, 1973; *An Introduction to Fiction*, Little, Brown, 1976, 2nd edition, 1978; *Literature*, Little, Brown, 1976, 2nd edition, 1979. Contributor of poetry to magazines; reviews and criticism to *New York Times Book Review, Atlantic, Nation, Saturday Review, Dissent*. Poetry editor, *Paris Review*, 1962-64. Editor and publisher (with Dorothy M. Kennedy), *Counter/Measures*, 1971-74.

SIDELIGHTS: "Writing verses and stories has preoccupied me since the age of nine or ten, when I was editing a weekly woman's magazine with a circulation of one: my mother. In seventh grade, I published home-made comic books—wretched stuff—on my gelatin-pan duplicator. Later

Here's a big bowl of black bolts and nuts you can crack,
Here's some cider to slide down your craw,
    Oh what fun it'll be
    While we roast that old tree—
■ (From *One Winter Night in August* by X.J. Kennedy. Illustrated by David McPhail.)

JOSEPH KENNEDY

on, after my kids were born, I would make up stories and rhymes to divert them. Whichever rhymes they liked I would keep in a bureau drawer, where they stayed until 1973, when Margaret K. McElderry, a sympathetic children's book editor, asked if I had any. A collection of the more nonsensical verses followed. (Before that, there was a section called 'For Children, If They'll Take Them' in my first book of verse for big people. I was encouraged, too, by the friendly support of Myra Cohn Livingston, the West Coast author of so many children's books, who struck up an inspiring correspondence.)

"For years I have been working on a novel for older children, whose plot originated during a family holiday without television, when each night I would spiel out a new installment. It concerns another world, whose ecology centers upon a gigantic moonflower. This story, if I ever get it done, will try to please those children known to me. Such kids do not like to be told that everything is all sweetness and light; for such a view, as even the youngest infant knows, is so much malarkey. The face of a world, however imaginary, has to have a few warts, if a child is going to believe in it; and must wear an occasional look of consternation, or foolishness. It also needs, I suspect, a good deal of poetry, and a bit of incredible beauty and enchantment, if at all possible."

The X in the name under which Joseph Kennedy publishes was reportedly chosen arbitrarily to distinguish the author from the better-known Kennedys.

FOR MORE INFORMATION SEE: A Controversy of Poets, edited by Paris Leary and Robert Kelly, Doubleday, 1965; *Contemporary Poetry in America,* edited by Miller Williams, Random House, 1973; *World Authors,* edited by John Wakeman, H. W. Wilson, 1975; *Fifty Contemporary Poets,* edited by Alberta T. Turner, McKay, 1977.

KESSLER, Leonard P. 1921-

PERSONAL: Born October 28, 1921, in Ohio; married wife, Ethel; children: Kim, Paul. *Education:* B.F.A., Carnegie Institute of Technology. *Residence:* Rockland County, N.Y.

CAREER: Author and illustrator. Began illustrating and designing children's books, 1951. Worked as camp director at summer camps for children. *Military service:* U.S. Army, Infantry, Second World War; became staff sergeant; awarded Purple Heart and Bronze Star. *Awards, honors:* Included among the *New York Times* choice of best illustrated children's books of the year, 1954, for *Fast Is Not a Ladybug* by Miriam Schlein, 1955, for *Heavy Is a Hippopotamus* by M. Schlein, and 1957, for *Big Red Bus* written jointly with his wife, Ethel Kessler.

WRITINGS: What's In a Line? (self-illustrated), W. R. Scott, 1951; *World without Color,* S. Gabriel Sons, 1953; (with John G. McCullough) *Farther and Faster* (self-illustrated), Crowell, 1954; (with wife, Ethel Kessler) *Plink, Plink! Goes the Water in My Sink,* Doubleday, 1954; (with E. Kessler) *Crunch, Crunch,* Doubleday, 1955; (with E. Kessler) *Peek-a-Boo: A Child's First Book,* Doubleday, 1956; (with E. Kessler) *Big Red Bus* (self-illustrated), Doubleday, 1957; *Art Is Everywhere,* Dodd, 1958; (with E. Kessler) *The Day Daddy Stayed Home* (self-illustrated), Doubleday, 1959, reissued, 1971; (with E. Kessler) *I Have Twenty Teeth—Do You?,* Dodd, 1959.

ETHEL and LEONARD KESSLER

(With E. Kessler) *Kim and Me,* Doubleday, 1960; (with E. Kessler) *Do Baby Bears Sit in Chairs?* (self-illustrated), Doubleday, 1961; *The Duck on the Truck,* Grosset, 1961; *I Made a Line,* Wonder Books, 1962; *The Worm, the Bird, and You: A Long and Short Look at the World about You,* Dodd, 1962; (with E. Kessler) *All Aboard the Train* (self-illustrated), Doubleday, 1964; *Here Comes the Strikeout* (self-illustrated), Harper, 1965; *Mr. Pine's Purple House* (self-illustrated), Wonder Books, 1965; *The Sad Tale of the Careless Klunks* (self-illustrated), Dodd, 1965; (with E. Kessler) *Are You Square?* (self-illustrated) Doubleday, 1966; *Kick, Pass, and Run* (self-illustrated), Harper, 1966; *Mrs. Pine Takes a Trip* (self-illustrated), Grosset, 1966; *Are We Lost, Daddy?,* Grosset, 1967; *Did You Ever Hear a Klunk Say Please?* (self-illustrated), Dodd, 1967; *Last One in Is a Rotten Egg* (self-illustrated), Harper, 1969; *Soup for the King* (self-illustrated), Grosset, 1969.

A Tale of Two Bicycles: Safety on Your Bike (self-illustrated), Lothrop, 1971; *On Your Mark, Get Set, Go! The First All Animal Olympics* (self-illustrated), Harper, 1972; (with E. Kessler) *Our Tooth Story: A Tale of Twenty Teeth* (self-illustrated), Dodd, 1972; *Paint Me a Picture, Mr. Pine* (illustrated by John Kuzich), Ginn, 1972; (with E. Kessler) *Slush Slush!* (self-illustrated), Parents' Magazine Press, 1973; (with E. Kessler) *Splish Splash* (self-illustrated), Parents' Magazine Press, 1973; *Who Tossed That Bat? Safety on the Ballfield and Playground* (self-illustrated), Lothrop, 1973; (with E. Kessler) *All for Fall* (self-illustrated), Parents' Magazine Press, 1974; *The Forgetful Pirate* (self-illustrated), Garrard, 1974; (with E. Kessler) *What's Inside the Box?,* Dodd, 1976; (with E. Kessler) *What Do You Play on a Summer Day?,* Parents' Magazine Press, 1977.

"A monster?" yelled Rabbit.
"Where? Where?" asked Duck.
■ From *What's Inside the Box?* by Ethel and Leonard Kessler. Illustrated by Leonard Kessler.)

"In the galley
in an old black pot,
is the secret map
that you forgot,"
sang the bird.
■ (From *The Forgetful Pirate* by Leonard Kessler. Illustrated by the author. Copyright © 1974 by Leonard Kessler.)

Illustrator: Miriam Schlein, *Fast Is Not a Ladybug,* W. R. Scott, 1953; M. Schlein, *Heavy Is a Hippopotamus,* W. R. Scott, 1954; M. Schlein, *It's about Time,* W. R. Scott, 1955; Hyman and Alice Chanover, *Pesah Is Coming,* United Synagogue Book Service, 1956; H. and A. Chanover, *Pesah Is Here,* United Synagogue Book Service, 1956; Lily Edelman, *Sukkah and the Big Wind,* United Synagogue Book Service, 1956; Lenore Klein, *What Would You Do, If?,* W. R. Scott, 1956; John Bryan Lewellen, *Tommy Learns to Fly,* Crowell, 1956; M. Schlein, *Deer in the Snow,* Abelard-Schuman, 1956; Maryalicia Crowell, *Horse in the House,* W. R. Scott, 1957; Jean Fiedler, *Teddy and the Ice Cream Man,* Abelard-Schuman, 1957; J. B. Lewellen, *Tommy Learns to Drive a Tractor,* Crowell, 1958; Franklyn Mansfield Branley, *A Book of Moon Rockets for You,* Crowell, 1959, revised edition, 1970; F. M. Branley, *A Book of Satellites for You,* Crowell, 1959, revised edition, 1971.

F. M. Branley, *Big Trucks, Little Trucks,* Crowell, 1960; Lucia and James L. Hymes, *Hooray for Chocolate and Other Easy-to-Read Jingles,* W. R. Scott, 1960; F. M. Branley, *A Book of Planets for You,* Crowell, 1961, revised edition, 1966; Mike McClintock, *What Have I Got,* Harper, 1961; Muriel Rukeyser, *I Go Out,* Harper, 1961; James Playsted Wood, *The Elephant in the Barn,* Harper, 1961; Carla Greene, *What Do They Do? Policemen and Firemen,* Harper, 1962; Jacqueline Harris Straus, *Let's Experiment! Chemistry for Boys and Girls,* Harper, 1962; F. M. Branley, *A Book of Astronauts for You,* Crowell, 1963; C. Greene, *Doctors and Nurses, What Do They Do?,* Harper, 1963; C. Greene, *Soldiers and Sailors, What Do They Do?;* C. Paul Jackson, *How to Play Better Baseball,* Crowell, 1963, reissued, Scholastic Book Service, 1971; C. Greene, *Railroad Engineers and Airplane Pilots, What Do They Do?,* Harper, 1964; L. and J. L. Hymes, *Oodles of Noodles, and Other Hymes' Rhymes,* Young Scott Books, 1964; Solveig Paulson Russell, *Indian Big, Indian Little,* Bobbs-Merrill, 1964.

Rochelle Scott, *Colors, Colors, All Around,* Grosset, 1965; F. M. Branley, *A Book of the Milky Way Galaxy for You,* Crowell, 1965; Augusta R. Goldin, *Ducks Don't Get Wet,* Crowell, 1965, reissued, 1976; C. Greene, *Where Does a Letter Go?,* Harvey House, 1966; L. Klein, *What Is an Inch?,* Harvey House, 1966; F. M. Branley, *A Book of Stars for You,* Crowell, 1967; C. Greene, *Animal Doctors, What Do They Do?,* Harper, 1967; C. Greene, *Truck Drivers, What Do They Do?,* Harper, 1967; L. Klein, *How Old Is Old?,* Harvey House, 1967; Harry Milgrom, *Adventures with a Straw,* Dutton, 1967; F. M. Branley, *A Book of Mars for You,* Crowell, 1968; C. P. Jackson, *How to Play Better Basketball,* Crowell, 1968; James Duncan Lawrence, *Binky Brothers, Detectives,* Harper, 1968; H. Milgrom, *Adventures with a Paper Cup,* Dutton, 1968; F. M. Branley, *A Book of Venus for You,* Crowell, 1969; L. Klein, *Just a Minute: A Book about Time,* Harvey House, 1969; Molly Whisman, *My Hideout,* Harper, 1969.

F. M. Branley, *A Book of Outer Space for You,* Crowell, 1970; J. D. Lawrence, *Binky Brothers and the Fearless Four,* Harper, 1970; Edna Mitchell Preston, *The Boy Who Could Make Things,* Viking, 1970; Henry Walker, *Illustrated Baseball Dictionary for Young People,* Harvey House, 1970; Mannis Charosh, *The Ellipse,* Crowell, 1971; M. Charosh, *Straight Lines, Parallel Lines, Perpendicular Lines,* Crowell, 1972; C. Greene, *Cowboys, What Do They Do?,* Harper, 1972; C. P. Jackson, *How to Play Better Football,* Crowell, 1972; Harley Knosher, *Basic Basketball Strategy,* Doubleday, 1972; Richard J. Margolis, *Homer the Hunter,* Macmillan, 1972, reissued as *Homer and the Ghosts,* 1976; Melvin Berger, *The New Water Book,* Crowell, 1973; F. M. Branley, *A Book of Flying Saucers for You,* Crowell, 1973; Peggy Parish, *Too Many Rabbits,* Macmillan, 1974; Anne-Catharina Vestly, *Hello, Aurora,* Crowell, 1974; F. M. Branley, *A Book of Planet Earth for You,* Crowell, 1975; Nina and Herman Schneider, *Science Fun for You in a Minute or Two,* McGraw, 1975; Nancy Jewell, *The Family under the Moon,* Harper, 1976; N. and H. Schneider, *Got a Minute? Quick Experiments You Can Do,* Scholastic Book Service, 1976.

SIDELIGHTS: Kessler first became interested in art as a young boy attending classes at a local neighborhood center. The illustrator's works were primarily done in black-and-white or two colors. One of the author-illustrator's earlier books was *What's in a Line?,* which introduced graphic art to young readers. "An original, stimulating book [—] it will give pleasure to the imaginative child . . . ," noted a *New York Times* critic.

Farther and Faster was written in collaboration with John G. McCullough and dealt with the history of transportation. "The book is most attractively and profusely illustrated . . . ," commented a reviewer for the *Chicago Sunday Tribune.* In reviewing the same book, a *New York Times* critic observed, "The educational theme is made exciting by an alert, lively approach and by illustrations which are dear, gay and humorous."

The author-illustrator jointly wrote *Big Red Bus* with his wife, Ethel. In this picture book the Kesslers described a ride on a bus for children. A reviewer for *Christian Science Monitor* noted, ". . . preschoolers should enjoy watching the journey as much as the one of their number who is taking it in big pictures that almost bounce and rattle on the page."

In *Art Is Everywhere* Kessler gave instructions in drawing and painting techniques. "[The author] writes well with a good understanding of the child's vocabulary and conceptual grasp. His little illustrations really work with the text, are aimed at children without being self-consciously childish . . . ," commented a critic for *School Arts.*

The Day Daddy Stayed Home was another joint effort by the Kesslers. In this book, the husband and wife team told what happened when a heavy snowfall kept daddy home for the day. "The story is appealing, and the illustrations are simple, good-natured, and childlike," described a reviewer for the *Chicago Sunday Tribune.* A critic for *Library Journal* noted, "Good feeling for the silence that comes with falling snow and the gaiety of youngsters and fathers playing together."

Kessler's book, *Here Comes the Strikeout,* told the story of a small boy who became discouraged because he was unable to make a hit in baseball. "A baseball story written humourously and convincingly, by a pro among easy-reading writers," observed a *New York Times* reviewer.

In *Did You Ever Hear a Klunk Say Please?* the author-illustrator wrote about the wild and disorderly lives of ill-mannered children. A critic for *New Yorker* commented, "[The book] is gay and brisk and lends itself to reading out loud. I think that children will find the book hilarious and not in the least edifying."

FOR MORE INFORMATION SEE: Lee Kingman, editor, *Illustrators of Children's Books: 1957-1966,* Horn Book, 1968.

KING, Martin Luther, Jr. 1929-1968

PERSONAL: Given name, Michael, changed to Martin when he was six years old; born January 15, 1929, in Atlanta, Ga.; son of Martin Luther (a minister) and Alberta (Williams) King; married Coretta Scott, June 17, 1953; children: Yolanda Denise, Martin Luther III, Dexter Scott, Bernice Albertine. *Education:* Morehouse College, A.B., 1948; Crozer Theological Seminary, B.D., 1951; Boston University, J. Louis Crozer fellow, Ph.D., 1955, D.D., 1959; Chicago Theological Seminary, D.D., 1957; special student at University of Pennsylvania and the department of philosophy, Harvard University.

CAREER: Ordained Baptist minister in his father's church in Atlanta, Ga., 1947; pastor, Dexter Avenue Baptist Church, Montgomery, Ala., 1954-60; founder and president, Southern Christian Leadership Conference (SCLC), Atlanta, Ga., 1957-68; Ebenezer Baptist Church, Atlanta, Ga., co-pastor with his father, 1960-68. Vice-president, National Sunday School and Baptist Teaching Union Congress of National Baptist Convention; president, Montgomery Improvement Association. *Member:* National Association for the Advancement of Colored People (NAACP), Alpha Phi Alpha, Sigma Pi Phi, Elks. *Awards, honors:* Selected one of 10 outstanding personalities of 1956 by *Time,* 1957; L.H.D., Morehouse College, 1957, Central State College, 1958; L.L.D., Howard University, 1957, Morgan State College, 1958; *Time* Man of the Year, 1963; Nobel Prize for Peace, October, 1964; Judaism and World Peace Award of the Synagogue Council of America, 1965; Nehru Award for International Understanding (posthumous), 1968; received numerous awards for leadership of Montgomery Movement. Two literary prizes were named in his honor by National Book Committee and Harper & Row.

WRITINGS: Our Struggle: The Story of Montgomery (originally appeared in *Liberation,* April, 1956), Congress of Racial Equality (CORE), 1957; *Stride Toward Freedom: The Montgomery Story,* Harper, 1958; *A Comparison of the Conceptions of God in the Thinking of Paul Tillich and Henry Nelson Wieman* (thesis), Boston University, 1958; *The Measure of a Man,* Christian Education Press (Philadelphia), 1959, memorial edition, Pilgrim Press, 1968; *Pilgrimage to Nonviolence,* Fellowship Publications, 1960; *"Unwise and Untimely?",* Fellowship of Reconciliation, 1963; *Strength to Love* (sermons), Harper, 1963; *Letter from Birmingham Jail,* American Friends Service Committee, 1963; *Why We Can't Wait,* Harper, 1964; *A Martin Luther King Treasury* (photographed by Roland Mitchell), Educational Heritage (New York), 1964; *Where Do We Go from Here: Chaos or Community?* Harper, 1967, new edition, introduction by Coretta Scott King, Bantam, 1968, published in England as *Chaos or Community,* Hodder & Stoughton, 1968; *Conscience for Change,* Canadian Broadcasting Co., 1967; *The Trumpet of Conscience,* foreword by Coretta Scott King, Harper, 1968; (author of introduction) William Bradford Huie, *Three Lives for Mississippi,* New American Library, 1968; Deloris Harrison, editor and author of commentary, *We Shall Live in Peace* (juvenile; excerpts from speeches), Hawthorn, 1968; *Speeches About Vietnam,* Clergy and Laymen Concerned About Vietnam, 1969; *A Testament of Hope,* Fellowship Publications, 1969; Sanders Redding, general editor, *Creative Encounters With "Dear Dr. King:" A Handbook of Discussions, Activities and Engagements on Racial Injustice, Poverty and War,* Buckingham Enterprises, 1969; *A Drum Major for Justice* (sermon), Taurus Press, 1969; Nissim Ezekiel, editor and author of introduction, *A Martin Luther King Reader,* Popular Prakashan (Bombay), 1969; *Words and Wisdom of Martin Luther King* (illustrated by Paul Peter Piech), Taurus Press, 1970; *Family Planning: A Special and Urgent Concern,* Planned-Parenthood World Population, 1971; *Speeches of Martin Luther King, Jr.,* commemorative edition, Martin Luther King, Jr. Memorial Center, 1972.

Other writings: "The Method of Non-Violence" (not published), 1957; (with others) *Crisis in Modern America* (a series of lectures on civil rights and economic life), edited by H. John Heinz, III, Yale University, 1959; "America's Greatest Crisis" (address for Transport Workers Union of America, AFL-CIO), [New York], 1961; "I Have a Dream" (speech delivered at the March on Washington), 1963; "Nobel Lecture," Clark & Way, 1964, Harper, 1965; "Address at Valedictory Service," University of the West Indies, Mona Jamaica, 1965; "Beyond Vietnam" (address sponsored by The Clergy and Laymen Concerned about Vietnam), Altoan Press, 1967; "A Declaration of Independence from the War in Vietnam," in *Ramparts,* May, 1967; "Sermon" (delivered at the Washington Cathedral), 1968. Delivered an average of 450 speeches a year throughout the country on behalf of the Black cause.

Records: "I Shall Die, But That is All I Shall Do for Death," (speeches by Martin Luther King included), Center for the Study of Democratic Institutions, 1969; "Remaining Awake Through a Great Revolution," Creed Records; "A Knock at Midnight" (a sermon delivered at the Mt. Zion Baptist Church in Cincinnati), Creed Records.

ADAPTATIONS: "Martin Luther King, Jr." (filmstrip with record), Miller-Brody Productions; "King;" starring Paul Winfield and Cecily Tyson was presented on NBC-TV, February 12-14, 1978; "Martin Luther King, Jr.: From

MARTIN LUTHER KING, JR.

Montgomery to Memphis" (26½ min. b/w), BFA Educational Media.

SIDELIGHTS: "On December 5, 1955, to the amused annoyance of the white citizens of Montgomery, Alabama, an obscure young Baptist minister named Martin Luther King, Jr., called a city-wide Negro boycott of its segregated bus system. To their consternation, however, it was almost one hundred percent successful; it lasted for 381 days and nearly bankrupted the bus line," a *Playboy* interviewer wrote.

From that time until his assassination on April 4, 1968, in Memphis, Tennessee, where he was organizing striking garbage workers, King stood on the front lines of a non-violent Black revolution against social injustice. King became the universally acknowledged leader of the American civil rights movement, and chief spokesman for the nation's 20,000,000 Blacks. He represented what the *New Yorker* called "a new kind of political leader in America."

Any progress he made was made the hard way. In the course of his civil rights work he was jailed at least fourteen times, stabbed once in the chest, and his home was bombed three times. He had to come to terms with the probability of his own violent death. He told Gerald Priestland in an interview: "I'm realistic enough to know that I can meet a violent end. I live every day under the threat of death, and I have no illusions about it. There are enough sick people in the world for me to come to a violent end just as other leaders have done."

King grew up in a middle income home in Atlanta and was fourteen before he himself experienced racial prejudice. He and a teacher were returning from Dublin, Georgia, where he had participated in and won an oratorical contest sponsored by the Negro Elks. He told the *Playboy* interviewer: "Mrs. Bradley and I were on a bus returning to Atlanta, and at a small town along the way, some white passengers boarded the bus, and the white driver ordered us to get up

(From the television special "King," starring Paul Winfield and Cicely Tyson. Copyright © 1978, NBC.)

and give the whites our seats. We didn't move quickly enough to suit him, so he began cursing us. . . . I intended to stay right in that seat, but Mrs. Bradley finally urged me up, saying we had to obey the law. And so we stood up in the aisle for the 90 miles to Atlanta. . . . It was the angriest I have ever been in my life.''

"King was a believer in nonviolence,'' a *Life* editorial states, "and perfected the technique, learned from Gandhi, of using it as a weapon in his war for social change. . . . King insisted on nonviolent means because he took the Sermon on the Mount seriously, and that can be a daring and unpopular thing to do.'' The *New Yorker* writer comments: "To the last, Dr. King assumed that when the legal and extra legal barriers to communication were hewn down, people would begin to see their brotherhood beneath the skin and begin to know 'the majestic heights of being obedient to the unenforceable.' . . . A refined civility ran through him to the core; he didn't need to dissemble, to conceal hatreds, for none smoldered within him—except the hatred of evil.'' King was never bitter, never spiteful, and so did not threaten whites.

King's books expressed his beliefs and opinions not only on civil rights, but on other issues as well. *Stride Toward Freedom,* his account of the 1958 Negro boycott of the Montgomery bus lines, is, according to Abel Plenn, "a document of far-reaching importance for present and future chronicling of the struggle for civil rights in this country.'' King told *Playboy* that he thought three important things came about as a result of *Letter from a Birmingham Jail,* which was written during one of the terms he served for civil disobedience, in reply to eight clergymen who had been critical of his work in Birmingham. "It helped to focus greater international attention upon what was happening in Birmingham,'' said King. "Without Birmingham, the march on Washington would not have been called. . . . It was also the image of Birmingham which . . . helped to bring the Civil Rights Bill into being in 1963.'' Stone says of *Why We Can't Wait:* "The book's logic and eloquence strike hard at the jugular veins of two American dogmas—racial discrimination, and that even more insidious doctrine which nourished it, gradualism.''

Herbert Warren Richardson calls King "the most important theologian of our time . . . because of his creative proposals for dealing with the structure of evil generated by modern relativism, *viz.,* ideological conflict. . . . King created not only a new theology, but also new types of piety, new styles of Christian living.'' Because the struggle against racism was a struggle against such an ideological conflict, King has to carry this struggle into other areas as well, and so was the first to join the civil rights struggle with the struggle against the Vietnam war. *Where Do We Go from Here: Chaos or Community* expressed his views on both subjects. He wrote: "The worth of an individual does not lie in the measure of his intellect, his racial origin or his social position. Human worth lies in relatedness to God. An individual has value because he has value to God.''

A reviewer for *Virginia Quarterly Review,* commenting on *The Trumpet of Conscience* writes: "King saw clearly, four months before he died, that the white man's hate and the rich man's dollar remain the West's most powerful forces, despite the preaching and example of his movement and the many moral outcries preceding him.''

Time said of King: "The nation may take greater heart from the luminous words he flung into the face of white America: 'We will meet your capacity to inflict suffering with our ca-

pacity to endure suffering. We will meet your physical force with soul force. We will not hate you, but we cannot in all good conscience obey your unjust laws. We will soon wear you down by our capacity to suffer. And in winning our freedom, we will so appeal to your heart and your conscience that we will win you in the process.' In his death, if not in life, Martin Luther King may have gone far toward that goal.''

King was originally buried in Southview Cemetery in Atlanta; he is presently buried in property adjacent to Ebenezer Baptist Church.

In April, 1970, a documentary entitled "King: A Filmed Record—Montgomery to Memphis'' played one time simultaneously in over 1000 theatres in North America and Europe. The proceeds, which amounted to about $3,500,000 went to the Martin Luther King, Jr., Special Fund, the purpose of which is to finance organizations carrying on Dr. King's civil rights work.

FOR MORE INFORMATION SEE: New York Times, October 12, 1958, April 12, 13, 1968; *America,* August 17, 1963; Lerone Bennett, Jr., *What Manner of Man,* Johnson, 1964; *Critic,* August, 1964; *Playboy Interviews,* Playboy Press, 1967; *New Yorker,* June 22, 1967, April 13, 1968; *Christian Science Monitor,* July 6, 1967; *Book Week,* July 9, 1967; *Christian Century,* August 23, 1967; *New York Review of Books,* August 24, 1967; *New York Times Book Review,* September 3, 1967; *Commonweal,* November 17, 1967, May 3, 1968; *New Statesman,* March 22, 1968; *Punch,* April 3, 1968; *London Times,* April 6, 1968; *Listener,* April 11, 1968; *Time,* April 12, 1968, October 3, 1969; *Life,* April 19, 1968, September 12, 1969, September 19, 1969; *Antioch Review,* spring, 1968; *Esquire,* August, 1968; *Virginia Quarterly Review,* autumn, 1968; Coretta Scott King, *My Life with Martin Luther King Jr.,* Holt, 1969; *Washington Post,* January 14, 1970.

(Assassinated April 4, 1968, in Memphis, Tenn.)

KNIGHT, David C(arpenter)

PERSONAL: Born in Glens Falls, N.Y. *Education:* Graduated from Union College, Schenectady, N.Y.; also attended the University of Paris.

CAREER: Employed in Berlin, West Germany, as a civilian employee with U.S. Military Intelligence; has also been a science editor for a New York publishing firm.

WRITINGS: The First Book of Sound: A Basic Guide to the Science of Acoustics, Watts, 1960; *Robert Koch: Father of Bacteriology* (illustrated by Gustav Schrotter), Watts, 1961; *Isaac Newton: Mastermind of Modern Science* (illustrated by John Griffin), Watts, 1961; *The First Book of Air: A Basic Guide to the Earth's Atmosphere,* Watts, 1961; *Science ABC* (illustrated by G. Schrotter), Watts, 1962; *Johannes Kepler and Planetary Motion,* Watts, 1962; *The Science Book of Meteorology,* Watts, 1964; *The First Book of Deserts: An Introduction to the Earth's Arid Lands,* Watts, 1964; *Copernicus: Titan of Modern Astronomy,* Watts, 1965.

The First Book of Mars: An Introduction to the Red Planet, Watts, 1966, revised edition, 1973; *Let's Find Out about Mars* (illustrated by Don Miller), Watts, 1966; *Let's Find Out about Insects* (illustrated by Henry S. Gillette), Watts,

You usually hear thunder a few seconds after the bolt of lightning that caused it. ■ (From *Let's Find Out About Sound* by David Knight. Pictures by Ulrick Schramm.)

1967; *The First Book of Berlin: Tale of a Divided City,* Watts, 1967; *Let's Find Out about Magnets* (illustrated by D. Miller), Watts, 1967; *Let's Find Out about Weather* (illustrated by Rene Martin), Watts, 1967; *Let's Find Out about Telephones* (illustrated by D. Miller), Watts, 1967; *Comets,* Watts, 1968; *The First Book of the Sun,* Watts, 1968; *Let's Find Out about Earth* (illustrated by D. Miller), Watts, 1968, revised edition, 1975; *The Whiskey Rebellion, 1794: Revolt in Western Pennsylvania Threatens American Unity,* Watts, 1968; *Meteors and Meteorites,* Watts, 1969; *Let's Find Out about Rocks and Minerals* (illustrated by Matthew Kalmenoff), Watts, 1969.

Let's Find Out about the Ocean (illustrated by R. Martin), Watts, 1970; *The Naval War with France, 1798-1800,* Watts, 1970; (compiler) *American Astronauts and Spacecraft: A Pictorial History from Project Mercury through Apollo 13,* Watts, 1970, revised edition published as *American Astronauts and Spacecraft: A Pictorial History from Project Mercury through the Skylab Manned Missions,* 1975; *Poltergeists: Hauntings and the Haunted,* Lippincott, 1972; *How to Identify 101 Popular Sailboats under 30 Feet,* Arco, 1973; *The Tiny Planets: Asteroids of Our Solar System,* Morrow, 1973; *From Log Roller to Lunar Rover: The Story of Wheels* (illustrated by Lorelle Raboni), Parents Magazine Press, 1974; *Thirty-Two Moons: The Natural Satellites of Our Solar System* (illustrated by Pamela Carroll and Ellen Cullen), Morrow, 1974; *Your Body's Defenses,* McGraw-Hill, 1974; *Those Mysterious UFO's: The Story of Unidentified Flying Objects,* Parents Magazine Press, 1975; *Let's Find Out about Sound* (illustrated by Ulrick, pseudonym of Ulrik Schramm), Watts, 1975; *Eavesdropping on Space: The Quest of Radio Astronomy,* Morrow, 1975; *Bees Can't Fly, But They Do: Things That Are Still a Mystery to Sci-*

ence (illustrated by Barbara Wolff), Macmillan, 1976; *Harnessing the Sun: The Story of Solar Energy,* Morrow, 1976.

SIDELIGHTS: The Tiny Planets is one of several new science books for young people by David C. Knight to be published in the last few years. A *Library Journal* critic wrote, "For young scientists interested in outer space, this book offers new information on a little-explored part of the universe—asteroids. Knight describes the irregular shapes and sizes of these solar system roamers found between the orbits of Mars and Jupiter . . . [and] discusses their possible usefulness as strongholds in future space exploration. . . ." *Horn Book* commented that the book, ". . . lies in the realm of pure astronomy. This is a good, workmanlike summary of the history, nature, and—believe it or not—usefulness of the asteroids. . . ."

"*Eavesdropping on Space,*" wrote *Horn Book,* "contains a history and a description of radio astronomy. The photographs are pertinent; the explanations clear and generally correct. . . ." *School Library Journal* noted, "Radio astronomy had its beginnings in the 1930's when radio waves emanating from celestial sources were first detected. Without going into much technical detail, Knight discusses the instruments, methods, and discoveries of radio astronomers as well as the various types of antennae used and the significance of the discoveries."

KNIGHT, Francis Edgar 1905-
(Frank Knight, Cedric Salter)

PERSONAL: Born in 1905, in London, England. *Education:* Attended schools in Croydon, Surrey, England.

CAREER: Served in the Merchant Navy, 1920-30, beginning as an apprentice at the age of fifteen, later obtaining his Extra Master Mariner's Certificate, 1929; during World War II served as a navigation instructor in the Royal Air Force in Britain and South Africa; sold yachts for a time after the war; later turned to a writing career.

WRITINGS—Under name Frank Knight; fiction: *The Albatross Comes Home* (illustrated by A. E. Morley), Hollis & Carter, 1949; *Four in the Half-Deck* (illustrated by S. Drigin), Thomas Nelson, 1950; *The Island of the Radiant Pearls,* Hollis & Carter, 1950; *The Golden Monkey* (illustrated by John Strickland Goodall), Macmillan, 1953; *Strangers in the Half-Deck* (illustrated by Robert Johnston), Thomas Nelson, 1953; *Acting Third Mate* (illustrated by R. Johnston), Thomas Nelson, 1954; *Voyage to Bengal* (illustrated by Patrick Jobson), St. Martin's, 1954; *Clippers to China* (illustrated by P. Jobson), St. Martin's, 1955; *Mudlarks and Mysteries* (illustrated by P. Jobson), Macmillan, 1955; *Family on the Tide* (illustrated by Geoffrey Whittam), St. Martin's, 1956; *The Bluenose Pirate* (illustrated by P. Jobson), St. Martin's, 1956; *Please Keep off the Mud* (illustrated by P. Jobson), St. Martin's, 1957; *He Sailed with Blackbeard* (illustrated by P. Jobson), St. Martin's, 1958; *The Partick Steamboat* (illustrated by P. Jobson), Macmillan (London), 1958, St. Martin's, 1959.

The Sea Chest: Stories of Adventure at Sea (illustrated by William Riley), Collins, 1960, Platt & Munk, 1964; *The Sea's Fool,* Ward Lock, 1960; *Shadows on the Mud* (illustrated by P. Jobson), Macmillan (London), 1960, St. Martin's, 1961; *Captains of the Calabar,* Ward Lock, 1961; *The Last of the Lallow's* (illustrated by William Stobbs), St. Martin's, 1961; *The Slaver's Apprentice* (illustrated by P. Jobson), St. Martin's, 1961; *Pekoe Reef*, Ward Lock, 1962; *Clemency Draper* (illustrated by W. Stobbs), St. Martin's, 1963; *The Ship That Came Home* (illustrated by Derrick Smouthy), Benn, 1963; *Up, Sea Beggars!,* Macdonald & Co., 1964; *Remember Vera Cruz!* (illustrated by H. J. Gorin), Macdonald & Co., 1965, Dial, 1966; *Olaf's Sword* (illustrated by Andrew Sier), Heinemann, 1969, F. Watts, 1970.

Nonfiction: *A Beginner's Guide to the Sea,* St. Martin's, 1955; *The Sea Story, Being a Guide to Nautical Reading from Ancient Times to the Close of the Sailing Ship Era,* St. Martin's, 1958; *Captain Anson and the Treasure of Spain,* St. Martin's, 1959; *A Guide to Ocean Navigation,* St. Martin's, 1959; *John Harrison: The Man Who Made Navigation Safe,* Macmillan, 1962; *The Young Drake* (illustrated by Azpelicueta), Parrish, 1962; *Stories of Famous Sea Fights* (illustrated by Will Nickless), Oliver & Boyd, 1963, Westminster Press, 1967; *Stories of Famous Ships* (illustrated by W. Nickless), Oliver & Boyd, 1963, Westminster Press, 1966; *The Young Columbus* (illustrated by Azpelicueta), Roy, 1963; *Stories of Famous Explorers by Sea* (illustrated by W. Nickless), Oliver & Boyd, 1964, Westminster Press, 1966; *The Young Captain Cook* (illustrated by Joan Howell), Parrish, 1964, Roy, 1966; *Stories of Famous Explorers by Land* (illustrated by W. Nickless), Oliver & Boyd, 1965, Westminster Press, 1966.

Stories of Famous Sea Adventures (illustrated by W. Nickless), Oliver & Boyd, 1966, Westminster Press, 1967; *Prince of Cavalier: The Story of the Life and Campaigns of Rupert of the Rhine* (illustrated by John Lawrence), Macdonald & Co., 1967; *Captain Cook and the Voyage of the Endeavour,* Thomas Nelson, 1968; *Rebel Admiral: The Life and Exploits of Admiral Lord Cochrane* (illustrated by J. Lawrence), Macdonald & Co., 1968; *The Hero: Vice-Admiral Horatio Viscount Nelson,* Macdonald & Co., 1969; *Russia Fights Japan* (illustrated by Roger Phillips), Macdonald & Co., 1969; *Ships,* Benn, 1969; *The Dardanelles Campaign* (illustrated by F. D. Phillips), Macdonald & Co., 1970; *General at Sea: The Life of Admiral Robert Blake* (illustrated by Douglas Phillips), Macdonald & Co., 1971; *The Clipper Ship,* Collins, 1973; *True Stories of Spying* (illustrated by Victor Ambrus), Benn, 1975; *The Golden Age of the Galleon,* Collins, 1976.

Under pseudonym Cedric Salter: *Flight from Poland,* Faber, 1940; *Try-Out in Spain,* Harper, 1943; *Introducing Spain,* Methuen, 1953, revised edition, 1967; *Introducing Portugal,* Methuen, 1956; *Two Girls and a Boat* (illustrated by Victor Bertoglio), Blackie & Son, 1956; *A Fortnight in Portugal,* Percival Marshall, 1957; *Introducing Turkey,* Methuen, 1961; *Portugal,* Hastings House, 1970; *Algarve and Southern Portugal,* Hastings House, 1974; *Northern Spain,* Batsford, 1975.

SIDELIGHTS: Knight's books covered various periods of navigation history. The author's *Voyage to Bengal* was based on the last sailing of the "East Indiaman" in the early 1800's. "Full of suspense as well as of authentic details . . . [the book] will appeal to all teen-age lovers of the sea," commented a *New York Herald Tribune Book Review* critic.

In his *Captain Anson and the Treasure of Spain,* Knight gave an account of George Anson's journey around the world during the eighteenth century. To keep the book factual, the author relied on information from the diaries, logs, and letters of the men who participated in this segment of British naval history. A reviewer for *Christian Science Monitor* wrote, "The long voyage with its incredible endurance

and splendor as well as its violence . . . is told with a clipped directness and economy that is exactly right."

In *Captain Cook and the Voyage of the Endeavor* Knight described James Cook's trip around Cape Horn to New Zealand. Knight based his work on Captain Cook's journal of the voyage with additional notes from other sources. A critic for the London *Times Literary Supplement* observed, "Helped by his knowledge and love of the sea, he [Knight] presents careful research, quietly correcting more romantic interpretations of fact in an admirable narrative style, direct and absorbing. . . ."

Knight's latest book, *The Golden Age of the Galleon,* followed the voyages of a sailing warship under the command of Sir Francis Drake. A critic for *Junior Bookshelf* noted, "As well as being a rousing tribute to some of the most famous Elizabethan seamen and their activities, this book is handsomely produced. . . ."

FOR MORE INFORMATION SEE: San Francisco Chronicle, November 15, 1953; *New York Herald Tribune Book Review,* February 13, 1955; *Christian Science Monitor,* February 5, 1960; Brian Doyle, editor, *Who's Who of Children's Literature,* Schocken, 1968; *Times Literary Supplement,* June 26, 1969; *Junior Bookshelf,* October, 1976.

LA FARGE, Phyllis

PERSONAL: Married Chester Johnson. *Education:* Graduated from Radcliffe College.

CAREER: Author. *Awards, honors: The Pancake King* was selected as one of the books in the American Institute of Graphic Arts Children's Book Show, 1971-72, and also as one of the American Institute of Graphic Arts Fifty Books of the Year, 1971.

PHYLLIS LA FARGE

She thought maybe she should climb out, but she was afraid that someone would see her and ask her what she was doing. ■ (From *Joanna Runs Away* by Phyllis La Farge. Pictures by Trina Schart Hyman.)

WRITINGS: (Translator, with Peter H. Judd) Jean Giraudoux, *Giraudoux: Three Plays, Volume 2,* Hill & Wang, 1964; *Kate and the Wild Kittens* (illustrated by Ingrid Fetz), Knopf, 1965; *The Gumdrop Necklace* (illustrated by Alan E. Cober), Knopf, 1967; *Jane's Silver Chair* (illustrated by Robin Jacques), Knopf, 1969; (editor) Stendhal, pseudonym of Marie Henri Beyle, *The Red and the Black,* Washington Square Press, 1970; *Keeping Going,* Harcourt, 1971; *The Pancake King* (illustrated by Seymour Chwast), Delacorte, 1971; *Joanna Runs Away* (illustrated by Trina Schart Hyman), Holt, 1973; *Abby Takes Over,* Lippincott, 1974; *A*

Christmas Adventure (illustrated by Ray Cruz), Holt, 1974; *Granny's Fish Story* (illustrated by Gahan Wilson), Parents Magazine Press, 1975.

Contributor to magazines, including *Harper's* and *Vogue.*

SIDELIGHTS: Phyllis La Farge was born in New York City and spent much of her early childhood in rural Connecticut, returning to the city when she was ten. "The result is that I am pretty nearly split between city mouse and country mouse. Or one might say that, like Joanna in *Joanna Runs Away,* I am a city girl with a longing for a green field.''

She wrote her first children's story when she was in the sixth grade, ''cribbing liberally from one of my favorite books.'' Before that she told stories to her younger sister, who remembers that they were about a somewhat effete princess called Fern. ''My heroines have become more plebian over the years and their names ordinary. I devoted my twenties to writing the sort of novels that end up in the back of closets or the bottom drawer of filing cabinets, not a very heartening activity. In recent years I have been writing essays and children's books. When I was in college it would not have occurred to me that I would find either form congenial—and I do.

''Like many country mice and city mice these days, I live in neither city nor country, but the suburbs. City traffic without city amenities. Supermarkets and death-of-the-heart shopping plazas. I rely on summer in New England to counterbalance. It is my 'green pasture.'''

LARSEN, Egon   1904-

PERSONAL: Surname originally Lehrburger; born July 13, 1904, in Munich, Germany; son of Albert David (a manufacturer) and Beatrice (Koenigsberger) Lehrburger; married second wife, Ursula Lippmann (a translator), July 3, 1940; children: (first marriage) Peter. *Education:* Educated in Munich, Germany. *Home:* 34 Dartmouth Rd., London N.W.2, England. *Agent:* Robert Harben, 3 Church Vale, London N.2, England.

CAREER: Self-employed author and journalist, 1928—. U.S. Office of Strategic Services, civilian staff, London, England, 1944-45; Radio Munich, London correspondent, 1954—; correspondent for *Suddeutsche Zeitung,* Munich, Germany, and for other Central European newspapers. *Member:* P.E.N. (English Centre, London; Centre of German-Speaking Authors Abroad). *Awards, honors:* Diesel Silver Medal, 1963.

WRITINGS: Inventor's Cavalcade (originally written in German but published in English), translation by Ernest W. Dickes, Lindsay Drummond, 1943, Transatlantic, 1946; *Inventor's Scrapbook,* Lindsay Drummond, 1947; *Spotlight on Films: A Primer for Film-Lovers,* Parrish, 1950; *Men Who Changed the World: Stories of Invention and Discovery,* Roy, 1952; *Radar Works Like This,* Roy, 1952, 3rd edition, Phoenix House, 1966; *An American in Europe: The Life of Benjamin Thompson, Count Rumford,* Philosophical Library, 1953; *Men Who Shaped the Future: Stories of Invention and Discovery,* Roy, 1954; *The Young Traveller in Germany,* Phoenix House, 1954, Dutton, 1955, 2nd edition, Soccer, 1961; *The True Book About Inventions,* Muller, 1954, published in America as *The Prentice-Hall Book About Inventions,* Prentice-Hall, 1955, 2nd edition (under original title), Soccer, 1961; *The True Book About Firefighting,* Muller, 1955, 2nd edition, 1962; *Men Under the Sea,* Phoenix House, 1955, Roy, 1956; *You'll See: Report from the Future,* Rider & Co., 1957; *Transistors Work Like This,* Roy, 1957, 2nd edition, Phoenix House, 1963; *Men Who Fought for Freedom,* Roy, 1958; *Atomic Energy: A Layman's Guide to the Nuclear Age,* Hennel Locke, 1958, also published as *Atomic Energy; The First Hundred Years: The Intelligent Layman's Guide to the Nuclear Age,* Pan Books, 1958; (editor) Franklyn M. Branley, *Solar Energy,* English edition, Edmund Ward, 1959; *Transport,* Roy, 1959; *Sir Vivian Fuchs,* Phoenix House, 1959, Roy, 1960.

EGON LARSEN

Power from Atoms, Muller, 1960, Soccer, 1961; *Ideas and Invention,* Spring Books, 1960; *A History of Invention,* Roy, 1961, revised edition, 1969; *The Atom,* Weidenfeld & Nicolson, 1961; *Film Making,* Muller, 1962; *The Cavendish Laboratory: Nursery of Genius,* F. Watts, 1962; (editor with Eric G. Linfield) *England vorwiegend heiter: Kleine Literaturgeschichte des britischen Humors* (originally written in English but published in German translation by Larsen and wife, Ursula Larsen), Basserman, 1962, reissued as *Laughter in a Damp Climate: 700 Years of British Humour,* Jenkins, 1963, Arc Books, 1965; *Atoms and Atomic Energy* (juvenile), John Day, 1963; (editor) Harry E. Neal, *Communication: From Stone Age to Space Age,* Phoenix House, 1963; (with son, Peter Larsen) *Young Africa,* Roy, 1964; *The Pegasus Book of Inventors,* Dobson, 1965; *Munich,* A. S. Barnes, 1966; (with Maurice F. Allward) *Great Inventions of the World,* Hamlyn, 1966; *The Deceivers: Lives of the Great Imposters,* Roy, 1966; *Great Ideas in Engineering,* edited by Patrick Pringle, Robert C. Maxwell, 1967; (editor with Linfield) *Great Humorous Stories of the World,* Arthur Barker, 1967; *First with the Truth: Newspapermen in Action,* Roy, 1968; *Carlo Pozzo di Borgo: One Man Against Napoleon,* Dobson, 1968; *Lasers Work Like This,* Roy, 1969.

Hovercraft and Hydrofoils Work Like This, Dent, 1970, Roy, 1971; (editor) Peter Larsen, *The United Nations at Work Throughout the World,* Dent, 1970, Lothrop, 1971; *Great Ideas in Industry,* Robert C. Maxwell, 1971; *Strange Sects and Cults,* Arthur Barker, 1971, Hart Publishing, 1972; *Radio and Television,* Dent, 1976; *New Sources of*

Energy and Power, Frederick Muller, 1976; *Weimar Eyewitness*, Bachman & Turner, 1977; *Telecommunications*, Frederick Muller, 1977; *Food: Past, Present and Future*, Frederick Muller, 1977.

Translator: Erich Weinert, *Stalingrad Diary*, I.N.G. Publications, 1944; *I Escaped from Nazi Germany: A French Deportee's Report*, I.N.G. Publications, 1944; *Free Germans in the French Maquis: The Story of the Committee "Free Germany" in the West*, I.N.G. Publications, 1945; Rene Felix Allendy and Hella Lobstein, *Sex Problems in School*, Staples, 1948; Franz Farga, *Violins and Violinists*, Rockliff, 1950; (with Joseph Avrach) Gustav K. H. Buescher, *The Boys' Book of the Earth*, Burke Publishing, 1960; (with Frank Pickering) Karl Stumpff, *Planet Earth*, University of Michigan Press, 1960. Editor of biographical series, "People from the Past," Dobson, 1963-73. Occasional writer for, and director of, documentary films.

WORK IN PROGRESS: A Candle in Barbed Wire: Amnesty International, for Frederick Muller, London.

SIDELIGHTS: "I have been a writer ever since publishing, single-handed, a school magazine at the age of twelve. Left Germany in 1935 after being banned from publishing anything by Nazi government. Lived in Paris and Prague before settling in London in 1938. I have been a London correspondent for Radio Munich and leading German newspapers since 1954. (Competence in German language.)"

Twenty-two foreign-language editions of Egon Larsen's books have appeared in twelve European countries, Israel, Japan, Burma, India (in Hindi, Tamil, Urdu, Telugu), Turkey, Malaysia (Chinese), Iran (Farsi), Nigeria (Hausa).

FOR MORE INFORMATION SEE: Times Literary Supplement, August 17, 1967; *Kürschners Deutscher Literatur-Kalender*, Germany, 1975.

LATHROP, Dorothy P(ulis) 1891-

PERSONAL: Born April 16, 1891, in Albany, New York; daughter of Cyrus Clark Lathrop (a businessman and founder of the Boy's Club in Albany) and I. Pulis Lathrop (a painter); sister of Gertrude K. Lathrop (the sculptress). *Education:* Graduated from Teacher's College, Columbia University; studied illustration at the Pennsylvania Academy of Fine Arts and the Art Students League. *Home:* Falls Village, Connecticut.

CAREER: Author and illustrator of books for children. Taught art at Albany High School for two years. *Member:* National Association of Women Painters and Sculptors. *Awards, honors: Hitty*, written by Rachel Field and illustrated by Dorothy Lathrop, was the Newbery medal winner, 1930; Caldecott Medal, 1938, for *Animals of the Bible;* Eyre Medal of the Pennsylvania Academy of Fine Arts, 1941; Library of Congress prize, 1946.

WRITINGS—All self-illustrated; all published by Macmillan: *The Fairy Circus*, 1931; *Who Goes There?*, 1935, reissued, 1963; *Bouncing Betsy*, 1936, reissued, 1964; *Hide and Go Seek*, 1938; *Presents for Lupe*, 1940; *The Colt from Moon Mountain*, 1941; *Puppies for Keeps*, 1943; *The Skittle-Skattle Monkey*, 1945; *Let Them Live*, 1951, reissued, 1966; *Puffy and the Seven-Leaf Clover*, 1954; *The Littlest Mouse*, 1955; *Follow the Brook*, 1960; *The Dog in the Tapestry Garden*, 1962.

DOROTHY LATHROP

Other writings: *The Little White Goat*, Macmillan, 1933; *The Lost Merry-Go-Round*, Macmillan, 1934; *The Snail Who Ran*, F. A. Stokes, 1934; *An Angel in the Woods*, Macmillan, 1947.

Illustrator: Walter de la Mare, *Three Mulla-Mulgars*, Knopf, 1919; William Henry Hudson, *A Little Boy Lost*, Knopf, 1920; W. de la Mare, *Down-Adown-Derry*, Constable, 1922; de la Mare, *Crossings*, Knopf, 1923; Hilda Conkling, .*Silverhorn*, F. A. Stokes, 1924; George MacDonald, *Light Princess*, Macmillan, 1926; Jean Ingelow, *Mopsa the Fairy*, Harper, 1927; G. MacDonald, *Princess and Curdie*, Macmillan, 1927; Rachel Field, *Hitty*, Macmillan, 1929, reissued, 1968; Sara Teasdale, *Stars Tonight*, Macmillan, 1930; Nathaniel Hawthorne, *Snow Image*, Macmillan, 1930; W. de la Mare, *Dutch Cheese*, Knopf, 1931; Caroline Dale Snedeker, *Forgotten Daughter*, Doubleday, 1933; *Animals of the Bible*, text by Helen D. Fish from the King James Bible, F. A. Stokes, 1937, reissued, Lippincott, 1969; Sant Ram Mandal, *Happy Flute*, F. A. Stokes, 1937; Hans Christian Andersen, *Little Mermaid*, Macmillan, 1939; W. de la Mare, *Bells and Grass*, Viking, 1942; de la Mare, *Mr. Bumps and His Monkey*, Winston, 1942.

SIDELIGHTS: **April 16, 1891.** Born in Albany, New York. Mother, a painter; sister, a sculptor; father a businessman. "My mother . . . is a painter. It undoubtedly was seeing her at work, being in her studio, and there encouraged to use her brushes and paints that gave me my interest in art. From her came much of my training in painting, and talk of art and artists was from a very early age part of my daily life.

"Perhaps it was from my paternal grandfather, who had a bookstore in Bridgeport, Connecticut, that I inherited most strongly my interest in books, which turned my drawing and painting in that direction. In fact during all those early years, I wrote far more than I drew. . . ."

1918. ''I began to illustrate in 1918 while I was teaching and have been illustrating pretty steadily from that time on. For years I did little writing except occasional articles and lectures on illustration, and a few book reviews.''

1919. First book illustrated, *Japanese Prints* by John Gould Fletcher for Four Seasons. The company went bankrupt before it could pay for the drawings.

1931. ''Encouraged by Louise Seaman of the Macmillan Company, I wrote and illustrated my first book, *The Fairy Circus*. I don't know where my ideas come from. Open your mind and they come! They develop as I work. Do I rework material? Of course! Do I try out my ideas on children? Never!''

1938. First recipient of the Caldecott Medal for illustrations in *Animals of the Bible*. ''I still get letters from children about the book; however, most of them are at the well-meant instigation of teachers. Adults write too. The book is still selling well, and I think—and hope—that new plates are about to be made to replace badly worn ones. *Animals of the Bible* is, perhaps, my favorite book because of the diversity of illustrations in it.''

There was a painful picture of a man being swallowed by a large fish. ▪ (From *Hitty: Her First Hundred Years* by Rachel Field. Illustrated by Dorothy P. Lathrop.)

He jumped, he reared, he kicked. ▪ (From *The Three Mulla-Mulgars* by Walter de la Mare. Illustrated by Dorothy Lathrop.)

1940. For years lived in Albany, with her sister, sharing a two-room studio in the back of the house. ''. . . We built [the studio] when we began to work seriously, since it was increasingly evident that my mother's studio could hardly hold comfortably three working artists at once. Our studio is set back among the apple trees, and there we can have all the animal models, permanent or transient, that we need. It is far enough from the heart of the city to be noisier with birds than with traffic, and many wild animal, bird, and flower models walk conveniently up to our windows.''

Lathrop said in her Caldecott speech: ''Yes, it is dangerous to love your models too much. On the other hand, unless you do, no one will love your pictures of them. I don't mean this in any esoteric or mystical way. I don't claim that you set into motion a force which flows between yourself and your public. That, too, may be so for all I know, but what I mean is something quite concrete. For a person who does not love what he is drawing, whatever it may be, children or animals, or anything else, will not draw them convincingly, and that, simply because he will not bother to look at them long enough really to see them. What we love, we gloat over and feast our eyes upon. And when we look again and again at any living creature, we cannot help but perceive its subtlety of line, its exquisite patterning and all its unbelievable intricacy and beauty. The artist who draws what he does not love, draws from a superficial concept. But the one who loves what he draws is very humbly trying to translate into an alien medium life itself, and it is his joy and his pain that he knows that life to be matchless.

(From *Animals of the Bible,* text selected by Helen Dean Fish. Illustrated by Dorothy P. Lathrop.)

DOROTHY LATHROP

"No one, I think, is more convinced of the unity of all life than the artist, who sits before its different phases so long and silently, seeing them in a great intimacy. He not only beholds the flower, but he feels the life that, even while he draws, unfolds the petals, senses the force that pushes new leaves from the ground. He traces a network of veins in leaf and flower akin to the veining which shows under his own skin. He knows that under the microscope it is hard to tell which veins are plant and which animal, and whether that is sap or blood flowing so steadily through those channels. In that deep silence in which drawings are made, he so projects himself into the personality of any living model before him, that he becomes strangely identified with it. He not only feels himself a brother to this creature whose atoms are held together by the same mysterious force or vibration, not only feels the same life surging through them both, but, such is his intensity of interest, he *becomes* that creature. Or, as the eastern philosophers put it, he 'sees all creatures in himself, himself in all creatures.'" [*Caldecott Medal Books: 1938-1957,* edited by Bertha Mahony Miller and Elinor Whitney Field, The Horn Book, Inc., 1957.]

FOR MORE INFORMATION SEE: (For children) S. L. Goldsmith, "Animal Artist Extraordinary: Dorothy Lathrop," in *Topflight Famous American Women,* edited by Anne G. Stoddard, Nelson, 1946; Walter J. Wilwerding, *Animal Drawing and Painting,* Watson-Guptill, 1946; Bertha E. Mahony and others, compilers, *Illustrators of Children's Books, 1744-1945,* Horn Book, 1947; (for children) Stanley J. Kunitz and Howard Haycraft, editors, *Junior Book of Authors,* 2nd edition revised, H. W. Wilson, 1951; Gertrude K. Lathrop, "Dorothy P. Lathrop," in *Caldecott Medal Books: 1938-1957,* edited by B. Mahony and E. W. Field, Horn Book, 1957; B. E. (Mahony) Miller and others, compilers, *Illustrators of Children's Books, 1946-1956,* Horn Book, 1958; Lee Kingman and others, compilers, *Illustrators of Children's Books, 1957-1966,* Horn Book, 1968; Lee Bennett Hopkins, *Books Are by People,* Citation Press, 1969.

LEE, Dennis (Beynon) 1939-

PERSONAL: Born August 31, 1939, in Toronto, Ontario, Canada; son of Walter and Louise (Garbutt) Lee; divorced; children: two daughters, one son. *Education:* University of Toronto, B.A., 1962, M.A., 1964. *Office:* c/o Macmillan of Canada, 70 Bond St., Toronto, Canada.

CAREER: University of Toronto, Victoria College, Toronto, Ontario, lecturer in English, 1964-67; Rochdale College (experimental institution), Toronto, Ontario, self-described "resource person," 1967-69; House of Anansi Press, Toronto, Ontario, co-founder and editor, 1967-72. Full time writer. *Awards, honors:* Governor-General's Award for poetry, 1972, for *Civil Elegies;* Canadian Library Association Award, and Hans Christian Andersen Honour List, 1976, for *Alligator Pie.*

WRITINGS: Kingdom of Absence (poetry), House of Anansi, 1967; *Civil Elegies* (poetry), House of Anansi, 1968; (co-editor) *The University Game* (essays), House of Anansi, 1968; (editor) *T. O. Now: The Young Toronto Poets* (poetry), House of Anansi, 1968; *Wiggle to the Laundromat* (children's poetry), New Press, 1970; *Civil Elegies and Other Poems,* Anansi, 1972; *Alligator Pie* (children's poetry), Macmillan, 1974, Houghton, 1975; *Nicholas Knock and Other People* (children's poetry), Macmillan, 1974, Houghton, 1977; *The Death of Harold Ladoo* (poetry), Kanchenjunga Press, 1976; *Savage Fields* (literary theory), Anansi, 1977; *Garbage Delight* (children's poetry), Macmillan, 1977. Co-editor of two high school poetry anthologies.

DENNIS LEE

In Kamloops

In Kamloops
I'll eat your boots.

In the Gatineaus
I'll eat your toes.

In Napanee
I'll eat your knee.

In Winnipeg
I'll eat your leg.

In Charlottetown
I'll eat your gown.

In Crysler's Farm
I'll eat your arm.

In Aklavik
I'll eat your neck.

In Red Deer
I'll eat your ear.

In Trois Rivières
I'll eat your hair.

In Kitimat
I'll eat your hat.

And I'll eat your nose
And I'll eat your toes
In Medicine Hat and
    Moose Jaw.

(From *Alligator Pie*, poems by Dennis Lee. Pictures by Frank Newfeld.)

SIDELIGHTS: Known at first for adult poetry in Canada, where his three volumes of verse have attracted critical acclaim, Dennis Lee started writing nursery rhymes and jingles when his own children were very young. "I don't write 'for' children, in the sense of concocting verses to improve or interest tiny minds. Instead I write 'as' children, proceeding from the impulses of the two-year-old or the ten-year-old which still persist in the adult's nervous system."

FOR MORE INFORMATION SEE: Fiddlehead, spring, 1968, March-April, 1969; *Canadian Forum,* March, 1968; *Saturday Night,* July, 1968, August, 1969.

LEVINE, Rhoda

PERSONAL: Born in New York. *Education:* Graduated from Bard College. *Religion:* Jewish.

CAREER: Began dancing in musicals and the New York City Opera's ballet company after college graduation; teacher at Yale Drama School, New Haven, Conn., Bard College, Annandale-on-Hudson, N.Y., and Curtis Institute, Philadelphia, Pa.; choreographer for television programs (NET Opera, NBC Opera, and DuPont specials), Broadway productions, and several opera companies, including City Center Opera and the Metropolitan Opera's National Company; directed operas in Belgium and the Netherlands; author of books for children.

WRITINGS: Arthur (illustrated by Everett Aison), Atheneum, 1962; *Quiet Story* (illustrated by Rosalie Richards), Atheneum, 1963; *Three Ladies beside the Sea* (illustrated by Edward Gorey), Atheneum, 1963; *Harrison Loved His Umbrella* (illustrated by Karla Kuskin; Junior Literary Guild selection), Atheneum, 1964; *He Was There from the Day We Moved In* (illustrated by E. Gorey), Harlin Quist, 1969; *The Herbert Situation* (illustrated by Larry Ross), Harlin Quist, 1970.

SIDELIGHTS: Rhoda Levine first became involved in live opera during a trip to Spoleto, Italy, in 1963. The choreographer found her background in theatrical productions an asset when she eventually began directing opera for the stage. "That transition was very easy, because really the problems in all theater are the same, in terms of character," revealed Levine in an interview for *Opera.* "Of course the emotional timing of things is often determined by the music. But when you have a librettist and a composer like Da Ponte and Mozart, they're so accurate that it's never a problem, only a help."

In December of 1975, she directed the world premiere of the opera "Der Kaiser von Atlantis, oder der Tot Dankt Ab" (The Emperor of Atlantis, or Death Abdicates) for the Netherlands Opera. The opera was written in 1940 by two prisoners in a German concentration camp, but was never before performed publicly because of its antitotalitarian message.

In addition to her work in the theater, Rhoda Levine has also written books for children. Her first book, *Arthur,* was about a bird who decided to brave the cold New York winter rather than fly south with his friends. "This story, with an Andersen quality, is for reading aloud in small bits as there is much more to it than most," commented a reviewer for the *San Francisco Chronicle.*

FOR MORE INFORMATION SEE: Deborah Seabury, "Rhoda," *Opera,* February 14, 1976.

LIPMAN, Matthew 1923-

PERSONAL: Born August 24, 1923, in Vineland, N.J.; son of William Leo (a manufacturer) and Sophie (Kenin) Lipman; married Wynona Moore (a New Jersey state senator), February 5, 1952; married Teri Smith, December 26, 1974; children (first marriage): Karen, Will. *Education:* Stanford University, student, 1943-44; Columbia University, B.S., 1948, Ph.D., 1953. *Home:* 40 Park St., Montclair, N.J. 07042. *Office:* Institute for the Advancement of Philosophy for Children, Montclair State College, Upper Montclair, N.J. 07043.

CAREER: Columbia University, New York, N.Y., instructor in philosophy, social science, and fine arts, College of Pharmacy, 1954-57, assistant professor, 1957-61, associate professor, 1961-66, professor of philosophy, 1966-75, research associate in Department of Philosophy, 1971-75, chairman of department of general education, College of Pharmacy, 1962-75, instructor in contemporary civilization, Columbia College, 1954-63. College of the City of New York (now City College of the City University of New York), adjunct associate professor of philosophy, 1953-75; Sarah Lawrence College, part-time member of faculty, 1963-64; Montclair State College, Upper Montclair, N.J., professor of philosophy, 1972—, Institute for the Advancement of Philosophy for Children, director, 1974—. *Military service:* U.S. Army, Infantry, 1943-46; became sergeant; combat duty in France and Germany, two bronze stars. *Member:*

MATTHEW LIPMAN

American Philosophical Association, American Society for Aesthetics, British Society for Aesthetics. *Awards, honors:* Fulbright scholar at Sorbonne, University of Paris, 1950-51; Matchette Prize for Aesthetics, 1956; American Council of Learned Societies grant, 1967; National Endowment for the Humanities grants, 1970, 1972; New Jersey Council for the Humanities grant, 1975.

WRITINGS: What Happens in Art, Appleton, 1967; *Discovering Philosophy,* Appleton, 1969, 2nd edition, Prentice-Hall, 1977; *Contemporary Aesthetics,* Allyn & Bacon, 1973; *Harry Stottlemeir's Discovery,* IAPC, 1974; *Lisa,* IAPC, 1976; (with Ann M. Sharp) *Instructional Manual to Accompany Harry Stottlemeier's Discovery,* IAPC, 1975; (with Ann M. Sharp and Frederick S. Oscanyan) *Philosophy in the Classroom,* IAPC, 1977; (with Ann M. Sharp) *Instructional Manual to Accompany Lisa,* IAPC, 1977; (editor, with Ann M. Sharp) *Growing Up with Philosophy,* Temple University Press, 1978; *Suki,* IAPC, 1978. Contributor to philosophy, psychiatry and aesthetics journals.

SIDELIGHTS: "My stories are about children's discoveries of their minds. Has this happened to you? I mean, was there a day when you'd been thinking about, say, your cat, and you'd been thinking about your house, and you'd been thinking about funny words—and then suddenly, there you were, thinking about thinking?

"Well, the children in my stories begin to realize that they have thoughts, and that they can think about their thoughts, just as they can think about stars and mud puddles—and as they can think about their own feelings of joy and anger and loneliness and pride in themselves. Have you ever had a thought you'd never thought of before? Did you stop and wonder at it: how wonderful it is to have a new thought? How precious it is—a thought all your own, just like getting a new toy for a present!

"But how do thoughts fit together with one another? Are they linked together in chains? Or do they fit together like the parts of a jigsaw puzzle? If we already have some thoughts, can we figure out others? These are some of the questions which the children in my books wonder about.

"Yet they do more than wonder: they also try to answer the questions that occur to them. And they discuss these questions and answers with one another, with their teachers, and with their families.

"By now you understand why our thoughts are so important to us, and why we treasure them so. For regardless of whether we come from families that are well-to-do or not so well-to-do, regardless of whether we ourselves do well in school or not so well, we always have our thoughts to think about. We can bring them to mind as often as we like, and we may feel that, whatever else happens, our thoughts can never be taken away from us.

"So the children in these stories discover thinking as they discover themselves and their worlds. They discover thinking at the same time that they begin to discuss with their friends what it is to have friends, to have minds, to have rights, and all the other things that are important to children.

"I think that children who read these books come away with a better sense of the intelligent discussions children can have with one another, and the excitement of good conversation. They find the world they live in meaningful and intensely interesting. Perhaps if you begin to reflect more on how you

think, and if you begin to develop your own ideas, you too will come to find the world you live in a more interesting and more meaningful one."

FOR MORE INFORMATION SEE: New York Times, October 20, 1974; *Time,* November 18, 1974; *Newsweek,* September 20, 1976.

LOW, Joseph 1911-

PERSONAL: Born August 11, 1911, in Coraopolis, Pa.; son of John Routh and Stella (Rent) Low; married Ruth Hull, October 21, 1940; children: Damaris, Jennifer. *Education:* University of Illinois, student, 1930-32; Art Students League, New York City, student under George Grosz, 1935. *Address:* Box 129, Cruz Bay, St. John, Virgin Islands 00830; and Box 272, Chilmark, Mass. 02535.

CAREER: Began his art career in 1933 by typesetting and printing his own work; freelance designer in New York City, beginning 1941; Indiana University, Bloomington, instructor in design and graphic art, 1942-45, also established the university's Corydon Press; worked for New York advertising agencies and editorial offices while living in Morristown, N.J., 1946-54; Eden Hill Press, Newtown, Conn., founder, 1959, and owner; author and illustrator of books for children. His works have been exhibited throughout the United States, Europe, and South America. Many of his prints are

JOSEPH LOW

The Wyvern is watching,
as well he might. . .

■ (From *A Beastly Alphabet* by George Mendoza.
Illustrated by Joseph Low.)

represented in permanent collections at numerous museums, libraries, and universities, including the Boston Museum of Fine Arts, the Library of Congress, and Princeton University. *Awards, honors: Mother Goose Riddle Rhymes* was one of the *New York Times* Choice of Best Illustrated Children's Books of the Year, 1953; *New York Herald Tribune* Children's Spring Book Festival Award, 1962, for *Adam's Book of Odd Creatures; The Mouse and the Song* by Marilynne K. Roach was selected as one of the American Institute of Graphic Arts Fifty Books of the Year in 1974, and was also chosen for the Children's Book Showcase in 1975; *Trust Reba* and *The Land of the Taffeta Dawn* (the latter written by Natalia M. Belting and illustrated by Low) were exhibited in the American Institute of Graphic Arts Children's Book Show, 1973-74; *Boo to a Goose* was a Children's Book Showcase title in 1976.

WRITINGS—All self-illustrated: (With wife, Ruth Low) *Mother Goose Riddle Rhymes,* Harcourt, 1953; *Adam's Book of Odd Creatures,* Atheneum, 1962; *Smiling Duke,* Houghton, 1963; *There Was a Wise Crow,* Follett, 1969; *Trust Reba,* McGraw, 1974; *Boo to a Goose,* Atheneum, 1975; *Five Men under One Umbrella, and Other Ready-to-Read Riddles,* Macmillan, 1975; *Little though I Be,* McGraw, 1976; *What If . . . ? 14 Encounters—Some Frightful, Some Frivolous—That Might Happen to Anyone,* Atheneum, 1976; *A Mad Wet Hen and Other Riddles,* Morrow, 1977; *The Christmas Grump,* Atheneum, 1977; *Benny Rabbitt and the Owl,* Greenwillow, 1978; *My Dog, Your Dog,* Macmillan, 1978.

Illustrator: Wendell William Wright and Helene Laird, *Rainbow Dictionary,* World Publishing, 1947, reissued as *The Rainbow Dictionary for Young Readers,* Collins-World, 1972; Milton Allan Rugoff, editor, *Harvest of World Folk Tales,* Viking, 1949; Olivia E. Coolidge, *Egyptian Adventures,* Houghton, 1954; Maurice Machado Osborne, *Rudi and the Mayor of Naples,* Houghton, 1958; Miriam Schlein, *The Big Cheese,* W. R. Scott, 1958; Walter de la Mare, *Jack and the Beanstalk,* Knopf, 1959; Helene Jamieson Jordan, *How a Seed Grows,* Crowell, 1960; Rose Laura Mincieli, *Pulcinella; or, Punch's Merry Pranks,* Knopf, 1960; *The Wren-Boy's Rhyme,* Eden Hill Press, 1961; Brian Burland, *St. Nicholas and the Tub,* Holiday House, 1964; Augusta R. Goldin, *Spider Silk,* Crowell, 1964; Jonathan Swift, *Directions to Servants,* Pantheon, 1964.

Clyde Robert Bulla, *More Stories from Favorite Operas,* Crowell, 1965; Marguerite (Harmon) Bro, *How the Mouse Deer Became King,* Doubleday, 1966; Maria Elena De La Iglesia, *The Cat and the Mouse, and Other Spanish Tales,* Pantheon, 1966; Judy Hawes, *Shrimps,* Crowell, 1967; Lloyd Frankenberg, editor, *Poems of Robert Burns,* Crowell, 1967; Bernice Kohn, *Telephones,* Coward-McCann, 1967; Barbara K. Walker, and Mine Suemer, *Stargazer to the Sultan,* Parents' Magazine Press, 1967; Nathan Zimelman, *To Sing a Song as Big as Ireland,* Follett, 1967; Constance B. Hieatt, *The Knight of the Lion,* Crowell, 1968; Howard Liss, *Friction,* Coward-McCann, 1968; Paul Showers, *Hear Your Heart,* Crowell, 1968; Alvin R. Tresselt, *The Legend of the Willow Plate,* Parents' Magazine Press, 1968; Daisy Aldan, editor, *Poems from India,* Crowell, 1969; Countee Cullen, *The Lost Zoo,* Follett, 1969; Sophia Harvati Fenton, *Greece,* Holt, 1969; George Mendoza, *A Beastly Alphabet,* Grosset, 1969; G. Mendoza, *Flowers and Grasses and Weeds,* Funk, 1969; *The Compleat Gamester* (limited edition), Barre, 1969.

Noblesse oblige, which means
I rely on
You to oblige me: Leo the Lion.

■ (From *The Lost Zoo* by Christopher Cat and
Countee Cullen. Illustrated by Joseph Low.)

When Jimmy leaned down to see if Rabbit was at home, Gus nipped him in a very tender place. ■ (From *Boo to a Goose* by Joseph Low. Illustrated by the author.)

Mark Twain (pseudonym of Samuel Langhorne Clemens), *The Notorious Jumping Frog and Other Stories,* edited by Edward Wagenknecht, Heritage Press, 1970; Myra Cohn Livingston, editor, *Speak Roughly to Your Little Boy: A Collection of Parodies and Burlesques,* Harcourt, 1971; Padraic Colum, *The White Sparrow,* McGraw, 1972; Sigmund Kalina, *Your Bones Are Alive,* Lothrop, 1972; Natalia Maree Belting, *The Land of the Taffeta Dawn,* Dutton, 1973; Mary Ann Hoberman, *The Raucous Auk: A Menagerie of Poems,* Viking, 1973; Henry Wadsworth Longfellow, *Paul Revere's Ride,* Windmill Books, 1973; Russell E. Erickson, *The Snow of Ohreeganu,* Lothrop, 1974; Marilynne K. Roach, *The Mouse and the Song,* Parents' Magazine Press, 1974; Franklyn Mansfield Branley, *Roots Are Food Finders,* Crowell, 1975; Dorothy O. Van Woerkom, *Meat Pies and Sausages,* Greenwillow Books, 1976; Myra Cohn Livingston, *A Lolligag of Limericks,* Atheneum, 1978.

SIDELIGHTS: Joseph Low's designs are primarily done in pen and ink with color washes. The author-illustrator collaborated with his wife, Ruth, on his first book, *Mother Goose Riddle Rhymes.* A *Saturday Review* critic described the collection of riddles as ". . . a perfect book for a rainy day to be shared with boys and girls of almost any age." A reviewer for the *New York Times* noted, "The pictures are beautifully drawn, reproduced in fresh colors."

A more recent book by the author-illustrator is *Trust Reba.* "A fanciful animal story has light treatment but a serious theme, appreciation of others, and is illustrated with pictures, that have soft colors, vitality of line, and interesting details of an old-fashioned country home," observed a critic for the *Bulletin of the Center for Children's Books.* A *Horn Book* reviewer commented, "An offbeat anthropomorphic story, its sweetness and highflown fantasy offset by the artist's spirited pen lines. . . . The words are colorful and concise, and the pictorial interpretation is engaging."

Low's *Five Men under One Umbrella and Other Ready-to-Read Riddles* is a humorous, but simple book for beginning readers. ". . . it is not the jokes that are truly humorous, but

the wonderfully spirited watercolor illustrations. . . . [Low's] characteristic line and wash captures the right note of gaiety . . . ," noted a *Horn Book* critic.

The author-illustrator's book, *Little though I Be,* told the story of a small boy's efforts to impress his father. A critic for *Publishers Weekly* commented, "The author-illustrator presents a rarity, a modern fairytale of earthiness and illusion."

HOBBIES AND OTHER INTERESTS: Sailing.

FOR MORE INFORMATION SEE: New York Times, November 1, 1953; *Saturday Review,* November 14, 1953; Lee Kingman, editor, *Illustrators of Children's Books: 1957-1966,* Horn Book, 1968; Doris De Montreville and Donna Hill, editors, *Third Book of Junior Authors,* H. W. Wilson, 1972; *Horn Book,* December, 1974, and June, 1975; *Bulletin of the Center for Children's Books,* February, 1976.

LUEDERS, Edward (George)   1923-

PERSONAL: Surname rhymes with "readers"; born February 14, 1923, in Chicago, Ill.; son of Carl G. (a businessman) and Vera (Simpson) Lueders; married Julia Demaree, June 5, 1946; children: Kurt, Joel, Julia Anne. *Education:* Hanover College, A.B., 1947; Northwestern University, M.A., 1948; University of New Mexico, Ph.D., 1952. *Home:* 3840 San Rafael Ave., Salt Lake City, Utah 84109. *Office:* Department of English, University of Utah, Salt Lake City, Utah 84112.

EDWARD LUEDERS

See how he swims
With a swerve and a twist,
A flip of the flipper
A flick of the wrist!
■ (From *Reflections on a Gift of Watermelon Pickle* by Stephen Dunning, Edward Lueders and Hugh Smith.)

CAREER: University of New Mexico, Albuquerque, instructor, 1950-53, assistant professor of English and speech, 1953-57; Long Beach State College (now California State College at Long Beach), assistant professor, 1957-60, associate professor of English, 1960-61; Hanover College, Hanover, Ind., professor of English and chairman of department, 1961-66; University of Utah, Salt Lake City, professor of English, 1966—, chairman of department, 1969-71. Voluntary specialist in poetry for United States Information Service, and director of seminar on American poetry at American Studies Research Centre, both in India, spring, 1971; poet-in-residence, School of the Ozarks, spring, 1972; writer-in-residence, Pennsylvania State University, fall, 1972. *Military service:* U.S. Army Air Forces, 1943-46; served in China-Burma-India Theater; became sergeant. *Member:* National Council of Teachers of English, American Studies Association. *Awards, honors:* Lewis Carroll Shelf Award for *Reflections on a Gift of Watermelon Pickle . . . And Other Modern Verse,* 1968.

WRITINGS: (Editor with Jane Kluckhohn) *Through Okinawan Eyes,* University of New Mexico Press, 1951; *Carl Van Vechten and the Twenties,* University of New Mexico Press, 1955; (editor) *College and Adult Reading List of Books in Literature and the Fine Arts,* Washington Square Press, 1962; *Carl Van Vechten,* Twayne, 1965; (compiler with Stephen Dunning and Hugh L. Smith, Jr.) *Reflections on a Gift of Watermelon Pickle . . . and Other Modern Verse* (*Horn Book* honor list), Scott, Foresman, 1966; (compiler with Dunning and Smith) *Some Haystacks Don't Even Have Any Needle, and Some Other Complete Modern Poems,* Scott, Foresman, 1969; (with Brewster Ghiselin and Clarice Short) *Images and Impressions: Poems by Brewster Ghiselin, Edward Lueders, and Clarice Short,* University of Utah, 1969; *The Gang from Percy's Hotel and Other Poems,* American Studies Research Centre (Hyderabad, India), 1971; (compiler with Primus St. John) *Zero Makes Me Hungry* (poems), Lothrop, 1976; *The Clam Lake Papers: A Winter in the North Woods,* Harper, 1977. Contributor of articles, poetry, and reviews to *New Republic, College English,* and other professional journals. Editor, *Western Humanities Review,* 1969-72.

SIDELIGHTS: "Young people today are much easier to approach with poetry than in generations past.

"I think there are two main reasons. One is the wide variety of kinds of poetry available . . . poems being written and read for all kinds of reasons on all kinds of subjects in their own time.

"I think television has given us a sense of the different voices in which people speak, and each poem has its own voice. In previous times all poems had the same voice—the English teacher's voice. Now, everybody can read for himself and listen to the sounds of the poems and the person speaking.

"In compiling, freshness is the first item in considering a poem.

"We selected poems with fresh images, for one thing—images from today's world. The old themes, such as love and loneliness, anger and compassion are there. But they are set in the context of now, a now which is often wild, zany, tense, tender, stark, violent. Finally, they are formed or shaped in a rich variety of ways.

"People usually begin by thinking that all poems must rhyme. But they are thinking mostly of jingles. When they read poems in freer forms, they often are more excited by what they find there because it's likely to be closer to their sense of the way thing are and their own language.

"After all, it's harder to write a good poem in traditional form that is really a poem rather than just a mechanical rhyme. It's much more demanding—anyone can make a rhyme, but rhyme doesn't necessarily make poetry.

"It's best to write what you really want to write, rather than just filling out traditional forms.

"Good free verse puts this premium on elements of poetry that are more normal to kids—speech rhythms rather than mechanical meter; strange words, or familiar words used strangely for the fun of it, not because they suit some predetermined form.

"Kids at all ages or levels are being encouraged more and more to write creatively themselves, and it makes them better creative readers of poetry.

"As in music and painting and the other arts, nobody expects everybody to be a great artist; but we all recognize the value of everyone trying his hand at drawing, coloring or singing."

HOBBIES AND OTHER INTERESTS: Jazz piano (played occasional professional engagements, 1940-66).

FOR MORE INFORMATION SEE: Deseret News (Salt Lake City), October 26, 1977; *Milwaukee Journal,* December 18, 1977; *Milwaukee Sentinel,* January 25, 1978; *San Francisco Examiner,* March 20, 1978.

MAAS, Selve

PERSONAL: Born in Estonia; came to the United States in 1949, naturalized citizen, 1956; married Leopold Maas (deceased). *Education:* Educated in Estonia, Germany, and Washington, D.C. *Politics:* "Always for the best man." *Religion:* Lutheran. *Residence:* Maryland. *Office:* Library of Congress, Washington, D.C. 20540.

CAREER: Library of Congress, Washington, D.C., librarian, 1957—. Between 1949 and 1957, worked as housekeeper, nurse's aide, bookkeeper, cashier, and language teacher. *Member:* American-Scandinavian Association, Finlandia Foundation, Washington Opera Society.

WRITINGS: (Translator) *The Moon Painters and Other Estonian Folk Tales,* Viking, 1971; (translator with Peggy Hoffmann) *Sea Wedding and Other Stories from Estonia,* Dillon, 1977.

Author of "Stories from the Moon Painters," first broadcast on WNYC-Radio in 1972. Contributor to Estonian-language magazines.

WORK IN PROGRESS: Translating stories from German and Estonian into English.

SIDELIGHTS: "I like to observe the curious behavior of human beings. Ambitions: Few. Hopes: Fewer. Expectations: None. Principal pleasure: Living."

HOBBIES AND OTHER INTERESTS: Travel (Europe, Canada, U.S., Bahamas, Puerto Rico), needlepoint, weekends at her cabin in the Blue Ridge Mountains of Virginia.

FOR MORE INFORMATION SEE: Horn Book, October, 1971.

They raised the ladder to the heavens and waited for the moon to make its appearance. ■ (From *The Moon Painters* by Selve Maas. Illustrated by Laszlo Gal.)

The castle was once the stronghold of the clan MacMorden. According to the legend, Callum, chief of the clan MacMorden, and Duncan, his personal piper . . . fought to the very last man defending the castle against the attack of invaders from across the North Sea. ■ (From *Island in the Mist* by Ellen Jane MacLeod. Jacket illustration by Arthur Fitzsimmons.)

MacLEOD, Ellen Jane (Anderson) 1916-
(Ella Anderson)

PERSONAL: Born May 17, 1916, in Glasgow, Scotland; brought to United States by parents in 1925; returned to Scotland in 1951; daughter of Francis (a traffic manager) and Mary Rae (Lawrie) Anderson; married Donald M. Mac-Leod (now a free-lance journalist), December 15, 1953. *Education:* Attended schools in Scotland and United States. *Religion:* Protestant. *Home:* 12 Montgomery Pl., Buchlyvie, Stirlingshire, Scotland FK8 3NF.

CAREER: Early dancing career ended by automobile accident, turned to singing, then library work; County Library, Vancouver, Wash., assistant, 1943-50; author, mainly of youth books, 1955—. *Member:* Society of Authors.

WRITINGS: The Seven Wise Owls, Pickering & Inglis, 1956; *Alaska Star,* Pickering & Inglis, 1957; *Adventures on the Lazy N,* Pickering & Inglis, 1957; *The Ski Lodge Mystery,* Moody, 1957; *The Crooked Signpost,* Pickering & Inglis, 1957; *The Hawaiian Lei,* Pickering & Inglis, 1958; *Jo-Jo,* Pickering & Inglis, 1959; *Mystery Gorge,* Pickering & Inglis, 1959; *The Mystery of the Tolling Bell,* Pickering & Inglis, 1960; *The Fourth Window,* Cowman, 1961; *The Vanishing Light,* Pickering & Inglis, 1961; *The Talking Mountain,* Pickering & Inglis, 1962; *Orchids for a Rose* (romantic novel), Arcadia House, 1963; *Island in the Mist,* Bethany, 1965; *Stranger in the Glen,* Arcadia, 1969; *Trouble at the Circle 'G',* Pickering & Inglis, 1970; *The Broken Melody,* Lenox Hill, 1970; *The Kelpie Ledge,* Lenox Hill, 1972; *Isle of Shadows,* Lenox Hill, 1974.

Scripts for British Broadcasting Corp. include "One Stormy Night" and a play, "Something Fishy"; has novelized picture scripts and written serials.

WORK IN PROGRESS: A radio serial about the American West; career book for girls (singing).

SIDELIGHTS: "Although I was born in the large city of Glasgow, Scotland, it wasn't until I came to the small western town of Vancouver, Washington that my vivid imagination really took hold. There could be no wider difference between the bustling city life and the quiet slower pace into which I was flung. I remember telling adventure stories to my Scottish cousins on Saturday nights when they visited us, and always broke off at an exciting point until resuming it the following Saturday. I often wonder where I got the plots from but they must have been interesting for my cousins never missed a Saturday visit.

"I was eight years of age when I moved to America and from that day on found American school life both stimulating and exciting, in such deep contrast to the more strongly disciplined school life in Glasgow. I loved every minute of it. Being an only child in a neighborhood where there were not many children, my playmates were the characters in the many books I read. Each book became a personal friend.

"When we were living in New York, I used to sit in the dark and look out at the apartment house across the street, trying to imagine the families behind the curtained windows and making up stories in my mind of what they were like and their relationship to one another.

"My parents and I traveled several times across America and those vivid memories of places, people and happenings

ELLEN JANE MACLEOD

were used later as background to my books. Today, my novels for older girls still have American characters but in a Scottish background.

"I am extremely lucky to have a husband whose work is similar to mine, being a free-lance journalist. His encouragement has often kept me going whenever I've had a story or play which wouldn't move. We work mostly at night and well into the wee sma' hours. Living in the lovely Loch Lomond area and with the mountains, or bens, as backgrounds we can relax and discuss plots and dialogue."

MAHY, Margaret 1936-

PERSONAL: Born March 21, 1936, in Whakatane, New Zealand; daughter of Francis George (a builder) and May (a teacher; maiden name, Penlington) Mahy; children: Penelope Helen, Bridget Frances. *Education:* University of New Zealand, B.A., 1958. *Politics:* "Anarchist." *Religion:* "Humanist." *Home address:* R.D. 1, Lyttelton, New Zealand. *Agent:* Mrs. H. H. Watts, 10 Waterside Plaza, Apt. 37F, New York, N.Y. 10010.

CAREER: Petone Public Library, Petone, New Zealand, assistant librarian, 1958-59; School Library Service, Christchurch, New Zealand, librarian in charge, 1967-76; Canterbury Public Library, Christchurch, New Zealand, children's librarian, 1976—. *Member:* New Zealand Library Association. *Awards, honors:* Esther Glenn Medal from New Zealand Library Association, 1969, for *A Lion in the Meadow,* and 1973, for *The First Margaret Mahy Story Book.*

WRITINGS—For children: *A Lion in the Meadow,* F. Watts, 1969; *A Dragon of an Ordinary Family,* F. Watts, 1969; *Pillycock's Shop,* F. Watts, 1969; *The Procession,* F. Watts, 1969; *Mrs. Discombobulos,* F. Watts, 1969; *The Princess and the Clown,* F. Watts, 1971; *The Railway Engine and the Hairy Brigands,* Dent, 1972; *The First Margaret Mahy Story Book,* Dent, 1972; *The Man Whose*

One day a small, quite ordinary boy, called Robert was coming home from school. He looked over his shoulder and there was a hippopotamus following him. ■ (From *The Boy Who Was Followed Home* by Margaret Mahy. Pictures by Steven Kellogg.)

Mother Was a Pirate, Atheneum, 1972; *The Boy with Two Shadows,* F. Watts, 1972; *The Second Margaret Mahy Story Book,* Dent, 1973; *Rooms to Let,* F. Watts, 1974; *The Witch in the Cherry Tree,* Parents' Magazine Press, 1974; *Clancy's Cabin,* Dent, 1974; *The Bus under the Leaves,* Dent, 1974; *The Rare Spotted Birthday Party,* F. Watts, 1974; *Stepmother,* F. Watts, 1974; *The Third Margaret Mahy Story Book,* Dent, 1975; *Ultra-Violet Catastrophe,* Parents' Magazine Press, 1975; *New Zealand: Yesterday and Today,* F. Watts, 1975; *David's Witch Doctor,* F. Watts, 1975; *Leaf Magic,* Parents' Magazine Press, 1976; *The Boy Who Was Followed Home,* F. Watts, •1976; *The*

MARGARET MAHY

Wind between the Stars, Dent, 1976; *The Pirate Uncle,* Dent, 1977; *The Nonstop Nonsense Book,* Dent, 1977. Author of scripts for "A Land Called Happy," a series on TV II-New Zealand.

SIDELIGHTS: "I have been interested in writing children's stories for many years. There are certain sorts of story and certain uses of language which seem most appropriate in stories intended for children. It is almost as if there are certain images left over, insufficiently assimilated during one's own childhood. All stories, even the simplest ones, seem to be little pieces of biography even if what one is recounting is only one's childhood games and dreams."

MANGURIAN, David 1938-

PERSONAL: Born July 18, 1938, in Baltimore, Md.; son of George Nishan (an aeronautical engineer) and Margaret (Barton) Mangurian; married Luz Maria Paltan (a biology professor), August 2, 1971; children: Christina Victoria. *Education:* Pomona College, B.A., 1961; Columbia University, M.S., 1966. *Home address:* 121 Hubinger St., New Haven, Conn. 06511.

CAREER: Ventura Star-Free Press, Ventura, Calif., reporter, 1963-65; *Oxnard Press-Courier,* Oxnard, Calif., deskman and reporter, summer, 1966; free-lance writer and photographer in Central and South America, 1967-73; WPLG-Television, Miami, Fla., television news reporter, 1973-74; free-lance writer and photographer, 1974—. Associate producer of documentary film, "Enriched Baloney and Homemade Bread," 1970.

EXHIBITIONS—Photographs: "Ten Years in America Latina" (one man show), Motal Custom Darkrooms Gallery, New York, N.Y., May-August, 1976; "Lito the Shoeshine Boy" (based on the book), Boston Children's Museum, Boston, Mass., October, 1976. *Awards, honors:* Pulitzer traveling fellowship, 1966, from Columbia University; *Lito the Shoeshine Boy* received all of the following: Best Books of 1975 by *School Library Journal,* Notable 1975 Children's Trade Book in the Field of Social Studies by the National Council for the Social Studies, Kirkus Choice for 1975, 1976 Children's Book Showcase Title by the Children's Book Council.

WRITINGS: Lito: The Shoeshine Boy (with author's photographs), Four Winds, 1975. Photographs have been used in many text books, especially Spanish language and social studies-geography. Articles and photographs have appeared in magazines and newspapers in the United States, Canada, and England, including *Life, Clipper, Signature, Medical World News, Life en Espanol, Time, The New York Times, Business Week, Saturday Review, Copley News Service, Newsday, Toronto Star* and *Manchester Guardian.*

WORK IN PROGRESS: A book about a family of Indians living on the Altiplano near Lake Titicaca, Peru, with own photographs; a photographic and very different Mother Goose.

SIDELIGHTS: "I have worked as a . . . folk singer and bluegrass musician, aircraft factory worker, peach picker. . . . Folk music I recorded in Arkansas in 1958 was later issued by Folkways Records as 'Music from the Ozarks.' I recorded an album of bluegrass music with a group including my brother in England, and one track on an album by blues singer Wade Walton for Prestige Records under the pseudonym 'Memphis Mango.'

"I have spent much of my time (now almost half my life) traveling to see how other people live. . . . I once traveled with a friend by canoe across the United States, paddling 1,300 miles down rivers from Denver to Memphis in three months. I have been traveling over ten years now in Mexico, Central and South America. I traveled by airplane, helicopter, train, boat, hydrofoil, bus, truck, car, dugout canoe, horse, burro, and foot accumulating nearly 200,000 miles and 50,000 photographs. In 1969, after the so-called Soccer War between Honduras and El Salvador, I was jailed twice in El Salvador and finally deported for allegedly being a spy. The Salvadoran government later apologized and invited me back.

"Two people were most responsible for *Lito* becoming a book. Originally I photographed the street life of Lito as a photo-story assignment for UNICEF. It was an unusual assignment for UNICEF to begin with, because, usually, UNICEF wants its programs, not specific people, photographed. But my assignment was simply to photograph the life of a child who had to work and could not go to school.

"UNICEF's photo editor, Jean Speiser, had more vision than most photo editors. When she got my material—photos and a five or six page text in Lito's own words—she saw it as a book and sent the material on to John Day, publishers.

DAVID MANGURIAN

Jean herself never did much with the material for UNICEF, except that there is one photograph of Lito on display with others of children at the United Nations (permanently, I think).

"The person who formed my material into book form was Mary Walsh, a former editor at John Day. She personally wanted the book published and had John Day pay for about fifty 8x10 prints and helped me with the text. Her greatness was that she guided me, didn't direct me. In the end, however, her business office turned the idea down as not profitable. I have since learned that Mary Walsh was extremely angry over the decision, because she wanted American kids to read about kids like Lito. But she lost, as far as John Day is concerned.

"The business office at John Day, it turned out, made a mistake. Having turned my photo-story into book form, naturally I couldn't let the idea drop. I sent the manuscript and pictures to several other publishers and about the fifth try, editor Judith Whipple at Four Winds Press, gave me a contract. Judy, fortunately for me, had been brought up in Latin America and has a genuine feeling for Latin Americans. She wanted to make *Lito* a quality book, and they used good paper and a good modern layout which later won us the awards.

"A word about how I work: before I got the assignment to do *Lito,* I had been traveling in Central America and writing newspaper articles for the Copley News Service and sometimes directly for newspapers. But I had been thinking about trying to work from tape recorded interviews (I prefer to call

them conversations, because my interviews are usually quite free) with ordinary people in Latin America who don't themselves have the opportunity to communicate directly with Americans. There is something wrong about Americans traveling abroad and coming back to write their impressions of what they saw and experienced instead of the people in those countries writing about themselves. The problem is, many poor people in developing countries cannot even write their own language, and certainly not English.

"So what I become is both a catalyst and a creator. I tape record two or three hours of conversation, then have it transcribed. Then I retype the transcript in short pieces on the right side of the paper and code each bit and piece with a heading word, like 'Breakfast' or 'Shining shoes' or 'Lito's shack.' I code each bit and piece, also, with the original transcript page number, so I can get back to the original if I later have a problem with the translation or meaning. Then I xerox the retyped transcript. Then I cut the xeroxes apart and paste all the bits and pieces with the same headings on blank pages. I use scotch tape or spray glue. I then xerox all that, to eliminate the tape.

"I try to structure my text by putting the different subject headings in some order. Then I begin to write, in Spanish, of course. I do two or three drafts in Spanish, and if I get it cut down short enough, I then translate what I have into English. Once in English, I have to cut further and smooth out some of the roughness caused by the translation.

"In some cases, when the subject tells the same anecdote several times, I will combine parts of each telling in my final

(From *Lito, the Shoeshine Boy* by Lito Chirinos, as told to and translated by David Mangurian. Photos by David Mangurian.)

story, sometimes even joining part of a sentence from one telling with another part from a different telling. But every word I use was actually spoken by the subject. What I do is give his words structure and form his anecdotes and thoughts into a readable story. Because the words are first person, they have more impact than if I were to write about them.

"My photographs are also honest. I have not yet resorted to darkroom tricks or double negatives to create something that I did not really photograph. That is not to say that I don't try to create with my camera, because I do. Sometimes I just record action. But sometimes there are specific pictures I know I want, and then I shoot two or three rolls to try to get the effect I want.

"Once I have shot the pictures, the real fun begins—deciding which pictures are best and laying them out in sequence. The process is much like editing a film. Pictures give the text that extra dimension and strength. But I do not view pictures as illustrations for the text, or as more important than the text. The text and pictures are wedded together and become a unit. As pictures give the text more strength, the text gives the pictures more strength.

"When I select which photographs to use, I do not pick pictures I think children will like—I pick what I think are the best photographs. American children are exposed to so many good pictures and good graphics in magazines and movies and television that you don't have to be conservative in the layout of a book and the use of pictures in it. I had to fight some with my publisher for some of the things we did in *Lito*—particularly in using sixteen frames from a contact sheet showing Lito playing with his best friend, Churro. I wanted the sprocket holes and frame numbers to show. I wanted kids to see that it was film and that the sequence showed was as filmed. I won out and kids love it.

"The only types of photographs I feel strongly that children will not accept are abstracts and arty photos used for arty effect. Children are too concerned with discovering the reality of the world they were born into to be attracted by abstract pictures. They don't relate to abstracts. As for arty photos, they should not be used just for 'effect' in any book. At least not in my work. Each photo is an integral part of the book, and if it does not add to the story it should not appear. In fact, everything (pictures or words) that does not help drive home the main point of the story should be edited out. This fundamental rule of strong editing I learned at the Columbia University Graduate School of Journalism.

"I am fluent in Spanish, conversant in Portuguese. Otherwise it would be impossible to do the kind of work from tape recordings I do and be honest and accurate."

HOBBIES AND OTHER INTERESTS: Music (plays country, folk and blues on guitar and mandolin), collecting Latin American folk music, collecting Latin American folk art, swimming and body surfing.

MARINO, Dorothy Bronson 1912-

PERSONAL: Born November 12, 1912, in Oakland, Ore.; daughter of a teacher-turned-bookstore owner; married John Marino; children: Nina. *Education:* Attended the University of Kansas and the Art Students League, New York City. *Residence:* Brooklyn, N.Y.

DOROTHY MARINO

CAREER: Author and illustrator of books for children. *Awards, honors:* Helen Dean Fish Award for *Little Angela and Her Puppy.*

WRITINGS—All self-illustrated: *Little Angela and Her Puppy,* Lippincott, 1954; *The Song of the Pine Tree Forest,* Lippincott, 1955; *That's My Favorite,* Lippincott, 1956; *Edward and the Boxes,* Lippincott, 1957; *Good-Bye Thunderstorm,* Lippincott, 1958; *Where Are the Mothers?,* Lippincott, 1959; *Fuzzy and Alfred,* Watts, 1961; *Good Night Georgie,* Dial, 1961; *Now That You Are 6,* Association Press, 1963; *Moving Day,* Dial, 1963.

"Buzzy Bear" series, published by Watts; all self-illustrated: *Buzzy Bear Goes South,* 1961; *. . . and the Rainbow,* 1962; *. . . in the Garden,* 1963; *. . . Goes Camping,* 1964; *Buzzy Bear's Busy Day,* 1965; *. . . Winter Party,* 1967; *. . . First Day at School,* 1970.

Illustrator: Nancy W. Smith, *Ghostly Trio,* Coward-McCann, 1954; Marie H. Bloch, *Tony of the Ghost Towns,* Coward-McCann, 1956; Helen D. Olds, *Miss Hattie and the Monkey,* Follett, 1958; Myra B. Brown, *Company's Coming,* Watts, 1959 (published in England as *We're Having a Party Tonight,* Heinemann, 1961); M. B. Brown, *First Night Away from Home,* Watts, 1960; M. B. Brown, *Benjy's Blanket,* Watts, 1962.

SIDELIGHTS: Dorothy Marino became interested in illustrating while studying art. Her illustrations are usually two colors, for which she prepares separations on acetate.

Little Angela and Her Puppy was Dorothy Marino's first book. A *New York Times* critic wrote, "Little children will enjoy this short story and its many pictures of someone as small as themselves. They will understand Angela's longing for a playmate and will have a fine feeling of satisfaction when she finds one at last." The *Chicago Tribune* said that the, "Story and pictures make Angela so lovable and appealing in her lonely and joyful moods that she will seem very real to other little girls."

Next the teacher had some of the bear children do arithmetic problems on the blackboard.
Buzzy couldn't do that.
He crouched down even more in his chair.
■ (From *Buzzy Bear's First Day at School* by Dorothy Marino. Illustrated by the author.)

The reviews of *Song of the Pine Tree Forest* were mixed. *Bookmark* called it, "A sensitive story in pictures and rhymes about a little boy who got lost from his brother and sister on a mountainside. Both the text and illustrations reflect a deep feeling for outdoor life." "A charming title, attractive pictures of mountain, forest, and animals," commented *Saturday Review*, "and a gentle rhythm in the telling of the story are the assets of this picture book for very small children." On the other hand, *Library Journal* noted, "Though there is a simple charm about the book, it lacks the essence of satisfaction with which all picture books should be endowed."

FOR MORE INFORMATION SEE: New York Times, April 11, 1954; *Bookmark,* November, 1955; *Saturday Review,* September 17, 1955; Bertha Mahony Miller and others, compilers, *Illustrators of Children's Books, 1946-1956,* Horn Book, 1958; Lee Kingman and others, compilers, *Illustrators of Children's Books, 1957-1966,* Horn Book, 1968.

PAULINE MARK

MARK, Pauline (Dahlin) 1913-
(Polly Mark)

PERSONAL: Born August 11, 1913, in Mayville, N.Y.; daughter of Charles John and Nettie (Dearing) Dahlin; married Herman John Mark (now a teacher), April 16, 1934; children: Charles B., Kathleen A. *Education:* Clifton Springs Sanitarium and Clinic, R.N., 1934; additional study at University of Rochester, Syracuse University, and three colleges of the State University of New York. *Politics:* Republican. *Religion:* Protestant. *Home:* 381 Palena Blvd., North Port, Fla. *Agent:* Kay Brion, 116 East 19th St., New York, N.Y. 10003.

CAREER: Served with her husband, under Methodist Board of Missions, in Singapore and Sarawak, 1950-55, teaching half of this time at a jungle mission school in Sarawak and conducting a small clinic for mothers and children; Chautauqua (N.Y.) Board of Education, school nurse-teacher, 1956-58; Penfield (N.Y.) Board of Education, junior high school nurse and teacher, 1958-72, now retired. *Member:* New York State Teachers Association, Penfield Education Association (secretary, 1965-66).

*WRITINGS—*All under name Polly Mark: *Tani,* McKay, 1964; *The Way of the Wind,* McKay, 1965; *Seaview,* Thomas Bouregy, in press.

WORK IN PROGRESS: The Jade Turtle, a story set in Singapore.

SIDELIGHTS: Around fifty native children lived with the Marks at the mission school at Kapit, Sarawak. The "small clinic" that Pauline Mark once held there has grown into the modern institution, Christ Hospital.

MARKS, Stan(ley) 1929-
(Martin King)

PERSONAL: Born April 25, 1929, in London, England; taken to Australia at the age of two; son of Sidney (in clothing business) and Sally (Bernstein) Marks; married Eve Maas (a designer of toys), July 15, 1951; children: Lee (daughter), Peter. *Education:* Attended University of Melbourne. *Home:* 348 Bambra Rd., Caulfield, Melbourne, Victoria, Australia 3162. *Office:* Australian Tourist Commission, St. Kilda Rd., Melbourne, Victoria, Australia 3004.

CAREER: Author for adults and young people. Began working for an Australian country newspaper at the age of seventeen; later a reporter and theater critic for *Melbourne World,* Melbourne, Australia; reporter for newspapers in England, 1951, and in Montreal and Toronto, Canada, 1952-53; correspondent for Australian newspapers in New York, N.Y., 1954-55; returned to Australia to become public relations officer of Trans Australia Airlines, 1965-67; Australian Broadcasting Commission, Melbourne, public relations supervisor, 1958-64; Australian Tourist Commission, Melbourne, public relations manager, 1968—. *Member:* Australian Journalists Association, Australian Society of Authors, Australian Fellowship of Writers.

WRITINGS: God Gave You One Face (novel), R. Hale, 1964; *Is She Fair Dinkum?* (scripts), 1968; (author of text; photographs by Brian McArdle) *Graham Is an Aboriginal Boy* (juvenile), Methuen, 1968, Hastings House, 1969; *Rarua Lives in Papua New Guinea,* Methuen, 1972; *Animal Olympics,* Wren (Australia), 1972; *Fifty Years of Achievement,* Maxwells Ltd. (Australia), 1974; *K'Tut Lives in Indonesia,* Methuen, 1976; *Boy of Indonesia,* Methuen, 1976. Work included in *Walkabout's Book of Best Australian Articles,* Lansdowne Press, 1968. Writer of three one-act plays, stories for two long-playing children's records, "Animal Olympics" and "Montague the Mouse Who Sailed with Captain Cook," and of a song with George Kraus, "Dreaming in the Outback." Author of television play "When A Wife Strikes," 1970, stage version written, 1972; writes nightly cartoon "Ms" for *Melbourne Herald, Auckland Star* and other papers. Contributor of feature stories and articles to Australian and overseas journals; some of the articles were published under the pseudonym Martin King.

WORK IN PROGRESS: A novel, *Who Speaks for Tommy?;* a three-act farce, "Everybody Out."

SIDELIGHTS: "I began writing at the old age of twelve with letters and small items in national journals. I managed to get out of school gardening by telling other classes stories, making them up as I went along. I was always, as I am today, fascinated by imaginery characters and creating people (the subject of where do ideas come from has always been one of my pet topics) and meeting real people and living with them. This is how I wandered into journalism, and reported the gamut of newspaper rounds around the world, including the first Ontario Stratford festival, and sat on the side of major and minor events. I was known for human interest stories, including ones about animals.

The first events are soon over. ■ (From *Animal Olympics* by Stan Marks. Illustrated by Jeff Hook.)

"My first play written at seventeen, was a one-act called "A Common Man at U.N.O." which gained third prize in a Brisbane, Australia, theatre competition. I was, and still am, an idealist. My friends call me a Don Quixote and have even bought me a print of the Picasso work. But it gets more difficult as one sees the world we live in, and the way lives, groups and whole nations are manipulated, bargained away and treated like pebbles. I keep saying more people should be willing to live for causes than die for them—sometimes it is harder to go fighting mentally too.

"My first novel was *God Gave You One Face*. I asked my wife at dinner one night, after being told a guest had been in the German S.S. and my wife, as a child, in a camp, what would you have done if he had been one of your guards? She replied 'Probably killed him—I don't really know.' I replied she could have then been charged with murder and who knows what would have happened . . . this led to my novel, dealing with the battle between legality and morality. People tell me it would still make a good film. I'm waiting.

"Researching my 'Children's Everywhere' books for Methuen and Hastings House have been amongst the most rewarding moments (mentally) of my life, knowing that I was contributing to a series popular the world over, and for

books used on schools' reading lists, as my first two are and hopefully my third, will be.

"One actually follows the youngsters about and does what they do, eat their foods, as I did in Central Australia (with aborigines), in New Guinea and Indonesia; especially in a Balinese village sampling the Hindu life including watching a cremation ceremony, youngsters of ten and eleven painting better than many whose works sell at inflated prices in Australia (and who take themselves too seriously as do many adult artists), looking for food in the Australian desert, sailing New Guinea style, and wandering through remote forests after being warned that evil spirits were lurking amid them. Learning new children's games, swimming a different-style and singing new tunes.

"These were the factors which showed me how cultures differed, and how I must TRY and tell other youngsters and, through them, their parents how different people live around the world and no one race has a right to dominate others or claim what is right or superior for the entire globe. I want adults to discuss the books and cultures with their youngsters. But, it has made me feel that we should be one world, in a federal form, with one world government (no, not as the United Nation runs) and separate states—like the United

STAN MARKS

and this includes both male-female on an equal level. Yes, I am for women's equality, but also for people's equality. I'm appalled at how cheap human life (in all its levels) has become world-wide, in large so-called sophisticated cities and smaller so-called unsophisticated ones. Life is made up of individuals. I subscribe to Tolstoy's theory that in the end all a person needs is six feet (or the right size) so we should stop thinking we are each individual gods, with the right to power, whether mental or physical, over others. I like to think, or hope, my writings foster better understanding, and help show that unfortunately we tend to look at things as we are rather than as things are. We need to change for all our sakes. Life is a matter of geography, environment and family, and it's time we realised this, and how luck, or whatever you want to call it, plays such a key role in determining our lives and views. I also subscribe to the theory that one can best avoid criticism and becoming involved by being nothing, doing nothing and saying nothing. But then, the same ones will be the first to complain when they get nothing, forgetting all those who have made sacrifices throughout centuries so they can enjoy life and freedom, which is being whittled away today. Don't opt out and expect others to keep you—live your life, but don't expect others to pay you for being nothing—be true to yourself!''

Stan Marks has a strong interest in arts and youth and promoting better understanding between nations. As early as 1951 he suggested that an All-British Commonwealth Arts Festival should be held regularly; later he began urging that a Youth Council be established at the United Nations to get the world's young closer to policy making. A Commonwealth Arts Festival eventually was held, and the Youth Council idea brought him an invitation to the 1960 White House Conference on Youth. He also has advocated an ''Ideas Bank'' for international peace, where people might send suggestions to be sifted for possible discussion (''just one good idea might save that button being pushed''). His books reflect those concerns and his interest in aborigines. While researching *Graham Is an Aboriginal Boy* he lived for ten days with the Arunta tribe near Alice Springs in the Northern Territory, learned to hunt with a boomerang and to enjoy a diet of bush bananas and figs.

States or Australia or Canada, with a central government but individual states or provinces. Otherwise what hope for peoplekind? We can learn from the various community set ups of the 750 New Guinea language groups or Temple communities of Bali, as I did.

''Where do I get my general ideas? Who knows—they just come. *Animal Olympics* while 'talking' to an otter at the zoo—my friends claim I really do talk to animals. ''Montague Mouse'' after retracing Captain Cook's original voyage up Australia's East Coast and, as with the nightly cartoon strip, from the way people act (including my own doings) and what they tell me and life itself which is the greatest drama of all—better than television, the movies or anything. I personally learn a great deal from the innocence of children. One can discover so much by being involved in life on all levels, even in their own community, and realise it's better than the general—but not all artificial world of television and films. In many ways, it is as though adults, not so many young people, have dropped out of life and become spectators, especially of violence. I am more and more finding that young people are taking up today's issues, relating with them (or discussing issues) and discovering.

''When I am asked about writing, I tell people to just sit down in front of a piece of paper and begin to write ... there's no other way. You might even surprise yourself. And it's more rewarding than words can describe—fancy a writer saying that.

''I would like to think my adult and young peoples works interchange and are really for all ages. The young will read adult works and adults will read younger works, and especially with younger folk—perhaps in this way help to bridge any generation gap and help better understand tomorrow's men and women, and above all, our leaders and planners,

MASON, George Frederick 1904-

PERSONAL: Born October 18, 1904, in Princeton, Mass.; married Dorothy M. Brooks; married second wife, Caroline; children: (first marriage) Cynthia Fay, George. *Education:* Attended Worcester Art Museum School and Clark University. *Residence:* Princeton, Mass.

CAREER: Worked as a political cartoonist for a newspaper; American Museum of Natural History, New York City, employed as a staff member, later became associate curator of its Department of Education; author and illustrator.

WRITINGS—All self-illustrated: *The Bear Family,* Morrow, 1960; *The Deer Family,* Morrow, 1962; *Ranch in the Rockies,* Morrow, 1964; *The Wildlife of North America,* Hastings House, 1966; *The Moose Group,* Hastings House, 1968.

''Animal'' series; all self-illustrated; all published by Morrow: *Animal Tracks,* 1943; ... *Homes,* 1947; ... *Sounds,* 1948; ... *Weapons,* 1949; ... *Tools,* 1951; ... *Clothing,* 1955; ... *Tails,* 1958; ... *Habits,* 1959; ... *Baggage,* 1961; ... *Teeth,* 1965; ... *Appetites,* 1966; ... *Vision,* 1968; ... *Feet,* 1970.

Most bears like to eat fish, and the black bear is no exception. ■ (From *The Bear Family* by George F. Mason. Illustrated by the author.)

Illustrator: Dorothy Stall, *Chukchi Hunter,* Morrow, 1946; Ivan E. Green and Alice Bromwell, *Woody, the Little Wood Duck,* Abelard, 1953; Joseph Wharton Lippincott, *Bun, a Wild Rabbit,* revised edition, Lippincott, 1953; J. W. Lippincott, *Little Red, the Fox,* revised edition, Lippincott, 1953; J. W. Lippincott, *Long Horn, Leader of the Deer,* revised edition, Lippincott, 1953; J. W. Lippincott, *Gray Squirrel,* revised edition, Lippincott, 1954; J. W. Lippincott, *Striped Coat, the Skunk,* revised edition, Lippincott, 1954; Marie H. Bloch, *Dinosaurs,* Coward, 1955; J. W. Lippincott, *Persimmon Jim, the Possum,* revised edition, Lippincott, 1955; Miriam Schlein, *Oomi, the New Hunter,* Abelard, 1955; Genevieve Gullahorn, *Zigger, the Pet Chameleon,* Abelard, 1956; Elizabeth Greenleaf, *Pricky, a Pet Porcupine,* Oddo, 1965; Dorothy Edwards Shuttlesworth, *The Wildlife of South America,* Hastings House, 1966, revised edition, 1974; D. E. Shuttlesworth, *The Wildlife of Australia and New Zealand,* Hastings House, 1967.

SIDELIGHTS: "Experience in the American Museum of Natural History gave me a good foundation for writing about animals for children. I realized the need for interpreting scientific wording into simple language that children could understand. Ideas for books came from observations of wildlife during museum expeditions in Alaska and Canada to study and collect specimens for constructing habitat groups in the museum.

"I enjoy illustrating my books, but writing is a tedious labor, probably due to the method I have of writing and rewriting a manuscript three or four times."

Mason's career was influenced by the farm environment he grew up in as a child and the contrasting city life he experienced as an adult. The author-illustrator's first book, *Animal Tracks,* identified the prints of forty-four common North American animals. A critic for the *New York Times* observed, "Boy Scouts or any young naturalist . . . will find this book useful and inspiring."

Animal Homes was Mason's second book about the unique characteristics of wildlife creatures. "An interesting and easily understood account of the native American animals and the homes that they make for themselves," commented a critic for *Saturday Review of Literature.*

In *Animal Weapons* Mason discussed the various devices used by animals to protect themselves in combat. A reviewer for the *New York Times* noted, "It does not matter at all whether the nature-lover is 10 years old or 60. The youngest will have no difficulty with this author's clear, terse prose and practical line drawings, while the mature reader will be humbled to realize how little he has understood the mechanism of animal weapons."

The success of Mason's nature books was partly due to his illustrations. The author-illustrator's drawings were generally done in pen-and-ink or dry brush. His book, *Animal Clothing,* studied the different structures and functions of the outer coverings of animals. In a review for the *Christian Science Monitor,* Elizabeth Yates wrote, "Mr. Mason's drawings are as informative as his text. . . ." A critic for *Saturday Review* commented, "Almost as valuable as the text are the line drawings which range from a comparison of a chrysalis with an Egyptian mummy to the reason why a frog's color turns from green to yellow."

In *Animal Habits* the museum curator studied the psychological reasoning behind animal behavior. "George Mason refuses to yield to misguided sentimentalism. . . . His book, is, therefore scientifically accurate, as befits his record of many years with the American Museum of Natural History," observed a reviewer for the *Chicago Sunday Tribune.*

Animal Feet is Mason's latest book. In reviewing the book, a critic for *Scientific American* commented, "Comparative anatomy, with its message of evolution, was filled with excitements 100 years ago in the hands of Thomas Huxley. Mason restores that quality in [*Animal Feet*]. . . . The book

GEORGE FREDERICK MASON

is personal in tone with the authentic ring of direct observation.''

FOR MORE INFORMATION SEE: New York Times, October 10, 1943; *Saturday Review of Literature,* November 15, 1947; *New York Times,* October 23, 1949; *Christian Science Monitor,* November 10, 1955; *Saturday Review,* November 12, 1955; *Chicago Sunday Tribune,* November 1, 1959; Lee Kingman, editor, *Illustrators of Children's Books: 1957-1966,* Horn Book, 1968; *Scientific American,* December, 1971.

MAYER, Ann M(argaret)   1938-

PERSONAL: Born August 5, 1938, in Schenectady, N.Y.; daughter of Harry F. (an electrical engineer) and Mary (Insley) Mayer. *Education:* Mount Holyoke College, B.A. (with distinction), 1960; Harvard University, Ed.M., 1964; State University of New York College at Geneseo, M.L.S., 1975. *Home:* 5 Stenwick Dr., Churchville, N.Y. 14428. *Office:* Fairbanks Road School, 175 Fairbanks Rd., Churchville, N.Y. 14428.

CAREER: Minneapolis-Honeywell, Wellesley Hills, Mass., technical writer, 1960-61; Boston Children's Hospital, Boston, Mass., director of out-patient rheumatic fever clinic, 1961-63; teacher of second grade, Medford, Mass., 1964-65; Churchville-Chili Central Schools, Churchville, N.Y., teacher of second and third grades, 1965—. *Member:* American Library Association, National League of American Pen

ANN MARGARET MAYER

Women, National.Education Association, Save the Children Federation, Friends of the Osborne and Lillian Smith Collections.

WRITINGS—All biographies for children: *Dag Hammarskjold: The Peacemaker,* Creative Educational Society, 1974; *Two Worlds of Beatrix Potter,* Creative Educational Society, 1974; *Sir Frederick Banting: Doctor Against Diabetes,* Creative Educational Society, 1974. Contributor of biographies for children to periodicals, including *Adventure, Highlights for Children,* and *Whenever Whatever.*

SIDELIGHTS: "From the time I was a child I have enjoyed writing. My greatest stimulus came at the age of fourteen when I won the first non-fiction award for a story submitted to the *American Girl's* 'By You' page.

''I first considered writing a children's book when I began teaching elementary school and found a lack of biographies appropriate for the primary grades. I was unable to pursue my interest until I applied for and received a year's paid sabbatical from the Churchville-Chili School District. During that year I traveled, researched and wrote my three biographies. In my work with children it has given me great pleasure to share my books and writing experiences with them.''

HOBBIES AND OTHER INTERESTS: Traveling and music.

McCLINTOCK, Theodore   1902-1971

PERSONAL: Born in 1902; married Lillian Lustig (an editor). *Education:* Graduated from Harvard University, 1924. *Home:* Croton-on-Hudson, N.Y.

CAREER: Author, editor, and translator. Editor for Allyn & Bacon, F. S. Crofts, and W. S. Freeman, all publishers.

WRITINGS: The Underwater Zoo, Vanguard Press, 1938; *Tank Menagerie: Adventures of the Little-Game Hunters of the Fenway,* Abelard-Schuman, 1954; *Animal Close-Ups* (a Junior Literary Guild selection), Abelard-Schuman, 1958;

(translator from the German and adapter) Hedwig Wimmer, *Maha and Her Donkey,* Rand McNally, 1965; (translator from the German and adapter) Rudolf Neumann, *The Very Special Animal* (translation from *Die Geschichte von dem Ganz Besonderen Tier;* illustrated by Sigrid Heuck), Rand McNally, 1965; (editor) Elizabeth C. Gaskell, *Cranford,* University of London Press, 1966.

SIDELIGHTS: Theodore McClintock's book, *The Underwater Zoo* was a clear and lively account for children of collecting and observing small creatures which live in the water. A *Horn Book* critic described it as, "An unusual book with a style so limpidly clear that the reader actually feels a part of all that is done and seen and the revelation and mystery of tiny everyday life is before us." *Library Journal* added, "The narrative is in the form of a journal which permits a lively, informal style marked with an enthusiasm which should be contagious. Although this is a new treatment of the subject matter, in its suggestion for an inexpensive, but fascinating hobby it suggests Mannix' Backyard Zoo."

Tank Menagerie: Adventures of the Little-Game Hunters of the Fenway is a retelling, in fictional form, of *The Underwater Zoo.* The *New York Herald Tribune* commented, ". . . it would have been better if not fictionalized, but the idea it carries out should interest many children under twelve who are fascinated by snails and tadpoles, and other tiny pond creatures." The *New York Times* added, ". . . such treatment is more of a hindrance than a help in snaring the interest of older children. Solid pages of conversation between a boy and a girl about damsel-fly nymphs, scuds, snails, and tadpoles are soon boring. Youngsters who have their own tanks and an avid interest in the subject may find the story fascinating, but most young readers above the nursery age prefer their science straight."

HOBBIES AND OTHER INTERESTS: Hiking, animals, and bird watching.

FOR MORE INFORMATION SEE: Obituaries: *New York Times,* November 22, 1971; *Publishers Weekly,* December 20, 1971.

(Died November 21, 1971)

The adult dragonfly has moved over to the edge of the pot and is almost ready to take off. ■ (From *The Underwater Zoo* by Theodore McClintock. Illustrated by the author.)

DONALD McCORMICK

McCORMICK, (George) Donald (King) 1911-
(Richard Deacon)

PERSONAL: Born December 9, 1911, in Rhyl, Flintshire, Wales; son of Thomas Burnside (a journalist) and Lillie Louise (King) McCormick; married Rosalind Deirdre Buchanan Scott, 1934 (divorced); married Sylvia Doreen Cade, 1947 (deceased); married Eileen Dee Deacon, October 4, 1963; children: (second marriage) Anthony Stuart. *Education:* Attended Oswestry School, 1925-30. *Religion:* Church of England. *Home:* 8 Barry Ct., 36 Southend Rd., Beckenham, Kent, England.

CAREER: Kemsley Newspapers, foreign correspondent in Northwest Africa, 1946-49; *Gibraltar Chronicle,* Gibraltar, managing editor, 1946—; *Sunday Times,* London, England, with foreign department, 1949-65, foreign manager, 1965-73. *Military service:* Royal Navy Volunteer Reserve, 1940-46; served in Combined Operations; became lieutenant commander.

WRITINGS: The Talkative Muse, Lincoln Williams, 1934; *Islands for Sale,* Garnett, 1949; *Mr. France,* Jarrolds, 1955; *The Wicked City: An Algerian Adventure,* Jarrolds, 1956; *The Hell-Fire Club: The Story of the Amorous Knights of Wycombe,* Jarrolds, 1958; *The Mystery of Lord Kitchener's Death,* Putnam, 1959; *The Identity of Jack the Ripper,* Jarrolds, 1959, new and revised edition, Arrow Books, 1970.

The Incredible Mr. Kavanaugh, Putnam, 1960, Devin, 1961; *The Wicked Village,* Jarrolds, 1960; *The Temple of Love,* Jarrolds, 1962, Citadel, 1965; *Blood on the Sea: The*

A sight dreaded by agents during World War II. ■ (From *The Master Book of Spies*, written and advised by Donald McCormick.)

Terrible Story of the Yawl "Migonette," Muller, 1962; *The Mask of Merlin: A Critical Study of David Lloyd George*, Macdonald & Co., 1963, published in America as *The Mask of Merlin: A Critical Biography of David Lloyd George*, Holt, 1964; *The Unseen Killer: A Study of Suicide, Its History, Causes and Cures*, Muller, 1964; *Peddler of Death: The Life and Times of Sir Basil Zaharoff*, Holt, 1965 (published in England as *Pedlar of Death: The Life of Sir Basil Zaharoff*, Macdonald & Co., 1965); *The Red Barn Mystery: Some New Evidence on an Old Murder*, John Long, 1967, A. S. Barnes, 1968; *Murder by Witchcraft: A Study of Lower Quinton and Hagley Wood Murders*, John Long, 1968; *Murder by Perfection: Maundy Gregory, the Man Behind Two Unsolved Murders*, John Long, 1970; *One Man's Wars: The Story of Charles Sweeney, Soldier of Fortune*, Arthur Barker, 1972; *How to Buy an Island*, David & Charles, 1973; *The Master Book of Spies* (young adult), Watts, 1974; *Islands of England & Wales: A Guide to 138 English & Welsh Islands*, Osprey, 1974; *Islands of Scotland: A Guide to 247 Scottish Islands*, Osprey, 1974; *Islands of Ireland: A Guide to 110 Irish Islands*, Osprey, 1974; *The Master Book of Escapes* (young adult), Watts, 1975; *Taken for a Ride: The History of Cons & Conmen*, Harwood-Smart, 1976; *Who's Who in Spy Fiction*, Taplinger, 1977.

Under pseudonym Richard Deacon: *The Private Life of Mr. Gladstone*, Muller, 1966; *Madoc and the Discovery of America*, Muller, 1967, Braziller, 1968; *John Dee*, Muller, 1968; *A History of the British Secret Service*, Muller, 1969, Taplinger, 1970; *A History of the Russian Secret Service*, Taplinger, 1972; *The Chinese Secret Service*, Taplinger, 1974, published in England under the title of *A History of the Chinese Secret Service*, Muller, 1974; *William Caxton: The First English Editor*, Muller, 1976; *Matthew Hopkins, Witchfinder General*, Muller, 1976; *The Book of Fate: Its Origins & Uses*, Muller, 1976; *The Israeli Secret Service*, Hamish Hamilton, 1977.

SIDELIGHTS: "I started to write by producing a monthly magazine in an exercise book which I compiled by hand myself and lent it to friends at twopence a time. Later, this became a quarterly, produced by typewriter with three copies made.

"I always had a passion for islands and was never happier than when on holidays in North Wales creating my own dream world in a miniature island in a shallow river where I built a hut and lit camp fires. But, it was not until many years later that I actually started to write about islands and to tell the stories of many I had visited.

"Spies only began to fascinate me much later when after World War II, I lived in the, then, International City of Tangier, which had been one of the world's major espionage centres, with all the Secret Services of the world jostling one another for information and sometimes (or so it seemed), with some of the spies being so greedy, that they sold the same information to two or three different countries. I had thought this could only happen in fiction. In Tangier, I found that the Secret Service of fact is much more fun than that of fiction and often much more fantastic. For this reason, perhaps, I have stuck to non-fiction in writing about espionage, though I have often felt there is enormous scope for a really good fictional spy story for children—indeed, a story of espionage carried out by children. Perhaps one day I shall write it: already the outline is done. Meanwhile, I have made a study of spy fiction, tracing the history of the spy story from Fenimore Cooper to the present day.''

Donald McCormick's special interests encompass North Africa, espionage, and islands "everywhere in the world," biography, nonfiction requiring the author to be detective as well as writer, and the bibliography of romance and romantic traditions, customs and cults.

FOR MORE INFORMATION SEE: Books and Bookmen, July, 1967, October, 1968.

MEDARY, Marjorie 1890-

PERSONAL: Born July 24, 1890, in Waukon, Iowa; daughter of a newspaper editor and publisher. *Education:* Attended Cornell University; Northwestern University, M.A.

CAREER: Teacher in the New England area, 1939-41, and in Indianapolis, Ind., beginning 1941; worked part-time in the Bookshop for Boys and Girls lending library, Boston, Mass.; became an editor of textbooks for a publishing firm in New York; author of children's books.

MARJORIE MEDARY

She stifled her laughter as she said, "Please, Mr. Straw Man, will you toss a pitchfork right this way?" Unfolding the big bag of ticking, she held it open at arm's length. ■ (From *College in Crinoline* by Marjorie Medary. Illustrated by William M. Berger.)

WRITINGS: Orange Winter: A Story of Florida in 1880 (illustrated by Harold Sichel), Longmans, Green, 1931; *Prairie Anchorage* (illustrated by John Gincano), Longmans, Green, 1933; *Topgallant: A Herring Gull* (illustrated by Lynd Ward), H. Smith & R. Haas, 1935; *College in Crinoline,* Longmans, Green, 1937; *Joan and the Three Deer* (illustrated by Kurt Wiese), Random House, 1939; *Edra of the Islands* (illustrated by Dorothy Bayley), Longmans, Green, 1940; *Buckeye Boy,* Longmans, Green, 1944; *The Store at Crisscross Corners* (illustrated by Janet Smalley), Abingdon-Cokesbury, 1946; *Prairie Printer,* Longmans, Green, 1949; *Each One Teach One: Frank Laubach, Friend to Millions,* Longmans, Green, 1954, reissued, McKay, 1966; *Under Many a Star,* Peter Pauper Press, 1975.

SIDELIGHTS: Marjorie Medary took an interest in writing at an early age. The budding author sent out manuscripts of her work throughout her young adult life, but didn't decide to devote her full time to a writing career until she attended a Bread Loaf Writers' Conference during a summer recess from her teaching position.

Medary is a direct descendant of pioneers who settled in Iowa in the 1850's. Several of the author's books were based on that eventful period when America's frontier was expanding. *Crinoline College* told the story of a young girl who attended a coeducational college in the mid-nineteenth century. "Here is a picture, replete with minute and vivid detail, of an important era in education. . . . Marjorie Medary has caught the flavor of the times in her portrait of very real young people . . . ," noted a critic for the *New York Times*.

The author's own childhood adventures also provided her with ideas for her books. The author's memory of her experiences on Grand Manan Island (off the southeastern coast of Canada) developed into *Joan and the Three Deer*.

Buckeye Boy told the story of a young orphan boy and his desire to learn the printing trade. A *Kirkus* reviewer observed, "[The book has] interesting bits of canal life, some good gang fights, a glimpse into the printing and politics of the day. . . ." In reviewing the same book, a *Saturday Review of Literature* critic wrote, "Clearer than any 'vocational' story, this vivid and well written tale . . . reveals the struggle and the growth of youth. . . ."

Prairie Printer was a sequel to *Buckeye Boy*. A reviewer for the *New York Herald Tribune Weekly Book Review* called it "an excellent piece of historical fiction. . . ." A critic for *Saturday Review of Literature* commented, "This is a thor-

oughly American story of struggle and final success . . . told against an excellent historical background." Meanwhile, a *Horn Book* reviewer wrote, "Her characterizations are excellent and a considerable bibliography is evidence of her extensive research."

FOR MORE INFORMATION SEE: New York Times, August 29, 1937; *Kirkus,* July 1, 1944; *Saturday Review of Literature,* December 9, 1944; *New York Herald Tribune Weekly Book Review,* August 14, 1949; *Horn Book,* September, 1949; *Saturday Review of Literature,* November 12, 1949; Stanley J. Kunitz, editor, *Junior Book of Authors,* revised edition, H. W. Wilson, 1951.

MEEKER, Oden 1918(?)-1976

PERSONAL: Son of Lawrence Meeker; married wife, Olivia (divorced, 1952); married Bertie Moore. *Education:* Princeton University, B.A., 1941. *Home:* Woodstock, N.Y.

CAREER: Writer and social welfare leader. *Paris Herald Tribune,* columnist with first wife Olivia, post-World War II period; Cooperative for American Relief Everywhere Inc.

A girl watches the frontier. ■ (From *Israel Reborn* by Oden Meeker. Photograph courtesy of the Israel Government Press Office.)

(CARE), chief executive, Laos, 1954-55, Hong Kong, 1956, India, 1957-60, Israel, 1965. *War service:* Worked for British Information Services in the United States, during the second World War. *Awards, honors:* Anisfield-Wolf award, 1955, for *Report on Africa;* National Council of Christians and Jews citation for promoting understanding between persons of diversified backgrounds.

WRITINGS—All published by Scribner, except as noted: (With wife, Olivia) *And Points South* (illustrated by Barney Tobey), Random House, 1947; *Report on Africa,* 1954; *The Little World of Laos* (photographs by Homer Page), 1959; *Israel Reborn,* 1964; *Israel: Ancient Land, Young Nation,* 1968.

Also contributor to numerous periodicals, including *The New Yorker* and *Harper's.*

SIDELIGHTS: Meeker travelled to 130 countries during his lifetime. Many of his writings were based on his trips abroad. His book, *And Points South,* was an account of a ten month trip through Latin America. A *Saturday Review* critic commented, "In this impressionistic book so full of gentle caricatures you may find here and there a strong commen-

tary. The authors give a truthful account of some peculiarities and eccentricities of the Latin American people, but the account is in no way offensive. . . ."

The world traveler recorded his observations of the economic, social, and political conditions of Laos in his *Little World of Laos.* A critic for the *New York Herald Tribune* wrote, "This reviewer found *The Little World of Laos* particularly pleasant going. A never failing sense of humor, the colloquial style of any good drawing room ranconteur, and original figures of speech play a large part in the effect. . . ."

Meeker's *Report on Africa* covered his trip to that continent in 1952. "The author is offering us a somewhat novel kind of reportage which, besides being immensely informative and genuinely enlightening, has the virtue of being consistently entertaining," noted a reviewer for *Atlantic.*

The author also lived in Israel for several years. In his *Israel Reborn,* Meeker dealt with a brief historical background of present-day Israel. "A fully illustrated objective study with well-organized, highly readable text in a notably superior format," described a *Horn Book* critic.

(From *The Little World of Laos* by Oden Meeker.   Photographs by Homer Page.)

Meeker's last book, *Israel: Ancient Land, Young Nation,* gave his impression of the land and people of the Jewish homeland. A reviewer for *Library Journal* commented, "Written in an engaging manner, both the land and her inhabitants come to life with their strengths and weaknesses."

FOR MORE INFORMATION SEE: (Obituary) *New York Times,* January 20, 1976.

(Died January 19, 1976)

MEYNIER, Yvonne (Pollet)   1908-

PERSONAL: Born in France in 1908; married Andre Meynier (a history teacher), August 20, 1927; children: Odette (Mrs. Maurice Touchefeu), Yvette (Mrs. Jean Delaunay), Daniele (Mrs. Yves Treguer). *Education:* Attended the Sorbonne, University of Paris. *Address:* 50 Rue de la Palestine, 35000 Rennes, France.

CAREER: Author. Has been a kindergarten teacher, and has worked in radio in France. *Awards, honors: The School with a Difference* won the Grand Prix de la Literature pour les Jeunes and the Enfance du Monde award.

WRITINGS: Maria de l'Assistance, Calmann-Levy, 1946; *Maluories,* Calmann-Levy, 1948; *Comme la Plume au Vent: Dix Ans de Radio* (with a preface by Georges Duhamel), [Blainville-sur-Mer], 1956; *Une Petite Fille Attendait* (illustrated by Pierre Le Guen), Editions G. P., 1961; *L'-Helicoptere du Petit Duc* (illustrated by Raymond Busillet), Magnard, 1962; *Un Lycee pas Comme les Autres* (illustrated by Daniel Dupuy), Societe Nouvelle des Editions G. P., 1962, translation by Patricia Crampton published as *The School with a Difference,* Abelard-Schuman, 1964; *Erika des Collines* (illustrated by Jacques Pecnard), Societe Nouvelle des Editions G. P., 1963; *La Bonheur est Pour Demain,* Societe Nouvelle des Editions G. P., 1965; *Ou es-tu Antonio?* (illustrated by Michel Gourlier), Magnard, 1970; (with Job de Roince) *La Cuisine Rustique, Bretagne, Maine, Anjou,* R. Morel, 1970; (with husband, Andre Meynier) *Les Cotes de France,* Arthaud, 1972; *Le Voyage Imaginaire* (illustrated by Colette Goulard), Magnard, 1973.

SIDELIGHTS: The School with a Difference, Yvonne Meynier's only work translated into English, was described by *Horn Book:* "The story is based on actual letters and diaries, and the plot comprises the tensions and conflicts inherent in wartime living. The potential impact of the correspondence is lessened by an almost superficial brightness, a uniform style unlikely in three different writers, and a translation intended for British writers. But American girls need to know about growing up in war-torn, occupied lands, and the letters . . . will serve that purpose well. For those whose parents knew such experiences the letters will be particularly meaningful." The *London Times* added, "In spite of an awkward and often oversentimental translation, *The School with a Difference* is at once an engrossing tale and an interesting piece of documentary for the library shelf. . . . Even through the slightly sententious note of the language—schoolgirls today will be able to see in the lively letter writers young people very much like themselves."

MORRIS, Desmond (John)   1928-

PERSONAL: Born January 24, 1928, in Purton, Wiltshire, England; son of Harry Howe (a writer) and Marjorie (Hunt) Morris; married Ramona Baulch (a writer), July 30, 1952;

children: Jason. *Education:* Birmingham University, B.Sc., 1951; Magdalen College, Oxford, D.Phil., 1954. *Politics:* None. *Religion:* None. *Home:* 78 Banbury Rd., Oxford, England. *Office:* Department of Psychology, Oxford University, Oxford, England; and Wolfson College, Oxford University, Oxford, England.

CAREER: Oxford University, Oxford, England, researcher in animal behavior in department of zoology, 1954-56; Zoological Society of London, London, England, head of Granada TV and Film Unit, 1956-59, curator of mammals, 1959-67; Institute of Contemporary Arts, London, director, 1967-68; full-time writer, 1968-73. Research fellow at Wolfson College, Oxford, 1973—. Has exhibited paintings in England, having had first one-man show in London in 1950. *Member:* Zoological Society of London (scientific fellow). *Awards, honors:* Statuette with Pedestal from World Organization for Human Potential, 1971, for *The Naked Ape* and *The Human Zoo.*

WRITINGS: The Reproductive Behaviour of the Ten-Spined Stickleback, E. J. Brill, 1958; *The Story of Congo* (juvenile), Batsford, 1958; (editor with Caroline Jarvis) *The International Zoo Yearbook,* Zoological Society of London, Volume I, 1959-60, Volume II, 1960-61, Volume III, 1961-62, Volume IV, 1962-63.

Introducing Curious Creatures, Spring Books, 1961; *The Biology of Art: A Study of the Picture-Making Behaviour of the Great Apes and Its Relationship to Human Art,* Knopf, 1962; *Apes and Monkeys* (juvenile), Bodley Head, 1964, McGraw, 1965; (with wife, Ramona Morris) *Men and Snakes,* McGraw, 1965; *The Mammals: A Guide to the Living Species,* Harper, 1965; *The Big Cats* (juvenile), Mc-

DESMOND MORRIS

DESMOND MORRIS

Graw, 1965; *Zoo Time* (juvenile), Hart-Davis, 1966; (with Ramona Morris) *Men and Apes,* McGraw, 1966; (with Ramona Morris) *Men and Pandas,* Hutchinson, 1966, McGraw, 1967; (editor) *Primate Ethology,* Aldine, 1967; *The Naked Ape: A Zoologist's Study of the Human Animal* (Book-of-the-Month Club selection), J. Cape, 1967, Mc-Graw, 1968; *The Human Zoo* (Book-of-the-Month Club selection), McGraw, 1969.

Patterns of Reproductive Behaviour: Collected Papers (all previously published in journals), J. Cape, 1970, McGraw, 1971; *Intimate Behaviour,* J. Cape, 1971, Random House, 1972; *Manwatching: A Field-Guide to Human Behavior,* Cape/Elsevier, 1977; (co-author) *Gesture Maps,* Cape, 1978. Contributor to journals, including *Behaviour, British Birds, New Scientist,* and *Zoo Life.*

WORK IN PROGRESS: Research in human ethology; planning another exhibit of his paintings; writing new book on prehistoric art.

SIDELIGHTS: "As a boy in the Wiltshire village of Purton, I used to breed small mammals and sell them to a local zoo. One day, while rummaging around in the attic, I came across a dusty mahogany box containing an ancient microscope and a large collection of slides which belonged to my great grandfather, an enthusiastic naturalist. A whole new world was opened up to me, not merely of scientific knowledge but of beauty in the abstract patterns of shapes and colours.

"As I grew up, my interest in art and natural history developed side by side and, when the time came to choose a career, I was undecided. After my National Service—a disastrous period in the Medical Corps then a lecturing post in fine arts—I went to read zoology at Birmingham University. Continuing to sketch what I saw under my microscope lens, I filled hundreds of books with drawings and, at the end of my first year as a science student, held a one-man exhibition in London.

"The turning point in my life came in 1950 when I attended a lecture on the emerging science of comparative ethology by the famous Dutch ethologist Niko Tinbergen. That was it, in one hour he converted me. Crash. It hit me like a ton of bricks. Gaining a first-class degree from Birmingham, I went on to join Tinbergen's animal behaviour group at Oxford and obtained my doctorate.

"In 1956, Granada Television and the London Zoo formed a special production unit to make films and television programmes about animals, and I was invited to lead the team.

That spring, I introduced the first edition of 'Zootime,' a weekly programme that was to last a record-breaking eleven years.

"In 1959, I left the unit to become Curator of Mammals at the Zoo. One of my research activities was to encourage a chimpanzee called Congo to paint, while at the same time taking up my own brushes. In three years, Congo produced 400 paintings (the dwindling of his creative urge coinciding with the attainment of sexual maturity) while my total was a mere 350.

"Another less successful project was the attempt at mating the giant pandas Chi-Chi and An-An. In Moscow to arrange the match, I was under suspicion as a spy—I was followed, my phone tapped and my hotel room kept under constant surveillance.

"The stress of over-work, together with the extreme cold of the Russian winter, brought about a breakdown in my health. Recovering from a serious illness, I decided to cut down on my many activities and concentrate on my curatorship, a fortnightly television programme and one book. That book was *The Naked Ape*."

Morris was already the author of fifty scientific papers and twelve books—including *The Biology of Art, The Mammals, A Guide to the Living Species* and (with his wife, Ramona) *Men and Snakes, Men and Apes* and *Men and Pandas. The Naked Ape* started out as a lighthearted remark to a publisher at a party and ended up as one of the international bestsellers of the decade. "Though the idea for a book like that had been in my mind for years, I never seriously considered putting it down on paper. To be honest, I was frightened of what people would say, how they would react to this cold, very objective treatment of themselves."

Published in twenty-three countries, in languages including Icelandic, Serbo-Croat and Turkish, the book sold more than eight million copies. In America, it was selling eight thousand copies a day at one time; in Canada it outsold Bond in three weeks.

Desmond Morris describes himself as "a rare and vanishing species of 20th-century man, an anti-specialist. I believe, you see, that one of the terrible blights of modern life is the need to specialize."

With *The Naked Ape, The Human Zoo,* and *Intimate Behaviour,* Morris drew favorable critical response for having made accessible to a wide audience scientific material that might otherwise have remained limited to a relatively small number of zoologists and ethologists. His style was often described as stimulating, entertaining, and even "racy," while his intent was described as a serious one—"to help us take a new look at ourselves, not against the backdrop of our accepted culture, but against the wider vistas of our biological heritage. This appeals to our desires, especially urgent today, to question the conventional norms and to take a hard look at the direction society is taking."

The Naked Ape was filmed by Universal and released in 1973.

Outside the stables, in the hills nearby, an angel went about telling the shepherds that a child of God had been born. ■ (From *Happy Birthday, Baby Jesus* by Charles L. Mee. Illustrated by Ken Munowitz.)

KEN MUNOWITZ

MUNOWITZ, Ken 1935-1977

PERSONAL: Born May 2, 1935, in Bronx, N.Y.; son of Morris and Regina (Fass; a diamond cutter) Munowitz. *Education:* Cooper Union, certificate, 1957. *Home:* 201 East 71 St., New York, N.Y. 10021. *Office:* Horizon Magazine, 10 Rockefeller Plaza, New York, N.Y. 10020.

CAREER: Horizon Magazine, New York, N.Y., art director, 1967-77. *Exhibitions:* Arras Gallery, New York, N.Y., March, 1973, December, 1976. *Military service:* National Guard, special services, 1957-64.

ILLUSTRATOR: Charles L. Mee, *Happy Birthday, Baby Jesus,* Harper, 1976; Charles L. Mee, *Moses, Moses,* Harper, 1977; Charles L. Mee, *Noah,* Harper, 1978.

(Died December 20, 1977)

NEILSON, Frances Fullerton (Jones) 1910-

PERSONAL: Born October 21, 1912, in Philadelphia, Pa.; daughter of William (a teacher) and Mary (Fullerton) Jones; descendent of John Knox; married Winthrop Cunningham Neilson, Jr., 1930; children: Winthrop, John, Mary. *Education:* Attended school in Philadelphia, Pa. *Religion:* Episcopalian.

CAREER: Began producing children's plays for settlement houses and hospitals, 1930's; became writer for several radio programs, including "Orgets on the Air" and "The Topaz Room"; also served as vice president of Holiday House (publishing firm). Helped establish libraries in service clubs and hospitals. *War service:* Nurses aid, and member of the

Writers' War Board. *Awards, honors:* New York Herald Tribune Honor Award, 1942, for *The Donkey from Dorking.*

WRITINGS: Donkey from Dorking (illustrated by Lidia Vitale and Janet Hopkins), Dutton, 1942; *Mocha the Djuka* (illustrated by Avery Johnson), Dutton, 1943; *Giant Mountain* (illustrated by Mary Reardon), Dutton, 1946; *The Ten Commandments ih Today's World* (illustrated by Nils Hogner), Thomas Nelson, 1946; *Look to the New Moon* (Junior Literary Guild selection), Abelard, 1953; *Storm on Giant Mountain,* School Book Services, 1975.

All with husband, Winthrop Neilson: *Dusty for Speed!* (illustrated by Hans Kreis), Dutton, 1947; *Bruce Benson: Son of Fame* (illustrated by Margaret Ayer), Dutton, 1948; *Bruce Benson: Thirty Fathoms Deep* (illustrated by John C. Wonsetler), Dutton, 1949; *Bruce Benson on Trails of Thunder,* Dutton, 1950; *Edge of Greatness,* Putnam, 1951; *Verdict for the Doctor: The Case of Benjamin Rush,* Hastings House, 1958; *Letter to Philemon: Novel of a Man's Search For Faith,* Thomas Nelson, 1962, reissued, Concordia, 1973; *Seven Women: Great Painters,* Chilton, 1968; *What's New—Dow Jones: Story of the Wall Street Journal,* Chilton, 1973; *The United Nations: The World's Last Chance for Peace,* New American Library, 1975.

SIDELIGHTS: Frances Neilson spent most of her childhood in Dorking, England, which provided the backdrop for her first book, *Donkey from Dorking.* The book told the story of Longears the donkey who was taught such entertaining tricks as riding a bicycle.

The author has traveled extensively through the West Indies, South America, Canada, Scotland, France, and Switzerland. *Mocha the Djuka* was inspired by an expedition into the jungles of Dutch Guiana. "While the jungle background is made vivid with color and sound, this is essentially a story of friendship. . . . It is written warmly and wisely. All friendly and eager youngsters will recognize themselves in this charmingly written and illustrated little book . . . ," observed a reviewer for the *Springfield Republican.*

In *Bruce Benson: Son of Fame* in collaboration with her husband Winthrop Neilson, told the adventures of a young boy traveling with his parents on an exploration of Central America. A critic for *Saturday Review* wrote, "Bruce is a well-drawn character and his growth as the story develops is well-described . . ." In a sequel to this book, the husband and wife writing team penned *Bruce Benson: Thirty Fathoms Deep.* A *New York Times* reviewer described the sequei as ". . . a moving yarn certain to hold the attention of eight to eleven-year-old boys. . . ."

Edge of Greatness was also jointly written by Frances and Winthrop Neilson. In this historical novel, the Neilsons re-created one day in the life of Benjamin Franklin. A reviewer for the *Christian Science Monitor* commented, "The build up of local and historical background, streets, buildings, actual persons, and weather . . . is done with fidelity. . . . The style is sincere, with ever so faint a grain of Rabelaisian spice. . . ."

Seven Women: Great Painters was a later book by the Neilsons. "The intention of this articulate, beautiful book is to provide 'an emphatic no' to the theory that women are not capable of matching men in creative ability. . . . The authors have accomplished much more than a disproof of the theory about women artists. They have created a valuable, illuminating contribution to art history collections . . . ," observed a *Library Journal* critic.

HOBBIES AND OTHER INTERESTS: Swimming, horseback riding, dancing, and gardening.

FOR MORE INFORMATION SEE: Current Biography Yearbook 1955.

NICKERSON, Elizabeth   1922-
(Betty Nickerson)

PERSONAL: Born June 26, 1922, in Fort Scott, Kan.; daughter of Clarence T. (a stonemason) and Helen (a caterer; maiden name, Smiley) Smith; married July 25, 1942 (divorced); children: Stephen, Michael, Marki (daughter). *Education:* Attended Oregon State University, 1939-42, and Goucher College, 1943-44; University of Utah, B.A., 1946; University of Manitoba, M.A., 1965; graduate study, McGill University, 1972. *Home:* Rideau Rd., Kars, Ottawa, Ontario, Canada K0A 2E0. *Office:* All About Us/Nous Autres, Inc., Box 1985, Ottawa, Ontario, Canada K1P 5R5.

CAREER: Canadian Broadcasting Corp. (CBC), Winnipeg, Manitoba, performer in television arts and crafts series, 1957-65; EXPO-67, Montreal, Quebec, consultant for "Man the Creator" exhibit, 1967; Man and His World (permanent exhibition), Montreal, director and exhibitor, 1968; All About Us/Nous Autres, Inc. (foundation for young Canadian writers and artists), Ottawa, founder and national coordinator, and project coordinator for literary quarterly, *Nous Journal,* 1972—. Consultant for "Education Through Art" project, United Nations Educational, Scientific, and Cultural Organization (UNESCO), 1967-68; member of Canadian national committee, United Nations Children's Fund (UNICEF), 1967-68, also conducted study tour of community development in India and Thailand; member of Advisory Committee on Human Rights. *Member:* Association of Cultural Executives (Canadian), Society for Education Through Art, Phi Beta Kappa. *Awards, honors:* India Council fellowship, 1967; British Council fellowship, 1968; Canada Council travel grant, 1972.

WRITINGS: How the World Grows Its Food, McGraw, 1966; *Celebrate the Sun,* Lippincott, 1969; *Chi: Letters from Biafra,* New Press (Toronto), 1970; (editor) *Girls Will Be Women,* All About Us, 1976.

WORK IN PROGRESS: Research on creativity in children; *Ring of Changes,* a book on cultural interaction in Canadian society, completion expected in 1979; *Ceremony in Aneverly,* a utopian novel of a society based on positive human interaction.

SIDELIGHTS: "Books have always been my magic window on the world. I grew up in a small Oregon town then surrounded by wonderful, mysterious forests alive with living, changing vistas and it had a Carnegie Library. In 1954 I came to Canada, as many people did during those troubled times, and have lived here ever since. I've had the opportunity to learn different ways living in Canada, and from travelling over most of the world. I have come to know people from everywhere, and that along with the forest and the library is why I began to write.

"My interests and concern for many years has centered around what people can do when they do their very best. This particularly applies to young people, and their creative

BETTY NICKERSON

efforts. When people try to do their very best, they create marvelous paintings, poems, structures, families, communities, and this, to me, is a vitally important survival skill. When human beings try to make things better, to make them beautiful or to make them work well, they are never destructive or hurtful to themselves, to others or to their environment.

"Needing a way to illustrate the important matters that human beings share, in 1957 I began to focus on children's art. This took the form of a weekly television series in Winnipeg in which I designed, hosted, scripted and collected material from young people. Through a strange series of events, I learned in a little town in Czechoslovakia where I was making a film for the television show, that the paintings and drawings of young people could communicate across huge barriers of language, distance, politics, etc. And I set to work to collect childrens' art from all over the world (some fifty-four countries sent paintings to me) they vividly show those things which we share as human beings.

"It was out of this collection that both my illustrated books for young people took shape. *Celebrate the Sun* includes paintings by children from thirty countries, and explores the festivals we all celebrate—the festivals of the seasons which are born of man's long need to mark the passage of time. Traditional holidays are called by many different names, but all of them celebrate the dawn of new phases of the year, and the myths and legends which human beings have developed to explain these grand natural phenomena. There is remarkable similarity in all the cultures of the world, so, guided by the paintings of children' I wrote both the *Sun* book, and *How the World Grows Its Food.* Young people have a great deal to tell all of us, young and old, about what they see as important in the world we share.

"For me, writing a book is very much like having a baby. It is there in my mind and body, growing, changing, shifting, and finally in one great burst of effort it all materializes. I write in terribly long sessions, lasting several days with very few breaks even for eating or sleeping. The ideas have been formed through the long gestation, and then the words well up in an overwhelming flow, and I can scarcely get them down on paper quickly enough to capture them. I've devised a funny 'writing machine' to accommodate this strange behaviour. It consists of a big roll of print-out paper, set in a shoebox using a fat knitting needle to carry the roll, and then I write. Sometimes it goes on for six, ten or even thirty feet of unbroken words, paragraph after paragraph. This is really very helpful as it seems great ideas can flee my mind just because it is time to change a sheet of paper! Another good idea is to take the phone off the hook.

JAPAN
AGE 10

As the great shrines move through the streets of the beautiful ancient city, musicians' melodies blend with the tinkle of hundreds of tiny golden bells, and the deep, rich sound of temple gongs.
■ (From *Celebrate the Sun* by Betty Nickerson. Artwork by children from many lands.)

"When the words dry up, and they do, I go back to the research or stop for a few days to work on my current tapestry, do some gardening indoors or out, or in rare fits of inspiration, a bout of housework, canning, sewing, whatever. Then when the words come back, I try the typewriter again. I have learned that I cannot force the words to take shape; they happen when the accumulation of information from research or thought reaches some critical mass. Or when I've observed, seen, sensed some new concept that supplies a part of the pattern. Looking for patterns, but mostly just looking at everything that one can possibly perceive is perhaps the most important skill a writer can acquire. The answers are around somewhere, awaiting discovery and a writer to place them in the scheme of things.

"Despite the ugliness, meanness, greed and hurt that surrounds us, I remain convinced that human beings have the power to make a paradise of beauty, caring, and growth. It could happen if we all did our best to make things better, so I try in whatever ways come to hand—only a little of it is writing. For the past four years I have directed a project to discover the creativity of young Canadians, kids of six to eighteen. And it has been a magnificent experience. My respect for young writers and artists, for the ability of young people to state the conditions, needs, hopes, joys and concerns of the world they are growing into increases daily.

"Kids respond to the idea of making responsible statements, and they appear willing to make the effort to act responsibly and with imagination. The real difficulty is in finding a way in which their ideas can enter the mainstream of society, and I'm certain that is true not only in Canada, but in all the world. If I can do anything to help bring that about, I do it. The world will be a reasonable place if we who live in it act reasonably—as individuals, citizens, workers, artists, parents—human beings. I believe that we could combine all our skills, customs and knowledge taking the best of them, and make a masterpiece of human achievement from our best pieces. These are the things I write about, especially for young people."

NIXON, Kathleen Irene (Blundell) (K. Nixon)

PERSONAL: Born in London, Eng.; married V. R. Blundell.

CAREER: Author and artist.

WRITINGS—Under pseudonym K. Nixon; all self-illustrated: *Pushti*, F. Warne, 1956; *Pindi Poo*, F. Warne, 1957; *Poo and Pushti*, F. Warne, 1959; (with Robert Foran) *Animal Mothers and Babies*, F. Warne, 1960; (with Maurice Burton) *Bird Families*, F. Warne, 1962; *The Bushy Tail Family*, F. Warne, 1963; *Animal Legends*, F. Warne, 1966; *Strange Animal Friendships*, F. Warne, 1967; *Animals and Birds in Folklore*, F. Warne, 1969.

To her horror and surprise out poured hundreds of insects. ■ (From *Animals and Birds in Folklore* by K. Nixon. Illustrated by the author.)

SIDELIGHTS: Books described Kathleen Nixon's drawings in *Animals and Birds in Folklore* as, "Realism and beauty in animal portraiture." The critic went on to say, "Here the pictures elevate a series of simple bedtime stories into an artistic experience, with a wide range of animals and birds moving with grace, power, and cunning across the page."

Publishers Weekly's description of *Strange Animal Friendships* included, "For children really to savor these true stories, it is important they be told they are true. Nevertheless, children will probably not find these unlikely friendships (those between a dog and a fox, a cat and a pigeon . . .) as amazing as the adults who may read the stories to them—children having always been world citizens before the UN was ever dreamed of. Both adults and children will enjoy Miss Nixon's accounts and her pictures which accompany them."

The artist-author has lived in India and has traveled extensively in America, Australia, Canada, China, and Japan. Her animal pictures have been exhibited in several cities, including Melbourne, London, and Paris.

ORMONDROYD, Edward 1925-

PERSONAL: Born October 8, 1925, in Wilkinsburg, Pa.; children: Evan, Kitt, Beth. *Education:* University of California, Berkeley, A.B., 1950. *Residence:* Newfield, N.Y.

CAREER: Author and librarian. *Military service:* Served on a destroyer escort in the Pacific during World War II. *Awards, honors:* Commonwealth Club of California Literature Award, 1957, for *David and the Phoenix.*

WRITINGS: David and the Phoenix (illustrated by Joan Raysor), Follett, 1957; *The Tale of Alain* (illustrated by Robert Frankenberg), Follett, 1960; *Jonathan Frederick Aloysius Brown* (illustrated by Suzi Spector), Golden Gate Junior Books, 1964; *Time at the Top* (illustrated by Peggie Bach), Parnassus, 1963; *Theodore* (illustrated by John M. Larrecq), Parnassus, 1966; *Michael: The Upstairs Dog* (illustrated by Cyndy Szekeres), Dial, 1967; *Broderick* (illustrated by Larrecq), Parnassus, 1969; *Theodore's Rival* (illustrated by Larrecq), Parnassus, 1971; *Castaways on Long Ago* (illustrated by Ruth Robbins), Parnassus, 1973; *Imagination Greene* (illustrated by John Lewis), Parnassus, 1973; *All in Good Time* (illustrated by Robbins), Parnassus, 1975.

SIDELIGHTS: Ormondroyd wrote his first book, *David and the Phoenix,* while he was a student at the University of California, but it took seven years before he could find a publisher for it. A reviewer for the *Chicago Sunday Tribune* observed: "Ormondroyd has written a stimulating, ageless story. It combines beautiful writing, topnotch adventure, and enchanting fantasy."

The author's *Time at the Top* was about a young girl and her unusual elevator ride. An *Atlantic Monthly* reviewer proclaimed: "A book not to miss, beautifully illustrated with black-and-white drawings." In reviewing the same book, a critic for *Junior Bookshelf* commented: "A fresh variation on the 'time slip' theme. The story moves quickly and is interesting, but fantasy of this kind must be carefully thought through, with all its implications, to be convincing."

In *Theodore,* Ormondroyd related the tale of a little girl and her affection for her toy bear. A critic for *Young Readers'*

EDWARD ORMONDROYD

Review wrote: "A recitation of the simple story line cannot do the book justice for the author and artist have really endowed this bear with a personality that is endearing. The very common but hard to capture affection between stuffed animal and child is excellently portrayed."

The author's *Castaways on Long Ago* told the story of three children and their adventurous vacation on a farm. A reviewer for the *Bulletin of the Center for Children's Books* commented: "With high dramatic sense, Ormondroyd saves the most exciting episode and the solution of an unusual mystery-fantasy until the very end of a very good book. What gives the book substance that goes beyond the plot is the quality of characterization: both the children and their farm hosts are highly individual, sharply drawn and consistent in behavior and dialogue, for which the author has a keen ear."

HOBBIES AND OTHER INTERESTS: Birdwatching, playing flute, making furniture, gardening.

FOR MORE INFORMATION SEE: Chicago Sunday Tribune, November 17, 1957; *Atlantic Monthly,* December, 1963; *Young Readers' Review,* January, 1967; *Bulletin of the Center for Children's Books,* February, 1974; *Junior Bookshelf,* June, 1976.

PALMER, C(yril) Everard 1930-

PERSONAL: Born October 15, 1930, in Kendal, Jamaica; son of Cyril (a farmer) and Vida Palmer. *Education:* Mico Training College, teaching diploma, 1955; Lakehead University, B.A. *Address:* P.O. Box 31, Nipigon, Ontario, Canada P0T 2J0. *Agent:* A. M. Heath, 35 Dover, London, England.

(From the movie "My Father Sun-Sun Johnson" from the story of C. Everard Palmer. Copyright, Learning Corporation of America.)

CAREER: Teacher in Ontario, 1965—.

WRITINGS—Juvenile: *A Broken Vessel,* Pioneer Press, 1960; *The Cloud with the Silver Lining,* Deutsch, 1966; *Big Doc Bitterdot,* Deutsch, 1968; *The Sun Salutes You,* Deutsch, 1970; *The Hummingbird People,* Deutsch, 1971; *A Cow Called Boy,* Bobbs-Merrill, 1971; *The Wooing of Beppo Tate,* Deutsch, 1972; *Baba and Mr. Big,* Bobbs-Merrill, 1972; *My Father Sun Sun Johnson,* Deutsch, 1974; *The Adventures of Jimmy Maxwell,* Ministry of Education, 1976; *A Taste of Danger,* Ministry of Education, 1976.

SIDELIGHTS: "I believe that one of the reasons I was pointed in the direction of writing lies in the fact that when I was young, I was too shy to speak and even when I spoke, I did it poorly. Words didn't come out of me easily. Another influence was Westerns. I was swept up by the raw action as well as by the style and drawls.

"I can remember clearly the day on which I vowed to become a writer. I had just put down a western. I began immediately to scribble stories in my school exercise books. Of course, they were nonsensical, but that did not deter me.

"My break came while I was in Teacher's College. My first short story appeared in the college magazine and won critical praise from the English teacher. I could write! A number of short stories followed, appearing in Jamaica's *The Sunday Gleaner.*

"One thing followed another. The Ministry of Education was about to launch its own publications: books for Jamaican children by Jamaicans. I answered their ad, was given the nod to write a book and out of that venture came *The Adventures of Jimmy Maxwell* and *A Taste of Danger.* Then came *A Broken Vessel,* an adult book.

"With that book I might have taken the road into writing exclusively for adults, but Andre Deutsch of London spotted the two Ministry publications and asked me to write a book for them, any book, provided it was realistic.

"And then again, the story might have been different had I stayed with *The Daily Gleaner,* for which newspaper I did a stint as trainee journalist. Crime was my beat, and the job not only took me into the seamier parts of Kingston, but gave me a first-hand look at crime. Had I stayed I might have written my stories around crime or police work.

"All the stories that I have written have been set in the small village in Jamaica in which I grew up. The people lived close to the earth and were, also, close to one another. Although the economy of the village was based largely on subsistence farming, which meant that many of the people were poor, they had a remarkable sense of humour, to laugh at themselves and at one another, and most of all they had the ability to endure. There was fun at all times, even fun in work and of all things fun even in death, in the form of the wake.

"This is the period of my life which has meant the most to me, the period which is most vivid, the phase that I remember most clearly, the part I like to borrow from to create my stories. None of the stories ever happened except in the fictional sense, but they are true to the colour and character of the village.

"I fished in the rivers, swam in them, milked cows, rode donkeys, climbed trees and, of course, watched the panorama of life pass before my eyes.

C. EVERARD PALMER

"Unlike many writers, I do not stick to a rigorous discipline. When I begin to write a story I begin with an idea, but rarely ever work the plot out to the end. I begin and if the characters come alive, they do have much to say in the way the story goes.

"Neither do I stick to a plan of work such as writing a specific number of hours per day. On some days, if the story is going good, I might write up to eight or ten hours, then next day I may not write at all.

"On one occasion I wrote a 20,000 word book in two days—mainly because I liked what I was writing and the words came rushing out. On the other hand, a book of similar length, pinned me down for three months because I did not like the way it was going and continued to put off working on it.

"The last book that I have produced, *My Father Sun Sun Johnson,* is different from the rest. The theme which is concerned with greed—what it can do to the victim and to the aggressor as well—remained the dominant element throughout. In the other works, my main concern was with plots and characters and fairly entertaining stories for boys and girls. So, from an artistic point of view, I have found *My Father Sun Sun Johnson* to be the most rewarding."

FOR MORE INFORMATION SEE: Times Literary Supplement, April 16, 1970; *Books and Bookmen,* May, 1970.

She must have noticed me standing with my hands locked behind me, gazing at the mountain of baked goodies, because she proceeded to give us samples of what she had baked. Her samples were good, very good. ■ (From *The Cloud with the Silver Lining* by C. Everard Palmer. Illustrated by Laszlo Acs.)

PARKER, Richard 1915-

PERSONAL: Born in 1915. *Address:* 36 Central Parade, Herne Bay, Kent, England.

CAREER: Formerly employed as a librarian and teacher; novelist and author of fiction for children.

WRITINGS: A Camel from the Desert (illustrated by Biro), Sylvan Press, 1947; *Penguin Goes Home* (illustrated by Biro), Chatto & Windus, 1951, reissued, Chivers, 1973; *Six Plays for Boys,* Methuen, 1951; *Only Some Had Guns,* Collins, 1952; *The Gingerbread Man,* Collins, 1953, Scribner, 1954; *A Moor of Spain: The Story of a Rogue* (illustrated by John Harwood), Penguin, 1953; *Seven Plays for Boys,* Methuen, 1953; *A Kind of Misfortune,* Collins, 1954, Scribner, 1955; *Harm Intended,* Collins, 1954, Scribner, 1956; *Draughts in the Sun,* Collins, 1955; *The Three Pebbles* (illustrated by William Ferguson), D. McKay, 1956; *The Sword of the Ganelon* (illustrated by W. Ferguson), Collins, 1957, D. McKay, 1958; *Brother Turgar and the Vikings* (illustrated by Joan Milroy), Ginn, 1959; *The Kidnapped Crusaders* (illustrated by Richard Kennedy), Ginn, 1959.

More Snakes than Ladders (illustrated by Jillian Willett), Brockhampton, 1960, published in America as *Almost Lost* (illustrated by Leonard Shortall), T. Nelson, 1962; *The Green Highwayman* (illustrated by R. Kennedy), Ginn, 1960; *Fiddler's Place*, P. Davies, 1961; *New Home South* (illustrated by Prudence Seward), Brockhampton, 1961; *Voyage to Tasmania* (illustrated by P. Seward), Bobbs-Merrill, 1961; *Lion at Large* (illustrated by Kurt Werth), T. Nelson, 1961; *A Valley Full of Pipers* (illustrated by R. Kennedy), Bobbs-Merrill, 1962; *Goodbye to the Bush* (illustrated by Kenneth Brown), Ginn, 1963; *The House That Guilda Drew* (illustrated by Mamoru Funai), Bobbs-Merrill, 1964; *Boy on a Chain,* P. Davies, 1964, published in America as *Killer,* Doubleday, 1964; *Perversity of Pipers* (illustrated by R. Kennedy), Van Nostrand, 1964; *Private Beach* (illustrated by Victor Ambrus), Harrap, 1964, Duell, Sloan, 1965; *The Boy Who Wasn't Lonely* (illustrated by James J. Spanfeller), Brockhampton, 1964, Bobbs-Merrill, 1965.

Second-Hand Family (illustrated by Gareth Floyd), Brockhampton, 1965, Bobbs-Merrill, 1966; *M for Mischief* (illustrated by Juan Ballesta), Constable Young Books, 1965, Duell, Sloan, 1966; *One White Mouse* (illustrated by Rene Hummerstone), Brockhampton, 1966, published in America as *No House for a Mouse* (illustrated by W. T. Mars), Follett, 1968 and as *The Impossible Pet,* Scholastic Book Services, 1972; *New in the Neighborhood,* Duell, Sloan, 1966; *The Punch Back Gang* (illustrated by John Plant), Harrap, 1966, reissued, White Lion, 1976; *The Hendon Fungus,* Meredith Press, 1968; *A Sheltering Tree,* Meredith Press, 1969; *The Old Powder Line,* T. Nelson, 1971; *Spell Seven* (illustrated by Trevor Ridley), T. Nelson, 1971; *Paul and Etta* (illustrated by Gavin Row), T. Nelson, 1973; *A Time to Choose,* Hutchinson, 1973, Harper, 1974; *Three by Mistake,* T. Nelson, 1974; *He Is Your Brother* (illustrated by G.

Standing in the moonlight just outside the front gate, the lion looked unusually large. ■ (From *The Midnight Beast* by Richard Parker. Illustrated by Kurt Werth.)

Floyd), Brockhampton, 1974, Nelson, 1976; *Snatched* (illustrated by Peter Kesteven), David & Charles, 1974; *Boy into Action* (illustrated by Trevor Parkin), Abelard-Schuman, 1975; *Beyond the Back Gate* (illustrated by Peter Dennis), Abelard-Schuman, 1975; *The Quarter Boy,* T. Nelson, 1976; *In and Out the Window,* Hutchinson, 1976.

SIDELIGHTS: Many of Parker's books for children, such as *Private Beach* and *Voyage to Tasmania,* have been based on incidents involving his own family—he has three daughters and twin sons. Others, such as *He Is Your Brother,* came out of his teaching experiences.

"I wanted to say a lot more about all the family, but it just sprawled and sprawled and in the end Jane and her father had to be pruned back to leave Mike and Orry more or less in the center.

"The story started way back when I happened to read a compulsive book by an American mother about her own autistic child. I was reminded of a girl I had in class many years back in a village school. The community was closely integrated and the parents came up to ask me if I would have their nine-year-old daughter in my class although by normal standards she was ineducable. The girl was just on the point

RICHARD PARKER

of breaking out of her shell. I took her on—or rather my class took her on—and we had a very exciting year.

"Every millimeter of progress was cheered and praised and encouraged by the kids, who kept up a nonstop stimulation program (arrived at instinctively and with only the slightest direction from me). Well, what with the memory of this and the book I had just read, I felt I had to do something about it. I made contact with a woman who ran a special unit for autistic children and spent a few afternoons as an unpaid helper. Orry emerged as a sort of combined character. When I started the story he quickly established himself as a person and the family just grew around him.

"As for the railway bit, I do happen to live right in the area of the first passenger railway in the world. And one of our normal Sunday afternoon walks is along the disused track to the mouth of the funnel designed by Stephenson himself, the digging of which cost six lives."

Gingerbread Man, one of Richard Parker's earliest novels, was reviewed by a *New York Times* critic, who wrote, "It's a fine job in every respect—off-trail, refreshing, and exciting. And the excellent depiction of the barely tangential worlds of children and adults may well stay in your mind as long as *High Wind in Jamaica. New Statesman & Nation* commented, "The formula is hackneyed; but Mr. Parker writes well enough to work up a continuous feeling of excitement."

"It's an excellent suspense story in every respect," wrote the *New York Times* of *Harm Intended,* "superlatively written and plotted, with fine examples of detection by the community as a whole. But what you'll remember most is the children, each a fully characterized individual, all wonderfully authentic and alive in their reactions to each other, to their parents, and to the threat of crime." Observed *Library Journal:* "A most satisfactory, literate thriller with a cinematic climax. For an extra dividend there are the children themselves, the sort of natural, inconsequent, endearing and sometimes infuriating youngsters created by such other British writers as E. Nesbit, Forrest Reid, Kenneth Grahame, and Arthur Ransome."

Commenting on *Lion at Large,* a critic for the *New York Times Book Review* wrote: "This story races along at a fine pace; the dialogue is good, much of it very funny, and there is intrigue, danger and a spine-tingling climax. Through it all the characters seem as real as the youngsters down the block. . . ." "Richard Parker is a vigorous writer with a strong feeling for situation," noted the London *Times Literary Supplement* in its review of *Private Beach.* "In the present book, whose plot is perhaps not intense enough for his energy, he experiments, not unsuccessfully, with that kind of apparently inconsequential spoken thought more usually associated with the style of William Mayne. . . ."

FOR MORE INFORMATION SEE: New Statesman and Nation, January 9, 1954; *New York Times,* July 25, 1954 and July 29, 1956; *Library Journal,* July, 1956; *New York Times Book Review,* May 14, 1961; *Times Literary Supplement,* July 9, 1964.

PARRISH, (Frederick) Maxfield 1870-1966

PERSONAL: Born July 25, 1870, in Philadelphia, Pennsylvania; son of Stephen (an artist) and Elizabeth (Bancroft) Parrish; married Lydia Austin (a painter), June 1, 1895; chil-

PARRISH in his early twenties

dren: John Dillwyn, Maxfield, Stephen, Jean. *Education:* Haverford College, student, 1888-1891; Pennsylvania Academy of Fine Arts, student, 1891-1894; Drexel Institute of Arts and Sciences, student under Howard Pyle; University of New Hampshire, A.F.D., 1954. *Home:* New Hampshire.

CAREER: Illustrator and commercial artist. Designed his first magazine cover for *Harper's Weekly,* April, 1895, followed by assignments to do pictures and posters for other popular periodicals, including *Century Magazine, St. Nicholas, Scribner's,* and *Collier's;* his works also became familiar to the public through his illustrations for calendars and advertisements. Noted for his use of rich colors, especially the shade of blue named for him, his most famous mural, *Old King Cole,* was hung in the Hotel Knickerbocker in New York, 1920, and later moved to the St. Regis Hotel, 1933; his paintings and drawings were exhibited in the Gallery of Modern Art in New York, 1964. *Member:* National Academy of Design (associate, 1905; academician, 1906), Society of American Artists, Philadelphia Water Color Club (honorary member), Phi Beta Kappa, Phi Kappa Sigma. *Awards, honors:* Honorable mention, Paris Exposition, 1900; silver medal, Buffalo Exposition, 1901; L.L.D., Haverford College, 1914; gold medal, Architectural League, 1917.

ILLUSTRATOR: Kenneth Grahame, *Golden Age,* Lane, 1900; Washington Irving, *Knickerbocker's History of New York,* Russell, 1900; K. Grahame, *Dream Days,* Lane, 1902; Eugene Field, *Poems of Childhood,* Scribner, 1904, reissued, 1974; L. Frank Baum, *Mother Goose in Prose,* Bobbs-Merrill, 1905; *Arabian Nights Entertainment,* edited by Kate Douglas Wiggin and Nora A. Smith, Scribner, 1909, reissued, 1974; Nathaniel Hawthorne, *Wonder Book [and] Tanglewood Tales,* Duffield, 1910; Francis Turner Palgrave, *Golden Treasury of Songs and Lyrics,* Duffield, 1911; Louise Saunders, *Knave of Hearts,* Scribner, 1925.

Collections: *The Maxfield Parrish Poster Book* (introduction by Maurice Sendak), Harmony, 1974; *Maxfield Parrish Prints: A Collector's Guide,* edited by M. S. Sweeney, Bauhan, 1975.

SIDELIGHTS: **July 25, 1870.** Frederick Parrish was born in Philadelphia. Later he took a family name, Maxfield, as his middle name.

1884-1886. In Europe with his family, he was in Paris at the time of Victor Hugo's funeral: "I was fifteen and climbed a tree on the Champs-Elysées. The avenue was jammed, but I scattered the crowd when a branch of my tree broke with a noise like a pistol shot. They thought it was the beginning of a nihilist demonstration."[1] [Coy Ludwig, *Maxfield Parrish,* Watson-Guptill Publications, 1973.]

He had other Parisian reflections: "Last Friday we all went to the Opera to see 'Faust' played. We enjoyed it immensely, and thought to see the house itself. When we went in we entered into a huge vestibule with carved stone ceiling and waxed floors. Then we waited here a few minutes and then went up the grand staircase ... It is perfectly magnificent made of polished marble and other different stones.

"This morning Papa and I took a walk through the long picture gallery at the Louvre, and I enjoy the pictures more and more each time I see them."[1]

All was not joy: "I have been to the dentist the last two Thursdays, and I don't mind it so much as he is a nice man and don't hurt much. You know when you are with Doctor Pugh, your mouth becomes rather full, after you have had the rubber dam on about half an hour, but this dentist puts a cyphon [sic] in your mouth so you don't mind it at all. And then he has the gas light back of a glass globe filled with water so as to magnify it, and it throws a strong light into your mouth."[1]

1881-1891. Student at Haverford College, a Quaker institution. "It would be going too far to state that art was in any way forbidden, yet there was a feeling in the air it was looked upon with suspicion, as maybe related distantly to graven images and the like.

"I was all for becoming an architect, and once, exploring in some forgotten corner of the library, discovered a number of giant French books of engravings of classic temples; books of wonder, smelling of old mouldy leather and long years of unuse. From the astonished librarian permission was obtained to take them one at a time to my room, where many hours were spent making tracings of capitals and things. . . .

"There may have been precious little art around, but there was surely a wealth of material for making it. For all there was Haverford, and the sheer beauty of the place was an influence and an education hard to equal.

"Lying under those copper beeches, when we should have been doing something else, looking into the cathedral windows above did a lot more for us than contemplation of the Roman Colosseum. There were grand trees in those days, and grand trees do something to you. It would be of great interest to know just what it was at college that influenced us most, that helped most to form our futures. Like enough it was not the big things on the front page, but possibly some small affair not mentioned in the catalog. . . .

"But then there were big things, and I think the biggest of them all was Dr. [Francis B.] Gummere. His room was like a temple, of music and beauty and all the best that man had written. Through the open window behind his desk were trees again, tall shafts of tulip poplars, and among them the thrushes singing. It would be good to be back there again, listening to the rich music and rhythm of this perfect rendering. . . . Indeed we were in the presence of great art then: it seemed to combine them all, the medium mattered little. Association with his personality and the magic of his teaching seemed to go hand in hand with the beauty of Haverford, a combination never to be forgotten."[1]

1892-93. Spent summers painting at Annisquam, Mass., under the guidance of his artist father. "I trust you will not be disappointed in the little work I have to show—but I have not gone in so much this time for quantity. I've worked as much and more than last year, but have painted over and scraped out—thinking I can gain more by practice and not keeping a lot of useless stuff. If I feel encouraged you will know it has not been in vain. You may be glad to know I use up my yellows very fast, which was not the case last year. I suffer from impatience more than anything else."[1]

While there, he wrote to his mother in Philadelphia: "Our studio is by this time all fixed and we are thoroughly enjoying the coziness of it. . . . Our divan being made of a bed-stead given by our landlady E. is quite a piece of furniture. We took away the stairs leading to the western platform as taking up entirely too much room, and put a ladder in their stead. We each have a good solid table, and have the floor covered with a large sail, which keeps the wind out, and makes a good surface to walk on. The stove is the greatest success. There are miles of pipe for a thimble of a stove at the other end. But what it lacks in quantity it makes up in quality, for put a match therein and the place is warm. Indeed I should sleep in it and live in it (the studio) were I alone here, although the chinks would no doubt let in much cold air in winter.

"About sculpture—thee might be right. An artist here declares my hands were cut out for a baseball player, so opinions differ. I truly love it, but it is not for me; as I care for color more than any other phase of art. And don't be afraid of my ever sticking to 'easel pictures' alone."[1]

In later years, he recalled these summers: "My own art school work was simply terrible. I didn't know what it was all about, only by actually doing it could I get anywhere. I got a lot from my father who was an artist, who called my attention to many hundreds of things in the visual world to which most of humanity are blind."[1]

1893. Parrish revealed a great mechanical aptitude, and wrote his mother: "And about the mechanical—it may come in handy some day, but at present I am wrestling with its evil tendencies as shown in my work, for it is hard to rid myself of the love of a good neat job, which doesn't improve artistic expression one bit."[1]

This very quality made it hard for him to dash off spontaneous drawings: "I'm no earthly good at the little telling sketch. The few strokes of the pencil were never my medium: couldn't even make a drawing on The Players' Club table cloths."[1]

1893. Parrish went to Chicago World's Fair. "Today has been trying to explain why this place is sometimes referred to as the 'windy city.' It has been blowing a gale, with a little

**All serious resistance came to an end as soon as I had reached the quarter-deck and cut down the
pirate chief. ■** (From *Dream Days* by Kenneth Grahame. Illustrated by Maxfield Parrish.)

(From *Poems of Childhood* by Eugene Field. Illustrated by Maxfield Parrish.)

rain and drizzle too. A stunning loose gray sky, just like Normandy, has made a beautiful picture all day long with the white buildings under it. Finer even than yesterday when all was a dazzling white under a clear ultra-marine sky. I have not been much in the buildings, though what things I have seen inside are simply marvels of handiwork. What I love to look at most is the conception of the whole thing. Look at it, and realize the possibilities of this effect and that. One often dreams of laying out ideal cities with unlimited means, but such mental recreations have to be remodeled after seeing this. These stupendous architectural groupings could scarcely be surpassed in fairy tales without becoming absurd. And one of the strangest things about it all is that it is almost impossible to imagine such things can ever be done again. It seems more fairy like when one knows it is all to come down in a few months.

"The people one never ceases to watch. Such characters and types were never collected before, and in themselves they are a Fair. One has only to come here to find that what is known as caricature is after all a literal rendering of truth. I am enjoying it all in a general way and though horses made of prunes are no doubt very wonderful, yet I prefer to see it as I like best. The Fine Arts building has seen me most. There are few fine, really fine things. That man Zorn from Seden is certainly a wonder. Tell Papa no pictures are hung in groups. The works of the same artist are scattered all over the place, the only limit being the U.S. section, France section, etc. His etchings are however all together and look very well. The medals were evidently given to a bootblack to confer on the things he liked best—most every other picture has a medal and it seems as much of an honour to be without one as to have one."[1]

1894. The young artist was commissioned to paint wall decorations for the Mask and Wig Club of the University of Pennsylvania. He wrote his father: "Work is coming on very well indeed, and all parties concerned thereby seem highly pleased.... I have one side nearly finished, and the other I think will go on much quicker since I will know just how to economize labor. It is great fun—and I have constantly to keep a check on myself. I get so excited and carried away with what I am doing that 'tis bad for one's nerves: but there is in it at times a wild fiendish delight which partakes of all sorts of sensations, of what is possible in art and in me and in everything. However as time goes on I am getting myself better under control I trust. I have sailed in knowing nothing whatsoever about fresco work and have been trying experiments of my own which I think are highly successful—and have a few wrinkles in store for Cornish which I think will be successful...."[1]

June 1, 1895. Married Lydia Austin. Both were Quakers, although Parrish was not devout, and his wife a member of another meeting. On his marriage, his meeting terminated his membership. The notice from Society of Friends to Maxfield Parrish read: "Frederick Maxfield Parrish who had a birthright in the religious Society of Friends married a person not in membership with us, and in the manner of his marriage violated our testimony in favor of the free ministry of the Gospel.

"He was visited by a Committee of this Meeting, but having exhibited a want of interest in our religious Society and no design to continue his membership therewith, we no longer consider him a member amongst us. Nevertheless we design that by attention to the Divine Witness he may experience preservation and know the reward of Peace."[1]

1895. Went to Europe for second time, to visit museums and salons. "[*Brussels*] I have been feasting on glorious pictures in a great gallery. Oh, the masters of the Dutch and Flemish schools knew how to paint! I only wish they showed up better in photos, but their charm is lost. They were a perfect revelation to me—the first time I had a chance to see the old fellows face to face. The van Eyck's, the van Orley's, the Memling's and a host of wonders. Spent last evening in a concert garden under great trees in company with a beautiful string orchestra, where one can sit at one's ease and be very happy and wish with all one's might that someone else were with him.

"[*Paris*] Here I am in Paris at last! And what a Paris it is: there seems a very magic in the name! How often it is that places we have visited in childhood seemed so grand and vast, and when seen again in later years have seemed so contracted and as though something were missing—but not so with Paris. Never has anything appeared to me so vast, so magnificent. When I arrived here at sunset the city burst upon me as nothing ever did. . . . The streets are endless and marvels of beauty: the palace of the Louvre seems simply stupendous, and all is on such a scale of splendor it takes one's breath away. I could not have come upon all this at a time when my appreciation was more keen and my eyes more open to let nothing escape them. I feel that I am seeing so much more than other people here: that they are missing half of it. It takes back all I said of Bruxelles: there is only one Paris, and this is it.

"I have been to both the salons and consider it a duty performed. The new salon at the Champs de Mars is very disappointing. I knew there would be lots of bad but I was expecting more good and one or two at least great things. The old salon is simply shocking. Of the Avenues and Avenues of pictures there is not one good thing: not one. The most interesting thing is to see what frightful subjects some have taken, and see which Frenchman had the most original idea of blood. There are many examples worth dwelling upon . . . one . . . is the canvas of a man who has gone straight to the slaughter house for his subject. There before us is a colossal representation of a newly cut-open ox, dripping, swimming, wallowing in crimson, animal blood! . . . I was certainly disappointed with the salons. May be it was too much of a shock coming right out of Bruxelles. However the new salon is not by any means without some mighty good things. Strangely enough it is very, very sane, and it is the old salon which abounds with modern horrors. . . .

"I had resolved not to enter the Louvre until I had thoroughly seen the salons; but Sunday as I passed one of the entrances the temptation was too much for me and in I went. As luck would have it the first room I entered was the Salon Carrée. I nearly fainted. If Chapman's Homer was to Keats what that was to me then his Sonnet gives some idea of my sensations. One had but to turn and there were Titians, Rembrandts, Botticellis, Correggios, van Eycks, all together, in one glorious mosaic of richness. What an awesome feeling it is to be in such a presence. I took a hurried walk all through the vast galleries just to see what was in store for me. That great Titian, 'La Mise au Tombeau' simply haunts me. I dream about beautiful reds and blues and greens and glorious whites. The color in that picture is pure magic. . . .

"[*Paris*] I am sitting in the Tuileries watching the twilight: a glorious place to be alone in and wish one were not. This evening is simply heavenly—such gray twilights! One does not wonder that the old masters put such beautiful ones behind their madonnas. Took lunch with Henri, Schofield and

Glackens and had a fine time. Have laid in a fine stock of photographs, too, but the Velasquez's of Madrid I cannot get. Maybe I can in London.

"[*London*] After breakfast I got on top of a bus in the drizzle and rode to morning services in Westminster Abbey. A thick yellow fog was rolling up making all like evening and very fascinating to be out in: and inside Westminster all morning were vast black places to look into, and where there was light it was a beautiful amber. I settled myself away over in the poets' corner, away from people, under Shakespeare and 'rare Ben Jonson' and listened to some charming choir boys singing. The rich warm blackness all around was most impressive and like a forest with nothing above but impenetrable gloom.

"When it was all over I buttoned up to the teeth and ploughed through the wet across Westminster bridge just as 'Big Ben' with a hoarse roar was striking twelve. What is that wonderful fascination about a bell? They are such human things hung up aloft in dark towers, silently waiting until their turn comes. You watch them hanging motionless and they seemed possessed of a subtle, quiet power: a being with a voice. And the great domes too, they are like great bells forever silent: they always impressed me as though they were living things but slumbering. Their very names 'bell' and 'dome' a ring, and you feel them reverberating when you say them. I shall carry back with me no sweeter, happier recollection than those glad, silvery chimes up in the Cathedral tower at Antwerp; pouring through the air their careless jangle of sweet sound. How fine to be a child and live under them; to look up into the dark tower and wonder what they were doing and saying when they were not ringing: to wonder what made them ring at all, and how fine it would be to be one of them and hang away up high among the dark rafters, in such happy company, and swing and ring when they did. . . .

"*Monday evening*. I had a grand sleep after my day in the wet; and the rain has left us for awhile. . . . I saw one more Annual Exhibition today namely The 'New Gallery' on Regent St. It was beastly bad of course, with the exception of John Sargent's portrait of Ada Rehan which was a stunner. My! but you never saw such rot! England is the most hopeless place there is, for her art community surround themselves with a wall, and they are satisfied. In every picture of 'the return of the sailor-lad' or mermaid playing with a tiger on the bank and such subjects, is written, satisfaction, we think this is beautiful and so do the people, what more do you want. And when such artists go to the National Gallery, if they go at all, I doubt if they are conscious of any contrast. I firmly believe now that America will in time have modern exhibitions to show that will outclass any on this side of the water: it will take a long time to be sure, but she has not as much to contend against as have England and France, though she has much more to learn. I trust I have deposited my last shilling on modern exhibitions here: I never saw so many at once, but London is a big place."[1]

1898. Began construction of "The Oaks," near Cornish, New Hampshire. The house was the subject of numerous magazine articles. "The place has been so photographed that the corners are getting rounded.

". . . as you descend some steps from the upper level to the house terrace, through old oak trunks and branches, through them and beyond them, you have a confused sensation that there is something grand going to happen. There is blue distance, infinite distance, seen through this hole and that, a

Bookplate, circa 1900-1905.

sense of great space and glorious things in store for you, if only you go a little further to grasp it all. It takes your breath away a little, as there seems to be just blue forms ahead and no floor. Then you come upon the lower terrace, and over a level stone wall you see it all: hills and woodlands, high pastures, and beyond them, more and bluer hills, from New Hampshire on one side and from Vermont on the other, come tumbling down into the broad valley of the Connecticut, with one grand mountain over it all.

". . . we had some epic parties here long, long ago. Judge Learned Hand to this day likes to talk them over, and to see Walter Lippmann and Felix Frankfurter unbend a bit was a day to remember. But we were all young then, and if we didn't quite understand W. L. we did not bother. Dining then was gay and often too big. Far better were modest lunches on the studio porch of a day in summer. . . .

"The summer rush is on and it's pretty gay. We are thinking of going down to New York to rest. The colony has become more or less literary, and a pretty good lot of fellows. Ethel Barrymore is with us for the summer, and all us fossils take a little longer selecting our neckties and brushing what hair we've got as though it made a damn bit of difference. I am hard at work on a big picture [*Old King Cole*] about the size of Texas to go over the bar in the Knickerbocker Hotel in New York."[1]

1901. Having contracted tuberculosis, Parrish spent the winter in Hot Springs, Arizona. "We never expected to find ourselves out here, but here we are and having the time of our lives. Century Co. sent me out to illustrate a series of

The Man in the Moon. ■ (From *Mother Goose In Prose* by L. Frank Baum. Illustrated by Maxfield Parrish.)

(From *Knickerbocker's History of New York* by Washington Irving. Illustrated by Maxfield Parrish.)

articles on the region, and though not exactly in my line, there were other inducements which made it hard to resist, and now that we have tried it the art part of it seems to be most enjoyable. . . . And air! You [have never] breathed such stuff in your life: it's right from the keg. We are twenty-five miles from a railroad in one of numerous canyons which cut this country in all directions, and wherever we go it is always on desert ponies. We ride to the tops of the mountains, and from there you see nothing but other mountains and not a sign of a human being anywhere. You get a sense of freedom and vastness here that I never imagined existed. . . .

"Lydia is a regular Annie Oakley, rides the desert horses astride, and is a crack shot with a six shooter. But shooting people is considered bad form here nowadays, so she has to content herself with targets. . . .

"Christmas day I sat on a Coroner's inquest, a new departure for me in celebrating that day. It was in a little cabin up in a gulch, not far from here, and Lord, I wish you could have seen the jury! We pushed back the bottles and sat on the bar, and took the oath while the chickens snuffled around the floor and sad eyed burros looked in at the door. The next day they buried him and put stones on top so the coyotes wouldn't dig him up. And the next day all but two of the jury took to drink and remained in an alcoholic trance for a week. Such is life out here. We shall stay here until April and then up to New Hampshire in time to plant."[1]

The Parrishes had four children: John Dillwyn (1904-1969), Maxfield, Jr. (1906), Stephen (1909), Jean (1911).

1912. He wrote his son, John: "This is not exactly a postal card is it. But the regular post card I found would be much too small to hold this beautiful picture. It is meant to show what we do with ourselves here when you are so far away. I admit it is a very poor picture, and but for being a wonderful likeness of your devoted dad, and the first letter I ever wrote to you, it isn't much, I must say. But when you come back to us again we will all go out and have a slide on the hen-house hill. When it is very good we start from the door where they keep the kerosine and bump into the door where you boys put on your coats and galligaskins. Sometimes Steve can go all the way down without falling off. When it comes time to pull the sled back Max discovers something wrong with his leg, something very serious and although he often gets the leg mixed up with the other one, you cannot help feeling sorry for him. The black cow and her black calf look over the fence at us and wonder what on earth we are trying to do. And the hens sit on the fence and say things about us. Then sometimes Max and I do 'stunts.' He will stand up behind me on the sled with his hands on my shoulders, and then I will lie flat on my tummy and Max will sit on my back and we will go down that way. Get well and strong very soon, Buddy dear, and come back to us, for the place is not the same without you. All your animals are waiting for you in the stable. Daddy."[1]

1909. The artist began planning murals for the New York residence of Mrs. Gertrude Vanderbilt Whitney. "As a companion tone to the rich brown of the wood work, I want to have a band of rich beautiful evening blue; those to be the two big notes of the room. I feel sure you will agree with me, that, outside of Niagara Falls there is nothing more beautiful in all nature than figures against a sky of r.b.e. blue. . . .

"The idea of the whole scheme has not changed in all these years, but will be sort of a fete or masquerade in the olden-

time. The real goings on will be in the loggia on the North wall, and the people will have sauntered off on to the other walls, as though it were a court or garden. They will all be youths and girls, as we would wish things to be.

"It is tremendously interesting to have this chance to revel in color as deep and as rich as you please. . . .

"The idea is simply this: don't light the decorations at all, but let them get what light they can after the room is lighted to suit living requirements. To my mind, decorations should decorate and they should not have attention called to them by specially directed light any more than wall paper or a rug or a piece of furniture."[1]

The Whitney murals were not entirely successful, and in later years he reflected: "I think I was once persuaded to try mural decoration, but I know only too well I was never meant for it, was never able to understand the requirements, or feel at home in it, as may be the case with smaller things. The panel in question is only too good a proof of it, for I . . . had a chance to study it longer than anything I had ever done, but to this day I do not know just why it is a failure."[1]

1910. Edward Bok asked him to paint some long, narrow wall panels for the women's dining hall at Curtis Publishing Company. "I will make a suitable painting for the south end of the room representing a carnival or masquerade. The scene will be in a white marble loggia: the foreground will be a series of wide steps extending across the entire picture, leading up to three arches and supporting columns. . . . On the steps and in the loggia in the gardens beyond and on the terraces will be crowds of figures . . . it will be my aim to make it all joyous, a little unreal, a good place to be in, a sort of happiness of youth. . . . In the narrow panels extending around the room, it is my intention to show figures coming to the fete or carnival.

". . . All the people are youths and girls; nobody seems old. It may be a gathering of only young people, or it may be a land where there is youth, and nobody grows old at all. . . . What is the meaning of it all? It doesn't mean an earthly thing, not even a ghost of an allegory: no science enlightening agriculture: nobody enlightening anything. The endeavor is to present a painting which will give pleasure without tiring the intellect: something beautiful to look upon: a good place to be in. Nothing more."[1]

Parrish had definite ideas about subjects for his murals in public places. Asked why he picked the Pied Piper for a bar mural, he replied: ". . . I don't exactly know, except that I must have thought it an attractive one, as I do now. Seems to me I heard somewhere that it was not a subject quite suited to increase the receipts of a bar, as guests in draining a glass were apt to note a child in the painting that resembled a little one at home and then and there cancel that wish for a second glass."[1]

But for private homes, he chose less definite subject matter. He rejected an idea for a music room mural of scenes from *Tristan* And *Parsifal.* "Scenes from any of these operas are grand, grand subjects.[1]

"Concerning them, I have just one little suggestion to offer. These are pictures made by music, and I am wondering if it is wise to attempt to render them in a medium that is so much inferior. They are pictures you feel and do not see, pictures of the mind, we'll say, and I think that music takes up the rendering of such things and thoughts where painting has to leave off and go no further.

"About the only thing painting could do with them would be to go beyond the limitations of the stage, have more heroic people, grander settings, and obtain greater beauty in form and composition and color, and place about them a real but imaginative nature."[1]

And he was adamant on the subject of titles for his murals. "I am the last one in the world to invent titles for pictures. I loathe titles even when they might fit, and in the case of the dining room murals, I threw up my hands. The panels are really sections of one large picture, technically what are known as fragments, and what to call each one—why, it's well nigh impossible.

"Could they be Opus No. 4, like music? Or, 'A Pair of Vases.' 'Another Pair.' 'Even Two More.' etc. . . . As to the sentimental titles for Heaven's sake let's not have that."[1]

1911. A poetry anthology, printed without his knowledge, claimed to be illustrated by Maxfield Parrish. Actually, the illustrations were reproductions of his *Collier's* covers. He then granted only magazine rights to *Life*. ". . . when they have served their purpose as covers, is it your intention to use them for anything else . . . ? The reason I ask is that I want to safeguard myself against a dreadful thing that happened to some of my work at Collier's, where the reproduction rights were sold to Duffield with which they illustrated Palgrave's *Golden Treasury of Lyrics*. The . . . bad taste of the thing we won't dwell upon here, but the worst of it was that a book is out over the world now, and for all the public knows, these old cast-off covers are my conception of these beautiful classic lyrics. It was about the worst ever. Never a word said to me. . . . I dare say Collier's were entirely within their rights from me, and felt they could do as they pleased with privilege . . . now, alas, too late I wish I had known a thing or two."[1]

Parrish did covers for *Life* until 1923. He enjoyed the work greatly, especially the covers executed in a simple, comic style which Parrish called his "odds and ends." Many of the comic figures have his own face in caricature. "I'll say right now that there is a lot of good fun doing these for your crowd down there that I like. I like the spirit of it, and work, I think, is the better for it."[1]

1914. Arranged with advertising executive Rusling Wood to do some paintings for various products, reserving the right to determine which products he thought would be suitable subjects.

"There are some ideas or subjects that would not interest me. . . . But—if you have an idea that IS interesting I should be very glad indeed to have a try at it. And by interesting, I mean something that can be made with a 'punch' to it, something the public will recognize wherever they see it. . . .

"If you have an idea you would like worked out, say something on the same order as the Dutch Boy on the Colgate soap ad, let me know about it: I will gladly undertake it, and if I do not see a result that will do justice to myself or to you or to the product advertised, I will tell you frankly that I do not want to undertake it.

"The art of pictorially advertising interests me very much, but I do think it is one of the most difficult arts to put across, and what makes success is an extremely subtle affair."[1]

However, he specified that he wanted to do only a small number of paintings for advertisements. "I only want a little of this kind of work, for I find that the way I do it does not pay anywhere near as well as what we may call my regular work: pictures for plain people, overmantel panels, etc. I like it as a relief and a variety, and it is that, but too much of it wouldn't be good business. . . ."[1]

1915. Parrish met Clarence Crane, a Cleveland candy manufacturer and the father of Hart Crane. The artist designed a candy-box cover for the elder Crane, who was delighted with it, and commissioned paintings for 1916 and 1917 holiday gift boxes. The subject for 1916 was Omar Khayyam, and for 1917, Cleopatra. Parrish was unhappy with the color reproduction of the *Rubaiyat* panel: "I cannot bear the Omar. The cook loved it, and I gave it to her.

"Cleopatra is welcome here, or any lady of history of undoubted charm. She was not particularly good looking they tell me, but had a 'way' with her. . . . Of course there are no end of subjects. All I care about is something that can hold color and be made effective."[1]

He was horrified to find that the candy-box bore the label "The Maxfield Parrish Package," and wrote to Crane: "You see, I do not mind your saying that the design is by me, but I somehow don't like the idea that the article sold, or rather its container is mine. Because if I did many things of this kind for different kinds of merchandise, I would become the god-father of each article. . . .

"I cannot promise to make one every year. To tell you the truth, some day soon I hope to give up this kind of work entirely. I mean, I've been looking forward to the day for years when I could do my own work, just the things I want to do, and no orders, nothing but just to try to express the things that are inside me. Landscapes mostly, or figures when I want to. The time isn't quite ripe yet, perhaps, but I feel it is coming along sooner than it was some years ago. . . ."[1]

1917. After a vacation with his wife at Saint Simons Island in Georgia, Parrish began the 1918 painting for Crane, on the subject of the Garden of Allah. These candy-box paintings were all reproduced widely as art-prints in later years, and brought in many thousands of dollars in royalties. "Now, maybe, I can sit down and write to you with a better imitation of intelligence than was possible down on that little lazy island. A picture goes off in an hour or so, rushed to death on it as usual, and believe me, right here, it is the last thing I will ever do that has to be rushed. To say nothing of wearing you all out, it makes bad work, and that makes you mighty unhappy.

"About the next one. You do seem to have an admiration for my work that is not entirely justified. I wonder how you would like one that I really liked? . . . I like your suggestion of the Garden of Allah, but I am quite sure what you mean. . . . There is a book about it which I have not read, but I think we have it here in the house. Then there was a silly play I saw in New York, beautifully given, with wonderful effects of desert and moonrise. Was it that you had in mind? To tell you the truth I am not very strong on subject pictures, historical affairs, like Cleopatra or Omar. I would much rather do things like ideal gardens, spring, autumn, youth, the spirit of the sea, the joy of living (if there is such a thing). And what is more, I think the vast public likes them better when the artist can get his idea 'across,' to borrow from Wordsworth. They are the hardest things in the world to do, and consequently the most interesting. I kind of wish you had seen the one I did for the General Electric people, a sort of calendar they are to bring out in the fall to remind the public that they make a good lamp.

"... I think I got a little of the spirit of the thing. Enough so anyway, to fool the G. E. people, who phoned and wired and wrote to tie me up for one every year till the crack of doom. Oh yes, it was rushed too, and it might have been better. Do you know what I mean by getting the spirit of the thing? I mean the spirit of the things in which we take most joy and happiness in life. The spirit of out of doors, the spirit of light and distance . . . that is a quality not lost on the public. I feel sure. . . .

"Now, here is another thing. Very sordid. I have a snug little income that dribbles in now and then from royalties, a by-product from the sale of prints. Where I have made paintings, and where the prints of them are offered for sale, the publishers divide one half the royalties with me: that is they take one half and send me the other half. These have always been offered to me. I have never asked for them, so that I have come to believe it is fair business to expect them. Now how would you feel about sharing the royalties with me on work I did for you that was put out for sale in print form? I never mentioned this to you because somehow it never occurred to me that you would sell the prints of the paintings. And right here, let me add that you had every conceivable right to do so. I would like to make some more covers for you, but if I do, they are to be done in advance and no rush whatsoever. I'll begin the next one sometime this summer for 1918 Christmas, if you wish to go on with them."[1]

Parrish was most excited by landscapes. Until late in his career he had to do other things for his livelihood; but he always worked in as many landscapes as possible. "... I have felt for a number of years that I have a better grasp on landscape than on any other subject."[1]

He did some landscapes for the Broadmoor Hotel in Colorado in 1920. "Should I ever be able to come out there and paint the place, I would do it just as I did the series on the Italian Gardens, make many photographs and studies on the spot and then paint the actual picture at my home. In some ways this is better, for with a certain temperment [sic], a literal rendering of the material facts can be avoided, and the part that stays in the mind can the better be brought out, the spirit and atmosphere of the place.

"I remember going out to Colorado Springs once to make a postery sort of picture for the Broadmoor Hotel. Besides the hotel they had two features of which they were very proud: an artificial lake and the Rocky Mountains. But you could not see all three from any one position. So what did we do but put the lake on the other side of the hotel, thus showing all three attractions in one picture. We did not dare drag in Pikes Peak, but took liberties only with what man had done.

"Strange as it may seem, I would much prefer to paint such pictures here, away from the actual place, because I feel that the most important qualities of such scenes are their sense of vastness, space, color and light, fleeting qualities, which can best be portrayed in retrospect.

"The magic and spirit . . . you feel instead of actually see, and if you don't get it in a painting a colored photograph would do as well, if not better. Just a faithful 'portrait' of a locality, factual, would never do. I feel sure all great landscape paintings were at least finished indoors, for there is no such thing as copying the more illusive qualities as light play-ing over the scene, the sense of air and space and color, distance and the great dome of the sky, for these things last but for a moment anyway. The material objects, 'stage properties' so to speak, one has to have to help get the message across, trees and rocks, hills and valleys, rivers and mountains, but unless you get the other, the thing is a failure."[1]

1920. Began illustrations for *The Knave of Hearts,* a play for children by Louise Saunders, wife of Scribner's editor, Maxwell Perkins. "Do you remember years ago I said I always had the longing to make pictures for another book? . . . This is just to say that the longing is still there, and of late the longing seems to be growing into something else. I wonder did you ever read a little play called *The Knave of Hearts* by Louise Saunders Perkins? . . . I have read it and seen it acted, and the thought will not down that it would be a most interesting thing to illustrate. . . .

"The reason I wanted to illustrate *The Knave of Hearts* was on account of the bully opportunity it gives for a very good time making the pictures. Imagination could run riot, bound down by no period, just good fun and all sorts of things.

"It figures out about fifteen pages in full color, a cover and a double page cover lining, a dozen headings and odds and ends, and . . . I dare say the size is too large for you, but of course, the larger the better, as far as pictures are concerned. . . .

"You must understand all this lay-out to be in gorgeous color. The landscape back of the figures in the cover lining—a very beautiful affair illuminated by a golden late afternoon sun: castles, waterfalls, rocks and mountains. . . .

"The next great question will be WHEN? Goodness only knows. As I will get no money until the book begins to sell, it will have to be worked in with other work, and I know I shall enjoy doing it that way, with a sort of rest in between."[1]

In his advertising work, Parrish was frequently asked to alter a painting to make it work for another product. He usually refused. For instance, the Fisk Tires "Yawning Boy" trademark was worked into his painting for Fisk, "There was an Old Woman Who Lived in a Shoe." Asked later to paint the boy out so that the painting could be used for an advertisement for cereal, Parrish replied that it would ruin his design to change it, and added: "Have you tried the Birth Control League? I should think it would make a grand poster for them."[1]

And in another instance, he wrote to Wood: "I hope you don't think I'm a crank about my ideas of changing the original design, but really I know I am right. There are a few of my architectural friends who seem to know what I am after, but I'm darn if anybody else does. You like my work, but I wonder if you know why you do. Well, putting modesty aside, I do think some of it, the best of it, has a quality of design about it that most of this kind of work lacks. By design, I mean a certain kind of studied subtle composition, a harmony of line and mass and color, just for all the world the stuff you find and enjoy in music. Now if you take a couple of bars out of *The Maiden's Prayer* and stick it in *The Star Spangled Banner* you are going to spoil both (though in this instance I am not quite sure). So that, in taking a figure out of the composition, out of his studied surroundings, and putting him somewhere else, something is going to suffer, believe me."[1]

He also did not like to be given fixed subjects, preferring, as most artists do, to select his own. In 1919, he was given a commission for a series to be entitled "Primitive Man." "I hope you will understand . . . it is foolish for me to do any commercial work which I am not interested in. I mean also that this, what we might call 'dictated' work is becoming more and more irksome to do, and as I make more money from the work that I really care for, and get far more enjoyment from it, naturally I cannot be blamed for disliking the other. . . . I would be ever so glad if I could give up the Primitive Man and the one to follow, because they are not the kind of thing that I would choose to do: I will do them, of course, as well as I know how, because I said I would, but I would make more money and be very much happier if they were pictures of my own choice."[1]

1923. The artist did agree to alter a painting, "The Spirit of Transportation," removing the trucks and leaving only the rocky landscape. It was then widely reproduced as an art print, renamed—not by Parrish—"The Royal Gorge." "I was amused at the title. . . . The tree was taken outside my studio window here: the brook was from the back of Windsor, the rocks were from Bellows Falls, and a mountain or two from Arizona. And yet I've heard some say they had been just to that spot."[1]

Parrish was finally able to abandon advertising, as his success in art-prints grew. He was then able to price himself out of the market for all but a few choice advertising posters. ". . . As I told you I want to get of advertising work on account of the endless interruptions it causes from men with the best intentions in the world coming to see me, or what is just as bad, making me spend days and days writing them letters telling them not to. I am perfectly sincere in this.

"Another thing. I am now very happy in the kind of work I am doing. Even making covers for *Life* is mighty good fun. They pay just as well as posters for only the reproduction rights: the originals come back to me, of which I have the exclusive print rights, should any be suitable for that purpose, and I can sell the originals. . . . I also want to do some serious painting for publication as prints for it would be a grand satisfaction to have an income three or four times the price of one poster for a number of years, and own the original as well. This is plain arithmetic, not to mention common business sense. . . .

"What I am doing nowadays, is to build up the print business. A successful print is a pretty good thing all round. In the first place I can paint exactly what I please, and then, if it's successful it means an income, a pretty big one, for a number of years. I have just finished an ambitious painting [*Daybreak*] for Reinthal and Newman, of whom I have a high opinion, and I'll wait and see what the picture is going to do for me. . . ."[1]

1917-1931. Among the commissions he retained was the series of Edison Mayda Calendars for General Electric, which made Parrish's name known to nearly everyone in the country. One calendar was "Dream Light," which Parrish called "Girl in a Swing." "In this particular one, I was fairly well satisfied with the girl, as telling the story, telling it quietly, naturally, without any frills. I was a little suspicious of it, however, when my carpenter Ruggles thought it the best thing I'd ever done. There was quite a 'varnishing day' here of people to see it before it was put in its box, and the popular appeal seemed very genuine, but that, of course, has nothing to do with the reception by more enlightened ones in more effete localities. . . . As a picture for this particular

MAXFIELD PARRISH

purpose I do not like it as well as the Bagdad one; that, with its brilliance and poster quality I think the best of the series.

"For the 1930 I would advise the picture to be shorter.

"Of late years I have been doing all my work on a layout, so to speak, of Dynamic Symmetry, a rediscovery on the part of Jay Hambidge of the old Greek method of making rectangles. Those familiar with this method consider that these dynamic rectangles are far more pleasing than just arbitrary rectangles, and not only that, but by their subdivisions they permit every feature of the picture to be a harmonious part of the whole panel. If done with intelligence there is a certain balance to the design which is of great value. . . .

"Now these dynamic rectangles are very simple things, but they are fixed, and you can have only certain ones, or compound ones.—This may sound like sheer lunacy, but take my word for it, there is a lot in it. . . ."[1]

1923. Parrish's most famous painting, "Daybreak," soared to unprecedented popularity. "News of *Daybreak* filters into these remote parts, and I am getting comments in almost every mail. I heard of a business man who carries a large sized framed print with him on his journeys to and from New York and the West. I wish there was some way to reach him and suggest that he buy two."[1]

The House of Art, New York art publishing firm for whom "Daybreak" was painted, asked him to write a few words about it. Parrish replied: "Alas, you have asked the very one thing that is entirely beyond me, to write a little story of *Daybreak,* or, in fact, of any other picture.

"I could do almost anything in the world for you but that. I know full well the public want a story, always want to know more about a picture than the picture tells them but to my mind if a picture does not tell its own story, it's better to have the story without the picture. I couldn't tell a single thing about *Daybreak* because there isn't a single thing to tell: the picture tells all there is, there is nothing more."[1]

1925. Still working for the House of Art, Parrish tried to duplicate the success of "Daybreak" without imitating the painting itself. "For the next, I have in mind the two upright panels. One, at least, should be a marked departure in color scheme, for we must not always have this tiresome M.P. blue in every print. They are to be a rich gold tone, and needless to say, as beautiful as possible, with a great landscape behind the figures. . . .

". . . the figure in the new one is of a younger girl, seated in profile. . . . There is something about the picture in the show I did not like: it was a bit realistic, looked a little like a real person. Whereas I think nudes (especially for our purpose) want to be idealized."[1]

1926. Parrish began work on "October," the last painting he did for the House of Art (which retitled the work "Dreaming"). "This particular painting was inspired by a fine old oak tree in rather wild country north of here. It looked centuries old, and growing almost entirely out of a rocky ledge had to send its roots in every direction for a living.

"This figure was the result of much study, and is the seventh figure I had in the picture before I got something to give satisfaction. I dared not have a larger figure, for as soon as I did, it destroyed the scale and grandeur of the tree. And having a small one, I realized much would go out of her features in the smaller reproductions, so that I concentrated particularly on her pose, her general silhouette or outline to tell the story.

"In the vast majority of figure painting the figure is featured, in the lime light, and her surroundings are treated merely as background. My own aim in this kind of work is to keep the figure in its place out of doors, not feature it, emphasize it any more than a rock or tree. If this is done you get a quality of reality and consequently a beauty of truth. . . ."[1]

By 1929, Parrish decided that it was futile to try again and again to duplicate the success of "Daybreak." He dropped out of the art-print market. "I am a commercial artist, who, ever since his beginning has made his living by having his work reproduced. People who like attractive pictures are going to cut them out and possibly frame them no matter in what form, illustrations in books, in magazines, calendars, etc.

"This whole question of pictures made to order is a darn peculiar form of merchandise. You know that. As a gamble, poetry and music and literature are not far off. A man makes a great hit, a best seller, with a novel. His publishers are frantic for him to repeat, and the chances are his first success proves to be his last. You may order another best seller from me, and god knows I'm willing enough, but—can I deliver the goods? I have given the matter no end of thought and analysis, for I am just as keen as the next one to make money and not one bit ashamed to own to it. . . .

". . . They [the public] all seem to like the tiresome M.P. blue, for one thing, and girls having a pleasant chat, for another. They must look pleasant. . . . The contemplative kind, such as *Hilltop,* not so popular.

". . . You know, and I know, that what people like is a beautiful setting with charming figures, clothed or otherwise, and probably no one special feature. Whatever it is, it's elusive. *Stars* did not have it, nor *Hilltop.* Needless to say the good art quality has no particular appeal: that is only for those who know. . . .

"There are countless artists whose shoes I am not worthy to polish whose prints would not pay the printer. . . .

"The question of judgement is a puzzling one. I am beginning to doubt my own. . . .

". . . this particular vein of mine may be petering out. It wouldn't be surprising. Maybe the public knows before the artist does. . . ."[1]

1931. Parrish decided not to paint any more "Girl-on-Rock" paintings, although he was by then famous for them. He said so in an Associated Press interview: "I'm done with girls on rocks. I've painted them for thirteen years and I could paint them and sell them for thirteen more. That's the peril of the commercial art game. It tempts a man to repeat himself.

"It's an awful thing to get to be a rubber stamp. I'm quitting my rut now while I'm still able.

"Magazine and art editors—and the critics, too—are always hunting for something new, but they don't know what it is. They guess at what the public will like, and, as we all do, they guess wrong about half the time.

"My present guess is that landscapes are coming in for magazine covers, advertisements and illustrations. . . .

"There are always pretty girls on every city street, but a man can't step out of the subway and watch the clouds playing with the top of Mount Ascutney. It's the unattainable that appeals. Next best to seeing the ocean or the hills or the woods is enjoying a painting of them."[1]

1934. The artist accepted an offer from a calendar and greeting card company, Brown and Bigelow, to paint some landscapes. In this second venture into art-prints, Parrish recalled the difficulties of following the success of "Daybreak." "I feel that the broad effect, the truth of nature's mood attempted, is the most important, has more appeal than the kind of subject. 'Broad effect' is a rather vague term, but what is meant is that those qualities which delight us in nature—the sense of freedom, pure air and light, the magic of distance, and the saturated beauty of color, must be convincingly stated and take the beholder to the very spot. If these abstract qualities are not in a painting it is a flat failure. You might just as well have the typical art calendar, a collection of familiar things around the 'Home Sweet Home:' the old well sweep, duck pond, barn yard gate, and the cows coming home.

"If *Peaceful Valley* is a success we must be careful not to repeat it. I would not advise having a quaint little village nestling among trees in every picture. . . . There is only one rubber stamp permitted, each and every picture must represent one grand good place to be in."[1]

When they put a white border around the 1941 calendar print, "The Village Brook," Parrish complained: "Of all things to put a white border on a dark picture! It simply kills it. It's the first thing that hits you bang in the eye; takes all the life out of the subject and leaves it dead. . . . You'd never

MAXFIELD PARISH in his studio at "The Oaks"

think of framing a dark picture in white to hang on a wall, and for that reason that applies equally well in a border to a print.

"You see it isn't a matter of taste, it is a matter of the laws of contrast and juxtaposition. My tiresome blue we seem to hear so much about is just ordinary blue you can buy around the corner, but what I put next to it is what makes it what it is. The gilt frames I use have to be toned away down from their original state, else they would blind the observer so he couldn't see the picture."[1]

Parrish is best known in New York for his mural "Old King Cole," which has been in the St. Regis Hotel since 1935. Of an early study for the mural, he wrote: "[It is a] watercolor drawing on manilla paper with here and there pieces of paper of various colors cut out and pasted on thus making many different qualities of tone. Between the glass and drawing is a sheet of transparent celluloid upon which is painted the sky."[1]

1943. Once again, a request for the story behind a painting, this time a landscape, drew the typical Parrish response: "There is nothing I dislike more than any kind of personal publicity, the so-called write up or 'story.' I've endured the torture for the past forty years and have only allowed it once in a while just to be decent, and now in my old age am thankful that there seems to be an end of it.

"There isn't any story here. So many in the past have tried to find one; jumped at the conclusion that because I painted pictures of a certain kind there must be something decidedly interesting about the artist: he must live in a tree, eat nuts and berries, or something. . . .

"If you are going in for interesting publicity give the public mystery. The Greta Garbo kind is the very best, and it keeps up. . . . I am happier in my work for you people than I have ever been, but if this publicity by-product has to be a part of it, it detracts a lot."[1]

July 25, 1950. For his eightieth birthday the neighbors gave him a surprise party, with a "birthday cake about the size of Connecticut, engrossed scroll of parchment setting forth unbelievable fairy tales and things, and it nearly finished me, congenital shrinking violet that I am."[1]

1950. "You ask for a description of my technique? Well—this method is very simple, very ancient, very laborious, and by no means original with me. It is somewhat like the modern reproductions in four color half tone, where the various gradations are obtained by printing one color plate over another on a white ground of paper. In painting it is an ancient process, as anyone can read in the many books written about the methods of the old masters, telling how each one had his own particular way of going about it: some by starting with a monochrome underpainting, some with a few colors, over which were glazed more or less transparent colors.

"Yes, it is rather laborious, but it has some advantages over the usual ways of mixing colors together before applying them. It is generally admitted that the most beautiful qualities of a color are in its transparent state, applied over a white ground with the light shining through the color. A modern Kodachrome is a delight when held up to the light with color luminous like stained glass. So many ask what is meant by transparent color, as though it were some special make. Most all color an artist uses is transparent: only a few

are opaque, such as vermillion, cerulean blue, emerald green, the ochres and most yellows, etc. Colors are applied just as they come from the tube, the original purity and quality is never lost: a purple is pure rose madder glowing through a glaze of pure blue over glaze, or vice versa, the quality of each is never vitiated by mixing them together. Mix a rose madder with white, let us say, and you get a pink, quite different from the original madder, and the result is a surface color instead of a transparent one, a color you look on instead of a transparent one, a color you look on instead of into.

"One does not paint long out of doors before it becomes apparent that a green tree has a lot of red in it. You may not see the red because your eye is blinded by the strong green, but it is there never the less. So if you mix a red with the green you get a sort of mud, each color killing the other. But by the other method, when the green is dry and a rose madder glazed over it you are apt to get what is wanted, and have a richness and glow of one color shining through the other, not to be had by mixing. Imagine a Rembrandt if his magic browns were mixed together instead of glazed. The result would be a kind of chocolate.

"Then too, by this method of keeping colors by themselves some can be used which are taboo in mixtures. Verdigris, for instance, is a strange cold green with considerable power, with an exceptional luminous quality, rare in greens. If in contact with coal gas it will change overnight, but when locked up in varnish it seems to last as long as any. Alizarin Orange, given up by color makers, is another. I have examples of both done forty years ago which show no signs of change.

"I used to begin a painting with a monochrome of raw umber, for some reason: possibly read that the ancient ones often began that way. But now the start is made with a monochrome of blue, right from the tube, not mixed with white or anything. Ultramarine or the Monastral blues, or cobalt for distance and skies. This seems to make a good foundation for shadows and it does take considerable planning ahead, and looks for all the world like a blue dinner plate. The rest is a build-up of glazes until the end. The only time opaque color is used is painting trees. The method of early Corots and Rousseau is a good one, suggested by nature herself, where a tree is first painted as a dark silhouette and when dry the outside or illuminated foliage is painted over it. This opaque may be a yellow or orange as a base to glaze over with green, as the problem may demand.

"It must be understood that when transparent glazes dry they look like nothing at all, and their glazes [color] must be brought back to life by a very thin coat of varnish. This varnish also protects one color from another should protection be called for. And it must also be understood that this varnishing is a craft all by itself and cannot be too carefully done. Hurry it, and put it on too thick and too cold, and disaster follows. Fortunately colors in their transparent state are dry when they feel dry, these glazes are extremely thin and have a chance to dry much faster than heavy impasto, whereas whites and opaque yellows seem to take forever to become thoroughly inert. Varnishing should be done in a very warm room where the painting and varnish have been exposed to the warmth for some hours. This is to drive off all invisible surface moisture and to make the varnish flow better and thinner, to be applied as thin as possible. Also, the varnished surface should remain warm until set. Days should be waited until this varnish coat is thoroughly dry: then a light rubbing of pumice flour and water takes off dust particles and makes a surface somewhat better to apply the next process."[1]

1952. Parrish wrote to a student his philosophy of landscape painting. "You mention 'realism:' that, I think, is a term which has to be defined: realism should never be the end in view. My theory is that you should use all the objects in nature, trees, hills, skies, rivers and all, just as stage properties on which to hang your idea, the end in view, the elusive qualities of a day, in fact all the qualities that give a body the delights of out of doors. You cannot sit down and paint such things: they are not there, or do not last but for a moment. 'Realism' of impression, the mood of the moment, yes, but not the realism of things. The colored photograph can do that better. That's the trouble with so much art today, it is factual, and stops right there."[1]

Further notes on landscapes: "I'll admit, moonlight in snow time is puzzling. Each time you go out to study it you find it is a different color.

"In my painting of trees my resemblance to those in nature is purely accidental.

"'Only God can make a tree.' True enough, but I'd like to see Him paint one."[1]

Asked if he painted leaves from nature, the artist replied: "No, that wouldn't do. It is purely imaginative, as Autumn leaves are not colored that way at all. That gets us into botany, and away beyond my depth."[1]

Not strictly a realist, Parrish was nevertheless no lover of abstract painting. "Modernistic-Abstractionist-Art . . . consists of 75% explanation and 25% God knows what!"[1]

1953. Lydia Parrish died.

March 30, 1966. Died at "The Oaks" at ninety-five. "Strange what keeps us going, isn't it, or did you ever take time enough out to speculate? Seems as though, for all the yesterdays are very much alike, it is the chronic curiosity of what tomorrow may have to offer. And, as a matter of fact, what more could one ask?

". . . I haven't a gray hair yet, the chief reason being they are all pure white. And yet it is rather interesting to be alive and think of things; to take delight in the trivial qualities of the material world around you, having discovered long ago you don't have to go so far afield to get it. I sometimes think the dawn of a new day, the magic silence of midwinter is about all there is, and however that may perhaps be, it is good to know no better."[1]

FOR MORE INFORMATION SEE: Current Biography, November, 1965; C. L. Ludwig, "From Parlor Print to Museum: The Art of Maxfield Parrish," *Art Journal,* Winter, 1965; G. Glueck, "Maxfield Parrish," *American Heritage,* December, 1970; Coy Ludwig, *Maxfield Parrish,* Watson-Guptill, 1973, an abridged version published as "Painting Techniques of Maxfield Parrish," *American Artist,* October, 1973.

Obituaries: *New York Times,* March 31, 1966; *Time,* April 8, 1966; *Newsweek,* April 11, 1966; *Publishers Weekly,* April 11, 1966; *American Artist,* June, 1966; *Britannica Book of the Year 1967,* 1967; *Current Biography Yearbook 1966,* 1967.

(Died March 30, 1966)

DAVID PASCAL

PASCAL, David 1918-

PERSONAL: Born August 16, 1918, in New York, N.Y.; son of Boucour and Carolina (Finor) Pascal; married first wife, Mary K.; married second wife, Theresa P. Auerbach (a biologist), August 24, 1962; children: (first marriage) Jeffrey B. *Education:* Attended American Artists School, 1937-38. *Residence:* New York, N.Y. *Office:* 60 West Eighth St., New York, N.Y. 10011.

CAREER: Free-lance author, cartoonist, and illustrator, 1941—. Instructor, School of Visual Arts, New York, N.Y., 1955-58; lecturer at museums, schools, and congresses in New York, France, Italy, Brazil and Argentina. Participant in overseas tours sponsored by U.S. Department of Defense, 1957, 1958, 1961. Exhibited work in one-man shows at Librarie Le Kiosque, Paris, 1965, Musee des Arts Decoratifs, 1967, Graham Gallery, New York, N.Y., 1973, and Museu de Arte, Sao Paulo, Brazil, "Man and His World," Montreal, Canada. Drawings have appeared in *New Yorker, Harper's, Saturday Review, New York Times, New York Herald Tribune, Punch, Ski, Look,* and other magazines in United States, and other countries. Chairman of cartoon shows given by National Cartoonists Society in New York Veterans Hospital; American organizer of First International Congress of Comics,. 1972. *Wartime service:* U.S. Merchant Marine, 1940-45.

MEMBER: International Comics Organization (American representative, 1970—), Immagine (Italy; American representative, 1970—), National Cartoonists Society (foreign affairs secretary, 1963—), Magazine Cartoonists Guild, Lucca International Comics Congresses (artistic counselor of board of directors, Italy, 1976—). *Awards, honors:* Second prize, Dattero D'Oro, in sixteenth Salone Internazionale Dell Umorismo, Bordighera, Italy, 1963; illustrator's award, National Cartoonists Society, 1969; Phenix award, Paris, 1971; Critics award, Eighth International Congress of Comics and Phenix award, 1972, both for *Comics: The Art of the Comic Strip.*

WRITINGS: (Illustrator) *The Art of Inferior Decorating,* text by Eddie Frederics, Chilton, 1963; (illustrator) Ivan Andreevich Krylov, *15 Fables of Krylov,* Macmillan, 1965; (self-illustrated) *The Silly Knight,* Funk, 1967; (author and illustrator) Jerzy Stanislaw Lec, *More Unkempt Thoughts,* Funk, 1969; (illustrator) Charles Issawi, *Laws of Social Motion,* Hawthorn, 1972; (editor with Walter Herdeg) *Comics: The Art of the Comic Strip,* Graphis Press (Zurich), 1972; "Goofus," Editions Jacques Glenat, 1975.

WORK IN PROGRESS: A children's book; "Comics, Paintings," based on the aesthetics of the comic strip.

HOBBIES AND OTHER INTERESTS: Tai-chi, swimming, and skiing.

PATTERSON, Lillie G.

CAREER: Library Services specialist and chairman of the Elementary Book Reviewing Committee for the Baltimore (Md.) public school system; teacher; author. *Awards, honors:* Coretta Scott King Award, 1970, for *Martin Luther King, Jr.: Man of Peace.*

**It was nice to relax
and meet things as they came
sort of comfy.**
■ (From *The Silly Knight* by David Pascal. Pictures by the author.)

Fred fished with Grandma Betsey as the two talked and sang together. ■ (From *Frederick Douglass: Freedom Fighter* by Lillie Patterson. Illustrated by Gray Morrow.)

LILLIE G. PATTERSON

WRITINGS—All published by Garrard, except as noted: *Booker T. Washington: Leader of His People* (illustrated by Anthony D'Adamo), 1962; *Meet Miss Liberty*, Macmillan, 1962; *Francis Scott Key: Poet and Patriot* (illustrated by Vic Dowd), 1963; *Halloween* (illustrated by Gil Miret), 1963; *Birthdays* (illustrated by Erica Merkling), 1965; *Frederick Douglass: Freedom Fighter* (illustrated by Gray Morrow), 1965; *Easter* (illustrated by Kelly Oechsli), 1966; *Lumberjacks of the North Woods* (illustrated by Victor Mays), 1967; *Christmas Feasts and Festivals* (illustrated by Cliff Schule), 1968; *Christmas in America* (illustrated by Vincent Colabella), 1969; *Martin Luther King, Jr.: Man of Peace* (illustrated by V. Mays), 1969; *Christmas in Britain and Scandinavia* (illustrated by K. Oechsli), 1970; (editor) *Poetry for Spring* (illustrated by K. Oechsli), 1973; *Sequoyah: The Cherokee Who Captured Words* (illustrated by Herman B. Vestal), 1975.

WORK IN PROGRESS: "A biography of Daniel Hale Williams, a pioneer in open heart surgery, and another on James Weldon Johnson—both individuals who should be better known to children."

SIDELIGHTS: "I grew up on the beautiful island of Hilton Head under the care of a grandmother, Cornelia Green, a great reader and singer. From my grandmother I captured a sense of the power of words. It was natural that I would follow a career in library media services, and later in writing. I gained a reputation as a storyteller, and helped to develop and coordinate educational radio and television programs for children.

"Out of my years of working with children, and training librarians, I feel that I have a solid background on children's reading interests, which grow more and more complex. My topics for writing grow out of gaps that exist in the juvenile book field, and out of my own beliefs in what children will read. Letters reach me weekly from young readers letting me know what one of the books I have written has said to a child. I enjoy research and will make my research as exhaustive for a simple text of less than 10,000 words as I would have done for a multi-volume work on a biographical subject. From this mass of information I try to capture something of the spirit of the individual so that young readers will take inspiration from the life and will be lead to more mature works."

HOBBIES AND OTHER INTEREST: Reading, sports of all kinds, music, walking, gardening.

FOR MORE INFORMATION SEE: New York Times Book Review, May 4, 1969; *Bulletin of the Center for Children's Books,* May, 1970

RITCHIE, Barbara (Gibbons)

PERSONAL: Born in Bemidji, Minn. *Residence:* Denver, Colo.

CAREER: Author, editor, and adapter.

WRITINGS: Ramon Makes a Trade (illustrated by Earl Thollander), Parnassus Press, 1959; *To Catch a Mongoose* (illustrated by E. Thollander), Parnassus Press, 1963; (adapter) Frederick Douglass, *Life and Times of Frederick Douglass,* Crowell, 1966; (adapter) F. Douglass, *The Mind and Heart of Frederick Douglass: Excerpts from Speeches of the Great Negro Orator,* Crowell, 1968; *The Ghost That Haunted the House That Culpepper Built* (illustrated by Richard M. Powers), Viking, 1968; (editor) *The Riot Report: A Shortened Version of the National Advisory Commission on Civil Disorders,* Viking, 1969; (adapter) Richard Hildreth, *Memoirs of a Fugitive: America's First Antislavery Novel,* Crowell, 1971.

SIDELIGHTS: Barbara Ritchie's picture story, *Ramon Makes a Trade,* is told in both English and Spanish. "This dual text," observed a *Kirkus* reviewer, "affords children of Spanish speaking backgrounds an incentive to increase their English vocabulary, while English speaking children will further be aided by the glossary of Spanish terms which accompanies Ramon's enterprising business adventure. A gentle story whose suspense is derived from an accurate understanding of the Mexican delight in bartering."

Another bilingual story is *To Catch a Mongoose,* written in both French and English. M. S. Libby observed in a *Book Week* review, "This is a satisfactory, simple story, but the particular glory of the book is charming water-color scenes of the island, its inhabitants, palm-fringed shore, streets and market places. They are large and well placed...." The *New York Times Book Review* noted, "...The story is well written with a fine economy of words, a swift sequence of simple events leading to a breathless and most satisfactory climax."

Ritchie has also adapted Frederick Douglass' autobiography, *Life and Times of Frederick Douglass.* "An editing of Douglass' lengthy autobiography has long been needed to find a modern audience," wrote a *Horn Book* critic. "This classic in American and Negro history has been little read because of its verbose, rambling style. Now the excesses have been eliminated and some sections transposed for brevity and clarity, but the original spirit remains. . . .''

Barbara Ritchie edited *The Riot Report,* which was reviewed by *Library Journal:* ''This shortened version of the *Report of the National Advisory Committee on Civil Disorders,* with its more handleable length, large print and attractive format, will reach interested young people who simply can not or will not plough through the original document. Although it would be easy to disagree with some of the editor's omissions, Miss Ritchie has done a creditable job. Deleted is the material on the actual events of the riots of 1967 (except for Detroit) as well as footnotes and statistical tables. What remains is basic information on life in the ghetto, history of the Negro, the civil rights movement, causes of the riots, and some of the Committee's conclusions. . . . This important, abbreviated document should be useful and made available to junior high and high school students.'' P. B. Edelman commented in the *New York Times Book Review,* ''How to explain the crisis of the American city to children? [This is] the book I would choose, if I could choose only one. . . .''

FOR MORE INFORMATION SEE: Kirkus Reviews, November 1, 1959; *New York Times Book Review,* April 12, 1964; *Book Week,* May 3, 1964; *Horn Book,* October, 1966; *New York Times Book Review,* May 4, 1969; *Library Journal,* July, 1969.

ROBBINS, Ruth 1917(?)-

PERSONAL: Born December 29, 1917 (or 1918, according to some sources), in Newark, N.J.; daughter of Louis Arnold and Bessie (Sofer) Robbins; married Herman Schein, February 21, 1941; children: Steven. *Education:* Graduated from Pratt Institute, Brooklyn, N.Y., 1939; attended School of Design, Chicago, Ill., 1939-41. *Residence:* Berkeley, Calif.

CAREER: Art director, U.S. Public Health Service, 1941-44, Office of Price Administration, 1944-46; U.S. Army, design consultant, 1946-48; free-lance designer for advertising and industry, 1948-56; Parnassus Press, Emeryville, Calif., founder, vice-president, and art director, 1956—; author and illustrator. *Member:* National Society of Art Directors, San Francisco Art Directors Club. *Awards, honors:* Caldecott Medal, 1961, for *Baboushka and the Three Kings.* Teaching a course in *Book Design and Production* at University of California Berkeley Extension, 1976—.

WRITINGS: Baboushka and the Three Kings (illustrated by Nicolas Sidjakov), Parnassus, 1960; *The Emperor and the Drummer Boy* (illustrated by N. Sidjakov), Parnassus, 1962; *Harlequin and Mother Goose; or, The Magic Stick* (illustrated by N. Sidjakov), Parnassus, 1965; *Taliesin and King Arthur* (illustrated by the author), Parnassus, 1970.

Illustrator: Anne B. Fisher, *Stories California Indians Told,* Parnassus, 1957; Adrien Stoutenberg, *Wild Animals of the Far West,* Parnassus, 1958; Josephine H. Aldridge, *A Penny and a Periwinkle,* Parnassus, 1961; Ernestine N. Byrd, *The Black Wolf of Savage River,* Parnassus, 1961; Theodora Kroeber, *Ishi, Last of His Tribe,* Parnassus, 1964; J. H. Aldridge, *Fisherman's Lock,* Parnassus, 1966; Ursula K. Le Guin, *A Wizard of Earthsea,* Parnassus, 1968; Charlotte Zolotow, *The Beautiful Christmas Tree,* Parnassus, 1972.

SIDELIGHTS: Ruth Robbins' Caldecott Medal-winning story, *Baboushka and the Three Kings,* was reviewed by a *Horn Book* critic who wrote, ''Mystery and dignity are in the retelling of the old Russian folk tale. Extraordinary modern drawings, some in rich colors, and a handsome type face which has not been popular for many years combine to make a beautiful picture book.'' Comments on the award-winning illustrations by Nicolas Sidjakov included this from the *Atlantic:* ''The pictures have a translucence and a stylized beauty that is interpretative of the legend.''

''Based on history, the author and artist responsible for *Baboushka and the Three Kings* have made another extraordinary book, harmonious in every aspect,'' wrote *Horn Book* concerning *The Emperor and the Drummer Boy.* ''There are no extra words in the direct prose, but no writing down. The pictures, for all their stylization, give a hint of the old books which might have furnished their subjects or been the inspiration for them. Mr. Sidjakov's use of many lines is most suitable in the pictures of ships and rigging and stunning in those of stormy seas. Red and blue are added most effectively. A beautiful book.'' A *New Yorker* critic observed: ''The most unusual and distinguished picture book of the year. The style, which is distinctly 'literary,' has the proper exalted tone of 'la gloire,' and is rich in useful phrases such as 'Back to your duties, all!' ''

FOR MORE INFORMATION SEE: Horn Book, December, 1960, December, 1962; *Atlantic Monthly,* December, 1960; *New Yorker,* November 24, 1962; *Saturday Review,* November 13, 1965; *New York Times Book Review,* November 28, 1965.

SADIE, Stanley (John) 1930-

PERSONAL: Born October 30, 1930, in Wembley, Middlesex, England; son of David (a textile merchant) and Deborah (Simons) Sadie; married Adele Bloom, December 10, 1953; children: Graham Robert, Ursula Joan, Stephen Peter. *Education:* Cambridge University, B.A., 1953, Mus.B., 1953, M.A., 1957, and Ph.D., 1958. *Home:* 1 Carlisle Gardens, Harrow, HA3 0JX, England. *Office: New Grove Dictionary of Music and Musicians,* Little Essex St., London WC2R 3LF, England.

CAREER: Trinity College of Music, London, England, lecturer, 1957-65; *Times,* London, England, music critic, 1964—; *Musical Times,* London, England, associate editor, 1966-67, editor, 1967—; *The New Grove Dictionary of Music and Musicians,* London, England, editor, 1970—. Commentator on music for British Broadcasting Corp. *Military service:* Royal Air Force, 1948-49. *Member:* Royal Musical Association (member of council), Critics' Circle (honorary secretary, music section, 1965-67; chairman, music section, 1967-70), American Musicological Society, International Musicological Society.

WRITINGS: Handel, J. Calder, 1962, Crowell, 1968; (with Arthur Jacobs) *Pan Book of Opera,* Pan Books, 1964, published in England as *The Opera Guide,* Hamish Hamilton, 1964, reissued in America as *Great Operas in Synopsis,* Crowell, 1966; *Mozart,* J. Calder, 1966, Grossman, 1970; *Beethoven,* Crowell, 1967; *Handel Concertos,* B.B.C., 1973. Contributor to *Gramophone, Musical Times, Opera,* and other musical publications.

WORK IN PROGRESS: Further studies on Mozart.

SIDELIGHTS: Travels as a music critic have taken Sadie to the United States and most European countries.

HOBBIES AND OTHER INTERESTS: Reading, watching cricket, playing bridge.

SCHNIREL, James R(einhold)   1931-

PERSONAL: Born October 26, 1931, in Geneva, N.Y.; son of Edwin R. (a contractor) and Charlotte (Beyer) Schnirel; married Shirley Birdwell (a teacher), June 22, 1957; children: Ben, Erica, John. *Education:* Delhi Agricultural and Technical Institute, certified in building construction, 1952; University of Oklahoma, B.S., 1959; Utah State University, M.S., 1975. *Home address:* Star Route, Box 155, Park City, Utah 84060. *Office:* Department of Technical Occupations and General Education, Utah Technical College at Salt Lake, 4600 South Redwood Rd., Salt Lake City, Utah 84107.

CAREER: Held various positions as carpenter, draftsman, designer, 1954-66; Utah Technical College at Salt Lake, Salt Lake City, Utah, instructor, 1962-67, division chairman, 1967-72, dean of technical occupations and general education, 1972—. Summit Park Homeowners Association, board member, 1970-74, president, 1974-76, Summit Park's representative to Summit County Council of Governments, 1974—; publisher of *Summit Park Newsletter,* a community newspaper, 1970-75; Citizens Committee—Planning & Zon-

JAMES SCHNIREL

ing for Summit County, 1976—; Park City Fire Protection District, chairman of the commission, 1976—; evaluator for Northwest Association of Secondary and Higher Schools. *Military service:* U.S. Navy, builder, 1953-1954.

MEMBER: American Vocational Association, American Technical Education Association, Utah Vocational Associational, Utah Industrial Education Association, Utah Adult Education Association, Utah Technical College Education Association (past president), Association for Non-Teaching Professionals at Utah Technical College at Salt Lake, Western Association of Cooperative and Work Experience Educators, American Institute of Architects (associate member). *Awards, honors:* OU chapter of American Institute of Architects (vice-president); designer of architectural pavilion for engineering open house competition; Kiwanis award, appreciation for outstanding service, 1975.

WRITINGS: (With Ron H. Jenkins) *Exploring Occupations in Communication and Graphic Arts* (for young people), McGraw, 1975; *Careers in Focus,* McGraw, 1975.

SIDELIGHTS: "Information relative to various careers has always been of interest to me and the aspect of the *Careers in Focus* program that I was involved in was especially interesting since it not only involved reading and studying a career but also involved an activity with each career exploration. This is important since those young people trying to gain an understanding of a career need to become more directly involved in what the career is all about ... I feel that career education is a necessity and is something that should be taught in one form or another from basic grades on up through the end of a high school career and further into adult life ... I feel that more work should be done in the adult career exploration area. Perhaps, this will be something I can look forward to working on in the near future."

HOBBIES AND OTHER INTERESTS: Photography, painting, sailing, skiing, music, pottery, and little theater.

SCOTT, John   1912-1976

PERSONAL: Name originally John Scott Nearing; born March 26, 1912, in Philadelphia, Pa.; married Maria Dikareva (a teacher), June 15, 1934; children: Leigh Scott Schumann, Elena Scott Whiteside. *Education:* Student at University of Wisconsin, 1929-31, Magnitogorsk Metallurgical Institute, 1932-37, Sorbonne, University of Paris, 1938-39. *Religion:* Protestant. *Home:* Peaceable Ridge, Ridgefield, Conn. *Office:* Time Inc., Rockefeller Center, New York, N.Y. 10020.

CAREER: Siberian steel mills worker, 1932-37; *Havas* (French news agency), Moscow correspondent, 1937-40; *London News Chronicle,* Moscow correspondent, 1940; *Time,* New York, N.Y., Japan correspondent, 1941, contributing editor, 1942, Washington correspondent, 1943, Stockholm bureau chief, 1944-45, Central European bureau chief, 1945-48, special assistant to publisher, 1948—. Radio and television commentator on foreign affairs; also programs for Radio Free Europe, Voice of America. *Member:* Academy of Political Science, Council on Foreign Relations, Overseas Press Club, Authors League.

WRITINGS: Behind the Urals, Houghton, 1942; *Duel for Europe,* Houghton, 1942; *Europe in Revolution,* Houghton, 1945; *Political Warfare,* Day, 1955; *Democracy Is Not Enough,* Harcourt, 1960; *China: The Hungry Dragon,* Par-

JOHN SCOTT

ents' Magazine Press, 1967; *Hunger: On Man's Struggle to Feed Himself,* Parents Magazine Press, 1969; *Divided They Stand,* Parents Magazine Press, 1973. Assistant to the Asia, Africa, Soviet Russia, China, Europe and the Common Market, and Latin America and the Alliance for Progress.

FOR MORE INFORMATION SEE: Time, October 8, 1956.

(Died December 1, 1976)

SHARFMAN, Amalie

PERSONAL: Born in Baltimore, Md. married (a government lawyer), Warren L. Sharfman, children: William Lee. *Education:* Attended Goucher College. *Home:* Washington, D.C. 2901 Cleveland Avenue, N.W. 20008.

CAREER: Radio announcer, moderator, and producer, author, and teacher. Producer and moderator of commercial & educational radio programs, Baltimore, Md. and Washington, D.C. Has taught nursery school at a private school, and at a day care center during World War II. Instructor in creative writing at Assumption College and Clark University, both in Worcester, Mass., and at George Washington University, Washington, D.C. First president, subsequently Executive Director Worcester Area Mental Health Association.

WRITINGS: A Beagle Named Bertram (illustrated by Tony Palazzo), Crowell, 1954; *Mr. Peabody's Pesky Ducks* (illustrated by Louis Darling), Little, Brown, 1957; *Papa's*

But from that day on, the entire world seemed so dark and gloomy, Jean-Pierre had the hopeless feeling that nothing would ever make it right again. ■ (From *Papa's Secret Chocolate Dessert* by Amalie Sharfman. Illustrated by Lillian Obligado.)

Secret Chocolate Dessert (illustrated by Lilian Obligado), Lothrop, 1972. Articles for a variety of publications.

FOR MORE INFORMATION SEE: New York Times, November 17, 1957.

SIMONETTA, Linda   1948-

PERSONAL: Born January 26, 1948, in Ann Arbor, Mich.; daughter of Stanley Gerald (a sales manager) and Frances (Raes) Richardson; married Sam Simonetta (an elementary school principal), April 4, 1971; children: Scott. *Education:* University of Northern Iowa, B.A., 1970. *Home:* 5113 Thistle Pl., Loveland, Colo. 80537.

CAREER: Elementary school teacher in the public schools of Englewood, Colo., 1970-74, and Loveland, Colo., 1974-75.

WRITINGS: (With husband, Sam Simonetta) *Trappers, Trains and Mining Claims,* Pruett, 1976.

SIDELIGHTS: "It was through our working with children in the elementary classroom that we became aware of the void in children's literature which dealt with Colorado history. There was a definite interest within the children as we read to them from adult books or told from memory of the colorful people who lived in Colorado's past. But nowhere was there printed material on the reading level of a ten-year-old which captured the excitement of early-day Colorado.

LINDA SIMONETTA

This fact, coupled with our own fascination for the state's history, served as the source of our inspiration to write *Trappers, Trains and Mining Claims*.

"Most of the actual writing was accomplished in a summer, but the research stretched back many years to our first encounter with the state. I suppose we actually began an extensive gathering of information two years before the book was written. At that time, we purchased a Jeep to further our access into the forgotten areas that once hosted mining camps. It was our policy to read as much of an area's history as could be learned. Then, with engine straining we would drive over wagon roads that had long since felt the bite of wheels to reach a destination which was seldom more than a clearing or a few fallen log cabins.

"History, in general, and Colorado history in particular, is fascinating for us. We have many pieces of antique furniture in our house which date back to the years that our book covers. Besides their beauty, it is good to help assure their continuance so that future generations may know the quality of earlier Americans' contribution to our country. I suppose this basically says that we appreciate the efforts of those who have come before, and that, hopefully, there will be those in the future who will feel similarly toward us."

HOBBIES AND OTHER INTERESTS: Collecting and refinishing antique furniture, hiking, skiing, gardening.

SIMONETTA, Sam 1936-

PERSONAL: Born January 7, 1936, in Easton, Pa.; son of Samuel and Erma (Riedinger) Simonetta; married Linda Richardson (elementary school teacher at time of marriage), April 4, 1971, children: Scott. *Education:* Miami-Dade Junior College, A.A., 1967; Florida Atlantic University, B.S., 1969; Western State College, Gunnison, Colo., M.A., 1972. *Home:* 5113 Thistle Pl., Loveland, Colo. 80537. *Office:* Centennial Elementary School, Loveland, Colo. 80537.

CAREER: Elementary school teacher in the public schools of Englewood, Colo., 1969-74; Loveland Public Schools, Loveland, Colo., assistant principal, 1974-76, principal of Centennial Elementary School, 1976—.

WRITINGS: (With wife, Linda Simonetta) *Trappers, Trains and Mining Claims,* Pruett, 1976.

SIDELIGHTS: See Simonetta, Linda.

HOBBIES AND OTHER INTERESTS: Collecting and refinishing antique furniture, hiking, skiing, gardening.

SAM SIMONETTA

COLIN SIMPSON

SIMPSON, Colin 1908-

PERSONAL: Born November 4, 1908, in Sydney, N.S.W., Australia; son of Henry F. V. (a tradesman) and Margaret (a nurse, maiden name, Langby) Simpson; married Estelle (Claire) Waterman (an artist), January 23, 1937; children: Julia Haden, Vivien Haden. *Education:* Attended University of Sydney, 1926-27. *Religion:* Atheist. *Home and office:* 4/13 Moruben Road, Mosman, N.S.W. 2088, Australia.

CAREER: Catts-Patterson Advertising Service, Sydney, Australia, copywriter and junior account executive, 1925-27; Paton Advertising Ltd., Sydney; advertising copywriter and account executive, 1925-28; journalist for Sydney newspapers and periodicals, with posts including associate editor of *Pix* weekly supplement editor for *Australian Women's Weekly,* and magazine editor for *Sunday Telegraph* and *Sunday Sun,* until 1947. Australian Broadcasting Commission, Sydney, radio documentary writer, 1947-50; full-time writer, 1960—. *Member:* Australian Society of Authors (vice-president, 1971-76), Australian Journalist Association (honorary life member).

WRITINGS—All published by Angus & Robertson (Sydney), except as indicated: (With Kenneth Slessor and Harley Matthews) *Trio* (poems), Sunnybrook Press, 1931; *Adam in Ochre,* 1951, Praeger, 1953; *Come Away Pearler,* 1952; *Adam with Arrows* (also see below), 1953; *Adam in Plumes* (also see below), 1954; *Islands of Men,* 1955; *Australian Image,* Legend Press, 1956; *The Country Upstairs* (also see below), 1956 (published in England as *Picture of Japan,* Angus & Robertson (London), 1957), published as *Japan: An Intimate View,* A. S. Barnes, 1962, revised edition, 1969; *Wake Up in Europe,* 1959, published as *Europe: An Intimate View,* A. S. Barnes, 1962; *Show Me a Mountain,* 1961; *Asia's Bright Balconies,* 1962; *Plumes and Arrows* (includes *Adam with Arrows* and *Adam in Plumes*), 1962; *Take Me to Spain,* 1963; *Take Me to Russia,* 1964 published in England as *This is Russia,* Hodder & Stoughton, 1965); *The Lusitania,* Ballentine, 1974; *The Viking Circle,* 1966, Morrow, 1968; *Katmandu,* 1967, Taplinger, 1968; *Greece: The Unclouded Eye,* 1968, Morrow, 1969; *The New Australia,* 1971, Dut-

ton, 1972; *Bali and Beyond,* 1971; *Off to Asia,* 1972; *This Is Japan* (incorporates *The Country Upstairs*), 1975; *Wake Up to New Zealand,* Reed, Sydney & Wellington, 1976.

SIDELIGHTS: "I write the kind of travel book that *I* should like to have read before going to a country as a tourist—or could only go to by armchair."

HOBBIES AND OTHER INTERESTS: Reading and sunning.

FOR MORE INFORMATION SEE: John Hetherington, *Forty-two Faces: Profiles of Living Australian Writers,* Chesire (Melbourne), 1962; Rohan Rivett, *Writing About Australia,* Angus & Robertson, 1969.

SIMPSON, Myrtle L(illias) 1931- (M.L. Emslie)

PERSONAL: Born July 5, 1931, in Great Britain; daughter of Hamish (British Army) and Kathleen (Calvert) Emslie; married Hugh W. Simpson (a pathologist), March 21, 1959; children: Robin, Bruce, Rona, Rory. *Education:* Educated in United Kingdom and India. *Politics:* Tory, "with overtones of Scottish Nationalist." *Religion:* Presbyterian. *Home:* 2 Kirklee Ter., Glasgow, Scotland. *Agent:* Winant Towers Ltd., 1 Furnival St., London E.C.4, England.

CAREER: Mountaineer and explorer; first woman to cross the Greenland ice cap. Trained as a radiographer in Edinburgh, Scotland, qualifying in 1953; went to New Zealand that same year, looking for higher hills to climb than those in the Scottish highlands; moved on to Australia, 1956, and spent two years traveling the continent, working at a variety of jobs "when out of pocket," including pearl diving and cooking for alligator hunters in the Northern Territory; re-

MYRTLE L. SIMPSON

turned to Scotland to help organize the Edinburgh Andean expedition in 1958; climbed the highest mountain in Peru and five other summits over 22,000 feet (married an expedition scientist the following year); member of the Scottish Spitsbergen expedition, 1960, two expeditions to Iceland, 1961 and 1962, and the Scottish Surinam expedition in South America, 1963; with her husband and two other men crossed the Greenland ice cap on skis, 1965. Lecturer and broadcaster on expeditions and personal experiences. *Member:* Society of Authors, P.E.N. *Awards, honors: Daily Telegraph* travel award, December 1967, for a Greenland trip the Simpsons made with their children the previous summer.

WRITINGS: Home Is a Tent (autobiographical), Gollancz, 1964: *White Horizons* (autobiographical), Gollancz, 1967; *Due North*, Gollancz, 1970; *Simpson the Obstetrician*, Gollancz, 1972; *Greenland Summer*, Gollancz, 1973; *Vikings, Scots and Scraelings*, Gollancz, 1977. Author under maiden name, M. L. Emslie, of "Far and Near Readers" on travel subjects, *Journey to Amazon, Black Fellows and Buffaloes, Lapland Journey, Spitsbergen Adventure, Three in the Andes*, all published by W. & R. Chambers, 1960. Articles have appeared in *National Geographic, Woman's Own, Sunday Express* (London), *Daily Telegraph* (London), *She, Guardian* and other periodicals and newspapers.

WORK IN PROGRESS: A biography of Sir James Y. Simpson; preparations for an expedition to the North Pole on skis.

SIDELIGHTS: Myrtle Simpson was born into an army family and from a very early age she was used to much traveling. Climbing and hill-walking in Scotland were always favorite pursuits, and at one time she emigrated to New Zealand—with thoughts of the mountains of that island very much in the forefront of her mind. In fact she did a lot of mountain climbing there, including an ascent of Mount Cook, the highest mountain in the Antipodes.

After three years in New Zealand she spent a further year travelling around the Australian outback and then returned to Scotland to help organise the Scottish Andean expedition. This was a memorably successful one, in which five new summits were climbed, including the 22,200 foot Huascaran, one of the highest mountains outside the Himalayas. Shortly after the expedition, she married Hugh Simpson, a lecturer in medicine at Glasgow University, and fellow member of the expedition. They now have four children, and their weekends are spent skiing, climbing and canoeing in the Scottish hills. Family expeditions have also been made to Spitzbergen, Dutch Guiana and Greenland, where she became the first woman to cross the 400 mile ice cap.

Believers in keeping the family together and exposing children to the simple primitive life, the Simpsons took their firstborn son, Robin, then an infant, on the Spitzbergen expedition, a four-month sojourn six hundred miles from the North Pole. When Bruce came along (1961) and Rona (1962), they too accompanied their parents on the 1963 Surinam expedition to South America, living for a time in a Wai Ana Indian village deep in the rain forest. The three children were left behind on the crossing of the Greenland ice cap, but flew to join their parents at Stromfjord and spent the summer living in an Eskimo encampment.

SMITH, Gary R(ichard) 1932-

PERSONAL: Born October 20, 1932, in Pocatello, Idaho; son of Alma Gibson, Sr. (a shoe store owner) and Maud

GARY R. SMITH

Bodell (Jensen) Smith; married Rita Ann Palmer, November 17, 1972; children: Andrew Gibson, Paula Jean, Jamie Ann. *Education:* Idaho State University, B.A. (business; honors), 1954, B.A. (business education; honors), 1959; University of Idaho, Ed. D. (highest honors), 1969. *Politics:* Republican. *Religion:* Church of Jesus Christ of Latter-day Saints (Mormons). *Home:* 990 East 2680 N., Provo, Utah 84601. *Office:* Department of Business Education, 359 Jesse Knight Building, Brigham Young University, Provo, Utah 84602.

CAREER: Public school teacher in Pocatello, Idaho, 1959-65; Utah State University, Logan, assistant professor of business education, 1967-69; Brigham Young University, Provo, Utah, associate professor of business education, 1969-77. professor, 1977—. Vice-president of Dale's Auto Supply, 1959—. *Military service:* U.S. Army, 1956-58.

MEMBER: American Vocational Association, National Business Education Association, Council of Distributive Teacher Educators, Western Business Education Association, Utah Business Education Association, Utah Distributive Education Teachers, Utah Vocational Association, Phi Delta Kappa, Phi Kappa Phi, Delta Pi Epsilon, Kentucky Colonels. *Awards, honors:* Named deputy marshal of Dodge City, Kan., 1974; outstanding service award from Utah Vocational Association, 1973; special recognition award from Distributive Education Clubs of America, 1975.

WRITINGS: Display and Promotion, McGraw, 1970, 2nd edition, 1978; (with Lindon K. Parks) *Profiles of Distinction*, Brigham Young University Press, 1975; (with Barbara Sethney Vorndran and Charles S. Winn) *Exploring Marketing Occupations,* McGraw, 1976.

WORK IN PROGRESS: Editing *Johnny Ain't No Rose.*

SIDELIGHTS: "I have long felt that we are too much concerned in education with knowledge and the regurgitation of facts. Students need to learn more about attitudes and learning how to enjoy life rather than how to recall facts. The materials in *Exploring Marketing Occupations* were designed to give students a hands-on experience at the junior high school level with actual job-related experiences. In *Johnny Ain't No Rose,* we have tried to express our personal philosophy of what education and teaching should be. We need more teachers who will express love and care for students rather than concern for subject matter. People count, things don't.

I suspect that this feeling for the individual was taught me most effectively by my parents. They have continually given of themselves in the service of others. We all need to be more that way. School would be much less painful for students if they knew they had teachers who would care and were concerned for them. Only when we become more people-oriented will we be able to achieve what we need to do in our educational system.

"As I have the experience of seeing my children grow, I am continually amazed at how readily they are able to give love to others. Yet as we grow older we seem to become more guarded and tend not to give ourselves to others or go out of our way to help them. We all need to become more childlike in our attitudes. We need to study the lives of little children and become like them. In short we need to follow Christ's admonition to become as little children. What a much better world this would then be."

SODERLIND, Arthur E(dwin) 1920-

PERSONAL: Born August 15, 1920, in Brooklyn, N.Y.; son of Arthur J. and Beda I. (Seaholm) Soderlind; married Dorothy A. Neumann (a registered nurse), August 7, 1948; children: Sheryl Soderlind-Jervis, Linda Turner, Deborah. *Education:* New York College for Teachers (now State University of New York at Albany), B.A., 1947, M.A., 1948; State University of Iowa, Ph.D., 1961. *Religion:* Lutheran. *Home:* 18 Simsbury Manor Dr., Weatogue, Conn. 06089. *Office:* Bureau of Elementary and Secondary Education, State Department of Education, 165 Capitol Ave., Hartford, Conn. 06115.

CAREER: High school teacher in Pawling, N.Y., 1948-49; Minot State Teachers College, Minot, N.D., supervisor of student teachers, 1950-52; State University of Iowa, Iowa City, supervisor of social studies student teachers, 1952-53; State University of New York at Albany, social studies supervisor of student teachers, 1953-61; Connecticut State Department of Education, Hartford, social studies consultant in bureau of elementary and secondary education, 1961—. Adjunct professor of history at University of Hartford. Member of board of directors, Lutheran Theological Seminary, Philadelphia, Pha., 1962-74. *Member:* National Council for the Social Studies (served variously as secretary, program chairperson, and president of Capital District council; secretary-treasurer of Iowa council; treasurer of New York state council; and member of board of directors of Connecticut council), Pi Gamma Mu, Phi Alpha Theta.

ARTHUR SODERLIND

WRITINGS: Colonial Histories: Connecticut, Thomas Nelson, 1976. Author of curriculum bulletins and National Council for the Social Studies bulletins; contributor to *Biographical Dictionary of American Educators.* Member of editorial board, "Connecticut History" series, Pequot Press, 1975.

WORK IN PROGRESS: A book on Roger Sherman of Connecticut.

SIDELIGHTS: "In the elementary and secondary schools of this state there is a renewed interest in local and state history as a result of the Bicentennial. This and the interest in ethnic studies has brought about an increased awareness of our heritage."

SOULE, Gardner (Bosworth) 1913-

PERSONAL: Born December 16, 1913, in Paris, Tex.; son of Edgar C. H. (a lawyer) and Floy (Perfect) Soule; married Janie Lee McDowell, September 20, 1940. *Education:* Rice University, B.A., 1933; Columbia University, M.S., 1936. *Home and office:* 517 West 113th St., New York, N.Y. 10025.

CAREER: Associated Press, New York, N.Y., reporter, editor, 1936-41; *PM,* New York, N.Y., photo editor, 1942; *Better Homes and Gardens,* Des Moines, Iowa, managing editor, 1946-50; free-lance newspaper syndicate and magazine writer, mainly on science, 1950-66. *Military service:*

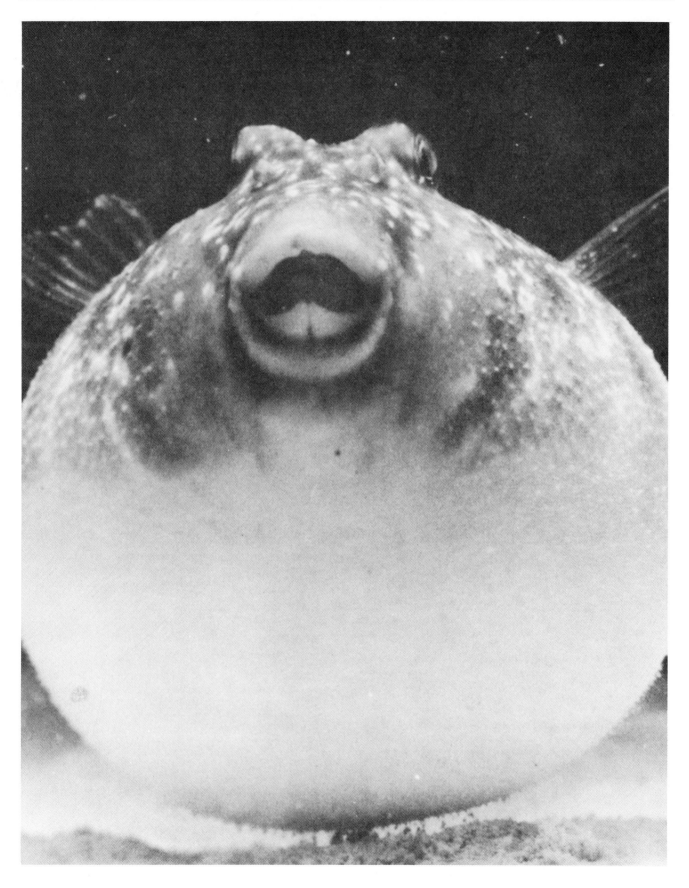

When an enemy tries to eat the blowfish, it simply puffs up so large it can't be swallowed.
■ (From *Remarkable Creatures of the Seas* by Gardner Soule. Picture courtesy of Miami Seaquarium.)

U.S. Naval Reserve, 1943-46; became lieutenant; officer-in-charge, *Training Bulletin,* U.S. Navy. *Member:* Marine Technology Society, International Oceanographic Foundation, Sigma Delta Chi, Columbia University Club.

WRITINGS: (Contributor) *The Complete Book of Press Photography,* 1949; (with Wilson Hicks) *This Is Ike,* Holt, 1952; *The Maybe Monsters,* Putnam, 1963; *Tomorrow's World of Science,* Coward, 1963; *Gemini and Apollo,* Duell, Sloan & Pearce, 1964; *The Mystery Monsters,* Putnam, 1965; *The Ocean Adventure: Science Explores the Depths,* Appleton, 1966; *Trail of the Abominable Snowman,* Putnam, 1966; *Sea Rescue,* Macrae Smith, 1966; *UFOS and IFOS: A Factual Report on Flying Saucers,* Putnam, 1967; (editor) *Under the Sea,* Meredith, 1968; *Undersea Frontiers,* Rand McNally, 1968.

Wide Ocean, Rand McNally, 1970; *The Greatest Depths,* Macrae Smith, 1970; *Strange Things Animals Do,* Putnam, 1970; *Surprising Facts,* Putnam, 1971; *New Discoveries in Oceanography,* Putnam, 1974; *Remarkable Creatures of the Seas,* Putnam, 1975; *Men Who Dared the Sea: The Ocean Adventures of the Ancient Mariners,* Crowell, 1976; *The Long Trail: How Cowboys and Longhorns Opened the West,* McGraw, 1976. Contributor of articles to *American Petroleum Institute, Esquire, Family Circle, Diner's Club Magazine, Elks' Magazine, Illustrated London News, McCall's, National Geographic, Popular Science Monthly, Boy's Life,* and other magazines and newspapers in the United States and England.

SIDELIGHTS: "Paris, Texas, where I was born, was a cotton town with a population of about 20,000. The people were as friendly as could be. From a very early age, I became interested in writing, partly because of the first school grades, partly because both of my parents were great readers, and partly because my Mother read to me.

"From Paris, we traveled a good deal. My father worked on the building of the Panama Canal; he was there for a number of years. The family spent two years in Cartagena, Columbia in South America and another year in Cardiff, Wales; at both of these places my father was American consul. He served in the Air Corps in World War I. Later he practiced law in Houston until his death. In Houston, where I went to high school (San Jacinto) and college (Rice), my Mother served, until retirement, as chairman of the romance language department (Spanish and French) at the University of Houston; she then became professor emeritus.

"My books published by Putnam's are aimed essentially at high school and junior high school students—but they increasingly are read by grade schoolers as well. Most of the other books are for adults. But I am basically a journalist, and so far as I can tell I write about the same in every case.

"I like to write about mysteries: the Loch Ness monster, the Abominable Snowman, Bigfoot, etc. I like to dwell on the wonder of the world around us (*Remarkable Creatures of the Seas*). I like to tell stories of men doing things. In *Men Who Dared the Sea,* I tried to tell of the first sailors and what they did—and how they affected all of us today. In *The Long Trail,* I tried to tell of the cowboys and what they did—and how they affected all of us today.

"I suppose my greatest love has been the ocean, which is to be always fascinating in all its aspects, and which so far has drawn nine books out of me.

"My effort, I suppose, is to be a careful observer, always an observer, and to put down on paper, as best I can, accurate (and if possible interesting) descriptions of what I have observed."

GARDNER SOULE aboard the miniature deep-diving submarine Star II.

SPELLMAN, John W(illard)   1934-

PERSONAL: Born July 27, 1934 in Tewksbury, Mass.; children: Suzanne Bharati, John Gilligan. *Education:* Northeastern University, B.A., 1956; University of Wyoming, graduate study, summer, 1956; School of Oriental and African Studies, University of Wyoming, graduate study, summer, 1956; School of Oriental and African Studies, University of London, Ph.D. (in ancient Indian history), 1960. *Home:* R.R. #2, Amherstburg, Ontario, Canada. *Office:* Department of Asian Studies, University of Windsor, Windsor, Ontario N9B 3P4, Canada.

CAREER: Wesleyan University, Middletown, Conn., visiting assistant professor of history, 1961-62; Kerala University, Trivandrum, Kerala, India, visiting assistant professor of politics, 1963-64; University of Washington, Seattle, assistant professor of history, 1964-67; University of Windsor, Windsor, Ontario, professor and head of department of Asian Studies. Lectured in Middle East, Pakistan, India and Japan. *Member:* American Oriental Society, Canadian Society for Asian Studies, Royal Asiatic Society of Great Britain and Ireland (fellow), Indian Political Science Association, Shastri Indo-Canadian Institute, Institute of Asian Cultures (president). *Awards, honors:* Ford Foundation fellow, 1958-61.

WRITINGS: (Author of introduction) *Kama Sutra of Vatsyayana,* Dutton, 1963; (co-author) *Studies in Social History* (modern India), edited by O. P. Bhatnagar, Allahabad, 1964; *Political Theory of Ancient India,* Clarendon Press, 1964; *The Beautiful Blue Jay and Other Tales of India* (*Horn Book* honor list), Little, Brown, 1967. Contributor of articles of professional journals. Advisory editor, *International Review of Politics and History.*

WORK IN PROGRESS: History of Political Crisis in Kerala, 1947-1965; *Sources of Ancient Indian Polity; Religion and Government in Ancient India; Development and Cultural Values in India.*

HOBBIES AND OTHER INTERESTS: Reading, gardening.

SPENCER, Elizabeth   1921-

PERSONAL: Born July 19, 1921, in Carrollton, Miss.; daughter of James L. (a farmer) and Mary J. (McCain) Spencer; married John Rusher (a credit manager) September 29, 1956. *Education:* Belhaven College, B.A., 1942, Vanderbilt University, M.A., 1943. *Politics:* Democrat. *Religion:* Episcopalian. *Home:* 2300 St. Mathieu, Apt. 610, Montreal, Quebec, Canada.

CAREER: Writer. *Awards, honors:* Women's Democratic Committee award, 1949; National Institute of Arts and Letters award, 1953; Guggenheim fellowship, 1953; Rosenthal Foundation award, American Academy of Art and Letters, 1956; Kenyon College Fellow in Fiction, 1957; first McGraw-Hill Fiction award, 1960; Bryn Mawr College Donnelly fellow, 1962; Henry Bellamann Award for Creative Writing, 1968; D.L., Southwestern University, 1968. Received writing fellowships to Bread Loaf Writers' Conference, 1951, Bryn Mawr, 1963, University of North Carolina, 1969, University of Indiana Summer Writers' Workshop, 1971, 1973, and Hollins College, 1973.

WRITINGS: Fire in the Morning, Dodd, 1948; *This Crooked Way,* Dodd, 1952; *The Voice at the Back Door,* McGraw, 1956; *The Light in the Piazza,* McGraw, 1960; *Knights and Dragons,* McGraw, 1965; *No Place for an Angel,* McGraw, 1967; *Ship Island and Other Stories,* McGraw, 1968; *The Snare,* McGraw, 1972. Contributor of stories to *Redbook, New Yorker, Atlantic, Virginia Quarterly Review, Texas Quarterly,* and to other publications.

WORK IN PROGRESS: A new novel.

SIDELIGHTS: "I began writing down stories as soon as I learned how to write; that is, at about age six. Before that, I made them up anyway and told them to anybody who was handy and would listen. Being a Southerner, a Mississippian, had a lot to do, I have later been told, with this impulse and with the particular mystique, importance, which attached itself naturally thereto and enhanced it.

"We had been brought up on stories, those about local people, living and dead, and Bible narratives, believed to be literally true, so that other stories read—the Greek myths, for instance—while indicated as 'just' stories, were only one slight remove from the 'real' stories of the local scene and the Bible. So it was with history, for local event spilled into the history of the textbooks: my grandfather could remember the close of the Civil War, and my elder brother's nurse had once been a slave.

"The whole world, then, was either entirely in the nature of stories or partook so deeply of stories as to be at every point inseparable from them. Even the novels we came later to read were mainly English nineteenth century works which dealt with a culture similar to our own—we learned with no surprise that we had sprung from it. Though I left the South

ELIZABETH SPENCER

(From the movie "Light in the Piazza," starring Olivia de Havilland and Rossano Brazzi. Copyright © 1962, Metro-Goldwyn-Mayer.)

in 1953, I still see the world and its primal motions as story, since story charts in time the heart's aspirations and gives central place to the great human relationships. It shows our experience to us in a form we can understand.''

FOR MORE INFORMATION SEE: New York Times Book Review, October 22, 1967.

STEINER, Stan(ley)   1925-

PERSONAL: Born January 1, 1925, in Brooklyn, N.Y.; son of Bernard (a designer) and Regina (Storch) Steiner; married Veronka Polgar (a university professor); children: Suki, Sanyi, Paul. *Education:* Attended University of Wisconsin for five months. *Politics:* "As little as possible." *Religion:* "Tribal." *Home and office:* 1000 Camino Rancheros, Santa Fe, N.M. 87501. *Agent:* Elizabeth McKee, c/o Harold Matson, Inc., 22 East 40th St., New York, N.Y.

CAREER: "None that I know of, or wish. Writing is not a career, it is a religion." Guest professor, Sorbonne (University of Paris), 1975-76; lecturer, University of Mexico, honors program and University of California, Berkeley, native studies. *Member:* National Association for Outlaw History, Padres (layman member), Seneca Tube (honorary member), Mark Twain Society, Chinese Historical Society, American

Indian Historical Society, Western Writers of America, National Congress of American Indians, National Indian Youth Council, Western History Association. *Awards, honors:* Anisfield-Wolf Award from *Saturday Review*, 1971, for *La Raza;* Golden Spur Award from Western Writers of America, 1973, for *The Tiguas*, 1977, for *The Vanishing White Man*.

WRITINGS: The Last Horse, Macmillan, 1961; *The New Indians*, Harper, 1968; *La Raza: The Mexican Americans*, Harper, 1969; *George Washington: The Indian Influence*, Putnam, 1970; (editor with Shirley Witt) *The Way: An Anthology of American Indian Literature*, Knopf, 1972; (editor with Luis Valdez) *Aztlan: An Anthology of Mexican American Literature*, Knopf, 1972; *The Tiguas: Lost Tribe of City Indians*, Macmillan, 1972; *The Islands: The Worlds of the Puerto Ricans*, Harper, 1974; (editor with Maria Teresa Babin) *Boringuen: An Anthology of Puerto Rican Literature*, Knopf, 1974; *The Vanishing White Man*, Harper, 1976.

Filmscripts: "The Water was So Clear the Blind Could See," for Vanishing Wilderness series, NET-TV, 1970; "The American Indian Speaks," Encyclopaedia Britannica, 1973; "Our Public Lands," Educational Television, 1977.

WORK IN PROGRESS: The Spirit Woman: The Notebooks of Wa Wa Chaw, Native American Publishing Pro-

STANLEY STEINER

gram, Harper; *Fusang: The Chinese in America,* for Harper; *The Machos: The Rise and Fall of the American Male; The Jaguar and the Petrol.*

SIDELIGHTS: "Concerned after World War II to escape the confusion of the city," wrote N. Scott Momaday, "[Steiner] set out to discover the source of his country and of himself. Now, after more than twenty years and 200,000 miles, he has come to know better than most men the American landscape and the people who are native to it. He has lived among the tribes and has written well of them."

Steiner, himself, told SATA: "The roots of America, which are its true heritage and will be its only salvation, are what I seek in my work. For these are my roots. And in seeking and finding them there is joy and peace. There is no other.

"More than that, I live on the sloping hills of the Sangre de Cristo Mountains (Blood of Christ Mountains) in Santa Fe. Quietly."

STERN, Madeleine B(ettina) 1912-

PERSONAL: Born July 1, 1912, in New York, N.Y.; daughter of Moses R. and Lillie (Mack) Stern. *Education:* Barnard College, A.B., 1932; Columbia University, M.A., 1934. *Religion:* Jewish. *Office:* Leona Rostenberg-Rare Books, 40 East 88th St., New York, N.Y. 10028.

CAREER: Teacher of English in high schools, New York, N.Y., 1934-43; writer, 1942—; partner, Leona Rosten-

berg—Rare Books, New York, N.Y., 1945—. *Member:* Antiquarian Booksellers Association of America, Modern Language Association of America, Authors League, Antiquarian Booksellers Association (England), Phi Beta Kappa. *Awards, honors:* Guggenheim fellowship, 1943-45.

WRITING: The Life of Margaret Fuller, Dutton, 1942; *Louisa May Alcott,* University of Oklahoma Press, 1950, 2nd edition, 1971; *Purple Passage: The Life of Mrs. Frank Leslie,* University of Oklahoma Press, 1953, 2nd edition, 1971; *Imprints on History: Book Publishers and American Frontiers,* Indiana University Press, 1956; *We the Women: Career Firsts of 19th-Century America,* Schulte, 1963; *So Much in a Lifetime: The Story of Dr. Isabel Barrows,* Messner, 1964; *Queen of Publishers' Row: Mrs. Frank Leslie,* Messner, 1965; *The Pantarch: A Biography of Stephen Pearl Andrews,* University of Texas Press, 1968; *Heads and Headlines: The Phrenological Fowlers,* University of Oklahoma Press, 1971; (editor) *Women on the Move,* four volumes, DeGraaf, 1972; (with Leona Rostenberg) *Old and Rare: Thirty Years in the Book Business,* Schram, 1974; (editor) *The Victoria Woodhull Reader,* M & S Press, 1974; (editor) *Louisa's Wonder Book: An Undiscovered Alcott Juvenile,* Central Michigan University, 1975; (editor) *Behind a Mask: The Unknown Thrillers of Louisa May Alcott,* Morrow, 1975; *Plots & Counterplots: More Unknown Thrillers of Louisa May Alcott,* Morrow, 1976. Contributor of articles on nineteenth-century American literature and Americana to scholarly journals.

WORK IN PROGRESS: Between Boards: New Thoughts on Old Books, with Leona Rostenberg.

SIDELIGHTS: "As I wrote in *Old & Rare: Thirty Years in the Book Business* (a collaboration with my partner, Dr. Leona Rostenberg): 'My first grand-scale exposure to printer's ink took place when I was seven. The experience proved addictive.'

"I have been writing, it seems, all my life—it is a compulsive discipline, I suppose. Even though I am actively engaged in the rare book business and travel abroad annually in search of rare books, I *must* find time to sit at the typewriter several hours a week. Mostly I write books about 19th-century Americana, especially feminist biographies and publishing history. I am drawn irresistibly to literary and biographical detective work.

"A great many books written for adults should also, I think, be read—and indeed are read—by children. Although only two of my books (*So Much in a Lifetime* and *Queen of Publishers' Row*) were consiously directed to a juvenile audience, I believe that many of my books would interest younger readers who wish to explore untraveled fields of the American past. Incidentally both those 'juveniles' were based upon 'adult' books I had written!

MADELEINE B. STERN

"Recently, my work with Louisa May Alcott has attracted the attention of both adult and juvenile readers. This was the editing of the blood-and-thunder thrillers she wrote before the success of *Little Women,* when she was struggling to earn a living and to express her rebellious attitudes toward life's many injustices. The story of the discovery of Alcott's pseudonym and well-kept secret by my partner, Dr. Leona Rostenberg, and an analysis of the strange and wild narratives so incongruous in Louisa Alcott are recounted in the introductions to *Behind a Mask* and *Plots & Counterplots.*

"In short, the more young people read, the better—especially when they make inroads into so-called adult literature."

As a rare book dealer, Stern specializes in sixteenth-, seventeenth-, and eighteenth-century volumes, published in French, Italian, Latin, and English; as a writer, she specializes in nineteenth-century Americana. Stern comments: "This dichotomy may lead to a split individuality, but it also leads to a very exciting life." Her books have been mentioned or used as a source in a number of other volumes, notably S. N. Behrman's *Portrait of Max,* Grace M. Mayer's *Once Upon a City,* John A. Garraty's *The Nature of Biography, Guide to United States Imprints,* and John Tebbel's *A History of Book Publishing in the United States.*

STEWART, John (William) 1920- (Jack Cole)

PERSONAL: Born October 1, 1920, in Chicago, Ill.; son of Ray Hiram Stewart and Mary Ethel (Holby) Stewart Cole; married Rose Elton Day, October 1, 1941 (divorced, 1945); children: Rosanne Margaret (Mrs. Alan Dean Wood), John William Dean. *Education:* Attended public schools in Gary, Ind., Alhambra and Huntington Park, Calif.; extension courses at University of California, Los Angeles. *Politics:* "Registered Democrat, but vote for man, not party." *Religion:* Presbyterian. *Home:* 629 Darfield Ave., Covina, Calif. 91724.

CAREER: Employed in brokerage firm, as private secretary, and by U.S. Government, prior to 1962; adult education teacher, San Gabriel Valley, Calif., 1962-72; now full-time writer. Co-founder and former president, San Gabriel Little Theatre, 1954; co-founder and president, Masque Players of Alhambra, 1962—. *Member:* Motion Picture Hall of Fame, American Film Institute.

WRITINGS—All for young people: *The Key to the Kitchen,* Lothrop, 1970; *Frederic Remington: Artist of the Western Frontier,* Lothrop, 1971; *Secret of the Bats: Exploration of the Carlsbad Caverns,* Westminster, 1972; *The Circus is Coming,* Westminster, 1973; *Winds in the Woods,* Westminster, 1975.

Adults: *Filmarama,* a six volume set of actor and actress screen credits: *The Formidable Years 1892-1919* (Vol. I), Scarecrow Press, 1975; *The Flaming Years 1920-1929* (Vol. II), Scarecrow Press, 1977.

Plays: "Leonora's Lost Love," first produced in San Gabriel, Calif. at San Gabriel Little Theatre, May, 1954; "Nobody's Perfect," first produced in Alhambra, Calif. at Masque Players Theatre, June, 1970; "The Waiting Room," first produced in Alhambra, Calif., at Masque Players Theatre, March, 1972. Also author of "Damnation" (screenplay), as yet unproduced.

JOHN STEWART

Contributor to *Alhambra Free Press and Post Advocate*. Field editor, *Offbeat*, 1959-60. Writer under name Jack Cole of column, "The Cole Shute," in *Offbeat* magazine, and a column in *Hollywood Studio* magazine.

WORK IN PROGRESS: The Golden Years 1930-1939 (Vol. III); *The Blue Years 1940-1949* (Vol IV); *The Dark Years 1950-1959* (Vol. V); *The Explosive Years 1960-1969* (Vol VI); all for Scarecrow Press.

SIDELIGHTS: "As an only child, I spent much of my early years reading. I could go anywhere in the world—be anyone I wanted to be through the magic of books. At the age of ten, I began putting into words my own wonderful world of make-believe. I always asked (and I still do) 'what if?' and let my imagination take over.

"Like most youngsters, my life was filled with school, friends, and adventures. Writing became a 'now-and-then' hobby. My first success was in my freshman year of high school. Instead of a composition for English class, I wrote a one-act play called 'Nancy Hanks Lincoln.' That play was used by the radio department for several years thereafter—and I received the only A in English I was to get, the rest were B's and C's.

"Today's youngsters lack imagination stimulation because of television. I have always been grateful for radio where we listened and formed pictures in our minds through imagination triggered by sound.

"The greatest value of writing lies in the author's ability to express feelings—to move the reader through emotions, the power to elicit emotional responses from readers is the key, not only to artistic writing, but to all forms of art. Too much dependence today is on the erotic. I turned to children's literature because I could get away from the use of four-letter words and sex scenes. The writer's role is to educate as well as entertain; in some respects to hold contemporary life up to gentle ridicule. Man has not changed in 2,000 years, yet his living conditions and morals have changed. Our first step out of diapers has taken place—the writer has a responsibility toward helping the 'infant' man take a good look at himself.

"There are three things a writer must have: a maniacal desire to write, self-discipline (a writer must MAKE the time to write, he will never FIND it), and self-confidence. Young people today have a greater opportunity to begin writing as must schools now have creative writing courses, unfortunately on the lower levels, it is taught by English teachers rather than professional writers.

"As a professional writer, I am often asked by various schools to talk to the students from the second grade up through high school. I find the lower grades much more receptive and open minded on the subject. After a brief talk, there is a question and answer period, then I put a word on the board and ask the youngsters to write whatever comes to mind. The results are fantastic! Teachers later tell me interest in both reading and writing improve. That is more rewarding than a check—well, almost!

"The most rewarding aspect of writing to me is when youngsters write saying how much they enjoyed my book and/or ask questions. Often the question asked is where do I get my ideas? Ideas are everywhere, all a writer has to do is ask himself 'what if?' regarding anything he sees, hears, tastes, smells, or touches—then allows that information to crawl slowly through his imagination until a story begins to evolve. Sometimes it is a matter of minutes and sometimes it may take a year or more. The next question is 'When can I start writing?' My answer is always 'right now—this very minute!' The wonderful thing about writing is that age does not matter. What matters is that you want to write and vital is the writing—the more you write the better you become."

HOBBIES AND OTHER INTERESTS: Acting, directing, traveling, any of the creative arts, collecting music of the 1920's, and working with young people on the subject of writing.

FOR MORE INFORMATION SEE: San Gabriel Valley Tribune Sunday Magazine, October 11, 1970.

STOIKO, Michael   1919-

PERSONAL: Born April 10, 1919, in New York, N.Y.; son of John and Pauline (Szumma) Stoiko; children: Jane Dallas, Michael Austin, Patty Houston. *Education:* Polytechnic Institute of Brooklyn, B.A.E., 1951. *Home:* 1217 Wine Spring Lane, Towson, Md. 21204. *Office:* SESMA STUDY, U.S. Naval Research and Development Center, Carderock, Md.

CAREER: Wright Aeronauticals, Woodbridge, N.J., development test engineer on Sapphire Jet, 1950-51; General Electric Co., Schenectady, N.Y., missile systems designer on Project Hermes, 1951-53; Martin-Marietta Co., Middle

MICHAEL STOIKO

River, Md., 1954-68, was field test engineer on Viking rocket, contributor to design study of Vanguard booster, project engineer on Nova launch vehicle, technical director on Project Gemini, Naval Research High Speed Ships Study, Naval Research and Development, Carderock, Md., chief of advance design, 1968—. *Military service:* U.S. Marine Corps, Aviation, 1940-45; became master sergeant. *Member:* American Institute of Aeronautics and Astronautics, Authors Guild.

WRITINGS: (With Donald Cox) *Spacepower: What It Means to You,* Winston, 1958; (with Cox) *Man in the Universe,* Winston, 1959; (with Cox) *Rocketry Through the Ages,* Winston, 1959; *Project Gemini: A Step to the Moon,* Holt, 1964; *Soviet Rocketry: Past, Present, and Future,* Holt, 1970; *Pioneers of Rocketry,* Hawthorn, 1974. Contributor to technical journals in United States, Mexico, and England.

WORK IN PROGRESS: A college text, *Rocket Booster Design;* adult nonfiction on space sciences.

SIDELIGHTS: "When I was in high school in New York in the thirties, I had a part time job sweeping out the hangar at Hoey Air Field, one of the first air fields in the country. I was caught up with flight and read a lot about it. I joined the Marine Corps in 1941 and during World War II, I got to fly. After the war I studied aeronautics at Polytechnic Institute of New York, and after college I was among the first engineers to work on the captured German-rockets brought over to the General Electric Company in Schenectady, New York.

"I knew we would go to the moon and beyond, and I wanted to be a part of it. I was lucky. I got to be one of the innovators and pioneers designing rockets for America's race for the moon. This creative and exciting experience I have been able to share with boys and girls who will share in an even greater advance into technology in the future of our country."

STOVER, Allan C(arl) 1938-

PERSONAL: Born June 28, 1938, in Cleveland, Ohio; son of Paul James (a railway clerk) and Blanche (Scramlin) Stover; married Elizabeth Bagaporo, September 6, 1971; children: Grace, Natalie. *Education:* Pacific State University, B.S.E.E. (with highest honors), 1962; Florida Institute of Technology, graduate study, 1964; Vanderbilt University, further graduate study, 1974—. *Residence:* South America. *Office:* Westinghouse Electric, MS 7600-FAV, P.O. Box 1624, Baltimore, Md.

CAREER: Pan American World Airways, Florida, systems project engineer, 1963-65; Philco Ford Corporation, engineer, 1966-71; RCA Service Company, planning installation engineer, 1972-73; Planned Systems International, engineer, 1973-74; Westinghouse Electric, Baltimore, Md., senior engineer, 1975—. Registered professional engineer in California; licensed able seaman (unlimited). *Military service:* U.S. Coast Guard, 1953-56.

MEMBER: Precision Measurements Association (senior member), Instrument Society of America (senior member), Institute of Electrical and Electronic Engineers, Precision Measurements Association of the Philippines (founder and first president). *Awards, honors:* Outstanding science book of the year award from National Science Teachers Association and Children's Book Council, 1974, for *You and the Metric System.*

ALLAN C. STOVER

A chief of some tribe may have realized the need for a unit of length after he settled a rash of disputes in his village. Human vanity being what it is, he most often selected a part of his body, probably his foot. ■ (From *You and the Metric System* by Allan C. Stover. Illustrated by Charles Jakubowski.)

WRITINGS: You and the Metric System (juvenile), Dodd, 1974. Contributor to technical journals.

WORK IN PROGRESS: A book on disasters; a science book on computers.

SIDELIGHTS: "I began to write late in life, at the age of thirty-two. . . . I write at night and on the weekends. I enjoy writing more than I would a hobby. I enjoy taking a complex subject and breaking it down so the casual reader will understand it. I want to write more books that people understand and enjoy.

"I helped the Philippine Government in their changeover to the metric system. This gave me the idea to write a book on the subject, since it was obvious the United States would soon change to metric. I also knew that many books on the subject would be difficult for the student and casual reader alike to understand. I wanted my book to be one that would be easy to understand . . . but still contain everything everyone should know about the metric system. I have visited many countries where metric units were used, so I had a feel for the system. I lived for nine years in the Philippines, almost two years in South America, and was assigned for two years to islands in the Pacific. I have visited Mexico, Okinawa, Taiwan, Japan, West and East Germany, Hong Kong, Nicaragua, Belize, Panama, Colombia, Ecuador, Zaire, South Africa, Antigua, Bahamas, Trinidad, Cuba, Jamaica, Haiti, Puerto Rico, Virgin Islands, Netherlands, Antilles. . . ."

STRACHAN, Margaret Pitcairn 1908-
(Caroline More)

PERSONAL: Born November 13, 1908, in Philadelphia, Pa.; daughter of Frank Russel and Margaret (Marcus) Pitcairn; married John E. Strachan, 1928 (died October 1, 1958); married Jack M. Alexander (president, Alexander Lumber Co.), February 9, 1963; children: (first marriage) Jacqueline (Mrs. Jack McCarthy), Bruce Pitcairn, John. *Education:* University of Pennsylvania, night student, 1929-30; University of Washington, creative writing seminars, 1946, 1947. *Religion:* Episcopalian. *Home:* 1936 S. Pinecrest Ave., Coupeville, Wash. 93239. *Agent:* McIntosh & Otis, 18 East 41st St., New York, N.Y. 10017.

CAREER: Seattle Times, Seattle, Wash., reporter, 1945-52; *Long Beach Press Telegram,* Long Beach, Calif., reporter, 1953; Sheraton-Gibson Hotel, Cincinnati, Ohio, publicity director, 1954; Better Housing League, Cincinnati, Ohio, publicity director, 1955-59; *Seattle Times,* reporter, 1961-64. Northshore School District, teacher of creative writing, adult education department, 1965. Served on board of Pacific Northwest Writers Conference, 1964-70, president, 1969. *Member:* National League of American Pen Women, National Federation of Press Women, Women in Communications, Inc., Seattle Freelances. *Awards, honors:* Sugar Plum Award from Washington State Press Women; short story awards from National League of American Pen Women; short story awards from National Federation of Press Women; award from Washington State Festival of the Arts founded by Governor Daniel J. Evans for appreciation of a Washington State's author's writing.

WRITINGS: Class President, Washburn, 1959; *Mennonite Martha,* Washburn, 1961; *Dolores and the Gypsies,* Washburn, 1962; *Patience and a Mulberry Leaf,* Washburn, 1962; (with Molly Cone under pseudonym Caroline More) *A*

MARGARET PITCAIRN STRACHAN

Batch of Trouble, Dial, 1963; *Summer in El Castillo,* Washburn, 1963; *Cabins with Window Boxes,* Washburn, 1964; *The Hop Ranch Mystery,* Washburn, 1965; *Where Were You That Year?,* Washburn, 1965; *Maria Takes a Fancy,* Washburn, 1966; *What Is to Be,* Washburn, 1966; *The Chinese Scroll Mystery,* Washburn, 1967; *Trouble at Torrent Creek,* Washburn, 1967; *Winds of Fate,* Washburn, 1968; *Two Families Make One,* Washburn, 1969; *Mystery of Blue Barn Stables,* Washburn, 1970; *Volunteering: A Practical Guide for Teenagers,* Washburn, 1971. Contributor of short stories, articles, and verse to family and juvenile magazines, and to newspapers. Contributor of rotogravure features on Pacific Northwest living to *Seattle Times.*

SIDELIGHTS: "I first wrote at about age six and still have those stories in a battered notebook. For many years I kept diaries, particularly during my mid-teens, but unfortunately when I became engaged at eighteen I burned these; not in fear of any lurid details, but in a fit of sentimentalism! They would be invaluable today in reminiscing of a teenager's feelings!

"At seventeen I went in training for a nurse, intending to become a second Mary Roberts Rinehart! Training then meant twelve hours on duty with classes at night; discouragement from supervisors and a good deal of stamina! Out of a class of fifty-eight, thirteen remained toward end of probation, one girl having tried to commit suicide. An experience I had with a mentally deranged patient, plus discovering I had all good marks, after being told I had all bad ones (!), was the last straw. I used those experiences years later in *Winds of Fate* for the heroine of that book.

"I resigned; went to Pierce's Business College in Philadelphia, took a year's course in five months, then worked a short time until I married at The Little Church Around the Corner in New York City. It was during the early years of my marriage I went to the University of Pennsylvania. After two babies and the Depression I gave that up! But I never stopped writing.

"Sheer stubbornness and encouragement from a family friend, Robert A. MacAlarney, former *Ladies' Home Journal* editor and professor of journalism at Columbia University kept me at it despite rejection slips. Gradually my short stories and articles began to sell. I always liked to know what 'went on the other side of the fence.' So I made many friends: Mennonites, Southern Mountaineers, Indians, Blacks, Orientals, a girl who owned and operated a hop ranch, a teacher of a one-room mountain school, and American girl living in Spain, and so on. It's a 'fun' life! I like writing mysteries, but find them extremely hard work! Both book-length and short stories. But once addicted, you can't stop!"

Margaret Strachan lived in Europe for six months in 1960, gathering material for juvenile fiction.

TABRAH, Ruth (Milander) 1921-

PERSONAL: Born February 28, 1921, in Buffalo, N.Y.; daughter of Henry and Ruth H. (Flock) Milander; married Frank L. Tabrah (a physician), May 8, 1943 (divorced, 1971); children: Joseph Garner, Thomas. *Education:* University of Buffalo, B.A., 1941; University of Washington, Seattle, graduate study, 1944-45. *Politics:* Democrat. *Religion:* Buddhist. *Home:* 106 Puako Beach Drive, Kamuela, Hawaii.

CAREER: Author, editor, and free-lance photojournalist; Hawaii School Advisory Council, elected member, 1962-66; chairman, 1964-66; Hawaii State Board of Education, elected member, 1966-78. National Association of State Boards of Education, vice-president of western division, 1968-72, director-at-large, 1971; consultant, U.S. Office of Education, 1969-72, The Consulting Organization, 1972—. Co-host, weekly series on Hawaii Public Television, "Hawaii Now." *Member:* P.E.N., Author's League of America, League of Women Voters, American Association of University Women, Phi Beta Kappa. *Awards, honors:* Distinguished Woman in Education Award from American Association of University Women, 1970.

WRITINGS: Pulaski Place, Harper, 1950; *The Voices of Others,* Putnam, 1959, published as *Town for Scandal,* Pocket Books, 1960; *Hawaiian Heart,* Follett, 1964; *Hawaii Nei,* Follett, 1967; *The Red Shark,* Follett, 1970; *Buddhism: A Modern Way of Life and Thought,* Jodo (Honolulu), 1970; *The Old Man and the Astronauts* (first appeared in *Cricket*), Island Heritage (Honolulu), 1975; *Lanai,* Island Heritage, 1976. Editor of Island Heritage's "Folktale Series," 1972-75 (which includes the Hawaiian legends *Puapualenalena, Kamapuaa, Kahala,* and *The Legend of Makaha;* the Japanese legends *Momotaro, Urashima Taro,* and *Issunboshi;* the Chinese legends *The Seven Magic Orders* and *The Magic Brush.* Contributor of magazine and feature articles nationwide.

WORK IN PROGRESS: A biography, *The Man Who Was Never Afraid* (Miklucho-Maklai). *The Legend of the White Serpent; Aloha Aina,* two-hundred years of Hawaiian history.

RUTH TABRAH

SIDELIGHTS: "I sold my first poem at age six to the 'Jolly Junior Sunbeam' column of the old *Buffalo Times* (N.Y.). Writing: poetry, novels, short stories, non-fiction, for adults and for children, for every and anyone—any way of sharing the color and depth and meaning of life and living—this is what has always been both compulsion and passion with me.

"When I moved to Hawaii in 1956, I began a new lifestyle, enjoying a mix of people and cultures, absorbing a more relaxed attitude towards both, appreciating an environment that is a mosaic of east and west.

"Like many of my generation, marriage and raising a family was a pleasant, deeply satisfying twenty-five year interlude. Now, I find living alone in my beach house on the Big Island of Hawaii, commuting by air to a studio-office-apartment in the heart of Honolulu, being an active part of Hawaii's political life statewide, and adventuring into the world of public television all stimulates that original passion of mine: to write books that will turn on readers to whatever turns on me.

"Since 1971, I've roamed bush villages in New Guinea (where *The Old Man and the Astronauts* were conceived), experienced a cold December in Siberia, explored Afghanistan by car, discovered the tranquil beauty and candor of India from Pondicherry in the south to the tiny Nepalese village of Lumbini where Gautama Buddha was born. In Spain, in Australia, in Japan, in Indonesia and Sri Lanka, I've had the good fortune to live among and make friends with all kinds of ideas and people. I have many books I want to write, and one of the next will be about China—the People's Republic of China, where I was a 'foreign friend' in Peking, Yenan, Sian, Soochow, Shanghai and Kwangchou during the last days of Chairman Mao. In the north Shensi mountains of China, I began once again to write poetry when I found myself part of a parade in Yenan, and differences of race and politics and language suddenly vanished. 'They do not know the word in English. We do not know the word in Chinese. By eyes and hearts we give each other the message. We are friends!'

"To me, this is what life—and the writing that explores and celebrates life is all about. My two sons, both happily grown and happily married here in Hawaii, agree."

Ruth Tabrah speaks French and German, and small amounts of Japanese and Spanish. She has travelled widely doing research for her books.

HOBBIES AND OTHER INTERESTS: Painting, skin diving.

TALBOT, Toby 1928-

PERSONAL: Born November 29, 1928, in New York, N.Y.; daughter of Joseph and Bella (Nager) Tolpen; married Daniel Talbot (a film distributor and exhibitor: New Yorker theater), January 6, 1951; children: Nina, Emily, Sarah. *Education:* Queens College, B.A., 1949; Brooklyn College,

M.A., 1952; Columbia University, doctoral program, 1953-55. *Home:* 180 Riverside Drive, New York, N.Y. 10024. *Agent:* Raines and Raines, 475 Fifth Avenue, New York, N.Y. 10016. Lynn Nesbit, International Creative Management, 40 West 57th St., New York, N.Y. 10019.

CAREER: Professor of Spanish and Latin American literature at Columbia University, Syracuse University, Long Island University, John Jay College, and of Latin American cinema at New School; education editor, *El Diario De Nueva York* (1950-53); director of film documentary, *Berimbau.*

WRITINGS—Juveniles: *I Am Maria,* Cowles, 1969; *My House is Your House,* Cowles, 1970; *Once Upon a Truffle,* Cowles, 1970; *Count Lucanor's Tales,* Dial, 1970; (editor) *The World of the Child,* Doubleday, 1970, Jason Aronson, 1976; *The Night of the Radishes,* Putnam, 1972; *The Rescue,* Putnam, 1973; *Away is so Far,* Four Winds, 1974; *Two by Two* (a bi-lingual book), Follett, 1974; *Coplas* (a bi-lingual book), Four Winds, 1974; *A Bucketful of Moon,* Lothrop, 1975; *Dear Greta Garbo,* Putnam, 1977.

Translations: José Ortega y Gasset, *On Love,* Meridean Books, 1966; Benito Pérez Galdós, *Compassion,* Ungar, 1968; Ortega y Gasset, *The Origin of Philosophy,* Norton, 1968; Félix Marti Ibáñez, *Ariel,* MD Publications, 1969; Roberto Cortés Conde, *The First Stages of Modernization in Latin America,* Harper, 1973.

He leaped out of the bed and flew out of the house. ■ (From *The Rescue* by Toby Talbot. Illustrated by Bert Dodson.)

TOBY TALBOT

TALMADGE, Marian

CAREER: Author. Has worked as a teacher at the University of Denver, director of a children's theatre and marionette troupe, and as a radio scriptwriter. *Awards, honors:* Winner (with Iris Gilmore) of the Boys' Life-Dodd, Mead prize competition, 1956, for *Pony Express Boy.*

WRITINGS—All with Iris Gilmore: *Pony Express Boy,* Dodd, 1956; *Wings of Tomorrow: The Adventures of a Cadet at the Air Force Academy,* Dodd, 1958; *Colorado Hi-Ways and By-Ways: Picturesque Trails and Tours,* Monitor Publications, 1959, reissued, Pruett, 1975; *Wings for Peace: A Story of Cadet Frank Barton of the Air Force Academy,* Dodd, 1959; *This Is the Air Force Academy,* Dodd, 1961; *Let's Go to the United States Air Force Academy* (illustrated by Robin King), Putnam, 1962; *Let's Go to a Truck Terminal* (illustrated by Albert Micale), Putnam, 1964; *NORAD: The North American Air Defense Command,* Dodd, 1967; *Six Great Horse Rides* (illustrated by Tran Mawicke), Putnam, 1968; *Emma Edmonds: Nurse and Spy,* Putnam, 1970; *Barney Ford: Black Baron,* Dodd, 1973.

SIDELIGHTS: Marian Talmadge's latest book, *Barney Ford: Black Baron* is a biography of a slave who escaped by means of the Underground Railroad and went on to become a successful businessman. A critic for *Library Journal* commented, " . . . Ford's biography should be a useful addition to literature on minorities."

HOBBIES AND OTHER INTERESTS: Collecting antiques and historical facts about the West.

TAYLOR, Carl 1937-

PERSONAL: Born January 3, 1937, in New York, N.Y.; son of Carl (a lawyer) and Pauline (Billings) Taylor; married Ching-Wen Pu (a teacher), March 20, 1970; children: May Tran. *Education:* Harvard University, B.A., 1959; Johns Hopkins School of Advanced International Studies, M.A., 1962. *Home address:* River Rd., Woodstock, Vt. 05091. *Office:* U.S. Department of State, Washington, D.C. 20520.

CAREER: U.S. Department of State, Washington, D.C., foreign service officer, 1962-64; Third Secretary, American Embassy, Jakarta, Indonesia, 1965-67; Vice Consul, American Consulate, Medan, Indonesia, 1967-69; Research Analyst for Burma and Thailand, Department of State, 1970-72; American Consul, Mandalay, Burma, 1972-74; First Secretary, American Embassy, Rangoon, Burma, American Political Science Association Congressional Fellow, 1974-75; Advisor, Office of Maritime Affairs, Department of State, Washington, D.C., 1976—. Special lecturer at University of Indonesia, 1963-64. *Military service:* U.S. Army Reserve, 1956-62. *Member:* American Foreign Service Association, Indonesia-America Friendship Association, Vermont Historical Society.

WRITINGS: Getting to Know Indonesia (juvenile), Coward, 1961; *Getting to Know Burma* (juvenile), Coward, 1962. Contributor to economics, history, and Asian studies journals.

WORK IN PROGRESS: Studying the history of the U.S. Airmail, with the aim of possibly writing a children's book on the subject.

Burmese dancing is very lively and graceful. The Burmese love to watch it for hours and most Burmese like to dance themselves. ■ (From *Getting to Know Burma* by Carl Taylor. Illustrated by Meg Wohlberg.)

CARL TAYLOR

SIDELIGHTS: Carl Taylor speaks Indonesian, Burmese, and German.

HOBBIES AND OTHER INTERESTS: Fishing, hiking, wood-chopping and gardening.

FOR MORE INFORMATION SEE: Asia, A Guide to Books for Children, The Asia Society, 1966; Robert O. Tilman, *Asian Specialists,* Interuniversity Southeast Asian Committee, Association for Asian Studies, 1969; *Cumulative Bibliography of Asian Studies,* Association for Asian Studies, 1969.

TERRY, Walter 1913-

PERSONAL: Born May 14, 1913, in Brooklyn, N.Y.; son of Walter Matthews and Frances Lindsay (Gray) Terry. *Education:* University of North Carolina, B.A., 1935; studied dance privately (with the view of becoming a critic, not a performer). *Office: Saturday Review,* 380 Madison Ave., New York, N.Y. 10017.

CAREER: Boston Herald, Boston, Mass., dance critic, 1936-39; *New York Herald Tribune,* New York, N.Y., dance critic and editor, 1939-42, 1945-66; *World Journal Tribune,* New York, N.Y., dance critic and editor, 1966-67; *Saturday Review,* New York, N.Y., dance critic and editor, 1967; *Saturday Review,* New York, N.Y., dance critic and editor, 1967—. Conductor of weekly radio programs, "Invitation to Dance," 1940—; lecturer on dance topics through-

out United States and abroad; dance consultant for national television shows, including "Camera 3," "Frontiers of Faith," and "Eye on New York," and for Cultural Exchange Program, Fulbright Fellowships, New York State Council on the Arts, Connecticut Commission on the Arts, Maine Council on the Arts, and the Rockefeller, Guggenheim and Ford Foundations. Own performances have been limited to dancing with a student company at University of North Carolina and as principal dancer in British production of "Rose Marie" at Royal Opera House in Cairo, 1943. Taught courses in history of dance and dance criticism at Adelphi University, Southern Connecticut State College, College of the City of New York, and Yale University. Advisor-contributor to dance collection, Library and Museum of the Performing Arts, New York Public Library at Lincoln Center. *Military service:* U.S. Army, 1942-45; stationed in Africa and Middle East, 1943-45; became master sergeant. *Member:* Newspaper Guild (New York), advisory commission for New York City's High School of Performing Arts. *Awards, honors:* Doctor of Fine Arts (honorary), Ricker College, Maine; made Knight of the Order of the Dannebrog by Command Queen Margrethe II of Denmark, 1976.

WRITINGS: (contributor) *Dance: A Basic Educational Technique,* 1941; *Invitation to Dance,* A. S. Barnes, 1942; *Star Performance: The Story of the World's Great Ballerinas,* Doubleday, 1945; *Ballet in Action,* photographs by Paul Himmel, introduction by George Balanchine, Putnam, 1954; *The Dance in America,* Harper, 1956, 1971; *Ballet: A New Guide to the Liveliest Art,* Dell, 1959; *On Pointe!: The Story of Dancing and Dancers on Toe,* Dodd, 1962; *Isadora Duncan: Her Life, Her Art, Her Legacy,* Dodd, 1963; *The Ballet Companion,* Dodd, 1968; *Ballet: A Pictorial History,* Van Nostrand, 1969; *Miss Ruth: The More Living Life of Ruth*

WALTER TERRY

St. Denis, Dodd, 1969; *Careers for the 70's–Dance,* Macmillan, 1971; (with Jack Rennert) *100 Years of Dance Posters,* Avon, 1973; *Frontiers of Dance: The Life of Martha Graham,* Crowell, 1975; *Ballet Guide,* Dodd, 1976; *Ted Shawn: Father of American Dance,* Dial, 1976. Contributor to *The Sunday Times* (London), *The Dancing Times, Politiken* (Copenhagen), *Dance Magazine, Dance News, Dance Perspectives, Ballet Annual, Playbill, Look, Horizon, Theatre Arts, Yankee, Pageant, Kenyon Review* and others. Reference works include *Encyclopaedia Britannica, Britannica Book of the Year, Compton Encyclopedia, The Dance Encyclopedia, Enciclopedia Dello Spettacolo* (Italy). Also dance definitions for various dictionaries.

TERZIAN, James P.   1915-

PERSONAL: Born October 12, 1915, in Adana, Turkey, of Armenian parents; came to United States in 1924; son of Paul (a pharmacist) and Sirouhi (Kalousdian) Terzian; married Mary Brodney (a librarian), February 14, 1938; children: Kathryn, Elizabeth. *Education:* University of Wisconsin, B.A., cum laude, 1943. *Home:* Scarborough Manor, Scarborough, N.Y. 10510. *Agent:* Robert P. Mills, 20 East 53rd St., New York, N.Y. 10022.

CAREER: Publicist and programmer for Madison (Wis.) Board of Education, 1939-41, and radio news editor and copywriter for radio station WIBA in Madison, Wis., 1941-43, while continuing education; U.S. Information Agency, Voice of America, New York, N.Y., 1946-54, began as news writer, then feature writer for documentary radio programs, and chief of World Wide English Service; Equitable Life Assurance Society of United States, New York, editor and writer, 1956-66; American Stock Exchange, director of publications, 1966-75; now retired. *Military service:* U.S. Navy, Seabees, 1943-46; combat correspondent in Pacific Theater. *Awards, honors:* Prize for best college short story, *Story* (magazine), 1944; cited in added index of distinctive short stories in *Best American Short Stories,* 1961, 1964; best short story award, *Ararat* (magazine), 1964.

WRITINGS: Caravan from Ararat (novel), Muhlenberg Press, 1959; (with Jim Benagh) *The Jimmy Brown Story,* Messner, 1964; *Defender of Human Rights: Carl Schurz,* Messner, 1965; *The Many Worlds of Herbert Hoover,* Messner, 1966; (with Kathryn Terzian) *Glenn Curtiss: Pioneer Pilot,* Grosset, 1966; *The Kid From Cuba: Zoilo Versalles,* Doubleday, 1967; *Pete Cass: Scramber* (novel), Doubleday, 1968; (with Kathryn Cramer) *Mighty Hard Road: The Story of Cesar Chavez,* Doubleday, 1970; *New York Giants,* Macmillan, 1973; (contributor) *The Gladiators: The Men of Professional Football,* Prentice-Hall, 1973. Writer of scripts for documentary albums, "The Second Elizabeth" and "Ike from Abilene," Abbey Records, 1952; writer of more than one hundred radio and television scripts and of film scripts for United Nations, National Council of Churches, and educational groups.

SIDELIGHTS: After a writing career of almost forty years, Terzian has chosen early retirement to devote himself to the study of other writers and their works.

Growers have continually failed to provide their workers with basic minimum living conditions.
■ (From *Mighty Hard Road* by James Terzian and Kathryn Cramer. Photo by George Ballis.)

JAMES TERZIAN

THELWELL, Norman 1923-

PERSONAL: Born May 3, 1923, in Birkenhead, Cheshire, England; son of Christopher and Emily (Vick) Thelwell; married Rhona Ladbury, April 9, 1949; children: David, Penelope. *Education:* Liverpool College of Art, national diploma of design, 1949, art teacher's diploma, 1950. *Religion:* Congregationalist. *Home:* Herons Mead, Timsbury, Romsey, Hampshire S95 ONE, England. *Agent:* Alan Delgado, 18 Temple Fortune Lane, London NW11 7UD, England.

CAREER: College of Art, Wolverhampton, Staffordshire, England, teacher of design and illustration, 1950-57. *Military service:* British Army, 1942-47; became sergeant. *Member:* Savage Club (London).

WRITINGS: Angels on Horseback, Methuen, 1957; *Thelwell Country,* Methuen, 1959; *A Place of Your Own,* Methuen, 1960; *Thelwell in Orbit,* Methuen, 1961; *A Leg at Each Corner: Thelwell's Complete Guide to Equitation,* Methuen, 1962, Dutton, 1963; *The Penguin Thelwell,* Penguin, 1963; *Top Dog,* Dutton, 1964; *Thelwell's Riding Academy,* Dutton, 1965; *Ponies,* Studio Vista and Watson-Guptill, 1966; *Thelwell's Compleat Tangler,* Methuen, 1967,

Dutton, 1968; *Thelwell's Book of Leisure,* Methuen, 1968, Dutton, 1969; *This Desirable Plot: A Dreamhouse Hunter's Nightmare,* Methuen, 1970, Dutton, 1971; *The Effluent Society,* Methuen, 1971; *Thelwell's Horse Box* (includes *Angels on Horseback; Leg at Each Corner; Thelwell's Riding Academy; Thelwell Country*), Dutton, 1971; *Penelope,* Methuen, 1972; Dutton, 1973; *Three Sheets in the Wind,* Methuen, 1973; *Belt Up,* Methuen, 1974; *Thelwell Goes West,* Dutton, 1975. Contributor to *Punch, Esquire, Tatler.*

SIDELIGHTS: "When the English satirist Norman Thelwell 'does' a subject," writes Arnold Gingrich, "whether cars or horses or dogs or gardens, it's done definitively and with zest." But, Gingrich adds: "Like all great humorists, Thelwell enhances your appreciation of the thing he makes you laugh at."

HOBBIES AND OTHER INTERESTS: Fly fishing on the River Test.

FOR MORE INFORMATION SEE: Punch, July 7, 1965; *Book World,* March 10, 1967; *The Irish Horseman,* December, 1970; *The Field,* November 18, 1971; *Guardian,* August 28, 1975; *The Horse,* Part 40, 1975; *Liverpool Post,* August 12, 1976.

NORMAN THELWELL

Shetland: The smallest and hardiest breed of all and perfect for introducing children to the problems of horsemanship. ■ (From *Angels on Horseback* by Norman Thelwell. Illustrated by the author.)

THIELE, Colin (Milton)   1920-

PERSONAL: Surname is pronounced Tee-lee; born November 16, 1920, in Eudunda, South Australia; son of Carl Wilhelm (a farmer) and Anna (Wittwer) Thiele; married Rhonda Gill (a teacher and artist), March 17, 1945; children: Janne Louise (Mrs. Jeffrey Minge), Sandra Gwenyth. *Education:* University of Adelaide, B.A., 1941, Diploma of Education, 1947; Adelaide Teachers College, Diploma of Teaching, 1942. *Home:* 24 Woodhouse Crescent, Wattle Park, South Australia 5066, Australia. *Office:* Wattle Park Teachers Center, Wattle Park, South Australia 5066, Australia.

CAREER: South Australian Education Department, English teacher and senior master at high school in Port Lincoln, 1946-55, senior master at high school in Brighton, 1956; Wattle Park Teachers College, Wattle Park, South Australia, lecturer, 1957-61, senior lecturer in English, 1962-63, vice-principal, 1964, principal, 1965-72; Wattle Park Teachers Center, director, 1973—. Commonwealth Literary Fund lecturer on Australian literature; speaker at conferences on literature and education in Australia and United States. *Military service:* Royal Australian Air Force, 1942-45.

MEMBER: Australian College of Education (fellow), Australian Society of Authors (vice-president, 1965), English Teachers Association (president, 1957), South Australian Fellowship of Writers (president, 1961). *Awards, honors:* W. J. Miles Poetry Prize, 1944, for manuscript of *Progress to Denial;* first prize in radio play section of Commonwealth Jubilee Literary Competitions, 1951, for "Edge of Ice," and also first prize in radio feature section; South Australian winner in World Short Story Quest, 1952; Fulbright scholar in United States and Canada, 1959-60; Grace Leven Poetry Prize, 1961, for *Man in a Landscape;* Commonwealth Literary Fund fellowship, 1967-68; a number of commendations in Australian Children's Book Council awards; *Blue Fin* was placed on the international honours list of the Hans Andersen Award; awarded the Companion of the Order of Australia in the national honours list, 1977.

WRITINGS: Progress to Denial (poems), Jindyworobak, 1945; *Splinters and Shards* (poems), Jindyworobak, 1945;

The Golden Lightning (poems), Jindyworobak, 1951; (editor) *Jindyworobak Anthology* (verse), Jindyworobak, 1953; *Man in a Landscape* (poems), Rigby, 1960; (editor with Ian Mudie) *Australian Poets Speak,* Rigby, 1961; *The Sun on the Stubble* (novel), Rigby, 1961; (editor) *Favourite Australian Stories,* Rigby, 1963; (editor, and author of commentary and notes) *Handbook to Favourite Australian Stories,* Rigby, 1964; *In Charcoal and Conte* (poems), Rigby, 1966; *The Rim of the Morning* (short stories), Rigby, 1966; *Heysen of Hahndorf* (biography), Rigby, 1968, Tri-Ocean, 1969; *Barossa Valley Sketchbook,* Tri-Ocean, 1968; *Labourers in the Vineyard* (novel), Rigby, 1970; *Selected Verse (1940-1970),* Rigby, 1970; *Coorong,* Rigby, 1972; (with Mike McKelvey) *Range Without Man,* Rigby, 1974; *The Little Desert,* Rigby, 1975; *Grains of Mustard Seed,* Education Department, South Australia, 1975; *Heysen's Early Hahndorf,* Rigby, 1976; *The Bight,* Rigby, 1976; *The Little Desert,* Rigby, 1976.

Children's books and school texts: *The State of Our State,* Rigby, 1952; (editor and annotator) *Looking at Poetry,* Longmans, Green, 1960; *Gloop the Glommy Bunyip* (children's story in verse), Jacaranda, 1962; (editor with Greg Branson) *One-Act Plays for Secondary Schools,* Books 1-2, Rigby, 1962, one-volume edition of Books 1-2, 1963, Book 3, 1964, revised versions of plays in the three books published as *Setting the Stage,* Rigby, 1969, and *The Living Stage,* Rigby, 1970; *Storm Boy,* Rigby, 1963, Rand McNally, 1966; (editor with Branson) *Beginners, Please* (anthology), Rigby, 1964; *February Dragon* (children's novel), Tri-Ocean, 1965; *Mrs. Munch and Puffing Billy,* Rigby, 1967, Tri-Ocean, 1968; *Yellow-Jacket Jock,* F. W. Cheshire, 1969; *Blue Fin* (children's novel), Rigby, 1969; *Flash Flood,* Rigby, 1970; *Flip Flop and Tiger Snake,* Rigby, 1970; *Gloop the Bunyip* (children's story in verse; contains material from 1962 book, *Gloop, the Gloomy Bunyip),* Rigby, 1970; (editor with Branson) *Plays for Young Players* (for primary schools), Rigby, 1970; *The Fire in the Stone,* Rigby, 1973, Harper, 1974; *Albatross Two,* Rigby, 1974, Harper, 1975; *Magpie Island,* Rigby, 1974; *Uncle Gustav's Ghosts,* Rigby, 1974; *February Dragon,* Harper, 1976; *The Hammerhead Light,* Rigby, 1976, Harper, 1977; *The Shadow on the Hills,* Harper, 1977. *The SKNUKS,* Rigby, 1977.

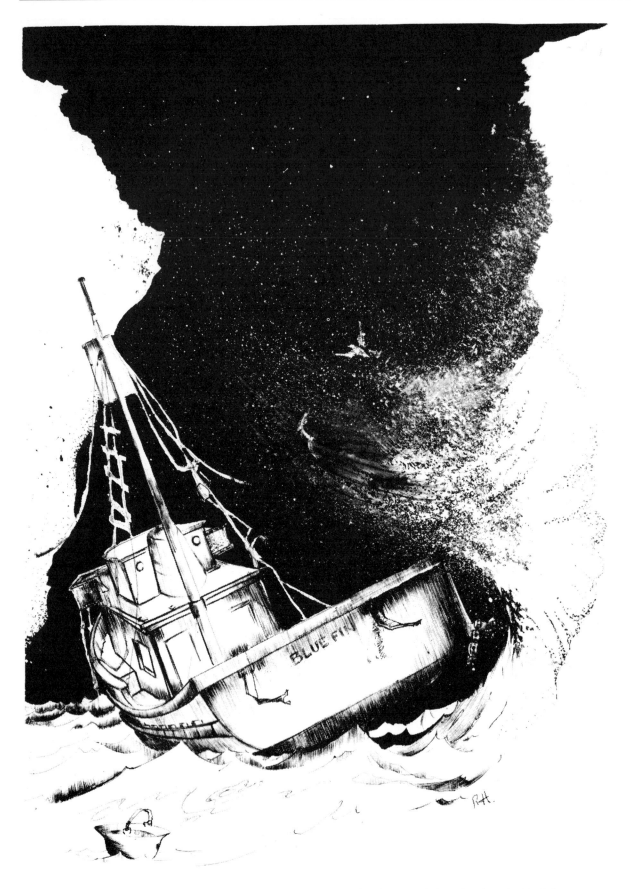

A great column of water rose out of the sea, thrust itself head and shoulders into the black fury of the vortex above, and began moving across the sea like a waltzing mountain. ■ (From *Blue Fin* by Colin Thiele. Pictures by Roger Haldane.)

Plays: "Burke and Wills" (verse), first performed at Adelaide Radio Drama Festival, 1949, and published in full in *On the Air,* edited by P. R. Smith, Angus & Robertson, 1959; "Edge of Ice" (verse), first performed on radio, 1952; "The Shark Fishers" (prose), first performed, 1954; "Edward John Eyre" (verse), first performed at Adelaide Radio Drama Festival, 1962.

Writer of other verse plays for radio, and radio features, documentaries, children's serials, and schools broadcasts programs; national book reviewer for Australian Broadcasting Commission. His poetry and short stories have appeared in many anthologies and journals; also contributor of articles and reviews to periodicals. *Storm Boy* was made into a feature film in 1976, and *Blue Fin,* 1973.

SIDELIGHTS: "I believe that almost every writer is influenced profoundly by his past life, especially his childhood and adolescence.

"I was still a boy in the primary school compulsorily memorising large tracts of Tennyson when I learned that all experience was an arch where through gleamed the untravelled world. And I was still a young university student when I learned that experience was a paddock full of burrs that clung tenaciously so that every time you looked back you saw too clearly the blundering tracks you were leaving behind. I suspect that for much of my life I have been caught between the twin urges to look forward and to look back—the one teasing and beckoning, the other revealing and illuminating.

"I don't know when I learned that experience needn't just cling, degenerating into mere reminiscence, but that it could shape, change and build in the most astonishing way, developing individual uniqueness. I certainly know it now. For experience varies not only in nature but in quality; and in the case of writers I believe this to be supremely important. Some events don't leave a trace. Not a ripple. At best they may be a kind of spiritual roughage, temporal bulk. But they don't add anything to make us grow into something more intensely and wholly us—you more you and me more me. They occur all the time, these non-events: the trivia of a neighbor's telephone call, the staleness of a minute's television, the banality of a comment or question.

"Conversely, and fortunately, there is experience that leaves us changed forever. It isn't necessarily sweeping or breathtaking, doesn't always come at us with histrionics; it may well come with silence or still small voic But, loud or soft, violent or gentle, its impact can shake us like fever. For just as experience itself varies greatly in quality so, I believe, does our response. And in youth and childhood, when the world can still be big and shining, when trust still lives and truth is not yet dead, these influences are often climactic. As is the seduction of that trust and the destruction of that truth.

"It is against convictions such as these that I tend to see my own early life. It was basically rural—farm and township, fallow and stubble, week-day and Sunday. But in being that it was much more. It was yabby creek and red gum hillock, candlelight and oven bread, mealtime grace and family Bible, Christening font and graveside coffin. It was ice on puddles and the fluffing of summer dust through barefoot toes; it was frost to the horizon and frogs in the flooded cellar and, literally, possums in the kitchen. It was draught horses straining in wagons, and early morning stars and Christmas and the stupendous cycle of the seasons. It was stallion and

COLIN THIELE

mare, bull and cow, boar and sow, gobbler and turkey hen, buck rabbit and doe—even man and woman. There was no need for elaborate sex education when every day teemed with copulation, conception and birth. As it also teemed with death.

"It was the miracle of living and the beauty and ugliness of the world. And above all else, it was solitude. Because I had no brothers or sisters near my own age I was thrown largely upon myself and—through the wisdom of country parents in those days when the world was still wide—I was given great freedom. Incredible freedom, now that I come to look back at it. Tending traps and roaming steep hills and valleys in the darkness long before dawn, trudging along sheep-walks up steep ridges in darkness long after sunset. And almost always alone. Alone to stand on the hilltops with the vast fall of the slopes before me down to the plains beyond, alone to see sunrise in a thousand ways, moonlight and starshine, storm and thunderbolt, snake's flash and eagle's strike, killer dog and wild cat. Alone to find rabbit kittens in burrows, hawks' nests in hollows, blue cranes in reeds, wattle buds breaking, sudden breathtaking new mushrooms in rings. Alone to think my own thoughts, enjoy my own happiness, nurse my own hurts. And, perhaps, to find my own self.

"There were *people* too—in farmhouses, schoolrooms, churches and sitting rooms for visitors. Fathers, mothers, relatives, neighbours, even occasional strangers. And, of course, a handful of teachers who contributed to my life in various ways. I remember one, for instance, who startled us soon after her arrival by asking us to bring a sprig of mallee leaves next day for drawing lesson. As soon as we got out-

(From the movie "Storm Boy," starring Greg Rowe, 1976.)

side we held a convocation to consider the incredible request. I could have pinpointed every tree and bush within ten miles of the place and I knew exactly where the nearest mallee was—a spindly specimen eight miles away down at the edge of the Flats beyond the hills. But, teachers being Law, I was nominated for the dash from Marathon. At four o'clock in the morning I was running in darkness and dew down the long slopes, over ridges and creek-beds, past sheoaks and gums and rabbit-warrens that I could have charted in my mind in the darkness—every furrow and hole. And finally reached the sick dwarf mallee, tore off a branch big enough to provide serves for my fellow-artists, and faced the long hard haul back to the uplands and the school. I staggered in before the bell, shirt drenched, thighs and calves quivering. And the teacher, sharper than iodine, blasted the lot of us for bringing such rubbishy specimens into class when the whole neighbourhood teemed with choice mallee leaves. No talk allowed, no timid word of explanation. Imposed silence. But I still remember the incredulous shock, the sudden destruction of an innocence, the realisation in me that even teachers could be desperately fallible—not only in their knowledge, but worse, in their sensibilities.

"Incidents like that may have confirmed still further my conviction of the value of solitariness, a conviction that has intensified throughout my life so that now I can feel only sadness and despair at today's vast uncontrolled populations. How can man any longer hope to find the solitude that is so essential to his spirit.

"Since boys grow and time is never static, I moved towards adolescence and found the shadows of adulthood reaching towards me. But I also felt the stirring strengths of youth, the enormous energies, the power of bodily resilience. The Great Depression had stricken the countryside and the nearest high school was at Kapunda more than twenty miles away. I went to Kapunda. Every day. Up at 5:30 in the morning, my mother and breakfast waiting in the kitchen, three miles on my bike to the railway siding, train to Kapunda, long walk to the high school on the hill, lessons all day, homework after school till train-time again, walk to the station at seven o'clock, slow haul back up the line to the local siding, ride home through the darkness, steaming dinner and mother both waiting in the kitchen at half-past eight, bedtime at nine. A rigorous, perpetual cycle. And I loved it.

"When the wind blew gales and the rain flung serpents and fish-fins in my face I didn't much notice their buffet and sting. I stood on the pedals of the cranky old bike and felt like Conrad's Marlow. I rode frost in the winter with my fingers unfeeling on the handle-bars, scattered limestones and boneshakers over the unmade roads in the dark, plunged as sodden as kelp through downpours and cloudbursts. And it was splendid. Exhilarating. Oh Youth!

"Because the train didn't leave Kapunda until seven in the evening I had three hours on my hands after school. It says something for the Headmaster that he entrusted me with the keys—so that I could do my homework. It astonished me that the warmth of human life fell away so quickly after four. The rush of departure, the desultory thud of the football for a while, the clip-clap of the Head's heels down the marble steps outside. For a little while longer, the cheery rattle of buckets and mops from the cleaner, and then the final slam of the front door. Silence. Solitude.

"I worked alone in the great rambling old building as darkness set in and the sounds of the night took over. Creaks on the stairs, the hush of wind in the chimney, unidentifiable shuffles next door. I don't think I was afraid. Though the building which had been Sir Sydney Kidman's old mansion contained underground stairways and catacombs, forbidden to us on pain of death, which teemed with stealthy ghosts and fearful imaginings, I believe that I worked unperturbed. And when I put out all the lights, slammed the front door, and walked down through the utter darkness of the front garden I wrapped myself round with my own thoughts as I always had, and lived in them until I reached the station.

"The daily trundle up and down in the train served many purposes. It gave me time to read. Most of Hardy I read that way, a twice-daily transformation that took me into Wessex and the superb isolation of Egdon Heath. Much of Dickens I read, too, and Conrad, and a good deal of poetry, and all kinds of many-splendoured things.

"The train also gave me a new view of the ebb and flow of life. It was like a hundred vantage points all in one, a moving crow's nest. The run of colour in the landscape, the subtle daily change of green, yellow, rust or brown, new furrows on the slopes, crops sprouting in myriad green wicks, ears of barley and wheat bursting as suddenly as bells, sunlight sharper than quince-juice, hills changing day by day like time-lapse photographs. At one moment clouds lowering around the carriage and rain lunging diagonally down the window, at the next the dust blowing off the fallow and the mud in the dry dams crazing in the heat.

"And the train gave me people. Not many, but enough to teach me a good many things about humanity. Talking, yawning, panting, sleeping people. People coming and going into the night, people laconic and garrulous, people with idiosyncracies of speech and phrase, people catching and missing trains, losing purses and tickets, over-shooting stations, wrestling their luggage, being met and not met, kissed and not kissed, farewelled, instructed, questioned, loved, abused and ignored. Perhaps it was a useful apprenticeship, for within a couple of years I was a university student in Adelaide, and people were pressing about me in greater numbers. Even then, however, I knew very few and usually worked alone. This sense of aloneness I have valued all my life. Even now nothing lifts my spirit more completely than a week or two by myself in a distant shack by the beach where I am sometimes lucky enough to be able to do some writing. Isolated, without telephones, with the wind-swept shores deserted in the winter, I can find again the verities of tide-fall and gull-cry and the nature of my own spirit—which are normally submerged by daily nonsense written on thousands of pieces of paper or by the madness of telephones connected for the most part with ridiculous human busy-nesses.

"I am not quite sure what I've been trying to say in this essay, except to reiterate simply that I believe a writer's past life is important to him. And that the particularity of that life, its intimate identity, moves in him forever. The quality of a man, always so much more important than his outward trappings, the individual struggle by which he has come to be himself, as often as not are rooted in his childhood. That's why I tremble at the task of parents and educators."

FOR MORE INFORMATION SEE: Australian Book Review, Children's Supplement, 1964, 1967, 1969; *Kirkus,* January 1, 1966; *New York Times Book Review,* May 1, 1966; *Library Journal,* May 15, 1966; *Young Readers Review,* September, 1966; *Bulletin of the Center for Children's Books,* Volume 20, November, 1966; *Childhood Education,* Volume 43, December, 1966 and Volume 43, April, 1967; *Books and Bookmen,* July, 1968.

ANN THWAITE

THWAITE, Ann (Barbara Harrop) 1932-

PERSONAL: Born October 4, 1932, in Hampstead, London, England; daughter of Angus John (a journalist and historian) and Hilda (Valentine) Harrop; married Anthony Thwaite (a writer), August 4, 1955; children: Emily, Caroline, Lucy, Alice. *Education:* Attended Marsden Collegiate School for Girls, Wellington, New Zealand, and Queen Elizabeth's Grammar School for Girls, Barnet, Hertfordshire, England; St. Hilda's College, Oxford University, B.A. (honors), 1955, M.A., 1959. *Religion:* Church of England. *Home:* The Mill House, Low Tharston, Norfolk NR15 2YN, England.

CAREER: Tokyo Joshi Daigaku (Women's University), Tokyo, Japan, part-time lecturer in English literature, 1956.

WRITINGS: The Young Traveller in Japan, Phoenix House, 1958; *The House in Turner Square,* Constable, 1960, Harcourt, 1961; *Toby Stays with Jane,* Constable, 1962; *A Seaside Holiday for Jane and Toby,* Constable, 1962; *Toby Moves House,* Constable, 1965; *Jane and Toby Start School,* Constable, 1965; *Home and Away,* Brockhampton, 1967, published in the United States under title, *The Holiday Map,* Follett, 1969; *The Travelling Tooth,* Brockhampton, 1968; *Allsorts, 1-5,* Macmillan, 1968-72; *The Camelthorn Papers,* Macmillan, 1969; *The Day with the Duke,* Brockhampton, 1969, World, 1970; *The Only Treasure,* Brockhampton, 1970; *Waiting for the Party: A Biography of Frances Hodgson Burnett* (adult), Scribner, 1974; *Allsorts, 6-7,* Methuen, 1974-75; *The Poor Pigeon,* Brockhampton, 1975, Children's Press, 1976; *Rose in the River,* Brockhampton, 1975, Children's Press, 1976; *Horrible Boy,* Brockhampton, 1975, Children's Press, 1976. Contributing editor to *Cricket,* 1974—.

WORK IN PROGRESS: Tracks, a children's novel to be published in 1978; *The Chatterbox,* a picture book to be pub-lished in 1978; a biography for adults of Edmund Gosse, to be published in 1981; *All Sorts of Poems,* an anthology.

SIDELIGHTS: "In the past I have reviewed and thought about other people's children's books a good deal. It is difficult for this not to make one self-conscious. This may have been one reason I spend a lot of my time now researching and writing adult biography. My children's novel, *The Camelthorn Papers,* is about expatriate children in Libya, has not been published in the United States, perhaps partly because I did not include an American child in the group.

"Most of my writing is closely related to real events, real life; for example, all three of the incidents I use in my early reading books, actually happened to my own children. I often go into schools through our Arts Association Writers in Schools Scheme and I find many of my stories are used by teachers to trigger off marvelous work—both art work and creative writing, particularly with children between eight and ten.

"One of the impulses behind my writing is undoubtedly preservation. I write very often to preserve places, experiences, insights and stages in our family life.

"I run a children's library in my own home for 150 children in this rural area and my greatest pleasure is when one of the members reads one of my books and returns it saying, 'That's just the sort of book I like.'"

FOR MORE INFORMATION SEE: Horn Book, February, 1975.

TICHENOR, Tom 1923-

PERSONAL: Born February 10, 1923; son of Jacob Marshall and Emma (Moore) Tichenor. *Education:* Studied at George Peabody College for Teachers. *Religion:* Baptist. *Home:* 310 Thompson Lane, Nashville, Tenn. 37211.

CAREER: Gave his first marionette show in Nashville, Tenn., as a teen-ager; puppeteer at Nashville Public Library, Nashville, Tenn., 1947-60; children's director of WKNO-TV (educational television), Memphis, Tenn., 1957-60, creating among other programs a weekly series of folk and fairy tales; creator of puppets for Broadway musical, "Carnival," 1961-62; performer on "Birthday House," WNBC-TV, New York, N.Y., 1964-67; puppeteer at Nashville Public Library, where he designed the story room, 1967—. Designer of stuffed toys and of stage costumes. *Military service:* U.S. Army, 1943-45. *Member:* American Federation of Television and Radio Artists, Screen Actors Guild, Actors' Equity Association.

WRITINGS—For children: *Folk Plays for Puppets* (five plays and directions for making puppets, scenery, and stage setting for each), Abingdon, 1959; *Smart Bear,* Abingdon, 1970; *Sir Patches and the Dragon,* Aurora, 1971; *Tom Tichenor's Puppets,* Abingdon, 1971; *Tom Tichenor Christmas Tree Crafts,* Lippincott, 1975.

Has also written plays for children's theaters. Contributor of plays, poems, stories, and articles to magazines, including *Good Housekeeping.*

SIDELIGHTS: "I grew up going to The Nashville Public Library, only in those days it was the Carnegie Library. The children's librarians were close friends and encouraged me

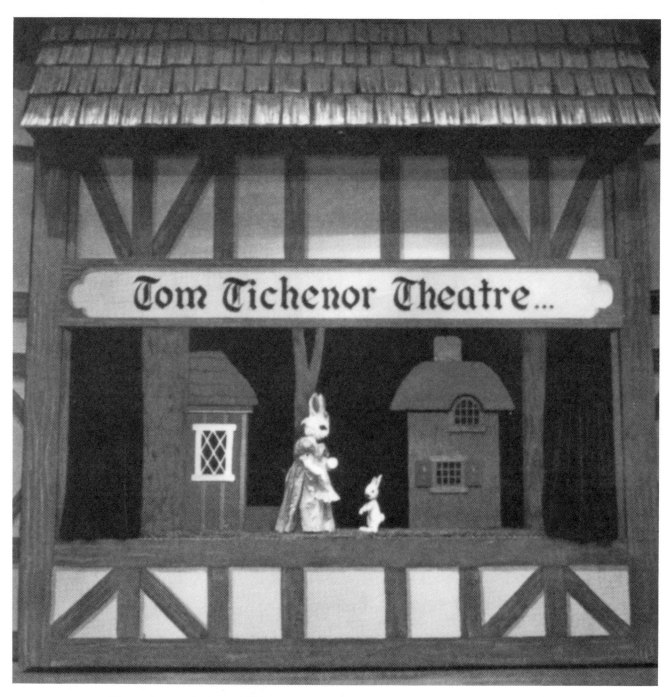

The marionette theater, Nashville Public Library. ■ (From *Tom Tichenor's Puppets* by Tom Tichenor. Drawings and photographs by the author.)

to 'follow my star' and dream my dreams. I wanted to act, but shyness kept me from taking part in school plays. Then when I discovered puppetry I could act and not be exposed. Naturally the puppet shows needed plays, so I wrote them. Before long I was writing radio scripts and acting, not only on radio but in children's theatre productions. Now it's difficult to say exactly what I am. I have to draw and design constantly, as well as write and perform. It's nice to be introduced as 'writer, puppeteer, artist,' but it is really a case of just doing what needs to be done.

"When I am forced to make a talk I always stress the importance of cultivating the imagination and having a dream. Plus

patience, determination and lots of plain old drudgery. For all my so-called living in a world of make-believe, none of it would come true if I didn't spend those long, hard hours in my workroom. It is the puppets and characters in my books that lead carefree lives and laugh through every adversity. Would that I had their attitude. 'It's your fault,' said Marco Polo Bear, looking over my shoulder. 'You shouldn't give it all to us. Save a little for yourself.' You know, he's right. But then, I've always said he was much smarter than I. Now, if he would only learn to type!''

FOR MORE INFORMATION SEE: Library Journal, July, 1970.

TOM TICHENOR

TOMPERT, Ann 1918-

PERSONAL: Born January 11, 1918, in Detroit, Mich.; daughter of Joseph (a farmer) and Florence (Pollitt) Bakeman; married Robert S. Tompert, March 31, 1951. *Education:* Siena Heights College, B.A. (summa cum laude), 1938; Wayne State University, graduate study, 1941-46. *Residence:* 141 Loretta Road, Marine City, Mich. 48039.

CAREER: Teacher; Freiburg, Mich., elementary, 1938-40; Clinton Township, Mich., elementary, 1940-42; Wheat School, St. Clair Shores, Mich., elementary, 1942-44; Lakeview School, St. Clair Shores, junior-senior high English, 1944-50; Grosse Pointe, Mich., elementary, 1950-51; Lakewood School, St. Clair Shores, elementary, 1952-53; East Detroit, Mich., elementary, 1953-59; writer, 1959—. *Member:* Society of Children's Book Writers.

WRITINGS—For children, except as indicated: *What Makes My Cat Purr?*, Whitman Publishing, 1965; *The Big Whistle*, Whitman Publishing, 1968; *When Rooster Crowed*, Whitman Publishing, 1968; *Maybe a Dog Will Come*, Follett, 1968; *A Horse for Charlie*, Whitman Publishing, 1969; *The Crow, the Kite, and the Golden Umbrella*, Abelard, 1971; *Fun for Ozzie*, Steck, 1971; *Hyacinth, the Reluctant Duck*, Steck, 1972; *It May Come in Handy Someday*, McGraw, 1975; *Little Fox Goes to the End of the World* (ALA Notable Children's Book), Crown, 1976; (editor) *The Way Things Were* (autobiography of a Marine City, Mich. pioneer; for adults), privately printed, 1976; *The Clever Princess*, Lollipop Power, 1977; *Little Otter Remembers*, Crown, 1977. Contributor to children's magazines, including *Jack and Jill*.

WORK IN PROGRESS: Badger Stories (tentative title), for Crown.

SIDELIGHTS: "I was reared on a small farm on the outskirts of Detroit where my father raised vegetables which were sold at a roadside stand in front of our house. . . . I suppose we were what would be called 'underprivileged' today, but we weren't aware of it. We had few toys so we made our fun. . . . But books were the most important things in my life.

"*The Crow, the Kite, and the Golden Umbrella* was written after I read in a newspaper about how the people in a Malaysian town were trying to rid themselves of a plague of crows. *What Makes My Cat Purr?* and *The Big Whistle* were also inspired by newspaper articles."

HOBBIES AND OTHER INTERESTS: Reading new writers, collecting paperweights and milkglass, working in her wildflower garden, caning chairs, sewing, needlework.

ANN TOMPERT

Little Fox's mother shivered and wrapped her shawl around her. ■ (From *Little Fox Goes to the End of the World* by Ann Tompert. Pictures by John Wallner.)

TOPPING, Audrey R(onning) 1928-

PERSONAL: Born May 21, 1928, in Camrose, Alberta, Canada; daughter of Chester Alvin (a Canadian diplomat) and Inga (Horte) Ronning; married Seymour Topping (managing editor of *New York Times*), November 11, 1949; children: Susan, Karen, Lesley, Rebecca, Joanna. *Education:* Graduated from Camrose Lutheran College, 1946, University of Nanking, 1946-48, University of British Columbia,

1948-49, and Berlin Art Academy, 1956-58. *Home and office:* 5 Heathcote Rd., Scarsdale, N.Y. 10583. *Agent:* Photo Research, 60 East 56 St., New York, N.Y.

CAREER: Free-lance writer, photographer, sculptor, film maker, and lecturer. Director, Foreign Policy Association; trustee, Fund for Peace; advisor, In the Public Interest; director, United Nations, Scarsdale Chapter. China photographs have been exhibited at Hallmark Gallery, Katonah

AUDREY TOPPING

Art Gallery, Neikrug Gallery, and Overseas Press Club (New York, N.Y.); work has also been shown in Berlin and London. *Member:* Westchester Art Society.

WRITINGS: (With husband, Seymour Topping, Tillman Durdin, and James Reston) *Report from Red China,* Quadrangle, 1971; *A Day on a Chinese Commune* (juvenile), Grosset, 1972; *Holiday in Peking* (juvenile), Grosset, 1972; *Dawn Wakes in the East,* Harper, 1973. Author of "China Today," a series of six film scripts and photographs for Spoken Arts; assistant producer of "The Forbidden City," for National Broadcasting Television. Contributor of photographs and articles to *New York Times, Vogue, Harper's Bazaar, National Geographic, Time, Life, World Book of Knowledge, Horizon, Art in America,* and *House and Gardens.*

WORK IN PROGRESS: The Walled in Kingdom, for Random House; an historical novel about American missionaries in China.

SIDELIGHTS: "My curiosity about China was first stirred when I was about two and was told by my sister Meme and brother Alton that they had been born in China and I had only been born in Camrose, Alberta, Canada.

"Although they seemed to accept this with incredible nonchalance, I was filled with wonder and envy. Because Meme and Alton were a few years older, I believed them completely when Alton told me he was digging a hole to China and Meme informed me that China lay just beyond the spruce trees we could see on our eastern horizon.

"Our childhood summers were spent on my Grandfather's farm in the Peace River District of northern Canada. Grandpa had spent over fifteen years as a missionary in China and my father and some of his brothers and sisters were born there. The farmhouse was surrounded by beautiful Chinese rock gardens and decorated inside with exotic treasures from the Orient.

"One day when I was five, Alton, Meme and I were exploring an old log house on the farm when we discovered a trap door in the ceiling. At that age trap doors are to open, so we found a ladder and Alton climbed up, slid the door partly open and came down.

"'O.K. Audrey,' he said, 'you go first.'

"I looked at Meme.

"'Go ahead,' she said. 'Don't be a sissy! We're right behind you.'

"So, as usual, I went first. I climbed through the dark hole and when they were sure I was still alive, they followed.

"It was pitch dark except for a faint light from the open door, but as our eyes became accustomed to the dark we saw a fearsome sight. There before us stood a huge golden-laquered Buddha with glass eyes staring straight at us. It was surrounded by smaller but no less terrifying images of fierce lions, dragons and weird monsters. A musty smell seeped from the carved camphor chests stacked under the sloping eaves.

"'Is this China?' I asked the authorities.

"'Yeah,' whispered Alton. 'This is China, but don't tell anyone we've been here.'

"That was my first trip to China. I have made six real visits since, first as a student and then as a photo-journalist, and each one has filled me with the same thrill I experienced in my Grandpa's attic.

"We have five children, some who have also been to China, and all of them are fascinated by the Orient. My books were written for them."

Audrey Topping's associations with China began with her grandparents, the first Lutheran missionaries in China, and continued with her father, Ambassador Chester Ronning, an old friend of Premier Chou En-Lai. Since her marriage, she and her family have lived in Saigon, London, Berlin, Moscow, India, and Hong Kong, and have visited China five times since the Communist revolution.

FOR MORE INFORMATION SEE: National Geographic, December, 1971, April, 1978; Seymour Topping, *Journey Between Two Chinas,* Harper, 1972; Chester Ronning, *Memoirs of China in Revolution,* Random House, 1974.

TRELL, Max   1900-

PERSONAL: Born September 6, 1900, in New York, N.Y.; son of Salomon and Sophia (Levin) Trell; married Bluma L. Popkin (a professor of classics, New York University), September 6, 1928; children: Max, Jr. *Education:* Columbia University, B.A., 1923; Sorbonne, University of Paris, graduate study, 1929-30. *Politics:* Democrat. *Home:* 110 Bleecker St., New York, N.Y. 10012; Park West Apts., London W.2, England.

CAREER: Zits Theatrical Weekly, New York, N.Y., reporter, 1924; *New York Daily News,* New York, N.Y., reporter, 1925-27; Warner Brothers, New York, N.Y., story editor, 1927-32; *Pictorial Review,* New York, N.Y., associate editor, 1934-39. Producer and director of films for Columbia Pictures, "Arrivederci Roma," 1960, and "The Making of Oliver Cromwell," 1970. *Military service:* U.S. Navy, officers' training, World War I; U.S. Army, Signal Corps, 1942-46; became captain. *Member:* Screen Writers Guild West. *Awards, honors:* Academy Award for original story and narration, 1947, for "Climbing the Matterhorn," a short subject; Freedoms Foundation Award, 1948, for story and continuity of "Dick's Adventures," a syndicated cartoon feature based on American history.

MAX TRELL

WRITINGS: Tom and Mot (juvenile), Cosmopolitan Book Corp., 1930; *Lawyer Man* (novel), Macauley, 1934; *Shirley Temple: My Life and Times,* Saalfield, 1938; *Now I am Eight: By Shirley Temple As Told to Max Trell,* Saalfield, 1938; *Prince Valliant* (text adaptation of cartoon strip created by the artist, Hal Foster), five volumes, Hastings House, 1951-54; *Just This Once* (novel), Cosmopolitan Magazine, 1950; *The Small Gods and Mr. Barnum* (novel), Saturday Review Press, 1971.

Author of original screenplays: "High Conquest," 1947; "Climbing the Matterhorn," 1947; "Sixteen Fathoms Deep," 1948; "New Mexico," 1950; "Hell Below Zero," 1954. Author of daily syndicated juvenile fiction for King Features, Inc., 1926-56, and continuity and dialogue for syndicated cartoon feature, "Dick's Adventures."

Original story credits for motion picture versions of "Lawyer Man," Warner Brothers, 1935; and "Just This Once," MGM, 1951.

WORK IN PROGRESS: Peter, a novel, concerning Peter the Great before greatness.

SIDELIGHTS: "What can I say of myself as a writer vis-à-vis young writers except what they already know or sense, not about me surely but about themselves? They know that writers write, must write, can do nothing but write, want to do nothing but write. We live out our hours on a sheet of blank paper. There is no escape, not for any of us, old or young.

"I was lucky.

"My first wish was to work on a New York newspaper. A big metropolitan New York newspaper. How to get there?

"Eighteen. I was in college. A newspaperman (I advised myself with the wisdom of ignorance) needs only to skim off the cream of the world's knowledge. He has no need to be a scholar. He needs to know something about everything, not everything about something. So I raced through the college catalogue like Robinson Crusoe racing around his island. English Literature, French literature, anthropology, philosophy, economics, history, art history, zoology, pre-med. I learned practically nothing about anything, but something about everything. Enroute through this jungle of world knowledge, I gathered up garlands of D's, a few stray A's. I never made the Dean's list. Columbia was glad to be rid of me. It was great fun.

"A few weeks after graduation, loaded with my smatterings and remnants of learning, I landed a job on a newspaper, not the metropolitan newspaper I had in mind, but an outback refuge for would-be and has-been newspapermen called the *Bronx Home News*. The editor eyed me as a heaven-sent gift. He promptly put me in charge of the obit column, with diversions embracing block parties, church raffles, small fires, and the doings and sayings of neighborhood merchants, school principals, preachers, etc. But it wasn't all that easy. The gang that sat around me, most of whom had come up through the obits and block parties years before, looked at me with pity coupled with astonishing good will. As with any journalistic idiot they offered me first aid whenever they saw me gibbering over my typewriter. I soon discovered that they handled the English sentence twice as succinctly and more than twice as fast as I did. I lasted about six months. The experience almost normalized me, like a nearly successful operation on the brain. The salary was $17 a week.

"Just about this time a college friend tipped me off about a job on *Zit's Theatrical Weekly,* a Broadway sheet that aspired to be a rival of the two great show business periodicals of the time: *Billboard* and *Variety*. Zit's specialized in vaudeville and had some bashful pretensions now and then to investigating and dishing out hot-blooded backstage scandal. The job paid $22 a week and had no obit column, so I took it.

"The editorial staff consisted of three young reporters and an editor. The editor was a seasoned Chicago newspaper hack, salty and cynical, rough as an alley cat, and in unguarded moments as tender hearted as a mother hen. He had more technical know-how about bringing out thirty or forty pages of readable newsprint week in and week out than whole schools of journalism. He was a great teacher who would have ridiculed you into the woodwork if you had ever called him one. One night every week the whole staff carried all the copy down to the printer's and hung around half the night laying out the dummy and proof-reading until the first damp copies started coming off the press. That was fifty years ago and I can still smell them.

"One of the three reporters was Mark Hellinger. He now has a theatre named after him. A former reporter was Walter Winchell. George Gershwin dropped around, so did Will Rogers and other actors, actresses, directors, managers, musicians, playwrights. They'd sit around in the editor's office chewing the fat and dropping snips and bits of backstage gossip (which became lead stories in next week's issue)—people with names you used to see in lights up and down Broadway, but never saw in street clothes, looking and talking and borrowing money like ordinary human beings.

"From Zit's, after a couple of years, I finally made it to the New York *Daily News*. It was just then beginning to settle in as New York's first big metropolitan tabloid. The city room was jammed with bright young men and women from all over the country (I was one of the few New York locals) and if I still nursed any fantasies of being a reincarnation of Mark Twain or Eugene Field they lost no time straightening me out. The fellow sitting behind me was Jack Kirkland who later did the stage version of *Tobacco Road*. In the adjoining sports department was Paul Gallico. The executive editor was Frank Payne who tried flying across the ocean behind Lindbergh as the first civilian plane passenger and who was going to write the story of his trip for the paper, only the plane went down and Frank Payne and the pilot are lying at the bottom of the Atlantic, their story still untold. Everyone on the paper was sorry it turned out that way. But it was all in the day's work. Everyone kept right on writing, writing, writing—news stories, short stories, novels, plays. The typewriters never stopped clacking out pages, meeting deadlines in every sense of that terrible word. From the *Daily News* I moved—mind you, I didn't say moved up, just moved—to motion pictures in New York and Hollywood, then back to New York to magazine writing, cartoon strip continuity and dialogue, the army, and last and best of all, to books.

"One more item. It started back in the 20's shortly after college, and kept running like a long golden thread for nearly forty years. It was a contract with King Features Syndicate to write a daily children's story for the Hearst newspapers and affiliates across the country and internationally. A daily story? A daily chore? Far, far from it. Forty years of absolute joy for me and (let me hope) for the children who listened to the stories being read to them and who grew up to read the stories to children of their own during those happiest of all my years. The income was modest by modern standards but it gave me and my darling wife a two year honeymoon and more schooling, for real this time of my life, in the great universities of Europe.

"Didn't I say I was lucky?"

TULLY, John (Kimberley) 1923-

PERSONAL: Born July 7, 1923, in Wolverhampton, England; son of John (an actor) and Ruby (an actress; maiden name, Kimberley) Tully; married Margaret Else; children: Richard, David, Katharine, Diana. *Education:* Attended school in North Wales. *Home:* 209 Jersey Rd., Isleworth, Middlesex TW7 4RE, England.

CAREER: Writer for newspapers and for television; author; free-lance broadcaster. *North Wales Pioneer,* Llandudno, reporter, 1947-49; *Daily Mirror,* Manchester, England, reporter, 1949, Leeds, 1949-50; West African newspapers, Nigeria and Gold Coat, London correspondent, 1950-53. *Military service:* Royal Air Force, 1940-45; became flight sergeant. *Member:* Writers Guild of Great Britain (vice-chairman, 1976-77).

WRITINGS—Juvenile: *The Crocodile,* BBC Publications, 1972; *The Raven and the Cross,* BBC Publications, 1974; *The Glass Knife,* Methuen, 1974; *The White Cat,* Methuen, 1975; *Johnny Goodlooks,* Methuen, 1977.

Film scripts: "The Man from Nowhere," Children's Film Foundation, 1976; "One Hour to Zero," Children's Film Foundation, 1976. Also documentary films for firms including Shell Oil Co., British Gas Council, and Midland Bank.

Television scripts include the adaptations "The Viaduct," 1972, "Thursday's Child," 1973, "Tom's Midnight Garden," 1974, "Kizzy," 1976, and "The Phoenix and the Carpet," 1977, original plays, including "The Crocodile," "The Raven and the Cross," "A King of Argos," "A Choice of Friends," and "The Jo-Jo Tree," and documentary programs, including material for "Going to Work," "Exploring Science," "Merry-Go-Round," and "Countdown."

WORK IN PROGRESS: "Mr. Selkie," a new film for the Children's Film Foundation.

SIDELIGHTS: "The BBC commissioned me to dramatise a children's novel. . . . Broadcasting dates were fixed. The studio facilities were lined up. All that was lacking was a suitable book to dramatise.

"There are many good novels written for children but few fit the precise demands of time, budget, scope, and aims of a particular TV series. Everyone in the department was reading books furiously, to no avail. At last the producer, in desperation, suggested to me, 'Why don't you write an original television play, and then write the novel to go with it?'

"I snapped up the idea and wrote 'The Crocodile'. . . . While the play was in production I started writing the book, with a traumatic realisation that if children were being advised to read it, this had better be good! Not just a 'book of the film' but something worth reading in its own right. I hope I succeeded.

"By the time I had completed a second, similar exercise, 'The Raven and the Cross' . . . I had caught the book-writing bug. What tales I could tell if I were not restricted by the mechanics of television! So why not write a book for its own sake, with no holds barred? The result was *The Glass Knife.* . . .

"Drama was and is, I suppose, my first love because I was brought up in the theatre, both sides of my family being up to

He resolved to hunt his own food in the forest when the dawn came. If necessary he would live there. He would show his father that he could look after himself. ■ (From *The White Cat* by John Tully. Illustrated by Victor Ambrus.)

their hairlines in greasepaint. My grandmother . . . was writing popular melodramas and touring them round England before I was born. My childhood memories are of plays, revues, variety bills, and backstreet digs.

"I have written for a number of adult TV series as well as many children's programmes and I have learned a curious fact, that popular 'adult' material is often the most 'childish.' It's the kids who want to know the truth about the world in ter as more thoughtful and sincere." Tully's books have been published in Denmark, and South Africa.

JOHN TULLY

TURNBULL, Agnes Sligh

PERSONAL: Born October 14, in New Alexandria, Pa.; daughter of Alexander Halliday and Lucinda (McConnell) Sligh; married James Lyall Turnbull, 1918 (died, 1958); children: Martha Lyall Turnbull O'Hearn. *Education:* Indiana State College, Indiana, Pa., student; University of Chicago, special courses. *Home:* 46 Claremont Ave., Maplewood, N.J. 07040. *Agent:* Paul R. Reynolds, Inc., 12 East 41st St., New York, N.Y.

CAREER: Taught high school English until her marriage. Author. *Member:* Phi Beta Kappa (honorary). *Awards, honors:* D. Litt., Westminster College, University of Pennsylvania, University of Indiana.

AGNES SLIGH TURNBULL

WRITINGS: The Rolling Year, Macmillan, 1936; *Remember the End,* Macmillan, 1938; *Elijah the Fish-bite* (juvenile), Macmillan, 1940; *Dear Me,* Macmillan, 1941; *The Day Must Down,* Macmillan, 1942; *The Bishop's Mantle,* Macmillan, 1947; *The Gown of Glory,* Houghton, 1950; *The Golden Journey,* Houghton, 1955; *Out of My Heart* (nonfiction), Houghton, 1957; *Jed, the Shepherd's Dog* (juvenile), Houghton, 1957; *The Nightingale,* Houghton, 1960; *The King's Orchard,* Houghton, 1963; *George* (juvenile), Houghton, 1964; *The Wedding Bargain,* Houghton, 1966; *The White Lark* (juvenile), Houghton, 1968; *Many a Green Isle,* Houghton, 1968; *The Flowering,* Houghton, 1972; *The Richlands,* Houghton, 1974; *Whistle and I'll Come to You,* Houghton, 1975; *Winds of Love,* Houghton, 1977. Author of many short stories.

SIDELIGHTS: "People—the characters—suggest a novel, and once they take hold of me they inevitably form the plot. I keep the story fluid to let them live. As they grow, I go along with them and develop the narrative.

"I might have a general idea of what I want to do—and hope it turns into something, though I usually begin a little pessimistically—but all the main incidents just occur. The characters go on living their own lives, like life itself. It is like not knowing what is around the next corner or as if my characters opened the door of my study and said, 'Here, we are. Let's get going.'

"[My childhood was passed in the horse-and-buggy days] which meant that, among our diversions, were sleigh rides in winter, drives around the countryside in summer, picnics, socials, lawn parties and, in general, calm and sunny years.

"[In my house, as in most of those in the village, there was very little money] but there were better things: plenty of love, a great deal of fun and always books. My mother and

father were of cheerful dispositions and of inquiring minds, which made for a happy and interesting home life. Looking back on these years, I feel that these shared experiences and intimacy with all types of people were of value to me as a writer.

"I attended the village school, certainly an odd one by present educational standards. However, we did have something which modern children do not have. This was the daily exercise in the old readers, in this case, Appleton's. Just as the literary taste of former generations was said to have been molded by the McGuffey Readers, so I believe Appleton's did much for ours. I remember wandering home on many an Indian summer afternoon, repeating favorite Appleton poems as I went."

FOR MORE INFORMATION SEE: Horn Book, January-December, 1948; *The New York Times,* November 26, 1972.

TURNER, Ann W(arren) 1945-

PERSONAL: Born December 10, 1945, in Northampton, Mass.; daughter of Richard Bigelow (a printer) and Marian (an artist; maiden name, Gray) Warren; married Richard E. Turner (a teacher), June 3, 1967. *Education:* Attended University of Manchester, 1965-66; Bates College, B.A., 1967; University of Massachusetts, M.A.T., 1968. *Politics:* Liberal Democrat. *Religion:* Protestant. *Home and office:* 19 High St., Haydenville, Mass. 01039. *Agent:* Craig Virden, Curtis Brown Ltd., 575 Madison Ave., New York, N.Y.

CAREER: High school English teacher in Great Barrington, Mass., 1968-69; writer, 1971—. Assistant house manager at a home for young women with drug problems; telephone operator for Northampton Hotline (crisis intervention center), 1973-75. *Awards, honors:* First prize from *Atlantic Monthly* college creative writing contest, 1967, for "Athinai."

WRITINGS: Vultures (nonfiction for children), McKay, 1973; *Houses for the Dead* (study of death in several cultures), McKay, 1976.

WORK IN PROGRESS: Rituals of Birth (tentative title), a book on birth rites in different cultures and times, for older children.

SIDELIGHTS: "My upbringing . . . influenced my writing. Possibly because my liberal family was somewhat 'different' from the New Englanders of our town, I grew up being interested in different peoples and cultures. Living in the country and having an artist for a mother gave me a certain way of seeing, an eye for beauty and interest in what others might think ugly or dull; dead weeds, old men and women, fat ladies at the beach, ancient and venerable crows, and vultures. I still live in the country, draw nourishment from it, and write about the seasons in my journal.

"I am concerned with the things that make each culture individual, and the traits that hold us together. To understand ourselves now, I feel we must know the Eskimos, the Aborigines, the ancient Chinese, and Paleolithic man. We are that strange tribe in the jungle; we are the people so old that only their bones and amulets are left. In strange and beautiful ways we are the same, yet different. That is what I write of, and will probably continue writing of for a long, long time."

The Indian black vulture plays a special part in the ecology of his home countries, for he regularly eats small carrion, cleaning up animals that other vultures might not eat. ■ (From *Vultures* by Ann Warren Turner. Illustrated by Marian Cray Warren.)

FOR MORE INFORMATION SEE: New York Times Book Review, August, 1976; *Daily Hampshire Gazette,* October 21, 1976.

ULYATT, Kenneth 1920-

PERSONAL: Born March 16, 1920, in London, England; married Patricia Brealey, August, 1945; children: Susan, Keith. *Education:* Educated in England; attended art school. *Politics:* Liberal. *Home and office:* 13 Market St., Poole, Dorsetshire BH15 1NA, England.

CAREER: Has worked for advertising agencies and for publishers, as designer and writer; currently employed by Book Club Associates in England. *Military service:* Royal Air Force, 1940-45; served in North Africa. *Member:* English Westerners, Western History Association of America, local historical societies.

WRITINGS—All juveniles: *North Against the Sioux,* Collins, 1965, Prentice-Hall, 1967; *The Longhorn Trail,* Collins, 1967, Prentice-Hall, 1968; *Custer's Gold,* Collins, 1971; *The Day of the Cowboy,* Penguin, 1973; *The Time of the Indian,* Penguin, 1975; *Outlaws,* Kestrel, 1977, Lippincott, 1978. Contributor of articles and stories to magazines.

WORK IN PROGRESS: An anthology of Western themes, for Penguin; *Comanche Captive* (tentative title—the story of Cynthia Ann Parker) for Collins; *A History of the West* for Longman; *Life of a Hussar of the Napoleonic War* for Flammarion, Paris—this book is in conjunction with artist Gino d'Achille.

SIDELIGHTS: "I have always been lucky enough to earn my living at the two things I most like doing—writing and drawing. And I have always been interested in the frontier days in America, both as a boy when I was a keen scout and camper and later, when I began reading the old history of the west rather than its fiction. When television came along my children would ask me: 'Was it really like that?' and as often as not I would have to say 'No.' And so I began to write my first western: a story in which the Indians did not bite the dust and the cavalry were defeated. It was a true story. And I think that because I researched my background carefully and tried to give the reader an impression of what life—in its everyday detail—was like on the frontier, the book was well received by schools and libraries here in England.

"I research all my backgrounds carefully and, on the last three books, have tried to use photographs and paintings by people who were on the spot at the time, rather than depend on modern artists to interpret the scene. I try to make the

In the eastern woodlands, the settlers, who wanted to farm and hold the land for their own, came face to face with the Indians, who loved to hunt and roam at will. W.H.D. Koerner's painting, "Sauk's Demand," dramatically illustrates the conflict between members of that tribe and the pioneers. Note the butter churn beside the door. ■ (From *The Time of the Indian* by Kenneth Ulyatt.)

KENNETH ULYATT

UNWIN, David S(torr) 1918-
(David Severn)

PERSONAL: Born December 3, 1918, in London, England; son of Sir Stanley (a publisher) and Alice Mary (Storr) Unwin; married Periwinkle Herbert, July 31, 1945; children: Phyllida Mary and Richard Corydon (twins). *Education:* Attended schools in England and Germany. *Politics:* Liberal. *Home:* St. Michaels, Helions Bumpstead, Haverhill, Suffolk, England. *Office:* George Allen & Unwin Ltd., 40 Museum St., London W.C.1, England.

CAREER: League of Nations Secretariat, Geneva, Switzerland, editorial assistant, 1938-39; Allen & Unwin Ltd. (publishers), London, England, art editor, 1940-43. Publisher's reader for Allen & Unwin and other firms. *Member:* Authors Society, P.E.N. *Awards, honors:* Authors Club First Novel award, 1955, for *The Governor's Wife.*

WRITINGS—Adult novels: The Governor's Wife, M. Joseph, 1954, Dutton, 1955; *A View of the Heath,* M. Joseph, 1956.

Juveniles, under pseudonym David Severn: *Rick Afire!,* John Lane, 1942, Houghton, 1946; *A Cabin for Crusoe,* John Lane, 1943; *Wagon for Five,* John Lane, 1944, Houghton, 1947; *A Hermit in the Hills,* John Lane, 1945; *Forest Holiday,* John Lane, 1946; *Ponies and Poachers,* John Lane, 1947; *Bill Badger and the Pine Martens,* Bodley Head, 1947; *Wily Fox and the Baby Show,* Bodley Head, 1947; *The Cruise of the Maiden Castle,* Bodley Head, 1948, Macmillan (New York), 1949; *Bill Badger and the Bathing Pool,* Bod-

DAVID S. UNWIN

past which I find so exciting, vibrant for present-day young readers, and to help them understand.

"I live in an old house (1722) in Poole, about five hundred yards up the street from the quay, a street built by the merchants who grew rich on the old Newfoundland trade in the late seventeenth century. I like this feel of history around me and hope to write something using Poole as a background one day.

"As regards the writing itself, I work in an attic room looking south towards the sea, although I can see only the occasional mast over the rooftops. Time is fairly equally divided between the book club work and the westerns . . . with a lot of leisure hours spent wandering in Dorset. This very old area of the country has a great number of pre-historic 'monuments'—the hill forts of the tribes who inhabited the south of England long before the Romans came. Climbing these hills on a clear day, wandering along the ramparts of perhaps Maiden Castle and wondering what happened there so long ago is a tremendous source of pleasure for both my wife and me.

"I made a trip to California a couple of years ago, touring up through the Sierras and collecting some material on the gold towns. I was also able to see Ruth Koerner's collection of her father's pictures, in Santa Barbara, which I have used extensively in *Outlaws* and on the covers of the Penguin picture books."

I was fifteen years old and I was my own master.
■ (From *Jeff Dickson: Cowhand* by David Severn. Illustrated by Patrick Williams.)

ley Head, 1948; *Wily Fox and the Christmas Party,* Bodley Head, 1948; *Treasure for Three,* Bodley Head, 1949, Macmillan (New York), 1950; *Dream Gold,* Bodley Head, 1949, Viking, 1952.

Wily Fox and the Missing Fireworks, Bodley Head, 1950; *Bill Badger and the Buried Treasure,* Bodley Head, 1950; *Crazy Castle,* Bodley Head, 1951, Macmillan (New York), 1952; *Burglars and Bandicoots,* Bodley Head, 1952, Macmillan (New York), 1953; *My Foreign Correspondent Through Africa,* Meiklejohn, 1951; *Drumbeats!,* Bodley Head, 1953; *Blaze of Broadfurrow Farm,* Bodley Head, 1955; *Walnut Tree Meadow,* Bodley Head, 1955; *The Green-Eyed Gryphon,* Hamish Hamilton, 1958; *The Future Took Us,* Bodley Head, 1958; *Foxy-Boy,* Bodley Head, 1959, published in America as *The Wild Valley,* Dutton, 1963; *Three at Sea,* Bodley Head, 1959.

Jeff Dickson: Cowhand, J. Cape, 1963; *Clouds Over the Alberhorn,* Hamish Hamilton, 1963; *The Girl in the Grove,* Allen & Unwin, 1974, Harper, 1975; *The Wishing Bone,* Allen & Unwin, 1977. Co-editor, *My Foreign Correspondent,* 1947—.

SIDELIGHTS: "To be a man and a novelist raises no eyebrows. Respected and respectable, you tread as secure a path in society as a bank manager or senior civil servant. Should it emerge, however, that you write your novels for *children,* the atmosphere changes. This is regarded as something distinctly odd. Even the youngsters tend to feel suspicious about it and occasionally take one to task. 'Why,' demanded a tough little miner's son at the close of a Book Week talk of mine in Nottingham, 'don't you write books about men your own age?'

"We are, I suppose, as a bunch, less than straightforward. Carroll, Grahame, Kingsley . . . curious characters, all of them, and the list could be extended. (I am talking, needless to say, of the *sensitivos,* the literary figures, not to be confused with the men of action, whom we can leave safely strapped into their cockpits or with their feet braced firmly on the deck.) Examining their lives, the interesting truth emerges that really successful writers for children are as often as not childless, and this should not surprise us. In a sense they are privileged for, in their case, imagination has

never had to tangle with reality and no tiny feet have trodden too hard on their dreams.

"My first books for boys and girls were published when I was in my twenties, and I was promptly criticised for my presumption. How could I understand children? I was not even a father. I was much too young. I had no idea, at the time, how confusing it was to find *actual* parenthood. Like Ransome before me, I had placed a pair of boy-girl twins at the centre of my early fiction, and when some years later they arrived in fact, their advantage to me, as writer, was not immediately apparent. The truth is, surely, that childhood—one's own, personally experienced childhood—is the mainspring of much creative writing. And the lot of us, spinsters and bachelors included, have a clear idea of what it is like to be a child.

"The books I wrote during the first decade of my son and daughter's existence barely, if at all, reflect their presence. They were still too young. (*Drumbeats!* and *The Future Took Us* were concerned with older children.) They had grown to be teenagers when I became entangled with *The Girl in the Grove.* Here, for the first time, are hints and glimpses—no more than this; certainly no portraits—of the boy and the girl who passed through their childhood under my scrutiny. But then, my books never begin with people. They invariably begin with a place. Or, to be exact, since they are woven from various strands, two or three different and distinct places. The landscapes appear first. Afterwards, people wander into them and where these people come from I really do not know. They puzzle me. Esther, for example, who tells the story of *Drumbeats!* What a self-assured, positive little person she is. Surely I must have met her?

"*Drumbeats!* was the product of a year-long journey through Africa and a visit—on the twins' behalf, although we did not send them there—to Dartington School. I drew also on recollections of my own schooldays. Out of the contrast between the green cow-meadows and cricket fields of England and the dusty African bush the book was born. The drama of contrast, in one shape or another (so I have just decided) seems to be at the root of most of my work. In *Dream Gold* I play the Cornish coast in winter, rocky cliffs and gales and breakers, against the white sands and lagoons of a south sea island. And in *Dream Gold,* as in *Drumbeats!* and *The Girl in the Grove,* the basis of the story is the contrast of natural and supernatural; the real with the unreal.

"The Grove I had discovered during the war. Bombers used to drone east at nightfall over the dark cap of evergreens; railings and an iron gate, chained and padlocked, made private the hilltop sanctuary. At the turn of the century a husband and wife had died within a day or two of each other and had been buried there, side by side, far from church or village, their simple headstones enclosed and protected by an over-arching circle of yews. Here was a place made for a ghost—and it haunted my mind for years.

"This was my shadowy strand, my other-wordly strand, but it was not, in itself, enough. I needed something material; something solid, and what is more material than pounds and pence? Who treads more solidly upon the earth than the man who has amassed a fortune? Just such a man unexpectedly paid us a visit.

"He was a fruit farmer. His orchards spanned the horizon, he had built up a mighty empire, but at the time of his arrival at our home his conscience was troubling him. He had distressed many people in the locality, he told us, and yet had

had no choice in the matter. In order to grow more fruit, he had cut down a wood. Economically, the action made sense and was justifiable, but it had not pleased the neighbours. Now I already knew a little—at second-hand—about the making of money. My father was a shrewd business man who relished yet, at heart, disapproved of his financial flair. Money-spinning he regarded as the least of his activities and he had brought me up to question the capitalist ethic. Our fruit farmer friend gave me the theme I needed.

"Perhaps I was in too much of a hurry to begin *The Girl in the Grove.* Always before I had plotted my books carefully to the last page. This time I could see only a short way ahead; had no very clear idea where I was going. Why I should have relied on instinct eludes me, yet possibly it was not the mistake I thought it was for the plot ramified, expanded, took unexpected directions and, most important of all, was influenced by events.

"I worked at *The Girl,* on and off, through the centre years of my life; the period when I appeared to be standing in the middle of a see-saw, motionless and unalterable, while my offspring swung up towards adulthood and my parents sank visibly downwards into extreme old age. As a result, the story spanned the generations, for I was concerned, during that time, not simply with the problems of growing up but with those of growing old.

"When I said, earlier, that the people who wandered into my landscapes came from I knew not where, I was referring to my child characters. Both my father and my mother are present in this last book, in the sense that they lend mental and physical attributes to composite adult characters. I should not have gained a clear idea of an old lady's illness had not my mother, a few years before she died, learned—like Mrs. Hunter—a little of what death was about; while my father's instinct for translating into financial terms any situation in which he happened to find himself led, without a doubt, to Bernard Hunter slapping his price tags on the oaks and beeches. But the young people? Paul and Laura, Henry and Jonquil? They are strangers to me although I know them well.

"Paul, of course—and this, too, has only just occurred to me—bears a strong resemblance to Guy Trelawney in *Dream Gold,* a tale conceived fifteen years before. Guy, like Paul, is small and dark, moody and brooding, of uncertain temper, in every sense *difficile.* Have I known such a boy or can fiction, in this case, have begot fiction? I suspect—indeed, it is very probable—that I met with their original between the covers of an earlier book. If this be so, then I must make a belated bow in the direction of Kathleen Hull and Pamela Whitlock, the talented young authors of *The Far Distant Oxus.* For did they not create a hero so magnificently heroic, so bafflingly and utterly intractable, that I can picture him still (although I would prefer not to test my memory by a visit to our cupboard of children's books) riding on some vital and mysterious mission across a moorland gilded by the setting sun.

"There are many stories like theirs which, read as a child, leave an indelible stamp on the mind. Because of this; because the writer for children has on the whole more power than the adult novelist to influence—or at least to suggest—thoughts and attitudes, his responsibility to be true to his public is a real one. Asked recently by my American publishers to define my goals, I told them that, in my view, while books for boys and girls should stimulate and give pleasure, they should above all enlarge their readers' experience. Any

book which succeeds in doing this must be regarded, not as a superficial adjunct to life, but as an aid and abettor in the fascinating, protracted business of growing up. A good book for young people must entertain: that goes without saying. But it should be looked upon, also, as an encouragement in the art of living."

FOR MORE INFORMATION SEE: Books for Young Children, May, 1975.

VANDER BOOM, Mae M.

PERSONAL: Born in South Dakota.

CAREER: Author and teacher. Taught school in South Dakota and Nebraska.

WRITINGS: Our American Orange (illustrated by Doris Reynolds), Didier, 1951; *Miracle Salt* (illustrated by Erwin Schachner), Prentice-Hall, 1965; *The Shepherd's Boy* (illustrated by Patricia Seitz), Augsburg, 1969.

SIDELIGHTS: Mae Vander Boom lived for a time in California. Her proximity to an orange grove inspired her to write her first book, *Our American Orange.* The author's next book, *Miracle Salt,* gave a wealth of information about the history and use of salt. In a review for *Horn Book* Isaac Asimov noted, "A restriction of subject matter most emphatically does not imply a restriction of interest." In reviewing the same book, a critic for *Saturday Review* wrote, "[Vander Boom's book] has an unusual amount of information; it will be fascinating to age groups above and below the 8-12 level, at which it is listed. . . ."

Zena Sutherland, writing in the *Saturday Review,* described *The Shepherd's Boy* as a Nativity story in which "a Jewish child is among the shepherds on the night of Christ's birth, and later dreams that his Roman friend worships with him."

VAN RENSSELAER, Alexander (Taylor Mason) 1892-1962

PERSONAL: Born in 1892.

CAREER: Editorial writer for several New York newspapers, including the *Sun* and the *Telegram;* joined the publishing firm of Henry Holt & Co. as advertising manager after the First World War; later served in the same capacity at Duffield & Co., Century, and later Appleton-Century. *Military service:* Served in the U.S. Army during World War I.

WRITINGS: (With Frank Butcher) *Yule Light: A Christmas Pageant,* Century, 1930; *Betcha Can't Do It!,* Appleton-Century, 1940; *Try This One!* (illustrated by George Anrig), Appleton-Century, 1941; the latter two books were published together as *Fun with Stunts,* Blackiston, 1945; *The Complete Book of Party Games* (illustrated by M. B. Thompson), Sheridan, 1952, reissued as *Party Fun and Games,* Fawcett, 1962; *Magic: A Family Activity Book* (illustrated by John N. Barron), Knopf, 1952; *Fun with Ventriloquism* (illustrated by J. N. Barron), Garden City Publishing, 1955; *Fun with Magic* (illustrated by J. N. Barron), Garden City Publishing, 1957; *The Picture History of America* (illustrated by Raymond Lufkin), Doubleday, 1961; *Your Book of Magic* (illustrated by J. N. Barron), Faber, 1966, Transatlantic, 1968.

The wand is used almost entirely for misdirecting the attention of the audience. A wave of the wand instantly catches the eyes of the audience and leads them away from a movement you do not wish them to see. ■ (From *Fun With Magic* by Alexander Van Rensselaer. Illustrated by John N. Barron.)

Also contributor to various magazines, including *Bookman* and *St. Nicholas*.

SIDELIGHTS: Van Rensselaer's study of palmistry, mind reading, and ventriloquism was the outcome of his lifelong dream to be a professional magician. Many of the author's books reflected his interest in the area of illusions and tricks. Van Rensselaer's book, *Betcha Can't Do It!*, contained more than one hundred stunts and practical jokes. A critic for *Books* commented, "Alexander Van Rensselaer is a student of stunts—with coins, matches, milk bottles, brooms, cards, and bewildered witnesses."

The author's *Magic: A Family Activity Book* described twenty-five tricks for young people to perform. A reviewer for *Atlantic* noted, "... any young person could master the tricks ... and the number of birthday parties which would be enlivened by their performance could easily reach fantastic proportions."

The art of throwing one's voice without moving the lips became the subject matter for Van Rensselaer's book, *Fun with Ventriloquism*. "The practical suggestions [offered in this book] ... should produce results and make pretty good ventriloquists out of young readers," wrote a *Kirkus* critic.

One of the author's later books, *Fun with Magic,* provided information about the materials and techniques required for

a successful magician. A *Library Journal* reviewer observed, "Each trick has helpful step-by-step illustrations.... Make-up and text far more appealing than [other] ... books on the subject."

FOR MORE INFORMATION SEE—Obituaries: *New York Times,* August 22, 1962; *Publishers Weekly,* September 10, 1962.

(Died August 20, 1962)

Van VOGT, A(lfred) E(lton)   1912-

PERSONAL: Born April 26, 1912, in Manitoba, Canada; son of Henry (an attorney) and Agnes (Buhr) van Vogt; married Edna Mayne Hull (a writer under name E. Mayne Hull), May 9, 1939 (died, January 20, 1975). *Education:* Attended schools in Manitoba, and subsequently took about thirty courses at adult education or college level. *Religion:* Rationalist. *Address:* P.O. Box 3065, Los Angeles, Calif. 90028. *Agent:* Forrest J. Ackerman, Ackerman Agency, 2495 Glendower Ave., Los Angeles, Calif. 90027.

CAREER: Professional writer, 1932—, chiefly of science fiction. MacLean Publishing Co., Toronto, Ontario, Canada, western representative of trade papers, 1935-39. First director of Hubbard Dianetic Research Foundation of California, 1950-51. *Member:* International Society for General Semantics, Authors Guild of the Authors League of America, Science Fiction Writers of America, International Dianetic Society (president, 1958—), California Association of Dianetic Auditors (president, 1959—).

WRITINGS—Fiction, except as noted: *Slan,* Arkham, 1946 (appeared serially in *Astounding Science Fiction,* 1940); *The Book of Ptath,* Fantasy Press, 1947, reissued in paperback as *200 Million A.D., World of A,* Simon & Schuster, 1948, reissued as *Ptath,* Zebra, 1976; *Pawns of Null-A* (sequel to *World of A*), Ace Books, c.1949, reissued as *The Players of Null-A* (original magazine title), Berkley Books, 1966.

The Voyage of the Space Beagle, Simon & Schuster, 1950, reissued as *Mission Interplanetary,* Macfadden, 1950; *The House That Stood Still,* Greenberg, 1950, slightly revised edition published as *The Mating Cry,* Galaxy, 1960; *The Weapon Shops of Isher,* Greenberg, 1951; *The Weapon Makers* (sequel to *The Weapon Shops of Isher*), Greenberg, 1952, reissued as *One Against Eternity,* Ace Books, 1954; *Away and Beyond* (collection), Pellegrini & Cudahy, 1952; *Destination: Universe!* (collection with introduction by the author), Pellegrini & Cudahy, 1952; *The Universe Maker* (original magazine title, "The Shadow Man"), Ace Books, 1953; (with wife, E. Mayne Hull) *Planets for Sale,* Fell, 1954; (with Charles Edward Cooke) *The Hypnotism Handbook* (nonfiction), Griffin, 1956; *Empire of the Atom,* Shasta, 1957; *The Mind Cage,* Simon & Schuster, 1957; *Siege of the Unseen* (original magazine title, "The Chronicler"), Ace Books, 1959; *The War Against the Rull,* Simon & Schuster, 1959.

The Wizard of Linn (sequel to *Empire of the Atom*), Ace Books, 1962; *The Violent Man* (novel; not science fiction), Farrar, Straus, 1962; *The Beast,* Doubleday, 1963; *Rogue Ship,* Doubleday, 1965; (with E. Mayne Hull) *The Winged Man,* Doubleday, 1966; *A Van Vogt Omnibus,* Sidgwick & Jackson, 1967; *Far-Out Worlds of A. E. Van Vogt,* Ace Books, 1968; *Silkie,* Ace Books, 1969; *Quest for the Future,* Ace Books, 1970; *Children of Tomorrow,* Ace Books, 1970; *The Battle of Forever,* Ace Books, 1971; *More Than Superhuman* (collection), Dell, 1971; *The Proxy Intelligence and Other Mind Benders* (collection), Paperback Library, 1971, reissued as *The Gryb,* Zebra, 1976; *M-33 in Andromeda* (collection), Paperback Library, 1971; *The Darkness on Diamondia,* Ace Books, 1972; *The Book of Van Vogt* (collection), DAW Books, 1972; *Future Glitter,* Ace Books, 1973; *The Money Personality,* Parker Publishing Co., 1973; *The Secret Galactics* (subsequently published as a paperback under title *Earth Factor X* by DAW Books), Prentice-Hall, 1974; *The Man with 1000 Names,* DAW Books, 1974; *The Worlds of A. E. Van Vogt,* Ace Books, 1974; *The Best of A. E. Van Vogt,* Pocketbooks, 1976; *Supermind,* DAW Books, 1977; *The Anarchistic Colossus,* Ace Books, 1977.

Between 1932 and 1935, wrote about two dozen "true confession" stories for magazines and about 50 radio plays.

Other books; dates of original and some subsequent editions not available: *Earth's Last Fortress* (original magazine title, "Recruiting Station"), Ace Books, subsequently published in hardcover with "The Changeling" as *Masters of Time [and] The Changeling,* Fantasy Press, 1950, both stories reissued separately by Macfadden, 1967; *Mission to the Stars,* Berkley books, hardcover edition published as *The Mixed Men,* Gnome Press, 1952; *Monsters* (story collection), Paperback; (with E. Mayne Hull) *Out of the Unknown* (collection of stories originally published in the magazine *Unknown Worlds*), Fantasy Press, 1948.

WORK IN PROGRESS: To Conquer Kiber, for DAW; an untitled science fiction novel for Doubleday; and an untitled science fiction novel for Pocketbooks.

SIDELIGHTS: "As a person, I am an experimenter—principally on myself. For example, thirty-odd years ago I began awakening with an alarm clock every ninety minutes, 300 nights a year. The purpose: to solve story problems by the dreaming process. Ten years ago, I decided the method had therapeutic possibilities; and so about half the 300 nights were subsequently devoted to dream therapy and half to dream creativity (with the difference, also, that, instead of an alarm clock, I used an industrial timer that turned on a cassette recorder with my voice on it to awaken me).

"In 1968, I began an exercise experiment—by which I was eventually able to have the second-wind experience in three minutes. In 1972, I became interested in learning unusual languages while exercising. Today, I am familiar with more than a dozen, including such oddities as Frisian and Raeto-Romanic.

"I am a person who makes studies, and eventually devises a systematic thought about the subject under examination. Thus, I studied general semantics—and wrote the Null-A novels. Studied the violent male—and wrote a non-science fiction novel, *The Violent Man.* Studied the qualities a person must have to make and keep money. Result: a nonfiction book *The Money Personality.* Studied hypnotism—and wrote *The Hypnotism Handbook* for a psychologist. And so on, many subjects, most of which have still to be written up.

"I am a method writer. I have to know how to do something before I can do it. Have to know it on a very precise level. Thus, I write my stories in 800-word scenes, each scene having five steps in it. I write in what I call fictional sentences, using either imagery or emotion in every sentence for ordinary stories, and a hang-up for the science fiction fictional sentence. Recently, I made my precise study of film and television script forms. As a consequence, I have sold my first original screen treatment. I shall do a science fiction novel based on it. The film and the book will both be titled: *Computerworld.*

"My agent and I working together and following up every lead, have managed to keep an average of twenty of my books in print, year in, year out. My world-wide best sellers are: *The World of Null-A, The Weapon Shops of Isher, The Voyage of the Space Beagle* and *Slan,* and, of more recent titles *Quest for the Future* and *The Silkie.*"

FOR MORE INFORMATION SEE: The Oral History Collection of Columbia University, Butler Library, Columbia University, 1964; Sam Moskowitz, *Modern Masterpieces of Science Fiction,* World Publishing, 1965; *Reflections of A. E. Van Vogt Fictioneer Books,* Lakemont, 1975.

VAUGHAN, Harold Cecil 1923-

PERSONAL: Born October 26, 1923, in New York, N.Y.; son of Harold Cecil and Anna (Gosler) Vaughan. *Education:* Columbia University, A.B., 1943, M.A., 1947, graduate study, 1947-48. *Politics:* Democrat. *Religion:* None. *Home:* 2200 North Central Rd., Fort Lee, N.J. 07024.

HAROLD C. VAUGHAN

CAREER: Brooklyn Friends School, Brooklyn, N.Y.; teacher of history and social studies, 1950-59; Ridgewood Board of Education, Ridgewood, N.J., teacher of history and social studies, 1959—. Lecturer to many organizations, including Colonial Dames, Daughters of the American Revolution, Contemporary Club, Junior League of New York, and Long Island Historical Association. *Military service:* U.S. Army Air Force, 1943-44.

WRITINGS: The Citizen Genet Affair, 1793: A Chapter in the Formation of American Foreign Policy, Watts, 1970; *The Hayes-Tilden Election,* Watts, 1971; *The XYZ Affair,* Watts, 1972; *The Monroe Doctrine, 1923,* Watts, 1973; *The Colony of Georgia,* Watts, 1975; *The Versailles Treaty, 1919,* Watts, 1975; *The Constitutional Convention 1787: The Beginning of Federal Government in America,* Watts, 1976.

WORK IN PROGRESS: Currently doing research on a new series of books dealing with the territorial growth of the United States.

SIDELIGHTS: In recent years Harold Vaughan has traveled extensively throughout Europe (Greece in 1971, Western Europe in 1973), Canada (1975), and the southern United States in 1976.

VAUGHAN, Sam(uel) S.   1928-

PERSONAL: Born August 3, 1928, in Philadelphia, Pa.; son of Joseph (a lineman) and Anna Catherine (Alexander) Vaughan; married Jo(sephine) Vaughan, October 22, 1949;

children: Jeffrey Marc, Leslie Jane, Dana Alexander, David Samuel. *Education:* Pennsylvania State College (now University), A.B., 1951. *Politics:* Independent. *Religion:* Episcopalian. *Home:* 23 Inness Rd., Tenafly, N.J. *Agent:* Sterling Lord Agency, 600 Madison Ave., New York, N.Y. 10022. *Office:* Doubleday & Co., Inc., 245 Park Ave., New York, N.Y. 10017.

CAREER: King Features Syndicate, New York, N.Y., editorial deskman, 1951; Doubleday & Co., Inc., New York, N.Y., 1952—, successively advertising manager, sales manager, senior editor, executive editor, publisher and vice-president, and president. *Military service:* U.S. Marine Corps, 1946-48.

WRITINGS—Juveniles: *Whoever Heard of Kangaroo Eggs?,* Doubleday, 1957; *New Shoes,* Doubleday, 1961; *The Two-thirty Bird,* Norton, 1965; *The Little Church,* Doubleday, 1969. Contributor to *New York Times Book Review, Wilson Library Bulletin, Famous Writers Magazine, Sunday Times* of London, *San Francisco Review of Books.*

SIDELIGHTS: "To write for children is a particular privilege and something of a mystery, even after you have done it. As with all fiction, it is difficult to know whether you are really writing fiction or just typing. My 'juveniles' were generously reviewed but the most telling was by a young lady of about seven who concluded her notice in *Junior Reviewers* by saying that mine was 'a good book to read once.'

"I wrote the first book for our children and on a dare. The second was to prove that the first was not a fluke and the third to prove that a publishing house other than my own would publish me. By that time, my children were older and tended to drift off as I read successive drafts to them so I concluded that (a) they were becoming insensitive or (b) they were right. Since then, my writings have been inflicted on adults, who are better able to defend themselves.

"The first story idea was inspired by a friend, Pyke Johnson,

SAM VAUGHAN

and a contest sponsored by Quantas, the Australian airline. A little girl who lived in an apartment in New York City won a live kangaroo. I just imagined what might happen to her and her family when the 'roo arrived to live with them. (As it turned out, what Leonard Weisgard, the illustrator, and I imagined and what really happened were similar.)

"The second book was in verse and was meant to express some of the joy and fear and excitement of Big Events in the life of Little Persons—a haircut, a visit to the doctor or dentist, an unexpected visitor, or a new pair of shoes. I wrote a lot of it in the subway. The verse reads that way. Resolved: never to write again in verse.

"The third was inspired, again, by a contest for kids on television in which one prize was a cuckoo clock. What would happen if the clock arrived and it really *was*—cuckoo, that is."

"For me, writing requires or demands story, style, surprise, humor, and a message or moral or meaning.

"My next book length writings will be pseudonymous—the only way to gain freedom.

"My father was a reader; my mother a believer in education and in suitable ambition; my wife is a caring, loving woman who feels what she reads; and our children are all readers and by God it looks as if some of them can even write, contrary to popular myth about television, etc.

RUTH VAUGHN

VAUGHN, Ruth 1935-

PERSONAL: Born August 31, 1935, in Wellington, Tex.; daughter of S. L. (a clergyman) and Nora (Knowles) Wood; married Bill Vaughn (a professor of speech and clergyman), February 14, 1955; children: Billy Edward, Ronald Charles. *Education:* University of Kansas, B.S., 1968, M.A., 1969; University of Oklahoma, doctoral candidate, 1972—. *Politics:* Republican. *Religion:* Church of the Nazarene. *Home:* 6151 West Fremont Dr., Littleton, Colo.

CAREER: Bethany Nazarene College, Bethany, Okla., assistant professor of speech and creative writing, 1968-76. *Member:* Theta Sigma Phi, Phi Delta Lambda. *Awards, honors: What I Will Tell My Children About God* was chosen "book of the year" by Church Schools Reading League, 1966.

WRITINGS: Fun for Christian Youth, Beacon Hill, 1960; *Lord, Keep the Ducks!,* Beacon Hill, 1961; *Choice Readings,* Broadman, 1962; *It's Fun to Be a Girl,* Beacon Hill, 1963; *Dreams Can Come True,* Beacon Hill, 1964; *God's Masterpiece,* Standard Publishing, 1965; *What I Will Tell My Children About God,* Beacon Hill, 1966; *Playlets and Skits,* Standard Publishing, 1967; *No Matter the Weather,* Beacon Hill, 1968; *Skits that Win,* Zondervan, 1968; *Silhouette of a Storm,* Latourette, 1969.

That First Year, Gatspel, 1970; *Foods Have No Miracles,* Beacon Hill, 1971; *Baby's Album,* Gospel, 1971; *Celebrate with Words,* Broadman, 1972; *Hey! Have you Heard?,* Zondervan, 1973; *Even When I Cry,* Moody, 1975; *Thank You for Caring,* Worldwide, 1975; *Proclaiming Christ in the Caribbean,* Beacon Hill, 1976. Author of "Lions Can't Eat Truth," a three-act play, and of several filmstrip and movie scripts; author of "I Will Lift Up My Eyes," a syndicated

newspaper column. Contributor of more than two thousand short stories and articles to religious publications.

WORK IN PROGRESS: "I have completed the script of a three-act musical which is an adaptation of *The Cross and the Switchblade.* The musician is now working on the score and publishers are working with the Wilkerson people in regard to the world premiere. I have two books of drama to be released this spring: one by Standard and one by Zondervan. I am in the midst of writing a series of books on the use of drama in Children's Church which we plan to incorporate in the church here. Included in that series will also be a book on the use of Mobile Theatre drama and one on the use of Children's Theatre and one on the use of Dinner Theatre within the church setting."

SIDELIGHTS: "I now have Addison's Disease (a dubious honor shared with John F. Kennedy). Because of my characteristic hyperactivity, I went into 'Adrenal Insufficiency Crisis with Pituitary Insufficiency' in October, 1975, and almost died. My physicians said I could never teach again. They advised my husband to change locations since the psychological adjustments to a life of limited activity in the same locale would be so difficult for me. For that reason, we moved to Denver, where my husband is associate pastor of Denver First Church of the Nazarene, which is the largest church of that denomination in the world. My hyperactivity got me in trouble again, so I again went into Crisis in November, 1976 and have since been hospitalized frequently. When out of the hospital, I am totally house-bound with no visitors allowed. I, who was a professor of speech and creative writing for eight years, now have the hope of more time for personal writing.

"There was a two-year period when my health went down (and my weight to seventy-five pounds) before a diagnosis of Addison's Disease could be made. During that long slow slide into death, I continued my teaching, my play directing, my writing, my home-making, etc., because of the steel will power that has made such an over-achiever. But deep inside, I knew that I was dying. And so I wrote letters to my two children trying to share with them the things I would want them to know in case of my death. Finally, when the doctors in Oklahoma City had given up their efforts to save my life, I was sent to Scott and White Clinic in Temple, Texas, where a team of endocrine specialists made the diagnosis and began replacement therapy in time to pull me out of death. Prior to my leaving for the Clinic, I put these letters in our lockbox in the bank. When we moved, I got them out and looked them over. I felt they would make a good book. As I struggled to come out of Crisis into life this second time, I decided that would be my major project. So that is the manuscript in which I have the most interest at the moment. My doctor still tells me solemnly that if I do not make my personality 'compatable with the disease,' death is imminent. I, of course, am striving to learn how to live as an Addisonian. But it is vital to me, right now, to polish this manuscript as a legacy to my sons.

"How did I come to write my books? I was born in a parsonage to a minister's family. I lived there eighteen years; went to college; promptly met and fell in love with a minister who happened to be a college senior. When he entered his first pastorate, I, at age nineteen, went with him as his bride. The challenge of the pastorage at that age was both overwhelming and exciting. And my work with youth especially gave me an urge to share with them some of the things I had learned about life so RECENTLY which would help them with their problems. I taught them in classes and in counselling sessions, but I wanted something more concrete. At age twenty-one, on an impulse, I sent an essay I had written in college to a magazine who promptly bought it and asked for more. That was when it first occurred to me that my urge to share could be done through writing. My first book was accepted for publication at age twenty-two and I have averaged writing more than a book a year since that time.

"In an intensely busy life, where I have served as a pastor's wife for thirteen years, a college professor and play director for eight years, written prolifically, spoken prolifically at everything from youth camps to preachers' wives seminars to state speech conventions, kept my own house, did my own cooking, cared for my own children, washed my own husband's socks, completed two degrees and the Ph.D., with the exception of the dissertation which timing coincided with this illness . . . I have ever, ever kept writing. Why? Why has that been so important? Why, now, when I realize that the hyperactivity, the over achieving can no longer be a part of my life if I live, does my writing continue on envelopes, napkins, newspaper margins, anything I can get my hands on? Because I can't help it! If I feel, I have to express it.

"My doctor now posits the question to me: Do you want to live or die? My answer is that I will live, if only for the three beloved people of my world, my husband and my sons. And if God grant that there be strength for an expression of that love, I would pray that it be through my writing.

"My world parameters have shrunk. If they only include loving three people, I accept. If they could include writing my emotions and reactions and thoughts in a 'new world,' I would be more than grateful.

"I am overly-articulate, ask me a question and I want to give you all the details. That, again, I believe is the writer instinct. Every part of me is alive and conscious of all colors, all sensations, all innuendoes, all levels of meaning and I want to capture it, look it over, understand it, and share it. Addison's Disease is such a rare and little-known disease that my doctors, who share my sorrow in my having a non-functioning pituitary gland, delight in my ability to articulate 'how it feels' to live inside an Addisonian body. This is something they cannot experience from their textbooks and laboratories."

HOBBIES AND OTHER INTERESTS: Bicycling, boating, skiing, reading, music.

VERNEY, John 1913-

PERSONAL: Born September 10, 1913; son of Ralph and Janette (Walker) Verney; married Lucinda Musgrave, March 29, 1939; children: two sons (one deceased), five daughters. *Education:* Christ Church, Oxford, history degree, 1935. *Home:* Runwick House, Farnham, Surrey, England.

CAREER: Painter, illustrator, and writer. Has had exhibits of his work at Royal Society of British Artists, London Group, and British galleries. Member of Franham Trust. *Military service:* British Army, served with North Somerset Yeomanry, Royal Armoured Corps, and Special Air Service Regiment; served in Middle East and Europe; received Military Cross, French Legion d'Honneur, mentioned in dispatches. *Awards, honors:* Created second baronet, 1959.

WRITINGS: Verney Abroad, Collins, 1954; *Going to the Wars,* Dodd, 1955 (published in England as *Going to the*

JOHN VERNEY

Wars: A Journey in Various Directions, Collins, 1955); *Friday's Tunnel* (juvenile), Collins, 1959, Holt, 1966; *Look at Houses,* Hamish Hamilton, 1959; *Every Advantage,* Collins, 1961; *February's World* (juvenile), Collins, 1961, Holt, 1966; *The Mad King of Chichiboo,* F. Watts, 1963; *Ismo* (self-illustrated juvenile mystery novel), Collins, 1964, Holt, 1967; *A Dinner of Herbs* (memoirs of World War II), Collins, 1966; *Fine Day for a Picnic* (novel), Hodder & Stoughton, 1968; *Seven Sunflower Seeds* (self-illustrated juvenile mystery novel), Collins, 1968, Holt, 1969; *Samson's Hoard* (juvenile), Collins, 1973. Illustrator of books by others. Contributor to magazines, including *Cornhill, National Review, English Review,* and *Elizabethan.*

WORK IN PROGRESS: A diary in picture-form of a visit to New York; a novel about English local government; painting decorative pictures on furniture and other objects.

SIDELIGHTS: "More recently I have become mostly involved with painting decorative pictures on furniture, usually of people's towns or houses, which has become my specialty in the past ten years—though I take on anything that offers, such as a large mobile in the tower of Nuffield College, Oxford, or a glass-fired mural in the Fairlawn Primary School in the London Education Authority."

(From *The Elephant War* by Gillian Avery. Illustrated by John Verney.)

My name is February Callendar and so many exciting things have happened recently to myself and my brother Fri., that I have decided to put them down in a book. ■ (From *Friday's Tunnel* by John Verney. Illustrated by the author.)

VERNON, (Elda) Louise A(nderson) 1914-

PERSONAL: Born March 6, 1914, in Coquille, Ore.; daughter of Herman Oscar (a teacher and miller) and Elda (Farlow) Anderson; married Cecil Charles Vernon, May 24, 1957 (died April 27, 1972). *Education:* Willamette University, A.B., 1936. *Home:* 4262 Haines Ave., San Jose, Calif. 95136. *Agent:* Georgia Nicholas, Nicholas Literary Agency, 161 Madison Ave., New York, N.Y. 10016.

CAREER: High school English teacher in Cove, Ore., 1936-37, Culver, Ore., 1937-38, Camas Valley, Ore., 1939-40, and Junction City, Ore., 1940-48; Rosicrucian Order (Ancient Mystical Order Rosae Crucis), San Jose, Calif., editorial assistant, 1949-52; employed as secretary, 1954-72. Teacher in Metropolitan Adult Education Program, 1963—. *Awards, honors:* First award for children's book with a Christian message, from National Association of Christian Schools, 1972, for *Ink on His Fingers.*

WRITINGS—Historical fiction for children: *Peter and the Pilgrims,* Review & Herald, 1963; *Strangers in the Land,* Review & Herald, 1964; *The Bible Smuggler,* Herald Press, 1967; *Ink on His Fingers,* Herald Press, 1967; *The Secret Church,* Herald Press, 1967; *Key to the Prison,* Herald Press, 1968; *Night Preacher,* Herald Press, 1969; *The Beggars' Bible,* Herald Press, 1971; *Doctor in Rags,* Herald Press, 1973; *Thunderstorm in Church,* Herald Press, 1974; *A Heart Strangely Warmed,* Herald Press, 1975; *The Man Who Laid the Egg,* Herald Press, 1977.

SIDELIGHTS: "When I was in the sixth grade the teacher said, 'I would like you to write a story about the Pilgrims. When they boarded the Mayflower to come to America, what did they say to the people they were leaving behind in Plymouth, England?' My story was chosen as second best, and the teacher sent the first and second best to a classroom across the hall. I read my story aloud. Thirty-three years later, my first book was *Peter and the Pilgrims.* By that time I had completely forgotten my sixth grade experience and only remembered it a few years ago. It reminded me of an important truth: Nothing is lost in the human mind. Furthermore, you never know when the seed of an idea will sprout and grow.

"A writer is two people in one. There is an artist who says, 'What a great idea for a story.' Then there is the critic who says, 'What a stupid idea. What makes you think you can write?' The critic should not make remarks like that. His real job is to say, 'Look, you used the wrong word here. Why don't you use this one?'

"My books are about real people, great leaders of church history, but to put facts into story form, I weave an imaginary child into the historical scene. For example, if someone set a church on fire, someone certainly shouted, 'The church is on fire.' even though no history book says so.

"Where does the creative urge come from? No one knows. I remember a church historian asked me how I happened to

LOUISE A. VERNON

write about Anabaptists. My truthful answer was, 'The word *Anabaptists* appeared in my mind.' I was curious about it, went to the library and looked it up, and found out how persecuted they were for their beliefs. That turned into my book *The Secret Church.* But first I had to experience a rejection. I had called the book *The Lost Church,* and the first version was turned down. I rewrote the book from another angle, and it was accepted.

"Many people think that if you write a book you start with chapter one, chapter two, and so on, but this is rarely true. Creativity has its own way of presenting material. For example, I was writing a story about the Huguenots. Suddenly a prison scene popped into my mind. The father and his small son were in prison together. I wrote the scene without having any idea where it would go in the book, but I knew it belonged somewhere. Later, when I arranged the scenes, the prison scene went in just as I had written it months before.

"When I was writing about Martin Luther, a friend accompanied me to East Germany. She could speak German and I could not. At the border between West Germany and East Germany the train stopped. Armed men stood on a platform, their guns ready to shoot. My friend and I had to leave the train with all our suitcases and fill out forms in a little office where a Russian woman was in charge. When we finished and headed toward the train again, all the passengers were leaning out of windows shouting at us. 'They're telling us to hurry and get on the train,' my friend said. 'It is about to leave.' Just as I swung up behind my friend the train started off. There was barbed wire on each side of us for many miles. However, we were able to go to all the cities we had planned and to walk down the street in Wittenberg where so many historical events occurred in Martin Luther's time.

"A writer has many adventures in finding material to write about. I have enjoyed the experiences very much."

HOBBIES AND OTHER INTERESTS: European travel.

"Exactly what I thought," he exulted. "There's a cave here." ■ (From *Doctor in Rags* by Louise A. Vernon. Illustrated by Allan Eitzen.)

Once there had been a great forest here where animals and birds had made their homes, but as the town grew, many trees were cut down. Now only a few remained among the buildings that rose high above them. ■ (From *Hello, Aurora* by Anne-Catharina Vestly. Illustrated by Leonard Kessler.)

ANNE-CATHARINA VESTLY

VESTLY, Anne-Cath(arina) 1920-

PERSONAL: Born February 15, 1920, in Rena, Norway; daughter of Aagot and Mentz Schulerud; married Johan Vestly. *Education:* Studied acting at Studioteatret, Oslo. *Home:* Noeklesvingen 36, Oslo 6, Norway.

CAREER: Actress and writer. *Member:* Norwegian Authors' Association, Norwegian Dramatists' Association, Association of Authors of Children's Books. *Awards, honors:* Awards from Norwegian Ministry of Education, 1955, for *Ole Aleksander faar skjorte,* 1957, for *Aatte smaa, to store og en lastebil,* and 1958, for *Mormor og de aate ungene i skogen.*

*WRITINGS—*For children: *Ole Aleksander Fili-bom-bom-bom,* Tiden Norsk Forlag, 1953; *Ole Aleksander paa farten* (title means "Ole Aleksander on the Run"), Tiden Norsk Forlag, 1954; *Ole Aleksander far skjorte* (title means "Ole Aleksander Has a Shirt"), Tiden Norsk Forlag, 1955; *Ole Aleksander og Bestemor til vaers* (title means "Ole Aleksander and Grandmother in the Air"), Tiden Norsk Forlag, 1956; *Aatte smaa, to store og en lastebil* (title means "Eight Children, Two Grownups and a Truck"), Tiden Norsk Forlag, 1957, English translation published as *Eight Children and a Truck,* Methuen, 1973; *Ole Aleksander paa flyttefot* (title means "Ole Aleksander Moves House"), Tiden Norsk Forlag, 1958; *Mormor og de atte ungene i skogen,* Tiden Norsk Forlag, 1958, English translation by Patricia Crampton published as *Eight Children Move House,* Methuen, 1974; *Marte og mormor og mormor og Motten,* Tiden Norsk Forlag, 1959.

En liten takk fra Anton, Tiden Norsk Forlag, 1960; *Mormors promenade,* Tiden Norsk Forlag, 1961; *Acht Kleine, swei Grosse und ein Lastauto,* Rascher, 1962; *Barnas store sangbok* (songbook; title means "Children's Big Songbook"), J. W. Cappelen, 1962; *Lillebror og Knerten* (title means "Lillebror and 'Rooty'"), Tiden Norsk Forlag, 1962; *Trofaste Knerten* (title means "Faithful Knerten"), Tiden Norsk Forlag, 1963; *Grossmutter und die acht Kinder im Walde* (title means "Grandmother and the Eight Children in the Woods"), Rascher, 1963; *Marte, Morten und Grossmutter,* Rascher, 1964; *Knerten gifter seg* (title means "Knerten Marries"), Tiden Norsk Forlag, 1964; *Knerten i Bessby* (title means "Knerten in Bessby"), Tiden Norsk Forlag, 1965; *Aurora i blokk z* (title means "Aurora in the Apartment House"), Tiden Norsk Forlag, 1966, English translation by Eileen Amos published as *Hallo Aurora!,* Longman Young Books, 1973, U.S. edition adapted by Jane Fairfax, published as *Hello, Aurora,* Crowell, 1974; *Aurora og pappa* (title means "Aurora and Daddy"), Tiden Norsk Forlag, 1967; *Aurora og den vesle blaa bilen* (title means "Aurora and the Little Blue Car"), Tiden Norsk Forlag, 1968; *Aurora og Sokrates,* Tiden Norsk Forlag, 1969, English translation published as *Aurora and Socrates,* 1973.

Aurora i Holland (title means "Aurora in Holland"), Tiden Norsk Forlag, 1970; *Aurora paa burtigruten* (title means "Aurora on the Express Liner"), Tiden Norsk Forlag, 1971; *Aurora fra Fabelvik* (title means "Aurora from Fabelvik"), Tiden Norsk Forlag, 1972; *Knerten og Forundringskpakken* (title means "Knerten and the Surprise Packet"), Tiden Norsk Forlag, 1973; *Knerten paa sykkeltur* (title means "Knerten on Bicycle Tour"), Tiden Norsk Forlag, 1974; *Guro,* Tiden Norsk Forlag, 1975; *Guro og nokkerosene* (title means "Guro and the Waterlillies"), Tiden Norsk Forlag, 1976.

WORK IN PROGRESS: Third volume of *Guro* series.

ELLEN K. VIERECK

I was alone in the council ring. The council fire was lighting up the entire area, and I could see no one. Then, from nearby came the muffled boom of a tom tom.... ■ (From *The Summer I Was Lost* by Phillip Viereck. Illustrated by Ellen Viereck.)

VIERECK, Ellen K. 1928-

PERSONAL: Born May 4, 1928, in Brookline, Mass.; daughter of Frederick Stillman (an architect) and Felicia (an architect; maiden name, Doughty) Kingsbury; married Phillip Viereck (an elementary school principal and children's book author), December 28, 1948; children: Jennifer Olaranna, Timothy Doughty, Pamela Neagus, Margaret Ann. *Education:* Vassar College, B.A., 1949; Plymouth State College, M.Ed., 1957. *Politics:* Democrat-Independent. *Religion:* Unitarian-Universalist. *Home address:* RFD 2, North Bennington, Vt. 05257. *Office:* Molly Stark School, Willow Rd., Bennington, Vt. 05201.

CAREER: Has held positions as teacher at Bennington College Nursery School, Bennington, Vt., with Alaska Native Service, King Island, Alaska, at Pine Cobble School, Williamstown, Mass., and Bennington School District, Bennington, Vt., 1969—. *Member:* National Education Association (life member), Vermont Education Association, Vermont Council on Reading, Vermont Association for Learning Disabled, Common Cause, United States Combined Training Association, United States Pony Club. *Awards, honors:* Honorable mention for illustrations, 1968, for *The New Land.*

WRITINGS—Illustrator of children's books by husband, Phillip Viereck; all published by John Day: *Eskimo Island,* 1962; *Independence Must Be Won,* 1964; *The Summer I Was Lost,* 1965; *The New Land,* 1967; *Let Me Tell You about My Dad,* 1971.

Illustrator: Irving Adler, *Groups in the New Mathematics,* John Day, 1967; Olive W. Burt, *The National Road,* John Day, 1968; Irving Adler and Ruth Adler, *Directions and Angles,* John Day, 1969; Irving Adler and Ruth Adler, *Energy,* John Day, 1970.

SIDELIGHTS: "Teaching Eskimos led to the writing of our first books, written for them and still in use in some Alaskan schools (it also fulfilled project requirements for M.Ed. degree).

"My special interest in my present public school teaching is helping children with learning problems and I have several such children assigned to me each year. It is such a deep satisfaction to succeed in teaching the ones who 'can not' learn. Of course, one doesn't always succeed, I enjoy the added challenge of the 'special' children.

"My husband and I live in an 18th-century farmhouse, keep a few chickens, beef cows, two horses, sometimes a pig, a large vegetable garden, a few hives of bees, a maple sugar bush. We enjoy being as self-sufficient as possible and heat our house entirely with wood cut off our own farm. Whenever we get a little spare time, we go hiking or canoeing in the summer, cross-country skiing in winter. But just teaching school and keeping the farm going takes most of our energy."

HOBBIES AND OTHER INTERESTS: Early New England and U.S. history, horses, and cross-country skiing, gardening, small scale farming, music, sewing, landscape painting.

Once there was a little girl and everyone called her Tollush. The house she lived in with her mother was very small and plain. It stood at the edge of the village where the potato fields began.

(From *The Rainbow Dress and Other Tollush Tales* by Ilse-Margret Vogel. Illustrated by the author.)

VOGEL, Ilse-Margret 1914-

PERSONAL: Born June 5, 1914, in Breslau, Germany; came to United States, 1950, naturalized, 1955; daughter of Sperling Erich and Margaret (Gaertner) Vogel; married Howard Knotts (an artist), June 1, 1959. *Education:* Educated in German schools; studied art in Berlin, Germany, prior to World War II, and in Basel, Switzerland, 1948. *Address:* Duell Rd., Bangall, N.Y. 12506.

CAREER: Co-founder and co-owner of Rosen Gallery, first gallery for modern art in Berlin, Germany, 1945-48; assistant to J. B. Neumann at New Art Circle (gallery), New York, N.Y., 1950-53; began designing toys and writing for *Humpty Dumpty* (magazine), 1954; head designer for Knickerbocker Toy Co., New York, N.Y. 1956-63; writer and illustrator of books for children, 1964—.

WRITINGS—Author and illustrator: *The Don't Be Scared Book,* Atheneum, 1964; *1 Is No Fun, But 20 Is Plenty,* Atheneum, 1965; *Willy, Willy, Don't Be Silly,* Atheneum, 1965; *Hello Henry,* Parents, 1965; *When I Grow Up,* Golden Press, 1968; *Come On Play Ball,* Golden Press, 1969; *Peek-A-Boo,* Golden Press, 1970; *1, 2, 3, Juggle With Me,* Golden Press, 1970; *My Little Dinosaur,* Golden Press, 1971; *The Bear in the Boat,* Golden Press, 1972; *Daisy Dog's Wake Up Book,* Golden Press, 1973; *The Rainbow Dress,* Harper, 1975; *My Twin Sister Erika,* Harper, 1976; *Dodo Every Day,* Harper, 1977.

Illustrator: *Bears Birthday,* Golden Press, 1964; *Little Plays for Little People,* Parents, 1965; *City Cats, Country Cats,* Golden Press, 1969.

Creator of activity books for children for Whitman & Dell. Regular contributor to *Parent's Magazine* and *Humpty Dumpty*.

WORK IN PROGRESS: A Christmas Story for Harper; *Wings* for Harper which will be illustrated by her husband, Howard Knotts.

SIDELIGHTS: "I was born in Sybillenort, Germany, in what is now Poland. In the late thirties I moved to Berlin to study art. I left the art schools after a few weeks, for I realized that they had nothing to teach me—this being the Nazi era. These schools labeled the art I was interested in 'degenerate' so my studies in the arts consisted of listening to and learning from artist friends whose brains and bookshelves were still full of pre-Nazi art and knowledge.

"During World War II our main occupation was the daily struggle for survival. With the German surrender, life began again. I owned nothing but the clothes on my back and had nothing to eat but potato peelings that a friend who worked in the kitchen of the occupation powers distributed among his friends. But in spite of all this, there was an indescribable feeling of exaltation.

"I helped establish and run the first gallery for modern art in postwar Berlin. We exhibited all those artists who had been called degenerate during the previous twelve years.

"When, in 1948, the Iron Curtain threatened to separate Berlin from the rest of the world, I left for Basel, Switzerland, where I studied art. I soon applied for a United States immigration visa. Earlier, my curiosity had been aroused about the country of Thornton Wilder, Ernest Hemingway,

Thomas Wolfe, and William Faulkner, for I read and loved their books.

"I arrived in New York City in 1950 and worked for an art gallery that handled contemporary European art. When the gallery closed in 1953, I turned to illustrating as a profession. For the birthday of a friend's child, I made a stuffed lion. Discovering that I had talent for toy making, I brought my designs to a manufacturer of toys and was promptly hired. I have also designed greeting cards and gift wrapping.

"I am married to Howard C. Knotts, a painter whose work I had admired even before meeting him. It feels wonderful to live and work among hundreds of paintings again. Having a painter for a husband is the next best thing to being one myself."

Ilse-Margret Vogel made extensive study trips to France, Germany, Italy, the Netherlands, Switzerland, and Spain, visiting museums, 1959-62.

HOBBIES AND OTHER INTERESTS: Gardening, travel, watching cats (has ten), cooking, watching birds, reading, and seeing the seasons change.

VOGT, Esther Loewen 1915-

PERSONAL: Surname is pronounced Vote; born November 19, 1915, in Collinsville, Okla.; daughter of Henry L. (a farmer and carpenter) and Agnes (Penner) Loewen; married Curt T. Vogt (a mechanic), May 24, 1942, died, 1975; children: Shirley Jean (Mrs. Gordon Adams), Ranney Lee, Noami Ruth (Mrs. Lee Eitzen). *Education:* Tabor College, student, two years. *Politics:* Republican. *Religion:* Mennonite. *Home:* 113 South Ash, Hillsboro, Kan. 67063.

ESTHER VOGT

The bank of gray clouds had suddenly boiled up into a greenish-gray mass, and the air had grown stagnant and breathless. ■ (From *Turkey Red* by Esther Loewen Vogt. Illustrated by Seymour Fleishman.)

CAREER: Teacher in rural areas of Marion, Kan., 1939-40, and Hillsboro, Kan., 1940-42; part-time nurses' aide in a retirement center. Free-lance writer, 1955—. Young Women's Christian Association, Hillsboro, Kan., program chairman, 1961, 1964, 1965. *Member:* Kansas Authors Club (fourth district president, 1964-66), Mentor Study Club. *Awards, honors:* First prize in Native Kansas Sons and Daughters factual story contest, 1958; Tabor College Alumni Merit Award for outstanding service, 1974; David C. Cook juvenile book contest honorable mention, 1975.

WRITINGS: Cry to the Wind, Zondervan, 1965; *The Sky is Falling,* Herald Press, 1968; *High Ground,* Herald Press, 1970; *Ann,* Herald Press, 1971; *Prairie Tales* (juvenile), Mennonite Brethren Publishing House, 1971; *I'll Walk Again* (biography), Herald Press, 1973; *Eight Wells of Elim,* Herald Press, 1974; *Turkey Red* (juvenile), David C. Cook, 1975; *Beyond These Hills,* Beacon Hill, 1977; *Harvest Gold* (juvenile), David C. Cook, 1978. Writer of over 700 short

stories, mostly to religious periodicals, including a drama, ''Upon This Rock'' for a church centennial celebration, 1976.

WORK IN PROGRESS: Mystery at Red Rock Canyon (juvenile); *Come North Wind, Come South Wind* (adult fiction); biography on Linda Light, former Miss Kansas (1961) and Miss Universe Multiple Sclerosis (1972).

SIDELIGHTS: ''As a child I read everything I could lay my hands on, and hoped some day to write the kind of stories I liked to read. Unlike John-boy Walton, I tried to keep my writing dreams to myself, for fear that family and friends would laugh at me . . . until one day Mom found me out. She was relieved that 'all' I was doing when I sneaked upstairs was writing, as though it would go away like a mild case of pink-eye. My high school and college English teachers insisted I had a flair for words, and encouraged me to develop my writing talent. It wasn't until God definitely prodded me to write, after I read the biblical account of the talents in Matthew:25 that I began to take my writing seriously. After I wrote my first book and it was published, I was hooked. It's like eating one salted peanut: there have to be more. The second book should have come easier but it didn't. There is no easy book. But the terror doesn't haunt you quite so much in the next one. Writing a book is sort of like sliding down the old-fashioned cellar door. There's the exciting wheeeeeee of going places; yet the splinters remind you that it costs something too. Once I slid down a cellar door and the splinter Mom had to pry from my fanny wasn't funny!

''I have tried to make my plots unique to avoid a stereotyped writing style; and as a result each of my books is sufficiently different from the preceding one.

''When I was a child, I thought as a child, I spoke as a child, but even though I've long been a woman grown, I can't put away childish things because my writing includes books and stories for juveniles.

''Much of my fiction stems from personal experience. Since I grew up on a farm, most of my settings are rural or small-town.

''Successful writing demands discipline and sometimes dedication to a deadline. For a writer who is serious, doesn't procrastinate; he agonizes, wears out typewriters—*and he writes!*''

Esther Vogt is fluent in German and Low German (Dutch).

WAGONER, David (Russell)   1926-

PERSONAL: Born June 5, 1926, in Massillon, Ohio; son of Walter Siffert and Ruth (Banyard) Wagoner; married Patricia Parrott, 1961. *Education:* Pennsylvania State University, B.A., 1947; Indiana University, M.A., 1949. *Home:* 1075 Summit Ave., East, Seattle, Wash. 98102. *Agent:* Russell and Volkening, 551 Fifth Ave., New York, N.Y. 10017. *Office:* University of Washington, Seattle, Wash.

CAREER: DePauw University, Greencastle, Ind., instructor, 1949-50; Pennsylvania State University, University Park, instructor, 1950-54; University of Washington, Seattle, associate professor, 1954-66, professor, 1966—. *Military service:* U.S. Navy, 1944-46; became midshipman. *Awards, honors:* Guggenheim fellowship, 1956; Ford fellowship, 1964; Zabel Prize of Poetry, 1967; award from National In-

DAVID RUSSELL WAGONER

stitute of Arts & Letters, 1967; Elliston Lecturer in modern poetry, University of Cincinnati, 1968; National Council on the Arts award, 1969; chosen by the U.S. Information Agency to read poems and lecture on modern American poetry in Greece, Turkey, and Lebanon, 1971; Emily Clark Balch Poetry Contest, second prize, *Virginia Quarterly Review,* 1974; Blumenthal Prize, poetry, Chicago, 1974; Fels Prize for poetry, Coordinating Council of Literary Magazines, 1975; Fels Prize for editing, Coordinating Council of Literary Magazines, 1975; nominated for National Book Award in Poetry, 1975.

WRITINGS: Dry Sun, Dry Wind, Indiana University Press, 1953; *The Man in the Middle,* Harcourt, 1954; *Money Money Money,* Harcourt, 1955; *Rock,* Viking, 1958; *A Place to Stand,* Indiana University Press, 1958; *The Nesting Ground,* Indiana University Press, 1963; *The Escape Artist,* Farrar, Straus, 1965; *Staying Alive,* Indiana University Press, 1966; *Baby, Come on Inside,* Farrar, Straus, 1968; *New and Selected Poems,* Indiana University Press, 1969; *Where is My Wandering Boy Tonight?,* Farrar, Straus, 1970; *Working Against Time,* Rapp & Whiting, Ltd., 1970; *Straw for the Fire: From the Notebooks of Theodore Roethke, 1943-63,* Doubleday, 1972; *Riverbed,* Indiana University Press, 1972; *Sleeping in the Woods,* Indiana University Press, 1974; *The Road to Many a Wonder* (ALA Notable Book), Farrar, Straus, 1974; *Tracker,* Little, Brown, 1975; *Whole Hog,* Little, Brown, 1976; *Collected Poems,* Indiana University Press, 1976. Editor, *Poetry Northwest,* 1966. Contributor of poems to literary journals.

WORK IN PROGRESS: A full length-play.

WALWORTH, Nancy Zinsser 1917-

PERSONAL: Born October 29, 1917, in New York, N.Y.; daughter of William H. and Joyce (Knowlton) Zinsser; married Edward H. Walworth, Jr., February 5, 1944; children: Edward Z., Joyce K., Seth, Cornelia J. *Education:* Smith College, A.B., 1938; Radcliffe College, A.M., 1940. *Home:* Oenoke Ridge, New Canaan, Conn. 06840.

CAREER: The Brearley School, New York, N.Y., student teacher in English, 1938-39; War Department, Washington, D.C., secretary to John J. McCloy, Assistant Secretary of War, 1941-44; Potomac School, Washington, D.C., teacher of English and social studies, 1944-45; Dwight School, Englewood, N.J., teacher of English and social studies, 1947-50. Trustee: Country Day School, 1958-60, New Canaan Library, 1960-64. New Canaan Citizens School Council, co-chairman of educational objectives committee, 1955-57; New Canaan board of selectman, member, 1971-74.

WRITINGS: (With Polly Schoyer Brooks) *The World Awakes: The Renaissance in Western Europe,* Lippincott, 1962; *The World of Walls: The Middle Ages in Western Europe,* Lippincott, 1966; *When the World Was Rome,* Lippincott, 1972. Various articles for *Junior Encyclopedia Britannica,* 1965-67.

SIDELIGHTS: "Mrs. Brooks and I started writing history books for young people when we found ourselves on a par-

NANCY ZINSSER WALWORTH

(From *The World Awakes: The Renaissance in Western Europe* by Polly Schoyer Brooks and Nancy Zinsser Walworth.)

ents' committee to investigate social studies curricula of the local public schools. We were dismayed to find a gap in reference material at the junior high level, particularly in history. Since our children were heading for the junior high at that time, we decided to try to plug the gap.

"We felt that young people would respond to biographies more than to straight chronological history, and so in our three books (covering about a 2300-year span from the beginnings of the Roman Empire to the end of the Renaissance) we tried to write in lively language about a wide mix of people: artists, soldiers, writers, priests, kings and queens, set against the important events of the time. Our publishers allowed us about eighty illustrations per book and we selected the most vivid contemporary art we could find. We used our children as critics; one of them, by then an architect, did some diagrams and drawings for our book on Rome.

"We have done much traveling to help us recreate historical scenes—to battlefields, walled cities, abbeys and castles, aqueducts, countless museums and innumerable ruins, accompanied by our enthusiastic husbands."

WARBURG, Sandol Stoddard 1927-
(Sandol Stoddard)

PERSONAL: Born December 16, 1927, in Birmingham, Ala.; daughter of Carlos French and Caroline (Harris) Stoddard; married Felix M. Warburg, April 2, 1949 (divorced, June 14, 1963); married William A. Atchley (a doctor), June 1, 1974; children: (first marriage) Anthony, Peter, Gerald, Jason. *Education:* Bryn Mawr College, A.B. (magna cum laude), 1959; San Francisco State College, graduate. study. *Home:* 1721 Mar West, Tiburon, Calif. 94920.

CAREER: Writer. *Awards, honors: The Thinking Book* chosen one of ten best picture-books of 1960 by *New York Herald Tribune; Saint George and the Dragon* named a distinguished book of 1963 by American Library Association.

WRITINGS: The Thinking Book, Atlantic-Little Brown, 1960; *Keep It Like a Secret,* Atlantic-Little, Brown, 1961; *Saint George and the Dragon,* Houghton, 1963; *My Very Own Special Particular Private and Personal Cat,* Hough-

SANDOL STODDARD WARBURG

WATSON, Pauline 1925-
(POLA)

PERSONAL: Born July 24, 1925, in New Iberia, La.; daughter of Luke and Rosalie (Catalano) Bennett; married Jimmy T. Watson, October 19, 1947; children: Cindy (Mrs. Scott Walling), Jim, Duke, Vicki, Mike. *Education:* Palmer Institute of Authorship, graduate. *Home:* 24420 Stuebner Airline, Turnball, Tex. 77375.

CAREER: Accountant and office manager for an automobile dealership in New Iberia, La., 1942-47; writer, 1950—. *Member:* Houston Writer's Workshop (president, 1970), Associated Authors of Children's Literature, Houston (president, 1975), International Toastmistress Club (secretary and publicity chairman of Houston's Noonday branch, 1968), Federated Woman's Club (Beaumont, Tex.).

WRITINGS—Children's books: *A Surprise For Mother,* Prentice-Hall, 1976; *Cricket's Cookery,* Open Court, in press; *A Day With Daddy,* Prentice-Hall, in press; *Curley Cat Babysits,* Harcourt, in press.

Writer of weekly column, "Post Oak Patter," in *Bellaire Texan,* 1969—, and of monthly columns, "Kitchen Klatter," 1972—, and "Washboard Wisdom" (under pseudonym POLA), 1974—, both syndicated by Features Unlimited. Work anthologized in *Cricket's Choice,* edited by Clifton Fadiman and Marianne Carns, Open Court, 1975. Contribu-

ton, 1963; *Curl Up Small!,* Houghton, 1964; *I Like You,* Houghton, 1965; *From Ambledee to Zumbledee,* Houghton, 1968; *Growing Time,* Houghton, 1969; *Hooray for Us,* Houghton, 1970; *On the Way Home,* Houghton, 1973; (under the name Sandol Stoddard) *Free,* Houghton, 1976; *The Hospice Movement* (adult), Stein & Day, 1977.

WORK IN PROGRESS: Adult non-fiction; filmscript of *I Like You.*

SIDELIGHTS: Growing Time has been translated into Japanese and made into a Japanese film, 1975; *Curl Up Small* is a John Korty film.

FOR MORE INFORMATION SEE: Lee Bennett Hopkins, *Books Are by People,* Citation Press, 1969.

That way sometimes we fall flat on our faces and we look pretty silly. ■ (From *Hooray for Us* by Sandol Stoddard Warburg. Illustrated by Jacqueline Chwast.)

Paul put the vase on the table. ■ (From *A Surprise for Mother* by Pauline Watson. Pictures by Joanne Scribner.)

PAULINE WATSON

tor of children's stories and poems to children's magazines, including *My Weekly Reader* and *Cricket,* and of adult stories, articles and fillers to popular magazines, including *Woman's Day, Southern Living, Reader's Digest,* and *Parents' Magazine.*

WORK IN PROGRESS: Short, short witch and ghost stories with fun endings for the very young.

SIDELIGHTS: "I try to learn something new everyday and to have a long range plan of study toward goals that I have privately set for myself. I have just completed a course on gagwriting which I thoroughly enjoyed."

WEBBER, Irma E(leanor Schmidt) 1904-

PERSONAL: Born August 16, 1904, in San Diego, Calif.; daughter of Eugene Arthur (a civil engineer) and Edna (Allen) Schmidt; married John Milton Webber (a botanist), May 13, 1927; children: Herbert Milton, Irma Jean (Mrs. M. Michael Appleman). *Education:* University of California, Berkeley, A.B. (honors), 1926, M.A., 1927, Ph.D., 1929. *Home:* 500 Arlington Ave., Berkeley, Calif. 94707.

CAREER: Carnegie Institute, Berkeley, Calif., research assistant in paleobotany, 1927-29; U.S. Department of Agriculture, Washington, D.C., agent with Division of Blister Rust Control, 1929-31; Citrus Experiment Station, Riverside, Calif., research assistant, 1932-33; U.S. Department of Agriculture, collaborator with Division of Western Irriga-

tion Agriculture, Bureau of Plant Industry, 1934, Division of Cotton and Other Fiber Crops, 1936-43, Bureau of Plant Industry, Soils, and Agricultural Engineering, 1943-50, botanist, 1950-51, collaborator, 1951-53, in Agricultural Research Service, 1953—. Collaborator with Revista Lilloa (Argentina), 1937—. Botanical art is included in the Kerlan Collection, Hunt Institute, and Carnegie-Mellon University.

MEMBER: California Botanical Society, University of California Alumni Association, Phi Beta Kappa, Sigma Xi, Phi Sigma.

WRITINGS—Self-illustrated children's books: *Up Above and Down Below,* William R. Scott, 1943; *Anywhere in the World,* William R. Scott, 1947; *Bits That Grow Big,* William R. Scott, 1949; *It Looks Like This,* William R. Scott, 1949, revised edition, 1958, reissued as *What Does It Look Like?,* Scholastic Book Services, 1969, International Society for General Semantics, 1976; *Thanks to Trees,* William R. Scott, 1952. Contributor to scientific journals and children's magazines, including *Jack and Jill* and *Horn Book.*

WORK IN PROGRESS: Work on plants.

SIDELIGHTS: "Many of my friends were botanists and I married a botanical classmate who was the son of a distinguished botanist. Such ties tended to reinforce my interest in botanical research until my young children taught me how eager they were to learn about their environment. Then I

IRMA E. WEBBER

No matter how hard the sun shines, animals can not make food from the air and from the earth.
■ (From *Up Above and Down Below* by Irma E. Webber. Illustrated by the author.)

began a search for children's books that presented simple, non-technical but factual information about plants and other facets of the environment in attractive form. The paucity of such material about plants prompted me to draw on my botanical background and parental experience to produce *Up Above and Down Below* and subsequent volumes.'' Irma Webber's books have been published in Pakistan, Iran, Japan, Italy, England, and France.

HOBBIES AND OTHER INTERESTS: Gardening, travel.

WEBER, William John 1927-

PERSONAL: Born September 8, 1927, in Cleveland, Ohio; son of Clarence J. and Edith (James) Weber; married Barbara Ann Haigh, December 23, 1951; children: William James, John Hunt. *Education:* Ohio State University, D.V.M., 1953, M.Sc, 1954. *Home address:* Route 1, Box 368A, Leesburg, Fla. 32748. *Office:* Leesburg Veterinary Hospital, 3600 West Main St., Leesburg, Fla. 32748.

CAREER: Leesburg Veterinary Hospital, Leesburg, Fla., owner and partner, 1954—. Member of advisory council to Florida State Board of Health, 1970. *Military service:* U.S. Air Force, 1945-47. *Member:* American Veterinary Medical Society, Wildlife Society (member of Florida executive board), Florida Veterinary Medical Association (president, 1964-65), Sigma Xi, Phi Zeta. *Awards, honors:* Gold star award from Florida Veterinary Medical Association, 1968, 1970, 1976, veterinarian of the year award, 1969.

WRITINGS—Juvenile: *Wild Orphan Babies, Mammals and Birds: Caring for Them, Setting Them Free* (with own photographs), Holt, 1975; *Wild Orphan Friends*, Holt, 1976. Photography has appeared on greeting cards and other material from Hallmark Cards and American Greetings, and on covers of magazines, including *National Wildlife, Ranger Rick's Nature Magazine, Florida Wildlife, Archery World, Four Seasons Trails, Veterinary Medicine,* and *Florida Veterinary Journal.* Contributor to nature studies, outdoor recreation, and children's magazines, and to veterinary journals.

Altricial Birds are born helpless. They are hatched in a weak condition and are, therefore, confined to the nest. ■ (From *Wild Orphan Babies* by William J. Weber, D.V.M. Photographs by the author.)

Someday maybe we can live in a good building like other peoples do. ■ (From *It's Wings that Make Birds Fly* by Sandra Weiner. Illustrated by the author.)

WEINER, Sandra   1922-

PERSONAL: Born September 14, 1922, in Poland; naturalized U.S. citizen in 1937; daughter of Oscar and Leah Smith; married Daniel Weiner, March 12, 1942 (died, 1959); children: Dore. *Education:* Attended public schools in New York, N.Y. *Home and office:* 30 West 60th St., New York, N.Y. 10023.

CAREER: Author-photographer. Worked for many years with her late husband, Dan Weiner, the noted photographer and journalist. Now teaches photography at City College and the International Center of Photography in New York City.

WRITINGS—Children's books illustrated with photographs by the author: *It's Wings That Make Birds Fly: The Story of a Boy,* Pantheon, 1968; *Small Hands, Big Hands,* Pantheon, 1970; *They Call Me Jack,* Pantheon, 1973; *The Dhammapada,* Knopf, 1976; *I Want to Be a Fisherman,* Macmillan, 1977.

WERSTEIN, Irving   1914-1971

PERSONAL: Born 1914, in Brooklyn, New York; died, 1971. *Education:* Attended New York University.

CAREER: Author of historical stories for children, and journalist. During the second World War, served in the U.S. Army as a field correspondent for *Yank* magazine.

WRITINGS—History: *July, 1863,* Messner, 1957, reissued as *The Draft Riots: July, 1863,* 1971; *Abraham Lincoln versus Jefferson Davis,* Crowell, 1959; *Danger at Dry Creek: Tales of Wells Fargo* (illustrated by Al Schmidt), Golden Press, 1959; *Marshal without a Gun: Tom Smith,* Messner, 1959; *The Blizzard of '68,* Crowell, 1960; *Man against the Elements: Adolphus W. Greely,* Messner, 1960, reissued, Washington Square Press, 1967; *The Battle of Midway,* Crowell, 1961; *The Many Faces of the Civil War,* Messner, 1961, reissued, G. A. Pflaum, 1967.

A Nation Fights Back: The Depression and Its Aftermath, Messner, 1962; *The Battle of Aachen,* Crowell, 1962; *Civil War Sailor* (illustrated by Albert Orbaan), Doubleday, 1962; *Kearny, the Magnificent: The Story of General Philip Kearny, 1818-1862,* John Day, 1962; *Guadalcanal,* Crowell, 1963; *Jack Wade: Fighter for Liberty* (illustrated by A. Orbaan), Doubleday, 1963; *The Many Faces of World War I,* Messner, 1963; *Massacre at Sand Creek,* Scribner, 1963; *The Long Escape,* Scribner, 1964; *Turning Point for America: The Story of the Spanish-American War,* Messner, 1964; *Wake: The Story of a Battle,* Crowell, 1964.

The Battle of Salerno, Crowell, 1965; *The Franco-Prussian War: Germany's Rise as a World Power,* Messner, 1965; *The General Slocum Incident: Story of an Ill-Fated Ship,* John Day, 1965; *The Great Struggle: Labor in America,* Scribner, 1965; *Tarawa: A Battle Report,* Crowell, 1965; *The War with Mexico,* W. W. Norton, 1965; *The Lost Battalion,* W. W. Norton, 1966; *I Accuse: The Story of the Dreyfus Case,* Messner, 1967; *The Plotters: The New York Conspiracy of 1741,* Scribner, 1967; *Sound No Trumpet: The Life and Death of Alan Seeger,* Crowell, 1967; *Ten Days in November: The Russian Revolution,* Macrae Smith, 1967.

Okinawa: The Last Ordeal, Crowell, 1968; *Over Here and Over There: The Era of the First World War,* W. W. Norton, 1968; *The Uprising of the Warsaw Ghetto: November 1940-May 1943,* W. W. Norton, 1968; *This Wounded Land: The Era of Reconstruction, 1865-1877,* Delacorte, 1968; *All the Furious Battles: The Saga of Israel's Army,* Meredith Press, 1969; *Betrayal: The Munich Pact of 1938,* Doubleday, 1969; *The Cruel Years: The Story of the Spanish Civil War,* Messner, 1969, reissued, Bailey & Swinfen, 1974; *The Cruise of the Essex: An Incident from the War of 1812,* Macrae Smith, 1969; *Labor's Defiant Lady: The Story of Mother Jones,* Crowell, 1969.

Pie in the Sky: An American Struggle the Wobblies and Their Time, Delacorte, 1969; *The Stars and Stripes: The Story of Our Flag,* Golden Press, 1969; *Strangled Voices: The Story of the Haymarket Affair,* Macmillan, 1969; *The Trespassers: Korea, June 1871* (illustrated by Joseph Papin), Dutton, 1969; *Year of Turmoil: 1939,* Messner, 1969; *A Proud People: Black Americans* (photos by Bob Adelman), M. Evans, 1970; *Shattered Decade: 1919-1929,* Scribner, 1970; *The Storming of Fort Wagner: Black Valor in the Civil War,* Scholastic Book Services, 1970; *The Supremo: Lord Louis Mountbatten and the Testing of Democracy,* Macrae Smith, 1971; *Land and Liberty: The Mexican Revolution, 1910-1919,* Cowles, 1971; *The Boxer Rebellion: Anti-Foreign Terror Seizes China, 1900,* F. Watts, 1971.

IRVING WERSTEIN

Billy had no idea how long he had been lying on the sandbar. He gathered the strength to stand up, but he was so weak, he hardly managed to stay on his feet. His teeth chattered and he was not able to stop shivering. The wet clothes he wore stuck to his skin and every gust of wind cut through him like a sharp knife. ■ (From *Civil War Sailor* by Irving Werstein. Illustrated by Albert Orbaan.)

Pictorial works: *1861-1865: The Adventure of the Civil War Told with Pictures,* Pageant Books, 1960, reissued, Cooper Square, 1964; *1776: The Adventure of the American Revolution Told with Pictures,* Cooper Square, 1962, reissued, 1965; *1914-1918: World War I Told with Pictures,* Cooper Square, 1964; *1898: The Spanish-American War Told with Pictures,* Cooper Square, 1966.

SIDELIGHTS: All the Furious Battles: The Saga of Israel's Army was described by the *New York Times* as having "enough background for an understanding of the modern Israeli army. It is a clear, crisp authoritative narrative." A *Library Journal* review of *Betrayal: The Munich Pact of 1938* said, "The swift narrative forcefully raises the problem of negotiation versus war; a timely subject when many automatically condemn war as the greatest of evils. . . . The material is as objective as hindsight will allow. . . . Possibly not enough attention has been given to the Russian position; however, overall, this is a thorough, memorable book." *The Trespassers: Korea, June, 1871* elicited the following observation from a *Library Journal* reviewer: "This story of the first direct confrontation between the U.S. and Korea is told mainly by the skillful use of verbatim quotes found in official documents and correspondence. Boys will enjoy this as an easily read, fast-paced, and exciting story of an ill-fated military expedition."

The reviews of *Year of Turmoil, 1939* were mixed. *Library Journal* said, "This fast-moving, entertaining account reads like on-the-spot reporting from *Time* and *Life* magazines.

The author shows how trouble was popping up in every area of the globe in 1939. . . . The whole book makes for lively reading, but also affords a clear understanding of the period which set the stage for the holocaust of World War II." On the other hand, the *New York Times* said, "[This] is presumably an introduction to World War II. It professes to give a 'taste' of 'one of history's most climactic years.'. . . Adults may find [it] an entertaining romp through memories of 1939, but the author fails to make his review valuable for young readers by not providing any significant evaluation of the events."

Of *Shattered Decade, 1919-1929,* the *New York Times* commented, "Werstein pulls the plug and lets the glamorous legend of the Roaring Twenties go down the drain in his swift-moving, clear-eyed history of those times. He doesn't altogether ignore the dazzle of that decade. There are glimpses of those fabulous people—Babe Ruth, Lucky Lindy, etc. Werstein's purpose is clear: to show today's young reader that the turmoil of the present did not happen spontaneously." *Library Journal* added, "This book will stimulate interest in the period, and thinking readers may find striking similarities between the 20's and the 60's."

FOR MORE INFORMATION SEE—Obituaries: *New York Times,* April 9, 1971; *Publishers Weekly,* April 26, 1971.

WESTHEIMER, David 1917-
(Z. Z. Smith)

PERSONAL: Born April 11, 1917, in Houston, Tex.; married Doris G. Rothstein, 1945; children: Fred, Eric. *Education:* Rice Institute, B.A., 1937; Columbia University, post graduate study in creative writing and radio writing. *Home:* 11722 Darlington Ave., No. 2, Los Angeles, Calif. 90049. *Agent:* Dorothy Olding, Harold Ober Associates, 40 East 49th St., New York, N.Y. 10017. *Office:* 407 North Maple Dr., No. 206, Beverly Hills, Calif. 90210.

CAREER: Houston Post, Houston, Tex., assistant amusement editor, 1939-41, 1945-46; radio-television and Sunday magazine editor, 1950, television-radio editor, 1953-60; Literary Projects Co., Beverly Hills, Calif., editor, 1960-62. *Military service:* U.S. Army Air Forces, 1941-46, 1950-53, became a major; awarded the Distinguished Flying Cross, Air Medal, U.S. Air Force Reserve, now lieutenant colonel. *Member:* Writers Guild of America (West), Authors League of America.

WRITINGS: Summer on the Water, Macmillan, 1948; *The Magic Fallacy,* Macmillan, 1950; *Watching Out for Dulie,* Dodd, 1960; (under pseudonym, Z. Z. Smith) *A Very Private Island,* New American Library, 1962; J. P. Miller's *Days of Wine and Roses* (novelization of screenplay), Bantam, 1963; *This Time Next Year,* New American Library, 1963; *Von Ryan's Express,* Doubleday, 1964; *My Sweet Charlie* (dramatization by Westheimer produced at Longacre Theater), Doubleday, 1965; *Song of the Young Sentry,* Little, Brown, 1968; *Lighter Than a Feather,* Little, Brown, 1971; *Over the Edge,* Little, Brown, 1972; *Going Public,* Mason & Lipscomb, 1973; *The Olmec Head,* Little, Brown, 1974; *The Avila Gold,* Putnam, 1974.

SIDELIGHTS: "When I was a boy, starting at age seven or eight, I was a voracious reader. My early favorites were fairy tales of all nations and Greek, Roman and Norse mythology (how I hated Loki the Evil One, who killed Baldur

DAVID WESTHEIMER

the Good). Then on to all the Tom Swift books and other series for boys, the Edgar Rice Burroughs novels, my oldest brother's Literary Guild selections and whatever caught my eye in the Houston Public Library, from *Dracula* and *Erewhon* to *Kristin Lavransdatter* and *The Wandering Jew.* There was also time for the 'pulp' magazines of the period—science fiction, detective stories, adventure stories, war stories (World War I; World War II was yet to come).

"When very young, I prowled the Norma Meldrum Children's Library section of the library and was gradually weaned to the adult section by the children's librarian, Harriet Dickson Reynolds, who took an interest in me and my reading habits. Mrs. Reynolds, now retired, later became head librarian for the whole city of Houston.

"There was a considerable period in my boyhood when, during summer vacations, I took the bus to the library to draw and read three books—the maximum allowed—twice each week every week until school started again. After college, my reading tapered off until a period when I found myself with more time on my hands than I really wanted. It was in

World War II. The B-24 Liberator bomber on which I was navigator was shot down by Italian fighter planes and I became a prisoner of war of first the Italians and then the Germans.

"There was a tiny library in the Italian prisoner of war camp and a larger one in Germany. And prisoners were allowed eleven pounds of books from home each three months. So I became a voracious reader again. How I was turned to reading, again, by Dickens' *Dombey and Son* is described in *Song of the Young Sentry,* though I was not, and am not, the central character, Steve Lang.

"This time it was Dickens, Thackeray, Tolstoi, Dostoevski, Dante, biography, mysteries. Anything I could get my hands on, with particular attention to books I thought I would never again have the time or inclination to read. *Moby Dick,* for example. I had started it many times earlier in life but had never been able to read it through to the end.

"In none of this was I consciously preparing myself to become a writer. In my boyhood, I had no thought of being a writer. A fireman, perhaps, or a chemical engineer. In college, I did begin to nurse ambitions to become a writer but was far more concerned with thoughts of getting a job and earning a living. By the time I was a prisoner of war and had worked for a newspaper the desire to write had crystallized but even then I had no idea I was doing research for the novel which almost twenty years later would prove to be the most widely read of the more than a dozen I have written to date—*Von Ryan's Express.*"

Von Ryan's Express was made into a motion picture, starring Frank Sinatra.

FOR MORE INFORMATION SEE: New York Times, December 25, 1966.

WEXLER, Jerome (LeRoy) 1923-
(Roy Delmar)

PERSONAL: Born February 6, 1923, in New York, N.Y.; son of Lewis (a tailor) and Rose (a clothing designer; maiden name, Leiberman) Wexler; married Gwen Schorr, June 24, 1951 (divorced January 10, 1975); children: Amy, Herbert. *Education:* Attended Pratt Institute and University of Connecticut. *Politics:* "Not interested in politics." *Religion:* Unitarian. *Home and office:* 4 Middle Lane, Wallingford, Conn. 06492.

CAREER: Agricultural Photo Library (stock photograph company), Wallingford, Conn., owner and operator, 1950-58; tool and parts inspector in New Haven, Conn., 1958-73; writer and photographer, 1973—. *Military service:* U.S. Army, 1943-46. *Awards, honors:* Writing awards include outstanding book awards from National Science Teachers Association, for *A Calf Is Born, The Harlequin Moth, Bulbs, Corms and Such, A Chick Hatches, Vegetables from Stems and Leaves,* and *The Carrot and Other Root Vegetables;* awards from National Science Teachers Association, for outstanding science trade books for children, 1973, for *The Apple and Other Fruits* and *My Puppy Is Born;* American Institute of Graphic Arts certificate of excellence, 1972, for *The Carrot and Other Root Vegetables; A Chick Hatches* was a Children's Book Showcase title, 1977.

WRITINGS: (With Carolyn Meyer) *Rock Tumbling: From Stones to Gems to Jewelry* (self-illustrated juvenile), Mor-

row, 1974; *How to Tumble Polish Gemstones and Make Tumbled Jewelry,* Gemac, 1977.

Illustrator (photographs)—All juveniles; all published by Morrow: Millicent E. Selsam, *Milkweed,* 1967; Selsam, *Maple Tree,* 1968; Selsam, *Peanut* (ALA Notable book), 1969; Selsam, *The Tomato and Other Fruit Vegetables,* 1970; Selsam, *The Carrot and Other Root Vegetables,* 1971; Selsam, *Vegetables from Stems and Leaves,* 1972; Selsam, *The Apple and Other Fruits,* 1973; Joanna Cole, *My Puppy Is Born,* 1973; Selsam, *Bulbs, Corms and Such,* 1974; (with Carolyn Meyer) *Rock Tumbling,* 1974; Selsam, *The Harlequin Moth: Its Life Story* (ALA Notable book), 1975; Cole, *A Calf Is Born,* 1975; Selsam, *Popcorn,* 1976; Cole, *A Chick Hatches,* 1976; Selsam, *The Amazing Dandelion,* Morrow, 1977; Selsam, *Mimosa Pudica: The Sensitive Plant,* Morrow, 1978. Agricultural photographs have been published under pseudonym Roy Delmar.

WORK IN PROGRESS: Photographs for *The Venus Flytrap* and *The African Violet Plant;* photographic essays on plants, animals, and insects.

SIDELIGHTS: "I don't know why but almost all nature photographers run around photographing plants only in their flowering and/or fruiting stage. My approach is to study, and photograph, its entire life cycle—from seed to seed. When this photo essay is unfolded in a book or in a slide show it entices the reader/viewer with something he can understand and gives me the opportunity of presenting a tremendous amount of botany without the reader/viewer realizing that he's being fed this, so-called, dull subject.

JEROME WEXLER

"The books are directed at children because I believe that if we can get them involved and interested in the world around them now they will never, as adults, be bored for there is always another plant, insect, or animal to raise and study.

"For many years I owned and ran a stock photo house. . . . I took all of the pictures and showed both good and bad agricultural practices. The pictures were used basically for educational purposes and about four thousand to five thousand were published throughout the world. At present I am a self-employed writer-photographer specializing in the photography of the world around us: plants, animals, and insects. These photo essays are used in books, magazines, film strips, etc. These pictures, like those for the Agricultural Photo Library, are used basically for educational purposes."

WHELAN, Elizabeth M(urphy) 1943-

PERSONAL: Born December 4, 1943, in New York, N.Y.; daughter of Joseph F. (an attorney) and Marion (Barrett) Murphy; married Stephen Thomas Whelan (an attorney), April 3, 1971; children: Christine Barrett. *Education:* Connecticut College, B.A., 1965; Yale University, M.P.H., 1967; Harvard University, M.S., 1968, Sc.D., 1971. *Home:* 165 West End Ave., 20D, New York, N.Y. 10023. *Agent:* Rhoda Weyr, William Morris Agency, 1350 Avenue of the Americas, New York, N.Y. 10019. *Office:* Demographic Materials, Inc., 165 West End Ave., New York, N.Y. 10023.

CAREER: New Haven Health Department, New Haven, Conn., member of staff, 1966-67; Massachusetts Depart-

ELIZABETH M. WHELAN

ment of Public Health, Boston, epidemiologist/vital statistician, 1968-71; Planned Parenthood-World Population, New York, N.Y., county study coordinator, 1971-72; demographic Materials, Inc., New York, N.Y., executive director, 1972—; Harvard School of Public Health, Boston, research associate, 1976—. Consultant to Child Welfare League of America, to Population Council, New York, N.Y., and other organizations. *Member:* American Public Health Association, American Medical Writers Association, Population Association of America.

WRITINGS: Sex and Sensibility: A New Look at Being a Woman, McGraw, 1974; *A Baby?—Maybe: A Guide to Making the Most Fateful Decision of Your Life,* Bobbs-Merrill, 1975; (with father-in-law, Stephen T. Whelan) *Making Sense out of Sex: A New Look at Being a Man,* McGraw, 1975; (with Fredrick J. Stare) *Panic in the Pantry: Food Facts and Fallacies,* Atheneum, 1975; *Boy or Girl?,* Bobbs-Merrill, 1977; (with Fredrick J. Stare) *Eating for Good Health,* Christopher, in press; *How to Avoid Cancer,* Norton, in press.

Contributor to *Social Biology, Studies in Family Planning, Journal of Marriage and the Family, Demography, Glamour, Cosmopolitan, Bride, National Review* and other publications. Member of editorial board, *Connecticut College Alumni News,* 1972—.

WORK IN PROGRESS: A look at the psychological aspects of pregnancy, tentatively titled *The Pregnancy Experience,* for Norton.

WHITE, Florence M(eiman) 1910-

PERSONAL: Born December 26, 1910, in New York, N.Y.; daughter of Morris and Anna (Siegal) Meiman; married Martin White, September, 1933; children: Donald, Lawrence, Judith. *Education:* Hunter College (now Hunter College of the City University of New York), B.A., 1933; graduate study at Columbia University, New York University, and University of California; St. Johns University, Brooklyn, N.Y., LL.B., 1938. *Residence:* Beverly Hills, Calif.

CAREER: Attorney. Has taught in elementary schools in minority neighborhoods of New York, N.Y. and Los Angeles, Calif.; teacher of adults in Los Angeles, Calif., 1950-56; teacher in film industry, 1960—. *Member:* P.E.N., Society of Children's Book Writers, California Writers Guild, Southern California Council on Literature for Children and Young People.

WRITINGS—For children: My House Is the Nicest Place, Golden Gate, 1963; *One Boy Lives in My House,* Whitman Publishing, 1965; *Your Friend, the Insect,* Knopf, 1968; *Your Friend, the Tree,* Knopf, 1969; *How to Lose Your Lunch Money,* Ritchie, 1970; *How to Lose Your Best Friend,* Ritchie, 1972; *Cesar Chavez: Man of Courage,* Garrard, 1973; *Hello, Sun,* Rand, 1974; *Malcolm X: Black and Proud,* Garrard, 1975.

Filmscripts: "Biography of Hidalgo," Stephen Bosustow Productions, 1971; "Biography of Juarez," Stephen Bosustow Productions, 1971; "How to Lose Your Lunch Money," BFA Educational Media, 1972. Contributor to *Childcraft, Life and Health,* and *Los Angeles Elementary School Administrators' Journal.*

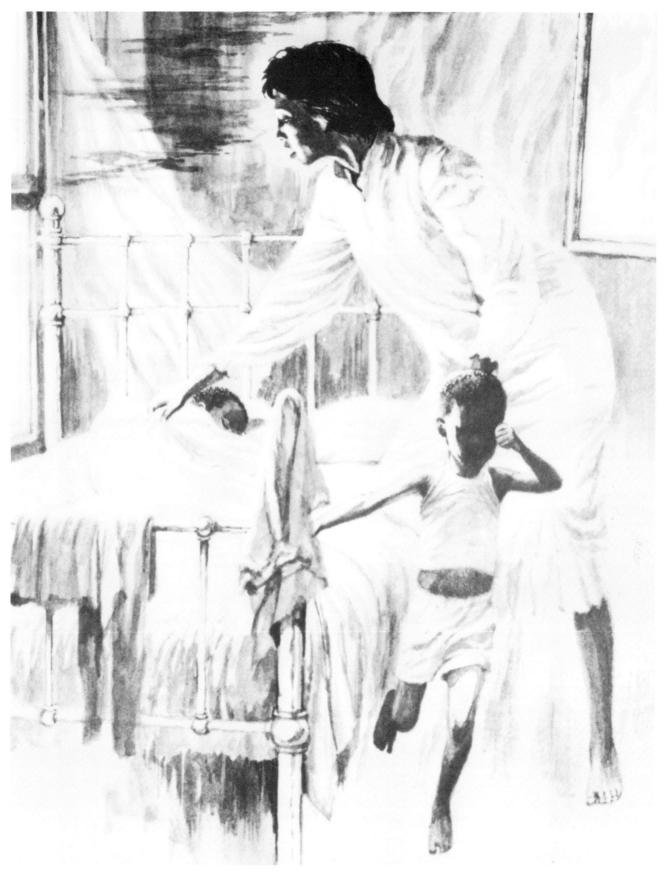

Four-year-old Malcolm was awakened by his mother's excited voice. She grasped his arm and pulled him out of bed. ▪ (From *Malcom X: Black and Proud* by Florence White. Illustrated by Victor Mays.)

FLORENCE M. WHITE

SIDELIGHTS: "I was born in and spent my youth in Manhattan, the heart of New York City, particularly in its libraries. Religiously, I went every Saturday afternoon to the library, frequently dragging with me a younger brother or sister. I loved walking through the aisles and browsing. Then I selected as many books as children were permitted to, and returned home to read them as quickly as possible. If it was summer time, I walked over to Central Park, found a large, shady tree near the 59th Street lake, sat down and read for hours.

"My favorite books were biographies. I was interested in people of great accomplishment. Perhaps, I thought, if I read enough about such people, I, too, could accomplish great things, perhaps become a judge, or congresswoman, or even president of the United States. I never dreamed then of becoming a writer.

"I went to Hunter College, and when I graduated I was prepared to teach. But by that time the Great Depression had set in, and the City of New York had 10,000 teachers waiting for jobs. So instead of teaching, I got married, my husband was a lawyer, and I began to study law. I practiced law until my second child was born. It wasn't until many years later that I began to teach.

"While I was teaching children, I thought it would be fun writing for them, too. So I began to write. My books are on a variety of subjects, but those that please me most are my biographies of Cesar Chavez and Malcolm X—two people who struggled against poverty and racial oppression to be-

come leaders of their people. I have plans for many more biographies of men and women who have helped to make the world a better place. I hope that these books will inspire young people to do what they can for their fellowmen.

"I also work part of the time in the movie and television studios as a teacher.

"I have two sons and a daughter. One of my sons is a professor of economics. He writes books, too, and we always send each other an autographed copy of a new book. With my book always goes a note: My books are easier to read than yours!

"So, enjoy, enjoy!"

HOBBIES AND OTHER INTERESTS: Travel (including East Africa and Eastern Europe), music, and most of all, people.

WHITEHOUSE, Arthur George   1895-
   (Arch Whitehouse)

PERSONAL: Born December 11, 1895, in Northampton, England; son of Joseph G. and Alice (Ryan) Whitehouse; married Ruth Elizabeth Terhune, 1922; children: Arthur Townsend, Patricia (deceased). *Education:* Attended grammar school in Livingston, N.J. *Home and office:* 63 Magnolia Ave., Montvale, N.J. 07645.

CAREER: Professional writer, cartoonist, 1919—, as a free lance, 1929—. Sports writer, cartoonist for *Passaic Daily News,* Passaic, N.J., 1922-23; sports editor, cartoonist for *Elizabeth Daily Journal,* Elizabeth, N.J., 1923-29; war correspondent in Europe during World War II; script writer in Hollywood for Metro-Goldwyn Mayer, 1945-47. *Military service:* British Army, 1914-1917; transferred to Royal Flying Corps as aerial gunner, 1917, became pilot, 1918, and ended service as acting-captain; credited with sixteen enemy planes; awarded Military Medal. *Member:* Royal Air Force Association, Quiet Birdmen, Royal Canadian Air Force Association, International Society of Aviation Writers.

WRITINGS: Wings of Adventure, John Hamilton, 1936; *Hell in the Heavens,* Chambers, 1938; *Hell in Helmets,* Jarrolds, 1939; *Crime on a Convoy Carrier,* World's Work, 1943; *Real Book of Airplanes,* Watts, 1952, 2nd edition, 1961; *Fighters in the Sky,* Duell, Sloan & Pearce, 1959; *Years of the Sky Kings,* Doubleday, 1959.

Years of the War Birds, Doubleday, 1960; *Tank-History of Armored Warfare,* Doubleday, 1960; *Bombers in the Sky,* Duell, Sloan & Pearce, 1960; *Combat in the Sky,* Duell, Sloan & Pearce, 1961; *Subs and Submariners,* Doubleday, 1961; *Squadrons of the Sea,* Doubleday, 1962; *Adventure in the Sky,* Duell, Sloan & Pearce, 1962; *Action in the Sky,* Duell, Sloan & Pearce, 1962; *Billy Mitchell,* Putnam, 1962; *Legion of the Lafayette,* Doubleday, 1962; *Amphibious Operations,* Doubleday, 1963; *Decisive Battles of the First World War,* Duell, Sloan & Pearce, 1963; *John J. Pershing,* Putnam, 1964; *Heroes and Legends of World War I,* Doubleday, 1964; *Espionage and Counterespionage,* Doubleday, 1964; *Squadron 44,* Doubleday, 1965; *The Early Birds,* Doubleday, 1965; *The Fledgling,* Duell, Sloan & Pearce, 1965; *Heroic Pigeons,* Putnam, 1965; *Frank Luke,* Universal Publishing, 1966; *Fighting Ships,* Doubleday, 1967; *The Zeppelin Fighters,* Doubleday, 1966; *Spies With Wings,* Putnam, 1966; *Fighting Ships,* Doubleday, 1967; *Scarlet*

Streamers, Putnam, 1967; *Heroes of the Sunlit Sky,* Doubleday, 1967; *Squadron Shilling,* Doubleday, 1968.

Playboy Squadron, Doubleday, 1970; *The Sky's the Limit,* Macmillan, 1971; *The Casket Crew,* Doubleday, 1971; *The Military Airplane,* Doubleday, 1971; *Hero Without Honor,* Doubleday, 1972; *Wings for the Chariots,* Doubleday, 1973. Stories in pulp magazines, 1928-38; stories and articles, some self-illustrated, in *American, Reader's Digest, Esquire, Coronet, Collier's, Saturday Evening Post, Liberty, True, Short Story, Adventure, Argosy,* and in British publications.

WORK IN PROGRESS: "I am now working on my complete autobiography, beginning with my birth in England through both World Wars and up to the present date."

SIDELIGHTS: "As noted above I was born in Northampton, England. I had a very happy life there, and loved my country very much. Then in 1905 after American labor-saving machinery was brought in to the Northampton shoe trade, a great number of our people were put out of work. As a result my father decided to emigrate to America (America meaning anywhere in the Northern Hemisphere).

"Shocked by this upheaval, I next found myself in Newark, New Jersey trying to figure out a way to get back to Northampton. Oh, we didn't all come to America to evade military conscription, freedom of prayer, or a cruel king. We came because we wanted work—not handouts.

"My schooldays in Newark were horrors. You see, I *spoke* English and was dressed like an English schoolboy and knew NOTHING about the Revolutionary War. A war that England apparently had lost. With that I began my writing career by sending reports of my life in America to our local paper. Fortunately for me, the Northampton editor carefully blue-pencilled some of the more outrageous statements, or there is no knowing where I might have wound up.

"I went to school here for only a few years. America was no better to my parents than England had been, so at fourteen I was pulled out of school and sent to work. I wound up in the famed laboratory of Thomas A. Edison and at times watched him trying to perfect talking motion pictures.

"When I was eighteen I got my first break in life. World War I broke out and I immediately worked my way back to England—on a cattle boat—and enlisted in my old county regiment, the Northamptonshire Yeomanry. I was also immediately trained as a machine gunner, and spent the next two years supporting all sorts of regiments in the ground war. Then one day I noticed an air battle in which a British Sopwith Pup shot down a German Albatross.

"Why I had never noticed this sort of thing before, I'll never know, but I did react and asked for a transfer to the Royal Flying Corps. Fortunately for me, the R.F.C. had been asking for volunteers to man the machine guns on their two-seater battle-planes. Within a very short time I was lifted from the ground and was doing daily patrols over the German lines—yes, and shooting down my share of the enemy Fokkers.

"A number of my letters back to my parents in America, were picked up by a neighbor who was working for the old New York *Sun*. In a few weeks I seemed to be getting more publicity than General Pershing who was to head the Ameri-

ARTHUR WHITEHOUSE

can Army when it came over to France to save us for something called Democracy.

"Well, that was the beginning of my literary (?) career. I got a sniff of printer's ink and it never left me. In the meantime, I won a commission in the field and became a Sopwith Camel pilot. Then just as I was seemingly headed for Glory, the Germans grabbed President Wilson's Fourteen Points, and quit cold. The Armistice finished me too.

"Oh yes, I had also been writing to a little American girl, a pleasure that lured me back to America, but America was not impressed with British ex-service men, and I found it tough to get a job or even eke out a living.

"I tried selling rat-poison, advertising space, and motor cars. You couldn't give cars away in 1919-20. So I decided I'd be a newspaper man and got a job as a sports cartoonist and sports writer on a Passaic, New Jersey paper. I taught myself cartooning from a book borrowed from the local library, and typing by the hunt-and-peck system, but I made it!

"With marriage came greater responsibilities, so I decided in 1928 to become a free-lance writer and contribute stories to the *Saturday Evening Post,* etc. etc. But I had to settle for *Flying Aces* and *Sky Birds* aviation pulps of the late 1920's. In no time I was working day and night turning out 5,000 words a day to keep up with the demand. It seems I was the only 'writer' who had ever flown a plane or fired a machine gun. I had the field practically to myself. But remember, I still had not gone past the eighth grade in school. But again the libraries came to my aid and I read and studied every volume on writing I could haul home.

"With the outbreak of World War II, I again volunteered to serve with Britain, but Britain did not want me. I volunteered with Canada and Australia. No soap. When the United States found itself in the war, I volunteered to serve in any capacity and almost made it until they found out I was the Arch Whitehouse who had been writing 'Battle of Britain' stories in the *Saturday Evening Post* (I had finally made it!). So they *ordered* me to get a United States uniform, put up War Correspondent strips under my R.A.F. wings and the ribbons of the medals I had gathered in World War I. Before I knew it I was in London covering the U.S. Eighth Air Force in their battles against Hitler and Berlin. I also covered the Ninth Air Force, and went into Normandy on the invasion. Through all this the British were asking me to have a look at some of their squadrons and do a story or two on them. No soap.

"Once we got to Paris, I resigned and left the war for Eisenhower to finish. On my arrival back home I was tagged by Metro-Goldwyn-Mayer to write a scenario on Daisy Neuman's best seller of that period: *Now That April's There.* Some little chit named Elizabeth Taylor was to star in it.

"I did my best, and my producer Sam Marx was delighted and I was offered a seven-year contract—which I later tore up. It turned out that Miss Taylor no longer wanted to play little girl parts, and wanted only formal dresses and romance. I was bounced around the Culver City lot for weeks getting $750 a week for banging out outlines for possible films. Tiring of that and wishing for sanity, I begged off and returned east and again took up magazine writing until I was kidded into trying a book on World War I. I had never written anything longer than a pulp novelette, but I found I could write millions of words, and had to be stopped at 85,000. The World War I book was a success and was also published in England. Many more of my forty volumes have been taken by foreign publishers—even the Germans see something in them and I draw good royalties from that country regularly.

"These military books required some sound background so the U.S. Army, Navy and Air Force co-operated beautifully, and I soon found myself aboard atomic submarines, flying off and onto aircraft carriers, and being bounced around in all sorts of tanks. Of course my early life in both World Wars fitted in beautifully. I also wrote novels based on characters I had met aboard the above tanks, subs and aircraft carriers.

"It may sound breathless and exhausting, but it hasn't been. I am now approaching my eighty-third year and am in splendid health, thanks to the girl previously mentioned. I maintain a stiff schedule of working every morning, trying to turn out 3,000 words. Then I go for a three-four mile walk every afternoon, or play a round of golf. At night I *read, read,*

"That's true Baru," said his mother. "When you've walked in the rain a few times, you'll be all black and gold once more--from your nose to the end of your tail." ■ (From *Once a Bright Red Tiger* by Alex Whitney. Illustrated by Charles Robinson.)

read, hoping some day to catch up on my limited formal education. Boston University has honored me by asking for my manuscripts, notebooks, and finished products which have been placed in their new Mugar Library—right alongside those of Robert Frost, of all people!

"Beyond this, there is very little to tell, and if any of our neighbors come across *Something About the Author* by accident, they'll probably be the most surprised individuals extant, because outside of our house, we never talk about writing, or what I work at. They simply know I once had something to do with flying in the First World War, and kid me about someone called Snoopy who is always hooting down Sopwith Camels.

"We let it go at that, knowing you can never beat down a rumor once it gets started."

WHITNEY, Alex(andra) 1922-

PERSONAL: Born October 8, 1922, in Flushing, N.Y.; daughter of John (president of American Spice Exchange) and Fanita (Moll) Clarke; married Roger Whitney (an industrial lighting designer), March 31, 1942; children: Susan A. (Mrs. George W. Lewis III). *Education:* Graduate of David Mannes College of Music, 1938-41. *Office:* David McKay Co., 750 Third Ave., New York, N.Y. 10017.

CAREER: Henry Z. Walck, Inc. (children's book division of David McKay Co.), New York, N.Y., promotion director, 1963-76, children's book editor, 1976—. *Member:* Publishers' Library Promotion Group (president, 1968-71), Publishers Ad Club, Children's Book Council.

WRITINGS—Books for children: *Once a Bright Red Tiger,* Walck, 1973; *Stiff Ears: Animal Folktales of the North American Indian,* Walck, 1974; *Voices in the Wind: Central and South American Legends,* McKay, 1976; *Sports and Games the Indians Gave Us,* McKay, 1977; *Pads for Pets: How to Make Habitats and Equipment for Small Animals,* McKay, 1977.

WILKINS, Frances 1923-

PERSONAL: Born October 15, 1923, in London, England; daughter of Frank (a government official) and Margaret (Freir) Bennett; married Frank James Wilkins (a lecturer), March 14, 1944; children: Penelope (Mrs. Macfarlane), Sally, Amanda. *Education:* Attended a girls' school in London, England. *Religion:* Roman Catholic. *Home:* 5 Dene Court, Chelmsford, Essex, England.

CAREER: Writer. Held various teaching positions since 1949. St. Philip's Convent School, Essex, England, teacher, 1974—.

FRANCES WILKINS

WRITINGS—For children: *Speaking and Moving,* Oxford University Press, 1957; *Speaking and Moving at Christmas Time* (rhymes and playlets), Oxford University Press, 1958; *Acting Is Fun: Short Plays for Children,* Blackie & Son, 1958.

Let's Write It Down: A New Approach to Spelling and Composition, University of London Press, 1960; *Six Great Scots,* Hamish Hamilton, 1961; *Six Great Archaeologists: Belzoni, Layard, Schliemann, Evans, Carter, Thompson,* Hamish Hamilton, 1961; *Five Nativity Plays for Junior School Or for Use in Parishes,* Mowbray, 1961; *President Kennedy,* Cassell, 1962; *Six Great Nurses: Louise de Maril-*

lac, Florence Nightingale, Clara Barton, Dorothy Pattison, Edith Cavell, Elizabeth Kenny, Hamish Hamilton, 1962; *The Young Traveller in Spain,* Phoenix House, 1962; *Mime and Rhyme,* Blackie and Son, 1964; *Wizards and Witches.* Oliver & Boyd, 1965, Walck, 1966; *Ancient Crete,* John Day, 1966; *Fairs,* Basil Blackwell, 1967; *Markets and Shops,* Basil Blackwell, 1968; *Unknown Lands,* Macdonald, 1969; *Let's Visit North Africa,* Burke Books, 1970.

Bridges in Britain, Basil Blackwell, 1971; *Castles,* Basil Blackwell, 1973; *The Entertainers,* Allman, 1973; *The Shopkeepers,* Allman, 1975; *Symbols and Signs,* Basil Blackwell, 1975; *Magna Carta, June 15, 1215,* Lutterworth, 1975; *The Sailing of the Mayflower,* Lutterworth, 1976; *Caves,* Basil Blackwell, 1977; *Growing Up in Tudor Times,* Batsford, 1977; *Let's Visit Egypt,* Burke Books, 1977.

WORK IN PROGRESS: Let's Visit Thailand.

SIDELIGHTS: "I am interested in going to the theatre especially to Gilbert and Sullivan operas; reading (especially *Punch*) and speaking Italian (very badly). I am also a practising and deeply committed Roman Catholic.

HOBBIES AND OTHER INTERESTS: Travel (Middle and Far East, Africa, Canada, the United States, the Soviet Union, all of Europe).

WILKINSON, Brenda 1946-

PERSONAL: Born January 1, 1946, in Moultrie, Ga.; daughter of Malcolm (in construction) and Ethel (a nurse; maiden name, Anderson) Scott; separated; children: Kim, Lori. *Education:* Attended Hunter College of the City University of New York. *Home:* 210 West 230th St., Bronx, N.Y. 10463. *Office:* Board of Global Ministries, 475 Riverside Dr., New York, N.Y.

CAREER: Writer. *Member:* Authors Guild of Authors League of America. *Awards, honors:* National Book Award nominee, 1976.

She knew that Lord Pengersec would have to return home this way, so she had decided to throw a spell across the drawbridge to make his mare pull up, and right in the mare's path she put a large tub of water. ■ (From *Wizards and Witches* by Frances Wilkins. Illustrated by Fritz Wegner.)

Ludell's throat felt extra dry, and her jaws grew tight. Heat encircled her eyes. How she wished she'd never called the others—and she and mama were alone, where she could put her aching face into mama's apron and just cry out all the pain.... ■ (From *Ludell* by Brenda Wilkinson. Jacket painting by Benny Andrews.)

BRENDA WILKINSON

WRITINGS—For children: *Ludell*, Harper, 1975; *Ludell and Willie*, Harper, 1976.

WILLARD, Mildred Wilds   1911-

PERSONAL: Born October 11, 1911, in New Kensington, Pa.; daughter of John Michael (a grocer) and Emma (Miller) Wilds; married Kester T. Willard (with United Air Lines sales department; now retired), October 13, 1934; children: John Michael, Thomas Gordon. *Education:* Allegheny College, student, 1928-30; Northwestern University, A.B., 1932; University of Chicago, graduate courses. *Religion:* Unitarian Universalist. *Home:* 4212 Linden Ave., Western Springs, Ill. 60558.

CAREER: High school English teacher in Lancaster, Wis., 1932-34; *Chicago Tribune*, Chicago, Ill., reporter, 1935-43; secondary and elementary teacher in Illinois schools, 1956-62. *Awards, honors:* First prize for short story, Midwest Writers Conference, 1950.

WRITINGS: The Man Who Had to Invent a Flying Bicycle, Stackpole, 1967; *The Cloud Crasher*, Transition Press, 1969; *The Magic Candy Mystery*, Transition Press, 1969; *The Luck of Harry Weaver*, Watts, 1971; *The Ice Cream Cone*, Follett, 1973. Contributor of forty short stories to confession and children's magazines; contributor to Childcraft Books and Science Research Associates multi-level reading program.

SIDELIGHTS: "My father, John Michael Wilds, a grocer, died when I was eleven months old. He left my mother, three sisters and a brother, much older than I was, the store to manage. When I hadn't yet learned to add and subtract enough to use the register or write in the charge accounts, I was given books to read, pictures to look at, and told to sit quietly behind the counter, behave and not be a nuisance to anyone. I liked this order because, between the book readings, I could hear true-to-life tales, told to my mother by the customers who needed a listening ear and sympathy. These tales included unhappy marriages, mistakes, happy times, sicknesses, death, recovery from harsh diseases, money concerns and unsuspected earnings.

"I learned to read the books before I went to school. This came about by helping my sisters fill orders by reading the labels on soups, canned vegetables, pickles and relishes. However, my family members were too busy to hear my troubles so I had to tell them to the horse, named Bird, who stayed in the stable until it was time to be hitched to the wagon and deliver the grocery orders.

"By the time I went to school, I had an urge to tell stories that I had made up. By the time I had accomplished the grammar lessons in the eighth grade, I wanted to be a writer. From then on, all teachers agreed that I should become one. Because an economic depression hit the country in the thirties, my sisters recommended that I become a teacher, rather than trying to get a job on a newspaper.

"I followed their advice and for the first two years after graduating from Northwestern, I taught English. I was shocked to discover that high school students in the majority didn't know a sentence from a sigh and a noun was a nothing ever heard about. They hated to write, finding it easier to talk and laugh, make fun of school, rather than to listen and learn.

"After two years of that, I'd had enough. I worked in Chicago on Montgomery Wards mail order catalogue, where a

MILDRED WILDS WILLARD

description of an item had to be reduced to enough words to fit under the picture. After a year of this, I was fortunately hired by the *Chicago Tribune* as a news and feature writer. Here for eight years I wrote all day and every day.

"When my two sons were too little to leave alone, I worked at home as a free-lance writer. Then again I was stunned to discover what editors thought would bring their publishers profit. They didn't consider the children's interests, only what would sell to librarians and parents. I have an unsold manuscript telling all about living and working in a grocery store at the time World War I brought so many changes. The editors that turned it down said that children weren't interested in history or stores.

"I travelled through Russia making notes on what the children's clubs were doing as projects to build their mother country. Editors turned this down on the assumption that children were not interested in Russia. However, in the Soviet Union all the children knew about the fifty states in America and the poor discipline in schools, the crime, and the fact that so many children here couldn't read or write. They pitied the children in a 'so-called democracy.'

"When my children were old enough to go to school, I returned to teaching but in the elementary grades to see what happened to the curiosity and desire to learn. I discovered that children were interested in history, more than in talking animals or folk tales, stories given to them in abundance. I also realized that very few writers can earn a living at free-lance writing. However, editors can not kill the curiosity of writers, nor their desire to share the stories they compose and experience. I keep on writing, although my files are filled with unsold manuscripts that the school children liked. I also have letters of praise from the children who have read the stories that were published. Also I have many complimentary letters from editors who would publish the manuscripts if the budget of their money-losing companies would so allow."

WILLIAMS, Eric (Ernest) 1911-

PERSONAL: Born July 13, 1911, in London, England; son of Ernest and Mary Elizabeth (Beardmore) Williams; married Sibyl Grain, April 1, 1948. *Education:* Attended Christ's College, London, England. *Home:* "Wherever he and his wife happen to be." *Address:* c/o Union Bank of Switzerland, Bubenbergplatz 3, Bern, Switzerland.

CAREER: Lewis's Ltd., London, England, interior architect, 1932-40, book buyer, 1946-49; London Films, London, England, scriptwriter, 1949; self-employed writer and journalist, 1949. *Military service:* Royal Air Force, 1940-46; bomber captain; shot down over Germany on 25th raid in December, 1942, escaped from Stalag-Luft III and returned to active service a year later; awarded Military Cross for the successful escape; member of Combined Anglo-U.S. Mission to recover Allied prisoners-of-war in Far Eastern theatre; demobilised as squadron leader, 1946.

WRITINGS: Goon in the Block, J. Cape, 1945; *The Wooden Horse,* Collins, 1949, Harper, 1950; *The Tunnel,* Collins, 1951, Coward, 1952, revised edition, edited for young readers, Collins, 1959, original version reissued as *The Tunnel Escape,* Berkley, 1963; (editor) *The Escapers: A Chronicle of Escape in Many Wars, with Eighteen First-Hand Accounts,* Eyre & Spottiswoode, 1953, published in America as *The Book of Famous Escapes: A Chronicle of Escape in Many Wars, with Eighteen First-Hand Accounts,* Norton, 1954; *Complete and Free: A Modern Idyll,* Eyre & Spottiswoode, 1957; *Dragoman Pass: An Adventure in the Balkans,* Coward, 1959, revised and reissued as *Dragoman,* New English Library, 1970; (editor and author of introduction) *Great Escape Stories,* Weidenfeld & Nicolson, 1958, McBride, 1959, reissued as *The Will to be Free: Great Es-*

That day the line was getting longer in front of the ice-cream stand. ▪ (From *The Ice-Cream Cone* by Mildred Wilds Willard. Illustrated by Józef Sumichrast.)

(From the movie, "The Wooden Horse," copyright 1950, British Lion Films, Ltd.)

cape Stories, Thomas Nelson, 1971; *The Borders of Barbarism,* Heinemann, 1961, Coward, 1962; (editor and author of introduction) *More Escapers in War and Peace, with Eighteen First-Hand Accounts,* Collins, 1968; *People: English in Action,* Edward Arnold, 1970; (editor and author of introduction) *Great Air Battles,* Pan, 1971. Contributor to film script, "The Wooden Horse," produced by Korda in 1951. Contributor to *Sunday Express* (London).

WORK IN PROGRESS: A sea story; a political thriller.

SIDELIGHTS: "I escaped from a prison camp in Germany during the Second World War. Home in England, I delivered fellow-prisoners' messages to their families and friends. These people were so anxious to know how their menfolk were faring that I began to write an article describing life behind barbed wire. The article grew into my first book, *Goon in the Block.* A British publisher accepted it on the spot and sold every copy within a fortnight of publication, but due to war time lack of paper he did not reprint. In *Goon in the Block,* because of military censorship, I had not been able even to mention the escape. As soon as the war was over I wrote the full story—of my time as RAF bomber captain, prisoner of war, tunneller and, ultimately, successful

escaper. This made two books, *The Tunnel* and *The Wooden Horse.*

"The worldwide success of *The Wooden Horse* enabled me to escape again, from the to-me-unsatisfactory life of a London businessman-commuter. After writing the script of the film I returned to Germany, neither prisoner nor fugitive, and supervised the building of a replica of Stalag-Luft III on location. Then I wrote the story of my peacetime escape, *Complete & Free;* and bought an old stone-and-slate house in an overgrown walled garden with seven acres of bracken-clad, rabbit-run cliffland overlooking the English Channel.

"Two publishers asked me to compile collections of the best escape stories, and I became an escapologist. In *The Escapers* I traced the development of the technique of escaping from enemy captivity through the centuries; while in *The Will to be Free* I highlighted the problems which faced escapers—and their helpers—in different campaign areas in modern wars. When later I was asked to compile *More Escapers,* I included accounts by men and women who broke the bonds of circumstance which had imprisoned them in peace as effectively as barbed wire imprisoned any prisoner of war. In all three books I introduce the protagonists and let them tell their own story, for I believe that only that person in that place at that time can convey truly what it was like, and involve the reader in his or her experience.

"My most recent book for young people, *Great Air Battles,* has a similar formula: I describe each battle and its place in history, then the combatants themselves tell of their fear and excitement, their dogfights and bombing raids, their exhaustion and, rarely, elation in victory.

"Life in the clifftop house was idyllic, but I needed more experience, more knowledge of the countries which lay beyond the sea that broke on the rocks below. Fortunately my wife shares my wanderlust and love of the outdoors. We sold house and furniture, and set off in a Land-Rover to travel the world. One adventure-packed summer which we spent camping behind the Iron Curtain in Hungary, Rumania and Bulgaria resulted in *Dragoman Pass;* three summers in Yugoslavia provided material for *The Borders of Barbarism.* We travelled on through Greece, Turkey and Cyprus, camping in the wilds from March to October and renting a house for the winter months wherever we happened to be.

"Many Greek islands and much of the Turkish coast are inaccessible except by boat, so we decided to take to the sea.

ERIC WILLIAMS

In all of Europe we could not find the craft we wanted. At last, in a fishing village on the Danish island of Fyn, a boat-builder undertook to build a motor-sailer of larch on oak to our design. She had to be small enough for the two of us to sail, big enough for us to live aboard year round. *Escaper*—out of London—was launched a year later. Her maiden voyage that fall was around the Baltic and through the Kiel Canal into the North Sea. In Wilhelmshaven we unstepped the mast, and headed South across Europe via the waterways of Holland, Belgium and France. Now we are slowly exploring the coasts and islands of the Mediterranean.

"I love the seafaring life: the loose democratic society of other seamen of many nationalities, and the friends one makes on excursions ashore; fishing with a trammel net from the dinghy; setting sail, taking soundings in strange anchorages, sleeping on deck under the stars; splicing rope—even painting the hull and varnishing the mast.

"When winter comes we base ourselves in a landlocked bay surrounded by pinewoods and olive groves where we gather berries, mushrooms, and wild spinach and asparagus. We comb the shore for driftwood to feed the small cabin stove, hunt boar and partridge in the steep rocky hills, and re-fit the ship in readiness for the spring.

"It is a demanding and sometimes dangerous life, never boring. It has given me the knowledge and experience for at least two more books. One is the story of *Escaper* and her wanderings, the other a thriller with a Mediterranean setting. Both will continue the theme, which runs through all my books, of individual man struggling for freedom and integrity in an increasingly 'civilised' world."

He expected every minute to hear the crack of a rifle and feel the tearing impact of its bullet in his flesh. ■ (From *The Wooden Horse* by Eric Williams. Illustrated by Martin Thomas.)

HOBBIES AND OTHER INTERESTS: Fishing and shooting, only "for the pot."

WILLIAMS, Selma R(uth) 1925-

PERSONAL: Born October 26, 1925, in Malden, Mass.; married Burton L. Williams (a lawyer), June 26, 1949; children: Pamela, Wendy. *Education:* Radcliffe College, A.B. (cum laude), 1946; Tufts University, Ed.M., 1964. *Politics:* "Independent-liberal." *Home:* 17 Dane Rd., Lexington, Mass. 02173.

CAREER: Harvard Law Record, Cambridge, Mass., executive director, 1946-50; Diamond Junior High School, Lexington, Mass., history teacher, 1964-67; Concord-Carlisle Senior High School, Concord, Mass., history teacher, 1967-68; Middlesex Community College, Bedford, Mass., lecturer in history, 1973—. Research coordinator, Cambridge Historical Commission Bicentennial Diorama; producer and lecturer on slide shows focusing on women in history. *Member:* Authors Guild, League of Women Voters (member of local executive board, 1955-60), New England Association of Women Historians, Organization of American Historians, American Historical Association, Essex Institute.

WRITINGS: Fifty-Five Fathers: The Story of the Constitutional Convention, Dodd, 1970; *Kings, Commoners, and Colonists: Puritan Politics in Old and New England, 1603-1660 (Horn Book* honor list), Atheneum, 1974; *Demeter's Daughters, the Women Who Founded America, 1587-1787,* Atheneum, 1976; (co-author) *Putting Women in Their Place, Report on American History High School Textbooks,* National Organization for Women, 1976; *Riding the Nightmare: Women and Witchcraft,* Atheneum, 1978.

WORK IN PROGRESS: A biography of Anne Marbury Hutchinson.

SIDELIGHTS: "In my undergraduate days I constantly bewailed missing out on the suffrage campaign. Only after teaching history to students of all ages, from junior high to university graduate level, did I finally discover what I wanted to be when I grew up—an activist uncovering deep female roots in history and spreading the word.

"Each book has led directly to the next. *Fifty-Five Fathers: Story of the Constitutional Convention,* made me seek the roots of our government in England and early Massachusetts, and resulted in *Kings, Commoners, and Colonists.* This book in turn led me to wonder about the role of women in colonization, and produced *Demeter's Daughters.* And a

Authentic reconstruction of a Salem house, c. 1630. Photographed at Pioneer Village, Salem, Massachusetts. ■ (From *Demeter's Daughters* by Selma R. Williams. Photo courtesy of the Board of Park Commissioners, Salem, Mass.)

SELMA WILLIAMS

chapter here on women and witchcraft inspired my present project—uncovering the reasons why hundreds of thousands, perhaps millions, of women were put to death as witches in Europe and America.

"At least once a week I lecture professionally to schools, colleges, and women's clubs. Trying out new, sometimes wild, ideas on a live audience before committing them to print, proves the best possible sounding board. Lecturing also provides a needed break in routine from the daily six-hour stint of writing, surrounded by silence, immersed in total isolation."

WILSON, (Leslie) Granville   1912-

PERSONAL: Born February 10, 1912, in Castleford, West Yorkshire, England; son of Smith (a carpenter) and Mary Ann (Shackleton) Wilson; married Irene Dunn, July 27, 1935; children: Joan (Mrs. Maurice Gray), Arnold Ley. *Education:* Educated in Castleford, England. *Home:* 6 Rosemoor Close, Hunmanby, Filey, North Yorkshire YO14 0NB, England.

CAREER: Journalist. *Wakefield Express* newspapers, Pontefract, Castleford, Wakefield and Yorkshire, England, reporter and feature writer, 1929-42; *The Yorkshire Post,* Leeds and Yorkshire, England, reporter, feature writer,

book reviewer, industrial correspondent, 1942-53; *Westminster Press,* London, England, industrial correspondent, 1953-54; *Evening Gazette,* Middlesbrough, England, chief editorial writer, feature writer, sub-editor, 1954-67. *Member:* Society of Authors, Crime Writers Association.

WRITINGS: The Gateway to Journalism, Alliance Press, 1946; *Jonathan Enters Journalism,* Chatto & Windus, 1956; *Formula for Murder* (adult), Brown Watson, 1960; *A First Look At Newspapers,* Watts, 1974; *A First Look at the Police,* Watts, 1976.

Author of television play "Death of an Editor."

WORK IN PROGRESS: A play set in the Yorkshire coal field where he was born; research on novelists as psychologists; *Charlie Among the Computers,* a science fiction novel for children, to be published by Stainer & Bell in 1979.

SIDELIGHTS: Granville Wilson comments that he is "a compulsive reader. Could read before I was aged five. Began collecting books when I was nine; still at it." He considers reading the most durable of pleasures, and feels that borrowing books is not enough; one should own them.

GRANVILLE WILSON

In 1870 something happened which was to change the whole style of newspapers. That was the passing of a law which said that all children must go to school. ■ (From *Newspapers* by Granville Wilson. Illustrated by Geoffrey Bargery.)

WILSON, Walt(er N) 1939-

PERSONAL: Born March 26, 1939, in Texas; son of John A. (a brickmason) and Mildred Wilson; married Linda D., September 3, 1960 (divorced, July, 1975); married Suzanne L. (a probation officer), June 12, 1976; children: (first marriage) Melanie, Walter N., Jr., Michele. *Education:* Howard Payne College, B.A., 1962; Chapman College, M.A., 1975. *Home:* 1865 East 8th St., Chico, Calif. 95926. *Office:* Table Mountain School, 51 County Center, Oroville, Calif. 95965.

CAREER: Ordained Southern Baptist minister; minister of Southern Baptist churches in Texas, 1958-63, and California, 1964-72; Table Mountain School, Oroville, Calif., teacher and principal, 1973—. Teacher and principal of school in Marysville, Calif., 1966-73; member of governing board of Youth Service Bureau of Yuba-Sutter Counties, 1969-71; member of Juvenile Court School Administrators Council (California), 1970—. *Member:* Correctional Education Association, Court School Educators of Northern California (president, 1974-75), Phi Delta Kappa.

WRITINGS: T.A. for Teens, privately printed, 1974; *Say Hello to Yourself* (transactional analysis for adolescents), Broadman, 1975. Contributor to religious magazines and *Scholastic.*

WORK IN PROGRESS: Editing *Love and Graffite,* an anthology of poems by juvenile delinquents.

SIDELIGHTS: "As an adolescent, someone reached out to me . . . he offered to trust me and gave his love unconditionally. That changed the course of my life. That person . . . was an educator in my high school. Mr. Mac . . . believed in me as a person and . . . gave to me the most valuable thing he could give . . . himself and his time.

"I decided that I wanted to help other juvenile delinquents. As a minister of churches in Texas and California, I worked with adolescents in camps, revivals, and youth programs. . . . My work with juvenile delinquents has been very rewarding. I have listened to their hearts; watched them grow; cried and laughed with them; hurt with them. . . . I hope to publish some [of their] poems soon which I've been collecting for the last ten years.''

WILTON, Elizabeth   1937-

PERSONAL: Born July 27, 1937, in Adelaide, Australia; daughter of J. Raymond (a professor of mathematics) and Winifred (a Young Women's Christian Association worker; maiden name, Welbourn) Wilton; married Charles F. Stevenson (a teacher), December 26, 1970; children: Daniel Charles, Richard Wilton, Catherine Elizabeth. *Education:* Attended Adelaide Teachers College. *Politics:* Australian Labor Party. *Religion:* Society of Friends (Quakers). *Home:* 4 Tindara Ave., Windsor Gardens, South Australia 5087.

CAREER: Education Department, Adelaide, Australia, senior assistant, 1956-64; Crippled Children's Association, Adelaide, Australia, teacher of children with cerebral palsy, 1965-67; Education Department, Adelaide, Australia, head teacher in special education and guidance, 1968-70. Teacher with local adult illiteracy program. *Member:* Australian Society of Authors.

WRITINGS—For children: *A Ridiculous Idea,* Angus & Robertson, 1967; *Riverboat Family* (Junior Literary Guild selection), Angus & Robertson, 1967, Farrar, Straus, 1969; *The Twins and the 'Tortle,'* Rigby Ltd., 1968; *The Twins and the Christmas Tree,* Rigby Ltd., 1968; *The Lost Bangle,* Rigby Ltd., 1968; *The Little Sea-Dragon,* Rigby Ltd., 1968; *Prettyfoot,* Rigby Ltd., 1968; *The Foolish Fairy,* Rigby, Ltd., 1968; *The Unknown Land,* Rigby Ltd., 1969; *Adventure Ahoy!,* Rigby Ltd., 1969; *Land of His Dreams,* Rigby Ltd., 1969; *A Remarkable Obstacle,* Rigby Ltd., 1969; *On the Banks of the Yavva,* Rigby Ltd., 1969; *Red Ribbons and*

ELIZABETH WILTON

Mr. Anders, Angus & Robertson, 1970; *Riverview Kids,* Angus & Robertson, 1971.

WORK IN PROGRESS: Face to the Wind; a history of western Victoria, Australia; a biography of Captain William Randall; studying Australian gold rushes; *An Ocean of Darkness,* a story of refugees from World War II.

SIDELIGHTS: ''I write because I have to—I cannot help it; it is a sort of disease. I feel it important to collect the stories that old people have to tell of their early days in this country—before those stories are lost forever. I try to emphasize attitudes toward peace, conservation. I am interested in history, children, and educational methods (particularly with reference to reading).''

HOBBIES AND OTHER INTERESTS: Listening to music, watching ballet, stamp collecting, gardening, Esperanto.

FOR MORE INFORMATION SEE: Marcie Muir, *A Bibliography of Australian Children's Books,* Deutsch, 1976; *Horn Book,* December, 1969.

WINDHAM, Kathryn T(ucker)   1918-

PERSONAL: Born June 2, 1918, in Selma, Ala.; daughter of James Wilson (a banker) and Helen (an insurance agent; maiden name, Tabb) Tucker; married Amasa Benjamin Windham, February 10, 1946 (deceased); children: Kathryn Tabb, Amasa Benjamin, Jr., Helen Ann. *Education:* Huntingdon College, A.B., 1939. *Politics:* Democrat. *Religion:* United Methodist. *Home:* 2004 Royal St., Selma, Ala. 36701.

CAREER: Alabama Journal, Montgomery, police reporter, 1940-42; U.S. Treasury Department, Birmingham, Ala., statewide promoter of war bonds, 1942-44; *Birmingham News,* Birmingham, Ala., state editor, general reporter, and photographer, 1944-46; *Selma Times-Journal,* Selma, Ala., reporter, 1960-65, city editor, 1965-68, state editor, 1968-72, associate editor, 1972-73; Area Agency on Aging, Camden, Ala., community services planner, 1973—. Member of board of advisers of Alabama State Historical Commission; member of Selma city school board, 1960-72. *Member:* National Association for the Preservation and Perpetuation of Storytelling (member of board of directors). *Awards, honors:* Best nonfiction award from American Library Association, 1975, for *Alabama: One Big Front Porch;* journalism awards from Associated Press and Alabama Press Association, for photography, features, and spot news.

WRITINGS—All published by Strode: *Treasured Alabama Recipes,* 1964; (with Margaret Gillis Figh) *Thirteen Alabama Ghosts and Jeffrey,* 1969; *Exploring Alabama,* 1969; *Jeffrey Introduces Thirteen More Southern Ghosts,* 1971; *Treasured Tennessee Recipes,* 1972; *Thirteen Georgia Ghosts and Jeffrey,* 1973; *Treasured Georgia Recipes,* 1973; *Thirteen Mississippi Ghosts and Jeffrey,* 1974; *Alabama: One Big Front Porch,* 1975; *Thirteen Tennessee Ghosts and Jeffrey,* 1976.

WORK IN PROGRESS: Collecting Southern ghost tales, games, folklore, and songs; photographing the changing South.

SIDELIGHTS: ''My desire is to preserve our Southern ghost tales—the true ones—before they are lost. I use a newspaper reporter's training to check the stories, verify

Because these lucky dogs have never hunted in the haunted hunting grounds at Sewell's Woods, they were able to pose for the above photograph peacefully. ■(From *Jeffrey Introduces 13 More Southern Ghosts* by Kathryn Tucker Windham. Photos by the author.)

KATHRYN WINDHAM

dates, names, places, etc. The sites of all the stories can be visited—but I make no promise that the ghosts can be seen! Jeffrey is the 'something' that lives in our house.''

WITHERS, Carl A. 1900-1970
(Robert North, James West)

PERSONAL: Born March 20, 1900, near Sheldon, Mo. *Education:* B.A., Harvard College (now University); graduate work at Columbia University.

CAREER: Writer and researcher in the field of anthropology and folklore. *Member:* American Folklore Society, American Anthropological Association (fellow).

WRITINGS: (Under pseudonym James West) *Plainville, U.S.A.,* Columbia University Press, 1945, reprinted, Greenwood Press, 1970; (with Alta Jablow) *Rainbow in the Morning* (illustrated by Abner Graboff), Abelard-Schuman, 1956; *Ready or Not, Here I Come* (illustrated by Garry Mackenzie), Grosset & Dunlap, 1964, a later edition published as *A Treasury of Games,* 1969; (adapter) *The Tale of a Black Cat* (illustrated by Alan Cober), Holt, 1966; (adapter) *The Wild Ducks and the Goose* (illustrated by A. Cober), Holt, 1968; (reteller) *Painting the Moon: A Folktale from Estonia* (illustrated by Adrienne Adams), Dutton, 1970; (reteller) *The Grindstone of God: A Fable* (illustrated by Bernarda Bryson), Holt, 1970.

Editor: *The Penguin Book of Sonnets,* Penguin, 1943; *Counting Out* (illustrated by Elizabeth Ripley), Oxford University Press, 1946, a later edition published as *Counting-Out Rhymes,* Dover, 1970; *A Rocket in My Pocket* (illustrated by Susanne Suba), Holt, 1948, reissued, 1968; (under pseudonym Robert North) *The Treasure Book of Riddles* (illustrated by Ruth Wood), Grosset & Dunlap, 1950; (with Sula Benet) *The American Riddle Book* (illustrated by Marc Simont), Abelard-Schuman, 1954; (with S. Benet) *Riddles of Many Lands* (illustrated by Lili Cassel), Abelard-Schuman, 1956; (with Ben Botkin) *The Illustrated Book of American Folklore: Stories, Legends, Tall Tales, Riddles, and Rhymes* (illustrated by Irv Docktor), Grosset & Dunlap, 1958; *I Saw a Rocket Walk a Mile* (illustrated by John E. Johnson), Holt, 1965; *A World of Nonsense: Strange and Humorous Tales from Many Lands* (illustrated by J. E. Johnson), Holt, 1968; (with A. Jablow) *The Man in the Moon: Sky Tales from Many Lands* (illustrated by Peggy Wilson), Holt, 1969.

SIDELIGHTS: Written under the pseudonym, James West, *Plainville, U.S.A.* describes life in a rural American community during the late 1930's and early 1940's. The *Annals of the American Academy of Political and Social Science* commented, ''Those who do not know American rural life, especially 'backwoods' rural life, will find this book as interesting as a novel, because the type of life that Plainvillers live will seem novel to them. The author leaves no phase of

I had a little dog, his name was Ball;
When I'd give him a little, he wanted it all.
■ (From *A Rocket in My Pocket* by Carl Withers. Illustrated by Susanne Suba.)

What is the easiest way to swallow a door?
--Bolt it.
■ (From the *American Riddle Book* by Carl Withers and Sula Benet. Illustrated by Marc Simont.)

life untouched or undescribed. Those who are interested in a highly analytical account of contemporary rural life will also read the book with interest, if for no other reason than to observe what among the commonplace an anthropologist considers significant." *Library Journal* added, "Well arranged, comprehensive and particularly pleasing in presentation. Interesting now as a detailed picture of life in a rural town and will be fascinating to future generations. Gradations in customs and manners are shown objectively and yet with a warmly human touch. In approach and interpretation, it sets a standard for these studies."

Horn Book described *A Rocket in My Pocket* as "... a large collection of the contemporary rhymes of American children, living folklore gathered by the well-known anthropo-

gist, Carl Withers, from cities, towns, and villages across the United States. . . . The book makes hilarious group reading and will open ears and eyes to a new interest available around us. The delightful illustrations by Susanne Suba are a perfect combination of naivete and sophistication. Another valuable feature of the book is the charming essay by Mr. Withers about this kind of folklore and its significance." *Booklist* noted, "Will be of more interest, probably to folklorists and to adults concerned with the social growth and development of children than to children themselves."

With Sula Benet, Withers compiled the *American Riddle Book*. The *New York Times* description included, "There are true riddles, conundrums, charades, puns, teasers—a compendium of fine nonsense and wit. The title refers to the audience rather than the sources, for some of these are centuries old, and one of the most interesting sections is that containing riddles from the Philippines, Persia, Latvia, and other unexpected sources." *Library Journal* added, "The compilers, who are folklorists and anthropologists, have chosen and classified the riddles in ways which are sure to interest and amuse children. . . ."

One of Carl Withers' most recent efforts was the retelling of a folktale from Estonia, *Painting the Moon*. *Horn Book*'s comments included, "The story is told in a matter-of-fact manner, the ludicrous proceedings being allowed to speak for themselves. But the artist [Adrienne Adams] has caught and emphasized all of the intrinsic humor, adding a gentle slapstick to her characteristically beautiful pictures, it is gratifying to the adult reader to find, unobtrusively at the end of the book, full bibliographic information on the source of the story." *Library Journal* noted, "Adrienne Adams' . . . full-color illustrations add much humor to the tale of the devil's decision to paint the moon black. Children—even young scientists who know the true explanation for the moon's spots—will appreciate the story, and storytellers will find the text eminently tellable."

(Died January 5, 1970)

Open your mouth and shut your eyes.
I'll give you something to make you wise.
■ (From *A Rocket in My Pocket* by Carl Withers. Pictures by William Wiesner.)

(From *Super Sam and the Salad Garden* by Patty Wolcott. Illustrated by Marc Tolon Brown.)

PATTY WOLCOTT

WOLCOTT, Patty 1929-

PERSONAL: Born September 26, 1929, in Lowell, Mass.; daughter of John Gilmore and Priscilla (Clapp) Wolcott; married Raoul Berger (a legal historian), April 22, 1967. *Education:* Wheelock College, B.S. in Ed. (with honors), 1952; Columbia University, M.A., 1963. *Religion:* Unitarian Universalist. *Home:* 140 Jennie Dugan Rd., Concord, Mass. 01742.

CAREER: Teacher in public schools in Arlington Co., Va., 1952-55, and Weston, Mass., 1955-56; Houghton Mifflin Co., Boston, Mass., editor of elementary textbooks, 1956-59; Artists & Writers Press, New York, N.Y., editor of children's trade books, 1960-61; teacher of kindergarten in Nassau, Bahamas, 1961-62, and at Teachers College, Columbia, New York, N.Y., 1963-66; assistant to author, Richard Lewis in New York, N.Y., 1966-67; full-time writer, 1969—. Volunteer teacher of creative writing to children in Dorchester, Mass., 1971. *Member:* Kappa Delta Pi. *Awards, honors:* *Tunafish Sandwiches* was selected by the National Science Teachers Association-Children's Book Council as one of the "Outstanding Science Trade Books for Children in 1975."

WRITINGS—Children's books; all published by Addison-Wesley, except as noted: *The Reef of Coral,* Singer-Random House, 1969; *The Cake Story,* 1974; *The Forest Fire,* 1974; *I'm Going to New York to Visit the Queen,* 1974; *The Marvelous Mud Washing Machine* (Scholastic Book Club selection), 1974; *Where Did That Naughty Little Hamster Go?,* 1974; *Beware of a Very Hungry Fox,* 1975; *My*

Shadow and I, 1975; *Pickle Pickle Pickle Juice* (Scholastic Book Club selection), 1975; *Super Sam and the Salad Garden,* 1975; *Tunafish Sandwiches,* 1975.

A filmstrip-cassette ensemble, built around all ten of Wolcott's "First Read-by-Myself Books" was published by Instructional/Communications Technology-Taylor Associates, 1978.

SIDELIGHTS: "My teachers college education gave me an invaluable insight into the child's mind, an appreciation of the child's world. After my graduation from college, I taught five and six year olds for a number of years. The children dictated stories to me while I was teaching them to read. I loved their stories, their language. Those dictations opened for me the minds and hearts of children. I started to look at children's books more closely and to contribute some of my experiences to children's books. Since then, I have been associated with them, editing and writing through the years. Though I devote full time to writing now, I try to be with young children whenever I can. I read my manuscripts to them, and they give me helpful and inspiring advice.

"My interest in children's books was stimulated by Professor Leland Jacobs at Teachers College, with whom I studied children's literature and writing for children, and became far more aware of the children's book as an art form.

"I wrote my 'First Read-by-Myself Books,' because as a teacher, I felt most published easy-to-read trade books had too many words for children at the very beginning of their reading lives, and that a means of exciting the interest of these children was essential. My other writing for children, including *The Reef of Coral,* mentioned above, is of a different style. There I attempt to write a story book with lyrical overtones."

FOR MORE INFORMATION SEE: Saturday Review/ World, November 30, 1974; *Reading Teacher,* April, 1975; *Learning,* May/June, 1975; *School Library Journal,* September, 1975.

WOOD, Edgar A(llardyce) 1907- (Kerry Wood)

PERSONAL: Born June 2, 1907, in New York, N.Y.; moved to Canada, 1909, naturalized citizen, 1973; son of William Campbell (an insurance agent) and Elizabeth (Callon) Wood; married Marjorie Marshall, February 10, 1936; children: Rondo (daughter), Heather Kathleen (Mrs. Patrick David F. Ion), Walden Gregory. *Education:* Attended public schools in Alberta. *Religion:* Protestant. *Residence:* Red Deer, Alberta, Canada.

CAREER: Full-time free-lance writer, 1924—. Local correspondent for five Alberta newspapers, 1926-36, columnist, 1926-73; archery tackle manufacturer, 1937-44; radio broadcaster and scriptwriter for Canadian Broadcasting Corp. (CBC) and independent stations, 1939-73; television scriptwriter for the programs "Rope Around the Sun" and "The Outrider," and host of programs "The Kerry Wood Storybook," "Outdoors with Kerry Wood," and "Playtime" for CBC, 1958-65. Secretary-treasurer of Red Deer Public Library board, 1930-45. *Member:* Alberta Natural History Society (life member; sanctuary chairman, 1936-64; former president, secretary-treasurer, and committee chairman), Alberta Federation of Naturalists (life member). *Awards, honors*—For books: *Cowboy Yarns for Young Folk* was named runner-up children's book of the year by the Canadian Library Association, 1951; Governor-General medals for juvenile literature, 1955, for *The Map-Maker,* and 1957, for *The Great Chief;* first Vicky Metcalf award from Canadian Authors Association, 1963, for "consistently good writing of material inspirational to Canadian youth." Other awards include grants from John S. Ewart Foundation, 1954 and 1957, and from Canada Council, 1960; Alberta Historical Society award of the year, 1965; LL.D. from University of Alberta, 1969; achievement award from Government of Alberta, 1975.

WRITINGS—All under name Kerry Wood; all juveniles, except as noted: (Self-illustrated with A. H. Short) *The Magpie Menace,* privately printed, 1936; *Robbing the Roost* (adapted from author's radio script), privately printed, 1938; *I'm a Gaggle Man Myself* (adapted from author's radio script), privately printed, 1940; *Three Mile Bend,* Ryerson Press, 1945; *Birds and Animals in the Rockies,* H. R. Larson, 1946; *A Nature Guide for Farmers* (adult), H. R. Larson, 1947.

Cowboy Yarns for Young Folk, Copp Clark, 1951; (self-illustrated) *The Sanctuary,* privately printed, 1952; *Wild Winter,* Houghton, 1954; *The Map-Maker,* Macmillan (Toronto), 1955; *Willowdale,* McClelland & Stewart, 1956; *The Great Chief,* Macmillan (Toronto), 1957; *The Queen's Cowboy,* Macmillan (Toronto), 1960; *Great Horned Mac Owl,* privately printed, 1961; *The Boy and The Buffalo,* Macmillan (Toronto), 1963; *Mickey the Beaver and Others,* Macmillan (Toronto), 1964; *A Lifetime of Service: George Moon,* privately printed, 1966; (self-illustrated) *A Corner of Canada,* privately printed, 1966; *A Time for Fun,* privately printed, 1967; *Samson's Long Ride,* Collins (Toronto), 1968; *The Medicine Man,* privately printed, 1968.

(Self-illustrated with wife, Marjorie Wood) *The Creek,* privately printed, 1970; *The Icelandic-Canadian Poet: Stephan G. Stephansson,* privately printed, 1974; (illustrated with photographs by the author and others) *Red Deer: A Love Story,* privately printed, 1975; (illustrated by M. Wood) *Bessie, The Coo,* privately printed, 1975.

Work represented in over seventy school texts and fifty anthologies. Writer of an estimated sixty-two hundred short stories, eight thousand magazine articles for Canadian, American, and British publications, nine thousand newspaper columns, and over three hundred television scripts.

WORK IN PROGRESS: Articles and short stories, "no books at the moment."

SIDELIGHTS: Wood decided to become a writer at the age of twelve and has been a full-time professional since the age of sixteen. His career began when a school administrator urged him to drop out of high school and spend the time writing. Since the day he left school in 1926, he has worn out nineteen typewriters and gained the distinction of being one of only three Canadian authors who were able to live off their writings during the Depression. A devoted naturalist, Wood is especially proud of helping to establish twenty-six wildlife sanctuaries across North America.

"My love of nature developed in early childhood and increased steadily. Through its study grew my interest in Indians and their history; personal friends among them added to my profound respect.

EDGAR A. WOOD

"My scholarly father encouraged and guided me through a wide course of reading, making sure that I understood the books. From him and helpful librarians came my determination to write, and the advice and confidence of a high school teacher precipitated the career. The family background of nine ministers and deaconesses, plus the absorbing responsibilities in the Scouting movement, perhaps, helped a natural tendency toward service.

"The writings of P. A. Taverner, ornithologist, Henry David Thoreau, naturalist-philosopher, plus those of Peter McArthur and Robert Stead were certainly influential.

"I have always felt that writing for children is an important part of my work. A writer should exhibit sincerity, a feeling of accurate knowledge throughout his book. There should be a story achievement, even though it may contain some sadness. It should have believably natural characters, usually some humor, be of interest to both children and adults, having values which endure regardless of age, locality or era. A book may instruct, entertain, or inspire. Nonsense and fantasy have some importance, but sarcasm and satire should never be used in children's literature.

"Two of the most gratifying honors that have come to me are the Vicky Metcalf Award, and the librarians' estimate in 1969 that 500,000 Canadian children annually read my books.

"Two of the most interesting audiences I have ever addressed were the New York State librarians in conference at Lake Placid, and a group of holidayers under the auspices of the Institute of the Blind at Sylvan Lake, Alberta. The former: listeners kept rising and leaving the hall, then returning with many more delegates in tow! The latter: I had gauged my talk to be attuned to their ears and what nature they were hearing, rather than to their eyes and what they might see around their camping area. Both groups' responses were tremendously enthusiastic.

"Of very great influence and help in my lifetime have been the members of my family: my elder brother, Thaddy, until his death in 1918, my father throughout his life, and my wife, Marjorie, and our three children. Marjorie's encouragement and assistance in our forty years of happy marriage have been of considerable strength to me."

HOBBIES AND OTHER INTERESTS: Walking, nature observations, nature-oriented handicrafts (especially archery and wood carving).

FOR MORE INFORMATION SEE: Calgary Herald, May 5, 1965; *Vancouver Sun,* February 10, 1967; *Ottawa Citizen,* September 20, 1969; *Western Producer,* August 30, 1973; *Red Deer Advocate,* June 2-June 15, 1976.

WOODARD, Carol   1929-

PERSONAL: Born January 19, 1929, in Buffalo, N.Y.; daughter of Harold A. and Violet (Landsittel) Young; mar-

CAROL WOODARD

Even Tickles the cat purred a song when Lori put some milk in her dish. ■ (From *It's Fun to Have a Birthday* by Carol Woodard. Illustrated by June Goldsborough.)

ried Ralph Arthur Woodard (an engineer), August 19, 1950; children: Camaron, Carsen, Cooper. *Education:* Hartwick College, B.A., 1950; Syracuse University, M.A., 1952; State University of New York at Buffalo, Ph.D., 1972. *Office:* State University of New York College at Buffalo, 1300 Elmwood Ave., Buffalo, N.Y. 14222.

CAREER: State University of New York College at Buffalo, associate professor of human development and early childhood, 1969—. Consultant to Lutheran Church in America. *Member:* National Association for Education of Young Children, Pi Lambda Theta.

WRITINGS—Adult: Ways to Teach 3's to 5's, Lutheran Church Press, 1965.

Juveniles: *Can I Help?,* Lutheran Church Press, 1968; *Time for Fun,* Lutheran Church Press, 1968; *The Busy Family,* Fortress, 1969; *The Very Special Baby,* Fortress, 1969; *It's Fun to Have a Birthday,* Fortress, 1970; *The Wet Walk,* Fortress, 1970; *It's Nice to Have a Special Friend,* Fortress, 1970.

Contributor to magazines.

WORK IN PROGRESS: Developing Concepts of Music and Movement, for Denison.

SIDELIGHTS: "Many of my books for young children concerned the activities and experiences which my own children enjoyed. My children also served as my chief critics and offered invaluable suggestions. My more recent writings concern early childhood material designed to assist the student teacher in the field setting. Teacher education and program development are my major areas of interest related to my vocation while reading and gardening are great for relaxation."

WORLINE, Bonnie Bess 1914-

PERSONAL: Born August 3, 1914, in El Dorado, Kan.; daughter of Robert H. (an attorney) and Grace (a teacher and social worker; maiden name, Miller) Worline; married Irvill Courtner King (a clergyman and teacher), March 27, 1937; children: Courtner Worline, April Marian (Mrs. Donald Schirmer), Waveland Irvill Robert. *Education:* University of Chicago, A.B., 1935; University of Pittsburgh, M.A., 1945; University of Kansas, further graduate study, 1951-60. *Politics:* Liberal. *Religion:* Protestant. *Home:* 279 J St., Brawley, Calif. 92227. *Office:* Department of English, San Diego State University, Imperial Valley Campus, 720 Heber, Calexico, Calif. 92213.

CAREER: Hammond Christian Center, Hammond, Ind., resident teacher, 1937; Rankin Christian Center, Rankin, Pa., resident teacher, 1938-40; KCKN-Radio, Kansas City, Kan., continuity editor, 1942-44; Gorham State College, Gorham, Maine, director of public relations and publications, 1946-51, instructor in English, 1946-51, head of department, 1946-51; University of Kansas, Lawrence, instructor in English, 1951-61; San Diego State University, Calexico, assistant professor of English, 1964-77. Director of special education for the high school in Brawley, Calif., 1961-70; director of Hipass Summer Camp for the Retarded; member of local Area Health Planning Commission and Mental Health Association. *Member:* National Council of Teachers of English, Brawley California Teachers Association (president, 1965-67), California College and University Faculty Association, Writers Group (Imperial Valley), Imperial Valley Association for the Retarded (organizer), Modern Language Association.

WRITINGS: Sod House Adventure (juvenile), Longmans, 1956, reissued as *The Children Who Stayed Alone,* Scholastic Book Services, 1965. Author of novelettes, published serially in *Chicago Daily News.* Contributor to magazines and newspapers. Editor of *IMP* (at San Diego State University, Imperial Valley Campus), 1974-76.

WORK IN PROGRESS: Sod Schoolhouse, a sequel to *The Children Who Stayed Alone; Mythology of the Western World,* for high school students; *Grease the Inside of the Pan!,* a manual for people who work with older retarded children; *What Color Is God's Skin?,* fiction; *Meredith,* novel; *Manzanita Chronicles,* novel; *Defender of Her People: A Biography; Primer of English Composition for Confused Adults.*

SIDELIGHTS: "I was born in Kansas of educated, pioneer-stock parents with a large, close-knit family clan in the background. Winters were spent in Kansas City, summers in the country at family homesteads sharing life with cousins, and at our own summer home in Missouri on the edge of the Ozark region, where I made friends with an entirely different group of people. Sharing daily activities with a large variety of friends, both adults and children, stimulated my interest in learning all sorts of facts and skills, and in telling about them. Always I wanted to write, always I did write, always I was encouraged by family and adult friends, including demanding but stimulating teachers. A rigorous two-year high-school journalism course drilled me in accurate observation, organization of material, and working under time pressure. I won some Quill and Scroll honors for feature stories and for a weekly humor column I wrote for the school paper.

BONNIE BESS WORLINE

"I was graduated from high school in June, 1930, when the Great Depression had just hit, and suddenly life became a matter of day-to-day survival. My covered-wagon grandmothers had preached and practiced that anyone can do anything, and I began to learn, by following their example, that one learns to do by doing. I held such widely varied jobs as children's life-guard, tutor to the blind, domestic worker, hospital social worker, translator from Latin to English for a Hungarian philosophy professor—and many, many others. Always through periods of discouragement I sustained myself with the reminder that it all was good copy for the future—grist for the mill in that dreamed-of-day when I would be free to write stories.

"At seventeen, a graduate of the local academic junior college, I entered The University of Chicago in 1932 with a full tuition scholarship, and $37.50 saved (after helping a suddenly impoverished family) from profits of a summer preschool I had organized and run with my sister in our home. In bread-line troubled, Capone-infested Chicago I earned my keep, graduated, landed a job writing catalogue copy for Montgomery Ward and Company, and with the urging of Thornton Wilder, my teacher and advisor at the university, I began to write and sell fiction to The Chicago Daily News Syndicate and various religious story papers.

"In 1937 I married a minister, and in the following years with him lived and worked as a Home Missionary in metropolitan and in company-towns and in rural settlement houses in various states, finished a master's degree in fiction technique, was a paid speaker for adult education and youth groups, edited small, mimeographed magazines for small community organizations, had two children, taught journalism and advertising in junior college, for five years headed

He dipped water into the washbasin on its low bench, made a great lather with the bar of homemade soap, and delighted the younger ones by blowing bubbles through his clenched fists. ▪ (From *The Children Who Stayed Alone* by Bonnie Bess Worline. Illustrated by Walter Barrows.)

the English department at Gorham State College (Maine) while functioning as a preacher's wife on Peak's Island, Maine, helping develop our small farm on the edge of Gorham, and commuting by ferry and car through the Maine winters.

"In 1951 we moved to Lawrence, Kansas where I taught English at the University of Kansas, studied for a Ph.D., had another baby, wrote and sold more story-paper serials and a few articles on educational methods. In the summer of 1953 my husband and son were at camp in Maine, and I asked my nine-year old daughter for special cooperation while I met a publication deadline. She agreed to get meals for both of us and keep the pack of neighboring faculty children out for the duration if, in turn, I would write a 'real' story for her. Not about stupid things like people getting married, but one that she would not be ashamed to show her friends. Specifically, she ordered a book in which (1) the main character was a girl, (2) she had a brother a little younger (hers was a little older), (3) there would be little brothers and sisters (she had none yet), (4) Palomino horses would be included.

"She did prepare us quite adequate meals. Unfortunately, I had not negotiated for dish-washing. We ate our last meal from muffin pans, the only clean containers left in the house. Together we did a TREMENDOUS dish-washing, and I faced the blank paper for my daughter's order. I had never

written a story for children. I had, indeed, told thousands and thousands, to groups as well as to my own children. But I could think of nothing to fit my new assignment. Rummaging in my memory, I suddenly recalled a story I had written in fifth grade, when I was ten, just about my daughter's age. It had been for my grandmother. She loved a picture of a coyote on a snowy prairie, howling toward a small cabin from which a feeble light shone through one small window. She had said it reminded her of her own early pioneering days. My father and aunt were giving her the picture for Christmas, and meanwhile it was hanging in our study at home. I had been fascinated by it, and began to wonder who was in that cabin? How did they feel as they listened to the coyote? How would I feel knowing I was so isolated in miles and miles of empty land?

"I had begun to answer my own questions on paper. A story grew which became my Christmas present to my grandmother. She thought it was wonderful. I was old enough to realize that that was because she was my grandmother. But I was warmed then by her enthusiasm.

"I had never tired of listening to her stories, and those of her friends, about their pioneering experiences; some of those people and their adventures began to come alive again. I discovered that my mother had a copy of my early story, and I used it almost unchanged for the focus of what became *The Sod House Adventure*. I added some preliminaries, and a supplement and conclusion, but the episode which has since proved most popular with readers, the knock on the cabin door in the middle of the night, is almost exactly as I wrote it when I was ten. I am not sure that this is an encouraging sign of artistic progress.

"The writing took a little over a week. My daughter was satisfied, a pride of neighborhood children sat on the floor with popcorn and listened to it and pronounced it good, and I was off the hook and went on to grade papers and write for newspaper-reading adults.

"In the fall, by request of some of the children who had heard it, the book was read to their classes by various elementary teachers. The next fall the teachers asked for it again; a janitor borrowed it and dropped it into the oil in the boiler room, and requested a copy for his mother when I had it retyped. The teachers urged that I publish it. I explained that getting a book published is a time-consuming art in itself, that I had no contacts for children's books, and probably no one would want it anyway. So I left the matter. My daughter, however, despite my pessimism, mailed it to Longmans, Green and Company because they had published her favorite book of the moment. They bought *Sod House* by return mail, eroding my authority in my daughter's eyes. In 1965 Scholastic reprinted it as *The Children Who Stayed Alone*, and it was again featured by them in January, 1976. In the fall of 1975 it had been listed as one of the all-time best sellers for its age group.

"Meanwhile, readers had regularly written to ask for more. But I was busy and delayed with teaching, studying, mothering, and community activities. *The Sod Schoolhouse*, a sequel, is now at last at Scholastic. Its origins are more complex. It includes material from tales of the pioneers, experiences of my father and his family as students in country school, of my grandfathers as administrators, of my mother and one grandmother as teachers, and of my own periodic attendance at the country school featured in the story. Also reflected are experiences of my husband as teacher in several such schools, and of my sons as students, one at a school in Maine, the other in California, and of my personal experiences as a teacher of methods with students who were teaching in one or two room country schools. I have been professionally involved with the entire gamut of educational theories and practices, and I increasingly am convinced that values attributed to the self-contained one-room, eight-grade elementary school, given an excellent teacher, are not mere nostalgia. Of interest, at least to me, is the fact that *Sod Schoolhouse* has circulated in manuscript among teachers, who have claimed to find in it some helpful insights into children's interests and ways of learning.

"In any event, the final push to get *Sod Schoolhouse* finished came when a child in the fifth grade class, my now grown daughter, was teaching brought her a book, saying, 'Mrs. Schirmer, I loved this, I think you should read it. But I wish there was another to tell what happened after the children started to school.' And there was her *Sod House Adventure,* in another cover, and under the name of *The Children Who Stayed Alone,* but still with my daughter listed in the dedication. She said, telling me about it, 'Mother, it is time you finished that sequel.'

WORTIS, Avi 1937-
(Avi)

PERSONAL: Given name is pronounced Ah-vee; born in 1937 in New York, N.Y.; son of Joseph (a physician) and Helen (Zunser) Wortis; married Joan Gabriner (a weaver),

AVI WORTIS

Seth studied his face for signs of generosity. ■ (From *Emily Upham's Revenge* by Avi. Illustrated by Paul O. Zelinsky.)

November 1, 1963; children: Shaun, Kevin. *Education:* University of Wisconsin, Madison, B.A., 1959, M.A., 1962; Columbia University, M.S. in L.S., 1964. *Home:* 89 West Bridge St., New Hope, Pa. 18938. *Agent:* Dorothy Markinko, McIntosh & Otis, Inc., 475 Fifth Ave., New York, N.Y. 10017. *Office:* Roscoe L. West Library, Trenton State College, Trenton, N.J. 08625.

CAREER: New York Public Library, New York, N.Y., librarian for Theatre Collection, 1962-70; Trenton State College, Trenton, N.J., librarian, 1970—. *Member:* Authors Guild of Authors League of America, Mystery Writers of America. *Awards, honors: Snail Tale* was named one of the best books of the year by British Book Council, 1973; *No More Magic* was a Mystery Writer's of America runner-up, 1975, for "Best Mystery of the Year."

WRITINGS—All for children; all under name Avi: *Things That Sometimes Happened,* Doubleday, 1970; *Snail Tale,* Pantheon, 1972; *No More Magic* (novel), Pantheon, 1975; *Captain Grey* (novel), Pantheon, 1977; *Emily Upham's Revenge* (novel), Pantheon, 1978. Contributor to library journals.

WORK IN PROGRESS: The Protecting of Ned, a novel for children, under name Avi; a history of American children's literature.

SIDELIGHTS: "I was born into a family with a writing tradition. Two great-grandfathers had been writers. My grandmother was a playwright. With a house full of books, being read to every night, a near-by library, the idea that writing was a splendid thing to do could hardly fail to make its mark on me.

"Not surprisingly I was a big reader, reading all sorts of things, children's books, adult books, and not the least, comic books. Beyond reading, my grandparents were excellent story tellers, and my mother read to me and my twin sister (the poet and critic, Emily Ledier) nightly. I can even recall telling my own tales of adventure to a slightly younger cousin when quite young. I do believe that if you want to be a writer you have to read a lot.

"Despite this background my first desire was to become an airplane designer, then a biologist. After my junior year in high-school my parents were informed that I was in desperate need of a tutor for somehow I had never learned to write or to spell.

"That summer I met every day with a wonderful teacher who not only taught me writing basics, but also instilled in me the conviction that I wanted to be a writer myself. Perhaps it was stubbornness! It was generally agreed that was one thing I could not possibly do!

"My journey to children's literature was not direct. First it was the theatre, playwriting. Then it was writing novels for adult readers. In the meantime I had all kinds of jobs: sign printer (sometimes with spelling mistakes), carpenter, theatre coach, a whole host of jobs I never did with much satisfaction or success.

"At last I found an opportunity to work in a library. I was home at last! There I found no conflict between my desire to write and the demands of good librarianship. Quickly, I enrolled in library school, attending night classes. I still work as a librarian as well as write, so I am surrounded by books, morning, noon and night.

"Even then it was only when I had children of my own and had begun to invent stories for them that I thought of writing children's books. Once begun I soon left other writing interests and concentrated on books for young people.

"While I am a fast writer, and never at a loss for ideas, I do a very great deal of re-writing, over and over again. I'm never convinced I can't improve a book, be it only a word or two.

"After writing my books a number of times I try them out on my children. Their reactions are always useful. More re-writing and my wife is asked to criticize. More re-writing and then visits to local school rooms. More re-writing! Then to my agent. More re-writing. Then to the publisher. Actually, I do my least re-writing then.

"The history of children's literature fascinates me, and from time to time I teach college courses or speak to groups about it. When I have the time I visit flea markets and used book stores for I am building up a collection of old and recent children's books. It makes me proud to put my own books in the midst of them all!"

WRIGHT, Judith   1915-

PERSONAL: Born May 31, 1915, in Armidale, New South Wales, Australia; daughter of Phillip Arundell and Ethel (Bigg) Wright; married Jack Philip McKinney (a philosophi-

JUDITH WRIGHT

cal writer); children: Meredith Anne. *Education:* Attended New South Wales Correspondence School and New England Girls' School; University of Sydney, arts degree. *Politics:* Swing voter. *Mailing address:* c/- Post Office, Braidwood, NSW 2622, Australia.

CAREER: J. Walter Thompson (advertising agency), Sydney, Australia, secretary, 1938-39; University of Sydney, Sydney, Australia, secretary, 1940-42; Australian Universities Commission, Brisbane, Australia, clerk, 1944-46; University of Queensland, Brisbane, Queensland, Australia, statistician, 1946-49. Part time lecturer in Australian literature at various Australian universities. President, Wildlife Preservation Society of Queensland, 1962-76. *Member:* Society of Authors (Australia; council member), Australian Academy of the Humanities (fellow). *Awards, honors:* Grace Leven Prize, 1953; D.Litt., University of Queensland, 1962, University of New England, 1963; *Encyclopaedia Britannica* Award, 1964.

WRITINGS—Poetry: *The Moving Image,* Meanjin, 1946, 2nd edition, 1953; *Woman to Man,* Angus & Robertson, 1949, 2nd edition, 1955; *The Gateway,* Angus & Robertson, 1953; *The Two Fires,* Angus & Robertson, 1955; *Birds,* Angus & Robertson, 1960; *Five Senses,* Angus & Robertson 1963, revised edition, 1972; *City Sunrise,* limited edition, Shapcott Press, 1964; *The Other Half,* Angus & Robertson, 1966; *Collected Poems,* Angus & Robertson, 1971, second edition, 1974; *Alive,* Angus & Robertson, 1972; *Fourth Quarter,* Angus & Robertson, 1976.

Editor: *Australian Poetry,* Angus & Robertson, 1948; *A Book of Australian Verse,* Oxford University Press, 1956, 2nd revised edition, 1969; *New Land, New Language: An Anthology of Australian Verse,* Oxford University Press, 1957; *Judith Wright* (poetry), Angus & Robertson, 1963; *Shaw Neilson* (biography and selected poetry), Angus & Robertson, 1963; (with Andrew Thompson) *The Poet's Pen,* Jacaranda, 1965; *Witnesses of Spring,* Angus & Robertson, 1968.

Other: *The Generations of Men,* Oxford University Press, 1959, new edition, 1966; *Kings of the Dingoes* (juvenile), Oxford University Press, 1959; *Charles Harpur* (biography and criticism), Lansdowne Press, 1963; *The Day the Mountains Played* (juvenile), Jacaranda Press, 1963; *Range the Mountains High* (juvenile), Lansdowne Press, 1963; *Country Towns* (juvenile), Oxford University Press, 1964; *Preoccupations in Australian Poetry* (history and criticism), Oxford University Press, 1965, new edition, 1967; *The River and the Road* (juvenile), Lansdowne Press, 1966; *Because I Was Invited,* Oxford University Press, 1975; *Charles Harpur,* Oxford University Press, 1977; *The Coral Battleground* (documentary), Nelson, 1977.

WORK IN PROGRESS: Research for a continuation of *The Generations of Men.*

SIDELIGHTS: "All my childhood was lived in the country, at a time when most people could ride and there were still few cars. My own ancestors had lived on the land ever since we first came to Australia early in the nineteenth century, and all of them were pastoralists running sheep and cattle on various stations—the Australian word for 'ranches.' My own family lived more than thirty miles from the nearest town, on a station called 'Wallamumbi.' So from the beginning I was taught to ride and to work with cattle and sheep. The nearest school was too far for us to ride there, so my two brothers and I did our lessons by correspondence, until I went to boarding-school at thirteen. After those years of freedom, I didn't much enjoy the experience.

"I had begun writing verse and stories before I went to school, and wanted to be a writer. My first book of verse was published in 1946 and since then I have published many. My books for children were really written for my daughter Meredith, and they all come from my own childhood and the stories I heard then of the days of early settlement in Australia. The first of them, *Kings of the Dingoes,* is about a little white Pomeranian dog I once had, and his friend Benbow, and their adventures with a wild dingo pack (dingoes are Australian native dogs). The second, *The Day the Mountains Played,* is based on an Aboriginal legend, and the third, *Range the Mountains High,* is about a bushranger (the Australian word for bandit) who used to hold up the gold escorts in New South Wales in the nineteenth century and was a local legend in the district where I grew up. The fourth, *The River and the Road,* is about an imaginary family who lived in a flourmill which my own great-grandfather used to run in the nineteenth century.

"I have only written one book of verse for children, about Australian birds. I love birds, and have worked for a long time as president of a wildlife preservation society. The strange and beautiful wildlife of Australia is disappearing fast as Australians clear their trees and change the lovely country that I remember in my childhood as full of birds and animals.

"So I suppose my books for children all come from what I remember of Australia when I was a child myself. We all loved horses and dogs, and some of the characters I like best in the stories are dogs and horses, and Australian wild animals. Now that most people live in cities, not many Australian children are lucky enough to know much about the kind of country life I had myself, or even about the history of Australia.

"Now that my daughter is grown up, I have stopped writing books for children. But I think I probably enjoyed writing those stories more than any of the other books I have written."

WYNTER, Edward (John) 1914-

PERSONAL: Born January 24, 1914, in England; son of Edward (a physiotherapist) and Ida (an actress; maiden name, Thomson) Wynter; married Norah Marsh, December 1, 1945; children: John Howard. *Education:* Attended Marine School of South Shields, 1930-35; Camden Teachers College, London, teachers certificate, 1947; College of Craft Education, M.C.C.Ed., 1953. *Politics:* "Moderate." *Religion:* Church of England. *Home:* 24, West Avenue, Three Bridges, Crawley, Sussex RH10 1SJ, England.

CAREER: Marine engineering apprentice in England, 1930-35; De Havilland Aircraft Factory, Watford, England, assistant planning engineer, 1943-44; Old Hale Way Boys' Secondary School, Hitchin, Hertfordshire, England, teacher, 1947-49; Westfield Boys' Secondary School, Hinckley,

EDWARD WYNTER

Leicester, England, teacher, 1949-50; The Player Secondary Boys' School, Nottingham, England, teacher, 1950-54; Hazelwick Comprehensive School, Crawley, Sussex, England, teacher, 1954-76, head of technical department, 1958-76, part time art teacher, 1976—. *Military service:* Royal Navy, engine room artificer, 1935-39; served in Norway, West Indies, and North and South America. *Member:* Assistant Masters Association.

WRITINGS—For young people: *Metalcraft,* Longman Group, 1966; (editor) Foong Kee Yoong, *Woodwork, Metalwork, and Related Drafting,* Longman Group, 1968; *Woodwork,* Longman Group, 1970; *Using Woodwork Tools,* A. & C. Black, 1974.

WORK IN PROGRESS: Reference Book of Tools, completion expected in 1978; *Technical Drawing,* 1979.

SIDELIGHTS: "During my early years in teaching, woodwork was the traditional, well established major craft taught in schools. There was a little elementary metalwork being taught in some schools but on the whole this was limited to simple work usually done in a corner of the woodwork room, and more of a sideline. . . . The school courses I planned were as broad as possible, bearing in mind the educational needs of the pupils. Wrought iron work, foundry work, tool making, art metalwork and jewelry were taken to various stages but the accent was on model engineering, and many simple working model steam engines and electric motors were made.

"I consider myself most fortunate to have enjoyed my work so much. The vocational interests of pupils have often been awakened and quite a lot of boys and a few girls have gone into industry to follow courses of training both at the bench and the drawing board.

"Man is a tool-using animal and most people enjoy using their hands and making things. Practical activity balances book learning and makes for a complete person. Increased leisure and mass production are two good reasons why people need to learn how to design and make things for themselves.

"It is a most satisfying and enjoyable experience to create beautiful objects, and a rewarding experience to arouse and guide this interest in others."

HOBBIES AND OTHER INTERESTS: Gardening, photography, drawing and painting (water colors and oils), "tinkering about at the workbench and country walks with my wife and our Yorkshire terrier."

ZALLINGER, Jean (Day) 1918-

PERSONAL: Born February 15, 1918, in Boston, Mass.; daughter of John Farquharson and Mabel (Souter) Day; married Rudolph Franz Zallinger (an artist; teacher), September 27, 1941; children: Peter, Franz, Kristina, Lisa. *Education:* Attended Massachusetts College of Art, four years; Yale School of Fine Arts, B.F.A., 1942. *Home and office:* 5060 Ridge Road, North Haven, Conn. 06473.

CAREER: Illustrator. Paier School of Art, Hamden, Conn., instructor, 1967—. Women's Auxiliary, Yale, New Haven Hospital, vice-president, 1969-70. *Exhibitions:* John Slade Ely Gallery, New Haven, Conn., 1971. *Member:* Peabody Museum Associates, Audubon Society, Qunnipiac Valley

Art Gallery Associates (Yale), Committee on Selection for Shows at John Slade Ely Gallery, New Haven, Conn. *Awards, honors:* Purchase Prize, Paint & Clay Club, 1948.

ILLUSTRATOR: Butterfly Puzzle, Springbook Co., 1962; Aileen Fisher, *Valley of the Smallest,* Crowell, 1966; Julian May, *They Live in the Ice Age,* Holiday, 1967; J. J. McCoy, *House Sparrows, Ragmuffins of the City,* Seabury, 1968; Ford, *Water Boatman's Journey,* Seabury, 1969; Jean George, *The Moon of the Deer,* Crowell, 1969; Seymour Simon, *Discovering What Earthworms Do,* McGraw, 1969; Seymour Simon, *Discovering What Frogs Do,* McGraw, 1969; Helen Hoke, *First Book of Arctic Mammals,* Watts, 1969; George Mendoza, *Digger Wasp* (AIGA Award Book), Dial, 1969.

Taylor Alexander, *Botany,* Western, 1970; Ross E. Hutchins, *The Mayfly,* Addison-Wesley, 1970; Joanna Cole, *Cockroaches,* Morrow, 1970; Seymour Simon, *Discovering What Goldfish Do,* McGraw, 1970; George H. Kimble, *Hunters & Collectors,* McGraw, 1970; Frances Behnke, *What We Find When We Look Under Rocks,* McGraw, 1971; Seymour Simon, *Discovering What Gerbils Do,* McGraw, 1971; Lewis W. Walker, *Survival Under the Sun,* Doubleday, 1972; Burke Davis, *Biography of a Leaf,* Putnam, 1972; Alexander Martin, *Weeds,* Western, 1972; Julian May, *Plankton: Drifting Life of the Waters,* Holiday, 1972; Gladys Conklin, *Insects Build Their Homes,* Holiday, 1972; Francine Jacobs, *Sea Turtles,* Morrow, 1972; Mary Adrian, *Secret Neighbors,* Hastings, 1972; Lisbeth Zappler, *The*

JEAN DAY ZALLINGER

(From *The Natural History of the Tail* by Lisbeth Zappler. Illustrated by Jean Zallinger.)

Natural History of the Tail, Doubleday, 1972; Alan M. Fletcher, *Fishes That Hide,* Addison-Wesley, 1973; Seymour Simon, *Discovering What Crickets Do,* 1973; Seymour Simon, *Birds on Your Street,* Holiday, 1974; Mary Adrian, *Wildlife on the Watch: A Story of the Desert,* Hastings, 1974; Alice Hopf, *Biography of an Ant,* Putnam, 1974; Alice Hopf, *Biography of an Armadillo,* Putnam, 1975; Gladys Conklin, *I Like Beetles,* Holiday, 1975; Francine Jacobs, *An Ocean Desert: The Sargasso Sea,* Morrow, 1975; Francine Jacobs, *Secret Language of Animals,* Morrow, 1976; Gladys Conklin, *I Watch Flies,* Holiday, 1976; Wong and Vessel, *My Snail,* Addison-Wesley, 1976; Morton, *Herbs & Spices,* Western, 1976. Has also illustrated National Wildlife Butterfly Stamps.

WORK IN PROGRESS: Biography of a Fish Hawk by Burke Davis.

SIDELIGHTS: "I work mostly in prism color on Hereulens—Mylar—direct contact method—color separated—also, for the field guides, watercolor."

FOR MORE INFORMATION SEE: Illustrators of Children's Books: 1957-1966, Horn Book, 1968.

ZWEIFEL, Frances 1931-

PERSONAL: Born May 26, 1931, in Hampton, Va.; daughter of Robert William (an air force officer) and Helen (Huber) Wimsatt; married Richard Zweifel (a museum curator), July 30, 1956; children: Matthew, Kenneth, Ellen. *Education:* Trinity College (Washington, D.C.), B.A., 1952; University of Arizona, M.A., 1956. *Politics:* Ambiguous. *Religion:* Roman Catholic. *Home:* 412 Glendale Rd., Northvale, N.J. 07647.

CAREER: Free-lance biological illustrator; American Museum of Natural History, New York, N.Y., scientific illustrator, 1956-58.

WRITINGS: (Self-illustrated) *A Handbook of Biological Illustration,* University of Chicago Press, 1961; *Bony,* Harper, 1977.

Illustrator: Evelyn Shaw, *Alligator,* Harper, 1972.

SIDELIGHTS: "Love of animals and drawing led to biological illustrating. I work at home, between motherly and household duties. I work mainly in ink, pencil, and some watercolor. Drawings for scientists must be accurate: proportions, backgrounds, other plants and animals in background.

"I feel that illustrations for children's books should be equally accurate, but also lively, because children and animals are fun.

"When I was young, I wanted to be a veterinarian. But I became allergic to furry animals, so now I draw them instead of doctoring them.

"My husband is a herpetologist, which makes our life the most interesting one I know of. We travel to wherever he does his field research, mainly the American southwest and Georgia. We have lizards and snakes and frogs (all non-furry) for pets. We all love the desert and the Western mountains. The children are good field assistants.

"In illustrating *Alligator,* I used photographs and drew from life at The Bronx Zoo. My husband's expertise was invaluable.

"In writing *Bony,* I based the story on a pet squirrel we once had. The mischievous incidents all really happened.

"My children are my best critics, perceptive and accurate and outspoken."

More and more babies come out of their egg shells. But they cannot get out of the nest. ■ (From *Alligator* by Evelyn Shaw. Pictures by Frances Zweifel.)

SOMETHING ABOUT THE AUTHOR

CUMULATIVE INDEXES, VOLUMES 1-14
Illustrations and Authors

ILLUSTRATIONS INDEX

(In the following index, the number of the volume in which an illustrator's work appears is given *before* the colon, and the page on which it appears is given *after* the colon. For example, a drawing by Adams, Adrienne appears in Volume 2 on page 6, another drawing by her appears in Volume 3 on page 80, and another drawing in Volume 8 on page 1.)

Illustrations Index

Something about the Author

AUTHORS INDEX

(In the following index, the number of the volume in which an author's sketch appears is given *before* the colon, and the page on which it appears is given *after* the colon. For example, the sketch of Aardema, Verna, appears in Volume 4 on page 1). This index includes references to *Yesterday's Authors of Books for Children.*

Bauer, Helen, *2:* 14
Baum, Willi, *4:* 23
Baumann, Amy (Brown), *10:* 9
Baumann, Hans, *2:* 16
Bawden, Nina. *See* Kark, Nina Mary, *4:* 132
BB. *See* Watkins-Pitchford, D. J., *6:* 214
Beach, Charles Amory [Collective pseudonym], *1:* 21
Beach, Edward L(atimer), *12:* 35
Bealer, Alex W(inkler III), *8:* 6
Beals, Carleton, *12:* 36
Beame, Rona, *12:* 39
Beaney, Jan. *See* Udall, Jan Beaney, *10:* 182
Beatty, Hetty Burlingame, *5:* 18
Beatty, Jerome, Jr., *5:* 19
Beatty, John (Louis), *6:* 13
Beatty, Patricia (Robbins), *1:* 21
Bechtel, Louise Seaman, *4:* 26
Beck, Barbara L., *12:* 41
Becker, Beril, *11:* 23
Becker, John (Leonard), *12:* 41
Beckman, Gunnel, *6:* 14
Bedford, A. N. *See* Watson, Jane Werner, *3:* 244
Bedford, Annie North. *See* Watson, Jane Werner, *3:* 244
Beebe, B(urdetta) F(aye), *1:* 23
Beech, Webb. *See* Butterworth, W. E., *5:* 40
Beeching, Jack, *14:* 26
Beeler, Nelson F(rederick), *13:* 11
Beers, Dorothy Sands, *9:* 18
Beers, Lorna, *14:* 26
Beers, V(ictor) Gilbert, *9:* 18
Behn, Harry, *2:* 17
Behnke, Frances L., *8:* 7
Behrman, Carol H(elen), *14:* 27
Beiser, Germaine, *11:* 24
Belknap, B. H. *See* Ellis, Edward S(ylvester), *YABC 1:* 116
Bell, Corydon, *3:* 19
Bell, Emily Mary. *See* Cason, Mabel Earp, *10:* 19
Bell, Gertrude (Wood), *12:* 42
Bell, Gina. *See* Iannone, Jeanne, *7:* 139
Bell, Janet. *See* Clymer, Eleanor, *9:* 37
Bell, Margaret E(lizabeth), *2:* 19
Bell, Norman (Edward), *11:* 25
Bell, Raymond Martin, *13:* 13
Bell, Thelma Harrington, *3:* 20
Bellairs, John, *2:* 20
Belloc, (Joseph) Hilaire (Pierre), *YABC 1:* 62
Bell-Zano, Gina. *See* Iannone, Jeanne, *7:* 139
Belting, Natalie Maree, *6:* 16
Belvedere, Lee. *See* Grayland, Valerie, *7:* 111
Benary, Margot. *See* Benary-Isbert, Margot, *2:* 21
Benary-Isbert, Margot, *2:* 21

Benasutti, Marion, *6:* 18
Benchley, Nathaniel, *3:* 21
Benchley, Peter, *3:* 22
Bendick, Jeanne, *2:* 23
Bendick, Robert L(ouis), *11:* 25
Benedict, Dorothy Potter, *11:* 26
Benedict, Lois Trimble, *12:* 44
Benedict, Rex, *8:* 8
Benét, Laura, *3:* 23
Benét, Stephen Vincent, *YABC 1:* 75
Benezra, Barbara, *10:* 10
Bennett, John, *YABC 1:* 84
Benson, Sally, *1:* 24
Bentley, Phyllis (Eleanor), *6:* 19
Berelson, Howard, *5:* 20
Berenstain, Janice, *12:* 44
Berenstain, Stan(ley), *12:* 45
Berg, Jean Horton, *6:* 21
Berger, Melvin H., *5:* 21
Berger, Terry, *8:* 10
Berkowitz, Freda Pastor, *12:* 48
Berliner, Franz, *13:* 13
Bernadette. *See* Watts, Bernadette, *4:* 226
Bernard, Jacqueline (de Sieyes), *8:* 11
Bernstein, Theodore M(enline), *12:* 49
Berrien, Edith Heal. *See* Heal, Edith, *7:* 123
Berrill, Jacquelyn (Batsel), *12:* 50
Berrington, John. *See* Brownjohn, Alan, *6:* 38
Berry, B. J. *See* Berry, Barbara, J., *7:* 19
Berry, Barbara J., *7:* 19
Berry, Erick. *See* Best, Allena Champlin, *2:* 25
Berry, William D(avid), *14:* 28
Berson, Harold, *4:* 27
Berwick, Jean. *See* Meyer, Jean Shepherd, *11:* 181
Best, (Evangel) Allena Champlin, *2:* 25
Best, (Oswald) Herbert, *2:* 27
Beth, Mary. *See* Miller, Mary Beth, *9:* 145
Bethancourt, T. Ernesto, *11:* 27
Bethell, Jean (Frankenberry), *8:* 11
Bethers, Ray, *6:* 22
Bethune, J. G. *See* Ellis, Edward S(ylvester), *YABC 1:* 116
Bettina. *See* Ehrlich, Bettina, *1:* 82
Betz, Eva Kelly, *10:* 10
Bevan, Tom, *YABC 2:* 8
Beyer, Audrey White, *9:* 19
Bialk, Elisa, *1:* 25
Bible, Charles, *13:* 14
Bierhorst, John, *6:* 23
Billout, Guy René, *10:* 11
Birmingham, Lloyd, *12:* 51
Biro, Val, *1:* 26
Bischoff, Julia Bristol, *12:* 52
Bishop, Claire (Huchet), *14:* 30
Bishop, Curtis, *6:* 24

Bisset, Donald, *7:* 20
Bixby, William, *6:* 24
Black, Algernon David, *12:* 53
Black, Irma S(imonton), *2:* 28
Blackett, Veronica Heath, *12:* 54
Bladow, Suzanne Wilson, *14:* 32
Blaine, John. *See* Goodwin, Harold Leland, *13:* 73
Blaine, John. *See* Harkins, Philip, *6:* 102
Blaine, Marge. *See* Blaine, Margery Kay, *11:* 28
Blaine, Margery Kay, *11:* 28
Blair, Ruth Van Ness, *12:* 54
Blair, Walter, *12:* 56
Blake, Quentin, *9:* 20
Blake, Walker E. *See* Butterworth, W. E., *5:* 40
Bland, Edith Nesbit. *See* Nesbit, E(dith), *YABC 1:* 193
Bland, Fabian [Joint pseudonym]. *See* Nesbit, E(dith), *YABC 1:* 193
Blassingame, Wyatt (Rainey), *1:* 27
Bleeker, Sonia, *2:* 30
Blegvad, Erik, *14:* 33
Blegvad, Lenore, *14:* 34
Blishen, Edward, *8:* 12
Bliss, Ronald G(ene), *12:* 57
Bliven, Bruce Jr., *2:* 31
Bloch, Lucienne, *10:* 11
Bloch, Marie Halun, *6:* 25
Bloch, Robert, *12:* 57
Block, Irvin, *12:* 59
Blough, Glenn O(rlando), *1:* 28
Blue, Rose, *5:* 22
Blume, Judy (Sussman), *2:* 31
Blyton, Carey, *9:* 22
Boardman, Fon Wyman, Jr., *6:* 26
Boardman, Gwenn R., *12:* 59
Bobbe, Dorothie, *1:* 30
Bock, Hal. *See* Bock, Harold I., *10:* 13
Bock, Harold I., *10:* 13
Bock, William Sauts Netamux'we, *14:* 36
Bodecker, N. M., *8:* 12
Boden, Hilda. *See* Bodenham, Hilda Esther, *13:* 16
Bodenham, Hilda Esther, *13:* 16
Bodie, Idella F(allaw), *12:* 60
Bodker, Cecil, *14:* 39
Boeckman, Charles, *12:* 61
Boesch, Mark J(oseph), *12:* 62
Boggs, Ralph Steele, *7:* 21
Boles, Paul Darcy, *9:* 23
Bolian, Polly, *4:* 29
Bolliger, Max, *7:* 22
Bolton, Carole, *6:* 27
Bond, Gladys Baker, *14:* 41
Bond, J. Harvey. *See* Winterbotham, R(ussell) R(obert), *10:* 198
Bond, Michael, *6:* 28
Bond, Ruskin, *14:* 43
Bonham, Barbara, *7:* 22

Nast, Elsa Ruth. *See* Watson, Jane Werner, *3:* 244
Nathan, Robert, *6:* 171
Navarra, John Gabriel, *8:* 141
Naylor, Penelope, *10:* 104
Naylor, Phyllis Reynolds, *12:* 156
Nazaroff, Alexander I., *4:* 160
Neal, Harry Edward, *5:* 139
Nee, Kay Bonner, *10:* 104
Needleman, Jacob, *6:* 172
Negri, Rocco, *12:* 157
Neigoff, Anne, *13:* 165
Neigoff, Mike, *13:* 166
Neilson, Frances Fullerton (Jones), *14:* 149
Neimark, Anne E., *4:* 160
Nelson, Esther L., *13:* 167
Nesbit, E(dith), *YABC 1:* 193
Nesbit, Troy. *See* Folsom, Franklin, *5:* 67
Nespojohn, Katherine V., *7:* 170
Ness, Evaline (Michelow), *1:* 165
Neufeld, John, *6:* 173
Neumeyer, Peter F(lorian), *13:* 168
Neurath, Marie (Reidemeister), *1:* 166
Neville, Emily Cheney, *1:* 169
Neville, Mary. *See* Woodrich, Mary Neville, *2:* 274
Newberry, Clare Turlay, *1:* 170
Newell, Edythe W., *11:* 185
Newlon, Clarke, *6:* 174
Newman, Robert (Howard), *4:* 161
Newman, Shirlee Petkin, *10:* 105
Newton, Suzanne, *5:* 140
Nichols, Cecilia Fawn, *12:* 159
Nickelsburg, Janet, *11:* 185
Nickerson, Betty. *See* Nickerson, Elizabeth, *14:* 150
Nickerson, Elizabeth, *14:* 150
Nicolay, Helen, *YABC 1:* 204
Nicole, Christopher Robin, *5:* 141
Nielsen, Virginia. *See* McCall, Virginia Nielsen, *13:* 151
Nixon, Joan Lowery, *8:* 143
Nixon, K. *See* Nixon, Kathleen Irene (Blundell), *14:* 152
Nixon, Kathleen Irene (Blundell), *14:* 152
Noble, Iris, *5:* 142
Nodset, Joan M. *See* Lexau, Joan M., *1:* 144
Nolan, Jeannette Covert, *2:* 196
Noonan, Julia, *4:* 163
Nordstrom, Ursula, *3:* 144
North, Andrew. *See* Norton, Alice Mary, *1:* 173
North, Captain George. *See* Stevenson, Robert Louis, *YABC 2:* 307
North, Robert. *See* Withers, Carl A., *14:* 261
North, Sterling, *1:* 171
Norton, Alice Mary, *1:* 173
Norton, Andre. *See* Norton, Alice Mary, *1:* 173

Norton, Browning. *See* Norton, Frank R(owland) B(rowning), *10:* 107
Norton, Frank R(owland) B(rowning), *10:* 107
Nowell, Elizabeth Cameron, *12:* 160
Nye, Robert, *6:* 174

Oakes, Vanya, *6:* 175
Oakley, Don(ald G.), *8:* 144
Oakley, Helen, *10:* 107
Obrant, Susan, *11:* 186
O'Connell, Peg. *See* Ahern, Margaret McCrohan, *10:* 2
O'Connor, Patrick. *See* Wibberley, Leonard, *2:* 271
O'Dell, Scott, *12:* 161
Odenwald, Robert P(aul), *11:* 187
Oechsli, Kelly, *5:* 143
Ofasu-Appiah, L(awrence Henry), *13:* 170
Offit, Sidney, *10:* 108
Ogan, George F., *13:* 171
Ogan, M. G. *See* Ogan, Margaret E. (Nettles), *13:* 171
Ogan, Margaret E. (Nettles), *13:* 171
Ogburn, Charlton, Jr., *3:* 145
O'Hara, Mary. *See* Alsop, Mary O'Hara, *2:* 4
Ohlsson, Ib, *7:* 171
Olds, Elizabeth, *3:* 146
Olds, Helen Diehl, *9:* 148
Oldstyle, Jonathan. *See* Irving, Washington, *YABC 2:* 164
O'Leary, Brian, *6:* 176
Olmstead, Lorena Ann, *13:* 172
Olney, Ross R., *13:* 173
Olschewski, Alfred, *7:* 172
Olsen, Ib Spang, *6:* 177
O'Neill, Mary L(e Duc), *2:* 197
Opie, Iona, *3:* 148
Opie, Peter, *3:* 149
Oppenheim, Joanne, *5:* 146
Orgel, Doris, *7:* 173
Orleans, Ilo, *10:* 110
Ormondroyd, Edward, *14:* 153
Ormsby, Virginia H(aire), *11:* 187
Osborne, Chester G., *11:* 188
Osborne, David. *See* Silverberg, Robert, *13:* 206
Osborne, Leone Neal, *2:* 198
Osmond, Edward, *10:* 110
Ousley, Odille, *10:* 111
Owen, Caroline Dale. *See* Snedecker, Caroline Dale (Parke), *YABC 2:* 296
Oxenbury, Helen, *3:* 151

Page, Eileen. *See* Heal, Edith, *7:* 123

Page, Eleanor. *See* Coerr, Eleanor, *1:* 64
Pahz, (Anne) Cheryl Suzanne, *11:* 189
Pahz, James Alon, *11:* 190
Paice, Margaret, *10:* 111
Paine, Roberta M., *13:* 174
Paisley, Tom. *See* Bethancourt, T. Ernesto, *11:* 27
Palazzo, Anthony D., *3:* 152
Palazzo, Tony. *See* Palazzo, Anthony D., *3:* 152
Palder, Edward L., *5:* 146
Palmer, C(yril) Everard, *14:* 153
Palmer, (Ruth) Candida, *11:* 19'
Pansy. *See* Alden, Isabella (Macdonald), *YABC 2:* 1
Panter, Carol, *9:* 150
Pape, D(onna) L(ugg), *2:* 198
Paradis, Adrian A(lexis), *1:* 175
Parker, Elinor, *3:* 155
Parker, Nancy Winslow, *10:* 113
Parker, Richard, *14:* 156
Parkinson, Ethelyn M(inerva), *11:* 192
Parks, Edd Winfield, *10:* 114
Parks, Gordon (Alexander Buchanan), *8:* 145
Parlin, John. *See* Graves, Charles Parlin, *4:* 94
Parr, Lucy, *10:* 115
Parrish, Mary. *See* Cousins, Margaret, *2:* 79
Parrish, (Frederick) Maxfield, *14:* 158
Parry, Marian, *13:* 175
Pascal, David, *14:* 174
Paschal, Nancy. *See* Trotter, Grace V(iolet), *10:* 180
Paterson, Katherine (Womeldorf), *13:* 176
Paton, Alan (Stewart), *11:* 194
Paton Walsh, Gillian, *4:* 164
Patterson, Lillie G., *14:* 174
Paul, Aileen, *12:* 164
Pauli, Hertha, *3:* 155
Paulson, Jack. *See* Jackson, C. Paul, *6:* 120
Pavel, Frances, *10:* 116
Payson, Dale, *9:* 150
Paz, A. *See* Pahz, James Alon, *11:* 190
Paz, Zan. *See* Pahz, Cheryl Suzanne, *11:* 189
Pearce, (Ann) Philippa, *1:* 176
Peare, Catherine Owens, *9:* 152
Pease, Howard, *2:* 199
Peeples, Edwin A., *6:* 181
Peet, Bill. *See* Peet, William B, *2:* 201
Peet, William Bartlett, *2:* 201
Pelaez, Jill, *12:* 165
Peltier, Leslie C(opus), *13:* 177
Pembury, Bill. *See* Groom, Arthur William, *10:* 53
Pender, Lydia, *3:* 157

Richards, Frank. *See* Hamilton, Charles Howard St. John, *13:* 77
Richards, Hilda. *See* Hamilton, Charles Howard St. John, *13:* 77
Richards, Laura E(lizabeth Howe), *YABC 1:* 224
Richardson, Grace Lee. *See* Dickson, Naida, *8:* 41
Richardson, Robert S(hirley), *8:* 164
Richoux, Pat, *7:* 180
Richter, Conrad, *3:* 171
Richter, Hans Peter, *6:* 191
Ridge, Antonia, *7:* 181
Riedman, Sarah R(egal), *1:* 183
Rikhoff, Jean, *9:* 158
Ringi, Kjell, *12:* 168
Rinkoff, Barbara (Jean), *4:* 174
Rios, Tere. *See* Versace, Marie Teresa, *2:* 254
Ripley, Elizabeth Blake, *5:* 158
Ripper, Charles L., *3:* 174
Ritchie, Barbara (Gibbons), *14:* 176
Riverside, John. *See* Heinlein, Robert A(nson), *9:* 102
Rivoli, Mario, *10:* 129
Roach, Marilynne K(athleen), *9:* 158
Robbins, Ruth, *14:* 177
Roberts, David. *See* Cox, John Roberts, *9:* 42
Roberts, Jim. *See* Bates, Barbara S(nedeker), *12:* 34
Roberts, Terence. *See* Sanderson, Ivan T., *6:* 195
Robertson, Barbara (Anne), *12:* 172
Robertson, Don, *8:* 165
Robertson, Dorothy Lewis, *12:* 173
Robertson, Jennifer (Sinclair), *12:* 174
Robertson, Keith, *1:* 184
Robins, Seelin. *See* Ellis, Edward S(ylvester), *YABC 1:* 116
Robinson, Adjai, *8:* 165
Robinson, Barbara (Webb), *8:* 166
Robinson, Charles, *6:* 192
Robinson, Jan M., *6:* 194
Robinson, Jean O., *7:* 182
Robinson, Joan (Mary) G(ale Thomas), *7:* 183
Robinson, Maudie (Millian Oller), *11:* 200
Robison, Bonnie, *12:* 175
Robottom, John, *7:* 185
Roche, A. K. [Joint pseudonym with Boche Kaplan]. *See* Abisch, Roslyn Kroop, *9:* 3
Rockwell, Thomas, *7:* 185
Rockwood, Roy [Collective pseudonym], *1:* 185
Rodgers, Mary, *8:* 167
Rodman, Emerson. *See* Ellis, Edward S(ylvester), *YABC 1:* 116

Rodman, Maia. *See* Wojciechowska, Maia, *1:* 228
Rodman, Selden, *9:* 159
Rogers, (Thomas) Alan (Stinchcombe), *2:* 215
Rogers, Frances, *10:* 130
Rogers, Matilda, *5:* 158
Rogers, Pamela, *9:* 160
Roland, Albert, *11:* 201
Rolerson, Darrell A(llen), *8:* 168
Roll, Winifred, *6:* 194
Rollins, Charlemae Hill, *3:* 175
Rongen, Björn, *10:* 131
Rood, Ronald (N.), *12:* 177
Rooke, Daphne (Marie), *12:* 178
Rose, Anne, *8:* 168
Rose, Wendy, *12:* 180
Rosen, Sidney, *1:* 185
Rosen, Winifred, *8:* 169
Rosenbaum, Maurice, *6:* 195
Rosenberg, Ethel, *3:* 176
Rosenberg, Nancy Sherman, *4:* 177
Rosenberg, Sharon, *8:* 171
Rosenblum, Richard, *11:* 202
Rosenburg, John M., *6:* 195
Rothkopf, Carol Z., *4:* 177
Rothman, Joel, *7:* 186
Rounds, Glen (Harold), *8:* 171
Rourke, Constance (Mayfield), *YABC 1:* 232
Rowland, Florence Wightman, *8:* 173
Roy, Liam. *See* Scarry, Patricia, *2:* 218
Ruchlis, Hy, *3:* 177
Rudomin, Esther. *See* Hautzig, Esther, *4:* 105
Ruedi, Norma Paul. *See* Ainsworth, Norma, *9:* 4
Rushmore, Helen, *3:* 178
Rushmore, Robert William, *8:* 174
Ruskin, Ariane, *7:* 187
Russell, Franklin, *11:* 203
Russell, Helen Ross, *8:* 175
Russell, Patrick. *See* Sammis, John, *4:* 178
Russell, Solveig Paulson, *3:* 179
Ruth, Rod, *9:* 160
Ruthin, Margaret, *4:* 178
Rutz, Viola Larkin, *12:* 181
Rydell, Wendell. *See* Rydell, Wendy, *4:* 178
Rydell, Wendy, *4:* 178
Ryden, Hope, *8:* 176

Sabin, Edwin Legrand, *YABC 2:* 277
Sachs, Marilyn, *3:* 180
Sackett, S(amuel) J(ohn), *12:* 181
Sadie, Stanley (John), *14:* 177
Sage, Juniper [Joint pseudonym]. *See* Brown, Margaret Wise, *YABC 2:* 9
Sage, Juniper. *See* Hurd, Edith, *2:* 150

Sagsoorian, Paul, *12:* 183
Saint, Dora Jessie, *10:* 132
St. Briavels, James. *See* Wood, James Playsted, *1:* 229
St. George, Judith, *13:* 187
St. John, Wylly Folk, *10:* 132
Salmon, Annie Elizabeth, *13:* 188
Salter, Cedric. *See* Knight, Francis Edgar, *14:* 112
Samachson, Dorothy, *3:* 182
Samachson, Joseph, *3:* 182
Sammis, John, *4:* 178
Samson, Anne S(tringer), *2:* 216
Samson, Joan, *13:* 189
Samuels, Charles, *12:* 183
Sandburg, Carl (August), *8:* 177
Sandburg, Charles A. *See* Sandburg, Carl (August), *8:* 177
Sandburg, Helga, *3:* 184
Sanderlin, George, *4:* 180
Sanderlin, Owenita (Harrah), *11:* 204
Sanderson, Ivan T., *6:* 195
Sandin, Joan, *12:* 185
Sandoz, Mari (Susette), *5:* 159
Sanger, Marjory Bartlett, *8:* 181
Sarg, Anthony Fredrick. *See* Sarg, Tony, *YABC 1:* 233
Sarg, Tony, *YABC 1:* 233
Sargent, Robert, *2:* 216
Sargent, Shirley, *11:* 205
Sarnoff, Jane, *10:* 133
Sattler, Helen Roney, *4:* 181
Saunders, Caleb. *See* Heinlein, Robert A(nson), *9:* 102
Saunders, Keith, *12:* 186
Savage, Blake. *See* Goodwin, Harold Leland, *13:* 73
Savery, Constance (Winifred), *1:* 186
Savitt, Sam, *8:* 181
Savitz, Harriet May, *5:* 161
Sayers, Frances Clarke, *3:* 185
Sazer, Nina, *13:* 191
Scabrini, Janet, *13:* 191
Scagnetti, Jack, *7:* 188
Scanlon, Marion Stephany, *11:* 206
Scarf, Maggi. *See* Scarf, Maggie, *5:* 162
Scarf, Maggie, *5:* 162
Scarry, Patricia (Murphy), *2:* 218
Scarry, Patsy. *See* Scarry, Patricia, *2:* 218
Scarry, Richard (McClure), *2:* 218
Schaefer, Jack, *3:* 186
Schechter, Betty (Goodstein), *5:* 163
Scheer, Julian (Weisel), *8:* 183
Scheffer, Victor B., *6:* 197
Schell, Orville H., *10:* 136
Scherf, Margaret, *10:* 136
Schick, Eleanor, *9:* 161
Schiff, Ken, *7:* 189
Schisgall, Oscar, *12:* 187
Schlein, Miriam, *2:* 222